SEXTUS PROPERTIUS

In 30–15 BC Sextus Propertius composed at Rome four books of elegies which range from erotic to learned to political and exhibit an unparalleled richness of themes, concepts and language. This book investigates their sources and motives, examining Propertius' family background in Umbrian Asisium and tracing his career as he sought through poetry to restore his family's fortunes after the Civil Wars. Propertius' progress within the Roman poetic establishment depended on his patrons – Tullus, 'Gallus', Maecenas and Augustus. Initially his poetry was influenced radically by his elegiac predecessor C. Cornelius Gallus, arguably also the 'Gallus' who jointly patronized Propertius' first book. New heuristic techniques help to recover the impact on Propertius of Cornelius Gallus' (mainly lost) elegies. Propertius' subsequent move into Maecenas', and then Augustus', patronage had an equally powerful, ideological, impact; in his latter books he became (alongside Virgil and Horace) a major and committed Augustan voice.

FRANCIS CAIRNS is Professor of Classical Languages at The Florida State University. He is the author of *Generic Composition in Greek and Roman Poetry* (1972), *Tibullus: A Hellenistic Poet at Rome* (1979) and *Virgil's Augustan Epic* (1989), as well as numerous articles on Greek and Latin poetry.

SEXTUS PROPERTIUS
THE AUGUSTAN ELEGIST

FRANCIS CAIRNS

CAMBRIDGE
UNIVERSITY PRESS

CAMBRIDGE UNIVERSITY PRESS

Cambridge, New York, Melbourne, Madrid, Cape Town, Singapore, São Paulo

Cambridge University Press
The Edinburgh Building, Cambridge CB2 2RU, UK

Published in the United States of America by Cambridge University Press, New York

www.cambridge.org
Information on this title: www.cambridge.org/9780521864572

© Francis Cairns 2006

First published 2006

Printed in the United Kingdom at the University Press, Cambridge

A catalogue record for this publication is available from the British Library

ISBN 0 521 86457 7 (hardback)
ISBN 978 0 521 86457 2 (hardback)

The Greek fonts used in this work are available from
www.linguistsoftware.com   ☏ +1-425-775-1130

for Ian Du Quesnay

Contents

Preface

This monograph relates the background and evolving career of Sextus Propertius to the nature, development and character of his writings. It tries to explain why, in the early years of Augustus' dominance, this poet from Umbrian Asisium composed and published at Rome elegies notably different from those of his surviving contemporaries, Tibullus and the Ovid of the *Amores*. The differences are multiple and radical: they reside in the exuberance of Propertius' language, *exempla* and sequences of thought, and in the multi-faceted nature, thematic diversity[1] and breadth of coverage of his elegies. Erotic, personal, literary, political, aetiological and encomiastic by turns or in combinations, and exhibiting corresponding shifts of style and expression, they are like nothing else in Latin poetry. Since the question addressed is how Propertius came to be this linguistically and emotionally exciting and varied poet, and since the answers proposed relate to his life and to his successive patrons, the monograph's subject-matter entails its methodologies: philology and metrics, generic and other techniques of literary analysis attested from antiquity, and the disciplines of ancient history, politics and sociology. Consequently some other approaches and certain *magna nomina* currently in vogue in Roman elegiac studies are little, if at all, represented.

Quotation from Propertius has been restricted to a necessary minimum; so the reader will need to have a Latin text of Propertius to hand and to be aware of any emendations etc. introduced by its editor. For those passages quoted (or commented upon) I have consulted the standard critical editions, especially Fedeli (1984) and Goold (1990/

---

1   Their diversity is best illustrated by the fact that, when (rarely) two elegies are comparable, the later piece is a sophisticated emulative variation on the earlier: e.g. 1.3 and 2.29; 3.12 and 4.3.

1999),[2] but have followed my own judgement in the choice of readings. As a result quotations (and commentary) are mainly based on the text of N (the Neapolitanus) with uncontroversial corrections. No Propertian scholar would deny that N contains errors, or that it offers a lacunose and muddled version of a substantial part of Book 2. But sound readings of N reflecting Propertius' hellenistic *doctrina*, allusivity, use of technical terminology and linguistic inventiveness, sometimes echoing Greek syntax, can all too easily be condemned as corrupt.[3] Similarly, proposed transpositions and interpolations are rarely convincing and often result from failure to comprehend Propertius' compositional techniques and his compressed and distorted sequences of thought. To judge from some recent forays in these fields,[4] the salutary effects of Smyth (1970), that cemetery of discredited emendations, transpositions and lacunae, have perhaps worn off too soon. The difficult and much debated question whether Propertius Book 2 was published as a single entity and, if not, where it divides, has been handled cursorily and mainly in footnotes, especially since my agnosticism about a two-part Book 2 has no essential bearing on the arguments of this monograph.

Propertian studies have made substantial progress over the last three decades. On any account the most significant contributor has been Paolo Fedeli, whose Teubner text (1984) is the best to date, and whose major commentaries on Book 1 (1980), Book 3 (1985) and most recently Book 2 (2005), have set a new standard in Propertian exegesis.[5] My debts to the work of Fedeli and his school will be obvious throughout.[6] Among monographs on Propertius from the 1960s on three stand out for the depth and range of their coverage: Boucher (1965), Stahl (1985) and Newman (1997). Although I take issue on some points with the latter two works, no-one should doubt my admiration for H.-P. Stahl's detailed and meticulous analyses of Propertian elegies, or for the breadth and intuitive empathy of J. K.

---

2   G. Giardina, *Properzio. Elegie. Edizione critica e traduzione* (Testi e commenti 19, Rome 2005) reached me too late for me to take account of it.

3   Hence the portions of Shackleton Bailey (1956) with lasting value are not those proposing emendations but those redeeming passages of Propertius from otiose suspicion of corruption.

4   E.g. Günther (1997); Georg (2001).

5   Fedeli's early commentary on Book 4 (1965) is also worthy of respect.

6   Fedeli has also produced valuable *ancillae* in the form of a facsimile of the MS N (*Propertius. Codex Guelferbytanus Gudianus 224 olim Neapolitanus*. Assisi, 1985), and, with Paola Pinotti, a Propertian bibliography for the period 1946–83 (Fedeli–Pinotti (1985)), while his pupils have published commentaries on several single elegies of Book 4.

Newman's engagement with Propertius. Two further modern works, although not often cited in this monograph, have been constantly informative and inspirational in the broader Augustan sphere: Zanker (1987/1988), which has enlivened and inspired every subsequent student of the Augustan age, and Galinsky (1996), the clearest and wisest account of that age. The bibliographies of Harrauer (1973), Fedeli–Pinotti (1985) and Holzberg (2004a) have all assisted. A final resource has been the various corpora of Greek and Latin texts and inscriptions now available in electronic form, without which my labours would have been considerably more tedious and protracted. I am uneasily aware, however, of the possibility that such corpora may be lacunose or in error, and of the consequent potential insecurity of certain statements made on their basis, particularly where the uniqueness or absence of terms, forms and the like is concerned.

The rise of Propertian studies has come accompanied by a correlative disadvantage – the sheer volume of recent secondary literature.[7] I have attempted to be aware of relevant material appearing up to the end of 2004; but, since my manuscript was substantially completed in the course of that year, I was unable to interact with some items as much as they deserved. I particularly regret this in the case of P. A. Miller (2004), a work which usefully overlaps in a number of ways with the present monograph. Where items dated 2005 are cited, these were usually accessible to me in pre-publication form, although the same limitations to interaction applied. For all my efforts, however, I have surely missed useful secondary literature, and have failed to recognize the merits of some items which I did encounter. For this I can only apologize, as for any further failure on my part to give full credit to works actually cited, and most of all for any inadvertent misrepresentation of other scholars' views.

All this said, I have made a conscious effort to abstain from excessive citation. I generally cite either to give credit for prior discovery, or to refer to supporting evidence, or (less frequently) to record agreement. Topics remote from the well-trodden highways of Propertian scholarship may be more fully documented, as may

---

7   Growth has been exponential over the past fifty years in every area of classics. Scheidel (1997) estimated that a classical scholar spending an entire working life on the secondary literature up to 1992 would have 'nine minutes to spare for each item' (288). One shudders to think what the allocation would now be: research assessment exercises, tenure and promotion binders, and university administrators who equate length with quality have much to answer for.

controversial matters: particularly when major scholars have advanced positions contrary to my own, dissent (which does not imply disrespect) may be expressed. One particularly difficult recurrent decision has been whether, when many valuable scholarly contributions have been made to a topic, to list all of them, or instead to cite a single recent item containing earlier bibliography, even if that item is perhaps itself of lesser value. While I have tried not to omit altogether references to older works of fundamental importance, I have often felt obliged to take the latter course. Internal cross-references are fairly frequent since it was necessary to treat the same texts at different places from different viewpoints. But, particularly later in the book, they may simply point to the Indexes.

Typographical codings are sometimes added to words within (mainly) Latin quotations so as to reduce the need for lengthy explanations.[8] For the most part words are so distinguished when lines of passages are being compared in order to reveal the influence of C. Cornelius Gallus upon succeeding poets. Because the available codings are limited in number, each set tends to operate only within its own section. However, bold italic may sometimes mark important terms already mentioned or established as Gallan but not necessarily specifically designated as such in the surrounding discourse.

Some further conventions found in this work (in addition to those listed in the preamble to the Bibliography) should also be mentioned. Abbreviations of the names of ancient authors and works used in footnotes aim at clarity rather than conformity to any standard system, and the numeration of the most accessible rather than the latest or most authoritative edition of an ancient text may be employed; hence, for example, reference is made to Courtney (1993) for all fragmentary Latin poets. Texts are cited by their editor's surname, and modern commentaries are referred to by page, not line, numbers. Homonymous modern authors are distinguished by their initials. Authors of encyclopedia articles *vel sim.* are named only when their authorship is significant. Finally two points *re* nomenclature: *pace* Butrica (1996c) 87–96, I have often referred to Propertius Book 1 as the Monobiblos; and I may not have observed meticulously the temporal distinction between Octavianus and Augustus.

Where Latin and Greek is quoted to make non-verbal points and no paraphrase is offered, English translations have been added at the

---

8   Reference is also made to this practice at a later point (p. 79 n. 50).

request of the press. Those not attributed are my own; they aim only to be literal.

I have cited my own previously published papers freely to minimize the amount of material reproduced from them; the two cited most frequently – Cairns (1983a) and (1993) – contain essential supplementary arguments. An earlier version of Chapter 9 was read at the Symposium Cumanum 'Vergil and Philodemus', held at the Villa Vergiliana, Cuma, Italy, in June 2000, and it appeared as Cairns (2004a);[9] and part of Chapter 7 was presented in 2002 at the Convegno Internazionale 'Properzio tra Storia Arte Mito', Accademia Properziana del Subasio, Assisi, and was published in Italian as Cairns (2004b). Other portions of this volume originated in oral presentations: part of Chapter 11 was the keynote lecture at the University of Virginia (Charlottesville) 2000 Graduate Conference; and part of Chapter 12 was presented at the University of Iowa and at Emory University, Atlanta, in 2002. I am grateful to the participants on these occasions for their feedback.

Over the long gestation period of this book (1990–2004) many friends have offered valuable advice and help. Guy Bradley allowed me to photocopy his unpublished doctoral thesis, which later appeared in revised form as Bradley (2000), and informed me on many aspects of Umbria. Francesco Santucci generously spent time and effort guiding me about and around Assisi, and he provided me with copies of his indispensable publications on Assisi and its environs. The late Giovanni Forni sent me his published epigraphic papers relating to Umbria, and Mario Torelli patiently corrected a number of misapprehensions on my part, and gave me valuable pointers to bibliography. Dominic Berry, Claudio Bizzarri, Larissa Bonfante, Roger Brock, Gabriele Burzacchini, Ted Buttrey, Giovanni Colonna, Ingrid Edlund-Berry, Jeff Fish, Gordon Howie, Eleanor Winsor Leach, David Levenson, Massimo Morandi, Hans-Friedrich Mueller, Harry R. Nielsen III, David Sedley, Marilyn Skinner and David Stone advised variously on philological, literary, philosophical, archaeological, artistic, numismatic and historical questions. John Beeby digitized maps and charts of Umbria, Jeffrey Petsis worked on checking and indexing, and Niklas Holzberg, Guido Milanese, Paola Pinotti and Marta Sordi assisted bibliographically or with publications. My colleagues Jeff Tatum and Nancy de Grummond provided information

9   The University of Texas Press has kindly granted me permission to re-use it here.

and advice over a number of years, read those portions of the manu-script relevant to their specializations and offered candid criticism. I am also indebted to Neil Adkin for subjecting the proofs to his unerringly accurate and incomparably learned oversight. My greatest debt, however, is to Ian Du Quesnay, who despite his strong dissent from some of my positions, laboured manfully to remove mistakes and unclarities from the entire penultimate draft. It should not, of course, be assumed that anyone who has assisted me endorses my views; for these, as for all errors in this book, I take sole responsibility.

I gratefully acknowledge the generous financial support for my research of the Florida State University Council on Research and Creativity COFRS grant, the Florida State University Research Foundation AHPEG programme, and the Florida State University Department of Classics. The Faculty of Classics and the University Library of the University of Cambridge have over the last six years provided me with library facilities, for which I tender my sincere thanks. Finally my gratitude goes to Michael Sharp, Peter Ducker and their colleagues at Cambridge University Press for their efficient and tolerant handling of this book.

FRANCIS CAIRNS

Department of Classics, The Florida State University
Faculty of Classics, University of Cambridge
October 2005

Abbreviations

Anth. Lat.	D. R. Shackleton Bailey (ed.), *Anthologia Latina* I.1. *Carmina in codicibus scripta.* Stuttgart 1982–
CAH	*The Cambridge Ancient History.* Cambridge 1923–
CIL	*Corpus inscriptionum Latinarum.* Berlin 1863–
CLE	F. Buecheler (ed.), *Anthologia Latina* II.1, II.2. *Carmina Latina Epigraphica.* Leipzig. 1895–7; E. Lommatzsch (ed.) II.3. Leipzig. 1926
ERAssisi	G. Forni (ed.), *Epigrafi lapidarie romane di Assisi.* Catalogo regionale dei beni culturali dell'Umbria. Perugia 1987
Encicl. Virg.	F. della Corte (ed.), *Enciclopedia virgiliana.* Rome 1984–91
EOS	*Atti del Colloquio Internazionale AIEGL su epigrafia e ordine senatorio. Roma, 14–20 maggio 1981* (2 vols) = Tituli 4–5. Rome 1982
GC	F. Cairns, *Generic Composition in Greek and Roman Poetry.* Edinburgh 1972
GL	H. Keil (ed.), *Grammatici Latini* (8 vols). Leipzig 1855–80
IG	*Inscriptiones Graecae.* Berlin. 1873–
LALE	R. Maltby, *A Lexicon of Ancient Latin Etymologies.* Arca 25. Leeds 1991
Hofmann–Szantyr	J. B. Hofmann and A. Szantyr, *Lateinische Syntax und Stilistik.* Handbuch der Altertumswissenschaft II.2.2. Munich 1965
LIMC	*Lexicon Iconographicum Mythologiae Classicae* (19 vols). Zurich 1981–99
LSJ	H. G. Liddell and R. Scott, rev. by H. S. Jones. *Greek–English Lexicon*, 9th edn. Oxford 1940
LTUR	E. M. Steinby (ed.), *Lexicon topographicum urbis Romae.* Rome 1993–2000

OCD[3]	S. Hornblower and A. Spawforth (eds.), *The Oxford Classical Dictionary*. 3rd ed. Oxford and New York 1996
OLD	P. G. W. Glare (ed.), *Oxford Latin Dictionary*. Oxford 1968–82
PIR[1]	*Prosopographia imperii romani saec. I. II. III.* 1st ed. Berlin 1897–8
PIR[2]	*Prosopographia imperii romani saec. I. II. III.* 2nd ed. Berlin 1933–
THPR	F. Cairns, *Tibullus: A Hellenistic Poet at Rome*. Cambridge 1979
RE	A. Pauly, G. Wissowa, and W. Kroll. *Real-Encyclopädie der klassischen Altertums-wissenschaft*. Stuttgart 1893–1980
SEG	*Supplementum epigraphicum graecum*. Leiden 1923–71; Alphen aan den Rijn 1979–80; Amsterdam 1982–
TLL	*Thesaurus linguae Latinae*. Leipzig 1900–
VJR	*Vocabularium iurisprudentiae romanae*. Berlin 1903–
VSD	'Vita Donatiana e vita Suetoniana desumpta', in G. Brugnoli and F. Stok (eds.) *Vitae Vergilianae Antiquae*. Rome 1997. [17]–[70]
Walde–Hofmann	A. Walde and J. B. Hofmann (eds.), *Lateinisches etymologisches Wörterbuch* (3 vols). Indogermanische Bibliothek. 1 Abt. Lehr- und Handbücher, 2 Reihe: Wörterbücher 1. 3rd ed. Heidelberg 1938–56

CHAPTER 1

The Propertii

It was once standard for commentaries and monographs on Greek and Roman poets to start with biographies, which drew, often uncritically, on the apparently personal revelations in their subjects' works, and which usually gave credence to ancient Lives where they existed.[1] Propertius did not escape such biographical treatment, even though no ancient Life of him survives.[2] The Renaissance fantasized freely about him;[3] and his name, birthplace, birth and early years, liaisons with Cynthia (and Lycinna!), and links with contemporaries continued to fill scholarly introductions up to the mid-twentieth century.[4] The last fifty years have seen a retreat from the excesses of such biographies, and for good reasons: ancient poets' accounts of their personal experiences are now generally recognized as actually or potentially conventional and fictional;[5] and the limited credibility of ancient Lives of poets is now well understood.[6] But, while the virtual disappearance of the biographical fallacy and the emergence of a more sophisticated approach to ancient biographical information are both welcome, another concomitant trend is not. This is a tendency to neglect the facts

1 For the acme (or nadir) of such biographizing see Becker (1898), combining a sentimental and novelistic 'life' of C. Cornelius Gallus (3–147) with useful *Realien* (151–523).
2 He is unlikely to have featured in Suetonius' *De Poetis* (cf. Rostagni (1964) xxiii–xxiv), perhaps because he was not popularly regarded as the leading Roman elegist: cf. Quint. *Inst. Orat.* 10.1.93.
3 Cf. Pizzani (1996).
4 Cf., e.g., Butler and Barber (1933) xviii–xxv – 'The Life of Propertius' under the subheadings 'His name', 'His birthplace', 'Birth and early years', 'The liaison with Cynthia', and 'The poet and his contemporaries'; for similar material in analogous categories cf. Ch. I (De Properti vita = I.3–16) of the Prolegomena of Enk (1946). Rothstein (1920–4) I.1–14 also treats Propertius' life and writings, but more soberly.
5 See below, pp. 66–8. This has long been generally understood: cf., e.g., already K. F. Smith (1913) 26–9, 43–58. Among recent reiterations of the unhistorical nature of Propertius' Cynthia see, e.g., Newman (1997) Ch. 7.
6 Thanks in particular to Fairweather (1974) and Lefkowitz (1981).

1

of ancient poets' lives, and even to deny that they have value for the understanding of the poets' works. There are of course notable exceptions to this trend: for example, among Republican and Augustan Latin poets Catullus has been well served,[7] and Ovid, because of the wealth of autobiographical and contemporary material in his poetry, has attracted major scholarly attention to his life and historical background.[8] But more such attention would have been welcome as a preliminary to the finest commentaries on Horace's *Odes* 1 and Propertius' Monobiblos,[9] particularly since they do comment meticulously and in detail on the historical aspects of individual poems. With authors such as Horace and Propertius the tendency goes no further than relative neglect. But outright denial reveals itself nakedly and unashamedly in an important study by a leading Virgilian scholar who writes: 'If we turn out to know next to nothing of Virgil's "life and times", that matters little if at all to our understanding of the poetry'.[10]

Experience with an ancient writer distant in time and location from Propertius but not alien to him suggests that this last attitude is an impediment to progress: in the case of Callimachus, investigations into his antecedents and social standing have thrown much new light on his works.[11] Propertius' interactions with some of the leading figures of his age also feature in his poetry, and, if anything, his life and ambience impinge more sharply on it. So, if Propertius' background can be further investigated, refusal to do so risks depriving Propertian exegesis of valuable new insights.

Three additional reasons further authorize such an investigation: first, up-to-date, detailed discussions of Propertius' life and background are unavailable;[12] second, there exists epigraphic, archaeological, and historical evidence relevant to the poet and his context which has been under-exploited of late by Propertian scholarship;[13] and third, even known facts about Propertius familiar to earlier

---

7   See esp. Wiseman (1969); (1974); (1979); (1985).
8   Esp. Syme (1978).
9   I.e. Nisbet and Hubbard (1970); Fedeli (1980).
10   Horsfall in Horsfall (1995) 1.
11   Meillier (1979); Cameron (1995) Ch. 1; S. A. White (1999).
12   The best post-1960 treatment is La Penna (1977) 5–15 (with bibliography), the best earlier account Rothstein (1920) I.1–14.
13   Among older Propertian scholars Hertzberg (1843–5) I.3–12 assembled such material, but among more recent commentators and monographists only Rothstein (1920) I.1–14 and Enk (1946) I.3–5 show more than mild interest in it. It naturally features more largely in such works as Elisei (1916) and Fortini (1931), where its main function is to support Assisi's claim to be the 'patria di Properzio'.

scholarly generations seem to be fading from currency as a result of the curiously casual attitude of some recent Propertian scholars towards Propertius' *vita*. For example, Propertius has in the last few decades been allocated at least four different birthplaces.[14] One scholar (on no grounds whatsoever) has him born in Urvinum Hortense.[15] Another, without citing any evidence, writes of 'Perusia, the home of Propertius's family',[16] a view which is, of course, incompatible with Propertius' own clear statements (quoted below) that he was born in Umbria.[17] 'Mevania [modern Bevagna], the birthplace of Propertius' asserts a third scholar.[18] The *communis opinio*, repeated by a fourth scholar, 'Propertius in fact came from Assisi',[19] is correct. The confusion has, of course, been fostered from the Renaissance on by the local patriotism of various towns in the region of Assisi;[20] but Propertian scholars once knew better.

Propertian scholars also agreed not so long ago on another point, that the relative social standing of the poet and the 'Tullus' to whom he dedicated four elegies of Book 1 and one of Book 3 meant that (Volcacius) Tullus was Propertius' patron in the Monobiblos. Of late, however, there has been dissension in print over this question: in addition to reassertions of this, which is in essence the correct view,[21] Tullus has been described as a 'friend' to whom the poems were written 'on terms of equality', since (allegedly) 'The Volcacii were of similar social standing to the Propertii' and 'They are not the poems of patronized to patron'. This approach stoutly maintains that 'Propertius did not address a patron in his first book'.[22] A third line of interpretation compounds these two views, and makes Tullus 'Propertius' main friend and patron'.[23] These differing assessments of the relationship between Propertius and Tullus, which will be discussed more

---

14   Rothstein (1920) I.1 noted that fourteen different towns had claimed Propertius!
15   Modern Collemancio, see Maddoli (1963).
16   Gold (1987) 143, presumably misled by Prop. 1.22.3.
17   The source of some of this confusion may be that, whereas Perugia is part of the modern Italian province of Umbria, ancient Perusia was part of Etruria.
18   Du Quesnay (1992) 77–8 and 234 n. 104, adducing *CLE* 803 (irrelevant) and Prop. 4.1.123, and perhaps basing his conclusion on a more complex misunderstanding of 4.1.121–6.
19   Lyne in G. Lee (1994) xi.
20   See Elisei (1916) *passim*; Salvatore (1965) 381–92.
21   E.g. Cairns (1983a) 91; Gold (1987) 143: 'Tullus, Propertius' earlier patron'.
22   The quotations are from Lyne in G. Lee (1994) x; see also Syme (1986) 359: 'a "sodalis" of equal years, not a patron' – as if age was the criterion.
23   Du Quesnay (1992) 76; cf. Stahl (1985) 49: 'friend', 79: 'probable patron'.

fully in Chapter 2, are, of course, in part terminological.[24] But they also in part reflect the current lack of consensus about fundamental details of the life of Propertius, and so illustrate further the need for more information about Propertius and his ambience.

Such information cannot, of course, in itself ensure a sensible assessment of the functions of Propertian elegy within its contemporary society: for this a sound understanding of the ways in which inter-personal relationships were described in antiquity is also required (see below, pp. 35–8), as is an awareness of the overall historical context of Propertius' works. All too many contemporary interpretations of Propertian elegies are fundamentally flawed because they start from anachronistic assumptions: it is just as essential to integrate literary approaches to his works with their historical background as to recognize the difference between truth and fiction in Propertian elegy. But it may be useful at this time to set down what facts can be established about Propertius, and to try to reconstruct further his family background, life, and personal contacts. Given the state of the evidence, this enterprise will inevitably involve speculative hypotheses. However, if the results of these converge with known facts and with each other, they can gain strength thereby, and at the end of the day even unconfirmable speculations may be preferable to absence of enquiry or to downright error.

Propertius' nomenclature and birthplace have been fought over so frequently since the late nineteenth century and the basic facts about them have been established so firmly that they would not even require restating were it not for the uncertainties of some modern scholarship; hence this area can be dealt with briefly, if dogmatically. The poet's first, i.e. personal, name (*praenomen*) was 'Sextus' and his second, i.e. gentile, name (*nomen*) was 'Propertius'. The additional *nomen* 'Aurelius', and the third name (*cognomen*) 'Nauta' conferred on him by certain manuscripts (AFPV) are pure absurdities which lack any authority.[25] Propertius originated in Umbria and he describes himself as Umbrian: at 1.22.9–10 he declares *Umbria .../ me genuit*; at 4.1.64 he calls Umbria *Romani patria Callimachi*; and his interlocuter Horus

---

24   Latin *amicus* can cover both 'friend', and 'patron/client': see below, pp. 36–7, where a further potentially complicating factor is also discussed.

25   They were 'authenticated' by two inscriptions (*CIL* XI 4443 and 5308) now generally recognized as forgeries: see Forni (1985) 205–7. 'Nauta' derives from O's reading (*navita*) at Prop. 2.24.38, which is usually corrected to *non ita*. The sympathy for this nomenclature implied by Newman (1997) Ch. 4 esp. 141 is unwarranted.

subsequently asserts *Umbria te ... edit* (4.1.121).[26] The claims to be the birthplace of Propertius advanced, sometimes even in recent scholarship, on behalf of towns other than Asisium have already been mentioned; there is not a scrap of genuine evidence to favour any of them,[27] and it is astonishing that they can still sometimes mislead.[28] Taken in combination the same three Propertian passages which designated the poet as Umbrian also establish Asisium unequivocally as his birthplace, with the third stating this explicitly:

1.   proxima supposito contingens Umbria campo
        me genuit terris fertilis uberibus. (1.22.9–10)

[Perusia's] neighbour, adjacent with its low-lying plain, Umbria, fertile with its rich lands, bore me.

2.   mi folia ex hedera porrige, Bacche, tua,
        ut nostris tumefacta superbiat Umbria libris,
        Umbria Romani patria Callimachi!
      scandentis quisquis cernit de vallibus arces,
        ingenio muros aestimet ille meo! (4.1.62–6)

Give me leaves from your ivy, Bacchus, so that Umbria may be swollen with pride at my books, Umbria native land of the Roman Callimachus! Whoever sees the citadels rising from the valleys, let him prize the walls because of my poetic genius.

3.   Umbria te notis antiqua Penatibus edit.
        mentior? an patriae tangitur ora tuae,
      qua nebulosa cavo rorat Mevania campo,
        et lacus aestivis intepet Umber aquis,
      scandentisque Asis consurgit vertice murus,   125
        murus ab ingenio notior ille tuo? (4.1.121–6)

      123 quam *O*: qua ϛ   125 Asis *O*: Asisi *Lachmann*

---

26   For this reason it is incorrect to claim that Propertius was an 'Etruscan' *simpliciter*: cf., e.g., 'un altro poeta etrusco dell'età augustea' (Sordi (1964) 100), although the characterization 'l'umbro etrusco Properzio' (Sordi (1981) 53, 56) accords with what is proposed (below, pp. 61–2) about Propertius' possible maternal ancestry.

27   See Elisei (1916); Salvatore (1965) 387–92, who records alternative candidacies more briefly ('a tacere di svariate altre ipotesi, più o meno assurde', 387), and refutes all of them; Forni (1985) 205–7; Pizzani (1996). Bonamente (2004) 70 n. 170 assembles some further bibliography.

28   In addition to the cases noted above see La Penna (1977) 15 and Gabba (1986) 101 n. 15, mentioning the suggestion of Maddoli (1963), and seeming to admit that some doubt is possible.

Ancient Umbria bore you to a distinguished house. Is this untrue? or have I touched on the boundary of your native land, where foggy Mevania spreads dew on the low-lying plain, and the Umbrian Lake sheds warmth from its summer waters, and the wall of rising Asisium mounts up on the summit, a wall more famous because of your poetic genius?

Strict attention to the contexts, syntax, and content of these passages, both here and in the complementary discussion of them below (pp. 54–9), is essential if erroneous inferences are to be avoided.[29] First (pseudo-)etymologies of *Umbria* feature largely in the passages: 4.1.123–4, with their references to 'clouds', 'dewing', the *lacus Umber*, and 'waters', manifestly evoke the standard ancient derivation of *Umbri* from Greek '*Ombrii*', possibly through the intermediacy of *imber*.[30] Again, Isidore's linkage of *ubera* with moisture (*humor*) at *Origines* 11.1.76 suggests that 1.22.9–10 contain a second derivation of *Umbria* from *uber*, referring to its fertile soil.[31] In addition *antiqua* (4.1.121) alludes to the (non-etymological?) claim of the Umbrians to be the 'oldest race in Italy'.[32] The physical topography of the Valle Umbra is sketched graphically in 4.1.65–6: anyone looking from the valleys (the plural perhaps refers to the different river valleys within the overall Valle Umbra) and seeing the citadels of the walled Umbrian towns rising all around it is invited to associate the height of those walls with Propertius' <towering> poetic genius (*ingenium*). In 4.1.125–6 Propertius' interlocutor Horus restricts this concept, applying it to Asisium proper: as the town climbs, the wall of Asisium rises on its summit, and, according to Horus, it is 'better known' because of Propertius' *ingenium*. As well as implying that Propertius has elevated Asisium above other Umbrian cities through his poetry, this characterization of Asisium is vivid and realistic.[33] The town is

---

29   See Salvatore (1965) 384–7 for a useful discussion of their syntactical difficulties.

30   For the Greek derivation of *Umbria/Ombria* cf. Plin. *NH* 3.112; Solin. 2.11; *LALE* s.vv. Umbri, Umbria; Stok (1996) 576–82; Santini (1996) 520–2. For the possible role of *imber* see *LALE* s.v. imber.

31   If so, Propertius' etymologizing would partly answer the question of Parker (1992) 89: 'Why does Propertius lay such stress on the *fertility* of Umbria …?' Hendry (1997) 602–3 proposes that Propertius is deriving *Umbria* from *umbra* (hence 'Land of Shades'), but this derivation is unattested and implausible.

32   *Umbrorum gens antiquissima Italiae existimatur* (Plin. *NH* 3.112). For further documentation of this and of other ancient beliefs about Umbria and its inhabitants see esp. Stok (1996).

33   Lest this account of the walls of the Umbrian cities (4.1.66) and of Asisium (4.1.125–6) seem laboured or obvious, I note that, according to Newman (1997) 269, the *arces* of 4.1.65 are those of Rome.

indeed markedly higher than its surrounding plains, and it possessed in Propertius' day a complete circuit wall: *murus*, 4.1.125, 126.[34] Propertius' repeated emphases on 'height', viz. *scandentis* (of *arces*, 4.1.65; of *Asis*, 4.1.125), *consurgit*, and *vertice* (4.1.125) suggest, however, that more is involved than an accurate description of Asisium. If etymology is again present, the toponym being glossed cannot be 'Umbria', but might be (?)*As/Asis/Asisium*, always provided that its Umbrian root meant 'high'.[35] Lachmann's emendation of *Asis* (NLF) to *Asisi* at 4.1.125 would be acceptable only if the town was always called *As(s)isium*. But a growing body of opinion favours the view that *Asisium* is a Romanization of an original Umbrian toponym *As* or *Asis* and that Propertius employed the latter form in line 125, thus in part fulfilling his declared intention to sing of 'the old names of places' (*cognomina prisca locorum*, 4.1.69).[36]

Whatever name Propertius gave to Asisium, his emphatic references to its wall in 4.1.125–6 bring us close to the *Realien* of Asisium. The wall of Asisium, which was of some antiquity even in Propertius' day,[37] must have been a major source of civic pride, justifiably since it was a considerable feat of construction extending for 2,500 metres, and hence not much less extensive than Perusia's wall of 2,900 metres. But the link Propertius makes between the wall and his own poetic genius hints that something more personal is also involved. To follow up this hint a brief digression on the second- and first-century BC epigraphic evidence for wall-building at Asisium is needed; it

---

34 On the wall of Asisium cf. Strazzulla (1985) 18–24; Manca (1996); Coarelli (1991); (1996) esp. 243–8.

35 There is no independent evidence of this, although Catullus' *altas ... Alpes* (11.9) and Virgil's *aërias Alpis* (*Georg.* 3.474), which show awareness that '*Alpes* is a Gallic word for high mountain' (O'Hara (1996) 53), reveal what would be a parallel interest.

36 Salvatore (1965) 389–92, although accepting Lachmann's emendation, offers useful parallel material from Tibullus and Ovid. See however Bonamente (1984) 121–4; Poccetti (1986), with additional linguistic confirmation; *ERAssisi* p. 18. For the form *Asis* cf. esp. *Aesis*, as an Umbrian river name (e.g. Strab. 5.1.11, etc.; Plin. *NH* 3.112), and as the ancient toponym of modern Iesi (= Romanized *Aesium* or (?)*Aesulum*), on which see Forni (1982) 24–5.)

37 For what follows see Bradley (2000) 163–71, with full bibliography, referring esp. to Coarelli (1991) and (1996), who challenges the view that most city-wall building in Umbria (and Italy in general) belongs to the mid-first century BC, proposes commencement dates in the later third century BC for a number of Umbrian city walls, including that of Asisium, and sees the invasion of Hannibal as the event which stimulated this activity rather than the troubled conditions of the first century BC. The concept that walls had become the 'indispensable and defining element entitling a human settlement to claim the status of a real city' ('l'elemento indispensabile e carratterizzante perché un insediamento umano si qualificasse con la dignità di vera città', Gabba (1972) 108) can, of course, easily be retrojected.

deserves its space since it will lead us directly to Propertius' family and its status.

Five of the six surviving early Latin public inscriptions of Asisium (two of them virtual duplicates)[38] concern wall construction.[39] Three indubitably concern work on internal terrace walls; the other two (the quasi-duplicates) are perhaps also more likely to be associated with terracing than with the city wall (below); but the distinction is not particularly significant since all five record actions taken by magistrates in their official capacities, and the city wall had an 'intimate connection ... with the terraces supporting the urban layout'.[40] The earliest[41] of the five inscriptions (*ERAssisi* 26), preserved *in situ* in the nave of the cathedral of S. Rufino, documents the construction by six named magistrates (*marones*) of 'a wall from the arch to the circus, and the arch and a cistern'.[42] This *murus* was a terrace wall, but part of it connected with a large tower and portico which has been plausibly interpreted as a monumental gateway leading to the *arx* of Asisium.[43] Next in chronological order – from between the Social War and the late republic – comes *ERAssisi* 29.[44] Its initial portion is missing, but it almost certainly named the members of a board of four *(quattuor)vi]r(i) i(ure) dic(undo)*; the preserved portion names a board of five *(quinque)vir(i)* and records that they *mu[rum faciundum* (or *reficiundum) curarunt probaruntque]*. The *quattuorviri* were in this period the supreme magistrates of Asisium; they probably had ultimate oversight of the building operations, while the *quinqueviri* had hands-on control of the work. Finally, from the late republican period there are the two quasi-duplicates, *ERAssisi* 27 and 28, which seemingly employ virtually the same formula as *ERAssisi* 29. They name four *(quattuor)vir(i) i(ure) d(icundo)* of Asisium and then five

---

38   *ERAssisi* 26, 27, 28, 29, 30. The sixth (*ERAssisi* 31, of Augustan date), records similar work (paving the forum) and names magistrates in groups analogous to those found in the other five.

39   It is assumed that 'repair' would have been memorialized as 'construction', and that the susceptibility of Umbria to earthquakes would have stimulated the process.

40   Bradley (2000) 167.

41   The date of this inscription and of the constructions to which it refers has been controversial. Estimates, based on architectural features, letter-forms and spelling, and the use of Latin rather than Umbrian, have ranged from the later second century BC to after the Social War (see below, p. 12 n. 59). But the controversy does not affect the present discussion.

42   *marones/ murum ab fornice ad circum et fornicem cisternamq(ue) d(e) s(enatus) s(ententia) faciundum coiravere.*

43   For further bibliography and discussion see Coarelli (1991); (1996); Bradley (2000) 167–8.

44   Found *in situ* on the perimeter wall of the forum which supported its highest elevation, and so again referring to an internal wall.

quinquevir(i) in charge of the work, and they record that *s(enatus) c(onsulto) murum reficiundum/ curarunt probaruntque.*[45] If the comparatively high survival rate of such inscriptions is not fortuitous, it reveals an on-going major programme of wall building and repair at Asisium. So the men named in these inscriptions are a sample of the magistrates – *marones, quattuorviri,* and *quinqueviri* – who made up the 'wall-building' elite of Asisium.

Propertius' family belonged to this class. The longest of the early Umbrian inscriptions of Asisium, *ERAssisi* 25, a boundary stone printed and discussed further below (p. 11), mentions four officials, two **ohturs** and two *marones*. One of the **ohturs**, **Ner. T. Babr( )**, is either the same man as Ner. Babrius T.f.,[46] a *maro* in the earliest of the Latin building inscriptions (*ERAssisi* 26), or they are grandfather and grandson.[47] The second **ohtur** of *ERAssisi* 25, **T. V. Voisinier**, is either the father or the son of another *maro* of *ERAssisi* 26, V. Voisienus T.f. One of the two *marones* of *ERAssisi* 25, **C. V. Vistinie**, has two relatives among the *quinqueviri* of another building inscription, *ERAssisi* 29: C. Veistinius C.f. Capito, who could be his son, and Cn. Veistinius Cn. f.; and the second *maro* of *ERAssisi* 25 is (in his Umbrian nomenclature) the first historically attested member of Propertius' family, **Vois. Ner. Propartie**. On the analogy of his three fellow officials of *ERAssisi* 25, this 'Propertius' *maro* will himself have served on wall building commissions and/or will have had relatives who did so over the first century BC. The poet's interest in the *murus* of Asisium suddenly acquires a new dimension: it can be seen to reflect the family pride of the Propertii in their part in the construction and maintenance of walls at Asisium.

Persons bearing the *nomen* 'Propertius(a)', both freeborn and freed slaves, appear epigraphically in many parts of the Roman world over the period 100+/– BC on,[48] but they are concentrated especially in three localities: Africa Proconsularis and Numidia, Rome, and Asisium. The African Propertii are the descendants of Italian emigrants or

---

45 Neither inscription was found *in situ*. *ERAssisi* 29, which uses the same formula, was found *in situ* on a terracing wall, which probably, but not certainly, indicates that *ERAssisi* 27 and 28 also concern, and were originally affixed to, such a wall.

46 In the Umbrian system of nomenclature the father's *praenomen* came immediately after the son's.

47 The usual assumption is that they are the same person, but for the other view see, e.g., Campanile (1996) 188–90. Another family member, C. Babrius C.f. Chilo, appears as an annual magistrate (a *quinquevir*) in *ERAssisi* 29, another wall inscription.

48 Forni (1985).

of their freedmen, or represent provincials who obtained citizenship through magistrates of that name.[49] The presence of one Propertius attested non-epigraphically in Rome around 60 BC was probably temporary (see below, pp. 14–16), but by the early principate at the latest there was a Roman branch of the gens *Propertia*, which belonged to the tribe *Fabia*, whereas the Propertii of Asisium belonged, like most other citizens of Asisium, to the tribe *Sergia*. Since there are very few known freeborn Propertii of Asisium and Rome in the first century BC, the most economic hypothesis is that all belonged to a single extended family.[50] The tribal difference is not an insuperable impediment to this conclusion: two other Umbrians (not from Asisium) domiciled at Rome were also of the *Fabia*, although no Umbrian city is known to have belonged to that tribe.[51] Their families, like the Roman Propertii, would either have gained their citizenship before the Social War or/and changed their tribal affiliation.[52] The *Fabia* was the tribe of the Iulii, and, if the Roman Propertii were of the Marian/ Caesarian persuasion, a reasonable supposition in view of their Caesarian allegiance under the early empire (see below, pp. 37–8, 44–50), their political loyalties could have motivated their enrolment in it.[53] The third and most numerous group of Propertii are found at Asisium, where they originated,[54] and where they continued to live for centuries.[55] The distribution of inscriptions from Umbria naming Propertii further confirms their origin in Asisium: there are sixteen published inscriptions of the Propertii from Asisium, plus, it seems, three more as yet unpublished,[56] but only two from Sentinum and one from Mevania.[57]

---

49   Forni (1985) 209.
50   Forni (1982) 26–7; (1985) 212–16.
51   Forni (1985) 215–16.
52   Forni (1985) 215–16 and Forni (1977) 90–1, listing examples of identical individuals with different tribal affiliations; Wiseman (1964) 131 noted the mutability of pre-Social War tribal affiliations, which suggests that at least the Roman branch of the Propertii gained citizenship before the Social War. On the process in general see Taylor (1960) 23, 280–2.
53   On Julius Caesar's interest in supplementing numbers in the Roman tribes and in creating local tribes in his new foundations cf. Weinstock (1971) 5, 158–62.
54   The historicity of the '*Rex Propertius*' of Veii recorded by Cato (*Origines* 2.17 Chassignet = Servius auct. on *Aen*. 7.697) cannot be assumed; the name 'Propertius' latinises an unknown (?)Etruscan name.
55   An Augustan period inscription (*ERAssisi* 56) documents as a town-councillor of Asisium Cn. Propertius T.f. Scaeva, and further underlines the family's commitment to the town.
56   On these see below, p. 30 and n. 143.
57   The Mevania inscription is of the Neronian/Vespasianic Sex. Caesius Sex. f. Propertianus, a Propertius adopted by a Sex. Caesius: see Cenerini (1985) 212–14; Forni (1985) 216–17,

As already noted, the earliest recorded member of the poet's family, **Vois. Ner. Propartie,** appears in an Umbrian language inscription of Asisium (*ERAssisi* 25). It is complete and reads:

> **ager emps et**
> **termnas oht**
> **c. v. vistinie, ner. t. babr**
> **maronatei**
> **vois. ner. propartie**   5
> **t. v. voisinier**
> **sacre stahu**

ERAssisi (p. 32) offers the Latin translation

> ager emptus et terminatus oht(retie)? C(ai) Veistinii V(--filii), Ner(--) Babrii T(iti filii), in maronatu Vois(--) Propartii Ner(--filii), T(iti) Voisieni V(--filii). Sacre sto.]

> This field was bought and its boundaries determined under the ohturship of C. Vestinius son of V(...), and of Ner(o?) Babrius son of Titus, in the maronate of Vois(...) Propartius son of Ner(o?) and of Titus Voisienus son of V(...). Sacred I stand.

This inscription shows a 'Propertius' holding high public office in Asisium in the late second or early first century BC. This much can be stated uncontroversially. It is also safe to conclude that the stone is not a state boundary marker of Asisium, but a private marker recording a purchase of land, a transaction between individuals (**ager emps et termnas** = *ager emptus et terminatus*, 1–2). However, the stone has two public aspects, its invocation of a religious sanction (**sacre stahu** = *sacre sto*, 7), and its naming of magistrates as dating and/or endorsing the sale. It is not important for the early history of Propertius' family whether the *marones* were, or were not, then the supreme magistrates of Asisium.[58] It is enough that **Vois. Ner. Propartie** held

220. Caesii are widely distributed – cf. Cenerini (1985); (1996) – and they are found at Asisium as donors of the so-called 'temple of Minerva' (actually a temple of the Dioscuri) in the Augustan period (cf. *ERAssisi* 9).

58 For various views of ohturs see, e.g., U. Coli (1964) 142–3; Prosdocimi (1981) 558–9; Campanile (1996) 183–5; Bradley (2000) 179–81. Most modern opinion holds that in *ERAssisi* 25 the *marones* (the magistracy was borrowed from Etruria by some Umbrian towns, including Asisium) are junior to the ohturs, whereas in *ERAssisi* 26 the six *marones* seem to be the supreme magistrates. On the *marones* of *ERAssisi* 26 see, e.g., Strazzulla (1983) 155; Prosdocimi (1981) 560; Campanile (1996) 182–4; Bradley (2000) 180: 'best seen as three pairs'.

high office there, which places the family socially in the top rank at Asisium in **Propartie's** time. Nor is it crucial whether that time was before or after the Social War;[59] **Vois. Ner. Propartie** belonged in any event to the generation of either the poet's grandfather or great-grandfather. His maronate has the further implication that, before they obtained Roman citizenship,[60] the Propertii of Asisium already possessed sufficient wealth[61] to qualify them for important local magistracies. This strengthens the view that, when Propertius wrote *notis Penatibus* at 4.1.121, he was thinking not just of Umbria's claims to high status but also (as at 1.22.1: *qui sint mihi, Tulle, Penates*), of the household of the Propertii, and of their claim to high status, and was in effect proclaiming the (local) *nobilitas*[62] of his own family. On this interpretation the assertion of *notis Penatibus* coheres with Propertius' further claim of a few lines later (126) that the wall (of Asisium) has become *notior* through his personal poetic genius (*ingenium*); compare the similar sentiment of 4.1.66.

Not only were the Propertii still among the most powerful families of Asisium in the poet's lifetime, but the presence of Propertii at Asisium throughout the early empire continued to be reflected epigraphically. *ERAssisi* contains 286 items. All are preserved by chance, and they come from several centuries, so the corpus is not a fit object

---

59 Umbrian *ERAssisi* 25 used to be dated to before the Social War, and Latin *ERAssisi* 26 to after it, on the assumption that Latin became the official language of Asisium after the Social War (cf., e.g., *ERAssisi* p. 32 on *ERAssisi* 25). More recent opinion, however, would allow Latin to have been used for some epigraphic purposes before the Social War and Umbrian (as possibly in *ERAssisi* 25) for others after it (much rests on how the relationships between the men of *ERAssisi* 25–9 are understood, on letter forms, and on when the transition from Umbrian to Roman magistracies took place). Hence Bradley (2000) dates *ERAssisi* 25 to 100–80 BC (286), and prefers a date of 110–90 BC for *ERAssisi* 26 (295); see also 178–81. Coarelli (1991) and (1996) had already reversed the chronology of the two inscriptions, and had judged the Latin inscription *ERAssisi* 26 to be from some decades before 100 BC and at most 30 years older than the Umbrian inscription *ERAssisi* 25.

60 This is on the presumption that the Umbrian nomenclature of **Vois. Ner. Propartie** means he was not a Roman citizen; this presumption may, however, be unwarranted, since in a local context a magistrate might perhaps have preferred to retain his epichoric appellation. Marius granted citizenship on the battlefield to two cohorts of Umbrian cavalry from Camerinum in 101 BC (Cic. *Pro Balb.* 46).

61 I.e. at least the *census equester*. The usage of the term '*eques*' has been a matter of lively scholarly discussion. It is used throughout this book in the non-technical sense of 'possessed of (at least) the *census equester*', not in the technical sense of '*eques equo publico*'. For a sensible view of the *equites* as a group and for documentation of relevant controversies see Berry (2003) 222–3.

62 On the etymological group to which *notus* belongs cf. *LALE* s.vv. nobilis; nobilito; nomen. For fuller discussion of such terms in the works of Cornelius Gallus and Propertius see Cairns (1983a) 84–6 with earlier bibliography, and below, Index II, s.v. *nobilis*.

for statistical analysis. But, interestingly, there are more inscriptions of the Propertii than of any other family of Asisium:[63]

PROPERTII	16
MIMI/ESII[64]	14 + 1(?)
VESPRII	10 + 2(?)
ATTII	10
PETRONII	9
V(E)ISTINII	8
ABURII	6 + 1(?)
ALLII	7
VOLCASII	7
VETURII	6

and the Propertii were also seemingly the first family to produce a senator – C. Propertius Q. f. T. n. Fab. Postumus[65] – although he was from the Roman branch with the 'Roman' *Fabia* tribal affiliation. The Mimi(e)sii were the next family from Asisium to enter the senate (in the reign of Tiberius?), in the person of Postumus Mimisius C.f. Sardus,[66] a man with the same *praenomen* and filiation as his presumed ancestor, one of the Mimesii *marones* of *ERAssisi* 26.[67] The Propertii and the Mimesii thus emerge as prominent survivors of the Civil Wars, proscriptions, and land confiscations: some other families of Asisium, such as the Babrii and Voisieni, who had been leading lights in the later second and earlier first centuries BC, clearly declined or disappeared under the early empire. Contrariwise other families with no early prominence, such as the Caesii and Petronii,

---

63 Only the families most often represented are included in the table, and inscriptions, not individuals, are counted. All inscriptions (but only those from Asisium) recording family members, freedpeople and adoptees are taken account of. Dubious cases are indicated (?); since judgement is involved, the totals differ slightly from those indicated by *ERAssisi* pp. 19–20. The few relevant inscriptions found since the publication of *ERAssisi* do not alter the overall picture.

64 For the 'bolli laterizi' of this family see Spadoni Cerroni (1996).

65 *PIR*² P 1010, on whom see also below, pp. 16–20, 22–4.

66 Wiseman (1971) no. 255; *EOS* II.262 (M. Gaggiotti and L. Sensi); *PIR*² M 592. His exact relationship to his ancestor remains to be determined. *CIL* XIV.3598.2 reveals that he was '*legatus Ti. Caesaris Augusti*' (*PIR*² thinks probably as a legionary legate); this is another of the Tiberian connections of Asisium.

67 T. Olius C. f. Gargenna of *ERAssisi* 31 may be the father or grandfather of T. Ollius, quaestor of AD 31 (cf. *EOS* II.252 (M. Gaggiotti and L. Sensi); Sensi (1983) 166–8), although *PIR*² O 96 prefers an origin for the latter in Cupra Maritima and regards the assignment to Asisium as made 'sine idonea causa'. If *PIR*² is wrong, the Ol(l)ii were the third family of Asisium to reach the senate, and another Tiberian link for Asisium emerges.

start to flourish under Augustus; they were probably late republican or Augustan incomers.[68]

Even over a century after the poet's lifetime, an important member of the Propertii was still residing at Asisium. Pliny *Epistulae* 6.15.1[69] describes a contemporary *splendidus eques Romanus*, Passennus Paullus, as a descendant and 'fellow-townsman' (*municeps*) of the poet; and this same man's full nomenclature appears in *ERAssisi* 47 = *CIL* XI 5405, found at Asisium near the church of S. Feliciano:[70] *C. Passennus C.f. Serg. Paullus Propertius Blaesus* – a Propertius adopted by a Passennus Paullus or with a maternal connection to the Passenni.[71] The *nomen* Passennus is otherwise attested at Asisium.[72] Passennus Paullus' tribe is the *Sergia*, which confirms Pliny's location of his (principal) residence at Asisium, as does the fact that *ERAssisi* 47 is his funerary inscription. One naturally wonders whether there is any significance in the fact that his second *cognomen* Blaesus is also that of Seianus' *avunculus*, Q. Iunius Blaesus, cos. suff. AD 10, of a family (like that of Seianus) from Etruscan Volsinii.[73]

The branch of the Propertii already established at Rome before the poet's advent there has already been mentioned, and there is a recorded presence of an individual Propertius at Rome in the generation preceding that of the poet and Propertius Postumus. He could, of course, have been one of the Roman Propertii, or another distant relative, but there is also the possibility that he was the poet's father: the Propertii of Asisium, because of their influential position there, must have had links with Rome independent of the *Fabia* branch. At *De Domo Sua* 49, as part of his claim that juries would on all occasions seek to slight Clodius, Cicero (addressing Clodius) gives a brief and opaque account of the activities of one of Clodius' agents, Aelius Ligus:

---

68 These may well be families which benefited from land redistributions in the aftermath of the Perusine War. The modern toponym of Petrignano d'Assisi (= *Petronianum*: see Santucci (1976) 225) presumably reveals the location of one of the estates of the Petronii.
69 Cf. also 9.22.1–2.
70 The find spot was recorded by Frondini: see Bonamente and Catanzaro (1996) 62.
71 Cf. also *PIR*² P 141; Forni (1985) 212–13, 220; and below, pp. 26, 31, 53–4.
72 *ERAssisi* 172.
73 On the consul (*PIR*² I 738) see Syme (1986) Index of Persons s.v. Junius Blaesus, Q. (suff. AD 10); on the connections between the Propertii and the Aelii Galli, the adoptive family of L. Aelius Seianus, see below, pp. 20–1, and for a summary of the other established and possible Tiberian links with Asisium, see below, pp. 24–5. It must, however, be emphasized that, although the Iunii Blaesi (cf. also *PIR*² I 737 and I 739) are the most prominent first-century AD bearers of the *cognomen* 'Blaesus', there are a number of others.

denique etiam ille novicius Ligus, venalis adscriptor et subscriptor tuus, cum M. Papiri, sui fratris, esset testamento et iudicio improbatus, mortem eius se velle persequi dixit. nomen Sex. Properti detulit. accusare alienae dominationis scelerisque socius propter calumniae metum non est ausus.

Lastly, even that upstart Ligus, who was always ready to sell you his signature and his support in a prosecution, when he had been disgraced and judgement passed on him by being left out of the will of his brother Marcus Papirius, said that he wanted to investigate Papirius' death, and accused Sextus Propertius in connection with it. But being partner to another man's wicked despotism, he did not venture to go on with the prosecution since he feared a conviction for false accusation. (tr. R. G. Nisbet, adapted)

The standard commentary on *De Domo Sua*[74] ignores the Sex. Propertius named here, but the suggestion that he might be the father of the poet was made long ago.[75] We know from Propertius himself (4.1.127–34) that his father died before the poet reached formal adulthood. But his death cannot be dated precisely, and the first sight we have of the poet is when he is already established at Rome in the early 20s BC, so his prior life can only be reconstructed from his own autobiographical remarks. However, the Sex. Propertius of *De Domo Sua* 49 could easily from a chronological standpoint be the poet's father, the date of the supposed events described there being around 60 BC;[76] and, although not too much should be made of this, the *praenomen* Sextus is comparatively[77] rare among the Propertii.[78] Whether or not Cicero's Sex. Propertius was the poet's father, *De Domo Sua* 49 could shed light on the political bias of the Propertii in 60 BC. At first sight it might appear to portray its Sex. Propertius as an ally of Cicero and so, in the context of *circa* 60 BC, as opposed to Clodius and Julius Caesar. But it probably reveals the reverse. The

---

74   R. G. Nisbet (1939).
75   See Rothstein (1920–4) I.4.
76   The alternative possibility that he was the poet's grandfather cannot be excluded but is less plausible.
77   The commoner attested *praenomina* of freeborn Propertii are: Gaius – Asisium: 14; Rome: 10; elsewhere: 14; Quintus – Rome: 8; Numidia: 1; Lucius – Africa: 7; see Forni (1985) 218–23.
78   I.e. the poet himself, the manumitter of a freedman buried at Rome, possibly the poet (see below, p. 28), his possible father of *De Domo Sua* 49, a Sextus at Asisium who manumitted a Tertia, again possibly the poet (see below, p. 29), one in Apulia (partly restored), and one in Numidia. The Sex. Caesius Sex. f. Propertianus epigraphically attested at Mevania (see above, p. 10 n. 57) could have derived his *praenomen* and filiation from his adopter.

story Cicero tells is, to say the least, peculiar. Aelius Ligus is alleged to have initiated a prosecution (*nomen detulit*) against Sex. Propertius, and then to have failed to carry the case forward (*accusare ... non est ausus*) because he was afraid that the jury would not convict and that he himself would be liable to prosecution for false accusation (*calumnia*). What Cicero fails to reveal is that Aelius Ligus was his own former ally, who in 58 BC had been bribed by Clodius to change sides and who then became a strenuous opponent of Cicero.[79] Since the events described were in train before 58 BC, the truth about Ligus' prosecution of Sex. Propertius is likely to be other than Cicero suggests. Ligus must have started it when he himself was an ally of Cicero; hence, if there was a political dimension to the prosecution, Sex. Propertius will have been on the side of Clodius and/or Caesar. A more plausible explanation of Ligus' discontinuation of his prosecution now presents itself than the one offered by Cicero: having been bribed to change sides, Ligus had no reason to continue proceedings against an adherent (Sex. Propertius) of his own new political master(s)! Cicero tells the story tendentiously against Clodius, and feigns good-hearted sympathy with Sex. Propertius as part of his strategy of blackening Clodius.

Various other contemporary or near-contemporary blood and marital relatives of Propertius also merit introduction. Of these his mother, a significant presence in Propertius 4.1.131–2, was dead by 25 BC (cf. Propertius 2.20.15); a speculation about her is offered below, pp. 61–2. The 'Gallus' of 1.21, arguably identical with his 'kinsman' (*propinquus*) of 1.22.7, is discussed below (pp. 49–50). Other relatives can be treated here; first there is the already mentioned C. Propertius Postumus (*PIR*[2] P 1010), whose funerary inscription is *CIL* IV.1501:

> C(aius) Propertius Q(uinti) f(ilius) T(iti) n(epos) Fab(ia) Postumus /
> IIIvir cap(italis) et insequenti anno pro / IIIvir(o) q(uaestor) pr(aetor)
> desig(natus) ex s(enatus) c(onsulto) viar(um) cur(andarum) pr(aetor) /
> ex s(enatus) c(onsulto) pro aed(ilibus) cur(ulibus) ius dixit pro
> co(n)s(ule)

Postumus' career under Augustus fits the expectations for someone of his background, a *novus homo* whose family came originally from an Italian *municipium*. He served twice in the same office in the vigintivirate (the initial stage of an aspiring senator's career), as *IIIvir capitalis*

---

and then as *proIIIvir capitalis*. Because this position involved holding court as a judge of common criminals it required some knowledge of the law,[80] and it was also, because of the sordidness of its duties, the least honorific among the positions open to *vigintiviri*. *Nobiles* avoided it, aspiring rather in the early empire to be moneyers, hence *IIIviri capitales* tended to be *novi*.[81] There was also a shortage of candidates for the vigintivirate in general, so a 'new man' like Postumus would have gained additional credit with Augustus by serving an extra year in the undesiderable role of *proIIIvir capitalis*;[82] his *cursus* inscription, with its emphatic *insequenti anno*, places due emphasis on this supererogatory service. An analogous pattern of an iterated year in the less desirable offices within the vigintivirate can be found in the early career of another *novus*, the poet Ovid, who served once as *IIIvir capitalis* and then again, probably as *Xvir stlitibus iudicandis*.[83] Ovid abandoned his political career for poetry, but Postumus persisted and subsequently became quaestor. After his quaestorship Postumus was designated praetor and served by special senate appointment as *curator viarum*. This position shows that Postumus had acquired imperial favour, probably because, typically of an imperial 'new man' and in contrast to young *nobiles* who expected high office as their heritage, he had shown himself willing to seek career advancement by assiduous performance of essential administrative tasks. An interesting sidelight on Postumus' role as *curator viarum* derives from the fact that Augustus personally took on the overall *cura viarum* in 20 BC and then delegated it to a group of *curatores viarum*. But Augustus continued in some sense to take special responsibility for the *via Flaminia*, the vital military road linking Rome and Ariminum, which he had reconstructed over its whole length.[84] It may be pure coincidence that Asisium lies near the *Flaminia*; but it is at least worth entertaining the possibility that Postumus' duties were those later performed by the formally named senatorial *curator viae Flaminiae*,[85] and that his appointment had something to do with the residence in Asisium of the

---

80   See Kenney (1969), 243–4, with bibliography at 244 n. 5.
81   On the status of the different posts in the vigintivirate in the late republic and early empire see Wiseman (1971) 147–53; Kienast (1982) Register: Namen und Sachen s.v. Vigintivirat.
82   Wiseman (1971) 152.
83   For the details of Ovid's legal experience, and his further roles as *centumvir* and *iudex* see esp. Kenney (1969) 243–9; *PIR*² O 180. For the view that in this period municipal aristocrats of equestrian status tended to show particular interest in jurisprudence see Frier (1985) 253–60.
84   Kienast (1982) 411; Eck (1996) 291–2.
85   Eck (1996) 291–2, 296–9.

other branch of the Propertii. Following this praetorian function, Postumus served as praetor, but once more in a judicial role,[86] and once more by special senatorial appointment. This time he stood in for a curule aedile, which again speaks equally of imperial favour and of the quality of his work. His *cursus* inscription then shows Postumus moving finally to a proconsulship in an unknown province. All in all Postumus enjoyed as much career success as a man of his background with 'civil' skills could have hoped for in this period.

The precise nature of Propertius Postumus' blood relationship to the poet cannot be recovered, but that they were fairly closely related (cousins in some degree?) seems likely.[87] It is also likely that, as most scholars have presumed, the 'Postumus' of Propertius 3.12 is the same man.[88] In particular the intimate ways in which Propertius refers to the relationship of Postumus with his wife (*uxor*, 37), who is named 'Galla' six times in the elegy, can best be explained on the hypothesis of a family relationship. The Postumus of Propertius 3.12 is represented as being on an Eastern expedition against the Parthians around 21 BC, as functioning on it in a military capacity, and as being in danger of death in action. Propertius then transmutes him into a deutero-Ulysses who will return from his travels to find his wife a second faithful Penelope. However, the expedition to recover the Parthian standards, although depicted as a great military adventure, not just by Augustan poets but by the senate which offered Augustus a triumph, in fact involved a pre-negotiated and staged concession on the part of the Parthians; the almost contemporary activities of Tiberius in Armenia were equally free of danger.[89]

Postumus' soldierly role is manifestly exaggerated in 3.12, as are for other purposes the bellicose aspects of the entire Eastern expedition in Propertius' description of its departure from Rome in 3.4. Propertius' account in 3.12 of Postumus' activities is full of elegiac clichés: it even employs the standard association of war and greed (3–6), and its conventional details are similar to those of Tibullus' version

---

86   Syme (1986) 308 suggested that Postumus' probable father-in-law, L. Aelius Gallus, was a
    relative of the late republican jurist C. Aelius Gallus, an interesting link in view of Postu-
    mus' possible legal specialization.
87   E.g., among numerous other scholars, Wiseman (1971) 254; Bonamente (2004) 34; *contra*
    only P. White (1993) 251. The fact that the *gens* was not widespread argues for a fairly
    close relationship.
88   Cf. also *PIR*² P 1010 (K. Wachtel), and Nisbet and Hubbard (1978) 223–5 (with earlier
    bibliography); only P. White (1993) 251 disagrees.
89   See, e.g., Syme (1978) 31–2; Kienast (1982) 282–4.

of Macer's soldiering in 2.6. The real-life C. Propertius Postumus may, of course, have served on at least one military campaign at the beginning of his career, and he may even have held a military tribunate before his vigintivirate, although this is not recorded in his *cursus* inscription. But even such positions could be mainly administrative, and Postumus' subsequent career shows no trace of the military. The presumption, then, must be that he was an administrator, possibly a legal specialist. Propertius *qua* elegist will have enjoyed transforming the peaceable Postumus into a great warrior, and this aspect of Postumus explains some of the make-up of the poem, in particular its hyperbolic Ulysses comparison:[90] with no possibility of seeing real action, Postumus can be lauded only via the reflected glory of the warlike Ulysses. Propertius associates Postumus' participation in the Parthian expedition with Augustus (2), not surprisingly since the whole enterprise was carried out under Augustus' auspices, and Augustus himself travelled to the East at this time. But, although Propertius' *Augusti fortia signa* (2) is both formally and historically correct, as well as tactful, Postumus may have accompanied Tiberius, not Augustus, to the East. He is not one of the four members of Tiberius' *cohors* featured in Horace *Epistles* 1.3,[91] but Tiberius must have had more than four *comites*. A possible confirmation of this suggestion will emerge below (pp. 22–4).

The addressee of Horace *Odes* 2.14 is also a 'Postumus', and the best commentators on Horace *Odes* 2 think it plausible that he is the same man as the epigraphic C. Postumus Propertius and the Postumus of Propertius 3.12.[92] The coincidence between Propertius' repeated stress on Postumus' wife's love and fidelity (despite its being partly dictated by Propertius' elegiac mandate)[93] and Horace's mention of Postumus' *placens/ uxor* (21–2) is striking, as is that between Propertius' use of *Odyssey* material (including the *katabasis*, 33) and Horace's emphasis on the underworld (7–12, 17–20). The only worthwhile argument which has been advanced against the identification is

---

90   For a more detailed analysis of 3.12 see *GC* 197–201. Propertius' treatment of Postumus in 3.12 is also similar (*mutatis mutandis*) to Horace's treatment of Iccius in *Od.* 1.29.

91   Hor. *Epist.* 1.9 recommends to Tiberius a Septimius who may have been another *comes* of this expedition.

92   Nisbet and Hubbard (1978) 223–5. Their remark apropos of Horace's reflections in *Od.* 2.14 on the underworld (7–12, 17–20): 'Perhaps Postumus had Etruscan associations' (230), is worth highlighting in the present context.

93   Similar sentiments appear in Prop. 4.3, where the couple are 'Lycotas' and 'Arethusa', but the circumstances could fit Postumus and Aelia Galla; 4.3 looks like a reworking of 3.12.

that the Postumus of Horace *Odes* 2.14 seems, at first sight, older than the Postumus of Propertius 3.12.[94] However, this argument is probably nugatory: whereas one might assume from Propertius 3.12 that Postumus is a young man recently married, there are other possibilities. Postumus' date of birth is unknown, as is the date at which he began his senatorial career. He might well have been older than the poet, or/and a late starter in his career, with a younger[95] (perhaps a second?) wife. Horace's Postumus is, as C. Propertius Postumus would have been, a man of property (cf. his well-forested estates, 22–4) and of wealth (his cellar contained expensive Caecuban wine, 25–8). His heir, mentioned by Horace (25), is discussed below, pp. 22–4.

Of the six occasions on which Propertius names the wife of his addressee Postumus in 3.12, five employ 'Galla' and one (in the manuscripts of Propertius) 'L(a)el(l)ia Galla'.[96] The latter combination is prosopographically most improbable;[97] and the editors of Propertius are very probably correct when they unanimously eliminate the initial L and identify Galla as an 'Aelia Galla' (*PIR*² A 294). Through Aelia Galla the poet is linked with two early Prefects of Egypt: she was the sister, daughter,[98] or niece of L.[99] Aelius Gallus (*PIR*² A 179), second *praefectus Aegypti* (26–24 BC).[100] This man adopted, probably around 20 BC, a son of L. Seius Strabo from Etruscan Volsinii (*PIR*¹ S 246);[101] and it so happens that L. Seius Strabo was later briefly *praefectus Aegypti* (AD 15).[102] The adopted son, L. Aelius Seianus (*PIR*² A 255), eventually emerged as the notorious favourite of Tiberius. The adoption of Seianus may have resulted from the tragic death at sea of 'Paetus', the subject of Propertius 3.7, if, as has been suggested, Paetus was the son of L. Aelius Gallus.[103] Paetus died on a voyage to Egypt, an understandable destination if his father was prefect there; and the tone of Propertius 3.7 lends further credibility to the sugges-

94 P. White (1993) 251. But the point was already answered by Nisbet and Hubbard (1978) 223.
95 This suspicion was voiced by Nisbet and Hubbard (1978) 223.
96 Galla: 3.12.1, 4, 15, 19, 21; L(a)el(l)ia Galla: 3.12.38.
97 The only significant Laelii of this period in *PIR*² are Laelii Balbi (L 46, 47, 48, 49, ?57, ?58). The only scholar who adheres to the reading 'Laelia Galla' is P. White (1993) 250.
98 Nisbet and Hubbard (1978) 223–4.
99 On his *praenomen* (L., not 'M.(?)' as in *PIR*²) see Syme (1986) 302 n. 25.
100 Stein (1950) 15–17; Bowersock (1965) 128–9.
101 On Seius Strabo and his relations see Syme (1986) Ch. 22 ('Kinsmen of Seianus'), and Table XIII; Nisbet and Hubbard (1978) 223–4; Salomies (1992) 23 n. 5.
102 Stein (1950) 24–5.
103 Syme (1986) 308.

tion that Paetus was Aelius Gallus' son, and so related by marriage to the poet. Lamentations and reproaches are, of course, conventional in an *epikedion*,[104] but Propertius criticises Paetus in ways which might have seemed inappropriate had Paetus been a stranger, but which can be paralleled in ancient laments for those near and dear.[105] With 3.7 may be contrasted 3.18, the *epikedion* for Marcellus, from which such reproaches of the deceased are absent. The dead man's *cognomen* Paetus will have been allotted to his son by L. Aelius Gallus with the intention of staking a family claim to descent from, or consanguinity with, the famous consuls of 201 BC (P. Aelius Paetus) and 198 BC (Sex. Aelius Paetus): a parallel indirect claim is made a little later among the Aelii Tuberones through the name Aelia Paetina.[106] Propertius' somewhat odd emphasis on the 'poverty' which his dead Paetus would have endured had he stayed on land (*pauper, at in terra*, 3.7.46) may hark back to another Aelian claim to fame: the *Aelia familia* of the early second century BC was celebrated for combining virtue, high status, extraordinary fecundity, and grinding poverty.[107]

The Etruscan origin of the Sei Strabones, coming on top of Propertius' early patronage by the Etruscan Volcacii of Perusia (see below, pp. 42–4, 59–62), is part of a more general pattern which will emerge among the relations and contacts of Propertius, and which probably played a part in the poet's entry into the circle of the Etruscan Maecenas in the mid-20s BC.[108] The mother of Seianus' natural father, L. Seius Strabo, was a Terentia A. f., and so either sister to, or at any rate related to, Maecenas' wife Terentia.[109] Seianus has a further link with Asisium if the family of one of his prominent partisans, T. Ollius, father of Nero's wife Poppaea, was from Asisium.[110] The prefecture of Egypt certainly has yet another connection with Asisium: Aelius Gallus' successor, the third *praefectus Egypti*

---

104 See Esteve Forriol (1962) 137–40; on Prop. 3.7, see 119–20.
105 See Alexiou (1974) 182–4, citing classical and Byzantine Greek examples.
106 Syme (1986) 306.
107 Val. Max. 4.4.8.
108 There may even have been a relationship of some sort between Propertius' earlier patron, Volcacius Tullus, and Maecenas: see Hammond (1980) and below, pp. 252–3.
109 Cf. above, p. 20 n. 101. Syme (1986) 301–4 convincingly recovers *CIL* XI.7285 for L. Seius Strabo (cf. also *CIL* XI.2707). The strangely mixed treatment of Maecenas by a client of Seianus, Velleius Paterculus (2.88.2–3), which combines emphasis on Maecenas' excellent family background, his 'effeminate' life-style, and his (unlauded) lack of ambition, could easily reflect Seianus' personal judgement of his relative Maecenas.
110 See above, p. 13 n. 67.

(from 25–21 BC), was P. Petronius (*PIR*² P 270)[111] from a family of Asisium;[112] a later inscription of Asisium (*ERAssisi* 51) associates the Petronii and a Propertius.[113] The prefecture of Egypt was a position of the highest trust in view of that province's strategic role in the Roman East and its economic role in the corn-supply of Rome; and it is compatible with the political commitment proposed in this and the following chapter for Propertius' family and for his native Asisium that they crop up so frequently in proximity to the prefecture. The links become even more intriguing when we consider on one hand the failure in loyalty of the first *praefectus Egypti*, C. Cornelius Gallus, who paid for it with his life, and on the other the strong influence of Gallan elegy upon Propertius and the probability (advanced below, pp. 42–3) that Gallus was also one of Propertius' first patrons.

Another Propertius is documented early in the reign of Tiberius, Propertius Celer (*PIR*² P 1007, *praenomen* unknown). Tacitus relates (*Annales* 1.75) that in AD 15 Celer applied to retire from the senate because of his poverty and that Tiberius assisted him financially with a gift of one million sesterces (thereby giving him the minimum senatorial *census*):[114]

> Propertio Celeri praetorio, veniam ordinis ob paupertatem petenti, decies sestertium largitus est, satis conperto paternas ei angustias esse.

Syme hinted that Tiberius was generous to Celer because he liked the poetry of Propertius, which might imply that he thought Celer was the poet's son.[115] However Celer is perhaps more likely to have been the son (and heir) of C. Propertius Postumus; like him Celer reached the praetorship, and Tacitus significantly makes Tiberius describe Celer's poverty as 'paternal'. Against this, Horace's ode to Postumus (2.14), in which he encourages Postumus to enjoy his wealth while he is still

---

111 Stein (1950) 17–18. For his *praenomen* (P. rather than C.) cf. *PIR*² P 270. He is another man with a Tiberian connection: the fact that his son or grandson, another P. Petronius (suffect consul 19 AD; *PIR*² P 269), was proconsul of Asia for six years under Tiberius (see also Syme (1986) 237) casts the Petronii as his long-term adherents and favourites. Other family members also reached the consulship: see Coarelli (1996) 258.

112 For the discussion of the family and its presence at Asisium see Coarelli (1996) 252–8, with a conjectural stemma at 258.

113 Cf. also Coarelli (1966) 255.

114 For the difficulties which some minor senatorial houses found in maintaining their status see Hopkins (1983) 74–8.

115 Syme (1986) 361.

alive, might easily be taken as the 'Epicurean' poet's conventional moralizing counsel to a miserly rich man, suggesting that Postumus was a skinflint rather than a spendthrift. But this would be a mistake: it is now recognized that, rather than proffer unsought and unwelcome advice to his patrons, Horace's injunctions in his *Odes* flatter the already established traits, interests and attitudes of his addressees.[116] The real-life Postumus may have had morbid preoccupations with death, and this could explain the engagement of *Odes* 2.14 with that topic.[117] But it should not be assumed that he was also pious, frugal, and intent on hoarding his wealth. Rather we should start from the assumption that Postumus was already doing what Horace was urging him to do, namely enjoying his riches and making sure that they did not descend to his heir (25). Postumus' *heres* might be a mere generalization; but he could be Celer, who, as an ex-praetor in AD 15, is of the right age to be the *heres* of Postumus if Postumus and Aelia Galla married in the mid to late 20s BC.[118] If so, the straitened circumstances of Celer would confirm that Postumus had been consuming his wealth without thought for his *heres* (*Odes* 2.14.22–4 might hint at heavy expenditure on arboriculture)[119] before Horace enjoined him to do so.

Tacitus' description of Tiberius' action in relieving Celer's 'poverty' looks like a paraphrase of Tiberius' very words in the senate as recorded in the *acta senatus*: in particular the expression *satis conperto paternas ei angustias esse* implies that Tiberius expressed his judgement on the extravagance of Celer's father in tactfully veiled terms by saying that Celer's poverty was inherited. We might well ask why Tiberius showed such tact, and indeed why he showed generosity towards Celer when, as Tacitus goes on to relate, he refused to follow up his grant to Celer with parallel aid to subsequent applicants (*Annales* 1.75). One reason which suggests itself is that, if Postumus, as proposed above, accompanied Tiberius, not Augustus, to the East in 21–20 BC, he would have been a former *comes* of the future emperor.

116 Cf. Nisbet and Hubbard on *Odes* 2.3 and 2.10, and esp. their remark 'In his paraeneses Horace normally advised his patrons to do what they are doing already' (157). Horace was thus able to simulate veracity by playing the Alcaic/hellenistic role of parrhesiastic preceptor to his addressees while avoiding giving offence to these same *laudandi*.
117 Cf. Nisbet and Hubbard (1978) 223–4, 229–33.
118 He may, of course, have been Postumus' son by an earlier marriage.
119 Propertius Postumus' *cura viarum* may also have been a costly office: *RE* Suppl. 13 s.v. Viae Publicae Romanae (G. Radke), esp. coll. 1473–5, which assemble some examples of individuals' expenditures on public roads.

Tiberius' long memory for favours and slights, and his loyalty to his friends were notorious.[120] Financial aid to the son of an old friend and tactful handling of an old friend's memory could account fully for the incident as related by Tacitus, and would also explain why Tiberius did not treat other senators similarly. If Celer was indeed the son of Postumus, it would not have harmed his case if he was also the son of Aelia Galla, daughter (or niece) of the adoptive father of L. Aelius Seianus, whose star began to rise in AD 14, when he was made joint Prefect of the praetorian guard along with his natural father, L. Seius Strabo.

The Tiberian connection with the Propertii and so indirectly with Asisium which would be evident here is consonant with those other links between Tiberius and Asisium which have so far been indicated only in passing. It involves Seianus (above, pp. 21–2) (and perhaps his *avunculus* Iunius Blaesus), the Aelii Galli (pp. 20–1), and various families of Asisium – the Propertii through Propertius Postumus (pp. 19, 22), the Petronii (p. 22 and n. 112), the Mimisii (p. 13 and n. 66), and possibly the Ol(l)ii (pp. 13 n. 67, 21). Other pieces of evidence fit the same pattern, starting with a pair of honorific inscriptions (*ERAssisi* 10 and 11) erected by the *seviri* of Asisium. The honorands are the consuls of 7 BC, the future emperor Tiberius and Cn. Calpurnius Piso, then a close associate of Tiberius, whose later involvement in the death of Germanicus would lead to his fall in AD 20. The intent of the inscriptions is clearly to record thanks for a significant benefit conferred by those consuls on Asisium. Its nature is unknown, but it has been pointed out that it would have been the outcome of an embassy to Rome led by representatives of the senatorial and high equestrian families of Asisium, among whom the Propertii, Petronii, Mimesii, and ?Ollii are likely to have featured.[121] Then there is the temple erected in the forum of Asisium, probably before 20 BC, by the (twin?) brothers Cn. and T. Caesius (cf. *ERAssisi* 9), for which a Tiberian link has also been hypothesized.[122] It was almost certainly dedicated to the twins Castor and Pollux, whose statues were later placed before it in a tetrastyle (cf. *ERAssisi* 3). This benefaction is similar to the dedication in AD 6 of the restored temple of the Dios-

---

120 E.g. Tac. *Ann.* 1.4; 2.42; 3.48; 4.15.
121 For these suggestions about the function and background of the two inscriptions see Eck (1996) 288–9. The date of Propertius Postumus' death is not known; if alive he would presumably have assisted the embassy or taken part in it.
122 By Coarelli (1991) 20, from whom what follows is derived.

curi at Rome by Tiberius, in his own name and in that of his dead brother Drusus, an action which has been linked with dynastic politics, the Dioscuri being emblematic of the two princes.[123]

The death of Propertius' father – whether or not he was Cicero's Sex. Propertius – before the poet reached formal manhood and the poet's later loss of family land have already been mentioned. In 4.1.127–34 the astrologer Horus addresses Propertius:

> ossaque legisti non illa aetate legenda
> patris, et in tenuis cogeris ipse lares:
> nam tua cum multi versarent rura iuvenci,
> abstulit excultas pertica tristis opes.   130
> mox ubi bulla rudi dimissast aurea collo,
> matris et ante deos libera sumpta toga,
> tum tibi pauca suo de carmine dictat Apollo
> et vetat insano verba tonare Foro.

And you collected your father's bones, which you should not have been collecting at that age, and you were constrained into a humbler home; for, although many oxen had ploughed your country estates, the grim measuring-rod took away your rich arable land. Presently, when the golden amulet was taken off your young neck and you put on the toga of an adult man before your mother's gods, then Apollo dictated some smatterings of his own song to you and forbade you to thunder your words in the insane law courts.

The linkage between the death of the poet's father and the confiscation of family land (129–30) some time after Philippi[124] (see also below, pp. 50–9), might imply that, if still alive, his father could have prevented this. Certainly the placement of the confiscation before Propertius' legal majority through his assumption of the *toga virilis* proclaims his own lack of responsibility for the loss. The normal age for this ceremony was sixteen, but civil unrest may have delayed it in Propertius' case. *mox* (131) is imprecise,[125] although in context it does not suit a date of much after 40 BC, and so points to 58–55 BC as his date of birth. The Monobiblos (28 BC?) displays considerable poetic maturity and much Greek and Roman learning, and it shows Propertius well established in his circle of patrons and friends at Rome.

---

123 For an overview of this area of imperial ideology see Poulsen (1991); on its application to Tiberius and Drusus, Schoonhoven (1992) 15–18; Bannon (1997) 178–9.
124 Keppie (1983) 178–9 dates to 41 BC the foundation of Hispellum, which was given some confiscated land of Asisium.
125 For the fact that *mox* does not mean 'soon', but 'in the future', see Rose (1927).

Thus it sits well with a poet into his later twenties.[126] It is clear that the loss of his father and of family land did not result in complete impoverishment for the young Propertius, although his implied dedication of his golden *bulla*[127] to his mother's gods and his assumption of the *toga virilis* before them (4.1.131–2) suggest *inter alia* that he was obliged to move to her house from his father's house, possibly to benefit from the protection of her relatives.[128] The Propertii continued to be wealthy and powerful both in Asisium and in Rome, with senators (Postumus and Celer) in Propertius' and the subsequent generation. Later C. Passennus C.f. Serg. Paullus Propertius Blaesus of Asisium (see also above, p. 14 and n. 71 and below, pp. 31, 52–3) associated on equal terms with Pliny the Younger; and other family members may have been prominent at Asisium, and also possibly at Rome.[129]

To explain their continuing wealth some recovery in the poet's family fortunes in the early principate can be assumed, but much must have remained to Propertius even immediately after the land-confiscation. A strong indication of this is that he was able to obtain an elite education. 4.1.133–4 itemises it: *vetat insano verba tonare foro* (134) clearly does not mean than the poet was already making speeches in the Roman forum; rather it indicates that he was being educated for this role in rhetoric and law. Similarly *pauca suo de carmine dictat Apollo* (133), although it might show Propertius already writing verses in his youth, has more to do with his early studies of Greek and Roman poetry. Attainment of a high educational level must have been costly in Rome of the first century BC,[130] since it required instruction first by competent schoolmasters, and then by learned literary and philosophical tutors (often Greeks) without whose expertise Greek (especially hellenistic) poetry and Greek philosophy

126 Propertius' various references to his *iuventa/us* (2.1.73; (?)2.3.33; 3.5.19; 3.9.57; 3.11.7) are unhelpful since 'youth' can extend to 40.

127 On the *aurea bulla* see Palmer (1989 [1998]). P. White (1993) 219 rightly notes that its mention 'is not sufficient to establish that Propertius was equestrian'; but in the light of other available evidence it seems hardly necessary to do this.

128 The excavated portion of the *Domus Musae* (see below, pp. 29–31) seems to be of Augustan date; see Guarducci (1985) 176. If it was the traditional home of the Propertii, some reconstruction in that period is implied.

129 These matters will not be clarified until the inscriptions found in the *Domus Musae* are published; for these see, most recently, Bonamente (2004) 72–4.

130 On fees see Bonner (1977) Index s.v. No reliable information about average tuition fees is available; the extraordinary rewards won by famous teachers like Verrius Flaccus and Remmius Palaemon were clearly not typical, although they do indicate the high cost of the 'best' education.

would have been opaque to a Roman. Attendance on Greek and Roman rhetors was another essential part of general education, all the more so if a young Roman aspired, as Propertius did, to legal practice. That aspiration also required pupilage to a jurisconsult. Paper and access to books, including those in libraries and private collections, and the services of slave readers and amanuenses would have added further to the expense of education. There were also costly prerequisites. One was freedom from the need to engage in business or other pecuniary acquisition; another was the possession and maintenance of a certain social standing and standard of living, since admission to a teacher's classes will have required the pupil to be socially acceptable not just to the teacher but to the families of other pupils. Wealth alone perhaps was not enough to ensure such social acceptability, but without wealth it would have been impossible. Propertius, then, as the Monobiblos elegies attest, had enjoyed the services of high-level, and therefore expensive, Greek and Latin instructors. One of them may even have been the former teacher of Virgil, of Helvius Cinna, and of Cornelius Gallus, the learned and prestigious Greek poet and scholar, Parthenius of Nicaea.[131] Propertius refers to him obliquely in his first elegy in the words *Partheniis ... in antris* (1.1.11), thus capping Virgil's similar allusion at *Eclogues* 10.57;[132] this could be a way in which former pupils of Parthenius signalled their relationship with him and with each other (see also below, pp. 131–6).

Of the two further elements of Propertius' early education documented in 4.1.133–4, his study of law is reflected in the many, and often well-informed, linguistic legalisms and legal allusions found in his elegies.[133] Since the young Propertius was not left isolated after his father's death but entered the protection of his mother's family and connections, his legal instructor(s) could have come from that larger circle.[134] Legal training was designed primarily to fit a young man,

---

131 Lightfoot (1999) 9–16 treats Parthenius' life and contacts, but the date of his death is, for lack of evidence, not discussed.

132 Hubaux (1930) 96 n. 1.

133 Cf. Cairns (2000), with some bibliography on the legal content of Roman elegy at 168 nn. 2–4 (n. 4 covers Propertius).

134 For Propertius' law teacher the jurist Volcacius is an outside possibility. Frier (1985) 253 n. 55 links him with the consular Volcacii (noting that Plin. *NH* 8.144 calls him a *nobilis*), and thinks he may be L. Volcacius *trib. pleb. ca* 68 BC. But the chronology is tight: the jurist Volcacius was either a pupil or a contemporary of Q. Mucius Scaevola, who died in 82 BC (see Frier (1985) 145 n. 26), so he may have been too early to have taught Propertius. Another possibility is the late republican jurist C. Aelius Gallus, if (cf. Syme (1986) 308)

particularly a *novus homo* from an Italian *municipium*, for a political career,[135] and the implication is that Propertius' family were preparing him for public life. The career of his cousin C. Propertius Postumus seems to illustrate the value of knowledge of the law in municipal new men who, like Postumus and (initially) Propertius, aspired to *honores*. The other educational element essential for a *novus* training for a public *cursus* was, as noted, rhetoric. Propertius' easy exploitation in Books 1 and 2 of genres ranging from progymnasmatic *nomos* (2.7) and *kataskeue* (2.12) through dicanic *defensio* (1.18) and symbouleutic *erotodidaxis* (1.9) to epideictic *propemptikon* (1.6 and 1.8) shows that he had been thoroughly grounded by his rhetorical teachers; and the hyper-rhetorical tones and content of Book 3 will reveal a later, new, and alluring rhetorical influence on Propertius, whose identity can be guessed with some plausibility.[136] By that time Propertius' patrons were the most affluent men in the Roman world, Maecenas and Augustus; but even in his early years he must have had solid finances behind him to obtain an excellent education in all these areas and to move, as his educational level would have demanded he move, in the society of senators' sons. Apart, then, from any assistance he received from his broader family circle, the land confiscation of which Propertius writes in 4.1 may not have been total, and the continued prosperity of Propertii of Asisium in succeeding generations could also suggest that the poet, like Horace and Virgil, at some point received from his wealthy patrons either compensation for his losses, or even possibly some restoration of land at Asisium.[137]

This survey of the family of Propertius can conclude with mention of two of the fairly numerous freedmen and freedwomen of the Propertii whose tombs are located at Rome and Asisium, their existence being, of course, another indication of the family's continuing prosperity. A Roman funerary inscription of the Augustan period: *Sex(ti) Propert[i Sex(ti)] / l(iberti) Antero[tis]* (*CIL* VI.25088) records the freed slave Anteros. Given the infrequency of the *praenomen* Sextus among the Propertii, the most economical conclusion is that Anteros was a freedman of the poet Propertius (or, less likely, of

---

he was related to L. Aelius Gallus, the probable father-in-law of Propertius' cousin Postumus.

135 The career of Ovid, about whose education more is known, again provides a clearer picture: see above, p. 17 n. 83.

136 I.e. the rhetor Volcacius Moschus: see below, pp. 63–5.

137 See also below, pp. 53–9.

his father). On similar grounds a tombstone found at Asisium, *Propertia Sex(ti) l(iberta) Tertia* (*ERAssisi* 190), could be that of a freedwoman of the poet, although its date is not secure.

However, no account of Asisium as the original home of the Propertii would be complete without mention of the *Domus Musae*,[138] the Roman house beneath the church of S. Maria Maggiore, the former cathedral of Assisi, and the Bishop's Palace. Trial soundings were made in 1864, but excavations did not start until 1948, and they ceased in 1975, although most of the *Domus* still remains uninvestigated.[139] Its ample proportions and construction reveal it as the home of a leading family of the town. The excavated portion[140] contains a number of wall-frescoes, some mythical in content;[141] beneath (in one case above) them were incised in antiquity in eight cases Greek elegiac distichs, in one case a Greek line which is possibly a dactylic pentameter, and in one case a line of Homer. The frescoes and inscriptions present an intriguing combination: the paintings include representations of recondite myths and mythical characters which overlap significantly with certain obscure mythical elements of Propertian elegy. Thus Galatea is shown, unusually, as won over by the musical and poetic skills of Polyphemus, exactly as Propertius describes her in 3.2.7–8.[142] Hercules is represented as a transvestite occupied with female tasks in the court of Omphale, again precisely as Propertius represents him in 4.9.47–50. Another fresco features Itys/Itylos, who is mentioned by Propertius at 3.10.10. In another Iamos is shown; his mother was an Evadne, and an Evadne appears twice in Propertius (1.15.21; 3.13.24). The Propertian Evadne is, however, a different mythical individual, the wife of Capaneus, and whether the Iamos fresco is the product of coincidence or confusion cannot be known. Also depicted in fresco is Marsyas finding the flute thrown away by Athena, a legend to which Propertius alludes (2.30.16–18). All this, together with the prominence of Apolline and Bacchic apparatus in other paintings, and the presence of the Greek

---

138 This section draws freely on Guarducci (1979) and (1985), to which reference should be made for undocumented statements; note, however, that certain of her earlier datings have been superseded.

139 For accounts of the archaeological activities at the house see Guarducci (1979) 269–71; Bonamente (2004) 70–1.

140 'Una specie di criptoportico con piccoli ambienti laterali' (Guarducci (1985) 163).

141 These were reported by Guarducci (1985) 164 to be 'oggi o distrutti o notevolmente svaniti'.

142 Leach (1992) 72–5, in a study of comparable iconography, ascribes both Propertius' version and the Assisi fresco to a 'dramatic tradition' (73). Keyssner (1938) 181 and n. 54 had earlier noted figurative parallels.

distichs, encouraged the conclusion that the house once belonged to the poet Sex. Propertius. Confirmation that this was the poet's house was seen in a graffito of AD 367 also found in the house in which a cultural pilgrim declared that he had 'venerated' the 'House of the Muse': *domum oscilavi Musae*. A further indication that the *Domus Musae* was the house of the Propertii is provided by the three still unpublished inscriptions of the *gens Propertia* which were found there, although these may have been brought from other location(s); their exact content has not been divulged.[143]

The incised inscriptions accompanying the frescoes were initially thought to be more or less contemporary with them, and it was even conjectured that Propertius himself might have composed the Greek distichs.[144] But it was subsequently recognized that they belong to the end of the first/beginning of the second century AD; hence the poet cannot easily have authored them. Whether the frescoes themselves are of the Augustan period is disputed.[145] But there seems to be agreement that the actual fabric of the excavated portion of the *Domus Musae* is Augustan;[146] and the funerary inscriptions of the Propertii found in a related and not too distant cemetery area outside Asisium (see below, pp. 52–3) are of varying imperial date. All this means that there is no hard evidence to show that the Propertii lived in the *Domus* before the principate. But, although as a juvenile the poet had to move to his mother's house after his father's death[147] and the land confiscation, there is no reason why the family as a whole should have changed their residence within Asisium at that time. So we can sensibly assume that before the principate they lived either in an earlier house on the same site or in earlier and as yet unexcavated parts of the *Domus*, that the house belonged to the poet, and that the *gens Propertia* used the same cemetery in republican times as they did later. All this fits with the view that the frescoes illustrate (at whatever remove) the recondite mythological tastes of the poet. As for the inscriptions, the best explanation for them is that they were incised by, or more likely since they are in different hands,[148] for a member of the

---

143 The adventures of these inscriptions up to 2003, and what is known of their contents, can be read in Bonamente (2004) 72–4.
144 Guarducci (1979) 293.
145 Guarducci (1985) 176 claimed that they are Augustan; Coarelli (2004) 105 dates them to around AD 100.
146 Coarelli (2004) 105 n. 27 writes of 'pavimenti chiaramente di età augustea'.
147 For the legal implications of such orphanage see Saller (1994) 181–203.
148 Guarducci (1985) 174.

gens Propertia who subsequently owned the house, who shared the poet's hellenizing tastes, and who was proud of the poetry of Sex. Propertius. Their date strengthens the possibility of that subsequent owner being C. Passennus C.f. Serg. Paullus Propertius Blaesus,[149] whose pride in his ancestor is documented. Given his own poetic pretensions,[150] Passennus may well also have authored the distichs.[151] The size and quality of the *Domus Musae* confirm the continuing prosperity of the Propertii (and the poet) in the Julio-Claudian period; and its location will contribute to discussion of the lands owned by the Propertii at Asisium (see below, pp. 53–4).

How, then, do the life and circumstances of Sex. Propertius compare with those of other Augustan poets? There is, of course, no such thing as a typical 'Augustan poet', but the major poets of the age from Virgil to Ovid do, for explicable reasons, have much in common. None of them were born in Rome, which reflects Rome's magnetic appeal to the sons of well-to-do families from all over Italy and further afield. No major poet, except possibly C. Valgius Rufus,[152] came from a senatorial family, which underlines the preoccupations, perils, and low fertility of the highest class. All the Augustan poets had sufficient family wealth to enable them to obtain the elite education essential for a *poeta doctus*. All were at least municipal *equites*, even Horace, despite his deceptive apparent claim to be a freedman's son,[153] and their takeover of the profession of poetry at Rome is no accident. On the earlier pattern poetry had either provided a living for men of lower social class such as Ennius and Laberius, or a leisure pursuit for the rich and powerful. In the first century BC C. Licinius Calvus and P. Helvius Cinna, from senatorial families, continued to exemplify the older pattern. However it was already beginning to break down: C. Valerius Catullus, from an international commercial background and with instant entrée to the highest circles at Rome but not from a senatorial family, anticipates the Augustan norm, as perhaps does T. Lucretius.

The takeover of poetry by equestrians in the first century BC is typical of their rise as a class. Seen as *viri boni* by those favouring

---

149   On this individual see above, pp. 14 and n. 71, 26, and below, pp. 52–3.
150   Cf. Plin. *Epist.* 6.15 and 9.22.
151   For these hypotheses see Guarducci (1985) 177–8; Coarelli (2004) also credits him with commissioning the frescoes.
152   Cf. Syme (1986) 395.
153   Cf. Williams (1995).

them, scions of the leading families of Italian towns invaded every attractive position at Rome in the last decades BC.[154] For poetry the dividing line is generally speaking the mid-40s BC, when the literary scene changed as the so-called *novi poetae* were either dead or were drawing to the end of their poetic careers. Of the fresh talents Virgil and Varius were studying Epicureanism in Naples in the mid-40s, Horace was about to leave for his philosophic studies in Athens, and Tibullus, probably younger, would not have begun his military career before the thirties. These, and the other poets who would emerge in the next two decades, were from families not yet senatorial but with senatorial prospects; they were wealthy in comparison with ordinary citizens but only moderately wealthy in comparison with the richest senatorial (and some equestrian) houses. The loss of land which many of them suffered in the forties seems to have created a situation different from that in the age of Catullus and one which would not persist, even for example in the case of Ovid. In order to rebuild their fortunes these poets of the forties and thirties appear to have been eager and willing to enter into close relationships, social and poetic, with patrons who could offer them substantial subventions, and who could donate or restore properties to them, as well as providing them with all the other advantages which poets in earlier and later times sought from patrons.[155] The new needs of this new group explain in particular the emergence of Maecenas as a patron. It is hard to imagine such an individual forming his own coterie of poets before the mid-40s BC, for all his vast wealth. Only then, when a new generation of equestrian poets needed such patronage, could a fabulously rich and influential *eques* be deferred to easily as *patronus* by his fellow equestrians.

But again, the homogeneity of Augustan poets should not be exaggerated, although apparent surface differences may mask yet further similarities. Only P. Vergilius Maro, for example, bears a *cognomen* showing that his ancestor (perhaps many of them) had occupied the maronate of Mantua; but a similar ancestral distinction is known for Propertius (see above, p. 11), and it might be conjectured with confidence for others. Only C. Cornelius Gallus held high civil and military

---

154 On the rise of this class see Syme (1939) Ch. 24; on their characterization as *boni viri*, 359–60 with 359 n. 3; on the sociological background of such transformations see Hopkins (1974) (the emergence of professionals); (1978) 74–96 ('structural differentiation'). Augustus himself was by birth not so distant from such origins.

155 See below, pp. 39–41.

offices, only C. Valgius Rufus eventually reached a (suffect) consul-ship,[156] only the family of Sex. Propertius produced a senator (Propertius Postumus) in the poet's own generation, and only P. Ovidius Naso was awarded the laticlave by Augustus;[157] but the underlying trends are not dissimilar. Q. Horatius Flaccus, with his self-imposed stigma of being a 'freedman's son', looks like the exception to everything, even though this 'biographical fact' has now been shown to be anything but fact.[158] Curiously, and as if in compensation, only he, as far as we know, had a genuine Greek education in Athens; but his *libertino patre natum* emphasis is mainly functional. It is a cloak for Horace's 'client' status vis-à-vis Maecenas, and no other Augustan poet was obliged by his choices of poetic forms to explore this rela-tionship so thoroughly and so frequently. On another level, only Albius Tibullus sprang from Latium, the historic heartland of the *Latini*;[159] but the families of some others may have originated in La-tium and moved thence to Roman *coloniae* and *municipia* elsewhere in Italy.

One recurrent factor in poets' biographies and autobiographies (Virgil, Horace, Tibullus and Propertius) is loss of property, suffered perhaps because of their families' adherence to a defeated party in the Civil (or earlier) Wars. Whatever truth resides in these alleged mis-fortunes, there is no reason to imagine that any of the poets became genuinely impoverished or déclassé. Virgil's great wealth is evi-denced.[160] As for Horace, incidentally the only Augustan poet who had personally fought against Augustus, his 'Sabine farm' was in fact a great *villa rustica* enclosing a *vivarium*, comparable with the Sir-mian villa of the Valerii Catulli.[161] Varius and Valgius too were far from poor,[162] and the fact that Ovid (a latecomer to this scene) had a senatorial son-in-law hardly argues for a straitened income.[163] Pro-pertius' circumstances are thus wholly analogous to those of his fellow poets.

This composite portrait of an 'Augustan poet' can usefully filter

---

156 In 12 BC: Syme (1986) Index of Persons s.v.
157 *Tr.* 4.10.29.
158 By Williams (1995).
159 Cf. Paci (1986).
160 *VSD* 13.
161 On Horace's villa see Centroni (1994) – with illustrations; Frischer (1995); on that of the Valerii Catulli, Wiseman (1987) 349–60.
162 Both possessed at least a senatorial *census*; Varius was given a million sesterces by Augustus as a reward for his *Thyestes* (Kl. P. s.v. Varius col. 1131).
163 He was Cornelius Fidus (*PIR²* C 1360).

out not only modern assumptions but also the poets' own deceptive statements. When one of them claims poverty or affects the simple life, our reaction should be disbelief. The conventions of elegy, already established in hellenistic epigram and 'neoteric' poetry and deployed by C. Cornelius Gallus, whose wealth must have been very considerable, demanded that the 'poor' elegiac poet-lover should have been ousted from the affections of his venal mistress by a richer rival; and a senatorial 'praetor' going out to (1.8) or just back from (2.16) his province, or who has departed perhaps with a higher rank to another (3.20) might indeed challenge a Sex. Propertius in his expenditure, just as M. Antonius was no doubt a better financial catch than Cornelius Gallus for the mime-actress Volumnia Cytheris.[164] But Propertius could probably have competed in cash terms if that was what he had really wanted, and if his scenario had in any case not in all likelihood been a fantasy invented on the analogy of Gallus' earlier plight. What the poets say about their material wealth, then, often joins what they say about their amours and sexual adventures in general as fiction or semi-fiction, not fact.[165] We must keep in mind firmly that these were well-educated, propertied, equestrians: they were wealthy enough not to need to engage in business, they were therefore able to devote themselves entirely to cultured activities, and they were in contact with the highest court circles, but they were nevertheless more than content to accept an increase in their fortunes from patrons from even higher social or financial strata. In this way historical errors about Augustan poets and consequent distortions of ancient realities can be avoided.[166] One example already mentioned is the claim that the elegies addressed by Propertius in Book 1 to Tullus are 'not the poems of patronized to patron' since 'The Volcacii were of similar social standing to the Propertii.'[167] The facts will emerge in a more nuanced form in Chapter 2.

---

164 On the 'affair' see Manzoni (1995) I Ch. 3.

165 A minor exception to this rule may be Propertius' cautious admission that he is 'quite wealthy' (*non ita dives*, 2.24.38), if this is how the corrupt *navita dives* of O should be emended.

166 E.g. the notion that when Horace lost his father's property after Philippi, the position he then obtained as *scriba quaestorius* in the *aerarium* 'marked a descent from what he had earlier achieved' (Nisbet and Hubbard (1970) xxvii), when in fact this post was a lucrative sinecure which cost a great deal of money to purchase (cf. Armstrong (1989) 18; Williams (1995) 304 with bibliography at n. 17).

167 Lyne in G. Lee (1994) x.

CHAPTER 2

The Volcacii Tulli and Others

Scholarly disagreement over whether the (Volcacius) Tullus who appears frequently in the Monobiblos was Propertius' friend, or his patron, was mentioned above (pp. 3–4, 34). A number of modern preconceptions have played a part in this debate.[1] In particular the notion that patronage was somehow inherently demeaning to the patronized may explain the vigour with which Tullus has sometimes been denied patron status. In fact patronage in its broadest sense – relationships of mutual support of many different types between persons of unequal status – was a central element of Roman life. Civil society in the modern sense did not exist in the Roman world, and no citizen could be protected or assisted under all circumstances solely by such laws and authorities as existed. Rather an individual's security and well-being derived in large measure from self-help combined with the protection of persons more powerful than himself,[2] and such protection had to be negotiated and renegotiated throughout an individual's life and over the generations of a family. The resulting structure was inevitably pyramidal: the meanest citizens might be the clients of one or more patrons of superior status; those patrons in turn were clients of others higher up the social structure, and so on. Patronage relationships were neither necessarily nor even characteristically exclusive, but they could, jointly or severally, be virtually all-embracing, providing support ranging from political to financial to legal to social. Although

---

1 The most authoritative studies of the language and realities of Roman patronage are Saller (1982) Ch. 1 and Saller (1989); the latter, which summarizes many of the essential facts about patronage, is a brief response to ill-founded criticisms of Saller (1982). I believe that my own position is in accord with that of Saller. For aspects of the *patronus/cliens* relationship as it applied to Augustan poets see also Horsfall (1981); and for a fine account of the relations between Maecenas and Horace, Du Quesnay (1984) esp. 24–7.

2 One perilous element of Roman life, against which patronage was an important protection, was the culture of delation prevalent from the later Republic on: see Lintott (2001–3).

35

non-egalitarian in that the client inevitably stood on a lower footing that the patron, they were not such that the dignity of the patronized was automatically affronted (although obviously clients could and did sometimes take affront). To begin with, a patron could benefit from his clients in aggregate as much as, or even more than, they might benefit from him. Not only were clients expected to uphold their patron politically and legally, but they could constitute a corps of respectful associates, including freeborn citizens, on whom the patron might call for personal attendance and assistance in all aspects of his life and business – from the well-documented areas of the *salutatio* and of political backing to less well-attested roles such as agents and procurators. Roman society did indeed offer further social support mechanisms, mainly for the lower classes, in the form of various associations – trade-guilds, cult groups, burial-clubs, and so forth. But these were neither intended to replace personal patronage nor capable of doing so.

Roman networks of patronage, and the loyalties which they engendered, reached upwards to leading citizens (*principes civitatis*) during the republic, and increasingly to the emperor under the principate. The latter development, the start of which can be seen in the literary area during the lifetimes and careers of Horace, Virgil, Propertius and other Augustan writers, ended with all Roman citizens, including men who in former ages would have headed their own patronage networks, being – at varying degrees of distance – dependants of the emperor. Links of patronage naturally originated in many different ways, with the initial mutual interests of patron and patronized being social, or political, or familial, or regional, or personal, or any combination of these. Once entered into, the relationship could persist over generations, but might change in nature as families and individuals progressed or regressed in status.[3]

A particularly elusive aspect of Roman patronage (and the source of some modern confusion about it) involves the language used of it in antiquity. Although for convenience I have so far written about Roman 'patrons' and 'clients' and will continue to do so, the terms *patronus* and *cliens* were in fact used relatively infrequently to de-

---

3   For example, the continuing association over many generations between the Valerii Catulli, presumably initially the socially superior family since they reached the consulship earlier (in AD 31), and the Veranii, as documented by Wiseman (1984), noting the presence of a member of both families among the four aristocratic attendants of the Arvales in AD 105.

scribe the relationship, and then often in specialized senses.[4] Patron-age was more often characterized in antiquity as *amicitia* ('friend-ship'), and the individuals engaged in it as *amici* ('friends'). This terminology makes perfect sense in the light of ancient theories of 'friendship', which explicitly distinguished between friendships of equal and unequal status and prescribed different reciprocal duties in each case.[5] The language of friendship enabled men of unequal social rank to cooperate in practical affairs within a society which regarded overt employee status as verging on the servile. By representing as 'friendship' what was in fact employment, Roman society legitimated the performance of services by inferiors to superiors and reciprocation by the latter in the form of rewards and protection. The language of friendship also helped to protect the client's dignity; and finally, and this aspect should not be undervalued, it could enable freeborn men of different stations in life to speak and think genuinely of each other as 'friends,' and to conduct their interactions within the broader and emotionally enriched inter-personal framework of *amicitia* while at the same time maintaining, where appropriate, their social distinctions.

A Roman poet entering a patronage relationship was in no essen-tial way different from any other Roman doing so. Literary patronage was a subset of patronage in general, and a poet who was a client incurred obligations analogous to those of any other client, and ex-pected analogous rewards. A primary obligation of a client was loyalty to his patron and to those to whom his patron owed loyalty. This is one reason why it makes no sense to look for genuine criticism of Augustus, overt or covert, in the works of Propertius.[6] Propertius' patrons in the Monobiblos, Tullus and Gallus, were both adherents of Augustus, while the patron of Books 2 and 3 was Maecenas, Augus-tus' close associate, and the patron of Book 4 Augustus himself. Pro-pertius therefore owed loyalty to the *princeps* throughout his poetic career; and if he had failed to show it at any point, his current patron(s) would certainly have reacted adversely to his behaviour. A Roman who showed disloyalty in word or deed within a patronage

---

4   Cf. Saller (1982) 8–11, pointing out that generally in the early Empire *patronus* 'was re-stricted to legal advocates, patrons of communities and ex-masters of freedmen' (9). Saller (1989) collects some interesting cases where *patronus* is used outwith these boundaries.

5   The locus classicus for ancient friendship theory is Aristot. *Eth. Nic.* 1155a–1172a. For an expansion of what follows see Saller (1982) 11–14.

6   There are, of course, many other reasons, ranging from simple self-interest to the fact that the Propertii had been Caesarians at least since the poet's father's generation, and probably longer: see also above, p.10, and below, pp. 44–50.

relationship would not only have risked social disapprobation, but might also be the recipient of a formal 'renunciation of friendship' (*renuntiatio amicitiae*) from his patron. A good illustration of the process is the fate of Timagenes, a Greek historian who was either not fully *au fait* with Roman expectations in this area or, more probably, regarded them as beneath his notice. Having entered Augustus' patronage Timagenes, who had a considerable reputation for his acerbic tongue, was unwise enough to employ it against Augustus, Livia and their family. When he refused to heed Augustus' warnings, he was expelled from the imperial household.[7] Timagenes was disciplined for his unbridled speech; a writer who offended his patron in his writings could expect even sharper reactions. Modern scholars sometimes appear to assume that Roman personal poetry equates with one side of a conversation, and that, just as the ideology of 'friendship' permitted the use of informal parrhesiastic speech by a client to a patron, so written criticism of a patron and the free expression in writing of viewpoints antipathetic to a patron would also have been tolerated. This is unrealistic: the circulated writings of ancient authors with powerful patrons were a quite different matter from the private conversations of writers with their patrons. Written attacks on a patron and subversion in writing of a patron's views would have had the potential to damage a patron politically and personally in the eyes of the world, and they would certainly have been regarded as a breach of the client's obligations to the patron, with consequences for the offending writer sure to follow. This is why it is intrinsically unlikely that any Propertian elegy is genuinely critical of imperial policy even if at first sight it looks like criticism.[8]

Some of the benefits which patrons might confer on their poet-clients were, of course, different from those expected by non-literary clients, but they were no less important in terms of the poets' careers. One valuable benefit was access to books in the patron's personal library and in those of his friends.[9] Asinius Pollio, an early patron of Cinna, Gallus and Virgil, established the first 'public' library at Rome,

7   Senec. *De Ira* 3.23.4–5, possibly somewhat tendentious; for further testimonia and discussion see Raaflaub and Samons (1990) 442–3, who accept Seneca's interpretation and credit Augustus with a more tolerant nature than his actions might seem to indicate; Bowersock (1965) 109–10, 125–7.

8   E.g. Prop. 2.7, seemingly critical of an early attempt by the *princeps* at marriage legislation, is in reality laudatory: see Cairns (1979a).

9   On the vital link between literature and libraries in the late republic see esp. Marshall (1976); on Cicero and Atticus in this connection, Shackleton Bailey (1965) 13.

and Augustus followed suit, eventually in the Palatine library.[10] It is unlikely that admission to such 'public' libraries was genuinely open: patrons no doubt gave preference to their own clients and their clients' clients.[11] A patron will also have been able to help a literary protégé by using his agents to make searches for specific books, particularly in the Greek provinces. Yet another service a patron might provide was to introduce a poet to other powerful figures who could offer ancillary patronage or subsidies. This is perhaps illustrated most vividly in the fresh crop of honorands who suddenly appear in Horace *Odes* 2, all of them doubtless contributors to Horace's increasing wealth. Maecenas too would have gained from sharing Horace's talents, not financially but in terms of *gratia* for the 'benevolence' with which he had permitted 'his' poet to honour other *laudandi*. An illustration of a patron's ability to further his client's contacts is the growing impact upon some of Maecenas' poets, i.e. Virgil, Horace and Propertius, of Augustus, who replaced Maecenas as the patron of their later works. Yet another benefit that a patron could confer on a poet was entrée to a cultured ambience in which the poet could associate freely with the intellectuals of all types, Greek and Roman, who formed part of the patron's circle. These contacts offered the poet access to multifarious sources of 'learning' and poetic stimulus. The wealth and political influence of Maecenas ensured that his circle offered these advantages to a high degree (see below, pp. 258–60). A patron could also offer opportunities and settings for poets to give readings of their works before influential and friendly audiences, and thus to establish themselves within Roman high society. Asinius Pollio (again) is credited by the elder Seneca[12] with introducing *recitationes* to Rome. Whatever this claim implies,[13] the association between Pollio and recitations clearly reflects Pollio's assiduity as a performer of his own work, and possibly also the distinction of his first poetic clients. A plausible setting for the performances of Maecenas' poets is their patron's house on the Esquiline, even though that part of it which was formerly described as an auditorium containing an *odeion* is no longer

10   Marshall (1976) 261–2, emphasizing the patronage element involved.
11   Plut. *Lucull.* 42 claims as an indication of Lucullus' generosity that his libraries were open to all. Whether or not this is historically accurate, Plutarch obviously thinks it exceptional.
12   *Controv.* 4 pr. 2: *Pollio Asinius numquam admissa multitudine declamavit, nec illi ambitio in studiis defuit; primus enim omnium Romanorum advocatis hominibus scripta sua recitavit.*
13   Pollio may have innovated by formally inviting his friends to come and hear his work; informal recitations over dinner are attested earlier, e.g. Cic. *Ad Att.* 16.2.6, 3.1.

universally identified as such.[14] Of course, poets, no less than other clients, obtained additional, more tangible, benefits from their patrons. These might consist of monetary subventions and gifts or restitutions of property. This aspect of a patron's potential beneficence towards his writers is illustrated by the 'poets' quarter' on the Esquiline constructed by Maecenas. He had regenerated the area to provide a site for his own mansion and tower, and by the later 20s BC Propertius and other poets of Maecenas' circle lived there when at Rome. This 'poets' quarter', proximate to his own establishment, will have been convenient for Maecenas when he wanted to show off his protégés to his guests. But it would also have been convenient and prestigious for the poets to live in such pleasant surroundings and in such close proximity to their influential patron, particularly since Maecenas was clearly either subsidizing their accommodation and living expenses, or had gifted them their houses.[15]

The benefits which patrons hoped to gain in turn from their poets were less tangible, but perhaps harder to acquire. The same ancient impetus towards self-memorialization which lay behind euergetism in all its forms, the epigraphic habit, and the construction of expensive funerary monuments, also fuelled literary patronage. Poets and their *laudandi* shared an aspiration for immortality through poetry, and the eagerness of patrons for poetic commemoration was underpinned by reflections such as:

> vixere fortes ante Agamemnona
> multi; sed omnes inlacrimabiles
>   urgentur ignotique longa
>   nocte, carent quia vate sacro.   (Horace *Odes* 4.9.25–8)

> Brave men there were before Agamemnon's time,
> A multitude, but buried in endless night
>   They lie unwept and unremembered,
>   All for the lack of a sacred poet.   (tr. Guy Lee)

Maecenas and Augustus were manifestly anxious to promote literature with a view to their own posthumous fame, and the other patrons of the age acted from similar motives. Patrons were also keen to recruit

---

14   However, Murray (1985) 43 and n. 16, with earlier bibliography, took a positive view of the 'auditorium' as a venue for recitations, as did *LTUR* 3.74–5 s.v. Horti Maecenatis. "Auditorium" (M. de Vos); most recently, Coarelli (2004) 107 firmly reasserts this role for it; see also below, p. 256 and n. 44.

15   On these topics, see further below, pp. 257–60.

writers of high quality: Augustus in particular must often have reflected on the well-known paradox that, for all he had conquered the
world, Alexander the Great was unable to find a poet equal to his
accomplishments.[16] Another overarching ambition of Roman culture
also played its part: Roman consciousness of their intellectual and
literary inferiority to the Greeks, coupled with their fierce nationalistic
pride in their *imperium*, demanded that Latin literature should attempt
to equal or surpass every Greek achievement in every literary genre.
From the viewpoint of Roman cultural chauvinism, then, it would
have been utterly self-defeating had Maecenas attempted to direct all
his poets into the composition of epics (cf. below, pp. 265–6). Prior to
the Propertius of Book 2 no elegist seems to have formed part of Maecenas' circle. Maecenas' recruitment of Propertius therefore plugged a
gap, and so must have made Propertius' adherence to Maecenas as
welcome to his patron as it was to Propertius himself (see below, pp.
252, 322).

A further personal motive must have induced patrons of literature
in the late Republic and early Empire to spend their resources on poets
rather than, or in addition to, using them for other forms of benefaction. When a politician was celebrated by a contemporary poet of
merit, his name and praises would percolate throughout Roman cultured society and thence to the literate Romanized population of the
imperium. He thus acquired an aura of glory which effectively aided
his career. An Asinius Pollio or a Volcacius Tullus, for example,
could scarcely have found a more practical mode of self-
advertisement; and even the patrician and *nobilis* M. Valerius Messalla Corvinus must have welcomed the additional splendour with
which Tibullus' poetry enveloped him. As for Maecenas, although he
already possessed immense wealth, and great power and influence,[17]
the eulogies of his poets endowed this Etruscan *eques* with a
prominence in the minds of his contemporaries which no other form of
publicity could have conferred on him. In the case of Augustus, the
praises of the poets legitimated his assumed semi-divine status and his
'divine parentage' at the highest cultural level.

Finally, the poetic patrons of the early empire enjoyed two benefits less material than those so far listed, but not to be underestimated
in the final summation: genuinely affectionate relationships with their

---

16 Cf. also below, pp. 265–6, 320 and n. 3.
17 On whether Maecenas lost influence with Augustus after 23 BC, see below, p. 279 and n.
   141.

protégés, and enjoyment of high-quality poetry which their own poetic aspirations and experiments enabled them to appreciate all the more. It is clear, for example, both from Horace's poetic interactions with Maecenas and from his non-poetic exchanges with Augustus,[18] that between Horace and his patrons there existed the close informal ties and personal interactions which constitute real friendship. *Mutatis mutandis* something similar can be concluded about Virgil and the same patrons (and also Pollio at an earlier period), and about Tibullus and Messalla. With Propertius and Maecenas we are less well informed, although Propertius' elegies addressed to Maecenas (2.1 and 3.9) do reveal something of the same ethos; and the close and friendly relations which Propertius enjoyed with Tullus and Gallus are manifest throughout the Monobiblos. The literary ambitions of Pollio, Messalla, Maecenas, and even, although to a lesser extent, Augustus, are well known, although none of them regarded poetry as their primary claim to fame. Their experience as practitioners of poetry would have given them not only the discriminating ability to recognize the superiority of the works of their poetic clients to their own products, but also a keener enjoyment of those works.

Propertius addresses or mentions a number of his contemporaries.[19] Some had a considerable impact on his poetry, and these deserve attention, especially if they are independently evidenced. One particularly prominent figure – the 'Gallus'[20] who appears in the Monobiblos as addressee/dedicatee of 1.5, 1.10, 1.13 and 1.20 – will be treated in Chapter 3. Apart from 'Gallus', the most notable Propertian contemporary in the Monobiblos is 'Tullus'. Like Gallus he is the addressee of four elegies (1.1; 1.6; 1.14; 1.22), and the curiously symmetrical arrangement of the poems dedicated to the two men hints that they were joint-patrons of Propertius, and also perhaps that they were linked socially and politically. Of the pair Tullus was, at least ostensibly, the more important *qua* patron, since the prologue and epilogue elegies of the Monobiblos are both addressed to him. The distinction may, however, be a social one:[21] Propertius 1.6 allows Tullus to be

18   See Galinsky (1996) 196–7.
19   For one or two likely acquaintances not mentioned in Propertius' elegies, see below, pp. 63–5.
20   Some scholars distinguish between the Gallus of 1.5, 1.10, and 1.13 on the one hand, and the Gallus of 1.20 on the other (see below, p. 78 n. 38), but it is hard to perceive a basis for this.
21   If Ch. 3 correctly identifies 'Gallus' as the equestrian C. Cornelius Gallus, then Tullus, from a consular family, was formally of higher status.

identified as (?)C. Volcacius Tullus,[22] nephew of L. Volcacius L. f.
Tullus, *consul ordinarius* of 33 BC.[23] The younger Tullus as depicted
in the Monobiblos is a lay figure, a conventionally strait-laced 'military man' utterly indifferent to love and devoted to the service of his
country. Such a *persona* provided a contrast useful for Propertius'
poetic purposes with two other, socially irresponsible *personae* of the
Monobiblos: the poet-lover himself, characterized by *nequitia*, and
another lover, the 'Gallus' of 1.5, 1.10, 1.13 and 1.20. The stress on
Tullus' military aspect is also honorific: in fact, like Propertius' cousin
Postumus celebrated in 3.12, the historical Tullus may have been more
of an administrator, in that his '*militia*' consisted in a special commission to accompany his uncle to the province of Asia in 29 BC with
praetorian status in order to oversee the return of looted temple
treasures.[24] Other elements of Tullus' real-life personality perhaps
diverged equally from Propertius' picture of him. In particular, since
he patronized an elegiac love-poet and was happy to be named
frequently in Propertius' erotic elegies, Tullus may not have been as
puritanical as he is depicted.

Scholars' doubts about Tullus' patronage of Propertius reflect not
just the misconceptions of the nature of Roman patronage discussed
above but failure to take proper account of the relative social status of
their two families. The Propertii were equestrian up to the poet's
generation, but the Volcacii had already been consular for two generations and senatorial for at least three. Senators and *equites* could and
did, of course, mingle socially, and marriages between members of
senatorial and wealthy equestrian families were not uncommon,[25] but
the social distinction always remained. The Volcacii Tulli came from
(Etruscan) Perusia,[26] the near neighbour of (Umbrian) Asisium. Propertius says as much on the only sensible interpretation of 1.22.1–4:

> Qualis et unde genus, qui sint mihi, Tulle, Penates,
> quaeris pro nostra semper amicitia.

22 *RE* Suppl. IX no.17 (col. 1837); *PIR*¹ V 624. His *praenomen* is more likely to have been C.
   than L. (rashly attributed to him at *GC* 4). L. and C. seem to have been the family preferences.
23 *RE* no.9, *RE* Suppl. IX no.18 (col. 1838); *PIR*¹ V 625.
24 Cairns (1974b) 159–63.
25 The possibility of such a marriage between the Propertii and a branch of the Volcacii is
   raised below, pp. 60–2.
26 See, e.g., Torelli (1969) 303–4; Harris (1971) 325. Wiseman (1971) 276–7 (No. 506) incorrectly rejects Syme's earlier assertions of a Perusine origin: cf. Syme (1979) 603–4; *EOS*
   II.283 (M. Torelli), reporting for the *velcha* (= Volcacii) a family tomb ('tomba gentilizia')
   at Perusia. On the family and its members see most recently Bonamente (2004) 44–54.

si Perusina tibi patriae sunt nota sepulcra,
Italiae duris funera temporibus ...

You ask, Tullus, in virtue of our perpetual friendship, my status and
race, and what my family is. If/since the Perusine graves of your native
land are known to you, those Italian deaths in the bad times ...

Following on Tullus' 'imaginary questions'[27] of lines 1–2 – for Tullus
was certainly aware of Propertius' social status, and he also knew that
Propertius' family originated in Perusia's neighbour, Asisium – Propertius responds in like measure with the ambivalent *si* clause of lines
3–4 ('if' or 'since'). This introduces *Perusina ... patriae ... sepulcra*
(3), which are naturally *nota* ('known') to Tullus. The transferred
adjective *Perusina* identifies the *patria* in question as Perusia; and,
because Propertius and Tullus are the only persons mentioned in lines
1–4, Perusia must be the 'native land' of one or the other of them. So,
since Propertius was from *proxima ... Umbria* etc. (9) (and specifically from Asisium),[28] it follows that Perusia is being identified as the
native land (*patria*) of Tullus.

The Volcacii achieved their first consulship in 66 BC in the person of L. Volcacius Tullus (*RE* s.v. Volcatius Tullus no.8), who continued his political career as a distinguished consular at least down to
46 BC. He was almost certainly not a 'new man'. Cicero in *De Lege
Agraria* 2.3 asserts that before his own consulship of 63 BC many
years had gone by without that of a *novus homo*. This must indicate
that L. Volcacius, whose consulship had been only three years earlier,
was not a *novus*.[29] His father and/or grandfather will therefore have
already achieved senatorial rank, and his family will have possessed
Roman citizenship certainly before the Social War and possibly since
early in the second century BC.[30] With occasional individual exceptions, and apart from areas of Sullan settlement and areas proximate to
Rome where the *latifundia* of Roman *nobiles* predominated, Etruria

---

27   For such 'imaginary questions' see *GC* 223–4 and nn.; for their possible correlative ('imaginary statements') see Martin (1998) 12.
28   See also above, pp. 6–7. By implying Asisium as Propertius' birthplace *proxima ... Umbria*
(1.22.9) answers at least part of Tullus' 'query'; on the boundaries of Perusia and Asisium,
and on the status of Arna, see below, pp. 56–7.
29   Cf. Wiseman (1971) 276 no.506, making this point; according to Du Quesnay (1992) 79, a
novus.
30   Cf. Harris (1971) 325; Valvo (1989) – on an inscription (mid-second to early first century
BC) of the haruspex C. Volcacius C. f., who was a citizen, as his father had been. On early
grants of citizenship to Umbrians see Bradley (2000) 138–45, 195–6.

was staunchly and consistently Marian/'*popularis*'.[31] Despite this fact, the earlier known actions of the consul of 66 BC provide little evidence of a firm or consistent political alignment.[32] In 66 BC L. Volcacius Tullus refused to accept Catiline's candidature for the consulship, and he favoured Cicero's suppression of the Catilinarians in 63 BC, although he was possibly more lenient when it came to sentencing.[33] In 56 BC Volcacius supported Pompey's commission to restore Ptolemy Auletes, but in 49 BC he remained in Rome instead of leaving with Pompey, and took part in Caesar's senate,[34] although in the same year he was in favour of opening peace negotiations with Pompey.[35] In 46 BC he was the only senator to oppose the pardon for Marcellus, an action which has been interpreted as 'sycophantic' towards Caesar.[36] It is possible to view these latter actions either as a move by L. Volcacius from the Pompeian to the Caesarian faction, or as a confirmation of Volcacius' previously unevident Caesarian loyalty, or as a resumption by him of a Marian/Caesarian posture which had been suppressed during Pompey's period of greatest influence, or finally as temporizing during and after the Civil War.

Another member of the family had clear Caesarian connections – C. Volcacius Tullus (*RE* s.v. Volcatius Tullus no.7), either the son or nephew of the consul of 66 BC, described by Julius Caesar as an *adulescens* in 53 BC.[37] C. Volcacius Tullus belongs to a recognizable group of professional soldiers active around the middle of the first century BC.[38] He served as a career officer under Julius Caesar in the

---

31   Terms like '*populares*' and '*optimates*' are sometimes regarded with suspicion, but, if used with caution, help to indicate broad and often continuous lines of political engagement over the last century of the Roman republic. On these concepts see *RE* s.v. *optimates* (H. Strasburger); *RE* Suppl. 10 s.v. *populares* esp. coll. 568–72 ("Wortgebrauch"); Tatum (1999) 1–31. The support of Etruria in general for Marius, Julius Caesar, and Octavianus (the '*causa popularis*') is demonstrated by Hall (1996b) 165–70; Zecchini (1998); and Bonamente (2004) 23–7; there were, of course, exceptions: see Zecchini (1998) 242–5.
32   For contradictory modern verdicts on his political allegiance see Du Quesnay (1992) 234–5 n. 117: 'The consul of 66 was a Caesarian' (citing Cic. *Ad Att.* 9.19.2 and possibly 10.3a.2); and Tatum (1999) 201, characterizing him as one of 'Pompey's intimate associates' in connection with his support for Caninius Gallus' law of 56 BC placing Pompey in charge of restoring Ptolemy Auletes (cf. esp. Cic. *Ad Fam.* 1.1.3).
33   This is, however, far from clear: cf. *Ad Att.* 12.21.1.
34   *Ad Att.* 9.10.7.
35   *Ad Att.* 9.19.2.
36   Berry (1996) on Cic. *Pro Sulla* 4.11.2; Shackleton Bailey (1968) 291–2 on Cic. *Ad Att.* 7.3.3.
37   *Bell. Gall.* 6.29.3.
38   For a list and background see R. E. Smith (1958) 59–66; for a wider-ranging study, Suolahti (1955).

Gallic War and he was also active on Caesar's side during the Civil War, a proof of his continuing loyalty. Nothing is heard of him after 48 BC, and he was presumably a casualty in the Civil War. The third prominent member of the family has already been mentioned – L. Volcacius L. f. Tullus, son of the consul of 66 BC, possibly brother of Caesar's officer C. Volcacius Tullus, and paternal uncle (*patruus*) of Propertius' patron (Propertius 1.6.19). He was *consul ordinarius* in 33 BC as Octavianus' colleague, and became proconsul of Asia in 29 BC. An earlier incident might be thought to show him as sharing the (original?) Pompeian adhesion of his father: following his praetorship in 46 BC he became governor of Cilicia in 45 BC and proved tardy in coming to the assistance of the governor of Syria, who was besieging the Pompeian Q. Caecilius Bassus in Apamea. But he might have had other reasons for his tardiness than Pompeian sentiments.[39] However that may be, L. Volcacius L. f. Tullus was obviously in high favour with Augustus from the late 30s BC on. There are a number of indications of this: his election as *consul ordinarius*, his sharing that honour with Octavianus, his subsequent governorship of Asia, one of the two most prestigious and lucrative provinces,[40] and finally the simultaneous appointment of his nephew as special commissioner with praetorian rank in the same province – an arrangement clearly intended to facilitate the work of both rather than set one magistrate against the other, but at the same time implying Octavianus' confidence in their loyalty.[41]

Since little is known of the family between 45 and 33 BC the reasons for the high standing of the Volcacii with Octavianus in the late 30s and early 20s BC can only be conjectured. The hypothesized death in Julius Caesar's service of C. Volcacius Tullus, especially if he was the brother of the consul of 33 BC, might have helped, as might the eventual political services to Julius Caesar of the elder L. Volcacius Tullus. But if the indications of Augustus' favour to the Volcacii require a more specific or more proximate explanation, then a question brought vividly to the fore by the two final elegies of the Monobiblos (1.21 and 1.22) might be raised: what was the role of the Volcacii in the siege of Perusia of 41–40 BC? As prominent Perusines, they can hardly have stood aside from the conflict, and the centrality of the

---

39   Du Quesnay (1992) 79 describes him in the 40s BC as 'Clearly a Caesarian ...'.
40   Bowersock (1965) 21 plausibly suggests that a factor in his appointment to Asia was his earlier eastern experience as legate in Cilicia.
41   Cf. also Du Quesnay (1992) 79.

siege to Propertius 1.21 and 1.22 strengthens this conclusion. 1.21 is placed in the mouth of a victim of the siege, another 'Gallus' (7) who seems to have been a relative of the poet;[42] and (as noted above, p. 44) 1.22, addressed to the younger Tullus, again refers directly to the war and its casualties as 'known' to Tullus (3–4). These two elegies are highly problematic, and 1.21 seemingly requires textual intervention at two places, and perhaps a third, before sense can be extracted from it.[43] But they offer the only surviving clues to the stance of the Volcacii from 46 BC on. The best treatment of 1.21 and 1.22 holds that in 41 BC the Volcacii adhered to L. Antonius and M. Antonius' wife Fulvia, who were besieged in Perusia.[44] This view has inherent plausibility: the Volcacii seem to have been identified with the Caesarian cause at least from the mid-40s BC on and probably earlier. But after Julius Caesar's murder the loyalties of his followers were confused and divided, and by no means all Caesarians automatically looked to the dictator's nephew and posthumously adopted son as the leader of their party.[45] As Caesar's principal lieutenant (and himself also kin to Caesar) M. Antonius had a strong counter-claim, and the Volcacii may well have followed him for a time, perhaps moving over to Octavianus in the 30s BC like M. Valerius Messalla Corvinus and many others when they could no longer stomach the influence on M. Antonius of Cleopatra and her entourage. There are many parallels for such a hypothesized conversion of the Volcacii and its results. Messalla Corvinus, Munatius Plancus and his nephew M. Titius, and the family of Domitius Ahenobarbus, who died before he could be rewarded in person for his defection from M. Antonius, all immediately come to mind.

If the Volcacii had been opponents of Octavianus but had then reversed their position and had provided him with political support at

---

42 On his identity with the *propinquus* of 1.22 cf., e.g., La Penna (1977) 9; and see below, pp. 49–50 and nn. 56, 58.

43 I.e. deletion of N's *ut* in 1.5, emendation of N's *ne* to *haec* vel sim. in 1.6, and possibly emendation of N's *ereptum* to *eruptum* in 1.7, on which see below, p. 49 n. 54. On 1.21 and 22 see also Parker (1991); (1992). Subsequent to Du Quesnay (1992), but without reference to it, Traill (1994), Heiden (1995), and Pellegrino (1995) also discuss various aspects of 1.21, including textual questions. For a prior treatment with copious earlier bibliography see Carratello (1991).

44 Du Quesnay (1992) 78–83, citing Bowersock (1965) 21 for the suggestion that L. Volcacius L.f. Tullus then joined M. Antonius in the East, albeit briefly.

45 On the situation after Philippi see Syme (1939) Chs. 16, 17.

Perusia and in the rest of Etruria,[46] this could explain their conspicuous rewards. The Perusine War was a particularly bloody and ferocious episode with an unusually vindictive aftermath: if even half the stories about Octavianus' treatment of Perusia after its surrender are true, he reacted to the threat which it had represented with uncharacteristic brutality. Hence Octavianus must have believed that the threat was deadly, and seen the stand of L. Antonius at Perusia as an attempt by M. Antonius to open up by proxy a second front on his flank.[47] Given the traditional attachment of Etruria and Umbria to the Marian/ Caesarian camp, he may also have regarded the lengthy defiance of Perusia as tantamount to treachery. Nevertheless Octavianus did show *clementia* to those who deserted the forces besieged there before the end, as he refrained from action against L. Antonius himself.[48] If the Volcacii were not among the die-hards, and even more if they then helped to negotiate the city's surrender to Octavianus, their favoured situation in the late 30s and early 20s BC can be better understood.[49] Propertius' failure to take a strong political line in any direction in 1.21 and 1.22, where he merely laments civil war in general (1.22.5) and exculpates Octavianus' troops for the death of 'Gallus' (1.21.7), arguably his own relative,[50] could reflect the confused state of Caesarian loyalties at the time of the siege. But the introduction of such a controversial topic so prominently at the end of the Monobiblos in direct relationship to Tullus and hence his family must indicate that

46 There was some continuing opposition to Octavianus in Etruria down to 36 BC, when Sex. Pompeius was defeated (Dio 49.15.1; Harris (1971) 302). Octavianus' initial disposition of Perusia after the siege was apparently, at least in part, restrictive (Dio 48.14.6, but see below, n. 49), although, as Augustus, he seems to have made efforts towards reconciliation: the town became Augusta Perusia (*CIL* XI.1924; XI.1929; XI.1930), he donated a building to it (Eck (1995) esp. 90), and he was honoured there with altars inscribed *Augusto sacr(um)/ Perusia restituta* (*CIL* XI.1923).

47 L. Antonius is sometimes viewed as a sincere republican and a champion of the dispossessed: e.g. Gabba (1971) 146–7; Roddaz (1988); Du Quesnay (1992) 53, 80–3. But, leaving aside questions such as his true character and the congruity of his alleged ideals with those of Octavianus, the simultaneous presence of Fulvia at Perusia argues that his main aim was to undermine Octavianus in the interests of his brother.

48 Appian *BC* 5.38, 48; Dio 48.14.3; Vell. Pat. 2.74.4.

49 For stress on the desertions of leading figures from L. Antonius during the siege of Perusia see Appian *BC* 5.38. For the survival and office-holding at Perusia of some local aristocrats see Harris (1971) 315–16, who regards them as partisans of Octavianus; among them was L. Proculeius A.f. Titia gnatus (*CIL* XI.1943), possibly related to C. Proculeius, Augustus' friend and Maecenas' brother-in-law (*RE* s.v. Proculeius 2) (Hanslik); *PIR*² P 985). Alternatively such survivors could have been pardoned through influence, or because they had changed sides promptly.

50 See below, pp. 49–50 and n. 56.

the Volcacii saw their conduct during the siege as justifiable.[51] The political stance of Propertius' own family at that time also requires brief consideration. The natural assumption must be that the patron-client relationship between Propertius and Tullus was familial, so that the Propertii were already in the *clientela* of the Volcacii before 41 BC. This assumption seems confirmed when Propertius pointedly refers to his *patrii amici* at 3.24.9, towards the end of his three books of erotic elegy. The context of this reference[52] unmistakably recalls Propertius' invocation of his *amici* in the introductory poem of the Monobiblos (1.1.25), an elegy dedicated to the younger Tullus. This most naturally identifies as among the *patrii ... amici* of 3.24.9 the Volcacii, who are thus 'paternal' or 'ancestral' patrons of the Propertii.[53] It would thus have been virtually impossible for the Propertii to be on one side in 41–40 BC and the Volcacii on the other; and indeed Propertius publicly proclaims in 1.21.7 that the Propertii had stood with L. Antonius at Perusia. The dying 'Gallus' in whose mouth 1.21 is placed has 'escaped' (or 'broken out'?)[54] of besieged Perusia only to be fatally attacked by brigands; and the elegy is addressed by the dying man to another soldier who has likewise fled wounded from the siege of Perusia. Gallus' declaration *pars ego sum vestrae proxima militiae* (4) not only signals military comradeship but points to a family relationship with the fleeing wounded soldier; then Gallus' reference to a *soror* (6) reveals that Gallus is the wounded soldier's brother-in-law and the soldier's *soror* his wife.[55] So, when Propertius then writes in 1.22.6–8 of a *propinquus* who died in the aftermath of the siege of Perusia, it makes sense to identify that *propinquus* with the dying Gallus of 1.21,[56] especially since 'Gallus' and

---

51 Du Quesnay (1992) 81 rightly emphasizes that, since the Perusine campaign showed Octavianus as a military commander worthy of his 'father', Julius Caesar, it was given its place among his achievements despite its discreditable aspects.

52 Propertius 3.24 and 25 (probably a single elegy) mirror the themes, and frequently the language, of 1.1: cf. Fedeli (1985) 672–5.

53 A similar implication may be found in Propertius 1.22.2: *quaeris pro nostra semper amicitia*. On this line, however, see also below, p. 62.

54 The consensus of the Propertian MSS (O) offers *ereptum* at 1.21.7. Du Quesnay (1992) 66–72 and 230–2 proposes the emendation *eruptum*. He treats the participle as 'medio-passive, past reflexive or intransitive' (232 n. 73); but the parallels offered for this interpretation of *eruptum* do not involve personal subjects, and the implication of *ereptum*, namely that 'Gallus' was somehow saved by divine intervention, is a tempting addition to the overall scenario.

55 Cf., e.g., Du Quesnay (1992) 66.

56 *Pace* Du Quesnay (1992) 75–6, who denies this on the ground that the dying Gallus of 1.21 gives instructions about finding his bones and thus (Du Quesnay presumes) would have been buried, whereas the *propinquus* of 1.22.7 has not been buried (8). This presumption

the *propinquus* are both mentioned in the seventh line of their respective ten-line elegies.[57] It is not possible to make further identifications of the individuals concerned,[58] but the clear proof offered by 1.21 and 1.22 that the Propertii, and by implication Asisium, supported L. Antonius in 41 BC helps to underpin other arguments which place the Volcacii too in his camp.

By 41–40 BC at the latest Propertius' father was dead: the poet writes of the loss of land which followed his death (4.1.129–30) as his own loss; so he was the sole heir. There is nothing to indicate that his father was a casualty at the siege of Perusia; if he was the Sex. Propertius of *De Domo Sua* 49,[59] he would have been over military age anyhow. Asisium may well have been earmarked to provide plots for triumviral veterans before the siege:[60] various cities joined L. Antonius precisely because they had already had land confiscated for veteran settlements or because they felt threatened by confiscations. The neighbouring *colonia* of Hispellum (modern Spello) was established at some point in the triumviral period and certainly by 40 BC,[61] hence by Octavianus, and it was awarded territory belonging to other cities, among them Asisium, including arable land belonging to Propertius.[62] The centuriation of Hispellum at that time was a matter of lively professional interest for Roman land-surveyors.[63] The grants to

may be invalid since despite his instructions the remains of Gallus may not have been found and buried; alternatively *contegis* in *tu nullo miseri contegis ossa solo* (1.22.8) could be taken, especially in the context of *perpessa es* (1.22.7), as a historic present (i.e. 'you did not cover his bones with earth' *sc.* 'when he died'), thus leaving open the possibility that the bones of the *propinquus* had later been found and buried. At the end of the day, *ossa non sunt multiplicanda praeter necessitatem*!

57   For modern readers the fact that the dead man of 1.21 bears the same *cognomen* as the addressee of four other elegies of the Monobiblos poses an immediate problem, and of course, some connection between the two men cannot be ruled out absolutely. But lack of evidence, the commonness of the *cognomen* Gallus, and our inability to judge whether the coincidence would have posed a problem for an ancient reader all preclude further conclusions.

58   Du Quesnay (1992) 76 proposed identifying the 'Gallus' of 1.21 as the father of the Gallus addressed in 1.5, 1.10, 1.13, and 1.20, whom he regards as an Aelius Gallus (77–8); for counter-arguments see below, pp. 70–1 and n. 6. The *propinquus* of 1.22.7 cannot, of course, be Propertius' father, since that is not how a Roman would refer to his father.

59   See above, pp. 14–16.

60   The strategic need to found a military colony at Hispellum may have been determinant, but Asisium's proximity to, and links with, Perusia, and Asisium's association with the cause of L. Antonius must have made matters worse: cf. Gabba (1986) 101.

61   Keppie (1983) 177–9.

62   On these confiscations and the centuriation of Hispellum see Forni (1982) 35–6; Manconi et al. (1996) 392–419; Campbell (2000) 142–3, 388–9 (*Constitutio Limitum*), 174–5, 410 (Hyginus *Liber Coloniarum*).

63   See Keppie (1983) 177–9; Manconi et al. (1996) 397–9. Campbell (2000) locc. citt. n. 62.

Hispellum included non-adjacent territory: a cippus found at Arna – twenty kilometres from Hispellum – seems to confirm the assignment to Hispellum of parcels of extraterritorial land there;[64] and the Younger Pliny relates that Augustus gave the inhabitants of Hispellum a bath-house on the river Clitumnus which they still possessed in his day.[65] This is confirmed, and additional land-allocations are revealed, by the presence in that area of centuriation on the *decumanus maximus* of Hispellum.[66] The veteran colony will have been sited at Hispellum so that Caesarian veterans could hold for Octavianus the vital network of roads and waterways (especially the *Via Flaminia*) linking the Tiber valley with the Adriatic coast and Cisalpina.[67]

The confiscations imposed on Asisium are reflected in the extent to which the *pertica* of Hispellum intruded into the territory of Asisium.[68] A substantial tract of land in the plain below the foothills of Monte Subasio on the Asisium side of the Rio Tabito, the natural boundary between Asisium and Hispellum,[69] is centuriated on the orientation of the *decumanus maximus* of Hispellum and therefore represents territory taken from Asisium and given to Hispellum. Similar phenomena, namely centuriations within Asisinate territory which do not follow the *decumanus maximus* of Asisium, can be seen in three further areas, and they are at least worth noting as possible sources of information about allocations of the lands of Asisium. First, a series of plots to the north-east of the ancient road running from Asisium to Vettona use that road for orientation rather than the *decumanus maximus* of Asisium (which is used by the plots on the other side of the road). The researchers to whom we owe this information regarded this anomaly as an agrimensorial *variatio*.[70] However, it is at least worth considering whether it might represent the grant of plots to veterans who moved into Asisium after 40 BC and obtained land there as a reward for their support of Octavianus. The possible significance of the other two non-standard centuriations in the territory of Asisium is discussed below, pp. 58–9.

---

64 Manconi et al. (1996) 393–4; Valenti (2000) 213–14.
65 *balineum Hispellates, quibus illum locum divus Augustus dono dedit, publice praebent, praebent et hospitium* (*Epist.* 8.8.6).
66 Manconi et al. (1996) 417–19.
67 Manconi et al. (1996) 419, explaining the strategic importance of Hispellum.
68 Manconi et al. (1996) 415, esp. 'si può parlare, in realtà, della evidente intrusione dell'orientamento della centuriazione di Hispellum in pieno territorio di Asisium'.
69 Manconi et al. (1996) 400 n. 87.
70 Manconi et al. (1996) 416.

Modern research into centuriation in the Valle Umbra has not yet revealed the location(s) of the lands of the Propertii at Asisium, and there are no praedials derived from the *nomen* Propertius to assist in this quest. But a combination of epigraphic and archaeological evidence at least points to interesting possibilities. The place at Asisium most securely associated with the Propertii is the *Domus Musae*, their house beneath S. Maria Maggiore and the Bishop's Palace (see above, pp. 29–31). Another such location is the adjacent cemetery area outside the city wall. Out of the fourteen funerary inscriptions of, or erected by, Propertii which are reported in *ERAssisi*, two (*ERAssisi* 182 and 186) have been lost, and no find-spots for them are recorded;[71] others, although preserved, also lack a recorded find-spot. Despite these gaps, a partial pattern presents itself:[72] *ERAssisi* 47, the funerary inscription for C. Passennus Paullus Propertius Blaesus (cf. above, pp. 14 and n. 71, 26, 31), was discovered near the present church of S. Feliciano, S-E of the (ancient) Porta Moiano, the gate of Asisium closest to the *Domus Musae*. Two other funerary inscriptions for Propertii (*ERAssisi* 51 and 185) were found near the same church. Yet another funerary inscription set up by a Propertius (*ERAssisi* 183) was discovered near the present Porta Nuova, in the same general area; and another for a freedman Propertius (*ERAssisi* 184) turned up at S. Angelo de Panzo to the south-east.

This scatter of funerary inscriptions of the Propertii suggests that the Propertii had a family burial-ground in the locality of S. Feliciano. The inscription of the wealthy and important Passennus Paullus is additionally suggestive: it was found at the imposing rectangular monumental tomb near S. Feliciano oriented (as such structures often are) on the cardinal points. The tomb's extant remains of *opus caementicium*, from which the ancient cladding has been removed, measure roughly three and a half by two and a half metres, and they are about three and a half metres high on its southern side. In its original condition it must have been a very prominent monument;[73] and it

---

71   The antiquarian Francesco Antonio Frondini, whose *Museo Lapidario Asisinate* was first published as Bonamente and Catanzaro (1996), often recorded find-spots where they were known; cf. also *ERAssisi*.

72   The reported find-spots of other inscriptions of the Propertii are unhelpful (e.g. near the Piazza S. Pietro (*ERAssisi* 56), Assisi(!) (*ERAssisi* 187), Bastia (*ERAssisi* 188)), as are their former 'luoghi di conservazione' (e.g. the 'asilo infantile' (*ERAssisi* 55, 163), casa Vennarucci (*ERAssisi* 189), casa Sermattei (*ERAssisi* 190)).

73   The remains of further such monumental tombs can be seen in the general neighbourhood, although all except one have been more or less levelled. The other survivor, on a lower level and near the ancient road from Asisium to Urvinum Hortense, has been incorporated

seems very likely that it was the tomb of Passennus Paullus.[74] The tomb's placement and orientation and the find spots of the funerary inscriptions of the Propertii cohere with yet another indication of where estates of the Propertii at Asisium, including some of the land which the poet lost, were situated. The broader, southern face of the tomb looks towards the area where the *pertica* of Hispellum intruded deeply into the centuriation of Asisium,[75] i.e. around modern Le Viole, Capitan Loreto, Massera and Capodacqua. This area has two toponyms on its *limites*, C. il Torricone and Torrione, both of which signal the presence of ancient boundary structures. These four factors, then, the site of the *Domus Musae*, the probable cemetery area of the Propertii at S. Feliciano, the presence and orientation of the monumental tomb there, and the location of the land of Asisium recenturiated with the *pertica* of Hispellum, all point to the same conclusion, namely that this is where the Propertii originally owned land, including at least some of the land they lost. A further pointer in the text of Propertius 4.1 is noted below (p. 56).

One of the two remaining anomalous centuriations of Asisium might contribute to the resolution of a different problem and open up a further line of enquiry about the location of lands belonging to the Propertii. The two final elegies of the Monobiblos, which refer to the siege and fall of Perusia (1.21 and 1.22), have already been discussed in part above (pp. 46–50). They were written a decade or so after the events of 41–40 BC and in the aftermath of the decisive defeat of the Antonians at Actium in 31 BC. In them Propertius expresses sorrow and regret for the suffering involved in the Perusine War, but he abstains from partisan sentiments, and the only personal loss which he mentions is that of his *propinquus*. However, not a mere decade but some twenty-five years after 41–40 BC, Propertius, now firmly established under imperial patronage, chose to include in the prefatory elegy of Book 4 an account of the confiscation of his family land in the late 40s BC, having said nothing at all about this in his first three Books. How can this be explained? Did Propertius decide to make public at last something which had rankled with him over his entire

---

into a house. Such tombs can be found throughout the territory of Asisium and neighbouring cities, and another will feature in the discussion below.

74 The tombstone of an *ancilla* of C. Passennus Fortunatus (*ERAssisi* 172), presumably a freedman of Passennus Paullus, was found near proximate S. Damiano.

75 Some of their lost land might also have lain in the area centuriated using the Asisium–Vettona road as DM (see above, p. 51). But it would have made more sense ergonomically for their house to have had easier access to their principal estates.

poetic career but which he had all the while suppressed? Nothing in Book 4, which was clearly intended to satisfy the aspirations of Maecenas and Augustus for elegiac glorification of Rome's past and present in the manner of Callimachus' *Aetia*, gives comfort to such a thesis.

A closer investigation of the relevant lines in context reveals their tone as somewhat dissimilar to the plangency detected in them by commentators, and this suggests that Propertius' motives were of a quite different order. The lines come just after the third of the three passages (treated above, pp. 5–7) in which Propertius wrote of Umbria and Asisium. A point to be borne in mind is that the first (1.22.9–10) and second (4.1.62–6) of these passages are triumphalist in tone: they express Propertius' pride in Umbria, in Asisium and in his own poetic role. At its start – and despite Horos' earlier warning (120) of 'new tears' in store for Propertius – the third passage (4.1.121–6, put in the mouth of Horos) exudes a similar pride:[76]

> Umbria te notis antiqua Penatibus edit.
>   mentior? an patriae tangitur ora tuae,
> qua nebulosa cavo rorat Mevania campo,
>   et lacus aestivis intepet Umber aquis,
> scandentisque Asis consurgit vertice murus,   125
>   murus ab ingenio notior ille tuo?

>   123 quam *O*: qua ς   125 Asis *O*: Asisi *Lachmann*

Then follow immediately the lines in which the tone changes as Propertius speaks of the death of his father and of the *pertica tristis* which took away his arable land:

> ossaque legisti non illa aetate legenda
>   patris et in tenuis cogeris ipse lares:
> nam tua cum multi versarent rura iuvenci,
>   abstulit excultas pertica tristis opes. (4.1.127–30)

Lines 121–6 have been erroneously regarded as providing evidence that Propertius' birthplace was other than Asisium (see above, p. 3). It is more useful to recall that, as a student of rhetoric,[77] Propertius was

---

76   This passage and the succeeding lines are printed again here for the readers' convenience. For translations see above, pp. 6 and 25.

77   It will be suggested (below, pp. 63–5) that Propertius continued his rhetorical studies at least into the later 20s BC.

familiar with the rhetorical exercises of antiquity, among which were 'praise of a land' and 'praise of a city'.[78] Lines 123–6 share three topoi with that pair of exercises: emphasis on the fertility of the place being praised, an account of its boundaries and a description of its situation. Recognition of these topoi in the Propertian passage is essential if it is to be interpreted correctly. Propertius conveys the fertility of Umbria in lines 123–4 by dwelling on its well-watered nature both through direct description and etymology (see above, p. 6). Here Propertius is close to the rhetorical model, which speaks of a country being λιπαρά καὶ εὔυδρος and εὔφορος καὶ πολυφόρος (Menander Rhetor 345.2–3, cf. 346.4–7; 347.7–9).[79] Propertius also treats in this and in the succeeding couplet the second topos, the boundaries of the territory of Asisium, having previously announced it in *ora* (122). The third topos, the situation of the town Asisium, comes in lines 125–6. Menander makes much of these two latter topoi in combination under 'praise of a city'. The city's location involves consideration of its boundaries – how it stands in relation to its own territory and to neighbouring territories: πρὸς τὰς περιοίκους χώρας καὶ πόλεις (347.6 Spengel); πρὸς τὴν περιοικίδα χώραν ... πρὸς τὰς ἀστυγείτονας χώρας (349.2–5 Spengel). The latter reference comes in the middle of a long passage which Menander devotes mainly to the city's position in its territory (348.15–351.19 Spengel), but which also covers its water-supply (349.25–30 Spengel).

The realization that in 4.1.121–6 Propertius is not so much interested in specifying his birthplace as in sketching the boundaries and location of Asisium directs our attention to the ancient topography of the Valle Umbra, which was very different from the modern scene. The territory of Asisium was not oriented on the cardinal points but ran roughly N-W to S-E. To the south its territory was bounded by that of Mevania (123, modern Bevagna); in antiquity this town was surrounded by marshland. To the west of Asisinate territory lay in Propertius' day the ancient *Lacus Umber*. Subsequently this area was canalized and drained, and in it the present rivers Topino and Ose now flow side by side before joining up and meeting the river Chiascio, and the Chiascio flows for some distance before entering the Tiber. In

---

78   The best general accounts of these exercises are 'Menander Rhetor': 344.15–346.25 Spengel ('praise of a country'), 346.26–351.19 Spengel ('praise of a city'). The treatise then discusses related but more specialized encomia. For other such encomia see Russell and Wilson (1981) 245.

79   Mist is also mentioned specifically in the 'praise of a city' (347.14 Spengel).

antiquity, however, this area was subject to permanent inundation.[80] The *Lacus Umber* thus constituted the western boundary of Asisium, and on the other side of it stood the small independent towns of Vettona and Urvinum Hortense. Because the outflow of the *Lacus Umber* joined the river Chiascio, which itself will have overflowed in winter, Propertius may have conceived of the *Lacus* as also marking the north[-western] boundary of Asisium, beyond which lay the territory of Arna (but see below). The urban centre of Asisium (mentioned in line 125) is sited on a spur of Monte Subasio, near the [north-]eastern limit of the arable land of Asisium. A good part of Monte Subasio with its abundant woods and pastures must have been controlled by Asisium, but in Propertius' mind the city of Asisium itself may have represented the north-eastern boundary – at least of its arable land.

The view that Propertius was thinking in terms of boundaries raises a question: why does he concentrate solely on Mevania as the southern boundary and on the *Lacus Umber* as the western (and northern?) boundary and make no mention of Hispellum? Of course a poet cannot be expected to be as literal-minded as a land-surveyor and necessarily to enumerate every boundary. But poetic omissions can sometimes be significant, and it should be remembered that this couplet is separated by only two others from Propertius' mention of the *pertica* (incidentally the only appearance of this word in extant Latin poetry) which took away his land. One possibility, then, is that Propertius omitted Asisium's boundary with Hispellum precisely because Hispellum had intruded into the territory of Asisium, in the process taking away land of the Propertii, so that this was a boundary which Propertius was emotionally unable to accept.[81] Something similar may be happening with regard to the north-western boundary, if the suggestion made above – that Propertius was thinking of the *Lacus Umber* as forming that boundary too – is incorrect. Arna (modern Civitella d'Arno), which lay in that quarter, also goes unmentioned by Propertius. Arna was a *municipium* independent of Perusia in the imperial period, and it has sometimes been held to have attained that status after the Social War.[82] But there is another view, namely that Arna belonged to Perusia up to 40 BC, when Octavianus gave it inde-

---

80   See De Albentiis (1986); Manconi et al. (1996) Tav. VII/b. These works supersede Salvatore (1965) 392–8, who had argued that the *Lacus Umber* is the river Clitumnus.

81   Similarly some modern political maps represent not the real boundaries of states but their territorial claims.

82   E.g. Forni (1982) 26, classifying Arna as 'municipio dopo il 90 a.C.'.

pendence and *municipium* status as part of his retribution for the revolt of Perusia, with some of its land also possibly being assigned extra-territorially to Hispellum.[83] If this latter view is correct, then the home towns of the Volcacii and Propertii were neighbours in the fullest sense during the boyhood of the poet; hence the removal of Arna from the control of Perusia in 40 BC could have been yet another fact to be expunged. It would not only have been unacceptable to Propertius' original patrons, the Volcacii, but perhaps also to the poet himself if, as will be suggested (below, pp. 61–2), he had a link with the Volcacii additional to patronage.

We can now confront the question why Propertius records his loss of land so long after the event, and why he does so just after an appar-ently prideful account of Asisium. Despite the land confiscations of the late 40s BC, Augustan Asisium was to all appearances a flourish-ing town, and the Propertii of Asisium seem to have suffered no per-manent damage to their fortunes. It is a fair conjecture that, just as steps were taken by Augustus to restore Perusia to something like its original status,[84] Asisium (and Propertius) may no longer by 16 BC have been feeling the full impact of the losses incurred in the trium-viral era. This cannot, of course, imply that Asisium was fully restored to its original boundaries, something impossible given the continued existence of Hispellum. But Asisium and the Propertii could have been compensated wholly or partly for their losses, possibly through part-restoration of their lands at Asisium and possibly through new grants of land in adjacent areas. Propertius' proud claim *murus ab ingenio notior ille tuo* (126) would have a deeper significance if it implied that his poetic genius (*ingenium*) had made the wall of Asisium *notior* not just by bringing his home town poetic fame but by influencing the restoration, or compensation, of some of the lost terri-tory of Asisium.[85]

That such compensation was a real possibility can be seen from the parallel experiences, real or imagined, of two other Augustan poets. Horace was on the losing side at Philippi, and he was later the recipient from Maecenas of an estate at Licenza in Sabine territory.[86]

---

83   Valenti (2000) 201–4, 212–14.
84   See above, p. 48 n. 46.
85   Asisium will, of course, have had additional influential supporters in Rome, esp. the poet's relative, C. Propertius Q.f. T.n. Postumus (on whom see above, pp. 13, 16–24), and his marital relations.
86   On Horace's 'Sabine farm', see also above, p. 33.

It has been suggested that this 'gift' was actually a restoration to the poet of paternal land which had been confiscated.[87] Alternatively Horace perhaps forfeited property in Venosa and was compensated at Licenza. Virgil moved from his native Mantua to Naples in troubled times and his family allegedly lost estates in his native city, although the evidence is thin.[88] Whether they did or not, Virgil died a rich man, leaving 10 million sesterces, the minimum census of ten senators, the bulk of it doubtless in houses and land, presumably donated by Maecenas and Augustus among others. So poetry could pay well, and Virgil's supposed loss and recovery of land, even if mere echoes of events in his *Eclogues*, may still reflect a common experience of the period. The confiscations and veteran settlements of those troubled decades were relatively haphazard;[89] this is not to say, however, that manifest injustices could not be corrected subsequently, particularly if a victim had influential friends, and especially if those friends made a practice of acquiring estates as the fruits of confiscations.[90] It is, therefore, at least a possibility that in 4.1 Propertius mentions his loss of land at Asisium as a way of implicitly thanking those patrons and friends who had helped him make good or compensate his losses – and those of Asisium. After all, it would be unrealistic to imagine that Propertius contributed three books of elegies to the greater glory of Maecenas and Augustus and got nothing in return except thanks and a few rounds of applause! Propertius' lament in 4.10 for the age-old destruction of Veii (a place also associated with the Propertii) provides a close conceptual parallel for what is proposed here: Veii was restored by Augustus (see below, pp. 291–2).

It may even be, although naturally this proposal is highly speculative, that one of the two remaining anomalous centuriations in the territory of Asisium represents the receipt by the city (and the Propertii) of compensation for lost land. This recenturiation involved the reimposition of the *pertica* of Asisium upon a tract of land, some of it on the Hispellum side of the Rio Tabito, the natural boundary

---

87   See Bradshaw (1989), with Cairns (1992b) 107–9.
88   It comes from *Catalept*. 8, the authenticity of which is dubious: cf. most recently Holzberg (2004b), and, for a brief but richly documented sceptical treatment of Virgil's entire biography, Horsfall (1995) Ch. 1.
89   See, e.g., Cornell (1992) 137–8: 'It is well recognised that the absence of any institutionalised mechanism for rewarding veterans on discharge was the principal cause of political conflict' (138).
90   The statement in *VSD* 12 that Virgil refused to accept from Augustus the confiscated property of an exile, even if without foundation, illustrates the practice. Maecenas accumulated estates wholesale: cf. below, pp. 253–4.

between the two towns – land which had previously been centuriated using the *decumanus maximus* of Hispellum.[91] The tract's new orientation must mean that it passed from the control of Hispellum into that of Asisium. The recenturiated land lies just to the south east of the area where the *pertica* of Hispellum continued to intrude into the territory of Asisium. What remained to Hispellum consisted of the less valuable land rising slightly towards Monte Subasio, a slope which nowadays carries a mixture of olives, vines and corn, whereas the recenturiated area consists entirely of arable plain. These factors make the scenario envisaged even more plausible. No date for the recenturiation has been proposed, but, if what Propertius says about his loss of land is really an allusive reference to its restoration, some of his lands were restored (or compensated) before 15 BC, and it could be that this was the area involved. The cemetery of the Propertii and the tomb identifiable as that of Passennus Paullus are oriented towards this land as well as towards the area where Hispellum intrudes. It might, then, have contained acreage lost to the Propertii in 40 BC and subsequently restored.[92]

A topic still to be considered is whether the links between the young Sextus Propertius and the Volcacii Tulli went beyond patronage. The proximity of Perusia to Asisium – the two towns may have been full neighbours before 40 BC (see above, pp. 56–7) – must have been a factor in the relationship of Propertius to his patrons, as must the common 'frontier culture' which existed along the border between Umbria and Etruria. That culture has been well documented

---

91   See Manconi et al. (1996) 405, who report that, on the basis of their field-work plus 'l'indagine a livello catastale' they were able (*inter alia*) 'individuare a NE del quintario di cui sopra [i.e. "nell'ansa più estesa dell'originario *Lacus Umber* drenata dal Rio Tabito"], oltre che una sovrapposizione di centurie appartenenti all'orientamento della pertica di Assisi (per qualche motivo successivamente estesa in «territorio» di Spello) anche …'.

92   The remaining recenturiation in the territory of Asisium was of another even larger area of land on either side of the ancient road connecting Asisium to Urvinum Hortense, which was used as DM in the resurvey; see Manconi et al. (1996) 416–17. It is bounded by modern Tor D'Andrea, Perticara,Torricone (the latter two toponyms signal pertication), and the bed of the ancient *Lacus Umber* at its lowest extent, where another such toponym, 'C. Perticoni', is found. Manconi et al. (1996) concluded that the original centuriation had been carried out at the same time as that of Hispellum; they do not say explicitly whether the earlier centuriation used the *pertica* of Hispellum or of Asisium, but their Tav. VII/b seems to show the presence only of that of Asisium. They hypothesized that the recenturiation was a fresh (post-Augustan) dispensation following waterlogging; the dating is offered without argument at 416 n. 126. A large ancient building existed at the head of the re-surveyed area, and the remains of a monumental tomb still stand at the point (Torricone) where the road from Asisium to Urvinum Hortense entered it; these will have belonged to the local magnate whose influence or resources achieved the land-reclamation.

in a number of archaeological studies which have shown it extending, for example, to funerary practices,[93] and it would explain perfectly well how the Propertius of the 30s BC, a young Umbrian local aristocrat of Asisium who had suffered some loss of property in the late 40s BC, came to be aided in his attempt to make a career as a poet in Rome by Etruscan social superiors from neighbouring Perusia. Moreover, certain features of Propertius 1.1, 1.21, 1.22 and 3.24 studied above (pp. 49–50) indicate that the relationship between the Volcacii and the Propertii was hereditary and of some standing: the concern of the two elegies with the siege of Perusia implies a shared background of harsh experience, and the genial irony of the 'imaginary question' attributed to Tullus – about matters which Tullus knows perfectly well – projects an air of long familiarity. The evident ability of the young Propertius to withstand the losses of family land and to gain a privileged education thus fits an established social context.

But it is still appropriate to ask whether the two families were more closely connected. The community of culture between Perusia and Asisium manifested itself partly through the presence in both cities of the same families under their respective Etruscan and Umbrian-Latin guises. Thus we find in Perusia the Vipi, Scaefi and Vuisi, and in Asisium their counterparts the Vibii, Scaefii and Voisieni.[94] The Volcacii too had their Umbrian branch in Asisium – the Volcasii. Volcacius and its variants (Volcatius and Vulcatius)[95] are Romanized equivalents of the Etruscan name Velχ vel sim.,[96] and Volcasius, Romanized via Umbrian, is the same *nomen*, since in Umbrian *k* 'becomes a sibilant' before *e* and *i*.[97] Members of this family also appear in the public inscriptions of Asisium as high magistrates, with C. and L. Volcasius being found among the *quinqueviri* in the late republican or early imperial duplicates *ERAssisi* 27 and 28, and another C. Volcasius (if indeed he is not the same C.) in some sort of official position in *ERAssisi* 30. Yet another Volcasius, probably of Asisium, began his senatorial career in the second century AD, reached the consulship, and was *patronus* of Tuder.[98] Persons bearing Etruscan and Roman versions and variations of the name Velχ/

---

93   See Verzar (1976) 119–20.
94   See Sensi (1983) 165.
95   On these interchangeable forms of the name (including Volcasius) see Schulze (1904) 377–8; *RE* s.v. Volcatius (H. Gundel); Bonamente (2004) 44–5.
96   Torelli (1969) 303–4.
97   Buck (1904) 89–90, cf. Pulgram (1978) 103.
98   *CIL* XI.4647, cf. Forni (1983).

Volcacius are found epigraphically throughout Etruria, including Perusia,[99] and, since the original Etruscan Velχ is a theophoric name,[100] they were not necessarily all related. But the pattern of linked Etruscan/Umbrian names found in proximate Perusia and Asisium (above) makes it likely that the paired families in the two cities started out as blood-relations. The closeness of Sextus Propertius to the Volcacii therefore prompts the question whether, as well as being in their patronage, Propertius was also related to them. An economic hypothesis would make his mother either a Volcasia of Asisium[101] or a Volcacia of Perusia, and so in either case a relation in some degree of the consular Volcacii of Perusia. Other marriages between families of Asisinate and Perusine origin are attested epigraphically, one being between another of the Propertii and a lady with a latinized Etruscan name.[102]

If Propertius was somehow related through his mother to the Volcacii, this would not have raised the poet to the social status of the Volcacii, particularly if their connection was not close, or if it was through the Volcasii of Asisium. Hence Tullus' status as Propertius' patron would not be in question, although a further nuance would accrue to it. However, the hypothesis would help to explain something which has intrigued, and sometimes misled, Propertian scholarship, namely the poet's extraordinary interest in things Etruscan, which will be discussed more fully below, pp. 271–93. It would also illuminate the poet's mention of his mother in 4.1.131–2: *mox ubi bulla rudi dimissast aurea collo,/ matris et ante deos libera sumpta toga*. She is, of course, introduced there in part because Propertius' father was dead by this time. But, if Propertius' mother was related to the Volcacii/ Volcasii, his introduction of her would explicate and offer thanks for the protection which he had enjoyed from his mother's family after his

---

99 Schulze (1904) 377–8.

100 See van der Meer (1987) 124–6; Rix (1998) 210–11, 215, documenting its derivation from Etruscan *Velchans = Volcanus*.

101 The Asisinate inscriptions of the Volcasii are listed at *ERAssisi* p. 119. Of the five tombstones of their freed slaves two (*ERAssisi* 247, 249) were found at S. Feliciano, the area hypothesized above (pp. 52–3) as a burial ground of the Propertii, as was *ERAssisi* 30. A tombstone of a freedwoman of the family (*ERAssisi* 248) is built into a wall at the adjacent S. Damiano, which may imply a nearby find-spot.

102 *ERAssisi* 56: *Cn(aeo) Propertio/ T(iti) f(ilio) Scaevae decurioni/ Avillia Aura/ uxor* (late first century BC) – on the *nomen Avi(l)lius* see Schulze (1904) 72 with n. 3; this relationship is noted by Feichtinger (1991) 206–7. Cf. also the more complex Augustan example, documented by Coarelli (1996) 252–8, of Galeo Tettius of Etruscan background married to Petronia C. f. of Asisium.

father's death. And, if the poet's mother had an Etruscan background, his reference to her would also reflect the high status of women in Etruscan culture, and the importance attached to matrilineal descent in Etruria.[103]

Indirect confirmation of a relationship of some sort between the poet and the Volcacii may, oddly enough, emerge from the two passages discussed above in which Propertius *qua* insane lover refers to his (*patrii*)[104] *amici* (1.1.25 in the Monobiblos prologue addressed to Tullus, and 3.24.9 in the counterpart epilogue of Book 3), and from Propertius' reference to his *amicitia* with Tullus in the epilogue of the Monobiblos (1.22.2). If Propertius' mother was a Volcacia or Volcasia, *amici/amicitia* in these key passages might equate with Greek φίλοι/φιλία and mean 'relations'/'kinship' as well as 'friends'/ 'friendship'.[105] Another epigraphic conjuncture might minimally assist the hypothesis of a family relationship between Propertius and his patron Tullus. In a tomb complex on the Via Statilia in Rome two freedmen and a freedwoman of the Propertii were buried: *C. Propertius C.l. Parmenon* (*CIL* VI.6646), *C. Propertius C.l. Corumbus* (*CIL* VI.6657) and *Propertia C.l. Rodine* (*CIL* VI.6657). Near them is the tomb of *L. Volcacius Tulli l. Hospes* (*CIL* VI.6671), a freedman, apparently, of the consul of 33 BC. How much can be made of this is not obvious[106] since the complex includes the tombs of freedmen of other *gentes*.[107] But, if this particular conjuncture is not fortuitous, literary patronage alone will hardly account for it: it would rather imply a familial link between the Propertii and the Volcacii, joint tombs of related families being particularly characteristic of funerary practice on the frontier between Umbria and Etruria.[108]

103 Cf. Sordi (1981); Newman (1997) 95–8.
104 The fact that *patrii* refers to Propertius' father, not his mother, is no obstacle: the relationship is thought of as 'inherited from his father' (*OLD* s.v. *patrius* 3), i.e. from his father's marriage. On the additional reference in *patrii* to Propertius' inherited patronage see above, p. 49.
105 Although an extended application of *amicus/amicitia* to relatives in some degree is not considered by *TLL* or *OLD*, this sense would explain an apparent conflict between Roman law and poetic assumptions. Roman law entrusted the *curatio* of mad people primarily to relatives, and under the Twelve Tables it was undertaken by agnates, and failing them by *gentiles* (although the praetor could appoint other curators): cf. Kroll (1959) 76; Buckland (1963) 168; A. Watson (1975) 76–8. Yet *amici* are involved in looking after a madman at Prop. 1.1.25 and 3.24.9–10, as they are at Cat. 41.5–6: *propinqui, quibus est puella curae,/ amicos medicosque convocate* (*re* a supposed madwoman).
106 Sensi (1983) 171 n. 58 highlights this conjunction as 'singolare', but it is unclear whether the evidence can bear so much weight.
107 R. Lanciani *Nsc.* 1877.314–21.
108 Verzar (1976) 119–20.

Contact between the poet Propertius and yet another contemporary 'Volcacius'[109] seems very likely. In the Monobiblos high-level genres such as the epideictic *propemptikon* (1.6; 1.8), *kletikon* (1.11) and *epibaterion* (1.17) account for much of Propertius' rhetorical content; and the Propertian elegies in which these genres feature seem additionally to remain close to their poetic predecessors, extant or lost.[110] But some elegies of Books 2 and 3 are qualitatively different: they are sophisticated but close reworkings of *progymnasmata* (e.g. 2.7; 2.12)[111] – i.e. of lower-level rhetorical exercises. Moreover, although Propertius did continue also to write in epideictic and in other advanced modes, some of his later elegies have a more overt declamatory feel to them, and they sometimes contain elements borrowed directly from the contemporary rhetorical schools (e.g. 3.11, 3.13, 3.19 and 3.22).[112] As already noted (p. 28), Propertius studied rhetoric in his youth as part of his preparations for a forensic career (4.1.134), and he will have encountered both progymnasmata and more advanced rhetorical genres, including notably epideictic genres, in the course of his youthful studies. But something new happened to Propertius in the period 28–20 BC which altered his taste in rhetorical poetry. Declamation in the schools of rhetors at Rome goes back to the early first century BC,[113] but it was only in the decades 30–10 BC that this activity first became a significant element in the social scene:[114] the Elder Seneca's *Suasoriae* and *Controversiae* preserve particularly vividly the ethos of the Augustan schools.[115] But the attraction of the schools in general may not adequately explain why Propertius, who had been trained rhetorically before declamation came into full vogue, subsequently moved so strongly in the direction of open homage to rhetoric. Might the influence of a powerful contemporary rhetor with a

109 Apart, that is, from the jurist Volcacius, with whom Propertius might have been acquainted, although the chronology is difficult; see above, p. 27 n. 134.
110 Propertius' *propemptika* (1.6, 1.8) have the best documented literary pedigree, starting with Parthenius' *Propemptikon*, on which see Lightfoot (1999) 114–15 (fr. 26) and General Index s.v. *propemptikon*, and continuing through Helvius Cinna's *Propempticon Pollionis* (see Courtney (1993) 212–18) and Gallus' *propemptikon* for Lycoris (on which see below, pp. 114–16).
111 On 2.7 see Cairns (1979a); on 2.12, Enk (1962) II.169–71.
112 For the rhetorical exercises of Propertius' third book see Underwood (1971).
113 Bonner (1949) 17–18; Fairweather (1981) Part II Ch. 2 'The history of declamation' illustrates the difficulties inherent in attempts to chart this topic, among them incorrect statements by the Elder Seneca.
114 Bonner (1949) 39–44.
115 For all aspects of declamation see Fairweather (1981) esp. Part IV; Fairweather (1984); and the relevant sections of Kaster (1995).

distinct style be suspected? Here is how a modern scholar (Fair-weather (1981) 294), who makes no reference to Propertius, charac-terizes one such rhetor active at Rome in the 20s BC:

> It is clear that he was a declaimer, much like Fuscus, with two styles: a dry style for narrative and argumentation (e.g. *Contr.* II.3.4; X.1.3; 2.17; 6.1) and the quasi-poetic descriptive manner which we find in *Suas.* 1.2:
>
> > Inmensum et humanae intemptatum experientiae pelagus, totius orbis vinculum terrarumque custodia, inagitata remigio vastitas, litora modo saeviente fluctu inquieta, modo fugiente deserta; taetra caligo fluctus premit, et nescio qui, quod humanis natura subduxit oculis, aeterna nox obruit.[116]

The ethos of the quoted Latin passage recalls that of the sea-scenes of Propertius 3.7, the *epikedion* for Paetus who drowned at sea, and the rhetor so characterized and quoted is Volcacius Moschus (*praenomen* unknown). Moschus was a Greek teacher of rhetoric from Pergamum who already enjoyed a high reputation in his home town before he came to Rome in the early 20s BC and set up a rhetorical school there.[117] The elder Seneca attended his declamations and had critic-isms to make of them.[118] Moschus clearly received his Roman citizen-ship along with his nomenclature from, or through the good offices of, the proconsul of Asia, L. Volcacius L.f. Tullus, and he may have been encouraged by him to move to Rome.[119] Moschus' subsequent career was varied and colourful: accused of poisoning, he enjoyed the distinction of having as his unsuccessful defence advocates at his trial in 20 BC the patrician Manlius Torquatus,[120] and the consular and triumphator C. Asinius Pollio. Both men were involved in the practi-cal rhetoric of the courts, and Pollio is also known to have practised declamation. They were, then, in some sense pupils of Moschus, and

---

116 'Boundless and unexplored by man is the sea: it girdles the whole earth: it guards the lands: it is a waste of waters untroubled by the oar: now its shores are unquiet under the raging billow, now they are desolate when the billow withdraws: a horror of darkness weighs on its waters, and, I know not how, what nature has denied to human eyes eternal night overwhelms.' (tr. W. A. Edward)

117 See *PIR*[1] V 621; *RE* Suppl. IX no.18; Fairweather (1981) General Index s.v. Volcacius Moschus; Kaster (1995) 327.

118 *Controv.* 10 *Praef.* 10–11, on which see Fairweather (1981) 293–4.

119 Rome was, however, in any case a magnet to learned Greeks in the late 30s and early 20s BC.

120 Addressee of Hor. *Epist.* 1.5: cf. *Moschi causam* (9).

they again exemplify the level of society at which Moschus and similar Greek instructors moved. Moschus had no monopoly of 'quasi-poetic' effects: another such rhetor was Ovid's teacher, Arellius Fuscus (compared to Moschus above),[121] and yet another was Fuscus' pupil, Papirius Fabianus, author of a parallel passage on Ocean (*Suasoriae* 1.4). But, particularly in view of Propertius' long-established connections with the Volcacii, it is very likely that he sat under Moschus among others, and learned from him and from similar rhetors some of the new declamatory techniques so apparent in Books 2 and 3. The failure of Moschus' two distinguished advocates to save him from condemnation and exile in Massilia, where he again taught and was made an honorary citizen, may have been due to his obvious guilt.[122]

Besides Tullus (and his uncle) and Gallus in the Monobiblos, and Maecenas and Augustus in later books, the other living[123] contemporaries introduced by Propertius under their real names are Bassus (1.4), Ponticus (1.7; 1.9), Virgil (2.34), Cornelia and her relatives (4.11), and (Propertius) Postumus and Aelia Galla (3.12). Bassus and Ponticus are both presented as literary figures, Ponticus overtly as an epic poet, Bassus more covertly, but unmistakably, as an iambist.[124] Both men function in their different ways as literary foils to Propertius the elegist. In Ponticus' case the opposition relies on the standard epic/elegy antithesis so often exploited by Propertius, while with Bassus two-fold tensions are at work. One is a straightforward confrontation between Propertian elegy and the iambic poetry of Bassus; it may embody Propertius' attitude to his part-predecessor Catullus, who indulged in both poetic forms. The other emerges on the hypothesis to be offered in Chapter 3 that 'Gallus' is the elegist C. Cornelius Gallus: on that assumption Propertius is also comparing and contrasting Bassus *qua* iambist and Gallus *qua* elegist in their attempts to separate him from his mistress Cynthia. Propertius may be insinuating (perhaps quite unfairly) that, whereas his own elegies aim only to retain the love of Cynthia once he has won her, the elegies of Gallus resemble the iambs of Bassus in that they are aggressively directed towards

---

121 By Fairweather (1981) 294.
122 However, if, as suggested below, pp. 75–7, the Volcacii ceased to enjoy Augustus' favour around 27 BC, Moschus' later condemnation could also have owed something to his earlier association with them.
123 Paetus (3.7) and Marcellus (3.18) are posthumously commemorated.
124 Cf. Suits (1976); Cairns (1983a) esp. 79–83.

alienating and seducing other people's partners. Such an insinuation would cohere with the doubtless equally unfair portrait of Gallus as a former heartless seducer presented at Propertius 1.13.5–8.[125]

Despite the multiple literary dimensions of Ponticus and Bassus, which make them such convenient foils for Propertian elegy, they are not fictional characters. Ovid mentions Ponticus as an epic poet and Bassus as an iambist, and he characterizes them as members of his own former literary circle (*Tristia* 4.10.47–8).[126] Nothing more, however, is known about the pair than is offered by their Propertian and Ovidian notices. The *cognomen*[127] 'Ponticus' does not designate a person of Black Sea origins,[128] but if anything might rather reflect interest in, or a military or commercial connection with, the Pontic region on the part of Ponticus' father. No known Ponticus of the Augustan period offers himself as a candidate. Martial often addresses, or writes of, a 'Ponticus' in uncomplimentary terms,[129] but he is not Propertius' friend *redivivus*; nor is the only other 'Ponticus' in Latin poetry, the addressee of Juvenal *Satire* 8. As for 'Bassus', the Augustan declaimer Iulius Bassus is a possible candidate in view of the descriptions of his character, style and interests in the Elder Seneca's *Controversiae*, which sit well with the 'iambic' *persona* attributed by Propertius to his 'Bassus'.[130] *Controversiae* 10 *pr.* 12 mentions Iulius Bassus' *amaritudo*, and 1.2.21 has him speaking *sordide* (cf. also 10.1.13–15). In addition a remarkable – even for rhetorical declamation – number of Seneca's quotations from his performances show him dealing with women, usually as their antagonist; and among the women he mentions two are described or characterized as *meretrices* (1.3.11; 9.2.4). On the other hand 'Bassus' is a common *cognomen*, so this identification cannot be more than a conjecture.

Little need be said about the other characters of Propertian elegy. The vividness with which Propertius presents his beloved has persuaded many that behind the pseudonym 'Cynthia'[131] lurks a real and

---

125 Cf. also below, pp. 117–18, 221–2.
126 His pairing of them presumably also alludes to their role in the Monobiblos.
127 'Ponticus' is also (inevitably) a slave name; but Propertius' Ponticus is manifestly not of servile status or origin.
128 For the principles see Solin (1993).
129 2.32.2; 2.82.1; 3.60.9; 4.85.1; 5.63.2; 9.19.2; 9.41.1, 10.
130 This speculation is reported by Suits (1976) 86 n. 1.
131 The name 'Cynthia' is Apolline, as are 'Delia' and 'Lycoris'; but, more significantly, their immediate derivation is from Callimachean epithets of Apollo.

possibly identifiable individual woman.[132] The mask of Cynthia may indeed conceal at some remove one or more real persons. But neither of the two identifications of Cynthia so far proposed is convincing. Apuleius' claim that she was a 'Hostia' does provide her with a *doctus avus* (cf. Propertius 3.20.8) in the person of the epic poet Hostius, but *Hostia* is not always metrically interchangeable with *Cynthia* in Propertius' verses, and Apuleius is in any case a poor witness.[133] It has been proposed to emend Apuleius' *Hostia* to *Roscia*, which would resolve the metrical problem and also supply her with another sort of *doctus avus*, the actor Roscius (from Lanuvium, cf. Cynthia's presence there in Propertius 4.8), but this is no more than a shot in the dark. And, even if an identification were possible, it would have little interpretational value for Propertian elegy given that the personality of Cynthia is highly fictionalized and visibly composite: at one time she seems to be a run-of-the-mill *meretrix*, at another she is more selective in her lovers; now she has a *mater/lena*, now she seems to be independent with her own house and slaves; at one point she must shin down a rope and make love with Propertius at the crossroads, presumably because she has a jealous *vir*, whereas mostly she can admit Propertius at will; and so on and so forth. The multiple models for the characterization and content of Roman elegy in different branches of earlier Greek and Roman literature are responsible for this farrago.[134] Cynthia's *doctus avus* is indeed initially a puzzling figure, but, since Propertius needed a *docta puella* to appreciate his learned poetry, and since professions tended in antiquity to run in families, he may have wanted to confirm Cynthia's 'learning' by giving her an invented 'learned ancestor/grandfather', especially since ancient poetic talent was in fact sometimes familial.[135] Such an invention would be in line with the exaggerated claims to exotic or noble antecedents sometimes

---

132 Boucher (1965) 441–74 gives an account of her *persona* from which the brief sketch below may be documented; see 460–8 for the emendation 'Roscia'; Fedeli (1985) 592–3 discusses the problem, and notes that F. Della Corte made the same proposal.

133 Apuleius (Apol. 10) is demonstrably weak *re* Ticidas' mistress. Her alleged 'real' name and pseudonym clearly derive from a misreading of Ovid, and little trust can be given to his other identifications: cf. Bright (1981). On this entire area, see now Maltby (2002) 42–6, discussing the nomenclature and existential status of all the beloveds of Roman elegy.

134 Cf. esp. Day (1938).

135 E.g. in the families of Simonides/Bacchylides, Sophocles, and a number of Greek comic poets.

made for lower-class individuals in Roman literature.[136] But, all in all, it is not worth pursuing Cynthia's 'real' identity,[137] any more than it would be worthwhile to enquire into those of her rival Chloris and her old nurse Parthenie of 4.7, or those of the *meretrices* Phyllis and Teia of 4.8.

However, the totals of the occurrences by name of the five women and single boy for whom the three surviving Roman elegists profess love perhaps tell a more interesting story:

Tibullus	Delia	15 (all prior to 1.7)
	Marathus	3 (1.4 and 1.8)
	Nemesis	5 (2.3–2.6)
Propertius	Cynthia	61 (Bk 1: 30, Bk 2: 23, Bk 3: 3, Bk 4: 5)
	Lycinna	2 (3.15 only)
Ovid *Amores*	Corinna	14

A beloved can, of course, be referred to without the use of her or his name. But the address by proper name is arguably more personal and intimate, and thus more diagnostic of the erotic involvement with that particular beloved being asserted by a poet and his poetry. Hence, although these are naive statistics, which would remain naive even if modified to take account of the relative lengths of the texts involved, they are nevertheless useful. They confirm, for example, that Ovid's interest in 'Corinna' was markedly less intense than that of his fellow elegists in their beloveds.[138] Again, they underline the transient character of Tibullus' attachment to 'Delia' in contrast with Propertius' longer obsession with 'Cynthia'. Finally, they throw an interesting light on Propertius' poetic development. Current orthodoxy tends to see Book 4 as beginning a completely new trend in his work; but these statistics rather highlight Book 3 as his real point of departure from erotic elegy.

The other *personae* of Propertian elegy have Greek names and can be dealt with summarily. The slaves Lygdamus (3.6; 4.7; 4.8) and Lycinna (3.15) are obviously stock characters out of Comedy.[139] Iole,

---

136 Cf. esp. Hor. *Od.* 2.4.13–16, where wealthy, and indeed royal, parentage is ironically claimed for the *ancilla* Phyllis. Nisbet and Hubbard (1978) cite a number of parallels, including two from comedy.

137 Coarelli (2004) 110–15, however, takes a different view, regarding Cynthia as a real Hostia, and proposing to identify her tombstone in a mutilated inscription from Tibur.

138 Here the greater bulk of the *Amores* vis-à-vis Tibullan elegy affects the judgement.

139 On Lycinna see Yardley (1974).

Amycle and Acanthis (4.5), Nomas, Petale, Lalage, Chloris and Parthenie (4.7), and Phyllis and Teia (4.8) look to be from the same stable. 'Lycotas' and 'Arethusa' appear in 4.3 in a self-imitative variation of the scenario of 3.12, where the protagonists were Postumus and Aelia Galla. It is unclear whether Propertius means us to think once more of that pair, or whether 'Lycotas' and 'Arethusa' are a generalized Roman officer and his wife. Demophoon (2.22) has several possible origins,[140] while Panthus (2.21) remains a mystery.[141] In Chapter 9 it will be argued that 'Lynceus' (3.24–25) is a pseudonym for the poet L. Varius Rufus.

140 He could be modelled on the mythical Demophoon, who deserted Phyllis, and who is mentioned in this very connection at Prop. 2.24.44 (on the Callimachean original see Puelma (1982) 237–8); or he might be the poet 'Tuscus', author of a poem on the pair (Ov. *EP* 4.16.20); or he may recall an otherwise unknown literary character.
141 The Trojan priest Panthus, who appears in Homer and Virgil, hardly seems relevant; see now, however, the discussion of the problem in Fedeli (2005) 611–12.

CHAPTER 3

'Gallus'

A 'Gallus' is the addressee of four elegies of the Monobiblos, just as four are addressed to the younger Volcacius Tullus, and there is a degree of symmetry in the placements of the elegies to 'Gallus' (1.5; 1.10; 1.13; 1.20) and those to Tullus (1.1; 1.6; 1.14; 1.22). These facts have already been referred to (above, p. 42) along with a conclusion drawn by me from them over two decades ago,[1] namely that these men were both patrons of Propertius in the Monobiblos and were associated in real life. I also assented to Franz Skutsch's view that 'Gallus' is the first 'prefect of Egypt' and the first major Roman elegist, C. Cornelius Gallus.[2] It is only fairly recently that these proposals have begun to receive greater attention, with more focus on the identity question, and less on the possibility that 'Gallus' was Propertius' patron and an associate of Tullus; and, although the view that 'Gallus' is indeed the poet Cornelius Gallus has steadily been gaining ground,[3] Syme's two alternative candidates, an Aelius Gallus and a Caninius Gallus, still command respect.[4] An Aelius Gallus might seem to acquire credibility both from the known relationship between the Propertii and that family,[5] and from the associations between Asisium and the prefecture of Egypt (cf. above, pp. 20–2). But would an Aelius Gallus have had sufficient prestige in the late 30s and early 20s BC to be paired as a patron with a Volcacius Tullus?[6] No such doubts could

1   Cairns (1983a) esp. 88–91, setting out in greater detail the reasons for, and consequences of, the conclusions mentioned here.
2   Skutsch (1901); (1906): see further below, pp. 77–8; on the other (dead) Gallus of 1.21.7–8 see below, p. 77 n. 31.
3   See, among recent monographs on Propertius, Janan (2001) Ch. 2; P. A. Miller (2004) 64–94; for earlier supporters of this view, see below, pp. 77–8.
4   Syme (1978) 99–103; cf. Du Quesnay (1992) 77–8.
5   So Du Quesnay (1992) 77–8.
6   Moreover, the head of the family, the prefect of Egypt (26–24 BC), on whom see above, pp. 20–1, was equestrian; hence an Aelius Gallus would be just as dubious a candidate for

70

arise with a Caninius Gallus: L. Caninius Gallus held the consulship in 37 BC, as his homonymous son was to do in 2 BC.[7] But – and this consideration excludes both of Syme's candidates – the 'Gallus' of the Monobiblos is manifestly a writer, one who closely resembles an elegist in the 'neoteric' tradition.[8] The 'Gallus' of Propertius 1.20 looks like an erotic poet who has written learnedly about the mythical Hylas (cf. Chapter 7); and the numerous and detailed parallelisms between 1.5, addressed to 'Gallus', and 1.4, addressed to the iambist Bassus,[9] make it clear that the 'Gallus' of 1.5 is also a literary figure, who again most resembles an erotic elegist.

This and the succeeding chapters will argue that Cornelius Gallus had a pervasive and often underestimated influence on Propertius, particularly in the Monobiblos, and that failure to take full account of it has led to a distorted view of Propertius' poetry. They will also presume, and further support, the identification of the 'Gallus' of the Monobiblos with the poet, and see this as enhancing the potential of Cornelius Gallus' fragmentary elegiacs, and of the other surviving evidence about him and his work, to throw light on Propertian elegy. Insights extend beyond the four Propertian poems which address 'Gallus' to the distinctive character of Propertius' language and concepts and the variety of his elegiac œuvre (both of which turn out to be considerably indebted to Cornelius Gallus), to the progress of his literary career, and to the figure of Cynthia, who is in certain respects modelled on Gallus' mistress Lycoris: on one occasion – 2.3.18, where Cynthia dances the part of Ariadne – Cynthia even practises Lycoris' profession of mime actress. However, since most of C. Cornelius Gallus' elegiac production has been lost, attempts to establish Propertius' poetic debts to him must quickly move into the realms of hypothesis, and outcomes will therefore necessarily be the product of speculation. Inevitably, too, there is a high risk of error, but the alternatives are either to decline the enquiry altogether or to seek knowledge even at that risk; and the risk will be diminished if hypotheses

---

the politico-social *nobilitas* which Syme demands of 'Gallus' as Cornelius Gallus. Aware of this problem, Syme asserts that Aelius Gallus 'might belong to a noble family that had lapsed from the career of honours' (Syme (1978) 101), and that 'Gallus, it follows, may derive from an old senatorial family' (Syme (1986) 308). There is no evidence of this.

7   The father: *RE* s.v. Caninius No.4. *PIR²* C 389; the son: *RE* s.v. Caninius No.5. *PIR²* C 390.

8   'Neoteric' is employed in this volume as an inaccurate shorthand way of referring to those Roman poets of the 60s–40s BC who espoused the ideals earlier paraded by Callimachus and some of his contemporaries; for ancient usage of the term see Tuplin (1976).

9   These are set out at Cairns (1983a) 62–79.

extrapolate from the known to the unknown, and if assent is limited to consistent and mutually supportive results. It should also be made explicit that at the end of the day the two propositions, i.e. the heavy influence of Cornelius Gallus on Propertius and the identity of the 'Gallus' of the Monobiblos with the elegist, although mutually comforting, do not stand or fall together. The impact of Cornelius Gallus can be seen in many elegies of Propertius besides those addressed to 'Gallus', and even if in the future new evidence were to disprove the identification, it would still be legitimate to track the presence of his elegiac predecessor in the poetry of Propertius.

The historical C. Cornelius Gallus has in the last fifty years been the subject of two painstaking monographs which more than adequately cover what is known of his life and career.[10] A few updates and qualifications of older views of him, plus a consideration of his possible interactions with the Volcacii Tulli may be useful before his poetic and patronal relevance to Propertius is considered. First his birthplace: according to Jerome, Cornelius Gallus was a 'Foroiuliensis', i.e. born in a 'Forum Iulii'. Various attempts have been made to identify the Forum Iulii of his birth among the many such locations,[11] with Syme sketching a colourful scenario around Fréjus in Gallia Narbonensis, and depicting Gallus as the son of a naval officer in the Roman fleet based there.[12] Unfortunately, places called Forum Iulii were not usually called Forum Iulii in the period of Gallus' birth (70 BC?), although older localities might of course have been renamed Forum Iulii from 60 BC on.[13] More damaging to the 'Foroiuliensis' view was the epigraphic discovery, published in 1963, that Cornelius Gallus himself, while he was Octavianus' *praefectus fabrum*, established a 'Forum Iulii' in Egypt.[14] This raised the possibility that Jerome's 'information' resulted from confusion, and it also provided a plausible reason for that confusion.[15] There is, then, in fact no reliable evidence about Gallus' birth-place. A guess, but no more, would be that, like many litterateurs of the late republic, he came from Cisalpina.[16] Gallus' career as a poet belongs to the 40s (and possibly the

---

10   Boucher (1966) esp. 5–65; Manzoni (1995) esp. 3–55.
11   See Manzoni (1995) 4–6.
12   Syme (1938).
13   The point is made by Manzoni (1995) 5.
14   Magi (1963); Salvaterra (1987); Manzoni (1995) 6–12.
15   Manzoni (1995) 12–15; Burgers (1997) 103.
16   Cf. Manzoni (1995) 6. Nothing, however, should be made of his *cognomen*: cf. Solin (1993) esp. 16–17.

early 30s) BC, and there is no evidence of poetic activity on his part thereafter. Hence suggestions that Gallus was still writing elegy in the late 30s and early 20s BC should be discounted,[17] and along with them the idea that Propertius in the Monobiblos was reacting to changes in the nature of Gallan elegy. Similarly, and more regrettably, on present evidence there is no way of deducing with confidence Gallus' contributions to the development of the Roman poetry book, or of sensibly conjecturing the proportional make-up in terms of learning, or love, or subjective and objective content, of the individual books of Gallus' elegiac poetry. It is not even fully certain what their title was, although I favour the traditional view that it was *Amores*, arguing that recent scepticism on this point is misplaced, and that further unnoticed evidence supports *Amores* (see below, pp. 230–2).

Next, Gallus' military contribution to the final defeat of Antonius and Cleopatra needs to be reevaluated, since it appears to have been more substantial than many surviving sources admit. They have been influenced by the deliberate down-grading of Gallus' role in the conquest of Egypt which followed his fall from Augustus' grace.[18] Gallus landed in Cyrenaica early in 30 BC and quickly won over the four legions posted there by Antonius to secure the western flank of Egypt. He then marched on Egypt, captured the frontier town of Paraetonium, foiled an attempt by Antonius to induce his four former legions to redefect, and trapped and destroyed Antonius' fleet in the harbour of Paraetonium. It was these military successes that allowed Octavianus to invade Egypt on its other, eastern, flank. Alexandria fell to Gallus on the first of August 30 BC, and Gallus' machinations then led to the capture of Cleopatra and her treasure.[19] Gallus' subsequent appointment as 'Praefectus Aegypti' was therefore a reward for services rendered as well as a demonstration of Octavianus' confidence in his loyalty and his military and civil competence.

Thirdly, Gallus' fall: its exact date, the precise reasons for it, and the details and chronology of the series of events which brought it about remain unclear.[20] Our sources reveal only that after his return to Rome from Egypt Gallus was subjected to numerous accusations, and

17 For this and other approaches rejected in this paragraph see Ross (1975) 49–50, 83–5, 102–3.

18 Cf. Manzoni (1995) 39–4. Cairns (1983a) 88–9 too readily accepted a minimalizing view of Gallus' military contributions in Egypt.

19 Cf. Manzoni (1995) 39–43.

20 Cf. Rohr (1994); Manzoni (1995) 49–55.

they offer diverse hints about what they were: financial misconduct involving peculation in Egypt, hubristic behaviour there, and verbal, possibly drunken, attacks on Augustus.[21] His support for Q. Caecilius Epirota, a freedman from the household of Agrippa's wife who was suspected of tampering with her, may not have been to his advantage.[22] In 27 or 26 BC a senatorial decree was issued against Gallus, either after or as part of a legal process in which he was condemned to exile and confiscation.[23] At some point Augustus renounced his 'friendship' with Gallus. The outcome of it all was Gallus' suicide. Augustus then complained, somewhat disingenuously, that 'he alone could not set what limits he chose to his anger with his friends'.[24] There is no evidence that Gallus was planning a revolt against Augustus during his prefecture of Egypt: the papyrus once thought to attest this does not in fact do so.[25] Gallus may well have expected higher honours or greater generosity from Augustus on his return from Egypt. His definitive role in its conquest after Actium, together with his suppression of a major revolt and his conduct of a successful frontier war during his tenure of office could have swelled his expectations. It seems, however, that Augustus was in these years hyper-sensitive to anything which might detract from his own image as the victor of the Civil Wars. This is shown by the steps he took to disallow the claim of the younger Crassus to dedicate *spolia opima*;[26] and in this climate Gallus may have felt that his military merits were being undervalued. If Gallus showed himself resentful about this or complained about Augustus' ingratitude, that would have sealed his fate.

On the hypothesis that C. Cornelius Gallus was one of Propertius' patrons, his fall and suicide will have deprived Propertius of his patronage, and been one of the factors in the poet's entry into the circle of Maecenas (cf. Chapter 8). Another dependant of Cornelius Gallus

---

21 Sueton. *Aug.* 66; Dio 53.23; Ov. *Am.* 3.9.63–4; *Tr.* 2.445–6; Ammian. Marcell. 17.4.5, on which see Schork (2004) 81–7, accepting that Gallus was accused of misappropriating Egyptian spoils.
22 Despite the matter of Agrippa's wife, the *temeratus amicus* of Ov. *Am.* 3.9.63–4 is undoubtedly Augustus.
23 On the quasi-judicial role of the Senate in Gallus' prosecution see Carter (1982) 188.
24 *quod sibi soli non liceret amicis, quatenus vellet, irasci* (Sueton. *Aug.* 66, tr. J. C. Rolfe).
25 Cf. Lewis (1975). Callegari (1999) discusses possible earlier datings for the events to which the papyrus refers.
26 For a useful summary cf. Raaflaub and Samons (1990) 422–3. More recently Rich (1996), in a review of all the evidence, has argued that Crassus did not in fact claim the right to dedicate *spolia opima*. But it is hard to reconcile his position with Augustus' documented pronouncement about the *spolia opima* and with the interest in this topic shown by other Augustan writers, including Propertius (cf. 4.10, and below, pp. 289–91).

whose fate *mutatis mutandis* paralleled that of Propertius was the learned freedman of Atticus, the *grammaticus* Q. Caecilius Epirota, already mentioned (p. 74) as suspected of sexual misconduct with the wife of Agrippa. Epirota was expelled from Agrippa's house, and taken in by Cornelius Gallus. The fall of Gallus compelled Epirota to earn his living, which he did by opening a school.[27] Propertius, who may have known Epirota, shared his lot in that by 27/26 BC he needed a new protector, whom he found in C. Maecenas. His need will have been enhanced if the Volcacii Tulli, who virtually disappear, not just from Propertian elegy but from the historical record, at exactly this time, simultaneously fell from Augustus' favour. Nothing more is heard of the consular uncle after his proconsulship of Asia (29 BC), and the nephew, who was so prominent in the Monobiblos, drops out of sight in Book 2. Apparently he remained in Asia after his uncle's term of office and was still there in the late 20s BC, when Propertius notes that he has been in Cyzicus 'for so many years' (*tam multos ... annos*, 3.22.1). A Roman of high birth and of praetorian rank, as Tullus was, would not normally have spent such a long time (6–8 years?) in Asia unless something was amiss. The very mention of Cyzicus as Tullus' residence in the province of Asia could be a tactful way of explaining to Propertius' readers that Tullus was no longer an imperial functionary in the province of Asia but an exile, actual or *de facto*, there: Cyzicus lies just beyond the 500 mile limit from Rome which exiles were required to observe, and it may have been well known as a preferred place of exile since Cicero, going into exile in 58 BC, repeatedly stresses in letters sent back to Rome that Cyzicus is his destination.[28]

An explanation for the fall of the Volcacii, if that was what it was, might be that they were either involved in those activities of C. Cornelius Gallus which led to his disgrace and suicide, or were too closely associated with the fortunes of Gallus in general. In that case

---

27 On all aspects of Epirota see esp. Kaster (1995) Index s.v. Caecilius Epirota, Q.
28 *Ad Att.* 3.6.1; 3.13.2; 3.15.6; 3.16 (the last three written at Thessalonika). For troubles at Cyzicus in the late 20s BC, which led Augustus to remove its status of 'free city' because of harm done to Roman citizens (Dio 54.7.6), see Bowersock (1965) 21, who suggests that Tullus could have lost his life in them. But one wonders whether the murder of an expraetor at this time in a city of Asia would have escaped the historical record. Tullus could, of course, have been stationed in Cyzicus precisely because it was a troubled city (for further unrest there in AD 25 see Bowersock (1965) 108), and have remained there after his official posting lapsed. Curiously Thessalonika seems to be the only location outside Italy where freedpersons of the Volcacii are epigraphically attested (*IG* X.2.1.399 – first century AD).

the Volcacii, both in their rise and fall, would parallel another figure just mentioned (p. 74), M. Crassus, the nephew of the triumvir. It was suggested (above, pp. 47–8) that the Volcacii were rewarded with an ordinary consulship and the prime province of Asia for transferring their allegiance from Antonius to Octavianus in the late 40s or 30s BC; even so Crassus defected from Antonius shortly before Actium, as his reward became *consul ordinarius* in 30 BC, and was given the proconsular military province of Macedonia the year after. Then Crassus' attempt to claim the *spolia opima* for personally killing an enemy chieftain offended Augustus and his career terminated.

Of course, alternative interpretations of the apparent eclipse of the Volcacii could be offered. It might, for example, be hypothesized that the elder Volcacius Tullus died soon after his return from Asia and that the younger Tullus liked life in Asia, lacked political ambition, did not want to marry, and lost interest in patronizing Propertius. Some *nobiles* certainly did decline to seek *honores*. But Tullus had already entered upon the *cursus*, and apparently he had glowing prospects, so it seems more likely that something went amiss with his career. Moreover, the only Propertian elegy later than Book 1 in which the younger Tullus features (Propertius 3.22) favours the notion that Tullus' long stay in Asia was not genuinely voluntary. It is a *kletikon* celebrating the *laudes Italiae* and inviting the younger Tullus to return from Asia. But behind the ostensible friendly invitation lie the elegy's public aspects: the elegy looks to be a concession on the part of Maecenas and Augustus to Propertius' residual duty towards his ex-patron, the poet being permitted to demonstrate that his change of patronage was not due to disloyalty to his former patron, and simultaneously a signal to Roman society that Tullus would be socially *persona grata* on his return to Rome.[29] If this is the true background to 3.22, then Tullus' public recall was also intended as an exercise of *clementia* by Augustus. Propertius holds out to Tullus (3.22.40–2) prospects of marriage, family, an oratorical career, and candidacy for an *honos* (i.e. a magistracy) appropriate to his family's status, hence in his case the consulship, since he was already praetorian. Tullus might therefore appear to have been fully rehabilitated, or never to have been in disgrace in the first place. But these lines are perhaps no more than face-saving consolatory

---

29   This last function is also that of Hor. *Od.* 2.7, where a 'Pompeius' who had fought on the losing sides in the 40s and 30s BC is welcomed back to Rome.

pretences. At all events, after Propertius 3.22 the younger Tullus and his family drop out of sight.[30]

With these historical points in mind the problem of the identity of Propertius' 'Gallus' can now be considered in greater detail.[31] In two monographs written in the first years of the twentieth century and focused around the early Virgil[32] Franz Skutsch advanced a number of novel proposals: one of them, made mainly on the basis of Virgil's sixth and tenth eclogues and various elegies of Propertius, especially 1.1, 1.8, 1.18, and 1.20, was to identify the 'Gallus' of the Monobiblos as the poet C. Cornelius Gallus. Skutsch's proposals were soon attacked, the main fire being directed at his now (almost universally) rejected theory that the *Ciris* is the work of Cornelius Gallus.[33] In the fray, however, the identification of Propertius' 'Gallus' as the poet also suffered, and, although it found at least one early supporter,[34] many important scholars of the twentieth century regarded it as unacceptable.[35] But attitudes have slowly been softening: Propertius 1.20 has always been an embarrassment to those wishing to expel Cornelius Gallus altogether from the Monobiblos,[36] so much so that some commentators on 1.20 opt for silence rather than enquiry;[37] but others have been willing to see the poet in the 'Gallus' of Propertius 1.20, an elegy with all the hallmarks of 'neoteric' poetry and unique in many respects within Propertius' œuvre (see Chapter 7), although without necessarily extending the identification to include 1.5, 1.10, and

---

30 There is a possible, but by no means certain, later family member in the Neronian senator 'Vulcacius/Volcacius' (*PIR*¹ V 623); Tac. *Hist.* 4.9 gives him the *cognomen* 'Tertullinus', but at *Ann.* 16.8 he is more plausibly 'Tullinus' vel sim. This man escaped condemnation in AD 65, and as tribune of the plebs in AD 69 vetoed a *senatus consultum*, but he failed to win high office. Torelli (1969) 303 notes the existence of a high-ranking Geminia Volcacia of the second century AD, and of a senator, C. Volcacius Gurges (the *cognomen* is possibly Etruscan) known to Pliny, but there is no indication of links between them and the Volcacii Tulli.

31 This account excludes the 'Gallus' who appears at Prop. 1.21.7–8. He was killed in the aftermath of the siege of Perusia in 40 BC, and he was identified (above, pp. 49–50) with the kinsman (*propinquus*) to whom Propertius refers in 1.22.7.

32 Skutsch (1901) and (1906).

33 Cf., e.g., Leo (1902); (1907).

34 Alfonsi (1943) 54. Boucher (1966) 84–101 did not expressly assent to Skutsch's theses, although his thorough exploration of them undoubtedly contributed to their revival.

35 Apart from its earliest critics, and the reviewers of Ross (1975) (below, p.78 nn. 39, 41), cf., e.g., Hubbard (1974) 25; La Penna (1977) 11; Syme (1978) 99–103; Fedeli (1980) 153; Fedeli (1981) 235–6; Du Quesnay (1992) 74–8.

36 See also below, p. 220.

37 E.g. Fedeli (1980) writes of 'l'amico Gallo' throughout his commentary on 1.20, although he rightly concludes (455) that Cornelius Gallus treated the Hylas myth.

1.13.[38] The turning point in the history of the 'Gallus' problem was the appearance in 1975 of David O. Ross Jr's monograph *Backgrounds to Augustan poetry: Gallus Elegy and Rome*, the central chapters of which revived and enlarged Franz Skutsch's thesis. Ross's treatment of 'Gallus' in Propertius did not find favour with most reviewers;[39] nevertheless, and despite certain difficulties which Ross's monograph presents,[40] his arguments were not received with total scepticism,[41] and over the intervening years they have gathered steadily increasing support.[42]

The main obstacle to the hypothesis that 'Gallus' is the poet C. Cornelius Gallus has always been Propertius 1.5.23–4, lines addressed to 'Gallus':

> nec tibi nobilitas poterit succurrere amanti;
> nescit amor priscis cedere imaginibus.

Nor will noble birth help you as a lover: love does not know how to defer to ancient masks.

On a literal reading of this couplet Propertius is attributing to 'Gallus' *nobilitas* and *priscae imagines*, possessed only by men whose ancestors had held senior magistracies.[43] But the historical C. Cornelius Gallus was an *eques*, so he was not *nobilis* and he did not have *imagines*.[44] Hence, the sceptics claim, 'Gallus' cannot be C. Cornelius Gallus. In an earlier attempt at a detailed refutation of this position I added new considerations to those advanced by earlier adherents of the identification.[45] Here I summarize the positions adopted there,

---

38   E.g. Bramble (1974) 87; Petrain (2000). Monteleone (1979) 38–53 explores in detail Gallan material in 1.20, while continuing to deny that its Gallus is the poet (38 n. 27).
39   Macleod (1975); Du Quesnay (1978); West (1978); Schmidt (1979).
40   These are mainly a consequence of the topic, which requires some repetitiousness and which demands a higher degree of indexing and cross-referencing than it received; hence the resultant criticisms of Schmidt (1979) are excessive.
41   See in particular Zetzel (1977), who, although doubtful or agnostic on a number of issues, presents a balanced assessment and adds many useful points.
42   E.g. Thomas (1979); King (1980); Cairns (1983a); Gall (1999) 181–91; Janan (2001) Ch. 2; P. A. Miller (2004) 78–83.
43   *nobilitas* can be a more flexible concept than is sometimes realised: for different approaches see Brunt (1982); Shackleton Bailey (1986); Cairns (1983a) 84–8; Giordano (1990); Burckhardt (1990); Levi (1998); and the question who was entitled to possess and display *imagines* (masks or representations of ancesters) is controversial: see Flower (1996) esp. 53–70 (with bibliography).
44   Syme (1978) 99–103.
45   Cairns (1983a) 84–8; the case made failed, however, to persuade Du Quesnay (1992) 76–7.

adding some supplementary remarks. I argued that the Propertian couplet is capable of a reading other than the reading it has usually received. First, the pentameter, which talks of love not giving way to *imagines*, does not directly attribute *imagines* to Gallus. Second, *nobilitas* in the hexameter, which Propertius asserts will not help Gallus' love-suit, may have here, not its politico-social sense but the non-technical sense 'celebrity', *nobilis* being linked with *nomen* and *notus* in popular etymology.[46] Gallus' *nobilitas* is therefore in effect the same thing as his *tantum nomen,* which two lines later Propertius says Gallus is in danger of losing: *quam cito de tanto nomine rumor eris* ('how quickly from being such a great name will you become mere gossip', 26). Why, then, does Propertius refer to the *nobilitas/nomen* of 'Gallus'? As will be argued below (pp. 97–9), C. Cornelius Gallus had claimed in his own verses to be 'well-known', and in doing so he had employed prominently a group of terms which became particularly emblematic of Gallan elegy.[47] These terms appear in profusion in Propertius 1.5: *nomen* (26), *notus, nota* (16), *noscere* (18), *nobilis/nobilitas* (23), and *ignotus* (5);[48] and it would seem that *nescire* (possibly imagined to be the negative of *noscere*) and *nescius* were also part of this same group (cf. 24).[49]

Moreover, Cornelius Gallus appears to have made prominent use of the term *imaginibus* at the end of one or more pentameters. The similarity between Propertius 1.5.24 and 1.14.8 has long been remarked on, and both lines have been identified as Gallan in inspiration:[50]

nescit Amor priscis cedere **imaginibus** (1.5.24)

nescit Amor magnis cedere divitiis (1.14.8)

---

46   *LALE* s.vv.

47   On the presence of these terms in 1.20, addressed to 'Gallus', where they are accompanied by numerous other Gallan features, see below, p. 226.

48   On these terms see Tränkle (1960) 24; Ross (1975) 73 and n. 1, 118 n. 2; King (1980) 213–14; Cairns (1983a) 85–6; Petrain (2000) 410; for the entire etymological background see Michalopoulos (2001) 128–30, 167. In 1.5 the Gallan flavour is reinforced by 28: *cum mihi nulla mei sit medicina mali,* on which see below, pp. 100–1.

49   Cf. the appearances of *nescire/nescius* in the Propertian examples which follow and the reappearance of *nescire* in Ov. *AA* 1.222, discussed below, p. 424.

50   By Tränkle (1960) 23, who also notes the resemblance between the ending of Prop. 1.5.23 *succurrere amanti* and those of Ov. *EP* 3.2.109 *succurrere amico* and *Ciris* 383 *succurrere amori.* Ross (1975) 68 n. 3, 95 n. 3 accepts Tränkle's suggestion. Here and elsewhere words in passages quoted are typographically coded to draw attention to verbal and/or conceptual parallelisms. Bold italic may be used without comment to indicate significant terms which have already been linked with Gallus.

Two more passages from the same stable (the first also addressed to 'Gallus'), but where the sense of *imaginibus* is different, can be added:

nescius undis

errorem blandis t̲a̲r̲d̲a̲t̲ **imaginibus**   (Propertius 1.20.41–2)

vanum nocturnis f̲a̲l̲l̲i̲t̲ **imaginibus**   ([Tibullus] 3.4.56)

More will be said about *imaginibus* as a Gallan line-ending in later chapters; but for the moment it is enough to observe that when composing these lines Propertius and ps.-Tibullus obviously had in mind either a single model or two related models. It, or one of them, was clearly very similar, if not identical, to Propertius 1.5.24. Given all the other evidence, can it be doubted that the author of the model line(s) was Cornelius Gallus? The problematic couplet can, then, be seen first as challenging Cornelius Gallus in 1.5.23 using Gallus' own Leitmotiv – his poetic fame – and then as quoting against Gallus in 1.5.24 (more or less) one of Gallus' own elegiac verses. The meaning of the couplet is therefore:

> Your 'celebrity' won't help you as a lover: <and, after all, it was you yourself who said> 'Love does not defer to distinguished pedigrees'.[51]

If this explanation is correct, then the couplet ceases to be a barrier to the identification of 'Gallus' as the poet Cornelius Gallus. Propertius' contemporary readers would have appreciated the fine irony of Propertius confuting his poetic mentor and probable patron Cornelius Gallus with words out of, or virtually out of, his own poetry.

Other aspects of this couplet must also have intrigued readers. False claims to distinguished descent were not infrequently made in Rome,[52] and no doubt were often flatteringly accepted, particularly since, even in the politico-social sphere, *nobilis* was far from stable in its meaning and applications (see above, n. 43). C. Cornelius Gallus is unlikely to have made a claim to politico-social *nobilitas* on his own behalf, and Propertius will certainly not have been implying any such thing here. Possibly, however, a shock effect was intended in lines 23–4, with readers initially misled or confused into imagining that such a

---

51   The precept of Ovid's *lena* Dipsas to her *meretrix* pupil (*nec te decipiant veteres circum atria cerae:/ tolle tuos tecum, pauper amator, avos, Am.* 1.8.65–6) perhaps reflects the Gallan line which Propertius reproduces.

52   See the bibliography at Cairns (1983a) 102 n. 80.

claim was being made, only to realize the truth at a second glance. The correctness of this entire explanation depends, of course, on the Gallan relevance of *nomen*, *nobilis* etc., and on line 24 being a quotation or near-quotation from Gallus. The first of these two prerequisites will be established later in the present chapter; the second of them has already been treated, and will be raised again in later chapters.[53]

Particularly if C. Cornelius Gallus is the addressee of four elegies of the Monobiblos, then it is reasonable to expect that his poetry exercised a strong influence on Propertius, especially in Book 1; and if Gallus was one of Propertius' first two patrons as well as his elegiac predecessor, then such influence can be anticipated to an even greater degree The question then arises how it can best be traced. It might seem an obvious approach to start with the sole explicit and fully assured (posthumous) reference to the historical C. Cornelius Gallus in Propertius:

> et modo formosa quam multa Lycoride Gallus
> mortuus inferna vulnera lavit aqua!   (2.34.91–2)[54]

And of late how many wounds did Gallus, dead of love for beautiful Lycoris, wash with the water of the underworld.

But this couplet does not offer a good starting point: Propertius is deliberately blurring the political nature of Gallus' suicide with the false suggestion that Gallus died in, or because of, love for Lycoris.[55] Doubtless these lines contain reminiscences of Gallus' own elegiac poetry, and one can be conjectured,[56] but they do not lead very far. Equally frustrating, at least initially, as a means of approaching Gallan influence upon Propertius are 1.5, 1.10, 1.13, and 1.20, poems which –

---

53 Gall (1999) 183–5 notes (as arguments for her thesis that *Ciris* is by Gallus) many coincidences between Prop. 1.5 and *Ciris* which can alternatively point to Gallus as a common source of both texts.

54 On Prop. 2.34 see below, n. 56 and pp. 112, 114, 213 n. 81, 215.

55 The equally sycophantic but more incautious formulation of Ovid may be contrasted: *tu quoque, si falsum est temerati crimen amici,/ sanguinis atque animae prodige, Galle, tuae* (*Am.* 3.9.63–4) – with Gallan *animae!* (Cf. below, p. 91 n. 77 and pp. 224–5). Less flattering to Gallus is *non fuit opprobrio celebrasse Lycorida Gallo,/ sed linguam nimio non tenuisse mero* (Ov. *Tr.* 2.445–6).

56 Commentators on Prop. 2.34.91–2 cite as a parallel Euphorion fr. 47 van Groningen: Κώκυτός <τοι> μοῦνος ἀφ' ἕλκεα νίψεν Ἀδωνιν. But, since Parthenius is 'highly likely' to have treated Adonis (Lightfoot (1999) 183; cf. also her General Index s.v. Adonis), Propertius may well be alluding here not only to Euphorion but also either to Parthenius' variation on Euphorion, or to a Gallan reprise of Parthenius, or to both; for a situation arguably similar see below, pp. 237–49.

on the hypothesis that their 'Gallus' is C. Cornelius Gallus – must be indebted to Gallan elegy. The obstacle here is that their representations of Gallus patently involve high degrees of *deformazione*.[57] As a result Gallus has a different *persona* in each of them (cf. also below, pp. 221–2), and this makes them a poor starting point for an enquiry into Gallus' influence on Propertius.

The lesson conveyed by this initial rebuff is that thematic pointers to Gallus in surviving Augustan poetry are not the easiest way to begin tracing the presence of Gallus in Propertius. They must eventually be used for that purpose, although always with caution; and the results obtained through them should, where possible, be confirmed by other, less dramatic but for that reason more reliable, markers of his presence. The lower-key Gallan markers are of two types: verbal, to be identified via certain lexical patterns which recur in Propertian and other Roman elegy, and metrical, i.e. features which distinguish Propertian elegy from most other Roman elegy and which can be traced to Gallus. These markers give fairly robust indications of Gallan influence, and, even though in isolation their interpretative value is often limited, they can be informative if combined with thematic evidence. This and succeeding chapters will exploit all three approaches – verbal, metrical, and thematic – stressing their confluence throughout. It is best, however, to start on the verbal level, and with Gallus himself, as represented by the Qaṣr Ibrîm fragment (= fr. 2 Courtney),[58] since it is Gallus' own lines which authorize a new heuristic methodology,[59] that of 'Gallan verbal complexes'.

Such complexes, some with an attested basis in Gallus' elegy, some assembled from later writings alone, will surface frequently in this volume; and arguments that single terms and themes are Gallan will sometimes be advanced in multiple contexts and from several viewpoints. Cross-referencing which is considered useful will be provided; otherwise pointers will be given to Index II (Index of Gallan Words and Concepts), or it will be assumed that the reader will consult that index for further evidence and information.

Since the Qaṣr Ibrîm fragment will frequently be cited elsewhere

---

57   Italian *deformazione* is left untranslated in this volume because it can cover both misrepresentation and assimilation. The closest English term, 'deformation', does not do so, and it has other, unwanted, overtones. For this type of approach cf., e.g., D'Anna (1981); (1987); Perkell (1996).

58   The sporadic attempts to deny Gallus' authorship of these lines are, I believe, entirely futile.

59   This methodology was employed in Cairns (2004b), an earlier part-version of Chapter 7.

in this volume, the translation given by its first editors, P. J. Parsons and R. G. M. Nisbet, is reproduced here, with line numbers appended:

(a) .... sad, Lycoris, by your misbehaviour. (1)

(b) My fate will then be sweet to me, Caesar, when you are the most important part of Roman history, and when I read of many gods' temples the richer after your return for being hung with your trophies. (2–5)

(c) At last the ... Muses have made poems that I could utter as worthy of my mistress. .... the same to you, I do not, Viscus, I do not, Cato, fear ...., even if you are the arbiter. (6–9)

(d) ... Tyrian ... (11).

To describe the construction and exploitation of Gallan verbal complexes as a 'new methodology' is not to deny that, long before the publication of the Qaṣr Ibrîm papyrus, scholars from Franz Skutsch on were constructing, without categorizing them as such, certain Gallan verbal complexes as part of their attempt to recover the verbal and thematic content of lost Gallan elegy from traces in his successors;[60] and some of these same complexes will reappear in this and succeeding chapters. But full consciousness of the methodology and of its implications could develop only in the wake of the Qaṣr Ibrîm Gallus. In particular the papyrus permitted recognition of the massive impact upon later Roman poetry of certain Gallan terms: *Romanae ... historiae, fecerunt, carmina digna,* and so forth.[61] That impact is fundamental to the validity of the methodology, and permits its extension to terms not represented either in the Qaṣr Ibrîm papyrus or in the single line of Gallus previously known (fr. 1 Courtney).[62]

The most helpful phrase in the Qaṣr Ibrîm papyrus is *Romanae ... historiae*: it provides the point of departure for this study because it provides unshakeable proof of the meaningfulness of the Gallan *historia* complex. The relevant couplet is:

> fata mihi, CAESAR, tum erunt mea dulcia, q u o m   t u
> ***maxima*** R̲o̲m̲a̲n̲a̲e̲ *p̲a̲r̲s̲* *e̲r̲i̲<s̲>̲* h̲i̲s̲t̲o̲r̲i̲a̲e̲   (fr. 2.2–3 Courtney)

---

60 See esp. Tränkle (1960) 22–4, 158, usefully tagging some likely Gallan terms and phrases and listing parallel passages. Pages 25–30, referring to the neoterics in general, contain some further terms which can be linked with Gallus in particular.

61 E.g. Anderson, Parsons and Nisbet (1979) 140–55; Newman (1980); (1997) Ch. 1 esp. 35–53; Barchiesi (1981); Hinds (1983); Cairns (1993).

62 Similar procedures involving hexameter formulae have long been applied to recover Ennian phrases and lines.

Gallus was not the first to employ *historia* in Roman poetry,[63] and its later poetic uses are not all indebted to Gallus. But in five of its seven Propertian appearances it manifestly imitates Gallus fr. 2.3 Courtney, and Propertius' imitations reveal four guiding principles which can help in the establishment of other such complexes:

1. The frequent maintenance of a term's original metrical *sedes*.
2. The possible presence of other elements from the passage being imitated.
3. The possible presence of elements from other passages of the author being imitated, which in turn may relate to other identifiable verbal complexes.
4. The absence of a requirement that the contexts in which the imitations appear should always reproduce the term's context from the model (if the model is known).

The five Propertian lines are:

t u quoque uti fieres *nobilis* **historia**	(1.15.24)
maxima de nihilo nascitur **historia**.	(2.1.16)
ite et <u>Romanae</u> consulite **historiae**!	(3.4.10)
et caput argutae praebeat **historiae**;	(3.20.28)
Famam, <u>Roma</u>, t u a e non pudet **historiae**.	(3.22.20)

All these lines maintain *historia* in its original Gallan *sedes* (principle 1); three contain other elements from the Gallan model: *maxima*,[64] *Romanae, Roma* (principle 2); and, when Propertius first employed *historia* (1.15.24), he combined it with Gallan *nobilis*, a key element of the Gallan *nomen* group so as to 'footnote' explicitly his borrowing of Gallus' *historia* (principle 3). Similarly Propertius confirmed the Gallan nature of his sixth use of *historia*, which he did not place in its known Gallan *sedes*, by qualifying it with another element of the *nomen* group, viz. *nota*: *narrant historiae tempora nota suae*

---

63   Cf. Lucilius 26 fr. 23 Charpin: *veterem historiam, inductus studio, scribis ad amores tuos.*
64   That *maxima* was meaningfully Gallan is shown by Virg. *Ecl.* 10.72: *vos* (i.e. *Pierides*) *haec facietis maxima Gallo*, where the use of *facere* (= ποιεῖν) of poetic composition and the presence of the Muses (cf. *fecerunt ... Musae*, Gallus fr. 2.6 Courtney) confirm beyond doubt Virgil's imitation of Gallus.

(4.7.64).[65] The context of 3.4.10 follows closely its Gallan forebear (cf. below, pp. 409–10), as does also, up to a point, 3.22.20, addressed to Tullus, Propertius' former joint patron with Gallus in the Mono-biblos. But the other three examples have little in common contextually with the surviving Gallan line (principle 4). They may well, of course, be indebted to further (lost) lines of Gallus ending in forms of *historia*.

Later examples of *historia* in Roman poets offer further lessons:

et te
raptum et R̲o̲m̲a̲n̲a̲m̲ flebimus **historiam**   (*Catalepton* 11.5–6)

Eubius, impurae c̲o̲n̲d̲i̲t̲o̲r̲ **historiae**   (Ovid *Tristia* 2.416)

non profecturae c̲o̲n̲d̲i̲t̲o̲r̲ **historiae**   (Ovid *Ibis* 520)

pars _erit_ **historiae** totoque legetur in aevo
(*Consolatio ad Liviam* 267)

primus R̲o̲m̲a̲n̲a̲ Crispus in **historia**   (Martial 14.191.2)

t u , *maxime* CAESAR
non sinis et L̲a̲t̲i̲a̲e̲ consulis **historiae**
(Sulpicius *Epigramma* ap. *VSD* 38 ll. 3–4)

et quidquid L̲a̲t̲i̲a̲ c̲o̲n̲d̲i̲t̲u̲r̲ **historia**   (Ausonius 11.22.14 Green)

novi R̲o̲m̲a̲n̲a̲e̲ quos memor **historiae**   (Ausonius 23.45 Green)

sparsa iacent L̲a̲t̲i̲a̲m̲ si qua per **historiam**
(Ausonius 22.1.4 Green)

The coded elements for the most part require little comment. But *Catalepton* 11.5–6 sound a warning for critics of Roman poetry: if the Gallan lines had not survived, it would be all too tempting to conclude that *Catalepton* 11.5–6 imitate Propertius. That this is not the case, and that they are in fact an imitation of Gallus, is quite certain: first *et te* (*Catalepton* 11.5) recalls Gallus' *quom tu*, similarly at the end of a hexameter (fr. 2.2 Courtney); second, *Catalepton* 11.4 begins with *fata*; cf. Gallus' *fata* (fr. 2.2 Courtney) in the same *sedes*. The Gallus-Catalepton link strikingly reveals the high level of intertextual sensitivity expected of their readers by Roman poets. The similar

65 The seventh Propertian line containing a form of *historia* (*hactenus historiae! nunc ad tua devehar astra*, 4.1.119) does not maintain the term's final *sedes* either; in both cases *historiae* precedes the caesura.

imitation of Gallus at *Consolatio ad Liviam* 267, guaranteed by *pars erit* (cf. Gallus' *pars eris*, fr. 2.3 Courtney), and probably also by *totoque legetur in aeuo*, which introduces an extension of the Gallan concept of universal fame,[66] teaches the same lessons.

On the other hand the imitation at Sulpicius *Epigramma* ap. *VSD* 38 ll. 3–4 presents an interesting dilemma. Its harking back to Gallus is clear, and indeed, of all the imitations listed, it alone reproduces Gallus' *Caesar*. But at the same time its use of *consulis* is reminiscent of Propertius 3.4.10: *ite et Romanae consulite historiae!* How is this to be interpreted? Did 'Sulpicius' conflate Gallus' couplet (fr. 2.2–3 Courtney) with Propertius 3.4.10, or did 'Sulpicius' take *consulis*, not from Propertius, but from another line of Gallus in which a form of *consulo* was employed, possibly again in combination with *historiae*? The latter view would imply that in 3.4.10 Propertius too had that other line of Gallus in mind. Neither interpretation can be ruled out, but on the whole the one involving conflation of Gallus and Propertius is less plausible: it will be argued in Chapter 12 that the Qaṣr Ibrîm fragments are parts of a single elegy which, like Propertius 3.4, looks prophetically to the future triumph of a departing general; and, if this is so, Gallus may well have written another (now lost) line which included a form of *consulo* and which said something analogous to Propertius 3.4.10. Other Gallan verbal complexes too give the impression of looking back to more than one original, and indeed the diverse manifestations of *historia* in Propertius suggest a fifth methodological principle, namely that, where within the work of one poet a feature known to derive from imitation of a predecessor manifests itself in markedly unconnected forms, a source for it in more than one passage of that predecessor should be suspected. Finally *conditor/conditur* (above) may have joined the complex in Ovid's late work and resurfaced in Ausonius, but indirect indications suggest (cf. Index II s.v. *condo/conditor*) an origin in another Gallan passage.

The pattern of authors observable in the *historia* complex has heuristic value and provides methodological guidance, since it recurs with variations in many hypothesized Gallan verbal complexes where the Gallan original does not survive. Often Propertius provides the initial clues to the complex. Sometimes, although not here, Tibullus offers

---

66   For this concept see below, pp. 97–9. Ovid also used the phrase *toto ... aevo* once in connection with his own poetic standing (*floreat ut toto carmen Nasonis in aeuo*, *Fast.* 5.377), and once in another context (*Tr.* 1.8.25). These uses reinforce the impression that *toto ... aevo* too is Gallan.

supplementary confirmation, particularly when his contrasting con-
text(s) seem to rule out any possibility of influence either way
between himself and Propertius. Then Ovid usually comes into play,
frequently as here with more than one reflection of the same Gallan
original(s). Poems from the *Appendix Vergiliana*,[67] especially *Ciris*
and *Culex*, make frequent and notable contributions; other minor
pieces of the first century AD also occasionally contribute. In general
the next prominent figure is Martial, who knew Augustan elegy well,
who had probably read Gallus' *Amores*, and who sometimes looks to
have consciously imitated Gallus. Then there is a gap before the key
terms reappear in the poets of late antiquity. Writers of that period
seem for the most part to have viewed classical Latin poetry as an
undifferentiated mine of vocabulary, so in general nothing much can
be made of their re-uses of relevant terms. Ausonius is cited occasionally in what follows if he seems close to earlier tradition, but such
'parallels' in late Latin will generally be ignored in the succeeding
chapters. Indeed the reader is warned that for economy's sake terms
may be described as 'unparalleled' in Latin poetry even if they do in
fact appear in late Latin but in circumstances which make it
impossible to deduce anything of value from their appearances there.

   Another phrase from the Qaṣr Ibrîm papyrus which uncovers a
Gallan verbal complex is *pars eri<s>* in the line already quoted:
maxima Romanae pars eri<s> historiae (fr. 2.3 Courtney). The
virtual[68] reprise of Gallus' *iunctura*, again in association with *historia*,
in *pars erit historiae totoque legetur in aeuo* (*Consolatio ad Liviam*
267) has already been mentioned. This imitation alone would demonstrate that *pars eri<s>* was a memorable phrase; but in fact the influence of the phrase was felt earlier and more widely. Cf.:

ibis, et accepti *pars eris* imperii	(Propertius 1.6.34)
pars ego *sum* vestrae proxima **militiae**	(Propertius 1.21.4)
hic *pars* **militiae**, dux *erat* ille ducum	(Ovid *Heroides* 8.46)
pars sis **militiae**; tumulo solacia posco	
	(Ovid *Metamorphoses* 7.483)

---

67 The dating problems of the *Appendix Vergiliana* are well known: see, e.g., *Encicl. Virg.*
    s.v. (A. Salvatore). *Catalepton* 5 and 8 are frequently held to be genuine; but, for sceptical
    views see, e.g., Horsfall (1995) 10–11; Holzberg (2004b).
68 Curiously the papyrus actually reads: *pars erit*. For a vigorous denunciation of this reading
    and insistence on the emendation *eris* see Anderson, Parsons and Nisbet (1979) 141.

nec, *pars* **militiae**, Telamon sine honore recessit
(Ovid *Metamorphoses* 11.216)

Of these lines only Propertius 1.6.34 equates in its grammatical forms
and their *sedes* to Gallus' line (fr. 2.3 Courtney), with of course *im-*
perii at its end instead of Gallus' *historiae*. Propertius may be evoking
the ethos of Gallus' *propemptikon*, probably addressed to Julius Caesar,[69] as a high compliment to his own propemptic addressee, Tullus.
But, as *Consolatio ad Liviam* 267 underlines, the minor variations of
tense, number and *sedes* in the other reminiscences should neither
conceal nor call into doubt their harking back to Gallus for *pars eris*.
Yet further confirmation of its Gallan origin comes from Propertius'
sly, first person insertion of the phrase into the mouth of a man called
'Gallus' at 1.21.4. As already stressed,[70] this 'Gallus' is not the poet,
but Propertius is revealing in this way his consciousnes of his allusion
to Cornelius Gallus' phraseology.

That the phrase *pars eris* vel sim. appeared in Gallus in other circumstances than fr. 2.3 Courtney is virtually assured by its association
in Roman poetry not only with the *historia* complex but with two
other Gallan verbal complexes focussed around *militia* and *imperium*.
These are not directly attested by the Qaṣr Ibrîm papyrus, but they are
reconstructable on the methodological basis revealed by the *historia*
complex:

armaque fraternae tristia **militiae**	(Propertius 1.7.2)
pars ego *sum* vestrae proxima **militiae**	(Propertius 1.21.4)
optavit lentas et mihi **militias**	(Tibullus 1.3.82)
horrida quid durae tempora **militiae**?	(*Catalepton* 9.42)
hic *pars* **militiae**, dux *erat* ille ducum	(Ovid *Heroides* 8.46)
pars sis **militiae**; tumulo solacia posco	
	(Ovid *Metamorphoses* 7.483)
nec, *pars* **militiae**, Telamon sine honore recessit	
	(Ovid *Metamorphoses* 11.216)

The first four examples place *militia* etc. in the final *sedes* of the pen-

---

69   For discussion of the identity of the 'Caesar' of the Qaṣr Ibrîm papyrus see below, pp. 408–
9.
70   Above, pp. 49–50, 77 n. 31.

tameter, and the two Propertian and the *Catalepton* lines all use the same form of *militia* (i.e. *militiae*), and they have similarly shaped second halves, with *militiae* preceded by a trisyllabic adjective or noun, which is itself preceded by an adjective agreeing with *militiae*.[71] Only one of the first four examples (Propertius 1.21.4) associates *militia* with *pars* and a form of *esse*, although all three Ovidian examples combine *pars* with *militiae* and two of them also employ a form of *esse*. Here a question arises analogous to that raised earlier by the lines of 'Sulpicius': *tu, maxime Caesar/ non sinis et Latiae consulis historiae*. Was Gallus' *maxima Romanae pars eri<s> historiae* his only use of *pars eris*, or did he also combine *pars* with *militia* in another, now lost, line which stuck in the minds of both Propertius and Ovid? Or did Ovid fixate solely on Propertius 1.21.4? This time the question is not so easy to answer. But the examples collected above, which show both Tibullus and *Catalepton* 9 presenting forms of *militia* in final position but without accompanying *pars*, and Ovid repeating *pars* plus *militiae* (and in two cases a form of *esse*) three times in divergent contexts, on the whole suggest that Gallus did use *pars*, a form of *esse*, and *militia(e)* somewhere else in his elegiacs. It is possible that the *militia* complex was ultimately inspired by Lucretius' *effice ut interea fera moenera militiai* (*De Rerum Natura* 1.29).[72] But, as often when terminology associated with Gallus is prefigured in earlier authors, all the post-Gallan examples point to Gallus as the vector for its later appearances.

The terms *miles, militia, mollis,* and *durus* play a major role in Propertius' etymologizing: his frequent introduction of them was motivated by the ancient 'etymology' which contrasted *militia* with *mollitia*; this antithesis then authorized a positive conceptual link between *militia/miles* and *durus* since *durus* is the opposite of *mollis*.[73] These are Latin 'etymologies', but there are clues which point to an ultimate Greek inspiration for it, and also to Gallus' probable role in transmitting it to Propertius. In line 10 of the programmatic first elegy of the Monobiblos Atalanta, who in the first mythical *paradeigma* of the Monobiblos stands for Cynthia, just as Milanion stands for Propertius himself, is described as *dura Iasis*. *dura* brings to mind her

---

71 Because of the limited metrical possibilities of the elegiac couplet, such features naturally have limited evidential value.

72 For the apparently general influence of Lucretius on the poetic vocabulary of Gallus see, e.g., below, pp. 91–2.

73 See Cairns (1984b), studying *inter alia* the manifestations of this etymology in Prop. 1.6.

proper name Atalanta because its Greek etymology derived 'Atalanta' from ἀ intensifying plus τλα from *τλάω – a reference to her hardihood. Since Gallus had also treated the Milanion/Atalanta myth, it has been suggested that Propertius found this etymology of 'Atalanta' in Gallan elegy.[74] That this was its transmission path is confirmed by the Gallan *militia* complex. The etymology shows up most clearly in *horrida quid durae tempora militiae?* (*Catalepton* 9.42), where *durae* etymologizes *militiae*. Then Propertius 1.6 reveals that the etymology and a use of *militia* went together in Gallus. Its line 30, *hanc me militiam fata subire volunt*, is one of the three Propertian examples of *militia* which do not obviously belong to the Gallan *militia* complex. But this line also contains Gallan *fata* (cf. fr. 2.3 Courtney) as well as *subire*, which can translate *τλάω*. Moreover the succeeding line *at tu seu mollis qua tendit Ionia* ... (31) etymologizes *militia* through its opposite *mollis*, and line 34, *ibis, et accepti pars eris imperii*, belongs to the Gallan *pars eris* complex.

This last line might be regarded as a simple calque on Gallus' *maxima Romanae pars eri<s> historiae* (fr. 2.3 Courtney). That would make the line-ending *imperii* Propertius' own invention. However, various lines of Ovid challenge this assessment:

corpore _pars_ nulla _est_, quae labet, **imperii**	(*Tristia* 2.232)
promovet A̲u̲s̲o̲n̲i̲u̲m̲ filius **imperium**	(*Ex Ponto* 2.2.70)
esse parem uirtute patri, qui frena rogatus saepe recusati ceperit **imperii**	(*Ex Ponto* 4.13.28)[75]

If *Tristia* 2.232, with its additional *pars* ... *est*, were the only Ovidian instance of *imperium(i)* in pentameter final position, it might easily be regarded as an imitation of Propertius 1.6.34. But the existence of three relevant Ovidian examples, the latter two of which do not resemble Propertius 1.6.34 except in their line-ending, creates doubt. That doubt is reinforced by *Carmen de Bello Actiaco* 24–5 Courtney: *cum causa fores tu maxima belli,/ pars etiam imperii*. In these lines *maxima* is additionally reminiscent of Gallus' *maxima Romanae pars eris historiae* (fr. 2.3 Courtney), and imitation of Gallus is patent.

---

74   Ross (1975) 62 and n. 2. On Gallus' use of the myth cf. also Rosen and Farrell (1986).
75   Martial's *quisquis et Ausonium non amat imperium* (6.61.4) can be left out of account here, since it looks like a reprise of *EP* 2.2.70.

Overall, then, it seems more probable that Gallus wrote a now lost line which combined *pars*, a form of *esse*, and *imperium(i)*. *carmina ... /... dicere ... digna* is not only securely Gallan, but is now the best known phrase of Gallus, even though it and the verbal complex which it reveals were, like the *historia* complex, recognizable as such only when the papyrus was published:

> tandem fecerunt c[ar]mina MUSAE
> quae *possem* domina **deicere digna** mea.   (fr. 2.6–7 Courtney)

The first editor noted the existence in other poets of some loci influenced by these lines, and subsequent studies have greatly expanded awareness of their presence in Roman poetry after Gallus.[76] Interestingly the *carmina ... dicere ... digna* complex started life not in Gallus but in two passages of Lucretius *De Rerum Natura*, although the terms are not combined there exactly as they are in Gallus:

> nunc age, nativos animantibus et mortalis
> esse animos animasque levis ut ***noscere possis***,
> *conquisita* diu dulcique *reperta* labore
> **digna** tua pergam disponere **carmina** vita.
> tu fac utrumque uno subiungas ***nomine*** eorum
> atque animam verbi causa cum **dicere** pergam,
> mortalem esse docens, animum quoque **dicere** credas
>
>   (3.417–23)[77]
>
> Quis *potis* est **dignum** pollenti pectore **carmen**
> condere pro rerum maiestate hisque *repertis*?
> quisve valet verbis tantum, qui fingere laudes
> pro meritis eius *possit*, qui talia nobis
> pectore parta suo *quaesita*que praemia liquit?   (5.1–5)

Some seemingly Lucretian baggage is visible in certain later examples of the combination.

> en erit umquam
> ille dies, mihi cum *liceat* tua **dicere** facta?

---

76   Anderson, Parsons and Nisbet (1979) 144; Barchiesi (1981) 155, 163; Hinds (1983). Cairns (1993) 109–12, suggesting *inter alia* that Lucretius found *dignum ... carmen* in Ennius, and that Gallus vectored the Lucretian reprise, and rebutting the attempt of Courtney (1993) 267 to deny that this *iunctura* is significant. There would also be room in the tradition for Varius Rufus' *De Morte*.

77   On *animam* (422) and *animum* (423), see also above, p. 81 n. 55 and below, pp. 224–5.

en erit ut *liceat* totum mihi ferre per *orbem*
sola Sophocleo tua **carmina digna** coturno?
(Virgil *Eclogue* 8.7–10)

MUSA, Palatini referemus Apollinis aedem:
res est, Calliope, **digna** favore tuo.
Caesaris in *nomen* ducuntur **carmina**: Caesar
dum canitur, *quaeso*, Iuppiter, ipse vaces.
(Propertius 4.6.11–14)

te mihi materiem felicem in carmina praebe –
provenient causa **carmina digna** sua.
carmine *nomen* habent exterrita cornibus Io[78]
et quam fluminea lusit adulter ave,
quaeque super pontum simulato vecta iuvenco
virginea tenuit cornua vara manu.
nos quoque per *totum* pariter cantabimur *orbem*,
iunctaque semper erunt *nomina* nostra tuis.
(Ovid *Amores* 1.3.19–26)

illa canenda mihi est. utinam modo **dicere** *possim*
carmina digna dea! certe dea **carmine digna** est.[79]
(Ovid *Metamorphoses* 5.344–5)

siqua tamen nobis, ut nunc quoque, sumpta tabella est,
inque suos volui cogere verba pedes,
carmina nulla mihi sunt scripta aut qualia cernis,
digna sui domini tempore, **digna** loco.
denique non parvas animo dat gloria vires,
et fecunda facit pectora laudis amor.
nominis et famae quondam fulgore trahebar,
dum tulit antemnas aura secunda meas.
non adeo est bene nunc ut sit mihi gloria curae:
si *liceat*, nulli cognitus esse velim.   (Ovid *Tristia* 5.12.33–42)[80]

The apparently Lucretian material could in fact have come to these
passages not through Lucretius but directly from Lucretius' Ennian
model, if he had one (see above, n. 76); but it too may have been
vectored by Gallus: the fact that both Virgil and Ovid blend *carmina
... dicere digna* with the Gallan concept of universal fame strengthens
the idea that Gallus was the main transmitter of *carmina ... dicere ...
digna*. Propertius and Ovid (twice) combine their versions of *carmina*

78   For the suggestion that Gallus as well as Calvus treated Io see Cairns (1993) 112–14.
79   Note that Ovid reproduces here the entire Gallan phrase, i.e. *carmina ... / possem ...deicere
      digna*.
80   Ov. *EP* 1.2.131–4 offers *et cecini fausto carmina digna toro* (132) and *domino* (134).

... *dicere digna* with Gallan *nomen*, but, although *nomen* is highly diagnostic of Gallus, its presence in these instances is less impressive
because *nomen* is also part of the Lucretian baggage. Ennius might, of
course, again be suspected of originating *nomen* in proximity to
dignum carmen.[81] Propertius also features the Gallan term *Musa* (cf.
fr. 2.6 Courtney), the Gallan Muse Calliope,[82] and *Caesaris ... Caesar*
(cf. fr. 2.2 Courtney), all within a brief four-line compass; similarly in
Tristia 5.12.33–42, Ovid alludes additionally to Gallus' use of *domina*
(fr. 2.7 Courtney), as well as showing his awareness of the entire
tradition (cf. the coded items).[83]

As we move on in time *Ciris* offers only

> ut *quiret* eo **dignum** sibi *quaerere* **carmen**
> longe aliud studium inque alios accincta *labores*   (5–6)

and *Culex* provides only the bald *digna ... carmina*, although accompanied by the 'neoteric' keyword *poliantur*,[84] and with *Musa* too in
evidence two lines earlier:

> posterius graviore sono tibi MUSA loquetur
> nostra, dabunt cum securos mihi tempora fructus,
> ut tibi **digna** tuo poliantur **carmina** sensu.   (8–10)

Other examples suggest that after, or even before, Ovid's late works
carmen/carmina dignum/digna had become a cliché,[85] and had lost
any necessary Lucretian/Gallan associations.

The combination *facere carmen* is found in the Qaṣr Ibrîm papyrus, in the phrase *tandem fecerunt carmina Musae* (fr. 2.6 Courtney).
But whether all later similar phrases are really Gallan is unclear. The
papyrus' first editor judged that '*fecerunt* is unconventional in such a
context' and suggested an allusion to ποιητής;[86] and it is true that
Gallus offers the first known instance of *facere carmen*. But the

---

81 *Ann.* 405 Skutsch offers a suitable context.
82 Cf. below, pp. 121–2, 125–6, 130.
83 These do not include the numerous personal pronouns and adjectives found in these
    passages, although their high frequency in Gallus fr. 2 Courtney (1, 2 (three), 4, 7, 8 (two),
    9) assures their significance.
84 Cf., e.g., Ov. *Tr.* 1.1.11; *EP* 1.5.61; and for *pumex* as another keyword for the topos, Cat.
    1.2; 22.8; Prop. 3.1.8.
85 E.g. *Catalept.* 9.16; Stat. *Silv.* 1.2.251–2; 5.1.208; *Carm. Priap.* 2.2 Bücheler; Mart. 7.63.2.
    Even in some Augustan loci it has the air of a cliché: e.g. Prop. 4.7.83; Hor. *AP* 91.
86 Anderson, Parsons and Nisbet (1979) 144.

combination is so common in later writers that its unconventionality may be doubted; and most of the contexts in which it recurs lack other pointers to Gallus. Only Virgil at *Eclogue* 9.32–3: *et me fecere poetam/ Pierides, sunt et mihi carmina* assuredly reflects Gallus with his varied combination of *facio, carmina* and the Muses, and with his explicit reference in *poetam* to the Gallan etymology *fecerunt = ποιητής*; but, particularly since it is hard to see the point of these lines as an imitation of Gallus fr. 2.6–7, it may be that Virgil had in mind another Gallan locus with similar terminology. A further passage repeating Gallus' very words is, if not delusory, a joke:[87] at *Tristia* 2.5 and 7 Ovid twice employs the phrase *carmina fecerunt*. But he means 'my poems brought it about'! Perhaps most significantly, in the sole Propertian example, *munera quanta dedi uel qualia carmina feci!* (2.8.11), only *munera* might show that Propertius had Gallus particularly in mind (cf. Index II s.v. *munus*). The explanation may be that Gallus' phrase had a now lost predecessor, one which diminished its link with Gallus. The possibility has already been considered that Ennius lies behind Lucretius *De Rerum Natura* 3.417–23 (quoted above, p. 91), a passage which contains *digna ... carmina* (420), *noscere* (418), *nomine* (421) and also the injunction *fac* (421), addressed to Memmius.[88] An Ennian use of *facere carmen* can therefore be suspected: cf. his contrived *pangit melos* (*Annales* 293 Skutsch).

More can be done with another term from the Qaṣr Ibrîm papyrus, the *nequitia* on Lycoris' part of which Gallus complains: *tristia nequitia ... a Lycori tua* (fr. 2.1 Courtney). *nequitia* is a favourite term of Propertius and Ovid in several metrical *sedes*, and it covers either the mistress' misbehaviour, as in Gallus, or that of the poet himself, or that of a third party. For Propertius and Ovid *nequitia* clearly functioned as shorthand for the elegiac life of love and social irresponsibility. But the term is absent from the vocabulary of both Catullus and Tibullus. So Gallus must have pioneered its use as an elegiac Leitmotiv, and passed it on to the two successors who followed most closely in his wake. The widespread use of *nequitia* by Propertius and Ovid implies that, in addition to its appearance in the Qaṣr Ibrîm papyrus, Gallus used the term in other contexts too:

---

87   The appearance of *Musas* in l.3 and *Caesar* in l.8 may argue for the latter judgement.
88   Despite the probable use by Gallus of *animus* and *anima*, the further presence in *DRN* 3.417–23 of four terms from the *animus* group, viz. *animantibus* (417), *animos animasque* (418), *animam* (422) and *animum* (423), may not be significant, given both the subject-matter of *DRN* and the high frequency of such terms in Lucretius.

hanc *animam* extremae reddere **nequitiae**	(Propertius 1.6.26)
nec tremis admissae conscia **nequitiae**?	(Propertius 1.15.38)
et *non ignota* vivere **nequitia**?	(Propertius 2.5.2)
nequitiaeque s u a e noluit esse rudis.	(Propertius 2.6.30)
non e g o **nequitiae** dicerer esse caput	(Propertius 2.24.6)
et sint **nequitiae** libera verba t u a e	(Propertius 3.10.24)
et rabidae stimulos frangere **nequitiae**	(Propertius 3.19.10)
ille e g o **nequitiae** Naso poeta m e a e	(Ovid *Amores* 2.1.2)
nequitiam vinosa t u a m convivia narrant	(Ovid *Amores* 3.1.17)
semina **nequitiae** languidiora facit	(Ovid *Amores* 3.4.10)
nequitiam fugio, fugientem forma reducit	(Ovid *Amores* 3.11.37)
est qui **nequitiam** locus exigat: omnibus illum	
	(Ovid *Amores* 3.14.17)
nec sint **nequitiae** tempora certa t u a e	
	(Ovid *Ars Amatoria* 2.392)
non e g o **nequitia** socialia foedera rumpam	(Ovid *Heroides* 4.17)
quae **tua nequitia** est, non his contenta fuisset	
	(Ovid *Heroides* 17.29)
nequitia est quae t e non sinit esse senem	(Ovid *Fasti* 1.414)
nequitiae: tolli tota theatra iube	(Ovid *Tristia* 2.280)

Apart from Gallan *animam* in Propertius 1.6.26 and *non ignota* in 2.5.2, *nequitia* in its Gallan *sedes* in two Propertian and three Ovidian examples, and *tuus* etc. in many cases, these lines contain little reminiscent of the Qaṣr Ibrîm papyrus. Some of them may, of course, be influenced by the other hypothesized and now lost Gallan uses of *nequitia*. Propertius 3.10.24 and Ovid *Ars Amatoria* 2.392 in particular seem to echo one other such Gallan use. They are contextually distant from the surviving line of Gallus, but have a close resemblance to each other, in that they begin *et sint* (P.) and *nec sint* (O.), and have identical genitive *nequitiae ... tuae* in *Sperrung* (cf. Gallus' *nequitia ... tua*, fr. 2.1 Courtney), enclosing *libera verba* (P.) and *tempora certa*

(O.). Moreover *libera verba* has independent claim to Gallan status.[89] It is found in all three later elegists, and in three of the four examples it has the same *sedes*:

nec tibi perpetuo **libera verba** fore	(Propertius 1.9.2)
vertet in offensas **libera verba** suas.	(Propertius 4.11.90)
ederet ut multo **libera verba** mero:	(Tibullus 1.9.26)
verbaque honoratus **libera** praetor habet.	(Ovid *Fasti* 1.52)

These examples suggest that Propertius' *et sint nequitiae libera verba tuae* (3.10.24) came closest to another (lost) Gallan line. But not all surviving elegiac uses of *nequitia* are likely to hark back to specific Gallan lines. Propertius and Ovid appear to have absorbed Gallus' concept of *nequitia* into their own erotic ideology and, without forgetting its originator, to have claimed it as their own.

(non?) vereor has been proposed (although not in so many words) as the basis of a Gallan verbal complex on two grounds: its appearance in the Qaṣr Ibrîm papyrus; and the repeated *non ego nunc ... vereor* of two Propertian lines which also feature the Gallan *non ego*:[90]

].atur idem tibi, **non ego**, Visce	
]Kato, *iudice te* **vereor**.	(fr. 2.8–9 Courtney)
non ego *nunc* Hadriae **vereor** mare noscere *tecum*	(1.6.1)
non ego *nunc* tristis **vereor**, mea Cynthia, Manis	(1.19.1)

The case for regarding *(non?) vereor* as specifically Gallan can be strengthened in several ways. First, one of the Propertian lines (1.19.1) contains the vocative *Cynthia*, while Gallus fr. 2.8–9 Courtney contains the vocative *Visce*, and perhaps also the vocative *Kato*. Second, the other Propertian line (1.6.1) has *tecum* while Gallus fr. 2.9 Courtney has *te*. Third, two more Propertian examples can be added as reinforcement to this complex:

non ego *nunc* **vereor** ne sim *tibi* vilior istis	(1.2.25)
quam **vereor**, ne *te* contempto, Cynthia, busto	(1.19.21)

---

89   Cf. also *sit modo libertas quae velit ira loqui* (Prop. 1.1.28). P. R. Hardie (2002) 125 n. 36, comparing Virg. *Ecl.* 1.27, suggests that Gallus used *libertas* in a prologue poem.
90   Cf. Noonan (1991) 122.

Fourth, an Ovidian couplet clinches the argument that *(non?)* *vereor* had a Gallan feel:

> sic illas **vereor**, quae, si *tua* gloria vera est,
> *iudice te* causam non tenuere duae   (*Heroides* 17.243–4)[91]

Even though *iudice te* is found in fr. 2.9 Courtney, it is not always indicative of Gallan influence.[92] But here – in combination with *vereor* – it is an indubitable reference to Gallus, as is Virgil's earlier variation on the same Gallan *iunctura*: *non ego Daphnin/ iudice te metuam* (*Eclogue* 2.26–7).[93] Further indications of the Gallan flavour of *(non?)* *vereor* in his successors comes from Ovid's coupling of *vereor* with a form of *nomen* at *Tristia* 4.5.15–16 and *Ex Ponto* 1.2.7–8.

The Gallan *nomen* complex was in effect already known in large part before the discovery of the Qaṣr Ibrîm papyrus, at least to those Propertian scholars who identified the 'Gallus' of the Monobiblos as C. Cornelius Gallus. The new fragments of Gallus did not *per se* extend its scope; but it can be set forth more fully here thanks to the methodologies deducible from the papyrus. Some examples of the *nomen* complex also embrace the 'East/West–morning/evening star' topos: East and West are taken as equivalent to the entire world, so the *nomen* becomes 'universal fame'.[94] The East/West–morning/evening star topos is, of course, not in origin Gallan: as an independent commonplace it goes back at least to Callimachus and perhaps earlier,[95] and indeed in Latin poetry *nomen* in its primary meaning 'name' is already found associated with East/West in Catullus 62.34–5:

> nocte latent fures, quos idem saepe revertens,
> Hespere, mutato comprendis **nomine** eosdem.[96]

---

91 The previous line (242) contains the term *tropaea*, probably a further indication of Gallan influence: for the triumphal interest of the Qaṣr Ibrîm elegiacs, and for the successor elegies which they inspired, see below, Ch. 12. For *tropaea* see Index II s.v. *tropaeum*.

92 E.g. it is found in Ter. *Hec.* 255, and Hor. *Od.* 1.28.14; and even many Ovidian examples seem to have no Gallan associations.

93 Cf. also Morelli and Tandoi (1984) esp. 101–5.

94 Cf. Ross (1975) 118.

95 *Hecal.* fr. 113 Hollis, with Hollis (1990) 296–9; cf. also *AP* 7.670 (Plato?); 12.114 (Meleager); Bosworth (1999) 5, discussing Ennius' influential use of it.

96 Schrader's emendation *Eous* is printed in place of *eosdem* (V) at Cat. 62.35 by modern editors. But Cinna fr. 6 Courtney (quoted below) might hint that *eosdem* should be retained

These Catullan lines, with or without Cinna fr. 6 Courtney:

> te <u>matutinus</u> flentem conspexit <u>Eous</u>
> et flentem paulo post vidit <u>Hesperus</u> idem.[97]

may have stimulated Gallus' imagination so that he vectored the combination – with *nomen* now in its secondary significance 'fame' – to later poetry, just as he vectored much Lucretian material. Ovid provides the best evidence for the specifically Gallan nature of the new, extended concept, complete with the East/West topos, since he twice associates it explicitly with Cornelius Gallus:[98]

> GALLUS et <u>Hesperiis</u> et GALLUS **notus** <u>Eois</u>,
> et sua cum GALLO **nota** <u>Lycoris</u> erit.
>
> (Ovid *Amores* 1.15.29–30)
>
> **nomen** habet Nemesis, <u>Cynthia</u> **nomen** habet
> <u>Vesper</u> et <u>Eoae</u> **novere** <u>Lycorida</u> terrae.
>
> (Ovid *Ars Amatoria* 3.536–7)

Ovid also applies the complex to his own situation in one of his later works, when, as will be seen,[99] he was envisaging himself in his exile as analogous to Gallus after his fall from the favour of Augustus:

> nostra per immensas ibunt praeconia gentes,
> quodque querar **notum** qua patet <u>orbis</u> erit.
> ibit ad <u>occasum</u> quicquid dicemus ab <u>ortu</u>,
> testis et <u>Hesperiae</u> vocis <u>Eous</u> erit.   (Ovid *Tristia* 4.9.19–22)

Propertius, writing of his Cynthia, but obviously recalling the same (lost) lines of Gallus to which Ovid refers in his two mentions of Lycoris, offers a more discreet variation. The whole world will fall in love with a portrait of Cynthia (who in one dimension is, of course, equated with Propertius' own poetry):

---

as an allusive 'etymology': the first of Cinna's two surviving lines ends in *Eous*, and the second with *idem*. Could Catullan imitation/emulation of Cinna have produced *eosdem* from those line-ends?

97   From Cinna's *Zmyrna* (fr. 6 Courtney), describing the heroine's sufferings.
98   Cf. Brugnoli (1983), noting as derived from Gallus a number of the passages discussed here.
99   Below, p. 208.

sive illam H̲e̲s̲p̲e̲r̲i̲i̲s̲, sive illam ostendet E̲o̲i̲s̲,
    uret et E̲o̲o̲s̲, uret et H̲e̲s̲p̲e̲r̲i̲o̲s̲.   (Propertius 2.3.43–4)[100]

The three Ovidian passages quoted above assign different quantities to the first *E* of *Eous*. Propertius 2.3.43–4 does likewise in a single couplet; presumably both poets are imitating Gallus in this.

East/West–morning/evening star has already been exemplified in Catullus 62.34–5 as a topos unconnected with the idea of universal fame; another pre-Gallan example of its independent use is Cinna fr. 6 Courtney (quoted above). Unsurprisingly there are yet other versions of this topos in Virgil, Ovid, and the *Ciris*. The Virgilian example has obvious Gallan associations; those of the others are less obvious:

te, dulcis coniunx, te solo in litore secum,
te v̲e̲n̲i̲e̲n̲t̲e̲ d̲i̲e̲, te d̲e̲c̲e̲d̲e̲n̲t̲e̲ canebat   (Virgil *Georgics* 4.465–6)

illam non udis veniens A̲u̲r̲o̲r̲a̲ capillis
cessantem vidit, non H̲e̲s̲p̲e̲r̲u̲s̲
                                        (Ovid *Metamorphoses* 5.440–1)[101]

quem pavidae alternis fugitant optantque puellae
H̲e̲s̲p̲e̲r̲i̲u̲m̲ vitant, optant ardescere E̲o̲u̲m̲.   (*Ciris* 351–2)

In addition to playing a part in the *nomen* group, *nota* = 'mark' seems to have enjoyed a life of its own in elegy, probably thanks to Gallus. The following lines bear witness to the existence of a Gallan verbal sub-complex with *nota* at its core, and with *collum* and *dens* as frequent concomitants:

nunc in amore tuo cogor *habere* **notam**	(Propertius 1.18.8)
det mihi plorandas per tua c̲o̲l̲l̲a̲ **notas**!	(Propertius 4.3.26)
imponitque **notam** c̲o̲l̲l̲o̲ *m̲o̲r̲s̲u̲q̲u̲e̲* cruentat	(Propertius 4.8.65)
oscula et in c̲o̲l̲l̲o̲ figere *d̲e̲n̲t̲e̲* **notas**.	(Tibullus 1.8.38)
et c̲o̲l̲l̲u̲m̲ blandi *d̲e̲n̲t̲i̲s̲ habere* **notam**.	(Ovid *Amores* 1.7.42)
factaque lascivis livida c̲o̲l̲l̲a̲ **notis**	(Ovid *Amores* 1.8.98)
c̲o̲l̲l̲a̲que conspicio *d̲e̲n̲t̲i̲s̲ habere* **notam**?	(Ovid *Amores* 3.14.34)

---

100 On this couplet see now Fedeli (2005) 149–50. In it Cynthia implicitly assumes the role which is attributed explicitly to Lycoris by Ovid.
101 Cf. also Ov. *Fast.* 1.139–40; Manil. *Astr.* 1.637–8.

Amores 1.7.42 and 3.14.34 both contain all the recurrent elements. An explanation which aimed to exclude Gallus as Ovid's influence might be that, in order to assemble these elements, Ovid combined Propertius 1.18.8 with Tibullus 1.8.38. But this explanation is hard to swallow, particularly since the context of Propertius 1.18.8 is very far from neck-biting. Rather this group of lines must have its ultimate origin in a predecessor of all three elegists, one who described erotic activites, who was interested in *nosco* words, and who probably used the line-ending *habere notam*. That predecessor can only be C. Cornelius Gallus, particularly since Propertius 1.5.16, from an elegy addressed to 'Gallus' and replete with *nosco/nomen/nobilis* material and other hints of Gallus, reads: *et timor informem ducet in ore notam* – the face in question being that of 'Gallus'!

It has long been held on the basis of Propertius 1.2.7–8 and 2.1.57–8 that the term *medicina* came to Propertius from Gallus.[102] *furor* too has been suspected of being Gallan because Virgil places a combination of the two words in the mouth of Gallus himself:[103] *tamquam haec sit nostri medicina furoris* (Virgil *Eclogue* 10.60). The *medicina* complex also involves the following passages (all from Propertius):

crede m i h i , *non ulla* t u a e *est* **medicina** FIGURAE:
nudus *Amor* FORMAE *non amat artificem.*   (1.2.7–8)

non ego tum *potero SOLACIA FERRE* roganti,
cum m i h i *nulla* m e i *sit* **medicina** MALI;   (1.5.27–8)

et *possum* alterius CURAS *SANARE* RECENTIS,
nec levis in *verbis* *est* **medicina** m e i s   (1.10.17–18)

omnis HUMANOS *SANAT* **medicina** DOLORES:
solus *Amor* MORBI *non amat artificem.*   (2.1.57–8)

t u (i.e. Bacchus) *potes* INSANAE *Veneris* COMPESCERE FASTUS,
CURARUMque t u o fit **medicina** mero   (3.17.3–4)[104]

The *medicina* complex visibly embraces a number of other terms, and where phrases are repeated or are very similar there is a high likelihood that they appeared in more or less the same form in Gallus too:

102   Tränkle (1960) 22–3; Ross (1975) 67–8, 91.
103   Cf. Ross (1975) Index rerum notabiliorum s.v. *furor.*
104   The last Propertian case of *medicina*, 2.14.16: *cineri nunc medicina datur* has no obvious link with the complex, despite the presence of *nota* in l.15.

mihi, non ulla tuae est medicina is very close to *mihi nulla mei sit medicina*, as is *curas sanare* to *sanat ... dolores*, and *curas* to *curarum*; and *nudus Amor formae non amat artificem* and *solus Amor morbi non amat artificem* are virtual twins. The line which succeeds Virgil's citation of Gallus' *medicina* statement – *aut deus ille malis hominum mitescere discat* (*Eclogue* 10.61) – is so close to much of the Propertian material collected above that it must also be Gallan in content, and possibly to some extent verbally too: in addition to *deus ille = Amor/Veneris, mitescere = solacia ferre/sanare/compescere* (similarly inceptive), *malis = mali* and *hominum = humanos*. All in all, the expanded version of the *medicina* complex, as set out above, can provide a model for this type of investigation.

A comment of Servius opens up an additional line of enquiry for Gallus:

> *exarsit in iras*: communis sermo habet 'ardeo in illa re', sed figuratius 'ardeo in illam rem' dicimus. et est specialis Cornelii elocutio. (ad *Aeneid* 7.445)

> *He flared up into anger*: ordinary language uses the expression 'I blaze in something', but we say more ornately 'I blaze into something'. And it is a specific idiom of Cornelius.

The most recent study of this passage correctly concludes that the Cornelius referred to is C. Cornelius Gallus:[105] it notes that Servius refers to all other Cornelii either by their *cognomen* alone, or by both their *nomen* and *cognomen*, while Cornelius Gallus is the one Cornelius who, as well as appearing in Servius as 'Gallus',[106] is referred to by Servius auctus ad *Eclogue* 9.10 simply as 'Cornelius'. That study also tends on the whole to regard Gallus' *specialis elocutio* as oratorical in nature. But it does consider the possibility that Servius' remarks might be based on several different Gallan loci, poetic loci not excluded, although it does not develop this approach. In fact a poetic locus for Cornelius Gallus' *elocutio* is assured by the appearance of phrases similar to Virgil's *exarsit in iras* in the very poets who otherwise seem to reflect Gallan influence. The relevant lines are:

talibus Allecto dictis **exarsit in iras**. (Virgil *Aeneid* 7.445)

---

105 Balbo (1999) esp. 242–3, cf. Balbo (2004) 28–9, 35–7, who observes (37) that the phrase *in eum furorem exarsit* is found in Liv. *Per.* 58.4.
106 Ad *Ecl.* 3.1; 6.64, 66, 72; 10.1, 2, 10, 46, 50, 74; *Georg.* 4.1.

igne cupidineo <u>proprios</u> **exarsit** <u>in artus</u>   (*Culex* 409)

tum vero <u>indomitas</u> **ardescit** vulgus <u>in iras</u>
                                                        (Ovid *Metamorphoses* 5.41)

o quam <u>terribilis</u> **exarsit** pronus <u>in iras</u>!   (Martial *Spectacula* 9.3)

The *Culex* poet replaced *iras* with *artus*, just as Ovid varied *exarsit* with *ardescit*. Only Martial reproduced the exact words found in Virgil – not, however, in Virgil's exact form but with *pronus* interposed between *exarsit* and *in*. There is a tendency in the non-Virgilian lines for a preceding adjective to govern the final noun of the line, i.e. *proprios ... artus/indomitas ... iras/terribilis ... iras*. The Gallan original too may have placed before *exarsit* an adjective agreeing with *iras*. The point of Servius' comment is that the *specialis Cornelii elocutio* involved using *ardeo* plus *in* plus the accusative rather than *ardeo* plus *in* plus the ablative. Ovid *Metamorphoses* 13.544–5 (*seque armat et instruit iram./ qua simul exarsit*) presents somewhat similar language. If the reading *iram* (MN¹) in 1.544 is correct,[107] then *qua simul exarsit*, in which *exarsit* is used with *qua* (ablative), is immediately preceded by *iram*, used as an accusative with *instruit*.[108] In that case Ovid looks to be slyly 'correcting' *Aeneid* 7.445. If so, then Servius' remark will have had a long history in Virgilian exegesis, and Virgil's usage of *exardesco* with the accusative will already have been characterized as odd in Ovid's day and explained as Gallan *imitatio*.

A more speculative but not unattractive possibility[109] can bring this chapter to an end. No fewer than four Propertian pentameters and one (possibly) Ovidian pentameter end in the striking quinquesyllabic *pudicitia(e)*:[110]

illis ampla satis <u>forma</u> **pudicitia**.   (Propertius 1.2.24)

occidit, Argivae fama **pudicitiae**.   (Propertius 1.15.22)

ianua Tarpeiae *nota* **pudicitiae**   (Propertius 1.16.2)

frange et damnosae iura **pudicitiae**   (Propertius 4.5.28)

---

107   Modern editors however read *ira*. Bömer (1982) 337 cites as parallels for *exardescere ira* Ov. *Met.* 1.724; 2.613; 12.102; 13.559 (*exaestuare*), but none is exact.
108   Ovid's fascination with this sort of language is also shown in: *protinus exarsit nec tempora distulit irae* (*Met.* 1.724).
109   Already adumbrated by Tränkle (1960) 141–2 n. 2.
110   Propertius also employs *pudicitia* earlier in a hexameter, viz. *templa Pudicitiae quid opus statuisse puellis* (2.6.25).

lis est cum *forma* magna **pudicitiae**   (Ovid *Heroides* 16.290)

Propertius 1.2.24 and Ovid *Heroides* 16.290 also share the further term *forma*. Apart from this, the similarities within this group all lie in their overall shape: dissyllabic nouns or adjectives always stand before *pudicitia(e)*, and these are preceded in three cases by adjectives of three long syllables, two of them proper adjectives, in agreement with *pudicitia(e)*. Despite the limitations of the Latin pentameter it is hard not to feel here the presence of a ghostly predecessor line, which was certainly not Catullan and hence was most likely Gallan. Martial's two pentameters ending in *pudicitia(e)* display not totally dissimilar line-shapes:

atque intrare domos iussa **Pudicitiast**   (Martial 6.7.2)

testis maternae nata **pudicitiae**   (Martial 6.27.4)

Finally, the term preceding *pudicitiae* in Propertius 1.16.2 is Gallan *nota*.

Further Gallan verbal complexes will be proposed in Chapters 4–7 in the course of other investigations. In addition study in Chapters 5 and 6 of metrical features seemingly indicative of Gallan influence will throw up new material relevant to already established Gallan verbal complexes, and will also raise new possibilities of such complexes. Even so, it must be emphasized that the discussion of Gallan influence upon Propertius and others in this volume makes no claim to be exhaustive: a multitude of proposals has been made over the last hundred years, not all of which are covered here and many of which are capable of further expansion and exploitation;[111] and there is major scope for future work in this area.

---

111 In addition to the works already cited cf., e.g., Yardley (1980); Kennedy (1982); (1987); Merriam (1990); Fabre-Serris (1995); Schmitzer (2002) Register 5.2 s.v. Gallus.

CHAPTER 4

Gallan Elegies, Themes and Motifs

DEFORMAZIONE

The concept of 'Gallan verbal complexes' was introduced in Chapter
3 to help reveal the lexical impact of Gallus on succeeding Roman
poetry; and metrical phenomena indicating Gallan influence will be
explored in Chapters 5 and 6. The present chapter reviews areas of
Propertius' œuvre where past scholarship has demonstrated or hypothesized thematic indebtedness to Gallus, offering supplementary
proposals where appropriate. The dangers inherent in this study are
evident: they have already been hinted at in Chapter 3 in connection
with those elegies of Book 1 in which 'Gallus' is the addressee (1.5,
1.10, 1.13, and 1.20) and which involve *deformazione*. In these direct
confrontations between Propertius and his predecessor *deformazione*
was the means whereby Propertius set about establishing his independent credentials as an elegist. Hence these, and the other Propertian
elegies where Gallus' personality is mediated through his mythical
analogues (e.g. 1.1 and 1.18), must be handled with particular caution.
When a theme or motif associated with Gallus surfaces in Propertius
without signs of a confrontation with Gallus, then *deformazione* may
be absent or less extreme: poetic themes and motifs often have a long
genealogy and they may be broad or general enough to allow each
poet who handles them to improvise within his own space. But even
here caution is required.

The parallel case of another Augustan erotic elegist, Albius
Tibullus, illustrates particularly well the perils of taking literally
accounts by one poet of another.[1] Had Tibullus' elegies perished like

---

1   This paragraph expands upon Du Quesnay (1978) 276: 'the difficulties of such an under-
     taking ... are easily grasped if one compares the picture of, say, Tibullus which emerges
     from the *testimonia* with that which emerges from the poems themselves.'

those of Gallus, and had Horace's two accounts of him been the only surviving testimonies to Tibullus and his work, the resulting reconstructions of Tibullan elegy can all too easily be imagined. The first stanza of *Odes* 1.33.1–4, written not later than 23 BC, would document an 'early Tibullus' (of 1.1–1.6?), portrayed (so Horace) in his obsessively repetitive elegies (1, 3) as wretched to a high degree (1–3), comparatively elderly (3), and the unsuccessful lover of an unyielding and faithless mistress named Glycera (2). The second and third stanzas of Odes 1.33 then introduce a number of other named individuals and their erotic relationships. It might well be assumed that these were linked with Tibullus, and indeed some *deformazione* of Tibullus 1.8 and 1.9 may be intended; but of the names only Pholoe (8) is genuinely Tibullan (1.8.69), and of the relationships nothing. Horace *Epistles* 1.4 would then document a new phase of Tibullus' literary career – Book 2(?), written under the influence of Cassius of Parma (3). In it Tibullus would abandon erotic poetry and compose elegies covering literary criticism (1) and, more prominently, philosophy (5–6, 9, 12–16). In these elegies Tibullus would be located in the countryside (2, 4), having presumably rejected the urban context in which he was Glycera's wretched lover. These later elegies would also break the elegiac mould in other ways by portraying Tibullus as rich (7, 11), influential (10), celebrated (10), and vigorously healthy (10). They would thus negate those elegiac conventions which make the poet-lover poor, of no social account, emaciated, and sickly.

Because Tibullus' entire œuvre has survived, this reconstruction can be seen to be sheer nonsense.[2] But it embodies the literal sense of Horace's words, and it shows how errors can arise from naive readings of sophisticated texts. The more informed reading of the two Horatian passages which the survival of Tibullan elegy facilitates may still miss some of their nuances, but enough can be grasped for present purposes of the differentiated friendly literary polemic which Horace, first as a lyricist and then as a philosophic epistolographer, directs against Tibullus. Some emphasis should perhaps be placed here on the qualification 'friendly' so as to avoid misunderstanding. Ancient literary polemic could, of course, sometimes be genuinely hostile: as far as they can be understood, Callimachus' attacks on the 'Telchines' were of this sort, as were Catullus' scabrous appraisals of Volusius'

---

2   Even had Tibullus' elegies been lost, the less outré account of him in *Am.* 3.9, Ovid's lament for his death, would have provided a corrective. *Am.* 3.9 also shows that such accounts need not involve severe *deformazione*.

Annales (36; 95.7–8). But in the latter half of the first century BC the 'polemics' which major Roman poets conducted among themselves were good-humoured and amicable: they were in reality means of acknowledging the influence on their own work of other poets and/or of expressing admiration for them, while asserting their own individuality. Much of this activity reflected the inter-generic or intra-generic clashes of the hellenistic period, but for the Romans these disputes were now reduced to intellectual games, and they were sometimes played between known friends such as Gallus and Virgil. In the present volume the terms 'polemic', 'criticism', and so forth, are (unless otherwise indicated) used to refer to this new brand of friendly interaction between poets.

In Horace's polemics against Tibullus, the two techniques of *deformazione* which he employs – misrepresentation and assimilation – can easily be recognized, and the two Horatian passages can be related to other literary polemics of the Augustan period.[3] The parallel polemic and *deformazione* practised upon Gallus by Virgil in *Eclogue* 10, and by Propertius upon Virgil in elegy 2.34 has not gone unnoticed.[4] In *Eclogue* 10 Virgil represents Gallus as abandoning his elegiac poetry and becoming a convert to the bucolic mode. But the conclusion that Gallus introduced a pastoral element into his elegy is unreliable: the entire trend of Virgil's *deformazione* of Gallan elegy was to bucolicize it.[5] Propertius in 2.34 reverses this process of *deformazione*: he subverts Virgil's *Eclogues* so as to transform the bucolic Virgil into an elegist.[6] If literary polemic and *deformazione* initially seem strange processes, a simple reflection may dissipate their strangeness: would it not be a gratuitous assumption, and one which flouts common sense, to imagine that contemporary Roman readers would gladly have perused straightforward rehashes of Gallus by

---

3   Nothing which follows undermines the possibility that some information about lost Gallan elegies can be derived from references to Gallus by Propertius and others. For example, Prop. 1.5, 1.10, 1.13, and 1.20 (on which see below, pp. 219–22) must to some extent reflect Gallus' *Amores*, but not straightforwardly.
4   E.g. D'Anna (1981) 289–95.
5   For the claim that Gallan elegy contained pastoral elements see Ross (1975) 48, 85–6, 160–1, referring to Franz Skutsch's earlier conclusions. In general Ross (1975) seems to have read Propertius (and Virgil) as paraphrasing Gallus; cf. Zetzel (1977) 259: 'Ross has discovered precisely what Virgil intended his readers to think about "Gallus," but the resemblance of Virgil's Gallus to the real one need not have been very close.' The 'pastoral hypothesis' is rejected by Zetzel (1977) 258–9 and Kennedy (1987) 49–53.
6   See below, pp. 313–14.

Virgil and Propertius, or of Virgil by Propertius, when they could read the works of Gallus and Virgil perfectly well for themselves?[7] Recognition that ancient writers employ *deformazione* on others' writings does not imply that the details and the nature of the literary works which they presuppose can always be recovered with full confidence. For example, does the full acceptance of the power of *Amor* attributed to Gallus in *Eclogue* 10 (*omnia vincit Amor et nos cedamus Amori*, 69)[8] imply that Gallus himself wrote something like this line in an elegy in which he admitted defeat by Love?[9] Or is Virgil simply claiming that Gallus *qua* love-elegist has been defeated by the very power he serves, and is therefore a failed poet in a failed literary form? Only the Nachleben of line 69's phraseology provides clues. Both of its key phrases – *vincit Amor* and *cedamus Amori* – return frequently, often with variations:

1.   **vincet amor** patriae laudumque immensa cupido

                                            (Virgil *Aeneid* 6.823)

    cedas: obsequio plurima **vincet amor**   (Tibullus 1.4.40)

    desere: non donis **vincitur** omnis **amor**   (Tibullus 1.5.60)

    quidquid erat medicae **vicerat** artis **amor**.   (Tibullus 2.3.14)

    huc ades et meus hic fac, dea, **vincat amor**

                                         (Ovid *Amores* 3.2.46)

    hac amor, hac odium; sed, puto, **vincit amor**

                                      (Ovid *Amores* 3.11.34)

    successore novo **vincitur** omnis **amor**

                                      (Ovid *Remedia Amoris* 462)

    non potuit Iuno **vincere**, **vincit Amor**   (Ovid *Heroides* 9.26)

    vicit Amor. supera deus hic bene notus in ora est

                          (Ovid *Metamorphoses* 10.26)[10]

    omnia **vicit amor**: quid enim non **vinceret ille**?   (*Ciris* 437)

2.   **cedas**: obsequio plurima vincet **amor**.   (Tibullus 1.4.40)

    nec vigilare alio *nomine* **cedat Amor**.   (Propertius 1.9.28)

    nescit **Amor** magnis **cedere** *divitiis*.   (Propertius 1.14.8)

7   So Nicastri (1984) 26.
8   Cf. Ross (1975) 70. In what follows the capitalization of *Amor* is fairly arbitrary.
9   For the suggestion of Gallan authorship see Perkell (1996) 135–7.
10   Cf. also the (related?) *victus amor(e)* – of Virg. *Aen*. 12.29; [Tib.] 3.6.4; Ov. *Am*. 3.10.29; *RA* 260; *Her*. 15.176; *Met*. 1.619; *Fast*. 2.585, and *vicimus ... Amorem* (Ov. *Am*. 3.11.5).

> *nescit* Amor priscis cedere *imaginibus.*   (Propertius 1.5.24)
> cede fatigato pectore, turpis amor.   (Ovid *Amores* 3.11.2)
> et mihi cedet Amor, quamvis mea vulneret arcu
>   (Ovid *Ars Amatoria* 1.21)
> cedit amor rebus; res age, tutus eris.
>   (Ovid *Remedia Amoris* 144)
> dum bene de vacuo pectore cedat amor.
>   (Ovid *Remedia Amoris* 752)
> vel timidus famae cedere vellet amor!   (Ovid *Heroides* 19.172)

The first group is not as striking in its implications as some other Gallan verbal complexes, but it probably authorizes the conclusion that an elegiac predecessor of Virgil initiated the phrase *vincit Amor*:[11] the concentration of examples of the key phrase towards the ends of pentameters is particularly suggestive. And if an elegist, who else but Gallus? The second group is more determinant since it contains two Propertian lines which are well attested as indebted to Gallus (1.5.24; 1.14.8);[12] and in Chapter 3 one of these (1.5.24) was argued to be either an actual line of Gallus or very close to one. Interestingly, however, only a single successor line (Tibullus 1.4.40) combines a form of *cedere* with *vincit amor* vel sim. This implies, at the level of probability, that Tibullus had *Eclogue* 10.69 as well as Gallan elegy in mind; and it also suggests that Gallus used the two phrases in two different contexts, from which they were extracted and conjoined with friendly malice by Virgil.

Many of the proposals about Gallan themes and motifs which follow claim no more than was claimed for the conclusions just reached, i.e. probability, and it perhaps goes without saying that each is stand-alone, so that the failure of one would not detract from the plausibility of others. The reverse, of course, does not apply: the more numerous the proposals which are deemed to succeed, the stronger the overall case becomes. First, those elegies of the Monobiblos which appear to have major debts to Gallus will be discussed briefly; then certain themes and motifs seemingly shared by Gallus and Propertius will be surveyed, and those Propertian elegies in which they appear in

---

11   Behind it lies an 'etymology' of Venus, transferred to *Amor*: cf. *LALE* s.v. Venus; Michalopoulos (2001) 171.

12   In addition Prop. 1.9.28 contains *nomine*, often a primary or confirmatory indication of the presence of Gallus.

strength will be highlighted. As already noted, this exercise draws considerably upon the work of earlier scholars, with the advantage that some topics can be handled summarily here thanks to earlier, more detailed treatments. However, no attempt is being made to provide a complete catalogue of past thematic proposals: the aim is only to reopen and enlarge debate about Gallus' *Amores* as a source for Propertius. Conclusions about Gallan influence on Propertian elegies and themes can often be materially strengthened by the co-presence of a figure, place, myth, commonplace, or lexical feature otherwise associated with Gallus; hence relevant supportive material from these areas will be deployed freely in asserting thematic dependence. This will mean invoking testimonia and later literary works whose debts to Gallus can reasonably be hypothesized, and also Gallan verbal complexes, both those already established and those which will be constituted as part of the ongoing argument. However, for the most part the metrical indicators of Gallan presence studied in Chapters 5–6 will not as yet be introduced. There are two reasons for suspending their introduction: first, they will later provide independent confirmation of certain hypotheses about the impact of Gallus made on other grounds; and second, it will turn out (below, pp. 216–18) that Propertius did not deploy these metrical indicators in a simplistic way. High concentrations of them sometimes annotate closeness to Gallus evident also on other grounds. But they can also serve to indicate Gallan imitation in places where it might otherwise have gone unobserved, at least by the unobservant, while lower concentrations are found when the presence of Gallus is obvious, e.g. in elegies addressed to 'Gallus' or with highly recognizable Gallan themes. One type of argument sometimes used to assert Gallan influence will be downplayed in what follows for a different reason: it has sometimes been implied or assumed that 'neoteric' style or language alone can justify claims of Gallan input into Propertian elegy in the absence of other, more specific indicators.[13] But Gallus had a number of neoteric predecessors, some of whom – in particular Catullus, Cinna, and Calvus – seem also to have influenced Propertius directly; so such an approach is not sustainable. On the other hand neoteric style or language can constitute a supplementary argument for the presence of Gallus in Propertius when that is backed by more direct evidence.

---

13   On the term 'neoteric' see above, p. 71 and n. 8. For the tendency cf., e.g., Ross (1975) Index rerum notabiliorum s.vv. neotericism, neoteric features of style.

GALLAN PRESENCE IN BOOK 1

Gallan influence starts very near the beginning of the Monobiblos. Its Meleagrian opening (1.1.1–4), which possibly genuflects to Catullus' invocation of Meleager in the identical location of his own first collection,[14] modulates after two more couplets into the myth of Milanion and Atalanta. There are many good reasons for thinking that this myth was treated by Gallus, and that its paradeigmatic appearance at 1.9–16 is indebted to Gallus and indeed makes programmatic reference to him.[15] The myth was presumably mediated to Propertius by Gallus from a Greek model, which was probably a work of Parthenius. The clue pointing to Parthenius as Propertius' and Gallus' source comes in line 11: *nam modo Partheniis amens errabat in antris*. There, at the start of a quatrain exhibiting pure Greek syntax transformed into Latin,[16] Propertius places his Milanion, facing 'wild beasts' (i.e. Centaurs, 12), on Mt Parthenius in Arcadia. The parallel reference to this toponym comes in a poem about the poetry and frustrated love of Gallus, and it shows Gallus in a similar context, hunting wild boars (Virgil *Eclogue* 10.57). There the reference is placed in the mouth of Cornelius Gallus himself: *aut acris venabor apros. non me ulla vetabunt/ frigora Parthenios canibus circumdare saltus* (57–8). Virgil's *Parthenios* has rightly been taken as reflecting a sophisticated compliment paid by Gallus in his *Amores* to his Greek poetic master, Parthenius,[17] specifically an acknowledgement of Parthenius as his source. Similarly Gallus may in his own version of the Milanion/Atalanta myth have placed Milanion on Mt Parthenius as a genuflection to his teacher. In that myth Gallus will either, like Propertius in 1.1, have analogized himself with Parthenius' Milanion, or even played the role of Milanion, as Propertius plays the role of Acontius in 1.18, and as Virgil has Gallus playing the part of Daphnis in *Eclogue* 10. Gallus' successors Virgil and Propertius, the first certainly and the second possibly also a pupil of Parthenius, may simply have been imitating Gallus' compliment as a way of footnoting their

---

14   Cat.1.1–3, cf. *AP* 4.1.1–4 (Meleager).
15   See Ross (1975) 59–70, 90–1. Despite the partial scepticism of Zetzel (1977) 253–4, Rosen and Farrell (1986) have now removed all doubts concerning the Gallan nature of Prop. 1.1 and 1.18.
16   For the hellenizing vocabulary and syntax of this passage see Cairns (1974a) 94–8; (1986); (1987).
17   By Hubaux (1930) 96 n.1.

own literary pedigree. But one could speculate that this type of allusion to a poet's name was a Parthenian method of honouring a master or source, and in that case Virgil and Propertius could have known of it independently of Gallus from Parthenius' own teaching and/or poetry, and they could have copied it to show that Gallus was not the only pupil of Parthenius who had attended to his lessons. Propertius' other employment of the same technique – to compliment Virgil in *Vergiliis* ('the Pleiads') of 1.8.10 with its anomalous prosody[18] – if not just a calque on Virgil's own practice might be another indication that the method has a longer history and goes back to Parthenius himself.[19]

Further elements of the Milanion exemplum of Propertius 1.1.9–16 seem to be specifically Gallan. Gallus will have written of his/Milanion's 'insanity' as a lover (cf. *Galle, quid insanis?*, Virgil *Eclogue* 10.22, and *insanus amor*, *Eclogue* 10.44), a concept which Propertius elevated into the full-blown description of his own *furor* (1.1.7, cf. *non sani pectoris*, 1.1.26) which occupies so much of this, his programmatic elegy. Gallus will also have represented Milanion (and himself?) as wandering about, and perhaps hunting;[20] and *antrum* meaning 'glen' probably appeared in Gallus before its (re-)appearance at Propertius 1.1.11.[21] The etymologizing adjective *dura* attached to Atalanta (1.1.10) is another good Gallan candidate in view of the widespread, and again probably Gallan, use in Propertius of the *mollis/durus/militia* etymology, and the ultimately Parthenian source of the etymology which seems assured by the Greek derivation of 'Atalanta' from ἀ-τλα.[22]

Lines 19–30 of 1.1 are concerned with a variety of *remedia amoris*, and it has been plausibly suggested that Gallan elegy treated this topic.[23] Gallus seeks *medicina furoris* at *Eclogue* 10.50–61, and ends by denying its ability to cure him. The *medicina* complex is diagnostic of Gallus,[24] and by proposing (?)different *remedia amoris* – magic, friends' assistance, branding, and travel – and by failing to describe them explicitly as ineffectual Propertius may be setting himself up *qua* elegist against Gallus, whose (ineffectual) remedies, at least on

---

18   Cf. Fedeli (1980) 204–5, 212–13.
19   See also below, pp. 131–6 on the Parthenian associations of *antra* etc.
20   Cf. Ross (1975) 62–4; Rosen and Farrell (1986) esp. 244–6; and below, pp. 140–3.
21   Cf. Ross (1975) 63 and nn.1–3, and see below, pp. 131–6.
22   Cf. Ross (1975) 62 and n. 2 and above, pp. 89–90.
23   Tränkle (1960) 22; Ross (1975) 66–8; Du Quesnay (1979) 61.
24   See above, pp. 100–1.

Virgil's account, were bucolic song, the wild countryside, inscribing on trees, and hunting. On the other hand, if the concluding verses of Propertius 1.1 (33–8) imply that Propertius' *remedia* also fail, then they will reflect that other topos 'there is no cure for love', for which, in view of *Eclogue* 10, Gallus is again likely to have been his source.[25] In this way Propertius would be retreating from his earlier pretensions and admitting that, like his poetic master, he too is beaten by love. That *deducere* occurred in Gallus and was the source of *deductae* (1.1.19) and *ducere* (1.1.24) is an interesting conjecture;[26] and the 'ends of the earth' topos (cf. Virgil *Eclogue* 10.65–8; Propertius 1.1.29) seems to be securely Gallan, given his use of similar commonplaces in his claim to universal fame, and given his attested interest in one such remote location, the Caucasus.[27] Two more concepts of 1.1 which have been proposed as Gallan are: 'natural solitude reflects in its desolation the situation of the unhappy lover' (cf. Virgil *Eclogue* 10.58–9; Propertius 1.1.29–30; 1.18; 1.20.13–14); and the lover 'dying of love' while others' 'attempts to offer words of comfort fail' (cf. Virgil *Eclogue* 10.9–30 and Propertius 1.1.25).[28] Neither concept seems alien to Gallus: Gallus' Milanion experienced the wilds of Arcadia, and Gallus, like Propertius in 1.18, placed himself in the shoes of Callimachus' Acontius, so he too shared Acontius' rustic solitude; as for dying of love, that is how Propertius in faux-naïf mode characterizes Gallus' death in 2.34.91–2, which suggests that this too featured in Gallan elegy. But to what extent Milanion and/or Acontius contributed to this motif (neither seem to have had comforters) is unclear; and in any case the influence of Theocritus' Daphnis (*Idyll* 1), at whatever remove, is obvious. That Gallus' Milanion appeared in a programmatic context similar to Propertius 1.1[29] can only be a conjecture, albeit an attractive one; and it is impossible to know whether Propertius' self-representation at 1.1.15–18 as a failure in love who contrasts with the successful Milanion is a straight imitation of Gallus or an inversion.

The succeeding elegies of the Monobiblos contain many indications of the presence of Gallus, and these will increase in number in Chapters 5 and 6. As things now stand they range from the *medicina*

---

25   Cf. Ross (1975) 67, and above, pp. 100–1 (on *medicina* as part of a Gallan complex).
26   Of Ross (1975) 66.
27   See below, p. 205 n. 53 and Index II s.v.
28   Cf. Ross (1975) 68.
29   As suggested by Ross (1975) 69.

complex exemplified in 1.2.7–8, to the Orpheus allusion of 1.3.42, to the plausibly Gallan ends of the earth of 1.6.3–4; in 1.6 the ends of the earth accompany a full-blown exploitation of the *mollis/durus/militia* etymology which is equally likely to derive from Gallus (25–36), and which also embraces manifestations of the Gallan *nequitia* (26) and *pars eris* (34) complexes. Another entire elegy (1.5) is addressed to Gallus, features his *nomen* group, and almost certainly contains a quotation from Gallus (24).[30] It would be easy too to hypothesize Gallan *erotodidaxis* as a background to 1.2 (see also below, pp. 116–18), and a *komos* by Gallus as the model that Propertius was playing off against in 1.3.[31] These reflections suggest that Gallan elements in Propertius' early elegies are not isolated features but the result of wholesale adoption by Propertius of Gallan themes. A further indication of this is the prominence in the early elegies of rivals to Propertius in his love-affair.[32] 1.4 casts Bassus in this role, while 1.5 features Gallus. Then comes the praetor of 1.8 (and of 2.16 and 3.20), who looks very similar to Gallus' rival for Lycoris since he is a *vir militaris* and since his wealth, and his use of it to attract Cynthia, is made very explicit (1.8.33–40, cf. 2.16; 3.20). It has been argued that Cornelius Gallus introduced the figure of the rich rival into Roman elegy, *inter alia* in the context of the *komos*.[33] On this hypothesis these early elegies of Propertius represent a series of direct and allusive reversals and *deformazione* of the œuvre of Gallus and of his poetic *persona*. Apart from the major elements of *deformazione* discussed elsewhere, there may be smaller, less intrusive touches: for instance, although *qua* rival Gallus is not overtly designated as rich in 1.5, a sly hint of his wealth may be present in 1.5.24: *nescit Amor priscis cedere imaginibus*, a line which is itself either Gallan or virtually Gallan (above, pp. 79–80): it is very like *nescit Amor magnis cedere divitiis*, addressed at 1.14.8 to Propertius' other patron, Tullus, and the resemblance could be interpreted as an ironically allusive characterization of Gallus too as '*dives*'. Again, like 1.2 and to some extent 1.1, both 1.4 and 1.5 are in their entirety erotodidactic, and thus must be indebted on a larger scale to Gallus' *erotodidaxis*.

---

30   Cf. also above, pp. 78–81 and below, pp. 229–30, 424–5.
31   Du Quesnay (1979) 60–1 hypothesized from Virg. *Ecl.* 2 the existence of at least one Gallan *komos*; see also below, pp. 118–19.
32   Catullus too had rivals for the objects of his affection (e.g. 21; 24; 37; 40; 81; 82), but he never develops the theme extensively.
33   By Du Quesnay (1979) 60–1, stressing the rival of Virg. *Ecl.* 2 (influenced by Gallus), esp. ll. 2, 57, and the link between *Ecl.* 10.22–3 and the indubitably Gallan Prop. 1.8.

Propertius' two *propemptika* of the Monobiblos reveal further strong links with Gallus, who composed the schetliastic *propemptikon* for Lycoris which lies behind 1.8.[34] 1.6, directed pointedly to Gallus' fellow patron, Tullus, is also a *propemptikon*, although it is excusatory and thus non-schetliastic. One might be tempted to explain 1.6's divergence in this respect from Gallus' known *propemptikon* to Lycoris by attributing it to originality on the part of Propertius: on this account Propertius was trying, by composing 1.6 in this variant mode, to demonstrate his own greater sophistication and superior rhetorical knowledge, while at the same time filling 1.6 with Gallan features so as to draw attention to the model which he was emulating. But, although Propertius' practice throughout much of the Monobiblos might seem to support such a surmise, Gallus fr. 2 Courtney imposes caution. If the later *propemptika* modelled on it (see Chapter 12) are to be trusted, the *propemptikon* of the Qaṣr Ibrîm papyrus was also excusatory and non-schetliastic. So Gallus was master of that *propemptikon* variant too. However this may be, Propertius' interactions with Gallus in 1.8 can be interpreted with greater ease: his 'polemics' there with his predecessor retain the schetliastic mode of Gallus' elegy for Lycoris and an analogous propemptic scenario: in both cases the poet's mistress has departed/will depart, supposedly to a cold region, with a rival who is a state official. In 1.8 Propertius' superiority to Gallus consists in the success of his *propemptikon*. Everyone knew that Gallus' *propemptikon* to Lycoris had failed and that despite it she went off with Gallus' rival;[35] on the contrary Propertius proclaims that his own *propemptikon* is successful and he shows it dissuading Cynthia from departing with his rival (1.8.27–46). Thus Propertius asserts his own superiority over Gallus *qua* lover, and hence the superiority of his elegy, as demonstrated by its erotic effectiveness, over Gallan elegy. Propertius also scores off Gallus when it comes to the routes which the two poets assign to their respective propemptic addresses: Propertius enhances the dangers facing Cynthia, and so enlarges both his prospects of success in dissuading her from leaving and the credit due to him for doing so, by giving her a more dangerous sea route, as opposed to the less dangerous, although just as chilly,

---

34   Cf., e.g., Pasoli (1977) with earlier bibliography; King (1980) 222; Fedeli (1980) 204–5; Manzoni (1995) 73–4.

35   Anderson, Parsons and Nisbet (1979) 153 enumerates and discusses the possible candidates for Gallus' rival.

land route allotted by Gallus to Lycoris.[36] The key passages for this interpretation are:

'Galle, quid insanis?' inquit. 't u a cura Lycoris
perque _nives_ alium perque horrida castra secuta est.'
(_Eclogue_ 10.22–3)

t u procul a patria (nec sit mihi credere tantum)
<u>Alpinas</u>, a, **dura** _nives_ et <u>frigora</u> Rheni
me sine sola vides. a, t e ne <u>frigora</u> laedant!
a, t i b i ne _teneras_ <u>glacies</u> secet <u>aspera</u> **plantas**!   (_Eclogue_ 10.46–9)

t u ne audire potes vesani murmura ponti
    fortis, et in **dura** nave[37] iacere potes?
t u **pedibus** _teneris_ positas fulcire <u>pruinas</u>,
t u potes insolitas, Cynthia, ferre _nives_?   (Propertius 1.8.5–8)

The shared (or varied) verbal details, as coded above, presumably reflect or emulate Gallus.[38]

Another question raised by Propertius 1.8 concerns the term _cura_ (1): its technical elegiac sense 'beloved' is definitely Gallan. This can be concluded first from Virgil's phrase _tua cura Lycoris_ (_Eclogue_ 10.22) with its word-plays on _cura_ = κούρη and κώρα = (Ly)-coris[39] and its context (_'Galle, quid insanis?' inquit. 'tua cura Lycoris/ ... '_); second from the appearance of _tua cura_ in the 'schema Cornelianum' at _Eclogue_ 1.57 (_raucae, tua cura, palumbes_); third from Propertius' frequent application of _cura_ to Cynthia; and fourth from Propertius' programmatic use of _cura_ meaning 'beloved' at 1.1.36.[40] Presumably Gallus wrote something like _mea cura Lycoris_. Confirmation comes from Statius' highly explicit _quid tuus ante omnis, tua cura potissima, Gallus,/ nec non noster amor ... ?_ (_Silvae_ 4.4.20–1), which refers to a Flavian individual named Gallus, and which is more than an echo of Virgil in that it footnotes Cornelius Gallus' original ownership of

---

36   On land and sea routes in _propemptika_ see Cairns (1992c), with earlier bibliography. A further (cultural) element of Propertius' superiority to Gallus derives from his knowledge of, and use of, _Ecl._ 10.

37   The additional 'irrational' partial overlap in sound between **nives** in _dura nives_ (_Ecl._ 10.47) and **nave** in _dura nave_ (Prop. 1.8.6) is instructive.

38   Cf. Fedeli (1980) 204–5; Manzoni (1995) 73–4.

39   This is the first appearance of _cura_ in this sense. Virgil is, of course, translating either Theoc. _Id._ 1.81–2 or a Greek imitator.

40   On all this cf. Ross (1975) 67–69.

Virgil's phrase.[41] But did Gallus describe Lycoris as *mea cura* specifically in his *propemptikon* addressed to her? There may be an oblique hint of this at Propertius 1.8.1, which focuses on the *iunctura* by perversely using *mea cura* (1) to mean not 'my beloved' but 'my love for you', in this way both evoking and emulating the Gallan/ Virgilian usage,[42] and possibly also 'correcting' Virgil's *tua cura*. A further complication arises from the appearance of *cura* in *Lydia doctorum maxima cura liber* (Ticidas fr. 2 Courtney), referring to Valerius Cato's *Lydia*, possibly a work celebrating a mistress of that name.[43] If this line is punning on *cura* ('concern' or 'beloved'), then Gallus did not invent the sense 'beloved' but vectored it,[44] as he often seems to have been the vector for others' phrases. However that may be, in later verse the feel of *cura* in the sense 'beloved' was specifically Gallan: it is never found in this sense in Tibullus, but, in addition to 1.1.36, Propertius employed it thus at 2.25.1, 2.34.9, and 3.7.21 (pluralized).

The influence of Gallus can also be suspected in many of the elegies of the Monobiblos which follow 1.8. Propertius 1.10 and 1.13, both addressed to Gallus, are very likely to have reworked elements of his elegy, including *erotodidaxis* and a description by Gallus of his own successful love-making. *Erotodidaxis* is ubiquitous in Augustan poetry, but in 1.10 and 1.13 (as in 1.5) Propertius is manifestly challenging Cornelius Gallus' prior activity as *magister amoris* and superimposing his own authority in that area. As for the notion that Gallus had described his own sexual success in his *Amores*, this has long been seen as the solution to an otherwise embarrassing problem in Propertius 1.10 and 1.13. In both elegies Propertius supposedly recounts how he saw (*vidimus*, 1.10.6; *vidi*, 1.13.14, 15) the love-making of 'Gallus' and his girl-friend. But voyeurism and exhibitionism are not well attested in Graeco-Roman culture, and it would seem that literary examples of this type of exhibitionism/voyeurism are later.[45] So, if 1.10 and 1.13 are taken literally, Propertius is depicting himself as the first known literary voyeur in the whole of antiquity and

---

41   For the reference to Virg. *Ecl.* 10.22 cf. Coleman (1988) 142–3.
42   Propertius might also have intended *mea cura* to convey the secondary meaning 'your love for me', but this again would not be equivalent to Virgil's *tua cura*.
43   For Cato's *Lydia* see Courtney (1993) 189–91. For further discussion and parallels, some of which involve the 'schema Cornelianum', see Manzoni (1995) 71–3.
44   *Lydia* could alternatively have been the title of a translation by Valerius Cato of Antimachus' *Lyde*.
45   See Krenkel (1977a); (1977b).

'Gallus' as the first Roman literary exhibitionist. How publicizing these activities could be reconciled with the social standing of these two Roman *equites* is anyone's guess! On the other hand, if 1.10 and 1.13 refer to a poem or poems written by C. Cornelius Gallus describing his own love-making,[46] perhaps along the lines of Propertius 2.15.1–24, then the embarrassment vanishes. The claim to have 'seen' or witnessed someone or something is made sufficiently frequently in Augustan poetry for it to be considered a standard motif.[47] Sometimes 'seeing' is intended to be taken literally.[48] But there is at least one other place where it has been correctly understood to mean 'reading': at *Eclogue* 10.26 the phrase *quem vidimus ipsi* (of Pan) has been interpreted as Virgil's claim to have read about Pan in the poetry of Gallus,[49] i.e. the phrase functions as a source-citation. In the light of *Eclogue* 10.26 Propertius' *vidimus* of 1.10 and repeated anaphoric *vidi ego* of 1.13 (cf. also *me ... teste*, 1.13.14) can all the more confidently be identified as parallel citations of Gallus' *Amores*, and a similar proposal will be made below (p. 232) about *visus* at Propertius 1.20.52.[50] The fact that Gallus is involved in all these passages suggests that he had made such conspicuous use of the 'seeing'/'reading' equivalence (and of *vidi/vidimus ipse/ipsi*) that later writers could evoke it as typical of his elegy.

If Propertius is following in 1.10 and 1.13 the emulative pattern observable in 1.8, then his treatment of his Gallan models can be surmised in outline: in 1.10 Propertius will be practising *aemulatio* of Gallus by posing as a more effective lover and 'teacher of love' than Gallus. The poetic master, Gallus, portrayed earlier in 1.5 as Propertius' erotic rival and a would-be seducer of Cynthia, has now himself fallen in love and so receives erotic instruction from Propertius, a former pupil who is now even more confident in his dealings with Gallus than he was in 1.5. Propertius' designation of his mistress Cynthia as the source of his erotic expertise may be an innovation intended to upstage an alternative claim made by Gallus. In 1.13

---

46 As was suggested by Skutsch (1906) 144, followed in the interval, knowingly or unknowingly, by many others.
47 Cf. Tränkle (1960) 24, identifying *vidi ego* etc. and *testis est* (below) as Gallan. Many other phrases featured in his Ch. II.1 may also be Gallan in origin.
48 E.g. Prop. 4.2.53; 4.5.61, 67.
49 Ross (1975) 98–9 n. 3. Elsewhere in Virgil (*Aen.* 1.584; 2.499), however, genuine autopsy is being claimed.
50 For another possible example of literary 'seeing' in elegy see Tib. 1.2.89; and for a wide-ranging discussion of *videre* and *meminisse* in similar terms with many new examples see Thomas (1999) 181–94.

Propertius admits that he has suffered a setback in his own love-affair, and that he has, for the time being at least, lost Cynthia. The reader, of course, already knows this, since it happened in 1.11+1.12. But Propertius nevertheless retains (or seizes from Gallan elegy?) the moral high ground: he portrays Gallus as rejoicing over this misfortune, while he himself is unwilling to wish a parallel fate upon Gallus. Indeed, despite Gallus' gloating, and even though Gallus is depicted as a former heartless seducer who has now fallen in love and has been successful in love, Propertius will continue to give Gallus precepts to help him to preserve his felicity. Thus Propertius also retains the erotodidactic high ground, in that he continues in the role of Gallus' *magister amoris*, which he had exercised in 1.10 and even earlier in 1.5. Oddly enough,[51] however, it is in the unitary elegy (i.e. 1.11+1.12),[52] which is sandwiched between 1.10 and 1.13 to inform Propertius' readers of his separation from Cynthia, that even more overt signs of Gallan poetic influence appear. Its learned first quatrain (1.11.1–4) eulogizing the Baiae region and ending with Gallan *nobilibus*(!) is surely derived from Gallus, one of whose poetic haunts was precisely that area: cf. *sive Gigantea spatiabere litoris ora* (1.20.9), addressed to 'Gallus'.[53] Then Gallus' own river Hypanis turns up at 1.12.4 (*quantum Hypanis Veneto dissidet Eridano*) along with another river, the Po, which might possibly stand for Gallus' *patria* (see above, p. 72). In 1.14 to 1.17 fewer Gallan touches are obvious at this stage of the investigation, although 1.14 again mentions the same area of known interest to Gallus, the Caucasus (*urgetur quantis Caucasus arboribus*, 6), and contains the securely Gallan *nescit Amor magnis cedere divitiis* (12), and 1.15 employs Gallus' *historia* line-ending, coupled with *nobilis: tu quoque uti fieres nobilis historia* (24). The most tempting, but also the most frustrating, elegy in this section of the Monobiblos is 1.16, a sophisticated *komos* which looks to be playing off against an earlier model. Since all three surviving elegists, and also Catullus in his elegiacs, wrote at length in this genre, the natural conclusion is that Gallus must have done so too;[54] but how 1.16 relates thematically to such hypothetical Gallan

---

51   Although what is observable here conforms with Propertius' overall practice in referencing
      Gallus overtly and covertly (see below, pp. 216–18).
52   For the unity of Prop. 1.11+1.12, see Butrica (1996a).
53   Cf. Ross (1975) 76 n.1, but commenting only on 'neoteric features'.
54   Cf. also above, p. 113 n. 31.

komoi cannot be conjectured. More Gallan aspects of 1.14 to 1.17 will, however, emerge in later chapters.[55]

The presence of Gallus in 1.18 is once more firmly grounded in past scholarship: despite the indisputable, and considerable, influence upon Propertius 1.18 of Callimachus' Acontius and Cydippe *aetion*,[56] it is clear that in his elegies Gallus had either narrated this myth or portrayed himself as an Acontius figure and that Propertius, in his parallel self-portrayal as Acontius in 1.18, accepted significant simultaneous input from that Gallan treatment.[57] 1.18, then, where the *persona* of Acontius is essentially Gallan, is parallel in this respect to 1.1, where Propertius exploited Milanion as a mask or analogue of Gallus.[58] When it comes to details derived from Gallus, degrees of certainty vary. 1.18.8's *cogor habere notam* is highly likely to derive from Gallus.[59] Likewise the thematic coincidences between *Eclogue* 10 and Propertius 1.18, and the occasional verbal correspondences, viz.

> certum est in silvis inter spelaea ferarum
> malle pati *teneris*que m e o s incidere amores
> **arboribus**:[60] crescent illae, crescetis, amores
> > (Virgil *Eclogue* 10.52–4)

and

> a quotiens *teneras* resonant m e a verba sub umbras,
> > scribitur et vestris Cynthia **corticibus**!   (Propertius 1.18.21–2)

imply that Gallus/Acontius too had inscribed his love on tree-bark, as did Callimachus' Acontius;[61] again the *moriens liber* of *Eclogue* 10.67 may recall that tree-bark.[62] Other claims are perhaps less cogent, but still plausible: the presence of Pan at Propertius 1.18.20 and Virgil *Eclogue* 10.26–7 should reflect Gallus, particularly since Pan is one of a group of rustic deities who certainly appeared somewhere in Gallan

---

55   For these, see below, pp. 206–12.

56   Cf. Cairns (1969), with references to earlier work.

57   Cf. Ross (1975) 71–4, 88–9; King (1980) 222–3; Rosen and Farrell (1986); Kennedy (1987) 51–2.

58   P. R. Hardie (2002) 122–8 offers some interesting speculations about further ways in which Gallus may have linked the two myths.

59   As first suggested by Tränkle (1960) 24; cf. the *nota* sub-complex (above, pp. 99–100).

60   Since Virgil began this hexameter with more general *arboribus* and since *arboribus* also has Gallan overtones at pentameter endings (cf. below, pp. 170–1 and 229), it is intriguing that Propertius instead used the more restricted *corticibus* at his pentameter ending.

61   Cf. Ross (1975) 73, 96 n.1.

62   Cf. Ross (1975) 96 n.1.

elegy (see below, pp. 122–3). The 'neoteric *a*' of Propertius 1.18.21, which crops up three times in Virgil *Eclogue* 10.47–9, twice along with postponed *ne,* could well have been a Gallan feature.[63] Finally, at lines 31–2 Cynthia's name will fill the woods and rocks: *sed qualiscumque es, resonent mihi 'Cynthia' silvae,/ nec deserta tuo nomine saxa vacent.* This is the last couplet of 1.18, and hence a suitable locus for an evocation of Gallus' *nomen* group, which functions there as a source-citation.[64]

Of the remaining elegies of the Monobiblos, 1.20, addressed to Gallus, has naturally been identified as a prime locus for Gallan influence.[65] But, since it is such a complex poem and since it plays such an important part in this enquiry, separate consideration of it will be reserved for Chapter 7, when all the approaches developed over Chapters 3–6 can be applied to it. The other later elegies of the Monobiblos have occasional elements which point clearly to Gallus. These, however, are mainly metrical and will be treated in Chapters 5–6. One elegy (3.4) from the remaining three Books can at present be linked indubitably, closely, and as a whole with Gallus' œuvre, but only thanks to the Qaṣr Ibrîm papyrus;[66] 3.4 will be be treated separately in Chapter 12 since it also offers important insights into the development of Roman elegy after Gallus. More elegies of Books 2–4 might well fall into the same category as 3.4 if more of Gallus' œuvre had survived; and, even as things are, it is worth attempting to link some of them with Gallus when they feature themes otherwise attested as Gallan.

POETIC INITIATION

The first such theme is poetic initiation.Virgil *Eclogue* 6.64–73 make it clear that, on at least one occasion, Gallus treated the theme of his own poetic initiation.[67] Cf.:

---

63   Cf. Ross (1975) 73 and n. 4; on this particle both in general and in Propertius see Kershaw (1980); (1983).
64   For this concept see, e.g., above, p. 117 and below, p. 143 and n. 124.
65   Esp. Ross (1975) 75–81, with earlier references.
66   Cf. Anderson, Parsons and Nisbet (1979) esp. 140–3, 151–5.
67   That the background to *Ecl.* 6 is in general Gallan is assumed in this volume; the technique used by Virgil in imitating Gallus is brilliantly hypothesized and paralleled by Yardley (1980). On these lines in particular cf. Ross (1975) 34–6 (referring to earlier bibliography);

tum canit, errantem Permessi ad flumina Gallum
Aonas in montis ut duxerit una Sororum,   65
utque viro Phoebi chorus adsurrexerit omnis;
ut Linus haec illi divino carmine pastor
floribus atque apio crinis ornatus amaro
dixerit: 'hos tibi dant calamos (en accipe) Musae,
Ascraeo quos ante seni, quibus ille solebat   70
cantando rigidas deducere montibus ornos.
his tibi Grynei nemoris dicatur origo,
ne quis sit lucus quo se plus iactet Apollo.'

Then he sings of Gallus wandering by Permessus' stream,
How one of the Sisters led him to Aeonia's mountains,
And how all Phoebus' choir stood up to greet a man;
How Linus there, the shepherd of inspired song,
His locks adorned with flowers and bitter celery,
Told him: 'The Muses give you this reed pipe (there, take it)
Which once they gave the old Ascrean, whose melody
Could draw the stubborn rowans down the mountainside.
Tell you with this the origin of Grynia's grove,
Lest any sacred wood be more Apollo's pride.' (tr. Guy Lee)

Not only does Virgil's placement of Gallus in a context of Heliconian literary initiation attest this, but the actors and events reported by Virgil differ sufficiently from those found in the Hesiodic/Callimachean tradition as we know it to indicate that a major new voice has contributed to that tradition. Of course, not all ancient initiation poetry has survived, and in particular the lost contribution of Philetas to the tradition must be responsible for some of the novel elements of *Eclogue* 6.64–73. But this is the poetic initiation of Cornelius Gallus; Gallus' own input to the stock scene, presumably made (at least in part) in his *aetion* of the Grynean Grove, was obviously regarded by him, and by Virgil, as a major achievement; and Virgil surely selected Gallus' innovations for special emphasis. These clearly consisted not in the presence of the *chorus* of Muses, including notably Calliope as *una Sororum* (65, below),[68] or of Apollo, but in the prominence of Linus as a forebear of Gallus. Orpheus is also present, if only in the background.[69] The older tradition is saluted by reference to Hesiod

Anderson, Parsons and Nisbet (1979) 151 (with earlier bibliography); Heyworth (1992) esp. 45–53.

68   On Apollo and Calliope in Gallus see Ross (1975) 60, 115, 121; Kennedy (1987) 53–4.
69   On Linus and Orpheus see Ross (1975) 21–31, 34–6, 36, 118–20. Gallus apparently associated Orpheus closely with the river Hebrus: cf. Ross (1975) 93–4; Kennedy (1987)

and by the placement of the event on Helicon, while the innovatory elements include mentions of the Permessus and of Gallus' poem on the Grynean Grove,[70] and the use of Silenus as speaker. The same, or another, Gallan initiation is reflected indirectly in *Eclogue* 4.55–9. These lines do not introduce an actual initiation, but they again link Orpheus and Linus,[71] as Gallus surely did:

> non me carminibus vincet nec Thracius Orpheus
> nec Linus, huic mater quamvis atque huic pater adsit,
> Orphei Calliopea, Lino formosus Apollo.
> Pan etiam, Arcadia mecum si iudice certet,
> Pan etiam Arcadia dicat se iudice victum.

> Linus will not defeat me in song, nor Thracian Orpheus,
> Though one should have his father's aid and one his mother's,
> Orpheus Calliope and Linus fair Apollo.
> If Pan too challenged me, with Arcady as judge,
> Pan too, with Arcady as judge, would own defeat. (tr. Guy Lee)

Here the mother of Orpheus (Calliope) and the father of Linus (Apollo) are both explicitly present and prominent. Calliope is named, and she is not just *una Sororum*, as she was in *Eclogue* 6.65. Both Calliope and Apollo are active in aiding their respective poet children. A similar train of thought must already have been present in Gallus. In *Eclogue* 6's initiation scene, Apollo was named both 'Phoebus' (66) and 'Apollo' (73), but here in *Eclogue* 4 he is 'Apollo'. To judge by these and other indications in the *Eclogues*,[72] Gallus was sometimes allusive and coy when it came to naming his characters in his account(s) of his initiation(s). There is no such coyness in Virgil's naming of characters in *Eclogue* 4.55–9, and indeed Pan's name heads two successive lines (58–9). Pan does not appear in the initiation of *Eclogue* 6, and his entrance at the end of *Eclogue* 4.55–9 has the air of

---

53–4; Manzoni (1995) 70. Wills (1996) 359–60 sees as Gallan certain anaphoras in passages about Orpheus by other poets, including Virgil. Ross (1975) 23 interpreted *ille* (67) as Orpheus. Zetzel (1977) 254 described this as 'scarcely Latin', while admitting that 'It is a problem to have Hesiod leading trees, but the mixture of two stories is a typical Alexandrian trait' and comparing Virgil's two Scyllas. No other text has Hesiod 'leading trees', but Gallus could have attributed this feat to Hesiod *qua* analogue of Orpheus (see also below, pp. 124–5).

70   Ross (1975) 21, 31, 79–80.

71   On the emphasis upon their parents cf. also Kennedy (1987) 53–4; for the version in which Orpheus and Linus were brothers cf. Ross (1975) 30 and n. 5. Gallus may well have exploited it.

72   Cf. also below, pp. 126, 129, 130.

an appendage. And yet lines 58–9, with their massive anaphoras, which include the topic of judging and the form *iudice* found in the Qaṣr Ibrîm papyrus (fr. 2.9 Courtney), help to give Pan good Gallan credentials, which are strengthened by two of his further appearances: at Virgil *Eclogues* 10.26–7 as one of Gallus' visitors in his erotic affliction (*Pan deus Arcadiae venit, quem vidimus ipsi/ sanguineis ebuli bacis minioque rubentem*), and again (unnamed) at Propertius 1.18.20 in an elegy of acknowledged Gallan derivation (cf. above, pp. 114–16).

A troublesome question then arises: if Pan too was featured in a Gallan scene of initiation, was it the same scene as is reflected in *Eclogue* 6, or did Virgil find him in a different Gallan context or contexts? Plausible arguments have been made for the presence in Gallus' works not only of Pan (or Pans), but also of Hamadryads/ Naiads etc., Silenus, Silvanus, and Pales.[73] But if any or all of these deities featured in a single Gallan account of his poetic initiation, that account was heavily populated. Three lines of the *Culex* appear to offer assistance; they unite 'Pans', sheep, Hesiod – and shepherds who rival him, a fountain and Hamadryads:

> o pecudes, o Panes et o gratissima tempe
> fontis Hamadryadum, quarum non divite cultu
> aemulus Ascraeo pastor sibi quisque poetae
> securam placido traducit pectore vitam.   (*Culex* 94–7)

As is often the case with *Culex* passages, these lines reflect Gallus,[74] and the phrase *Ascraeo ... poetae* looks very much like confirmation that Pan and the Hamadryads had roles in an initiation scene in Gallus. It could be argued that it was the *Culex* poet who put all these characters together, particularly since Hamadryads must have featured in Gallan elegy elsewhere than, or in addition to, an initiation scene.[75] On the other hand Pan reappears along with Silenus (and the Muses) in a Propertian poetic initiation quite certainly indebted to Gallus (3.3.29–30) and in a context which makes it unlikely that their joint appearance is merely a tribute to Virgil's *Eclogues* (see below, pp. 126–7).

---

73   See Ross (1975) 24–5, 28, 30, 71–2, 95 and n. 4, 98–9, 137 n. 4; Kennedy (1982) esp. 377–89.
74   Cf. also *Culex* 115–18 (Pans, Satyrs, Dryads, Naiads, Orpheus, Hebrus), and see Kennedy (1982), esp. 377–81 with acute remarks on Gallus' Hamadryads as 'surrogate Muses'.
75   They must, for example, have appeared in Gallus' Hylas poem (see below, pp. 222–3).

Propertius was multiply influenced by Gallus' initiation poem(s). They contributed to 2.13.3–8:

> hic me tam gracilis vetuit contemnere Musas,
> iussit et Ascraeum sic habitare nemus,
> non ut Pieriae quercus mea verba sequantur,
> aut possim Ismaria ducere valle feras,
> sed magis ut nostro stupefiat Cynthia versu:
> tunc ego sim Inachio notior arte Lino.

> He (Love) forbade me to despise so slender Muses, and told me to live in the grove of Ascra – not that Pierian oaks should follow my words or I should have the power to lead wild beasts in the valley of Ismarus – but rather that Cynthia should be enchanted by my verse. Then I would be more celebrated in my art than Argive Linus.

Here the characters and scenery of *Eclogue* 6 largely reappear: the Muses (the *chorus* of Apollo), the grove of Ascra (an allusion to Hesiod), Helicon, Orpheus, and Linus. However Propertius' context, unlike that of Virgil's reprise of Gallus' initiation scene, is strongly elegiac in that the *hic* (3) who dictates Propertius' choice of literary form is *Amor* (2), not Apollo. Interpretation of this feature is problematic: is Propertius reasserting – by returning it to its original elegiac form – a Gallan concept which Virgil had polemically subjected to epic/bucolic *deformazione* in *Eclogue* 6? Or is Propertius 'correcting' both Gallus and Virgil when he insists that the proper divinity to organize the initiation of an elegiac love-poet is *Amor*, not Apollo? In another elegy redolent of Gallan initiation Bacchus joins with Apollo to support Propertius in his erotic endeavours (3.2.9–10, see below, p. 128);[76] this might suggest that 2.13's innovation was Propertian. But Bacchic material in Propertius reflects Philetas (below, pp. 127–31), possibly mediated by Gallus.

It was suggested above (pp. 121–2 n. 69) that *Eclogue* 6.70–1, where Hesiod is 'leading trees', can be explained on the assumption that Gallus attributed to Hesiod the Orpheus-like ability to 'lead trees'. This suggestion may gain some support from Propertius 2.13.3–8, where Propertius is told by Apollo to 'live in the <Hesiodic> grove of Ascra, not that [*or* not on the condition that(?)] the oaks of Pieria should follow my words, or I should have the power to lead beasts in the valley of Ismaros' (5–6). Here Propertius (emulating or negating

---

76   In *Am.* 1.1 Ovid also presents *Cupido/Amor*, not Apollo, as controlling his literary choices. For a full discussion see McKeown (1989) 7–11.

Gallus?) disclaims for himself the power which Virgil had attributed to Hesiod. Propertius makes a close connection between the specifically Hesiodic character of the grove in which he is to live – *Ascraeus* always recalls Hesiod – and the notion of 'leading beasts and trees'; and *Pieriae* is neatly bifunctional in context as the birthplace of the Muses (mentioned in line 3), and as a region of northern Greece which complements *Ismaria*, another location in that area, and so underscores the allusive reference to Orpheus. It might, of course, be argued that in these lines Propertius is simply expanding upon Virgil's remarks in *Eclogue* 6 – and he does have these in mind as well. But Propertius' expansion can better be accounted for on the assumption that he was also drawing on the Gallan concept which lies behind Virgil's words, i.e. that because Hesiod was an Orpheus figure, he like Orpheus could lead trees, and perhaps also beasts. Propertius adds a further erotic twist to the concept, one parallel to his assignment of the role of poetic initiatory deity to *Amor* rather than to Apollo: whereas Propertius cannot lead trees and beasts, Cynthia is to be *stupefacta* 'amazed and dumbstruck' by his verse (7).[77] In other words Propertius will retain the power to 'lead' Cynthia.[78] Propertius also elevates himself as a poet above Gallus in a slyly indirect way: whereas in *Eclogue* 6 Linus had initiated Gallus, Propertius declares (8) that, if he can control Cynthia through his poetry, he would be *notior* ('more celebrated' – Gallus' own boast) than Linus, and hence 'more celebrated' than Gallus.

A Gallan initiation poem also seems to underly a single couplet of Propertius 1.2, i.e. *cum tibi praesertim Phoebus sua carmina donet/ Aoniamque libens Calliopea lyram* (27–8). This couplet features not just Phoebus and Calliope but also Calliope's *Aonia lyra*, with its reference to Helicon, and the gifting to Cynthia by Phoebus of his songs and by Calliope of that instrument – a key topos of literary initiation. Two other isolated Propertian couplets probably have the same pedigree: *non haec Calliope, non haec mihi cantat Apollo:/ ingenium nobis ipsa puella facit* (2.1.3–4), and *nondum etiam Ascraeos norunt mea carmina fontis,/ sed modo Permessi flumine lavit Amor* (2.10.25–6). There can be no doubt that the water of Permessus in the latter couplet is associated particularly with Gallus, as Virgil too

---

77   Virgil's use of this term at *Ecl.* 7.3 perhaps comes closest. There lynxes are *stupefactae* at the song of the rustics, which also halts rivers (3–4). These powers are those of Orpheus (e.g. Prop. 3.2.3–4).

78   Prop. 3.2 enshrines a similar concept, which climaxes at 3.2.9–10.

associates it with him at *Eclogue* 6.64. However, the further implications of Propertius' reference to Permessus are disputed (see below, pp. 329–32).[79]

Virgil's references to Pan, his use of Silenus as speaker, and the problem of whether Gallus' initiation featured rustic deities and if so which, have already been mentioned. Propertius 3.3,[80] in which he himself is initiated, may throw some further light on these matters. In 3.3 Propertius is dreaming; he is on Helicon (1–2) and he receives a pep-talk from Apollo of the standard restrictive sort (15–24). Apollo then directs him to a *spelunca*, where a second, booster lecture is delivered by Calliope (39–50). The *spelunca* and its contents are described in some detail:

> dixerat, et plectro sedem mihi monstrat eburno,   25
>   quo nova muscoso semita facta solo est.
> hic erat affixis viridis spelunca lapillis,
>   pendebantque cavis tympana pumicibus,
> orgia Musarum et Sileni patris imago
>   fictilis et calami, Pan Tegeaee, tui;   30
> et Veneris dominae volucres, mea turba, columbae
>   tingunt Gorgoneo punica rostra lacu;
> diversaeque novem sortitae iura Puellae
>   exercent teneras in sua dona manus:
> haec hederas legit in thyrsos, haec carmina nervis
>   aptat, at illa manu texit utraque rosam.   (3.3.25–36)

He (Phoebus) finished speaking, and with his ivory plectrum shows me a place where a new path has been made in the mossy ground. Here there was a green cave with attached mosaics; and tympana, the sacred implements of the Muses, hung from the hollow pumice and a clay bust of father Silenus, and your pipes, Pan of Tegea. And the birds of my mistress Venus, my flock, doves, dip their red beaks in the Gorgonian pool. And the nine maiden Muses, each with her different allotted power, apply their young hands to their own accomplishments. One gathers ivy to make thyrsi, another fits tunes to the lyre's strings, and that one with both hands weaves rose-garlands.

Lines 27–32 allude to Bacchus and refer to the Muses, Silenus, Pan, and Venus. But none of these deities is physically present at this point, and, of them, only the Muses – named first as *Musae* (29), and then on

79   Cf., e.g., Ross (1975) 117–20; Anderson, Parsons and Nisbet (1979) 151; Tatum (2000).
80   On the literary-programmatic aspects of 3.3 cf. Ross (1975) 120–2, 137 n. 3, and esp. Fedeli (1985) 110–15.

their second appearance as *Puellae* (33) in coy Gallan(?) fashion –
will actually come on stage in the elegy. Lines 27–32 are a catalogue
of attributes, or in one case an image, of these gods: *tympana* (28),
which allude to Bacchus via their Dionysiac associations; either *orgia*
(mystic implements?) or *organa* (musical instruments?) of the Muses
(29);[81] a clay image (or mask?) of Silenus (29); panpipes (30); and the
doves of Venus (31–2).[82] All these, except the doves, are offerings
dedicated in the *spelunca*. Line 33 then introduces a quatrain offering
a more detailed description of the activities of the Muses (*Puellae*),
one of whom is gathering ivy for *thyrsi* (35), again a manifestly
Bacchic motif.

External evidence and Propertius' own final 'footnote' to the
elegy (*Philetea ... aqua*, 52) suggest that his *spelunca* and its contents
derive ultimately from Philetas, and probably from a context of poetic
initiation in Philetas' works.[83] But Gallus too was undoubtedly an influence on this initiatory scene. Propertius' cave, although manifestly
artificial,[84] is specified as a cave, not a grove, so it is clearly part of the
debate over the meaning of terms for caves, glades and groves discussed below (pp. 131–6). Again, Propertius' rustic deities and
scenery, although they may have originated in Philetas, were obviously transmitted by Gallus: although the details are obscure, Propertius' cave is also reminiscent of the *antrum* of Silenus in *Eclogue* 6.
There Silenus lay drunk (*inflatum ... Iaccho*, 15), two *pueri* and a
Naiad entered it, and from it Silenus' song, which included an account
of the poetic initiation of Gallus on Helicon, issued and caused Fauns,
beasts, and trees to move in rhythm (27–8).[85] It is these analogies
which once more open up the possibility of a second poetic initiation
in Gallus' works. Gallus could well have recounted not only his
Hesiodic/Callimachean encounter with the Muses and higher deities
on the open ground of Helicon (in a *nemus*?); he could also have

---

81 On the textual problem of this line (where O offers the impossible *ergo*), the reasons for
   preferring *orgia* over other emendations and the various interpretations of the phrase, see
   Fedeli (1985) 137–8. It is unclear whether *orgia* stands asyndetically in apposition to
   tympana, or has a different reference.

82 Line 31 exemplifies the 'schema Cornelianum': cf. *raucae, tua cura, palumbes* (Virg. *Ecl.*
   1.57). The closeness of the two lines suggests a Gallan original: cf. Ross (1975) 69 n. 2.

83 Cf. Boucher (1965) 205–26, 307–8. The presence of *pumicibus* (28) hints that this programmatic keyword goes back to Philetas.

84 On these elements of Roman landscape architecture see Lavagne (1988); on references to
   them in Propertius, 497–503.

85 The detail that the Naiad Aegle will receive 'another reward' from Silenus than his song
   (26) hints that Gallus, like Propertius, did not neglect to stress his role as a love-poet.

asserted another, lower-key, Philetan(?) initiatory experience involving a cave (*spelunca*) in which he met rustic gods and other deities not part of the Hesiodic/Callimachean tradition.

Propertius 3.1 and 3.2 belong to the same introductory cycle of elegies as 3.3 with its major account of Propertius' poetic initiation. So it is not surprising that they too should contain further hints of Gallus' initiations and other Gallan material.[86] 3.1.1–2 has Propertius seeking admission to the sacred grove (*nemus*) of the heroized Callimachus and Philetas (2). *orgia* are mentioned here (4), as they probably are in 3.3.29, and there is an *antrum* shared by Propertius' two Greek predecessors (5). These features deserve attention and comparison with the other relevant passages, especially in view of the possibility that Gallus described more than one poetic initiation. 3.1 also highlights the Muses (10–14, 17–20). The latter passage alludes to Propertius' own poetic initiation: his '*opus*' comes down from Helicon, the Muses are '*Pegasides*', and they are asked to garland Propertius. Finally, the last line of the elegy refers briefly to 'Lycian' Apollo as the protector of Propertius' future fame.[87] 3.2.3–4 mentions Orpheus and the power of his music, implying that Propertius draws girls as Orpheus and his ilk drew beasts, rivers, and stones (cf. 2.13.5–8 and above, pp. 123–5). The further attractive suggestion has been made that Amphion (3.2.5–6) and Polyphemus (3.2.7–8) were also, like Orpheus, Gallan themes, and that Propertius is cataloguing these as such in lines 2–8.[88] Elegy 3.2 then goes on to combine Bacchus and Apollo as protectors of Propertius (9), and it claims the Muses as his *comites* and Calliope as 'worn out by my dances' (15–16).[89]

Past discussions of the impact of Gallan initiation poetry on Propertius have made little or nothing of another Propertian elegy which shows definite signs of such influence. This is 2.30, in which Propertius imagines himself and Cynthia visiting Helicon together, seeing the Muses and hearing them sing of the loves of Jupiter (25–40):

> libeat tibi, Cynthia, mecum   25
> rorida muscosis antra tenere iugis.

---

86 Cf. Ross (1975) 121–2.
87 Cf. Callim. *Aet.* fr. 1.22 Pf. The presence of Callimachus (along with Philetas and Gallus) is assumed rather than underlined in the present discussion since it has featured largely in past treatments of these elegies.
88 Du Quesnay (1979) 220 n. 212; cf. also below, p. 201 (*re* Antiope) and Prop. 3.15.
89 For the further possibility that the same Gallan original lies behind Prop. 3.2 and the central portion of Ov. *Am.* 1.3 see Cairns (1993) 114–15.

illic aspicies scopulis haerere Sorores
  et canere antiqui dulcia furta Iovis,
ut Semela est combustus, ut est deperditus Io,
  denique ut ad Troiae tecta volarit avis.   30
quod si nemo exstat qui vicerit Alitis arma,
  communis culpae cur reus unus agor?
nec tu Virginibus reverentia moveris ora:
  hic quoque non nescit quid sit amare chorus,
si tamen Oeagri quaedam compressa figura   35
  Bistoniis olim rupibus accubuit.
hic ubi me prima statuent in parte choreae,
  et medius docta cuspide Bacchus erit,
tum capiti sacros patiar pendere corymbos:
  nam sine te nostrum non valet ingenium.   40

May you desire, Cynthia, to occupy with me a dewy cave in the mossy
mountains. There you will see the Sister Muses sitting on the rocks
singing the sweet love-affairs of Jupiter of old, how he was fired by
Semele, how he lost himself over Io, and last how he flew to the
rooftops of Troy as a bird. But, if no-one exists who has conquered the
arms of the winged love-god, why am I alone charged with a fault
shared by all? Nor should you speak reverently to these maiden Muses:
this band too is not unaware of the meaning of love, if
(notwithstanding) one of them lay long ago on the rocks of Bistonia
embraced by the shape of Oeagrus. Here, when they will place me at
the front of their dance, and Bacchus with his poetic thyrsus will be in
the midst, then I shall allow the sacred ivy-berries to hang down my
head. For without you my poetic genius has no power.

The presence of the Muses indicates that the scene is Helicon, but it is
a Helicon different in a number of ways from that of Hesiod and
Callimachus. Its focus is the *rorida ... antra* of line 26, which appear
to be, not an open glade or glades or a *nemus*, but rather, as in 3.3.25–
52, a 'cave'. This is suggested not just by *rorida* but by *muscosis ...
iugis* (26): even so 3.3 indicates that its *spelunca* of line 27 is really a
cave by combining *muscoso ... solo* (26) with *cavis ... pumicibus* (28).
Here in 2.30, then, the contemporary debate about terms for caves,
glades and groves (see below, pp. 131–6) is again in full swing. Other
noteworthy features of the Heliconian visit of 2.30 are the allusive
naming of characters – the Muses are first introduced as *Sorores* in
coy (?)Gallan parlance (27, cf. *una Sororum, Eclogue* 6.65) – and the
participation by Bacchus and the poet in the dance of the Muses.
Another novel touch, perhaps attributable to Propertius rather than

Gallus, is the eroticization of the entire encounter between Propertius, Cynthia and the Muses. This starts with the Muses' songs, which celebrate the love-affairs of Jupiter (27–30). The first mentioned is his liaison with Semele; her son by Jupiter, Bacchus, hints of whom have appeared in the other poetic initiations discussed, will round off the elegy (38–40). Then comes Jupiter's affair with Io, subject of a famous poem by Calvus and possibly also a Gallan theme,[90] and finally Jupiter's abduction of Ganymede. A curious verbal/conceptual link between *avis* (30, the eagle sent by Jupiter to bring him Ganymede) and the, again coyly named, *Ales* (31), i.e. winged *Amor, en-courages* Propertius to protest about being reproached as a lover (31–2) and to make the point that the Muses – now called, not only coyly but paradoxically, *Virgines* (33) – are also personally acquainted with love (33–4). For proof he points to Calliope, who bore a son. She is not named, but she is identified allusively as the mother of Orpheus in the conspicuously learned periphrastic couplet 35–6, redolent of neo-tericism, and almost crying out its derivation from Gallus.[91] Finally Bacchus, not generally an actor in Heliconian initiation scenes, pre-sides with his 'learned' thyrsus over the Muses' dance in place of Apollo, and – another unusual touch – Propertius himself joins in the dance of the Muses,[92] wearing *corymbi*, symbolic both of Bacchus and Philetas (37–40).[93] The elegy ends with Propertius linking his poetic genius (*ingenium*) with Bacchus (40). The cave setting, the absence of Apollo, the presence of the Muses and Bacchus, and the footnoting allusion to Philetas in *corymbos* (39), again in the final couplet of the elegy, all point to the influence of a Gallan initiation of the second, more low-key type outlined above, one for which Gallus probably

---

90   Cf. above, p. 92 n. 78.
91   *accubuit* (36) is very likely to be Gallan (cf. also Prop. 1.3.3; Tib. 1.9.75; Ov. *Met.* 12.457), as is *accubuisse* (cf. Prop. 2.32.36; 3.15.12; 4.4.68), and possibly *accubuere* (cf. Ov. *Fast.* 1.402; *Met.* 8.663). In all Propertius employs forms of the verb six times, Tibullus once, and Ovid in elegiacs three times (in *Met.* twice), a pattern perhaps characteristic of Gallan *imitatio*.
92   I.e. with O's reading *me* in 1.37. Guyet's *te*, preferred by some editors, risks eliminating a genuine Propertian element: cf. 3.5.19–20: *me iuvat in prima coluisse Helicona iuventa/ Musarumque choris implicuisse manus*, and [Tib.] 3.8.24, where 'Sulpicia' writes of her-self *dignior est vestro nulla puella choro* (i.e. of the Muses). At 2.30.37 Propertius is not, however, thinking of himself as *choregus* (as perhaps at 3.3.16: *et defessa choris Calliopea meis*), since that is Bacchus' role; for Muse(s) joining the dance of the comic chorus (comic poet?) cf., e.g., Aristoph. *Pax* 774–6 (from Stesichorus); *Ran.* 675–8; fr. 334 (*Thesm. Deut.*).
93   Cf. *cera Phileteis certet Romana corymbis* (Prop. 4.6.3).

drew on Philetan rather than on Callimachean models.[94] This will be the same Gallan initiation as was seen to lie behind Propertius 3.3.25–52.

CAVES, GLADES, AND GROVES

Caves, glades, and groves have already cropped up in connection with Gallan initiation poetry.[95] It was observed that, when Propertius in his first elegy writes allusively of his mythical analogue Milanion, who had served Gallus comparably, as 'wandering' *Partheniis ... in antris* (1.1.11), he is capping Virgil's *Parthenios saltus* (*Eclogue* 10.57) and the Gallan original of both phrases, which doubtless employed *antrum*. How can the diverse expressions employed by Virgil and Propertius (Gallus) be explained? And why is it that *antris* in Propertius 1.1.11 must mean 'glades', given that it makes little sense for Milanion to be wandering in caves and perfect sense for him to be wandering in glades?

Greek ἄντρον covers any hollow or depression, although its standard early meaning was 'cave'; but in the hellenistic period ἄντρον seems to have been extended to include the area in front of a cave proper, or indeed to have been used simply to refer to a 'glade'. The cave of Polyphemus illustrates this development. Homer calls it both a σπέος and an ἄντρον in *Odyssey* 9, and he clearly means a cave proper:

> ἔνθα δ' ἐπ' ἐσχατιῇ σπέος εἴδομεν ἄγχι θαλάσσης,
> ὑψηλόν, δάφνῃσι κατηρεφές· ἔνθα δὲ πολλά
> μῆλ', ὄϊές τε καὶ αἶγες ἰαύεσκον· περὶ δ' αὐλή
> ὑψηλὴ δέδμητο κατωρυχέεσσι λίθοισι
> μακρῇσίν τε πίτυσσιν ἰδὲ δρυσὶν ὑψικόμοισιν.
>
> (*Odyssey* 9.182–6)

There at the most outlying point we made out a cave close to the sea, with a high entrance overhung by laurels. Here large flocks of sheep and goats were penned at night, and round the mouth a yard had been built with a great wall of quarried stones and tall pines and high-branched oaks. (tr. E. V. Rieu, adapted)

---

94 Dance in scenes of initiation (e.g. Prop. 2.30.37; 3.2.16) is again unCallimachean. In combination with *Culex* 18–19 and 115–20 (quoted below, p. 136 and n. 107), and Virg. *Ecl.* 6.66 (quoted above, p. 121) these passages hint that Gallus mediated this concept from Philetas.
95 See above, pp. 127–30, and Ross (1975) 62–4.

It was 'shaded by bays' and it had in front of it a yard full of pines and oaks.[96] However, Theocritus' Cyclops refers to his dwelling-place as an ἄντρον, which is clearly something different:

> ἄδιον ἐν τῶντρῳ παρ' ἐμὶν τὰν νύκτα διαξεῖς.
> ἐντὶ δάφναι τηνεί, ἐντὶ ῥαδιναὶ κυπάρισσοι,
> ἔστι μέλας κισσός, ἔστ' ἄμπελος ἁ γλυκύκαρπος,
> ἔστι ψυχρὸν ὕδωρ, τό μοι ἁ πολυδένδρεος Αἴτνα
> λευκᾶς ἐκ χιόνος ποτὸν ἀμβρόσιον προΐητι.   (*Idyll* 11.44–48)

... you will pass the night more pleasantly in the cave with me. There are bays and slender cypresses; there is dark ivy, and the sweet-fruited vine, and icy water, which wooded Etna sends forth for me from her white snowfields, a draught divine. (tr. A. S. F. Gow, adapted)

The combination of ἐν τῶντρῳ (44, 'in the *antron*') and ἐντί (45, 'there are') ... τηνεί (45, 'there'), along with repeated ἐντί (45) and the three examples of ἔστ'/ἔστι (46–7), shows that Theocritus' Cyclops conceives as being inside his ἄντρον not just bays but cypresses, ivy and vines, as well as a spring. In other words the Cyclops' ἄντρον includes what in Homer was distinguished from the cave as the 'yard', so that it also includes a 'grove'. It must be significant that the first appearances of *antrum* in Latin are in Virgil's *Eclogues*.[97] Its conjunction, in its new sense 'glade' or 'grove', with the name of Parthenius at Propertius 1.1.11 strongly suggests that Parthenius had featured ἄντρον as 'glade', thus equating it with *saltus* and *nemus*, and that Parthenius' pupils then started to use *antrum* in Latin not only in the old sense of Greek ἄντρον ('cave') but also in the new sense of ἄντρον – 'glade' or 'grove' – to which Parthenius had introduced them, and which they therefore associated with Parthenius.[98] Virgil's *saltus* of *Eclogue* 10.58 will then be the relatinized equivalent of *antra* in its new (Greek) sense 'glades'.

96   The similar situation at the cave (σπέος) of Calypso is described more extensively at Hom. *Od.* 5.57–73.

97   1.75; 5.6, 19; 6.13; 9.41. *decessit Olympius antro* is spurious (Ennius *Spuria* 15 Skutsch). Du Quesnay (1979) 220 n. 212 speculated that Polyphemus was a Gallan theme (see above, p. 128). If so, Polyphemus' cave in a Gallan elegy is another possible source for *antrum*; there is, however, no trace of Polyphemus in extant Parthenius.

98   Propertius' contemporaries would have regarded Greek and Latin ἄντρον /*antrum* as the same word, particularly since the theory that Latin was a form of Greek closest to the Aeolic dialect was then in vogue, although not unchallenged: cf. Maltby (1993). Propertius had recourse to this theory in his next line (1.1.12), where *feras* represents Aeolic φῆρας ('centaurs'): see Cairns (1974a) 97–8; (1986) 34, 36–8.

If Parthenius did feature ἄντρον as 'glade' or 'grove' (as well as cave?), one possible location in his œuvre, which would help explain his procedure, is his influential *propemptikon* (fr. 26 Lightfoot, cf. frr. 28, 29), which looks to have featured the Cilician 'Corycian cave'.[99] Strabo's description of that same 'Corycian cave' uses ἄντρον to mean both 'glade' and 'cave':

> ... τὸ Κωρύκιον **ἄντρον**, ἐν ᾧ ἡ ἀρίστη κρόκος φύεται. ἔστι δὲ κοιλὰς μεγάλη κυκλοτερὴς ἔχουσα περικειμένην ὀφρὺν πετρώδη πανταχόθεν ἱκανῶς ὑψηλήν· καταβάντι δ' εἰς αὐτὴν ἀνώμαλόν ἐστιν ἔδαφος καὶ τὸ πολὺ πετρῶδες, μεστὸν δὲ τῆς θαμνώδους ὕλης ἀει-θαλοῦς τε καὶ ἡμέρου· παρέσπαρται δὲ καὶ τὰ ἐδάφη τὰ φέροντα τὴν κρόκον. ἔστι δὲ καὶ **ἄντρον** αὐτόθι ἔχον πηγὴν μεγάλην ποταμὸν ἐξιεῖσαν καθαροῦ τε καὶ διαφανοῦς ὕδατος, εὐθὺς καταπίπτοντα ὑπὸ γῆς· ἐνεχθεὶς δ' ἀφανὴς ἔξεισιν εἰς τὴν θάλατταν· καλοῦσι δὲ Πικρὸν Ὕδωρ. (Strabo 14.5.5)

> ... the Corycian cave, in which the best crocus [saffron] grows. It is a great circular hollow, with a rocky brow situated all round it that is everywhere quite high. Going down into it, one comes to a floor that is uneven and mostly rocky, but full of trees of the shrub kind, both the evergreen and those that are cultivated. And among these trees are dispersed also the plots of ground which produce the crocus. There is also a cave here, with a great spring, which sends forth a river of pure and transparent water; the river forthwith empties beneath the earth, and then, after running invisible underground, issues forth into the sea. It is called Picrum Hydor [Bitter Water]. (tr. H. L. Jones)

Strabo initially applies the term Κωρύκιον ἄντρον to the large depression in which saffron, for which Corycos was famous, was grown. This area contained woods as well as saffron-beds, and so was not a 'cave' but a 'grove'. Then Strabo writes of an ἄντρον, a cave proper, situated inside this larger glade. Strabo's description reads like something from a tourist brochure. A similar description could have been available to Parthenius, and if it transmitted the two senses of ἄντρον to that section of Parthenius' *propemptikon* which treated the 'Corycian cave', this might illuminate what we see in Virgil and Propertius. As noted, the sense 'glades' for *antris* is essential at Propertius 1.1.11; 'glades' must also be the correct rendering at 1.2.11 (*surgat et in solis formosius arbutus antris*), since the arbutus tree can

---

99 Cf. Lightfoot (1999) 114–19, 169–70, 181–5, and, for a broader-ranging discussion of the Corycian cave, Leigh (1994) esp. 183–92.

hardly be growing in 'caves'. This line, only one couplet away from the Gallan *medicina* and *artificem* of lines 7–8, may likewise be indebted to a Parthenian/Gallan description of the Corycian cave. Strabo insists that the wood inside the large depression there is 'cultivated' (ἡμέρου). Propertius negates this concept: his *arbutus* is 'uncultivated' – is this *imitatio cum variatione* at some remove? The same natural–artificial contrast is found in an *antrum* = 'grove' context at Propertius 4.4.3–5: *lucus erat felix hederoso conditus antro,/ multaque nativis obstrepit arbor aquis/ Silvani ramosa domus*, and it may reflect the same source – cf. too Strabo's emphasis on the spring in the Corycian cave. Other Propertian loci where 'glade' (or 'grove') is appropriate are 2.32.39, where apples are being collected,[100] and 4.9.33, where the topic is the 'grove' of the Bona Dea, described as a *nemus* at line 24: *lucus ab umbroso fecerat orbe nemus* (note also the spring of line 35). The other meaning of *antrum*, 'cave', appears in Propertius at 2.30.26 (on Helicon), 3.1.5 (of Callimachus and Philetas), 3.2.14 (*operosa antra*), 3.5.43 (of Cerberus), and 4.9.9 and 12 (of Cacus). Sometimes the sense must be arbitrated: at 3.13.33, the *antra* where lovemaking takes place could have either meaning; and at 4.1.103 *antrum* is the grove(?) where the oracle of Ammon is situated, i.e. the oasis of Siwa. Propertius uses *spelunca* only once, at 3.3.27 where a genuine but probably artificial cave is described; he does not use *spelaeum*.[101] That term, first found at *Eclogue* 10.52 in the mouth of Gallus, would seem to have encountered strong disfavour: it was reused by the *Ciris* poet (467), and then never employed again in surviving Latin verse until late antiquity. It is hard to tell whether Gallus had infelicitously adopted the word during the *antrum* debate, or whether Virgil's attribution of it to Gallus in *Eclogue* 10 is *deformazione* verging on defamation.[102]

In Augustan poetry *antrum* and its quasi-synonyms must always have carried with them a reminiscence of Parthenius and a hint of the learned 'problem' or dispute which he initiated. But the topic is complex, as Virgil's usage illustrates: in *Eclogue* contexts otherwise unconnected with Gallus Virgil may have used *antrum* both in its

---

100 This passage is rich in Gallan associations: Hamadryads (37); Sileni and Silenus himself (38); a Naiad (40): cf. Kennedy (1982) 379–80, who adds the attractive suggestion that Gallus treated the myth of Paris and Oenone.

101 Lucretius uses only *spelunca*, never *spelaeum* or *antrum*.

102 The *Ciris* poet's bad taste or/and over-dependence on Gallus would seem to be in evidence.

Parthenian sense 'glade' (1.75; 5.6, 19)[103], and in its old sense 'cave' (6.13; 9.41).[104] On the other hand, where Gallus was his subject, Virgil seems to have wanted to emphasize the distinction between 'caves' and 'glades' by calling the former *spelaeum* and the latter *saltus* or *nemus*. The literary 'polemic' already observed in the *Parthenios saltus* of *Eclogue* 10.57 also reveals itself immediately after the introductory passage of *Eclogue* 10:

> quae nemora aut qui vos saltus habuere, *puellae*
> NAIDES, indigno cum Gallus amore peribat?   (*Eclogue* 10.9–10)

Here the two old Latin terms for 'glade' are set against Gallus and his emblematic Naiads. The polemic is also visible in the earlier, more muted, but in context equally transparent, countering of Gallan practice in the last of the three cases of *saltus* in the *Eclogues*:

> claudite NYMPHAE,
> Dictaeae NYMPHAE, nemorum iam claudite saltus
> (*Eclogue* 6.55–6)

Virgil's polemic is unlikely to be directed against Parthenius, as Virgil's own adoption of Parthenian practice in non-Gallan contexts shows, and this makes it even harder to assess his intentions. Is the polemic in part inter-generic, reflecting the 'conflict' between bucolic and elegy which animates Virgil's entire treatment of Gallus? Might there also be a rejoinder to Gallus, based on linguistic purism and raising the question whether his elegy (as opposed to Virgil's bucolic) should have seen fit to hellenize by using *antrum* rather than *spelunca*, and in particular by adopting Parthenius' new sense of *antrum*?[105] This would not be inconsistent with Virgil's own continued use of *antrum* elsewhere in his hexameter poetry.

Propertius, on the other hand, obviously had no qualms about *antrum* = 'glade'/'grove', a sense which in his eyes Gallan usage would have endowed with good elegiac credentials. We might even

---

103 For *Ecl.* 5 the proof is: *sive antro potius succedimus. aspice, ut antrum/ silvestris raris sparsit labrusca racemis* (6–7) – wild vines do not grow inside caves.

104 However, Ross (1975) opines (63 n. 2), perhaps correctly, that *antrum* always means 'grove' in the *Eclogues*.

105 If this was Virgil's point, then it had no impact: *spelunca* is found only three times in elegy: Prop. 3.3.27; Ov. *Am.* 3.1.3 (both perhaps referring to the same (?)Philetan original); and Ov. *Fast.* 1.555.

conclude that Propertius was attempting counter-polemic on the side of Gallus and against Virgil in his early and emphatic uses of *antrum* in 1.1.11 and 1.2.11. If so, this polemic and counter-polemic was observed by at least one later critic, the *Culex* poet. Below is his implied comment on the terminological battle. It is set within an invocation of Gallus' Naiads, and it ends with a line reminiscent of Propertius' *errabat in antris* (1.1.11), and doubtless of that line's Gallan model too. It contains *nemora, silvae, saltus*, and *antra*; it also refers to the Heliconian spring as *Pierii* (cf. Propertius 2.13.5 of oaks, *Aetna* 7 of the spring); and it mentions *Sorores* (here the Naiads, but the term is used at Virgil *Eclogue* 6.65, Propertius 2.30.27, and *Aetna* 7 of the Muses);[106] *chorea* (cf. Propertius 2.30.37); Pales; and *cura* (cf. above, pp. 115–16). The passage's pandectic character implies that the 'bucolic' hexameter of the *Culex* has the right to incorporate all the relevant terminology of both epic and bucolic:

> quare, Pierii laticis decus, ite, Sorores
> Naides, et celebrate deum ludente chorea.
> et tu, sancta Pales, ad quam ventura recurrunt
> agrestum bona fetura – sit cura tenentis
> aerios nemorum cultus silvasque uirentes:
> te cultrice vagus saltus feror inter et antra.   (*Culex* 18–23)[107]

WILD SURROUNDINGS

Caves, groves, and woods, however named, are only some of the elements of untamed scenery plausibly attributable to Gallan elegy. A number of passages of the *Appendix Vergiliana*, especially from the *Culex*, *Ciris*, and *Aetna*, embodying 'wild surroundings' have in the past been exploited to confirm indications of Gallus in Augustan poets.[108] For example *Eclogue* 10.13–15:

---

106   The Gallan status of this term in reference to the Muses is guaranteed by *Aonas in montis ut duxerit una Sororum* (*Ecl.* 6.65).

107   Another *Culex* passage brings together some of the characters who populated Gallan elegy (including Orpheus, named only by his patronymic: cf. Prop. 2.30.35): *hic etiam viridi ludentes Panes in herba/ et Satyri Dryadesque chorus egere puellae/ Naiadum in coetu. non tantum Oeagrius Hebrum/ restantem tenuit ripis silvasque canendo,/ quantum te, pernix, remorantem, diva, chorea/ multa tuo laetae fundentes gaudia vultu* (115–120).

108   See esp. Kennedy (1982), where 387 n. 91 highlights 'wild surroundings'; (1987). Ross (1975) occasionally comments on such material (e.g. 77).

illum etiam lauri, etiam flevere myricae,
pinifer illum etiam *sola* sub **rupe** iacentem
Maenalus et ge̲l̲i̲d̲i̲ fleverunt **saxa** Lycaei.

has been shown to be Gallan in origin,[109] with the *Ciris* and *Culex*
contributing usefully to the demonstration:

infelix virgo nequiquam a morte recepta
incultum *solis* in **rupibus** exigit aevum,
rupibus et **scopulis** et *l i t o r i b u s* d̲e̲s̲e̲r̲t̲i̲s̲   (*Ciris* 517–19)

scrupea d̲e̲s̲e̲r̲t̲a̲s̲ haerebant ad cava **rupes**   (*Culex* 51)

Further indications that Gallus lies behind all this have been seen in *si
modo sola queant saxa tenere fidem* (Propertius 1.18.4) and in a
Pompeian graffito possibly quoting Gallus: *illum in desertis montibus
urat Amor.*[110] The recurrent key terms in these passages are *rupes,
litus, saxum, solus* and *desertus*,[111] cf. also *scopulus*.

These are not the only noteworthy elements of the complex. *Ciris*
517's *infelix virgo* is reminiscent of *a virgo infelix*, with its conspicuous 'neoteric *a*'. This combination is first known from a fragment of
Calvus which addresses Pasiphae (fr. 9 Courtney). It then becomes a
virtual cliché, but one of its two applications to Pasiphae in *Eclogue* 6
continues: *a, virgo infelix, tu nunc in montibus erras* (52) and so probably also reflects the same Gallan model as influenced *Ciris* 517–19.
'Deserted', 'lonely', and 'empty' shores and lonely/deserted figures
on those shores feature largely in Latin poetry from Catullus on. The
combination of *desertus* and *litus* found at *Ciris* 519 (above) is also
very common. Cf.:

perfide, d̲e̲s̲e̲r̲t̲o̲ liquisti in *l i t o r e*, Theseu   (Catullus 64.133)

huc se provecti d̲e̲s̲e̲r̲t̲o̲ in *l i t o r e* condunt.   (Virgil *Aeneid* 2.24)

d̲e̲s̲e̲r̲t̲o̲s̲que videre locos *l i t u s*que relictum   (Virgil *Aeneid* 2.28)

d̲e̲s̲e̲r̲t̲a̲que *l i t o r a* Cretae   (Virgil *Aeneid* 3.122)

d̲e̲s̲e̲r̲t̲a̲m̲ *vacuo* Minoida *l i t o r e* questus?   (*Aetna* 22)

---

109 Lyne (1978) 313 on *Ciris* 518–19; Kennedy (1987) 51–3.
110 *CIL* 4.1645.2–3, as suggested by G. Lee (1982) 124; (1990) 132 on Tib. 1.6.51–2.
111 On *solus* and *desertus* cf. Kennedy (1987) 52.

> languida <u>desertis</u> Cnosia *l i t o r i b u s*   (Propertius 1.3.2)[112]
>
> <u>frigida</u> <u>deserta</u> *l i t o r a* turre peto   (Ovid *Heroides* 18.116)
>
> *l i t o r e* destituit. <u>desertae</u> et multa querenti
>   (Ovid *Metamorphoses* 8.176)

The persistence of this language and these concepts has something to do with the fame of Catullus' complaint of Ariadne, the influence of which is clearly visible in some of the later passages quoted above. But the unique example of the variant *solus + litus* at Virgil *Georgics* 4.465 is securely linked with Gallus, since its context is a description of the self-consolatory singing of that thoroughly Gallan figure Orpheus after his loss of Eurydice:

> ipse cava solans aegrum testudine amorem
> t e , dulcis coniunx, t e *solo* in *l i t o r e* secum,
> t e *veniente* die, t e *decedente* canebat.   (*Georgics* 4.464–6)[113]

'Lonely' mountains and crags and 'lonely' individuals on them are even more surely Gallan. In addition to the Virgilian examples quoted below, Propertius 2.19.7, which combines both notions, is a powerful indication, particularly since it occurs in his imagined hunting, which on other grounds can be associated with Gallus (see below, pp. 141–3):

> ibi haec incondita *solus*
> **montibus** et <u>silvis</u> studio iactabat inani   (Virgil *Eclogue* 2.4–5)
>
> pastorum et *solis* exegit **montibus** aevum   (Virgil *Aeneid* 11.569)
>
> *sola* eris et *solos* spectabis, Cynthia, **montes**   (Propertius 2.19.7)

Then there is the related concept that someone, or some group, alone can do something in the mountains:

> **montibus** in nostris *solus* tibi certat Amyntas.   (Virgil *Eclogue* 5.8)

---

112 Lieberg (1997–2000) esp. 156–7 regards Propertius' source for 1.3.2 as Virg. *Ecl.* 10.14–15 (where Virgil's Gallus is weeping *sola sub rupe*), but does not bring Cornelius Gallus' poetry into the equation.

113 On these lines cf. Thomas (1988) 227–8 (with 204), seeing 'the lone lament beside water' as Gallan. Note also Wills (1996) 358–61, arguing that anaphoras of *dum, nec, hic,* and, as here, (personal pronoun) *te,* reveal Gallan influence.

tristis at ille 'tamen cantabitis, Arcades,' inquit
'**montibus** haec vestris; *soli* cantare periti
Arcades   (Virgil *Eclogue* 10.31–3)

The latter example is particularly suggestive since it comes from the
mouth of Gallus himself. Finally another part of the fourth *Georgic*'s
account of Orpheus provides a further indication of the Gallan
associations of high places with 'loneliness': Orpheus weeps 'beneath
a high cliff by the wave of the lonely Strymon' and 'plays' *gelidis* ...
sub antris:

> septem illum totos perhibent ex ordine mensis
> **rupe** sub aëria <u>deserti</u> ad Strymonis undam
> flesse sibi, et <u>gelidis</u> haec evoluisse sub <u>antris</u>
> mulcentem tigris et agentem carmine quercus
> (Virgil *Georgics* 4.507–10)

Further elements of 'wild surroundings' with a probable Gallan
origin can easily be proposed. The first quatrain and the last three
couplets of the securely Gallan Propertius 1.18 are rich in them. Here
are unpeopled and 'silent' places, an empty grove and lonely rocks (1–
4), springs and a chill crag, a hard(!) night's sleep, a speaker alone,
woods to echo the lover's words, and woods and *deserta ... saxa*
(echoing *sola ... saxa* of line 1) to resonate with Cynthia's *nomen*
(27–32):

> haec certe <u>deserta</u> loca et taciturna querenti,
>   et *vacuum* Zephyri possidet aura <u>nemus</u>.
> hic licet occultos proferre impune dolores,
>   si modo *sola queant* **saxa** tenere fidem.   (1–4)
>
> pro quo divini fontes et frigida **rupes**
>   et datur inculto tramite *dura* quies;
> et quodcumque meae *possunt* narrare querelae,
>   cogor ad argutas dicere *solus* aves.
> sed qualiscumque es, resonent mihi 'Cynthia' <u>silvae</u>,
>   nec *deserta* tuo *nomine* **saxa** vacent.   (27–32)

There are clear analogies between these passages and the wilderness
scenario of Propertius 1.20.13–14, addressed to Gallus (cf. below, pp.
223, 227–8): *ne tibi sit duros montes et frigida saxa,/ Galle, neque
expertos semper adire lacus*. The not dissimilar Arcadian setting of

the Gallan Milanion-Atalanta myth of Propertius 1.1.9–16, with its *antris* and *rupibus*, is germane too, as is *Eclogue* 10.55–61, where Gallus hunts in Arcadia and where *frigora, saltus, rupes*, and *lucos* all feature. All in all, then, it is reasonable to hypothesize that there were various wilderness landscapes in Gallus' elegies – a single landscape is unlikely to have been so rich in detail – and that they influenced the Propertian passages listed above and also the wilderness of 2.19 into which Propertius says that he will go to hunt, with its two species of *flumina* (25, 30), its *solae ... silvae* (29), and its *muscosis ... iugis* (30), the last detail also reminiscent of two of Propertius' Gallan initiation scenes (2.30.26 and 3.3.26). That yet another element of the Gallan prototype(s) was *tacitus/taciturnus* is implied by the *iunctura*, unparalleled outside Propertius, but found in *molliter in tacito litore compositam* (1.11.14, cf. the *durus/mollis* complex) and *litore sic tacito sonitus rarescit harenae* (3.15.33).[114] And there were presumably more elements in such Gallan scenes. It is not credible, for example, that Virgil derived his combination of *litore* (unqualified) and *ingrato* qualifying *cineri* in *Aeneid* 6.212–13 (*nec minus interea Misenum in litore Teucri/ flebant et cineri ingrato suprema ferebant*) from Propertius 1.17.4 (*omniaque ingrato litore vota cadunt*). They must rather have had a common source; and, given the evidence assembled here, can that source have been other than Gallus?

HUNTING

The notion, which goes back to Franz Skutsch, that hunting was a Gallan motif[115] has already cropped up in this chapter. Hunting has several functions in Roman elegy and in ancient literature in general: *inter alia* it can be a means of achieving proximity to a beloved and performing services for a beloved in the hope of erotic reward; equally it can be a species of displacement therapy, a substitute for love; or, finally, it can be intended as an out-and-out cure for love.[116] At

---

114 Cf. also: *orbata est avibus, mutoque* in litore *tantum/ solae desertis adspirant frondibus aurae* (Petron. *Satyr.* 119.1 ll. 37–8). The cure for the textual problem of Prop. 3.15.33 cannot, then, be (with Goold (1990) 316 = (1999) 276) to emend *tacito*.
115 Skutsch (1901) 15–16; Ross (1975) 85, 90 n. 1 (but seemingly sceptical).
116 Cf. Kölblinger (1971) 87–122.

Eclogue 10.55–61 Virgil makes Gallus resolve to go hunting, and then reject the notion that hunting would cure his love:

> interea mixtis lustrabo Maenala Nymphis   55
> aut acris venabor apros. non me ulla vetabunt
> frigora Parthenios canibus circumdare saltus.
> iam mihi per rupes videor lucosque sonantis
> ire, libet Partho torquere Cydonia cornu
> spicula – tamquam haec sit nostri medicina furoris   60
> aut deus ille malis hominum mitescere discat.

> But meanwhile with the Nymphs I'll range on Maenala
> Or hunt the savage boar. No frosts will hinder me
> From drawing coverts on Parthenium with hounds.
> Already I see myself explore the sounding rocks
> And groves, already long to shoot Cydonian darts
> From Parthian horn. – As if this remedied our madness,
> Or that god learnt from human hardship to grow mild! (tr. Guy Lee)

The Gallan 'wild surroundings' elements in this passage have just been related to hypothesized descriptions in Gallus' elegies; and other Gallan features of this passage were mentioned earlier, including the Nymphs (55), *Parthenios* (57), and *medicina furoris* (60).[117] Since hunting is not a normal bucolic activity, Gallus' aspiration to go hunting in *Eclogue* 10 is most unlikely to have been generated *in toto* by Virgil's bucolicization of Gallan elegy. Hence Skutsch's hypothesis that Gallus himself stands behind these lines seems assured. Skutsch pointed to Tibullus 1.4.49–50 for confirmation of his view that hunting was a Gallan topic: *nec, velit insidiis altas si claudere valles,/ dum placeas, umeri retia ferre negent.* An even surer indication that Gallus imagined himself hunting comes from Propertius 2.19.[118] There Cynthia will go off without Propertius into the countryside (1–16), and Propertius will engage in hunting around the springs of the Clitumnus (17–26), not (like Virgil's Gallus) in an attempt to cure his love, but to occupy himself in Cynthia's absence. Propertius clearly had both *Eclogue* 10 and its Gallan model in mind; and, although we do not know what sort of hunting Gallus had proposed for himself, or exactly how Virgil employed *deformazione* with regard to Gallus' hunting, some conclusions can at least be drawn about Propertius' interactions with

---

117 See above, pp. 100, 110, 123, 131–6. Another such feature, the learned combination of Parthian bow and 'Cydonian' arrows (59–60), will be discussed below, pp. 275, 277–8.
118 Curiously Skutsch (1901) 15–16 does not mention Prop 2.19.

Virgil. In *Eclogue* 10 Virgil represents Gallus as soldiering (44–5), and as aspiring to hunt boars with hounds and (probably) deer with bow and arrows (56–60). Propertius' self-portrait as a hunter in 2.19 is clearly playing off against the vigorous programme laid out for Gallus by Virgil.[119] At first Propertius depicts himself as in every respect like Virgil's Gallus: he confidently envisages himself as capturing wild beasts, as dedicating horns on a pine-tree (19–20), which means that he will hunt deer, and as setting on hounds, presumably implying that he will go boar hunting. But then Propertius changes his mind: his next couplet (21–2) proclaims that he would not 'dare' to tackle lions (not in fact a prey commonly encountered in Roman Italy!) or wild boars. Then he downgrades himself even further as a hunter: his 'daring' will consist in catching 'soft' (*molles*, 23) hares with nets (*excipere*, 24), and birds with a limed pole (*figere*, 24). The pole (*calamo*, 2.19.24) of course pathetically matches the arrows of Virgil's Gallus (*spicula*, *Eclogue* 10.60).

It would seem that, in addition to wielding the Gallan *miles/mollis* etymology against Virgil (cf. above, pp. 89–90) – for hunting was the *Romana militia* (Horace *Satires* 2.2.10–11) – Propertius is engaging in further literary polemic here. His three couplets are an elegiac variation, underlined by *molles*, a term which elsewhere describes elegiac verses,[120] upon the boar and deer hunting of *Eclogue* 10. The literary polemic with which Propertius responds to Virgil takes the form of a 'correction', and Propertius announces his intent by introducing a set of terms which encapsulate standard concepts from 'Alexandrian' literary programmes. Apart from *molles* (23), and innovative 'daring' (*ausim*, 21; *audacia*, 23),[121] Propertius flags and rejects two other notions which were anathema to the neoterics: size (*vastos*, 2.19.21, of lions); and rusticity (*agrestes*, 2.19.22, of boars). Propertius' 'correction' of Virgil consists in setting out in lines 21–4 the proper mode of hunting for an elegist. He then closes his hunt (25–6) with a personal reference to celebrated 'wonders' of his own neighbourhood, the springs of the Clitumnus and its famous breed of cattle, thus putting his own personal (and Callimachean?)[122] mark on the controversy which he has been conducting with Virgil.

The co-presence in 2.19 of Gallus' original elegy along with

---

119   Cf. now Fedeli (2005) 560–1.
120   Domit. Marsus fr. 7.3 Courtney; Ov. *EP* 3.4.85.
121   Cf. e.g. Ennius *Ann.* 210 Skutsch; Lucr. *DRN* 1.66–7; Cat. 1.5.
122   Cf. Callim. frr. 407–11 Pf.

Virgil's pastiche of it is assured in a number of ways: apart from matters already noted, there is a whiff of Gallan 'wild surroundings' throughout much of 2.19;[123] and there are a few linguistic traces of Gallus. *monere* (20) recalls the prominent *monemus* of Propertius 1.20.1 addressed to 'Gallus' and the reinforcing *monitus* of 1.20.51, its penultimate line;[124] and there is also a hint of the *nomen* group in the penultimate line of 2.19 (a citation?): *quin ego in assidua mutem tua nomina lingua* (31). Moroever the last word of line 2.19.28: *venturum paucis me tibi Luciferis* is reminiscent of Gallus' interest in East/West, given the poetic interchangeability of these quadrants with the morning/evening star. One question, however, which cannot be answered with confidence is whether, when Propertius is polemicizing against Virgil, he is taking the side of Gallus by reestablishing a Gallan elegiac norm for hunting, or whether he is also criticizing Gallus for not having adhered to that elegiac norm. The only clue comes from the fact that Propertius does not hunt in 2.19 to escape love; this implies that he is a successful love-elegist, which was his stance in the elegies of the Monobiblos addressed to Gallus, and it might suggest that in 2.19 too Gallus is the object of Propertius' broader polemic.

In this chapter the influence of Gallus has several times been detected in Propertian literary polemical contexts. The implication, namely that Gallus himself indulged in this kind of discourse, is strongly reinforced by the settings of Gallus' two appearances in Virgil's *Eclogues*. *Eclogue* 6, which introduced Gallus to Virgil's public, is a *recusatio*; and *Eclogue* 10, although not primarily recusatory, makes much of the clash and confluence of Virgilian bucolic and Gallan elegy. It would seem, then, that Gallan elegy embraced literary polemic, including *recusatio*, and this hypothesis meshes with conclusions arrived at on other grounds about the imprint of Gallus on a number of further Propertian elegies;[125] it also permits the influence of Gallus to be seen as crossing over from the Monobiblos into the early elegies of Book 2. Thus 2.1, prologue of a book dedicated to a new patron who ostensibly sought epics from all his poets, is an overt *recusatio*. The presence of Gallus has been detected[126] in its third line in the

---

123 Note esp. *solae … silvae* (29) and *muscosis … iugis* (30), and cf. Index II s.vv.
124 Cf. also Prop. 1.1.35: *hoc, moneo, vitate malum* (in the final quatrain, where allusive citations may be in place). See below, p. 230 and n. 39.
125 Cf. Ross (1975) Index rerum notabiliorum s.v. *recusatio*.
126 By Ross (1975) 115–17.

conjuncture of Orpheus' parents, Apollo and Calliope, and also in the couplet *omnis humanos sanat medicina dolores/ solus amor morbi non amat artificem* (57–8)[127] and in the learned mythical paradeigmata of lines 51–70.[128] Two further Gallan reminiscences in 2.1 will be proposed below (pp. 266–7). It is no accident that the prologue to Book 2 is so full of Gallus since the epilogue (2.34) contains his death-notice (91–2). A reference to Aganippe, the spring that fed the Permessus, in 2.3.19–20 continues this strand by recalling Gallan/Callimachean Heliconian scenery; and the Gallan Leitmotiv of East/West (= universal fame) surfaces in the same elegy (43–4).[129] Mention of Europe and Asia at 2.3.36 reminds us of Gallus' known interest in the Hypanis, a river that divided these two continents. It is in 2.10, however, another *recusatio*, that Helicon first emerges in all its glory in Propertius' œuvre, and along with Helicon memories of Gallus return in abundance. The presence of Gallus in the cryptic final couplet of this difficult elegy is indubitable, but does not lead to scholarly agreement about 2.10 or about its ending.[130]

Another Gallan elegy of Book 2, namely 2.13, will feature more extensively in Chapter 8 (pp. 274–9). Its lines 3–8, discussed above (pp. 124–5), have long been regarded as Gallan in inspiration;[131] but the Gallan nature of the balancing quatrain (53–6) which precedes 2.13's final couplet has not been observed. Lines 53–6 are devoted to the death of Adonis and to Venus' reactions to it. The pentameter of Propertius' death-notice for Gallus (2.34.91–2), *mortuus inferna vulnera lavit aqua* (92), closely resembles a line of Euphorion about the Cocytus, a river of the underworld, washing the wounds of the dead Adonis; and it has been suggested that Gallus too had imitated that line of Euphorion.[132] If Gallus did imitate that line, or if, as proposed earlier, he modelled his own line on an imitation of Euphorion by

---

127 See above, pp. 100–1.
128 Paradeigmatic groups are likely to have been prominent in Gallus' *Amores*, given the mythical company kept by Gallus in his Virgilian epiphanies; if so, their appearances in Propertius will *per se* be diagnostic of Gallan influence. It cannot be coincidental that such paradeigmatic groups are much rarer in Tibullus, in whose work Gallan influence can in general be detected less frequently.
129 Cf. Ross (1975) 117–8.
130 Cf. Ross (1975) 119–20; see below, pp. 326–37.
131 Cf. Ross (1975) 34–6, 118.
132 See esp. Du Quesnay (1979) 62 and 220 n. 215, who on this basis referred to Prop. 2.34.91–2, and, noting the repeated formula *nec te paeniteat* of Tib. 1.4.47, Virg. *Ecl.* 2.34 and Virg. *Ecl.* 10.17, observed that the last of these lines is immediately followed by a reference to Adonis, and so concluded that Gallus had treated this myth.

Parthenius,[133] then the prominence of Adonis and Venus towards the end of 2.13 will also reveal a debt to Gallus. The only other elegy of Book 2 containing Heliconian material, 2.30, has already been discussed (above, pp. 128–31), and a full treatment of 2.34, where Gallus is named and further literary *deformazione* is visible, will be reserved for Chapter 9.

In 3.1.1–2 Callimachus and Philetas are invoked directly by name and asked to admit Propertius to their poetic company. This is not their first appearance in his elegy: Callimachus was named programmatically in both the prologue (2.1.40) and the epilogue (2.34.32) of Book 2, in the second instance along with Philetas (2.34.31), but it is only in Book 3 that Propertius begins the process of identification which leads eventually to his claim to be 'Callimachus Romanus' (4.1.64).[134] 3.1.1–2 advertise the fact that the two older hellenistic masters are now explicitly present as major players in Propertius' third elegy book. Despite this, Gallus is not absent from Book 3: the fact that 3.4 is predominantly of Gallan inspiration (see below, pp. 404–12, 433–40) is proof enough of this; and distinctly Gallan motifs have been identified in some numbers in the three programmatic elegies with which Book 3 begins. Nevertheless, as Book 3 and even more as Book 4 progresses, Gallus does begin to fade, with fewer Gallan motifs and verbal complexes making their appearance. The same will be found true of those metrical features which, as Chapters 5 and 6 will seek to show, are indicative of the presence of Gallus.

As promised, some of the topics of this and of the previous chapter will be revisited in Chapter 7 in a study of Propertius 1.20, and in Chapter 12 when Propertius 3.4, its Gallan antecedent, and its Ovidian successor are compared and contrasted. But, as is also the case with Gallan verbal complexes, there will still remain even after those additional investigations considerable scope for further proposals about the thematic and topical influence of Gallus upon Propertius.[135]

---

133 On the possible intermediacy of Parthenius see above, p. 81 and n. 56.

134 The role of Philetas in Propertian elegy (cf., e.g., Prop. 3.3.52) should not be undervalued just because far less of his work has survived. He is named again in Book 4 (4.6.3) along with (unnamed) Callimachus (4.6.4).

135 E.g., the themes of war and peace might be a fertile field, in view both of *Ecl.* 10's portrait of Gallus as a lover torn between these two activities and of the juxtaposition of Prop. 3.5 with the undoubtedly Gallan Prop. 3.4. Du Quesnay (1979) 60–3, 219–20 also offers further attractive suggestions, as does Schmitzer (2002), esp. 216–28.

CHAPTER 5

Gallan Metrics I
Polysyllabic Pentameter Endings

When Propertius' pentameters are compared metrically with those of his contemporaries,[1] they emerge as anomalous in at least two interesting ways. They exhibit proportionately many more polysyllables, defined for present purposes as words of four or more syllables, at their line-ends;[2] and a higher proportion of them terminate in trisyllables. These anomalies raise the prospect of yet another technique for detecting the presence of Gallus in Propertian elegy. In Chapters 3 and 4 certain polysyllables appeared repeatedly at the end of Propertian pentameters in which the influence of C. Cornelius Gallus was suspected on other grounds – they are assembled summarily below. Past scholarship has occasionally linked some of these lines with Gallus,[3] but the notion that Propertius' polysyllabic (and trisyllabic) pentameter endings in general might – at least to some extent – be associated with Gallan influence does not seem to have been raised.[4] Indeed a quite different explanation of one of these features of Propertian elegy is commonly accepted,[5] and it is now so well established that it is sometimes stated as a fact. This is that polysyllabic endings are a sign of earliness of composition.[6] For the most part commentators go no further and simply characterize Propertian elegies in which polysyllabic endings occur in some numbers as 'early';

1 Ceccarelli (2002) usefully summarizes twentieth-century studies of Propertius' metrics, providing relevant bibliography and comparisons with the practice of other elegists.
2 For the restricted interpretative value of Propertius' polysyllabic hexameter endings, see below, pp. 158–9.
3 See below, p. 163 and nn. 51, 52.
4 The concept was, however, deployed in Cairns (2004b).
5 On the other, subsidiary explanation sometimes offered ('Alexandrianism'), see below, p. 151.
6 E.g. Skutsch (1963) 239; Barsby (1974), with reservations; Jones (1992) 306; Ceccarelli (2002) 157–62, summarizing a broad swathe of earlier studies. Ross (1975) 81 and n. 1 protests against earliness as a blanket explanation of polysyllabic endings in Prop. 1.20.

although at least one attempt has been made to use frequencies of polysyllabic endings as a basis for the relative dating of individual elegies of the Monobiblos.[7] The earliness explanation is, of course, up to a point correct: earlier Roman taste obviously regarded polysyllabic pentameter endings as learned and elegant, and this is one reason why they are frequent in Roman elegiacs prior to Propertius;[8] and, when it comes to Propertius himself, polysyllabic endings are indeed common in his early elegies. Further underpinnings for this approach will emerge below, but even at a superficial level earliness is clearly not the whole story: Propertius 2.1 and 2.34 have a higher proportion of such endings than many elegies of the Monobiblos. Again, Tibullus precedes Propertius in Ovid's elegiac canon (*Tristia* 4.10.51–4); this may be because Tibullus was older than Propertius, and/or because he came to prominence as an elegist before Propertius.[9] But Tibullus uses proportionately far fewer polysyllabic pentameter endings than Propertius. Yet again, Ovid in his first elegiac books (*Amores, Ars Amatoria* and single *Heroides*) has no pentameters terminating in a word longer than a dissyllable; but he revived the use of polysyllabic endings in his later elegiac works, especially *Tristia, Ex Ponto*, and the double *Heroides* (see below).[10] So, given that earliness alone cannot be the full explanation of this phenomenon, a more detailed examination of the facts seems worthwhile.

An obligatory, although somewhat inconvenient, starting point for this examination is the table of polysyllabic pentameter endings in Roman elegy constructed by Maurice Platnauer in what has become the standard English-language handbook of Roman elegiac verse:[11]

---

7 Skutsch (1963). Keyser (1992) applies statistical analysis to the length of Propertius Book 2 and to the distribution within it of dissyllabic pentameter endings in an attempt to show that statistics alone do not lend credence to attempts to divide Book 2.

8 In the earliest Latin epigrams, by Valerius Aedituus, Porcius Licinus, and Q. Lutatius Catulus (printed by Courtney (1993) 70–1, 77), out of 12 couplets 5 end with a quadrisyllable and 3 with a trisyllable. However, in the five elegiac couplets of M. Tullius Laurea, written within Cicero's lifetime, all the pentameters end in a dissyllable: see Courtney (1993) 182–3, who notes this feature as of interest.

9 See now Knox (2005), arguing that the elegies of Tibullus 1 are earlier than those of the Monobiblos. The commonly accepted publication dates of their two first collections are far from firm, and, *pace* Lyne (1998), there is no conclusive evidence of influence of the one on the other in their first books.

10 The double *Heroides* are accepted by the majority of Ovidian scholars as genuine, and believed to be later than the single *Heroides*. For a dissentient voice *re* authorship, see Courtney (1998).

11 Platnauer (1951) 17: cf. also 15–16 (on trisyllabic endings).

Note on polysyllabic endings in the pentameter[12]

	(a)	(b)	(c)
	7 syllables	5 syllables	4 syllables
Tib. I and II[1]	–	5	18
Tib. (Lygd.)[1]	–	3	4
Corp. Tib.[1]	–	2	1
Propertius[2]	2	21	166
Ovid (excluding later *Heroides*)[3]	–	12	31

[1] Five only of *(b)* and *(c)* in Tibullus are proper nouns.
[2] Four of *(b)* and 42 of *(c)* are proper nouns.
[3] Three of *(b)* and nine of *(c)* are proper nouns.

Its inconvenience arises from the convention employed by Platnauer: he reckoned the combination of a preposition or conjunction and a noun as a single 'word'. Thus, for example, he treated *inter Hamadryadas* (Propertius 2.34.76) as a seven-syllable word. Platnauer's convention is, of course, technically correct, and any departure from it introduces its own distortions. But, if pushed to its logical limit, it becomes counter-instinctual and indeed confusing: do we really, for example, want to classify *et in armis* (Propertius 3.1.29) as a quadrisyllabic hexameter ending? It is therefore simpler to follow for the most part[13] the approach of Jost Benedum, who categorized line-endings by reckoning a typographical word as a 'word'.[14] Another advantage of Benedum's analysis (129–133, 190–1) is that, in addition to covering Propertius, Tibullus, and Ovid (and indeed Martial), he also takes account of Catullus' pentameters, which Platnauer did not. Tabulated,[15] the relevant portions of Benedum's statistics (190) are:

---

12   The table is as in Platnauer (1951) 17; in it 'later *Heroides*' means the double *Heroides*.
13   The statistics in Chs. 5 and 6 follow Benedum's system except that prodelided *es/est* is regarded as part of the preceding word. Hence e.g. *perfidia est* (Prop. 1.15.34) is counted as a quadrisyllabic pentameter ending, which adds one to Benedum's totals.
14   Various footnotes of Benedum (1967) 129–189 usefully underline the difficulties, not just of methodology but of choice of manuscript readings, which are inherent in the assembling of such statistics; they also note minor differences, insignificant for the present study, in the counts offered by previous scholars.
15   They were set out in slightly different form by Benedum, and in the case of Propertius they are modified to take account of the factor mentioned in n. 13 above.

Poet	Syllables				
	7	6	5	4	All 4–7
Catullus	1	0	18	94	113
Tibullus 1	0	0	2	13	15
Tibullus 2	0	0	0	8	8
Tibullus 1–2	0	0	2	21	23
[Tib.] Lygdamus	0	0	2	5	7
[Tib.] Sulpicia	0	0	0	1	1
Propertius 1	0	0	9	89	98
Propertius 2	0	0	7	51	58
Propertius 3	0	0	1	10	11
Propertius 4	0	0	1	4	5
Prop. 1–4	0	0	18	154	172
Ovid *Tristia* & *Ex Ponto*	0	0	9	31	40
Ovid *Ibis*	0	1	0	1	2
Ovid *Heroides*	0	0	2	1	3
Ovid *Fasti*	0	0	0	2	2

As this table shows, Benedum arrived at a total of 23 polysyllabic pentameter endings in the genuine works of Tibullus. Platnauer offered the same result as Benedum for Tibullus. Benedum actually offered a total of 88 4-syllable pentameter endings in Book 1 of Propertius, possibly because he regarded *perfidia est* (1.15.34) as two words, whereas I have treated them as a single quadrisyllabic word (see above, p. 148 n. 13). For Propertius Platnauer offered a higher total (189) as a result of his decision to count prepositions and conjunctions as part of the succeeding word.[16] On the basis of the pentameter line counts given by Benedum, occasionally modified in the light of those of Platnauer,[17] and taking my own independent count of 172 for Propertius' quadrisyllabic endings, we arrive at the following table:

Poet	Pentameters	Polysyllabic endings	Percentage
Propertius	2,003	172	8.59%
Tibullus	618	23	3.72%
Ovid	10,994	47	0.43%

As noted, almost all the Ovidian examples occur in *Tristia*, *Epistulae ex Ponto* and the double *Heroides*; they reflect special circumstances to be discussed below.

16   Barsby (1974) 647 offers a total of 219.
17   Platnauer (1951) 1–2.

These tables can be seen to provide yet further evidence in support of the conventional earliness explanation of the four- and five-syllable pentameter endings in Propertius' elegies, and they also reveal indirectly that the practice is due to Greek influence: the percentage of polysyllabic pentameter endings in Catullus' elegiac poems (35.2%)[18] is even higher than in Propertius' Monobiblos (27.48%), and it is close to the percentage found in Greek elegy, especially that of the fifth century BC and later. Luque Moreno[19] (1994) 68–9 assembled the relevant statistics for Catullus and Greek elegy from various sources, giving three different figures for different combinations of Catullus' elegies.[20] Of these the figure of 34.56% for the most comprehensive Catullan grouping (65–68, 76, 86, 89, 101) is very close to the 34.1% of post-Theognidean Greek elegy. The statistics are:

Poet/Period	Percentage of 4–7 syllable endings
pre-Theognis	39.60%
Theognis	31.20%
post-Theognis	34.10%
Catullus 65–8, 76, 86, 89, 101	34.56%
Catullus 65–7	44.20%
Catullus 68	20.00%
Catullus 69–116	35.90%

It might, of course, have been suspected in any case that, when Roman poets started to compose elegiacs, they would imitate the metrical practice of their nearest contemporaries, the hellenistic Greek elegists and epigrammatists, who employed polysyllables freely at pentameter ends. But it is useful to have statistical confirmation of this, and hence a clearer understanding of why, generally speaking, polysyllabic endings are early. Another set of statistics, this time for Propertian elegy, illustrates subsequent development in this area from around 30 BC to around 15 BC, i.e. a steady move in his elegiac corpus away from polysyllabic towards dissyllabic endings in pentameters, a move which again confirms the (partial) correctness of the earliness explanation. Propertius is the only practical source for such figures since

---

18   Based on Benedum (1967) 190.
19   The percentage frequency statistics for the different pentameter endings in both Greek and Roman elegy presented by Luque Moreno (1994) 68–72 derive from the publications of earlier investigators, among whom Benedum (1967) is not numbered.
20   Benedum (1967) 190 amalgamated the Catullan elegiacs for his purposes. His consolidated proportion comes out at 35.20%.

there are not enough polysyllabic endings in Tibullus to be statistically informative. In Propertius the movement can be seen vividly in the progressive reduction both in the numbers and in the percentages of polysyllabic pentameter endings throughout his four books:[21]

	Polysyllabic Pentameter Endings	Total Pentameters	Percentage
Book 1	98	353	27.76%
Book 2	58	681	8.52%
Book 3	11	494	2.23%
Book 4	5	475	1.05%

The reason for this and for the overall movement towards dissyllabic endings is usually and correctly said to be an increasing desire on the part of elegists to achieve coincidence of word-accent and ictus in the second hemistich of their pentameters.[22] Such coincidence was presumably not only aesthetically satisfying but helped to advance the reader or hearer smoothly into the next hexameter, whereas a monumental ending to a couplet impeded this.[23]

But despite this evidence in favour of the earliness explanation of polysyllabic pentameter endings, other additional considerations need to be kept in mind. One is 'neotericism' (= Alexandrianism), which has also sometimes[24] been associated with this phenomenon. Catullus led the way here: like those of Propertius, many Catullan polysyllabic endings consist of learned Greek proper names. Catullus clearly encountered many of these in the same metrical *sedes* in his Greek sources: this can be concluded from a comparison of three of the polysyllabic pentameter endings of Catullus 66 (*Coma Berenices*) with their originals in Catullus' Greek model, Callimachus *Aetia* fr. 110 Pf.

καὶ πρόκατε γνωτὸς Μέμνονος Αἰθίοπος   (52)

lugebant, cum se Memnonis Aethiopis   (52)

α.[   ]. Ὑδροχ[όος] καὶ[Ὠαρίων   (94)

proximus Hydrochoi fulguret Oarion   (94)

---

21 Cf. Benedum (1967) 190, whose figures these are. The steady parallel decline in trisyllabic endings suggests that the two phenomena are related.
22 E.g. Maltby (2002) 70–1.
23 Cf. Benedum (1967) 134–5.
24 E.g. by Ross (1975) 81 and n. 1.

πρόσθε μὲν ἐρχομεν ... μετοπωρινὸν Ὠκ]εανόνδε   (67)

qui vix sero alto mergitur Oceano   (68)

The last example, in which a Greek hexameter ending has been transformed into a Latin pentameter ending by stripping off an enclitic, is
tantalizingly similar to the many cases in Roman poetry where the
same polysyllabic word is found both with attached enclitic (-*que* or
-*ve*) as a hexameter ending and without an enclitic at the end of a
pentameter. The relevant Roman hexameter endings now survive
mainly in Lucretius, and the identical pentameter endings (without the
enclitic) appear in Catullus and later elegists.

However, although Catullus followed Callimachus in the three
cases above, he did not feel obliged to end a pentameter with a polysyllabic proper name just because his source line had done so. In
translating ἵππο[ς] ἰοζώνου Λοκρίδος Ἀρσινόης (54) Catullus did not
scruple to place Arsinoe's name at the end of the first hemistich:
obtulit Arsinoes Locridos ales equus (54). He showed equal adaptive
freedom in his transference of Berenice's name from the end of a
hexameter, †η με Κόνων ἔβλεψεν ἐν ἠέρι τὸν Βερενίκης (7), again
to the pre-caesural position of a pentameter: *e Bereniceo vertice*
caesariem (8). One polysyllabic common noun pentameter ending in
Catullus 66 has a genesis similar to the three proper noun examples
listed above, i.e. it follows its Callimachean model: *Graia Canopitis*
incola litoribus (58) = Κ]ανωπίτου ναιέτις α[ἰγιαλοῦ (58). This is a
particularly valuable example since *litoribus* later became a popular
pentameter ending in Propertius, presumably (*inter alia*)[25] because its
origin in Catullus' line endowed it in re-use with a ready-made allusive literary history of a type appreciated by Roman poets and readers,
namely its pedigree 'by Catullus 66 out of Callimachus' *Coma Be-*
renices'. In another polysyllabic pentameter ending derived from
Callimachus Catullus matched his source's verb closely: ἀμνά]μϙ[ν
Θείης ἀργὸς ὑ]περφέ[ρ]ετ[αι (44) = *progenies Thiae clara super-*
vehitur (44).

If the Callimachean *aetion* had survived entire, it would surely
have been possible to identify more polysyllabic proper and common
noun, verb, and other pentameter endings of Catullus 66 as derived
from Callimachus. Even in the present state of *Aetia* fr. 110 Pf. some
pentameter endings of Catullus 66 where the Callimachean original is

25   For its further, Gallan resonances, see below, p. 172.

lost might look like attractive candidates for Callimachean inspiration. In particular, those which recur in Propertius and in later elegy thrust themselves forward, i.e. *temporibus* (4, 60), *discidium* (22), *adulterio* (84) and *muneribus* (92). However, a major difficulty stands in the way of this approach: most of these terms have no obvious Greek equivalents metrically suitable as pentameter endings, so their genesis may have been more indirect. The processes by which they may have been generated are visible where *Aetia* fr. 110 Pf. does survive: sometimes the paired Greek and Latin lines both have polysyllabic endings, but the Latin ending does not translate the Greek ending. Either it renders freely the general sense of the Greek line, e.g. πρῶτοι καὶ τυπίδων ἔφρασαν ἐργασίην (50) and *instit ac ferri stringere duritiem* (50), where *duritiem* and ἐργασίην are not at all equivalent. Or the Latin ending translates a different term in the Greek line: cf. ἀ]σχάλλω κορυφῆς οὐκέτι θιξόμεν[ος (76) and *afore me a dominae vertice discrucior* (76). Here *discrucior* renders not final (οὐκέτι) θιξόμεν[ος, which is represented by *afore*, but initial ἀ]σχάλλω. It may, then, be that polysyllabic pentameter endings of Catullus 66 like *temporibus* and *muneribus*, which later achieved some popularity, started off in one of these two categories. What is at all events clear is that poem 66 must overall have played a major role in transmitting polysyllabic pentameter endings to Catullus' elegiac successors: it has an astonishingly high proportion of them, 29 out of 47, i.e. 61.7%. A tantalizing question is whether this proportion mirrors the metrics of the Callimachean *aetion* in its complete form or whether Catullus was hyper-Graecizing to advertise his learning. A third situation in which Catullus failed to translate Callimachus' Greek suggests that the latter alternative is more plausible: in *devotae flavi verticis exuviae* (62) Catullus departs from the metrics and indeed the sense of καὶ Βερ]ε-νίκειος καλὸς ἐγὼ πλόκαμ[ος (62) and creates a polysyllabic pentameter ending *exuviae* with no parallel in Callimachus.[26]

Another different consideration applies only to Latin polysyllabic pentameter endings of five or more syllables, e.g. *amicitia* or *pudicitia*: their length means that a poet had few options about their placement in a pentameter. Logically speaking, then, neither earliness nor 'neotericism' would need to be invoked to explain the location of such terms at the end of a pentameter. However, the very fact that poets chose to employ them despite their metrical intransigence, when

---

26   See also below, p. 155 n. 31.

synonyms or circumlocutions might have been substituted, hints that a purely mechanical explanation of their placement is inadequate. These very long words must have had literary associations which helped to outweigh their metrical inconvenience. Moreover the very location of such words at a pentameter ending probably confirmed their allusivity by mimicking their original placement. Even greater exercise of poetic freedom must be conceded when quadrisyllables end pentameters, since these can more easily occupy other *sedes*, which makes their appearance as polysyllabic pentameter endings more a matter of poetic discretion.[27]

Catullus' seminal role in the transmission of polysyllabic pentameter endings to later elegists has already been mentioned. It is, of course, only one facet of his influence on Roman elegy, for, despite his absence from the Ovidian and Quintilianic canons,[28] Catullus' elegiac writings – poems 65–116, ranging from long elegies to brief epigrams – were vitally inspirational for succeeding elegists, as they themselves recognized.[29] Above all Catullus created much of the conceptual and emotional vocabulary of Roman elegy.[30] However, when the polysyllabic pentameter endings of Catullus are compared with those of Propertius, some puzzlement results. Many, indeed most, of the Catullan endings do not recur in Propertius – or in subsequent elegy. A minority do recur in Propertius, either in identical form or as inflections of the same words; and these overlaps cannot be dismissed as fortuitous since the terms involved are neither trivial or commonplace. But, and this is where the puzzlement strikes hardest, the contexts, verbal and conceptual, in which Propertius (and indeed other later elegists) employ these identical or similar pentameter endings usually bear little relation to the contexts in which they are found in Catullus. This can easily be illustrated first from the endings *temporibus*, *litoribus*, and *muneribus*, and then from an alphabetical listing of the other endings shared by Catullan elegy and Propertius. In the comparanda which follow quinquesyllables are marked '(5)', and emboldenings indicate the same grammatical form in Catullus and Propertius:

---

27   Cf. Benedum (1967) 139–41.
28   Ov. *Tr.* 4.10.51–4, cf. 5.1.17–18; Quint. *Inst. Orat.* 10.1.93.
29   Prop. 2.25.4; 2.34.87–8; Ov. *Am.* 3.9.61–2; *Tr.* 2.427–30 (always accompanied by Calvus). Tibullus does not mention Catullus, but has many links with him: cf. Maltby (2002) index locorum notabiliorum s.v. Catullus.
30   His achievement is well illustrated by his omnipresence in Pichon (1902).

temporibus (in both senses, i.e. 'times' and 'temples')
Catullus **66.4** (times)   ut cedant certis sidera **temporibus**
Catullus **66.60** (temples)   ex Ariadnaeis aurea **temporibus**
Propertius 1.3.22 (temples) ponebamque tuis, Cynthia, **temporibus**
Propertius 1.22.4 (times)   Italiae duris funera **temporibus**

litoribus
Catullus **66.58**   Graia Canopitis incola **litoribus**.
Propertius 1.2.18   Eueni patriis filia **litoribus**
Propertius 1.3.2   languida desertis Cnosia **litoribus**
Propertius 1.11.2   qua iacet Herculeis semita **litoribus**
Propertius 1.17.28   mansuetis socio parcite **litoribus**
Propertius 2.34.64   iactaque Lavinis moenia **litoribus**

muneribus
Catullus **66.92**   sed potius largis affice **muneribus**.
Propertius 1.2.4   teque peregrinis vendere **muneribus**
Propertius 1.16.36   victa meis numquam, ianua, **muneribus**

The single lines quoted provide sufficent context for the verdict to be clear: the Propertian examples share little if any conceptual content with their Catullan forebears; and any grammatical similarities between them are non-significant, particularly since the practice of qualifying a final noun with an adjective, often a proper adjective, usually placed before the caesura, is a stock feature of Roman elegiac verse.

The rest of the polysyllabic pentameter endings shared by Catullus and Propertius convey a similar impression, namely that, when he re-used those previously employed by Catullus, Propertius was not thinking of Catullus or of the Catullan context(s) in which they had appeared:[31]

adulterio (5)
Catullus **66.84**   sed quae se impuro dedit **adulterio**
Catullus 67.36   cum quibus illa malum fecit adulterium.
Catullus 78.6   qui patruus patrui monstret adulterium.
Catullus 113.4   singula. fecundum semen **adulterio**.
Propertius 2.29.38   spiritus admisso notus **adulterio**

---

31 In one case (*ut domus hostiles praeferat exuvias*, 1.1.54) Tibullus re-uses a Catullan ending not found in Propertius. But again there is no contextual link with the Catullan examples: *quam de virgineis gesserat exuviis* (66.14); *devotae flavi verticis exuviae* (66.62).

amicitia (5)

Catullus 77.6	vitae, eheu nostrae pestis amicitiae
Catullus 96.4	atque olim iunctas flemus amicitias
Catullus 100.6	perspecta est igni tum unica[32] amicitia
Catullus 109.6	aeternum hoc sanctae foedus amicitiae
Propertius 1.22.2	quaeris pro nostra semper amicitia[33]

articulis

Catullus **99.8**	guttis abstersti mollibus **articulis**
Propertius 2.34.80	Cynthius impositis temperat **articulis**

auriculam

Catullus 67.44	speraret nec linguam esse nec auriculam
Propertius 1.16.28	percussas dominae vertat in auriculas

auxilium

Catullus 68.66	tale fuit nobis Allius auxilium
Propertius 1.1.26	quaerite non sani pectoris auxilia[34]

coniugio

Catullus 68.84	posset ut abrupto vivere coniugio
[cf. Catullus 66.80	non prius unanimis corpora coniugibus]
Propertius 2.15.28	masculus et totum femina coniugium

discidium

Catullus **66.22**	sed fratris cari flebile **discidium**
Propertius 1.11.28	multis ista dabunt litora **discidium**

flagitia

Catullus 67.42	solam cum ancillis haec sua flagitia
Propertius 2.34.12	posses in tanto vivere flagitio

(h)insidias

Catullus **84.2**	dicere, et insidias Arrius **hinsidias**
Catullus **84.4**	cum quantum poterat dixerat **hinsidias**
Propertius 1.20.30	et volucres ramo summovet **insidias**

---

[32]   The central portion of this line is hopelessly corrupt in the MSS, and *est igni tum unica* (a combination of emendations) has little claim to represent what Catullus wrote.

[33]   Cf. also Domit. Mars. fr. 1.6 Courtney: *novit, deposuit alter amicitiam* (*novit*: Bücheler, Courtney; *non vult*: codd).

[34]   In this sole case a direct link between Catullus and Propertius is arguable, since both lines involve a friend or friends' help to the distressed poet. But even here the link is more probably indirect, i.e. through Gallus.

invenies
    Catullus 89.6   quantumvis quare sit macer invenies
    Propertius 1.4.28   nec quicquam ex illa quod querar inveniam

(H)ionios
    Catullus 84.12   iam non Ionios esse, sed Hionios
    Propertius 3.11.72   Caesaris in toto sis memor Ionio

Oceano
    Catullus **66.68**   qui vix sero alto mergitur **Oceano**
    Catullus 88.6   nec genitor Nympharum abluit Oceanus
    Catullus 115.6   usque ad Hyperboreos et mare ad Oceanum
    Propertius 2.9.30   aut mea si staret navis in **Oceano**

officium
    Catullus **68.12**   neu me odisse putes hospitis **officium**,
    Catullus 68.42   iuverit aut quantis foverit officiis
    Catullus 68.152   pro multis, Alli, redditur officiis
    Propertius 1.20.40   proposito florem praetulit officio
    Propertius 2.18.14   invitum et terris praestitit **officium**

saevitiae
    Catullus **99.6**   tantillum vestrae demere **saevitiae**.
    Propertius 1.3.18   expertae metuens iurgia **saevitiae**

Cf. also Catullus 116.8: *at fixus nostris tu dabi' supplicium* and Propertius 1.16.4: *captorum lacrimis umida supplicibus.*
    Ancient poets can, of course, imitate terms used by their predecessors out of context, but intend *imitatio* nevertheless. However, if Propertius was really harking back to Catullus in the polysyllabic pentameter endings which they share, surely something more of Catullus would have accompanied those endings in at least a few cases. Since apparently nothing ever does, the implication is that Propertius was not directly influenced by Catullus in his use of these endings. Another indication of this is the low proportion of Catullan polysyllabic endings which reappear in Propertius. Catullus composed 113 pentameters ending in polysyllables;[35] they represent 89 roots. But, as shown, only 25[36] of Propertius' 172 polysyllabic pentameter endings overlap with those of Catullus; and this figure includes the five

35   Benedum (1967) 190.
36   On the most generous definition, which would match *supplicium* with *supplicibus* (above).

Propertian examples of *litoribus*, and the two each of *muneribus*, *temporibus*, and *officio/officium*. Hence the two poets' endings share only 18 roots. This rather small overlap is another strong argument against the notion that Catullus was a dominant influence on Propertius in this area. It rather indicates that, when they do share endings, either both were indebted to a common source, or Propertius got those endings not from Catullus but from an intermediary between Catullus and himself. Given that Catullus came early in the Roman elegiac tradition, the latter is by far the more likely alternative; and since Gallus is manifestly the source of the five Propertian pentameters terminating in *historia*, it seems pointless to look further. This conclusion will be confirmed by examination of many other Propertian pentameters ending in polysyllables.

The hypothesis being formulated, then, is this: as well as being signs of earliness of composition, and of 'neotericism', and possibly in a few cases the consequence of the sheer length and metrical awkwardness of a desiderated term, the polysyllabic pentameter endings of Propertius reflect and signal his imitations of earlier elegists, and especially of Cornelius Gallus. Quinquesyllabic pentameter endings, which are mainly confined to Propertius Books 1 (9) and 2 (7), may be hyper-indicative of Gallan influence.[37]

Before this hypothesis is tested, something needs to be said about those Propertian hexameters which end in polysyllables. These will play a relatively minor part in the discussion which follows, mainly because Propertius employs few of them:[38] there are only 13, of which 11 employ Greek words – six proper names (1.8.35; 1.13.21; 1.20.31; 2.34.33; 3.7.13; 4.4.71), three forms of *heroine* (1.13.31; 1.19.13; 2.2.9), *terebintho* (3.7.49) and *hyacinthos* (4.7.33). Only when a case is being made on other grounds for Gallan influence upon a passage of Propertius will their presence be noted. This is not to say that some of these polysyllabic hexameter endings might not in themselves be pressed to yield information about Propertius' sources. The triple recurrences of *heroine* and the repetition of *Orithyiae* (1.20.31; 3.7.13) could reflect an influential Roman poetic predecessor who had employed these terms at the end of a hexameter, and who could be Gallus. Similarly the two Latin polysyllabic hexameter endings *increpitarent* (2.26.15) and *formosarum* (2.28.49) may well reproduce or

---

37   There is only one example in Book 3 (23.20), and one in Book 4 (5.28).
38   Another reason is that the ancient 'generic' distinction between epic and elegy weakens the value of analogies drawn between their hexameters.

recall the final words of famous hexameters.[39] A particularly intriguing question is posed by:

> sed thyio thalamo **aut Oricia** terebintho
> ecfultum pluma versicolore caput   (Propertius 3.7.49–50)

together with:

> aut collo decus aut capiti, vel quale per artem
> inclusum buxo **aut Oricia** terebintho
> lucet ebur   (Virgil *Aeneid* 10.135–7)

Both passages present as the identical second hemistich of their hexameters *aut* plus the rare proper adjective *Oricia* and the rare noun *terebintho*. Moreover in both contexts there is mention of a 'head'; so coincidence can be ruled out. It seems improbable that Virgil was imitating Propertius; on the other hand, since Propertius did have some foreknowledge of the *Aeneid*,[40] there is an outside chance that this half-line stuck in his memory from a recitation. But the overlap is much more likely to reflect the impact on both poets of a Greek predecessor line, and an easy conjecture would point to Parthenius as its author. But one wonders whether Virgil and Propertius would, independently and in the absence of a Latin intermediary (?Gallus), have both rendered that line as they did.[41] A less striking, but not altogether insubstantial, case could be made for Gallan influence on final *hyacinthos* at Propertius 4.7.33.[42]

As a first step, then, towards testing the hypothesis of widespread Gallan influence on Propertian pentameters with polysyllabic endings, those which have already been linked with Gallus in previous chapters will be assembled with brief comment:

1.   The most important and most indicative examples – because their Gallan pedigree is confirmed by the Qaṣr Ibrîm papyrus (fr. 2.2–

---

39   *ast hic quem nunc tu tam torviter increpuisti* (Enn. *Ann.* 93 Skutsch) may be a remote ancestor of one of them.
40   Cf. Cairns (2003) and below, p. 405.
41   For similar cases, see above, p. 140 and below, pp. 204, 228–9. An alternative argument could be made for the influence of Varius' *De Morte* since Prop. 3.7 is about death, and Virgil and Varius were both writing in hexameters. But *Oricos* at Prop. 1.8.20 argues for Gallus.
42   Based on Virgil's quintuple, but mutually unrelated, uses of various forms of it at hexameter endings (*Ecl.* 3.63; 6.53*; *Georg.* 4.137*, 183; *Aen.* 11.69*, of which the three asterisked combine it with forms of *mollis*), and its reappearance at the end of *Ciris* 95.

3 Courtney) – are (as already noted above, pp. 83–4) the five Propertian lines ending in parts of *historia*:

tu quoque uti fieres nobilis historia	(1.15.24)
maxima de nihilo nascitur historia	(2.1.16)
ite et Romanae consulite historiae	(3.4.10)
et caput argutae praebeat historiae	(3.20.28)
famam, Roma, tuae non pudet historiae	(3.22.20)

2.   Two other Propertian pentameters ending in the polysyllables *imaginibus* and *divitiis* have long been recognized as Gallan in origin (cf. above, pp. 79–80, and Index II):

nescit Amor priscis cedere imaginibus	(1.5.24)
nescit Amor magnis cedere divitiis	(1.14.8)[43]

With the first, compare also:

nescius undis	
errorem blandis tardat imaginibus	(Propertius 1.20.41–2)
vanum nocturnis fallit imaginibus	([Tibullus] 3.4.56)

3.   Of the seven Propertian pentameters containing the quadrisyllable *nequitia*, which also features, although not as a pentameter ending, in the Qaṣr Ibrîm papyrus (fr. 2.1 Courtney), four employ the term in final position (cf. above, pp. 94–5):

hanc animam extremae reddere nequitiae	(1.6.26)
nec tremis admissae conscia nequitiae?	(1.15.38)
et non ignota vivere nequitia?	(2.5.2)
et rabidae stimulos frangere nequitiae	(3.19.10)

4.   Two more Propertian pentameters, which belong to the *medicina* complex and which end with quadrisyllabic *artificem*, have also been identified by earlier scholarship as Gallan in inspiration (cf. above, pp. 100–1):

---

43   Cf. also Prop. 1.6.14: *atque Asiae veteres cernere divitias*.

nudus Amor formae non amat artificem   (1.2.8)

solus Amor morbi non amat artificem   (2.1.58).

5.   The fact that the iunctura *pars eris* is indubitably Gallan (fr. 2.3 Courtney) draws attention to Propertius 1.21.4: *pars ego sum vestrae proxima militiae*, and hence also to Propertius 1.7.2: *armaque frater-nae tristia militiae*. Together these lines suggest that Gallus too had employed *militiae* as a pentameter ending. This view is further strengthened by the recurrences of forms of *militia* as final poly-syllables at Tibullus 1.3.82: *optavit lentas et mihi militias*, and at *Catalepton* 9.42: *horrida quid durae tempora militiae?* In addition to their linkage at Propertius 1.21.4, *pars* and inflections of *militia* crop up a number of times in combination in Ovid.[44] Gallus too may have combined *pars* and inflections of *militia*. (Cf. also above, pp. 87–9.)

6.   Propertius 1.18 is generally acknowledged to derive its inspi-ration from Gallus as well as from Callimachus.[45] It contains the pen-tameter *scribitur et vestris Cynthia corticibus* (22), and the act of inscribing a beloved's name on tree-bark is known from Virgil *Eclogue* 10.53–4 to have been specifically associated with a poem of Gallus, doubtless the one containing his adaptation of the Acontius *aetion* of Callimachus.[46] All this combines to support the notion that Gallus too had used *corticibus* as a pentameter ending (cf. above, p. 119). The appearance in the same Propertian elegy of a further con-spicuous and suggestive quadrisyllabic pentameter ending (*quod mihi das flendi, Cynthia, principium*, 1.18.6) makes *principium* another excellent candidate for Gallan status, especially since Propertius re-uses this term in another inflection at 2.6.16: *his Troiana vides funera principiis*.[47]

7.   It is overwhelmingly likely that Gallus is a major presence in Propertius 2.30 (cf. above, pp. 128–30). Lines 35–6 of 2.30, *si tamen Oeagri quaedam compressa figura/ Bistoniis olim rupibus accubuit* (35–6), reflect on the parents of that archetypal Gallan figure,

---

44   *hic pars militiae, dux erat ille ducum* (*Her.* 8.46); *pars sis militiae; tumulo solacia posco* (*Met.* 7.483); *nec, pars militiae, Telamon sine honore recessit* (*Met.* 11.216). Cf. also *EP* 1.2.81–2, combining *pars* and *militis*, and the wittily indecent *Am.* 3.7.65–9, where Ovid's *membra* (65) = *pars* (69) fail to perform their *militia* (68).

45   Cairns (1969); Ross (1975) 71–4.

46   Ross (1975) 71–4; Rosen and Farrell (1986).

47   The frequency of *principiorum* as a Lucretian hexameter ending is perhaps significant; cf. also the overlaps between Gallus and Lucretius noted above, p. 91.

Orpheus, while the next couplet but one reads *tum capiti sacros patiar pendere corymbos:/ nam sine te nostrum non valet ingenium* (39–40). There is a possibility, then, that *accubuit* echoes a pentameter ending of Gallus,[48] and a virtual certainty that *ingenium* does, given the number of times its various inflections appear in this position in the elegiacs of Propertius, Ovid, Martial, and others (see below, p. 169).

8.   Propertius 1.6 (a *propemptikon* to Tullus) is the companion poem to 1.8 (a *propemptikon* to Cynthia). 1.8 is recognized as drawing on Gallus' *propemptikon* to Lycoris, and it was suggested (above, p. 114) that 1.6 echoes some of the ethos of the Qaṣr Ibrîm papyrus. Hence in *ibis et accepti pars eris imperii* (1.6.34), the line-ending *imperii*, which is accompanied by the assuredly Gallan *pars eris*, is very likely to be another bow to Gallus, particularly in view of Ovid's three late pentameters: *corpore pars nulla est, quae labet, imperii* (*Tristia* 2.232); *promovet Ausonium filius imperium* (*Ex Ponto* 2.2.70) and *saepe recusati ceperit imperii* (*Ex Ponto* 4.13.28), the first also featuring *pars ... est*. (Cf. above, pp. 90–1).

9.   Propertius 2.19, with its hunting motif of arguably Gallan ancestry, contains the line *venturum paucis me tibi Luciferis* (28). The term *Luciferis* looks suspiciously like a portion of, or variant upon, Gallus' notorious East/West interest.[49] (Cf. above, pp. 97–8.)

10.   The fact that no less than four Propertian pentameters (1.2.24; 1.15.22; 1.16.2; 4.5.28) end in the quinquesyllabic *pudicitia(e)* (see above, pp. 102–3) raises the strong possibility that this term originated as an ending in Gallus and that Propertius regarded it as a particularly striking way of alluding to Gallus. *pudicitia(e)* is also found as a pentameter ending at *Heroides* 16.290 and at Martial 6.27.4, and in the combination *pudicitia est* at Martial 6.7.2. Some of the Propertian contexts where it occurs contain further hints of Gallus: at 1.2.24 it sums up a series of illustrations from nature and myth intended to bolster the point, made at 1.2.7–8 through invocation of Gallan *medicina*, that natural beauty is best. The presence of Gallan *nota* along with *pudicitiae* in 1.16.2 has already been underlined.[50]

---

48   See above, p. 130 n. 91 and below, p. 197.
49   *exoriente novo roscida Lucifero* (*De rosis nascentibus* 12) is too late to be relevant.
50   *Attalicus*, a favourite term of Propertius – his are four of the seven classical examples, one of which (2.32.12) ends a pentameter – appears at Prop. 4.5.24, four lines before Prop. 4.5.28 (ending in *pudicitiae*).

11. Finally two Propertian elegies in which polysyllabic pentameter endings have been associated with Gallus may be mentioned. Propertius 1.20, addressed to 'Gallus', has 11 out of its 26 pentameters ending in polysyllables, and 3 more ending in trisyllables (see also below, pp. 234–5). This has been noted, and has been associated as a stylistic feature with its addressee.[51] Again, the 'rapid succession of mythological exempla and the formality of the language' in 2.1.47–78, the latter including the 'two polysyllabic pentameter endings (both proper nouns) *Iliada* (50) and *Phillyrides* (60)' have been linked with 'the manner and style of Gallan elegy'.[52]

A note of caution should be injected here, and a point made earlier reiterated: despite the indications that many Propertian polysyllabic pentameter endings are indebted to Gallus, confirmatory evidence is always needed if the proper names and adjectives, almost all of them Greek, found in that position in Propertius are to be credited to Gallan influence. To be recognized as a *doctus poeta* Propertius was obliged to introduce such learned Greek terms irrespective of who had, or had not, employed them previously; and their metrical shapes often gave him limited options about where to locate them. Indeed, like Catullus, Propertius may have found some such terms at pentameter endings in a Greek source, and have been influenced by that source in his own placement of them. Hence, when a polysyllabic Greek (or indeed Latin) name or nominal adjective otherwise unconnected with Gallus appears at the end of a Propertian pentameter, the first question to be asked is whether it is paralleled or unparalleled in this position in Propertius or in other Latin elegiac verse. If it is unparalleled little more can usually be said about it. The same procedure should also be applied to polysyllabic common nouns and adjectives which appear at Propertian pentameter endings and which have no obvious Gallan link. One further point to be made is that not all apparent Latin parallels are of value when the possible influence of Gallus is being sought. Pre-Propertian Roman elegiac parallels are naturally valid, as are those from Propertius himself and from the other Augustan elegists. The same applies to parallels in Martial's epigrams and in those of other (minor) poets of the first century AD, although these obviously

---

51   Ross (1975) 81 n. 1; Petrain (2000) 415 n. 19.
52   Ross (1975) 116 and n. 5, detailing also many other linguistic features indicative of Gallan influence; the passages of Virg. *Ecl.* 6 in which Virgil summarizes mythical themes of probable Gallan origin are useful comparanda for many of them.

carry less weight. Contrariwise, however, what may seem to be parallels in Latin poets of the second century AD on are likely to have little or no significance, since, as was mentioned earlier in a similar context,[53] writers of that period generally treated their classical predecessors as storehouses of raw material from which they could borrow words, phrases, and line-endings without regard for their original contexts.[54]

In line with these caveats the unparalleled Propertian polysyllabic pentameter endings *Antinoo* (4.5.8), *Apidano* (1.3.6), *Arabiae* (2.10.16), *Attalicis* (2.32.12),[55] *Cymothoe* (2.26.16), *Dulichiae* (2.14.4), *Eridano* (1.12.4),[56] *Inachidos* (1.3.20), *Lampetie* (3.12.30), *Ortygia* (2.31.10), *Quintiliae* (2.34.90),[57] *Tantalidos* (2.31.14), *Telegoni* (2.32.4) and *Tyndaridas* (1.17.18) cannot at present be linked with Gallus, although Gallan associations for some of them will emerge later.[58] On the other hand certain unparalleled proper nouns and adjectives at Propertian polysyllabic pentameter endings are found in already established Gallan contexts, so conclusions can justifiably be drawn about them without further ado. *A fortiori* this is true of when Propertian proper nouns and adjectives are repeated at pentameter ends within passages known to have been influenced by Gallus. Some examples from these two latter categories are: *Iasidos* (1.1.10) in the Gallan Milanion exemplum; *Ascanius* (1.20.4)/*Ascanio* (1.20.16), and *Thessalia* (1.5.6) in elegies addressing 'Gallus'; the quadrisyllabic *Adryasin* (1.20.12), and the quinquesyllabic *Hamadryasin* (1.20.32)[59] and *Hamadryadas* (2.34.76), all at pentameter line-endings, whose Gallan nature is confirmed not just by the appearance of the first two in 1.20, addressed to 'Gallus', but by Cornelius Gallus' established interest in Dryads/Hamadryads;[60] *Menoetiaden* (2.1.38), which crops up in 2.1, an elegy heavily influenced by Gallus;[61] the three endings *Iliadas* (2.1.14); *Iliada* (2.1.50) and *Iliade* (2.34.66),

---

53   Above, p. 87. Hence Propertian polysyllabic pentameter endings are sometimes described in this volume as 'unparalleled' even where there are such later 'parallels'.
54   The pentameter endings of late Latin poets are studied by Marina Sáez (2003).
55   However, on *Attalicis* (2.32.12), cf. above, p. 162 n. 50.
56   Only otherwise in Ennodius *Carm*.1.8.20 (d. AD 521).
57   Since the subject of the couplet is Calvus and Quintilia, this pentameter ending presumably also featured in Calvus' *epikedion* for her, on which see Courtney (1993) 207–9.
58   Although also unparalleled, *Borysthenidas* (2.7.18) is in a different category in view of Gallus' known Caucasus interest, for which see Index II.
59   This is a humanist emendation, but it (or something similar) is secure.
60   Cf. esp. Kennedy (1982) 377–82 and Index II s.vv.
61   Cf. Ross (1975) 59, 67, 115–17; J. F. Miller (1981).

whose multiplicity might have excited speculation about their source even without the Gallan context of 2.1; the repeated *Leucothoe* (2.26.10) and *Leucothoen* (2.28.20), which should similarly arouse suspicions; and the triple appearance at Propertian pentameter endings of inflections of '*Callimachus*', additionally paralleled in other Latin poetry (below).

Again, two further, paralleled Propertian quadrisyllabic endings can also be linked independently with Gallus.The metrically strained *Vergiliis* (1.8.10) appears in a *propemptikon* undoubtedly influenced by Gallus' *propemptikon* to Lycoris as metamorphosed by Virgil's *deformazione* of it in *Eclogue* 10, and it functions as an allusion to both predecessors of Propertius. *Hesperios* too (2.3.44) is manifestly Gallan, since it appears in the East/West topos securely associated with Gallus: *sive illam Hesperiis, sive illam ostendet Eois,/ uret et Eoos, uret et Hesperios* (43–4).[62] It is methodologically useful to note that before late antiquity the only parallels for *Vergiliis* and *Hesperios* in this metrical position are Martial's *Vergilio* (11.52.18; 14.195.2), referring to Virgil, and *Hesperidum* in Martial *Spectacula* 21.4. Further indications will emerge below that Martial was acquainted with the works of Cornelius Gallus.

Yet another category of polysyllabic pentameter endings in Propertius consists of proper names not otherwise associated with Gallus but paralleled in this position in later poetry in circumstances which hint that Gallus was the source for both Propertius and his successor(s). Some of the relevant parallels are (again) found in Martial, and again in settings unrelated to those of Propertius – which of course points to a source for Martial other than Propertius. One such example is *anxia captiva tristius Andromacha* (Propertius 2.20.2): no other poets besides Propertius and Martial placed her name in this position; and Martial did so twice: *cum possis Hecaben, non potes Andromachen* (3.76.4); *quo tibi vel Nioben, Basse, vel Andromachen* (5.53.2), in utterly dissimilar contexts. The triple Propertian appearances of *Callimachus* as a pentameter ending: *intonet angusto pectore Callimachus* (2.1.40), *et non inflati somnia Callimachi* (2.34.32), and *Umbria Romani patria Callimachi* (4.1.64), are again echoed only in Martial: *nec te scire: legas Aetia Callimachi* (10.4.12). That they too are Gallan in origin seems likely in view of their multiplicity in Propertius, of the Gallan setting of the first Propertian

---

62   Cf. above, pp. 97–9.

example, and of the lack of similarity between Martial's context and those of Propertius.

Other places where Martial offers the sole parallel, always in a different case, to a Propertian proper name polysyllabic ending are *Andromede* (1.3.4) = Martial *Spectacula* 27.10: *Andromedan*, *Hermionae* (1.4.6) = Martial 3.11.4: *Hermione* (and cf. also *Ciris* 472: *Hermionaea* at a hexameter ending), *Pasiphae* (2.28.52) = Martial *Spectacula* 27.8: *Pasiphaes*, and *Pirithoum* (2.6.18) = Martial 10.11.4: *Pirithoi*. The last example is suggestive of complex *imitatio*/*variatio*: three lines earlier (10.11.1) Martial had ended a hexameter with *Pirithoumque*; Virgil did this too at *Aeneid* 6.393 and 601, and indeed Martial's hexameter replicates the *iunctura* of *Aeneid* 6.393: *Thesea Pirithoumque*. But it is unlikely that Virgil was Martial's only source: rather the Ovidian line: *Pirithoum Phaedrae Pirithoumque tibi* (*Heroides* 4.112) perhaps indicates that this entire group of lines originated in a passage (of Gallus?) which contained *Pirithoum* and *Pirithoumque*. Ovid offers far fewer verbal and uncontextualized parallels to proper name/adjective polysyllabic endings in Propertius than does Martial. Some of the Ovidian offerings seem to be reasonable indicators of a common source in Gallus, e.g.: *Erichthonius* (Propertius 2.6.4 = Ovid *Tristia* 2.294, *Erichthonium*; *Ex Ponto* 2.9.20), *Ausoniis* (Propertius 2.33.4[63] = Ovid *Tristia* 1.3.6, *Ausoniae*).[64]

Just as non-repeated and unparalleled polysyllabic proper names and adjectives at pentameter endings in Propertian elegy can be linked confidently with Gallus only if further evidence is available, so it is with those unique polysyllabic common nouns or adjectives, or verbs, which end Propertius' pentameters. For example, of those beginning with 'c', only *canitiem* (1.8.46), *cardinibus* (1.16.26), *compositam* (1.11.14), *corticibus* (1.18.22) and *cupidinibus* (1.1.2) come from contexts where Gallan influence can be argued for on other grounds.[65] However, when such endings are repeated and/or paralleled, they can sometimes be traced back to Gallus in the same ways as can proper names/adjectives. The methodologies exemplified in certain of the Gallan verbal complexes constructed in Chapters 3 and 4 again come

---

63   *Ausonius*, used frequently at pentameter endings by the poet Ausonius, plays on his own name. His pentameter endings also include some of the other proper names discussed here, but nothing can be based on them.

64   Doubt arises when the only parallel comes from a minor epigrammatist, e.g. *Penelope* (Prop. 3.13.24), also found at the end of a pentameter by Petronius: see Courtney (1991) 61 (= *Anth. Lat.* 477.10 R = 475.10 SB).

65   For *corticibus* see above, p. 161, and for the others see Index I.

into their own here, and may allow new complexes to be established around such endings. In addition certain of the Gallan verbal complexes already proposed can be extended by focussing on further significant polysyllabic terms which crop up within them at the end of pentameters.

The factors which can point to Gallan input into a polysyllabic pentameter ending in Propertius, not all of which will manifest themselves in any single case, have now emerged. They are: a multiplicity of Propertian examples; a possible antecedent in Lucretius, where the key terms usually have -*que* appended so that they form hexameter endings, or in Catullus; parallel(s) in one or more of Tibullus, later Ovid, the *Appendix Vergiliana* and Martial; and finally verbal and/or contextual associations with Cornelius Gallus and/or his elegy. The reasons why the late Ovid and Martial were students of Gallus' elegies should perhaps be spelled out. A line from Ovid's own 'epitaph' for himself – INGENIO PERII NASO POETA MEO (*Tristia* 3.3.74) – which exploits *ingenium*, a term with probable Gallan connections (below, pp. 168–9), explains why Ovid's *Tristia* and *Ex Ponto* return so markedly to this element of the metrical practice of Propertius and Gallus: Ovid, while in exile in Tomi, was identifying with Gallus, and was perhaps rereading the works of Gallus, and trying to imply to the world an analogy between himself, allegedly 'destroyed by his poetic genius', and Gallus, also an elegiac poet and also the author of his own self-destruction. The implication was, of course, tendentious since Gallus certainly, and Ovid probably, fell for reasons of state. There may also be an element of covert, or even subconscious, defiance in Ovid's metrical trend, which perhaps intensified as Ovid came to realize more and more that his chances of recall to Rome were fading. Martial's motivation was probably purely literary: much as Lucan sought the spirit of his *Bellum Civile* in pre-Virgilian epic, so Martial will have been searching for novelty and inspiration in the preclassical, i.e. the Gallan, era of elegy, before elegy achieved its canonical metrics in the work of Ovid.

An example may now be given of how a Propertian pentameter with a common noun polysyllabic ending can help to enlarge a known Gallan verbal complex, or indeed point to the existence of an additional new complex which is also plausibly Gallan. Of the two Propertian lines beginning with plausibly Gallan *nescit Amor*, one ends not with *imaginibus* but with *divitiis*: *nescit Amor magnis cedere divitiis* (Propertius 1.14.8). This ending belongs to another Gallan complex, and Propertius has seemingly substituted it here for *imaginibus* (whether or not Gallus himself had already done this). The *divitiae* complex may have started life in Lucretius. Cf:

| servitium contra paupertas divitiaeque | (*De Rerum Natura* 1.455) |
| sanguine civili rem conflant divitiasque | (*De Rerum Natura* 3.70) |

It certainly includes *verum illi domino tu quoque divitiae* (*Catalepton* 8.2), along with the three (in all) Propertian pentameters ending in forms of *divitiae*, the others being:

| atque Asiae veteres cernere divitias | (1.6.14) |
| cum pagana madent fercula divitiis | (4.4.76) |

Here, as often, multiple examples indicate a source. Once again Martial too exemplifies the line-ending in *hoc vestrae mihi sunt, Castrice,*[66] *divitiae* (6.43.6), cf. *dantur opes nullis nunc nisi divitibus* (Martial 5.81.2). Gallus' line *fixa legam spolieis deivitiora tueis* (fr. 2.5) directly documents his interest in 'riches', but that line is not the source of the *divitiae* complex,[67] although it did give rise to Ovid's *oppida sunt regni divitiora mei* (*Heroides* 16.34), and *textaque fortuna divitiora sua* (*Ex Ponto* 3.4.110). *imaginibus*, the other polysyllabic ending of a Propertian line beginning with *nescit Amor*, also has a Nachleben at pentameter ends – yet again in Martial:

| atriaque immodicis artat imaginibus | (2.90.6) |
| quidquid et hirsutis squalet imaginibus | (9.47.2) |

For the most part, however, the additional Gallan verbal complexes suggested by Propertian polysyllabic pentameter endings need to be established in the same way as those constituted earlier. One such complex centres around *ingenium.*[68] Propertius was very

---

66   Castricus, on whom see Galán Vioque (2002) 66, crops up again below (p. 172) in connection with another Gallan pentameter ending at Mart. 7.42. Was he perhaps an admirer of the work of Cornelius Gallus?

67   Outside the complex, but undoubtedly significant, is the first word of Tibullus' entire elegiac œuvre, *divitias* (1.1.1), which presumably picks up and reverses Gallus' term. Tibullus' other uses of the term are at 1.1.41 (*-as*) and 1.9.19 (*-is*).

68   Already linked with Gallus by Morelli (1985) 178, citing Mart. 8.73.6: *ingenium Galli pulchra Lycoris erat*; Ov. *Am.* 2.17.34; 3.12.16.

interested in this term: it appears twelve times in his elegies in the related senses 'poetic genius', 'poetic inspiration', and 'poet of genius'. In three of these appearances (again multiplicity!) it constitutes a quadrisyllabic pentameter ending:

tunc ego Romanis *praeferar* **ingeniis**	(1.7.22)
nam sine te nostrum *non valet* **ingenium**	(2.30.40)
hoc ego, quo tibi nunc *elevor*, **ingenio**	(2.34.58)

Like many such pentameter endings *ingenio* is prefigured by *ingenioque* as a Lucretian hexameter ending (*De Rerum Natura* 3.745, 5.1111). The other ancient examples of *ingenium* (alone) as a pentameter ending follow the (by now) recognizable pattern:

<u>materiae</u> gracili *sufficit* **ingenium**	(Ovid *Ex Ponto* 2.5.26)
<u>materiam</u> vestris adferat **ingeniis**	(Ovid *Ex Ponto* 4.13.46)
plectar et *incauto* semper ab **ingenio**	(Ovid *Ex Ponto* 4.14.18)
o quantum est subitis casibus **ingenium**	(Martial *Spectacula* 14.4)
o dulce invicti principis **ingenium**	(Martial *Spectacula* 20.4)
et cor solus habes, solus et **ingenium**	(Martial 3.26.4)
ipse tuo *cedet* Regulus **ingenio**	(Martial 5.63.4)
antiquis hospes *non minor* **ingeniis**	(*Catalepton* [16].2)[69]

The *divitiae* and *imaginibus* complexes both suggest that a polysyllabic Gallan term at a pentameter ending was often in itself enough to communicate an allusion to Gallus. Hence an inflection of *ingenium* in that position probably also sufficed to do this. It looks, however, as though other concepts such as the strength of the poet's *ingenium* and its standing vis-à-vis other *ingenia*, echoes of which appear in some of the examples listed here, were also present in Gallus' uses of final *ingenium* (see the codings above). The allusive strength of the term was perhaps due to Gallus having been the first Roman poet to vaunt his poetic 'genius' at pentameter end using *ingenium*, and to Propertius having followed him on three occasions. Ovid's uses of

---

69   The status of *Catalept.* [16] is suspect, and the eight Ausonian examples are, as often, unreliable.

ingenium at pentameter end in his exile poetry seem to reflect wryly on his own changed circumstances and on their analogy to Gallus' fate (esp. *Ex Ponto* 4.14.18). It is impossible to know whether *materia/ materiam* in two of his *Ex Ponto* examples also reflect Gallus or whether they are Ovid's own contribution.

divitiae and *ingenium* as pentameter endings left their clear mark on Propertius' successors. *imaginibus* did so to a more limited extent: as noted, it is paralleled later in this position only in Martial. And yet it is as certain as anything can be that *imaginibus* is Gallan and diagnostic of Gallus.[70] Other terms with final -*ibus* can be counted in some numbers among Propertian polysyllabic pentameter endings, but again they are rarely, if ever, exemplified in later (or even earlier) poetry, although interestingly some of them are occasionally paralleled in Tibullus. An instructive case is *aequoribus*, which ends three pentameters of Propertius and is therefore likely to echo a predecessor line – very probably by Gallus since 1.8 is indebted to a Gallan *propemptikon* and since 1.15.10 also contains the Gallan term *desertis*:[71]

accipiat placidis Oricos aequoribus!	(1.8.20)
et legitur Rubris gemma sub aequoribus	(1.14.12)
desertis olim fleverat aequoribus	(1.15.10)

But there are no post-Augustan examples of *aequoribus* in final pentameter position. There is, however, a Tibullan case: *prodigia indomitis merge sub aequoribus* (2.5.80). Since all the Propertian examples are from the Monobiblos, which definitely predates Tibullus Book 2, one might be tempted to characterize the Tibullan line as an imitation of Propertius. On the other hand, apart from the *sub* which it also shares with 1.14.12, and the possible antonymity of *placidis* and *indomitis*, the Propertian examples are not close to the line of Tibullus. The safest conclusion, then, is that both poets are imitating a predecessor, who is likely to be Gallus. This conclusion is supported by the Propertian and Tibullan occurrences of another polysyllabic pentameter ending, *arboribus*, which is discussed at greater length below in Chapter 7 (p. 229). Here it may be noted that its two Propertian uses can both be linked independently with Gallus: *urgetur quantis Caucasus arboribus* (1.14.6) refers to the Caucasus, a major Gallan

---

70 See Index II s.v.
71 See Index II s.v. *desertus.*

motif (cf. below, p. 205); and *roscida desertis poma sub arboribus* (1.20.36) comes from the most clearly Gallan of all Propertius' elegies (see below, Chapter 7) and *arboribus* is qualified by Gallan *desertis*. The two Tibullan examples:

cui dulcia <u>poma</u>
Delia selectis <u>detrahat</u> **arboribus**   (1.5.31–2)

<u>pom</u>aque **non notis** <u>legit</u> ab **arboribus**   (1.7.32)

are not imitations of Propertius. They obviously derive, like Propertius 1.20.36, from a single line by a predecessor about *poma*;[72] and *non notis* (Tibullus 1.7.32) virtually repeats the announcement of Propertius 1.20.36 that this predecessor is Gallus. There is only one post-Augustan example of *arboribus* as a pentameter ending.[73]

Yet another informative case is *carminibus*. It appears no less than four times in Propertius as a polysyllabic pentameter ending:

posse †cythalinis† ducere **carminibus**   (1.1.24)

sint modo fata t u i s *mollia* **carminibus**   (1.7.4)

sustulit e n o s t r i s , Cynthia, **carminibus**   (1.11.8)

nobilis obscenis tradita **carminibus**   (1.16.10)

In the first example *ducere carminibus* plays with Gallus' *carmina .../ ... deicere* of the Qaṣr Ibrîm papyrus (fr. 2.6–7 Courtney); cf. also Propertius 4.6.13 (*ducuntur carmina*, above p. 92). In the second, Gallan *mollis/durus* is present.[74] The third displays *nostris* in the same *sedes* as *tuis* in the second, and the fourth contains Gallan *nobilis*. There is a single example in Tibullus:

ter cane, ter **dictis** despue **carminibus**   (1.2.54)

which again plays, this time more closely, with Gallus' *carmina .../ ... deicere*; and Martial uses *carminibus* twice in this location:

---

72 The frequency of 'gathering' and 'offering' *poma* in Propertius, and the locations of these concepts (1.3.24; 1.20.36; 2.1.66; 2.32.39) would in themselves constitute a good case for Gallan inspiration, even if 2.32.39 was not accompanied by Hamadryads (37), Sileni and Silenus (38), and a Naiad (40) – see above, p. 134 and n. 100, and even if Tibullus' lines were not about gathering *poma*.

73 Mart. 13.42.2: *de Nomentanis sed damus arboribus*.

74 See Index II s.vv.

inque t u i s nulla est mentula **carminibus**   (3.69.2)

audeat hic etiam, Castrice,[75] **carminibus**   (7.42.2)

It is not easy to believe that Tibullus is imitating Propertius, or vice-versa, or that Martial is imitating either of them: the contexts of the different writers' examples are distinct, whether the *carmina* are poems or magical incantations. So the implication, particularly in view of the Gallan elements noted above in some of these lines, is that there was a common Gallan source for them, or more probably several such sources since Gallus may well have used the ending *carminibus* more than once.

The same approach again proves illuminating with *litoribus*, exemplified no less than five times in Propertius at the end of a pentameter (see above, p. 155). Each occurrence of *litoribus* is accompanied by its descriptive adjective, two of which, *Herculeis* (1.11.2) and *Lavinis* (2.34.64), derive from proper names, while a third (*patriis*, 1.2.18) refers to the preceding proper name *Eveni*. Another is Gallan *desertis* (1.3.2), and the last is *mansuetis* (1.17.28), like *desertis* a perfect participle passive in form. It seems very likely that all these lines have a common origin in a line or lines of an earlier poet. As observed (above, p. 152), their only surviving predecessor is Catullus 66.58: *grata Canopitis incola litoribus*, from his translation of Callimachus' *Coma Berenices*, where Callimachus wrote Κ]ανωπίτου ναιέτις α[ἰγιαλοῦ (*Aetia* fr. 110.58 Pf.). Although the Catullan line also has an accompanying adjective derived from a proper name (*Canopitis*), it seems unlikely to have generated all, or indeed any, of the Propertian lines; and the only later appearance of *litoribus* in this position comes in a pseudo-Senecan epigram: *cinctaque inaccessis horrida litoribus* (34.2 Prato). This pentameter exhibits the same syntactical pattern as its predecessors but its content is remote from anything in Propertius, unless *inaccessis* is meant to echo *desertis*. That the true source of this complex is indeed Gallus may be confirmed by a line of the *Ciris* already discussed (above, p. 137) as indebted to Gallus. It does not have *litoribus* in final position but it does reproduce the form *litoribus*, and, like Propertius 1.3.2, it accompanies *litoribus* with the Gallan *desertis*:

---

75   On Castricus, see above, p. 168 n. 66.

rupibus et scopulis et litoribus desertis (519).[76]

The other common nouns ending in *-ibus* which Propertius uses as polysyllabic pentameter endings and which are paralleled in relevant Latin poetry can be dealt with summarily:

1. *alitibus* (1.16.46): its hexametric precursor ending *alitibusque* is found at Catullus 64.152, and *fulserit hic niveis Delius alitibus* appears at [Tibullus] 3.6.8.

2. *harundinibus* (2.34.68) reappears at *Copa* 8.

3. *libidinibus* (2.16.14) is only found elsewhere at Martial 14.23.2.

4. *muneribus* (above, p. 155) features twice in Propertius (1.2.4; 1.16.36), but it is paralleled earlier only at Catullus 66.92.[77]

5. *temporibus* (above, p. 155) is exemplified twice in different senses in Propertius (1.3.22; 1.22.4). It is anticipated in both senses by Catullus (66.4, 60) but occurs later only at Martial *Spectacula* 18.4.

Of those terms without parallel outside Propertius as pentameter endings, one appears three times in his elegies (*luminibus*: 1.3.32; 1.15.40; 2.7.10),[78] and two are represented twice: *aggeribus* (1.21.2; 2.13.48), and *uberibus* (1.22.10; 2.34.70). Other terms end pentameters only in Propertius and only once: *cardinibus* (1.16.26); *corticibus* (1.18.22); *cupidinibus* (1.1.2); *militibus* (2.16.38); *nobilibus* (1.11.4); *papaveribus* (1.20.38); *pollicibus* (2.5.24); *pumicibus* (3.3.28); *sideribus* (1.3.38); *supplicibus* (1.16.4); *textilibus* (1.14.22); *verticibus* (2.2.14). Links between Gallus and two of these endings (*corticibus*, *nobilibus*) have already been proposed. Others, where the context is independently Gallan, will be treated further in Chapters 6 and 7.

The distribution at pentameter endings within Propertius' four books of polysyllabic nouns terminating in *-ibus* is striking, although it does not appear to have attracted much comment. There are thirty-two examples in Book 1, nine in the longer Book 2, only one in Book

---

76 The gratuitous spondaic ending may be another indication of its origin. Lyne (1978) ad loc. discusses possible sources and suggests, but without conviction, Gallus. The Catullan line *perfide, deserto liquisti in litore, Theseu* (64.133) may well be the ultimate source of all such collocations (cf. Lyne (1978) ad loc.), but it does not fully account for them.

77 The further parallel at Apul. fr. 4.8 Courtney is not significant.

78 Tibullus' otherwise unparalleled *liminibus* (*et dare sacratis oscula liminibus*, 1.2.86) may evoke *luminibus*, just as Propertius' *ducere carminibus* (1.1.24) plays with Gallus' *carmina/ ... deicere* (see above, p. 171).

3, and none in Book 4. Even given the steady decline in polysyllabic pentameter endings throughout Propertius' œuvre, this is a dramatic slump which demands an explanation. One might be that Roman taste changed rapidly in the later 20s BC, and that words of this shape in final position in a pentameter began to be regarded as clumsy or ugly. In the small, and functionally oral, culture of the Roman literary elite of this period such a feeling could have gained ground rapidly, and it could have had an immediate effect on poets through audience re-actions at their recitations: if their audiences began to hiss or titter when they heard such line-endings, poets would have abandoned them quickly. This hypothesis could explain the steep decline in the number of such endings in Propertius Book 2, their absence with one (doubt-less highly allusive) exception in Book 3, and their complete absence in Book 4. It would also explain why there are only two examples in the whole corpus of Ovidian elegy[79] of a polysyllabic pentameter ending in -ibus, even though Ovid became more open to the use of pentameters ending in polysyllables in his late works. Tibullus, who died in 19 BC, has 15 polysyllabic pentameter endings in Book 1, of which 6 end in -ibus, and 8 in Book 2, of which 3 end in -ibus.[80] These lower figures, although less dramatic, show a decline consonant with the trend observable in Propertius. Martial's later free adoption of polysyllabic pentameter endings, including those ending in -ibus, would, then, reflect a reaction (based on a change either in pro-nunciation or in fashion?), not just against Ovidian 'rules' but against a specific canon of taste established around 20 BC.[81] Finally, an interesting aspect of -ibus polysyllables is that so few of them (only 5, one of them found twice) end Catullus' pentameters, despite his high proportion of polysyllabic pentameter endings in general: virginibus (65.2); temporibus (66.4, 60); litoribus (66.58); coniugibus (66.80); muneribus (66.92). Earliness alone, then, will not explain Propertius' addiction to this type of pentameter ending in his Monobiblos, and it was not Catullus who created the trend towards polysyllabic endings

---

79 Both occur in the later books of the *Fasti*: *fluminibus* (5.582) and *funeribus* (6.660). *fluminibus* is paralleled at [Senec.] *Epigr.* 2.4 Prato; *funeribus* is unparalleled.

80 If, as suggested here, endings in -*ibus* were a conspicuous feature of Gallus' poetry, that could help to account for Quintilian's criticism of Gallus for 'harshness' (*Inst. Orat.* 10.1.93), which was no doubt the *communis opinio* of Quintilian's day.

81 It is unlikely that such endings became unpopular merely because they were associated with Gallus. If this had been the case, we might expect that Ovid would have revived them as part of his late, Gallan pose. That he did not shows that the objection to them was aesthetic.

in -*ibus*. So the trend-setter was probably intermediate in time between Catullus and Propertius, and, if so, who else could he have been but Gallus?[82]

Since both the view that Propertian polysyllabic pentameter endings in general can be exploited to reveal Gallan influence and the techniques for doing so introduced in this chapter appear to be novel, a resumé of the global scenario envisaged may be useful at this point. The first Roman 'elegists', Catullus and his contemporaries and predecessors in elegy and epigram, who encountered numerous Greek, especially hellenistic, pentameters ending in polysyllables, employed such endings copiously in their own works. Hence in these writers they are a mark both of earliness and of 'neotericism'. Similarly too, Catullus, along with Lucretius, terminated some hexameters polysyllabically by adding -*que* or -*ve* to terms later found as polysyllabic pentameter endings. In the succeeding decades Propertius was more sparing in the use of polysyllabic pentameter endings; Tibullus was less given to them, and the early Ovid avoided them altogether. Martial and other epigrammatists of the first century AD returned to them, as had also, to a small but significant degree, the late Ovid.

An element of Catullan influence upon certain of the later polysyllabic pentameter endings of Roman elegy seems certain, but it often appears to be indirect, since there is much in Propertius and Tibullus and other relevant writings which cannot be explained solely or at all as due to Catullus. Since Gallus is known to have employed one polysyllabic pentameter ending (*historia*) which continued in use accompanied by its context in the work of his successors, it makes sense to hypothesize that Gallus could have been the source of other such endings in later elegy, and that he vectored some of those introduced by Catullus. Many further polysyllabic pentameter endings in Propertius with otherwise attested Gallan links support this hypothesis; and the verbal complexes which can be constructed on the analogy of the lines influenced by Gallus' *historia* ending allow yet more polysyllabic pentameter endings in Propertius to be associated with Gallus. Thus Gallan influence, and not earliness or 'neotericism', is the primary motivation for this phenomenon in Propertius.

Roman taste moved away from polysyllabic pentameter endings in the later 20s BC, and there was a particular growing dislike for such

---

82 The statistics for Tibullus (above) are consonant with the overall impression that he was influenced less overtly by Gallus.

endings in -*ibus*. Tibullus was further to the fore in these metrical matters than Propertius, and Propertius' eventual adoption of the new modes must have owed something to Tibullan influence,[83] as well as being part of his own gradual retreat from Gallan elegy. Ovid's *Amores*, at least in their current second edition, show him embracing the new practices without exception, and he may have been a leader in the field. Ovid began to tolerate a few polysyllabic pentameter endings in his later work: a handful in the *Fasti*, more in the double *Heroides*, *Tristia*, *Ibis*, and most in the *Epistulae ex Ponto*. But he continued – except in two cases in the *Fasti*[84] – to shun endings terminating in -*ibus*. Many of the later Ovid's polysyllabic pentameter endings repeat those of earlier elegists. This again confirms the suspicion that Gallus stands behind many of them, and it shows Ovid, another victim of Augustus, identifying with Gallus and perusing Gallan elegy in Tomi.[85] Martial and other later minor epigrammatists once more accepted polysyllabic pentameter endings readily, including those found earlier, and even including forms in -*ibus*. Martial may well have studied Gallus as well as the surviving Augustan elegists, and he may have noted the late Ovid's mutation in practice.

Because Martial and other later epigrammatists frequently display continuity of usage with earlier elegy in their polysyllabic pentameter endings, it may be possible to exploit even them in order to construct verbal complexes which do not include Propertian examples but which could nevertheless point back to Gallus. Since this procedure is manifestly dangerous, one example will suffice. It will be left uncommented, although much that has been observed before in other complexes can also be perceived in it:

nomine, ne tollat rubra **supercilia**	(Catullus 67.46)
nec sedeo *duris* torva **superciliis**	(Ovid *Heroides* 17.16)

---

83   Cf. Maltby (2002) 70–1.
84   See above, p. 174 and n. 79.
85   Another factor may have contributed: *Ex Ponto* 4 was written under Tiberius, an admirer of learned hellenistic poets, including Parthenius, the *cliens* and teacher of Gallus and another influence on Propertius (see below, pp. 237–49). The interpretation offered here of Ovid's polysyllabic endings is paralleled by the metrics of *Am.* 3.9, his *epikedion* for Tibullus. In it Ovid employs Tibullan 3w caesurae, grouping them so as to draw attention to them; two of the relevant lines contain the name Tibullus, see McLennan (1972). For another Tibullan metrical feature of *Am.* 3.9 see Luque Moreno (1995). Helzle (1989) 67 explains the use of polysyllabic pentameter endings in *EP* 4 as 'a return to the less polished verse of his predecessors' to achieve 'lack of *munditia* ... to express the effect the rough surroundings had on the poet'.

terrarum dominum <u>pone</u> **supercilium**	(Martial 1.4.2)
cuius et ipse times triste **supercilium**	(Martial 1.24.2)
quod tibi prolatum est mane **supercilio**	(Martial 9.37.6)
et *Palatinum* ROMA **supercilium**	(Martial 9.79.2)

conveniens LATIO <u>pone</u> **supercilium**
(Carmina Priapea 1.2 Bücheler)

mentula subducti nostra **supercilii**
(Carmina Priapea 49.4 Bücheler)

scribere *patricio **digna*** **supercilio**
([Seneca] Epigrammata 39.2 Prato)

a pereat cui sunt prisca **supercilia**	(*Copa* 34)

Yet another type of verbal complex involving polysyllabic pentameter endings can be exemplified at this point: it includes at least one line from Propertius plus lines of other poets, but apart from the line-endings not much additional common ground can be detected within the complex. One explanation might be that a plurality of sources outside the known group influenced it; another might be the possibility, already considered, that a polysyllable used at a pentameter line-ending was in itself so striking that it could enjoy an allusive *Nachleben* divorced from any specific context. Three cases (the first two involving quinquesyllables) will sufficiently exemplify this phenomenon:

1.	sed quae se <u>impuro</u> dedit **adulterio**	(Catullus 66.84)
	cum quibus illa <u>malum</u> fecit **adulterium**	(Catullus 67.36)
	qui patruus patrui monstret **adulterium**	(Catullus 78.6)
	singula. fecundum semen **adulterio**	(Catullus 113.4))
	spiritus admisso ***notus*** **adulterio**	(Propertius 2.29.38)
	arguor <u>obsceni</u> doctor **adulterii**	(Ovid *Tristia* 2.212)
	in quibus ipse suum fassus **adulterium est**	(Ovid *Tristia* 2.430)
	scaenica vidisti lentus **adulteria**	(Ovid *Tristia* 2.514)

dum nova divorum cenat **adulteria**
(Versus populares fr. 7.4 Courtney)

hic ubi vir non est, ut sit **adulterium**.   (Martial 1.90.10)

adulterium is used four times by Catullus as a pentameter ending, and his employment of it as such was certainly known to, and imitated by Ovid, one of whose own three uses of it (2.430 terminating in *adulterium est*) actually refers to Catullus: Catullus is the *ipse* who 'confessed his adultery' in his poems (427–30). The three Ovidian examples all appear in *Tristia* 2, where Ovid was defending himself at length against the accusations which supposedly led to his exile, and another of them (2.212) specifically handles the charge that in *Ars Amatoria* Ovid had been an 'instructor in adultery'. All this, together with the multiplicity of the Catullan examples, might seem to tag Catullus clearly as the vector for this line-ending.

However, Propertius' 'footnote' to his single pentameter ending in *adulterio* (2.29.38) points in a different direction: *adulterio* is immediately preceded by Gallan *notus*, which suggests that Gallus too employed this ending. If he did, Ovid will have been aware of this, so one naturally looks to see whether Ovid's pointers to Catullus might also conceal a sly hint at Gallus. Of the four Catullan pentameters ending in *adulterium/o* one (67.6) concerns a certain 'Cornelius' who is committing adultery (*adulterium*); and another comes from an epigram (78) reviling a 'Gallus' who promotes adultery (again *adulterium*) within his family. It was, of course, a pure coincidence that Catullus was writing about two individuals whose names together happen to make up 'Cornelius Gallus', and it might be claimed that this thought never crossed Ovid's mind. But, as part of Ovid's imitation of this particular group of Catullan endings, in which he clearly took a keen interest, he referred directly to Catullus. So one has to ask whether a poet so generally obsessed with his literary predecessors and with intertextuality would have failed to notice the Catullan coincidence, or have failed to exploit it allusively in order to tell a fuller story about this line-ending. If Ovid did pick up and did refer to the Catullan coincidence, his explicit reference to Catullus at 2.430 was a way of footnoting his covert allusion to the place of Gallan elegy in the genealogy of this pentameter ending, and perhaps also a way of alluding to the analogy between his own fate and that of Gallus.

2.   hunc vexare pudorem, hunc vincula **amicitiai**
                              (Lucretius *De Rerum Natura* 3.83)

          vitae, eheu n o s t r a e pestis **amicitiae**   (Catullus 77.6)

atque olim missas flemus **amicitias**	(Catullus 96.4)
perspecta ex igni est unica **amicitia**	(Catullus 100.6)
aeternum hoc sanctae foedus **amicitiae**	(Catullus 109.6)
quaeris pro n o s t r a semper **amicitia**	(Propertius 1.22.2)
novit, deposuit alter **amicitiam**	
	(Domitius Marsus fr. 1.6 Courtney)[86]
indeclinatae munus **amicitiae**	(Ovid *Tristia* 4.5.24)
paene puer puero iunctus **amicitia**	(Ovid *Ex Ponto* 4.3.12)
per non vile t i b i *nomen* **amicitiae**	(Ovid *Ex Ponto* 4.13.44)
ut sim tiro t u a e semper **amicitiae**	(Martial 3.36.8)
orabat cana *notus* **amicitia**	(Martial 4.67.2)
quod colit ingratas pauper **amicitias**	(Martial 5.19.8)
esse putas fidae pectus **amicitiae**	(Martial 9.14.2)
ille t u a e cultor *notus* **amicitiae**	(Martial 9.84.4)
i, liber, absentis pignus **amicitiae**	(Martial 9.99.6)
et praetextata cultus **amicitia**	(Martial 10.13.4)
t e que t u a s numeres inter **amicitias**	(Martial 10.44.10)
esse t i b i ueras credis **amicitias**	(Martial 11.44.2)
quam 'regum solas effuge **amicitias'**	
	([Seneca] *Epigrammata* 17.2 Prato)

amicitia is again used multiply by Catullus as a line-ending, and only once by Propertius, but, as with *adulterium*, there is little to suggest that most of the later examples look back to Catullus[87] – or indeed to Propertius. Only Martial's hemistich *semper amicitiae* (3.36.8) might be a Propertian echo (of 1.22.2), but equally well both Propertius and Martial could be following Gallus here. Ovid seems to footnote one of his examples (*Ex Ponto* 4.13.44) as Gallan by combining *nomen* with *amicitiae*, and Martial twice writes *notus amicitia(e)* (4.67.2; 9.84.4) with similar intention. Of course, either or both of these combinations might itself be Gallan.

---

86 novit *Bücheler, Courtney*; non vult *codd.*
87 The unuseful exception is Ausonius, two of whose four endings in *amicitia* (*Epiced.* 22; *Prof.* 13.12) do have a Catullan flavour.

3.	hic timor est ipsis *durior* **exsequiis**	(Propertius 1.19.4)
	plebei parvae <u>funeris</u> **exsequiae**	(Propertius 2.13.24)
	nec qui det maestas munus in **exsequias**	(Tibullus 2.4.44)
	Dareique docent <u>funeris</u> **exsequiae**	(Ovid *Tristia* 3.5.40)[88]

exsequiae has no Catullan antecedent; and its distribution as a pentameter ending over all three surviving Roman elegists, and the absence of contextual links between their uses of it, are in themselves good indications of a Gallan origin. The fact that Ovid repeated the entire Propertian phrase *funeris exsequiae* might suggest that he had Propertius' line in mind, but equally it might indicate that this phrase goes back in its entirety to Gallus. There is some confirmation of this: the author of the *Consolatio ad Liviam*, who definitely knew his Gallus,[89] employed the same combination, although with variations in case, order, and line position, twice in pentameters:

<u>funeris</u> **exsequiis** adsumus omnis eques	(460)
et sensi **exsequias** <u>funeris</u> ipse mei	(202)

Ovid's complete avoidance of polysyllabic pentameter endings in his earlier works, and his increased tolerance of them in his later works, have already been mentioned, and the change has been explained, not as one of taste on the part of the poet or his audience, but in the main as a result of Ovid's self-identification with Gallus. The analytic listing (below) of the polysyllables Ovid used at the end of pentameters in his different works may help to solidify this and other hypotheses so far offered about the history and the significance of these line-endings. In the table an asterisk means that the word is unparalleled in this position in Latin elegiac writings up to and including Martial. Where such parallels exist they are noted after the key term; they may be different grammatical forms of it. Where an unparalleled polysyllabic pentameter ending is a virtual synonym of another, paralleled, polysyllabic ending, the latter is added. In the third column the number in brackets following 'Ov.' indicates how often the word appears in Ovid in this position.

---

88   The late elegist Maximianus may have recognized this as a typical elegiac pentameter line-ending when he wrote: *me velut expletis deserit exsequiis* (5.154).
89   See below, pp. 434–6, 439.

Polysyllabic pentameter endings in Ovid

Fasti (2)

5.582	fluminibus	[Senec.] *Epigr.* 2.4 Prato
6.660	funeribus*	

Heroides (3)

16.290	pudicitiae	Prop. 1.2.24; 1.15.20; 1.16.2; 4.5.28; Mart. 6.7.2; 6.27.4
17.16	superciliis	Cat. 67.46; Mart.1.4.2; 1.24.2; 9.37.6; 9.79.2; *Carm. Priap.* 1.2; 49.4 Bücheler; [Senec.] *Epigr.* 39.2 Prato; *Copa* 34
19.202	deseruit*	

Tristia 1 (3)

1.3.6	Ausoniae	Prop. 2.33.4
1.4.20	Italia*	(=Ausonia?)
1.10.34	Cyaneas*	(=Symplegades?)

Tristia 2 (6)

2.212	adulterii	Cat. 67.36; 78.6; 113.4; Prop. 2.29.38; Vers. Pop. fr. 7.4 Courtney; Ov. (3); Mart. 1.90.10
2.232	imperii	Prop. 1.6.34; Ov. (3); Mart. 6.61.4
2.294	Eric<h>thonium	Prop. 2.6.4; Ov. (2)
2.416	historiae	Gallus fr. 2.3 Courtney; Prop. 1.15.24; 2.1.16; 3.4.10; 3.20.28; 3.22.20; *Catalept.* 11.6; Mart. 14.191.2; Sulpic. *Epigr.* ap. *VSD* 38 l.4
2.430	adulterium est	see *Tr.* 2.212
2.514	adulteria	see *Tr.* 2.212

Tristia 3 (3)

3.5.40	ex<s>equiae	Prop. 1.19.4; 2.13.24; Tib. 2.4.44
3.9.2	barbariae	Ov. (2)
3.10.4	barbaria	see *Tr.* 3.9.2

Tristia 4 (2)

4.5.24	amicitiae	Cat. 77.6; 96.4; 100.6; 109.6 (cf. Lucr. *DRN* 3.83); Prop. 1.22.2; Domit. Mars. fr. 1.6 Courtney; Ov. (3); Mart. 3.36.8; 4.67.2; 5.19.8; 9.14.2; 9.84.4; 9.99.6; 10.13.4; 10.44.10; 11.44.2; [Senec.] *Epigr.* 17.2 Prato
4.10.2	posteritas*	

Tristia 5 (1)

5.6.30	obsequium	Prop. 1.8.40

Ibis (2)

506	Berecyntiades*	
518	historiae	see *Tr.* 2.416

Ex Ponto 1 (1)

1.2.68	patrocinium*	

Ex Ponto 2 (7)

2.2.6	perlegere*	
2.2.70	imperium	see *Tr.* 2.232
2.2.76	Dalmatiae*	(= Illyria?)
2.3.18	articulis	Cat. 99.8 (cf. Lucr. *DRN* 3.697); Prop. 2.34.80
2.5.26	ingenium	Prop. 1.7.22; 2.30.40; 2.34.58 (cf. Lucr. *DRN* 3.745; 5.1111); Ov. (3); *Catalept.* [16].2; Mart. *Sp.* 14.4; *Sp.* 20.4; 3.26.4; 5.63.4
2.9.20	Erichthonius	see *Tr.* 2.294
2.9.42	Alcinoi	Ov. (2)

Ex Ponto 3 (1)

3.1.166	aspiciant*	(last word of poem – cf. aspiceret, [Senec.] *Epigr.* 15.6 Prato)

Ex Ponto 4 (16)

4.2.10	Alcinoo	see *EP* 2.9.42
4.3.12	amicitia	see *Tr.* 4.5.24
4.3.54	Anticyra*	
4.5.24	officio	Cat. 68.12; 68.42; 68.152; Prop. 2.18.14
4.6.6	alterius	Cat. 78.2
4.6.14	auxilium	Cat. 68.66; Prop. 1.1.26; Tib. 1.8.24; Ov. (2)
4.8.62	Oechalia*	(=Thessalia?)
4.9.48	utilitas*	
4.9.80	Danuvium*	
4.13.28	imperii	see *Tr.* 2.232
4.13.44	amicitiae	see *Tr.* 4.5.24
4.13.46	ingeniis	see *EP* 2.5.26
4.14.4	invenies	Cat. 89.6; Prop. 1.4.28; Mart. 8.31.6
4.14.18	ingenio	see *EP* 2.5.26
4.14.56	imposuit	Mart. 4.40.10; 5.36.2
4.15.26	auxilium	see *EP* 4.6.14

Jost Benedum was aware of the known antecedents and Nachleben of Ovid's polysyllabic pentameter endings.[90] His demonstration that Ovid, and in some cases Propertius, could, without altering the words of a line, have avoided polysyllabic endings in a number of instances by reordering them[91] is especially valuable since it confirms that these endings are the result of free choice on the poet's part. When it comes to explaining why in each particular instance Ovid made that choice, Benedum is perhaps overall less felicitous, but again he makes good remarks about the finality and closure which such endings can confer,

---

90 Benedum (1967) 129–186. To his useful collection (137–8) of 3 sing. perf. ind. act. polysyllabic pentameter endings in -*uit*, add two Catullan examples: *lux autem canae Tethyi restituit* (66.70); *quae sese toto corpore prostituit* (110.8).

91 Benedum (1967) 139–41.

and he notes instances where they occur in the last line of a poem.[92] Observations of this type have been made earlier in this chapter and they will recur in the discussion of 'significant locations' in Chapter 6. Many of Benedum's comments on individual polysyllabic endings are also worthy of respect. At no point, however, does Benedum raise the possibility of general Gallan influence.

92   Benedum (1967) 134–6.

CHAPTER 6

Gallan Metrics II

TRISYLLABIC PENTAMETER ENDINGS

This chapter begins by directing attention towards the trisyllabic pentameter endings of Roman elegy. The aim of the enquiry is to try to determine whether, and if so to what extent, these endings can contribute towards revealing Gallus' influence on his elegiac successors, and on Propertius in particular. Both positive and negative indications emerge from the material. As it turns out, the trisyllabic endings are, for a number of reasons which will emerge below, much less impressive as pointers to Gallus than are the polysyllabic endings. Nevertheless, they can, particularly in combination with the latter and with other indications of Gallus' presence, make useful contributions to the overall project.

Benedum offered statistics for trisyllabic pentameter endings in Roman elegy down to and including the *Corpus Tibullianum.*[1] I have combined these with the figures for pentameters in Tibullus and Propertius which terminate in *-ibus* to form the table overleaf. The totals of trisyllabic endings in the different poets, the proportions of their *-ibus* endings, and the distribution, both of trisyllables and of *-ibus* endings, over the four books of Propertius, are all more or less in line with the statistics for polysyllabic pentameter endings. But there are many fewer trisyllabic than polysyllabic pentameter endings in Roman elegy. Catullus has the highest proportion (83 trisyllabic as against 113 polysyllabic), but with Propertius the figure is much lower, i.e. 49 trisyllabic and 172 polysyllabic endings.

---

1 Benedum (1967) 190. Platnauer (1951) 15–16 also dealt with this phenomenon, but Platnauer's practice of regarding prepositions and conjunctions as part of the succeeding word led him to conclude that Ovid used only three such endings, all in *Ex Ponto*. Benedum reports no trisyllabic endings in *Heroides, Fasti, Ibis,* or *Tristia.*

Table I: Trisyllabic Pentameter Endings

Poet/Work	All trisyllabic pentameter endings	All ending in -ibus	% ending in -ibus
Catullus	83	0	
Tibullus 1	12	3	25.00%
Tibullus 2	10	4	40.00%
[Tib.] Lygdamus	3	0	
Sulpicia	2	0	
Propertius 1	32	12	37.50%
Propertius 2	16	2	12.50%
Propertius 3	1	0	
Propertius 4	0	0	
Ovid *Ex Ponto*	5	0	

The paucity of trisyllabic endings in Propertius is the first reason why they are less useful than polysyllabic endings in helping to determine external influence upon him. Another negative factor is that a number of his trisyllabic endings are unparalleled in this position in Roman poetry, e.g. *sociis* (1.6.20), *opere* (1.14.2), *chalybe* (1.16.30), *Zephyro* (1.16.34), *gradibus* (1.16.42), *umero* (1.20.44), *calice* (2.33.40), *laqueis* (2.34.48) and *Helena* (2.34.88). Other Propertian trisyllabic pentameter endings are paralleled only once, e.g. *melius* (1.2.10, cf. Martial 4.83.2), *pueri* (1.3.10, cf. Papinius? Pomponius? fr. 1.2 Courtney: *puerum*), *cubitum* (1.3.34, cf. Martial 3.63.10: *cubiti*), *calamo* (2.19.24, cf. Apuleius fr. 4.12 Courtney); and little can be said in most such cases either. The same sometimes applies when there is a unique parallel in Propertius' own work, e.g. *thalamo* (1.15.18 and 2.15.14). However, unparalleled *animo* at Propertius 1.20.2 is perhaps more hopeful: elegy 1.20 is addressed to Gallus, Gallus appears in the vocative in line 1, *animo* is conspicuous at the end of the first couplet, and the term has Gallan credentials on other grounds (see Index II s.v. *animus*). But, although *Venere* at Propertius 1.14.16 and Tibullus 1.10.66[2] could point to a predecessor, it could be the product of coincidence since the lines have little else in common.

However, when there is a multiplicity of Propertian examples and/or external parallels, the situation is more encouraging. This is a not infrequent situation since six terms, all externally paralleled,

2   *nulla mihi tristi praemia sint Venere* (Prop. 1.14.16); *is gerat et miti sit procul a Venere* (Tib. 1.10.66).

constitute 22 (44.8%) of the 49 Propertian trisyllabic pentameter endings: they are *manibus* (8), *lacrimis* (5), *foribus* (3), *pedibus* (2), *tunica/is* (2) and *dominam/ae* (2). Of these three – *lacrimis*,[3] *tunica/is*[4] and *dominam/ae*[5] – have a Catullan pedigree, but, as will emerge when they are considered in detail, the resemblances between the relevant Catullan and Propertian lines and their contexts are, apart from the actual line-endings, very limited. This, together with the fact that the other two commonest endings, including the most frequent in Propertian elegy (*manibus*), have no Catullan antecedent, suggests an alternative source for the entire group.[6] That source may have been fascinated with the idea of using trisyllabic endings to refer to body parts, since in addition to *manibus* (8 times in Propertius, never in Tibullus) and *pedibus* (twice in Propertius, three times in Tibullus), we find *umero* (Propertius 1.20.44), *latere* (three times in Tibullus) and *capite/i* (twice in Tibullus, but also twice in Catullus).[7]

The Propertian examples of *manibus* are:

Cynthia non certis nixa caput **manibus**	(1.3.8)
nunc furtiva cavis *poma* dabam **manibus**	(1.3.24)
Cynthia et insanis ora *notet* **manibus**	(1.6.16)
et flere iniectis, Galle, diu **manibus**	(1.13.16)
ut tibi suppositis exciderent **manibus**	(1.15.36)
pulsata indignis saepe queror **manibus**	(1.16.6)
debitaque occultis vota tuli **manibus**	(1.16.44)
sed quos ipse suis fecit Amor **manibus**	(2.29.18)

Propertius was clearly enchanted with the pentameter ending *manibus*, which must have some specific significance for him, and there are several indications, cumulatively persuasive, that it was originally a

---

3   But only in the diminutive form *lacrimulis* (Cat. 66.16).
4   Cat. 67.22; 68.134; 88.2; 95.8.
5   Cat. 68.68, 158.
6   Outwith Propertius *manibus* is paralleled as a pentameter ending only in *Catalept.* 14.6: *ornabo, et puris serta feram manibus*. It is perhaps an added measure of Propertius' liking for this ending that it is absent from Tibullus.
7   The elegists' interest in terminating pentameters with a body part also extends to dissyllabic endings: e.g. final *pede* is frequent in Tibullus and Ovid, although found only once in Catullus (68.70) and once in Propertius (2.4.4); final *pedem* and *latus* appear in all three Augustan elegists, and final *caput* and *manu* are common in all (*manum* less common).

Gallan ending. To begin with, all these Propertian lines except 2.29.18 come from the Monobiblos, where the influence of Cornelius Gallus was at its strongest – and 2.29 is a palpable reworking of 1.3,[8] in which there are two pentameters ending in *manibus*. Moreover, for what it is worth, all the Propertian lines have the same structure, with an adjective or participle agreeing with *manibus* standing before the main caesura. This is a common structure in Latin pentameters, and so cannot in itself be regarded as a pointer to Gallus in particular; but its omnipresence in this group could help to make the case that they share a common source or sources. Then there is a direct clue to a Gallan origin for the group when at 1.13.16 *manibus* ends a line addressing Gallus by name. Further indirect clues are Gallan *poma* (1.3.24) and *notet* (1.6.16).[9] Finally, all the elegies in which this ending occurs have other links to Gallus which are discussed elsewhere.[10]

The case of *pedibus*, with its two Propertian and three Tibullan examples, is in some ways similar:

et caput impositis pressit Amor **pedibus**	(Propertius 1.1.4)
laesus, et invitis ipse redit **pedibus**	(Propertius 2.25.20)
expressa incultis uva dedit **pedibus**	(Tibullus 1.7.36)
sera tamen *tacitis* Poena venit **pedibus**	(Tibullus 1.9.4)
abdita quae senis fata canit **pedibus**	(Tibullus 2.5.16)

These lines are even closer in structure: not only does an adjective/ participle in agreement with *pedibus* stand in each before the caesura, but each contains a dissyllabic 3 sing. ind. act. verb which in all but one case (1.1.4) immediately precedes *pedibus*. If the lines were being examined independently of the present discussion, it might provoke argument about the influence of Tibullus on Propertius, or vice-versa. But, given all the other indications which have emerged in this and earlier chapters, indebtedness to Gallus by both Tibullus and Propertius seems a likelier explanation, even though none of the lines, except Tibullus 1.9.4, contains an established signal of Gallan presence.[11]

---

8   Cf. Cairns (1977).
9   Similar clues accompany Propertius' uses of *lacrimis* (below) and *animo* (see below, pp. 224–5, 424–5).
10 See Index I.
11 It might be possible, however, to develop further arguments based on the adjectives/ participles attached to *manibus*.

In the group embodying *lacrimis*, the second most common tri-syllabic pentamer ending in Propertius, the same structure of pre-caesural adjective/participle in agreement with final noun is again visible, and all the Propertian lines are from the Monobiblos. But this group also sends out further signals of its Gallan origin, and that despite the simultaneous presence of two, albeit inexact, overlaps between Catullus and Propertius:

frustrantur falsis *gaudia* **lacrimulis**	(Catullus 66.16)
affueram vestris conscius <u>in</u> **lacrimis**	(Propertius 1.10.2)
non nihil aspersis *gaudet* Amor **lacrimis**	(Propertius 1.12.16)
surget et invitis spiritus <u>in</u> **lacrimis**	(Propertius 1.16.32)
lumina deiectis turpia sint **lacrimis**	(Propertius 1.18.16)
ne soror acta tuis sentiat <u>e</u> **lacrimis**	(Propertius 1.21.6)
si quis adest iussae prosiliunt **lacrimae**	(Martial 1.33.2)

The Catullan/Propertian overlaps come in *gaudia/gaudet* and *lacri-m<ul>is*. But against any notion that Propertius was looking to Catullus 66.16 for this ending stand two (or perhaps three) Gallan indications within the group. First, Propertius 1.10.2 is addressed to Gallus, and it is part of an elegy which, on other grounds, has been argued (above, pp. 116–17) to reflect Cornelius Gallus' descriptions of his love-making in his *Amores*; second, 1.18.16 comes from an elegy of almost certain Gallan derivation (pp. 119–20). The possible third indication is that 1.21.6 comes from the elegy in which another, dead, 'Gallus' speaks. Other signs of the presence of Cornelius Gallus in that elegy have been noted (pp. 87–9), but lack of evidence makes it impossible to connect the 'Gallus' of 1.21 with the poet Cornelius Gallus.[12]

The *foribus* group (again all the Propertian lines are from the Monobiblos) does not contain as many pointers to Gallus, but it exemplifies the interpretative principle noted above in connection with the Tibullan and Propertian lines ending in *pedibus*:

alterius <u>clausis</u> expulit e **foribus**?	(Propertius 1.3.36)
quid mihi tam *duris* <u>clausa</u> *taces* **foribus**?	(Propertius 1.16.18)

---

12   For earlier discussion of the 'Gallus' of 1.21 see above, pp. 49–50 and nn. 56, 58.

quae solum *tacitis* cognita sunt **foribus**?   (Propertius 1.18.24)

frustra <u>clavis</u> inest **foribus**   (Tibullus 1.6.34)

Here the balance is reversed, with three of the lines being Propertian and only one Tibullan; but the temptation to think that Tibullus took the ending *foribus* from Propertius should be resisted. The Propertian lines all have the same structure, they all conclude questions, and they all clearly derive from a source which was interrogative, and in which the concepts of exclusion (*clausis expulit/duris clausa*) and silence or unresponsiveness (*taces/tacitis*) accompanied *foribus*, as both concepts do in Propertius 1.16.18. In his other two exploitations of that source Propertius has 'distributed' these two concepts, allocating *clausis expulit* to 1.3.36 and *tacitis* to 1.18.24, which comes from an elegy well established as Gallan (above, pp. 119–20); analogous 'distribution' can be seen in the indubitably Gallan *historia* complex. Moreover, two of the Propertian lines ending in *foribus* come from *komoi* (1.3 and 1.16), already suspected of derivation from one or more Gallan examples of the genre.[13] Tibullus' line does not correspond in structure with the Propertian lines, and it might appear to exemplify neither of the accompanying concepts hypothesized for Propertius' source. But this appearance is deceptive: Tibullus' *clavis* must be intended to invoke *claudo* etymologically. Cf.:[14]

<u>clavis</u> dicta quod <u>claudat</u> et aperiat (Isidore *Origines* 20.13.5)

<u>clausum</u> a claustris et <u>clavibus</u> dicitur (Isidore *Differentiarum Appendix* 158)

<u>clam</u> a <u>clavibus</u> dictum, quod his, quae celare volumus, <u>claudimus</u> (Paulus Festus 66)

<u>claudere</u> et <u>clavis</u> ex Graeco descendit (Paulus Festus 56)

con<u>clavia</u> dicuntur loca, quae una <u>clave</u> <u>clauduntur</u> (Paulus Festus 38)

con<u>clave</u> est separatior locus in interioribus tectis, vel quod intra eum multa loca <u>clausa</u> sint ut cubicula adhaerentia triclinio (Donatus ad Terence *Eunuchus* 583)

That Tibullus had the same source as Propertius is shown by three phrases which he employed elsewhere: (1) *tacito clam venit illa pede*

---

13   Cf. above, pp. 113 and nn. 31 and 33, 118–19.
14   Cf. *LALE* s.vv. clam; clavis; claudo; conclave, from which these texts are assembled.

(1.10.34 – of death), where *clam* is accompanied by *tacito* – cf. *taces* and *tacitis* above; (2) *clam taciturna manus,/ haec foribusque* (1.6.60–1 – a more indirect allusion); and (3) *et strepitu nullo clam reserare fores* (1.8.60), where *reserare* is the antonym of *claudere*. The latter two passages, in which *taciturna* and *strepitu nullo* are prominent and in which *foribus/fores* reappear, are, like Tibullus 1.6.34, found in komastic contexts reminiscent of Propertius 1.16; they too may be indebted to the same hypothesized Gallan model (above and n. 13). In view of the prominence of *manibus* and *pedibus* in earlier discussion it is also worth remarking on the *taciturna manus* of 1.6.60 and the *tacito ... pede* of 1.10.34, where *manus* and *pes* again provide (this time dissyllabic) pentameter line-endings.

The final two repeated trisyllabic pentameter endings of Propertius (*dominam/ae* and *tunica/is*) are each interesting in a different way. *domina*, as the Qaṣr Ibrîm papyrus revealed, was used by Gallus of his mistress Lycoris (fr. 2.7 Courtney); there it is found at the end of the first hemistich of a pentameter. However, *dominus/a* appears often in Roman elegiacs at the ends of pentameters:

isque d̲o̲m̲u̲m̲ nobis isque dedit **dominam**	(Catullus 68.68)
et d̲o̲m̲u̲s̲ <ipsa> in qua lusimus et **domina**	(Catullus 68.156)
atque aliquid *duram quaerimus* in **dominam**	(Propertius 1.7.6)[15]
ut promissa suae verba ferat **dominae**?	(Propertius 2.23.4)
nec fugiam *notae* s̲e̲r̲v̲i̲t̲i̲u̲m̲ **dominae**	([Tibullus] 3.19.22)
deliciae populi, quae fuerant **domini**	(Martial *Spectacula* 2.12)
vendidit ancillam, nunc redimit **dominam**	(Martial 6.71.6)
par d̲o̲m̲u̲s̲ est caelo sed minor est **domino**	(Martial 8.36.12)
tot **dominos**, at tu, Condyle, nec **dominum**	(Martial 9.92.6)
umbellam luscae, Lygde, feras **dominae**	(Martial 11.73.6)
non arsit pariter quod d̲o̲m̲u̲s̲ et **dominus**!	(Martial 11.93.4)

Martial 8.36.12 and 11.93.4 imitate Catullus' twice repeated combination of *domus* and *domina* (substituting *dominus* for *domina*), but there is nothing to connect any of the other lines with those of

---

15   The hexameter (1.7.5) ends in *amores*, which, if not a coincidence, possibly alludes to Gallus' title, on which see below, pp. 230–2.

Catullus. In [Tibullus] 3.19.22 'Lygdamus' employs Gallan *notae*, perhaps to draw attention to his imitation of a lost Gallan use of *domina* at a pentameter end; and his emphasis on *servitium* may also be Gallan, since it links his line with the hexameter <u>*ingenuus*</u> *quisquam alterius dat munera <u>servo</u>* (Propertius 2.23.3), which immediately precedes one of Propertius' two examples of *domina* at pentameter ending (2.23.4). Finally in Propertius 1.7.6 the adjective *duram* calls to mind the *mollis/durus* etymology which has been associated with Gallus. The evidence is not strong, but Gallus' attested use of *domina*, along with the pattern visible in these pentameter line-endings, make it possible that Gallus also ended a now lost pentameter with *domina*, and that it contributed to what we see in his successors.

The range of *tunica/is* as a pentameter ending is more restricted:

numquam se mediam sustulit ad **tunicam**	(Catullus 67.22)
fulgebat *crocina* candidus in **tunica**.	(Catullus 68.134)
prurit et <u>abiectis</u> peruigilat **tunicis**?	(Catullus 88.2)
et laxas scombris saepe dabunt **tunicas**	(Catullus 95.8)
visa, neque *ostrina* cum fuit in **tunica**	(Propertius 2.29.26)
mundus <u>demissis</u> institor in **tunicis**	(Propertius 4.2.38)
et dedit: ille pedem sustulit, hic **tunicam**	(Martial 10.81.4)
pedicant miserae, Lesbia, te **tunicae**	(Martial 11.99.2)

Again it is Martial who returns to the influence of Catullus, three of whose four examples are also obscene/abusive. Propertius seems remote from that ethos, although he is close to Catullus 68.134 in his *ostrina=crocina* and *demissis=abiectis*. It might therefore be supposed that at 2.29.26 Propertius is alluding directly to Catullus and is transferring to Cynthia the ornate *tunica* which belonged to Cupido in the Catullan line. But 2.29 is Propertius' reprise of his own 1.3 with its heavily Gallan input;[16] so some intermediacy of Gallus must remain a suspicion. As for Propertius 4.2.38, although Vertumnus has marginal racy characteristics, he rates high approval from Propertius, and so is quite unlike Catullus 88's Gellius, for whom Catullus consistently evinces hatred and contempt; hence direct imitation of Catullus by Propertius again seems questionable.

16 Cf. also above, pp. 113, 138, 186–7, and below, p. 197.

Examination of two repeated Tibullan trisyllabic endings exemplified in Catullus but not re-used by Propertius produces an even more uncertain outcome:

suscitat a *cano* volturium **capiti**	(Catullus 68.124)
non si demisso se ipse voret **capite**	(Catullus 88.8)
dicere nec *cano* blanditias **capite**	(Tibullus 1.1.72)
plena coronato stare boues **capite**	(Tibullus 2.1.8)[17]

All these lines have in common the ending *capiti/e* and the balancing pre-caesural adjectives/participles; and two of them (Catullus 68.124 and Tibullus 1.1.72) also share *cano*. While Tibullus would obviously not have wished to evoke the obscene associations and context of Catullus 88.8, Catullus 68.124 does look like an attractive model for Tibullus 1.1.72, particularly since old men are the subject in both cases. But again, Tibullus 2.1.8 seems unconnected with either Catullan line. The choice, then, is to see Tibullus as looking directly to Catullus for one, but only one, of his lines, or to postulate an intermediary; and there is little comfort in either choice. The same uncertainty emerges from Tibullus' unparalleled triple use of *latere* in final pentameter position.

primus et i̱ṉ tenero *fixus* erit **latere**.	(Tibullus 1.5.62)
haesura i̱ṉ nostro t̲e̲l̲a̲ gerit **latere**.	(Tibullus 1.10.14)
cantat, et a̱ pulso t̲e̲l̲a̲ sonat **latere**.	(Tibullus 2.1.66)

Here there is no Catullan line to serve as a possible model; yet it would be hard to suppose that Tibullus lacked a model, and simply conceived an unmotivated affection for *latere* in this *sedes*. Rather the relative paucity of trisyllabic pentameter endings in Tibullus argues that he had special allusive reasons for those few he chose to employ. Moreover, the Tibullan lines ending in *latere* have other significant elements in common apart from their generally similar shape: two share *tela*, two have the phrase *in ... latere*, two exhibit the concept of

---

17   Since the *De rosis nascentibus* of the *Appendix Vergiliana* belongs to a much later period, *mucronem absoluens purpurei capitis* (28) is irrelevant.

'being fixed'/'clinging to' and one has Gallan *tener*. So it seems probable that Tibullus had a model or models for them in Gallus, although there is little hint of Gallus in these lines or in their contexts. Ovid may have avoided trisyllabic pentameter endings in his early works in part because those terminating the pentameters of Propertius and Tibullus often end in *-ibus*;[18] his avoidance would thus have helped him to steer clear of this shape. As for Ovid's later works, the few trisyllabic endings admitted in them help little towards reconstructing the history of this practice since not many parallels can be found for them. *scelus est* (*Ex Ponto* 1.6.27), *liceat* (*Ex Ponto* 1.8.40), and *tegeret* (*Ex Ponto* 4.9.26) are unparalleled as pentameter endings; *recitent* (*Ex Ponto* 3.5.40) can only be compared with Martial 2.88.2: *recites*, and 3.18.2: *recitas*; and there are four unimpressive parallels for *videor* (*Ex Ponto* 3.6.46), viz: Porcius Licinus fr. 7.4 Courtney (*video*); Martial 2.38.2 (*video*); [Seneca] *Epigrammata* 25.10 Prato; 42.2 Prato (both *videor*). Nothing in the contexts of the parallels to *recitent* and *videor* suggests that any of his successors had Ovid or any predecessor of Ovid particularly in mind, and with most of Ovid's trisyllabic pentameter endings there is a marked absence of Catullan antecedents. This leaves open the possibility that Ovid could have found them in Gallus, but he could have invented them himself or looked for them outside the elegiac tradition which began with Catullus. However, *liceat* (*Ex Ponto* 1.8.40) might be Gallan (see Index II s.v. *licet*), as might be *faciet* (*Ex Ponto* 1.1.66): Catullus 68.50 has *faciat* in this position, Catullus 75.4 and 81.6 end in *facias*, and Catullus 74.2 ends in *faceret*. A pseudo-Senecan epigram provides another parallel (*faciam*, 25.2) and Martial seven.[19] The distribution of parallels for Ovid's *faciet* is thus similar to other distributions which earlier pointed to Gallus, and, for what it is worth, we know that Gallus featured *fecerunt* (fr. 2.6 Courtney). All in all, then, despite the uncertainties which surround most of Ovid's trisyllabic pentameter endings, some progress has been made with the trisyllable pentameter endings of Propertius and Tibullus: these two elegists admit a much smaller proportion of such endings than did Catullus, they tend to repeat endings, and, although the contexts of some of their endings overlap partially with those of their Catullan predecessors, most do not. Hence the impact on them of an intermediary may be hypothesized,

---

18   For a discussion of the history of polysyllabic line-endings in *-ibus*, see above, pp. 173–6.
19   *facio* (10.25.6; 10.64.6); *facies* (12.86.2); *facias* (3.71.2; 4.40.8; 11.55.4); *facient* (2.16.2). Martial also places *facies/em* = 'face' in this position.

and, although his visibility is sometimes poor, it is hard to think of a good overall candidate other than Gallus.

POSITIONING AND CLUSTERING

The supposition that Gallus provided most of the inspiration for Propertius' polysyllabic and (more doubtfully) trisyllabic pentameter endings finds confirmation in the locations and numbers of these endings within particular elegies. The 98 polysyllabic and 32 trisyllabic pentameter endings of the Monobiblos are not evenly distributed throughout the text. Because there are more polysyllables than trisyllables, the unevenness shows up more clearly when the spotlight is placed on polysyllables: poems 15 (12), 16 (11) and 20 (11) together contain 34 (i.e. 35%) of the 98 polysyllables in Book 1. The same pattern is visible in Book 2, with its 58 polysyllabic and 16 trisyllabic endings: here the smaller numbers involved produce an even more impressive statistic, with only two elegies – 2.1 (7) and 2.34 (11) – between them accounting for 18 (i.e. 31%) of the book's polysyllables.[20] The unevenness in distribution also extends to clustering within individual elegies: in 2.34, for example, all but three of the eleven polysyllabic endings congregate within lines 58–80. These concentrations of course relate, but only in part, to the subject-matter of the lines involved.

More widespread is the placement by Propertius of polysyllabic endings at intrinsically significant locations within an elegy. Propertius' fondness for a polysyllable at one such location, the end of an elegy, has been observed, and it has been suggested that he placed them there because the weight of a polysyllabic ending gives the last couplet closural force.[21] No less than 8 of the 22 elegies of the Monobiblos end in this way (1.2; 1.4; 1.8; 1.14; 1.15; 1.16; 1.17; 1.22); and since 1.22 is the final elegy of the Monobiblos, the entire book terminates with a polysyllable (*uberibus*). On the traditional poem divisions Book 2 has fewer (3) elegies ending in a polysyllable (2.20; 2.30; 2.32) – 2.18 ends with a trisyllable; and Book 3 has only

20   This should perhaps be borne in mind in discussions of whether Book 2 is really one or two books.
21   See Benedum (1967) 135–6, listing elegiacs of Catullus, various epigrams, Tib. 1.4, Ov. *EP* 3.1, and Propertian elegies with polysyllables as their final word. He also notes the final trisyllable of Prop. 2.18.

one elegy terminating in a polysyllable (3.11), a decline consistent with the overall reduction in numbers of polysyllabic endings from Books 1 to 3. The air of finality given to the last couplet of an elegy by a polysyllabic ending is undeniable; but it is also worth considering whether such an ending might also be functioning as a 'footnote' implicitly acknowledging the influence of a predecessor on the elegy which it closes. This view gains support from the presence of Gallus, arguable on other grounds, in some of the elegies ending in a poly-syllable discussed above, and it is strengthened in particular by the certainty of Gallus' presence in 1.8.

The ultimate position in an elegy is, however, by no means the only significant location for polysyllabic (and trisyllabic) pentameter endings. Another is the close of the first couplet of an elegy. The pro-logue of the Monobiblos (1.1) employs the quinquesyllabic *cupidi-nibus* in that location (1.1.2). If 5–syllable endings are particularly indicative of Gallan influence, that could explain its choice for first position, not only in the first elegy but in the entire Monobiblos.[22] The same phenomenon is found at 1.3.2 (*litoribus*), 1.7.2 (*militiae*), 1.8.2 (*Illyria*), 1.11.2 (again *litoribus*), 1.15.2 (*perfidia*), 1.16.2 (*pudicitiae*), 1.17.2 (*alcyonas*), 1.21.2 (*aggeribus*) and 1.22.2, the final elegy of the Monobiblos (*amicitia*). Thus 10 out of the 22 elegies of Book 1 seize the first possible opportunity to present a polysyllabic pentameter ending; and *amicitia,* the final example in the Monobiblos, is, like the first, quinquesyllabic. Three later elegies, two in Book 2 and one in Book 3, also end their first couplet with a polysyllable – (2.5.2 with the indubitably Gallan *nequitia*, 2.20.2 with *Andromacha*, and 3.14.2 with *gymnasii*), a decline in numbers parallel to that of polysyllabic final words of elegies. A polysyllabic pentameter ending placed in the first available position in an elegy might plausibly be thought to have annunciatory intent, and to mark the elegy which it introduces as indebted to Gallus. Where both first and ultimate positions are occupied by a polysyllable, this could be seen as double emphasis: out of the 13 elegies with their first couplet terminating in a polysyllable, six (1.8; 1.15; 1.16; 1.17; 1.22; 2.20) also have one at the end of their final couplet.

The second available position in an elegy (i.e. the fourth line) also

---

22   The first four lines of the Monobiblos render the first two couplets of an epigram of Meleager (*AP* 12.101.1–4). Propertius' impulse to acknowledge his debt to Gallus may therefore have been all the stronger, particularly if Gallus had not rendered Meleager in his Milanion elegy.

seems to have been significant in Propertius' eyes when it came to positioning polysyllabic pentameter endings. This is probably because his elegies often fall easily into quatrains, as those of Gallus perhaps did;[23] and quatrains seem to have constituted for Propertius a standard unit of meaning. Propertius places a polysyllable in second position in 11 elegies of the Monobiblos: 1.2†, 1.3*, 1.4†, 1.6, 1.7*, 1.11*,[24] 1.16*†, 1.19, 1.20, 1.21*, 1.22*†, and in 4 elegies of Book 2: 2.6, 2.14, 2.32† and 2.33 (those asterisked also have a polysyllable in first position, and those daggered a polysyllable as their final word).

The third possible position for a polysyllabic pentameter ending, i.e. line 6, might *a priori* seem likely to have no more significance than any other internal location. But in fact third position is used more frequently than any other in the Monobiblos except first and last – 7 times (1.1*, 1.3*%, 1.4%†, 1.5, 1.14†, 1.15*† and 1.18), but nowhere in the later books. It sometimes (as marked) accompanies other significant locations, i.e. first position (*), second position (%) or ultimate position (†). Propertius may have regarded this location as significant because, although his elegies often fall into quatrains, he sometimes employs a verse-paragraph of six lines. That is not to say, however, that Propertius places a polysyllabic pentameter ending in third position only when a unit of sense concludes there.

The final sections of elegies display phenomena similar to those found at their beginnings: an antepenultimate or/and penultimate couplet may end in a polysyllable, whether or not the final couplet also does. These locations are again used more frequently than others within the body of an elegy. The significance of a polysyllabic ending to a penultimate couplet can probably be admitted more easily, whereas greater doubt may attach to the importance of such endings in antepenultimate couplets. Three elegies of the Monobiblos (1.7, 1.9 and 1.15) present polysyllables at the end of antepenultimate couplets. In 1.7 and 1.15 they are accompanied by at least two other such endings in significant locations within the elegy (see below, pp. 203, 207–9). Polysyllabic *blanditias* ending 1.9.30 in antepenultimate position is the sole pentameter ending in 1.9 longer than a dissyllable, but 1.9 is

---

23   The modern scholarly debate about whether the Qaṣr Ibrîm fragments of Gallus are part of a single elegy or consist of 4-line epigrams is unresolved. If, as I believe (see below, pp. 410–12), the fragments come from a single elegy, Gallus too could sometimes have organized his material in quatrains.

24   Prop. 1.12.4 ends in a polysyllable, but is excluded from consideration because 1.12 very probably continues 1.11; cf. Butrica (1996a).

an attractive candidate for Gallan status because of its erotodidactic content,[25] and the isolated use in it of *blanditias* must be due to some special import that the term possessed. *blanditiae* appears six times in Propertian elegy (but never in Catullus), and, of these six appearances, three are at pentameter endings – in two of which *blanditiae* are 'unsafe'/'to be shunned':

> quisquis es, assiduas aufuge **blanditias** $(1.9.30)^{26}$
>
> o nullis tutum credere **blanditiis**   (ending the elegy – 1.15.42)
>
> arguta referens carmina **blanditia** $(1.16.16)^{27}$

Of the three elegies which contain these lines, 1.15 and 1.16 are in general replete with metrical and other indications of Gallan influence (below, pp. 207–10). *blanditiae* also crop up four times in Tibullus, although not at pentameter endings,[28] and no fewer than twenty times in Ovid's elegiac works. Clearly the term was absolutely expressive of the elegiac ethos: cf. esp. Ovid *Amores* 2.1.21: *blanditias elegosque levis, mea tela, resumpsi.* Virgil never uses it,[29] and Lucretius only once (*De Rerum Natura* 5.1018). It is almost unthinkable that this distribution could have come about if Gallus was not the vector for this term.

A similar verdict can be reached on the basis of evidence presented earlier (pp. 177–8) which indicated that the quinquesyllabic ending of 2.29.38 (*adulterio*) is likely to derive from a Gallan line, and elegy 2.29 is on other grounds too highly suggestive of Gallus.[30] Quadrisyllabic *accubuit* (2.30.36) closes the penultimate couplet of 2.30, which details the parentage of that Gallan hero, Orpheus; and, since much of 2.30 can be linked on other grounds with Gallus (above, pp. 128–31), and since its ultimate position is occupied by quadrisyllabic *ingenium* (40) – a Gallan term[31] acting as a source-citation – *accubuit* too seems likely to be directly inspired by Gallus (above, p. 130 n. 91). The fact that in 2.30 the entire penultimate couplet so

---

25   On possible Gallan *erotodidaxis* see above, pp. 116–18.
26   On the unacceptability of the emendation *a fuge* often printed here see Kershaw (1980) 71. On the reasons why elegies of Gallan inspiration may sometimes be conspicuously lacking in polysyllabic endings see below, pp. 216–18.
27   The other Propertian examples are: 2.19.4; 3.13.33; 4.6.72.
28   1.1.72; 1.2.91; 1.4.71; 1.9.77.
29   Although Ovid (characteristically) imports it into his *Metamorphoses* (9 occurrences).
30   *Inter alia* since it is a reprise of the theme of 1.3, on which see above, p. 191 and n. 16.
31   Cf. above, pp. 162, 168–70.

clearly points to Gallus also strengthens the case for believing that antepenultimate position in general is significant.

ephemeridas, another Propertian antepenultimate polysyllabic ending unparalleled as such, presents a more complex problem:

> me miserum, his aliquis rationem scribit *avarus*
> et ponit *duras* inter **ephemeridas**   (Propertius 3.23.19–20)

This is because *inter ephemeridas* also crops up at the beginning of an Ovidian couplet, *Amores* 1.12.24–5:

> inter **ephemeridas** melius tabulasque iacerent,
> in quibus absumptas *fleret avarus* opes

Ovid quite certainly had the Propertian antecedent in mind: in 3.22 Propertius was bewailing the loss of his *tabellae* (1, 11), cf. Ovid's *tabulasque*; and, apart from the presence of *inter ephemeridas* in the two couplets, an *avarus* is prominent in both poets' imaginary scenarios, and *ponit* and *iacerent* are conceptually related. Moreover *duro* appears in the Ovidian line (23) which precedes this couplet, cf. Propertius' *duras*. But does Ovid, who would of course have known if something in Gallus' poetry lies behind Propertius' couplet, provide any clue pointing to Gallus? The only known Gallan pointers are the Propertian *fleret* and the Propertian and Ovidian *duras/duro,* so we have to rely on earlier arguments that these were Gallan features, together with the general notion that antepenultimate position often carries a literary implication. It may be that the omnipresence of ring-composition, both verbal and conceptual, in Propertian elegy gave added significance to this position (as, of course, to the penultimate and ultimate positions) since ring-structures may align these with third, second and first positions.

We are on firmer ground when hypothesizing hints of Gallus in some polysyllables at the end of certain Propertian penultimate couplets. There are five examples of this feature in the Monobiblos: in 1.6, 1.12,[32] 1.14, 1.15, and 1.16; and in each case there are other proximate polysyllables to provide confirmation. The four Propertian examples of this feature from later books lack the company of other polysyllables, and two of them have no known Gallan reference:

---

32   With the traditional poem divisions this occurs also in Prop. 1.11, but see above, p. 196 n. 24.

2.2.14 (*verticibus*) and 2.31.14 (*Tantalidos*), both unique in this location. On the other hand 2.7.18 (*Borysthenidas*) is close to Gallus' known Caucasus interest, and Ovid *Ex Ponto* 4.10.45–60 offers further confirmation. This passage describes the rivers flowing into the Black Sea, and lines 53–4 list three of them, including *Borysthenio ... amne* (53). Then follows: *quique duas terras, Asiam Cadmique sororem,/ separat et cursus inter utramque facit* (55–6). This couplet is an unmistakable paraphrase of Gallus' surviving line about the river Hypanis: *uno tellures dividit amne duas* (fr. 1 Courtney).[33] *Borysthenidas*, then, can be regarded as securely Gallan, and indeed *qua* quinquesyllable as particularly indicative of Gallan influence. Over the final example, 3.20.28 (*historiae*), there can be no argument, since Gallus' own *historiae* and the entire *historia* complex cries out against scepticism.

Another feature of polysyllabic (and trisyllabic) pentameter endings in Propertius already noted is that not infrequently they come in clusters, and indeed sequences. These have particular value for this study, but an overall assessment of their role must be preceded by an investigation of their presence in individual elegies, particularly those of the Monobiblos, and of their relationships with the significant locations already discussed. Their patterns are highly varied. 1.1 has polysyllables in first (*cupidinibus*, 2 – a quinquesyllable) and third (*consilio*, 6) positions, and a trisyllable (*pedibus*, 4) in second position. There is thus an initial sequence of three non-dissyllables. Presumably it announces the Gallan content of the elegy, and so acts as a precursor of the Gallan Milanion exemplum. *Iasidos* (10) and *ingemuit* (14), both within the Milanion paradeigma, should allude directly to the language of Gallus' earlier treatment of it. Then the short sequence *carminibus* (24) and *auxilia* (26) most likely points to Gallan lines in which someone was 'leading' stars and streams. The very probable appearance in Gallus of Orpheus (and perhaps Hesiod) in such a role inevitably comes to mind.[34]

Elegy 1.2 has a polysyllable (*muneribus*, 4) in second position and another (*luxuriae*, 32) in ultimate position. The couplet 7–8, long recognized as Gallan (above, pp. 100–1), ends with quadrisyllabic

---

33 The line was influential, notably on Ovid: Knox (1985) 497 notes his echoes at *Her.* 19.142 and *EP* 4.10.55–6. Mariotti (1963) 613 n. 88 had already pointed to *Her.* 18.126 and 19.142. Knox also records the suggestion of Boucher (1966) 83–4 that Gallus' line appeared in his *propemptikon* for Lycoris.

34 Cf. above, pp. 121 n. 69, 124–5.

artificem, and there are other polysyllabic pointers to him: *litoribus* (18) stands in the midst of a set of three mythical paradeigmata, and the quinquesyllabic *pudicitia* (24, cf. above, pp. 102–3) ends Propertius' summing up of the import of those myths. Finally there are two trisyllablic endings, *melius* (10) and *tabulis* (22). The influence of Gallus can be suspected on the paradeigmatic group of myths of lines 15–20, as well as on the sudden evocation of Apollo, Calliope, and the gift of Apollo's songs and Calliope's lyre to Cynthia at 27–8.[35] Gallus' Heliconian visit may lie behind this. Cynthia's own visit to Helicon in 2.30, itself containing much obviously Gallan material (above, pp. 128–31), is also worth remembering in this context.

1.3 is even more impressively polysyllabic (and trisyllabic) than its predecessors: it begins with a sequence of no less than five such pentameter endings, the first three of them quadrisyllables: in first position *litoribus* (2), already employed as a polysyllabic pentameter ending at 1.2.18; in second position *Andromede* (4); and in third *Apidano* (6). The latter two are Greek proper names, and although (as noted) it may be difficult to locate such names in a pentameter other than at its end, their placements in 1.3 cannot be accidental, particularly since they are then followed at 8 and 10 by the trisyllabic *manibus* and *pueri*. Just as *litoribus* in 1.2.18 stood in the second of three mythical exempla, each allocated one couplet, so in 1.3 *litoribus* introduces three such couplets recounting paradeigmatic myths. The implication that these couplets too look to Gallus is plain. Another sequence of quadrisyllables presents itself after a brief interval in *saevitiae* (18), *Inachidos* (20), and *temporibus* (22); they are then followed by trisyllabic *manibus* (24). The central of the three couplets with quadrisyllabic endings refers to the myth of Io, a topic famously associated not with Gallus but with Calvus. However, I have proposed elsewhere that Gallus too treated the myth of Io, probably in connection with her encounter with Prometheus in the Caucasus.[36] If that proposal, which gains further support from 1.3.19–20, is correct, then Propertius is alluding in this couplet to Gallus' treatment of Io. The last sequence of pentameters in 1.3 with endings longer than a dissyllable stretches from line 27 to line 38 with one interruption, the dissyllabic ending of line 30: *auspicio* (28), *luminibus* (32), *cubitum* (34), *foribus* (36), *sideribus* (38). The first part of this passage describes the

---

35   For Calliope as a likely presence in Gallus, and for the Gallan origin of Propertius' Heliconian visits, see above, pp. 121–31.
36   See Cairns (1993) 112–14, and below, p. 205 n. 53.

final moments before Cynthia wakes up, when Propertius is gazing upon her and fantasizing (27–30); then moonlight awakes Cynthia (31–3), and she starts to upbraid Propertius (33ff.). Elegy 1.3, a complex *komos*[37] which makes considerable use of the figure of the *'fanciulla abbandonata'*,[38] dedicates its first lines to a paradeigmatic triad describing the sleeping Ariadne, Andromeda and Maenad, each of them approached by a would-be lover. All this is highly redolent of Gallus, and the later lines 27–38 have the air of a reprise of a longer passage from an earlier treatment of one of these mythical figures; presumably, then, at least one of them appeared in Gallus' *Amores*, and Propertius may be adverting to some of his lines.

With elegy 1.4 the tempo changes: polysyllables appear only at second (*servitio*, 4), third (*Hermionae*, 6), and ultimate positions, the last word of the elegy being *inveniam* (28). The early polysyllables may footnote Gallan treatments of the two myths of lines 5–6 (those of Antiope[39] and Hermione), and the ultimate *inveniam* could well footnote other Gallan colour in 1.4. That such material does lurk in 1.4 is virtually assured by the fact that 1.4 is one of a matched pair with 1.5, which is addressed to Gallus; but precisely because of this pairing Propertius may not have felt much need for metrically explicit pointers to Gallus in 1.4. The decline in the number of polysyllabic pentameter endings in 1.4 perhaps also reflects the advent of a new set of themes in the Monobiblos: in 1.4 Propertius initiates the series of 'polemical' elegies which surround the central elegy of the book (11+12):[40] there are 'literary polemics' against Bassus the iambist (1.4), against Gallus the elegist (1.5; 1.10; 1.13), who receives the most attention, and against Ponticus the epic poet (1.7; 1.9). These are interspersed with 'life-style polemics' (1.6; 1.14) against Propertius' other patron, Tullus. The equation of life-style with choice of poetic mode is standard in Roman elegy, so the high dominance of 'polemics' at the core of the Monobiblos would not have gone unnoticed by Roman readers. The two elegies which might not appear to embrace the same discourse in fact do so. 1.8 celebrates Propertius' success in dissuading Cynthia from abandoning him and going off to the East with a *praetor*; his success was due to his *preces* (28) and *carmen*

---

37   Cf. Cairns (1977) 325–37.
38   For the description see Alfonsi (1964).
39   For the proposal that Gallus had written about Antiope's son, Amphion, see above, p. 128; note also Prop. 3.15, featuring *in extenso* the myth of Antiope.
40   On the assumption that Butrica (1996a) is correct to argue for the unity of 1.11 and 1.12.

(40), i.e. his elegies; and literary polemic shows itself in 1.8 in the implicit contrast it sketches with the failure of Gallan elegy to prevent Lycoris leaving Gallus and going off with her soldier (above, pp. 118–19). The central elegy of the Monobiblos (1.11+1.12) portrays a humbler Propertius whose efforts to lure Cynthia back from Baiae to Rome have failed, but who will continue to love her. Thus it heralds those other elegies of the second half of the Monobiblos in which Propertius' love for Cynthia will once again experience set-backs and difficulties (1.15; 1.17; 1.18; 1.19).

Elegy 1.5 has an even smaller number of polysyllables at pentameter ends than 1.4 – only *Thessalia* (6) in third position and *imaginibus* (24), the latter not in a significant location. And yet 1.5 is addressed to and concerns Gallus; and of the two polysyllables at least one[41] – the quinquesyllabic *imaginibus* – is highly relevant to Gallus, since it is the heart of a Gallan verbal complex, and probably stands here in a direct quotation from Gallus (above, pp. 79–81). The question why there are so few polysyllabic pentameter endings in 1.5 will be confronted below as part of an overall assessment of their presence and frequency.

In terms of polysyllabic and trisyllabic endings elegies 1.6 and 1.7 offer a slightly less modest impression than 1.5, although they are by no means as rich in such features as were 1.1, 1.2, and 1.3. 1.6 is framed by polysyllabic endings in two significant locations: second position *Memnonias* (4) and penultimate position *imperii* (34). The 'house of Memnon' is an 'end of the earth', and Gallus was interested in such geographical entities;[42] and the Gallan credentials of *imperii* have already been discussed.[43] Two further quadrisyllabic pentameter endings, *divitias* (14) and *nequitiae* (26), enhance the Gallan flavour of 1.6, since both connect with the Qaṣr Ibrîm elegiacs. The ensemble, augmented as it is by 1.6's three trisyllabic pentameter endings (*manibus*,16; *sociis*, 20; and *patriae*, 22), has a clear emulative function. It comments on the fact that Propertius is imitating Gallus' *propemptikon* of the Qaṣr Ibrîm papyrus and so underlines the complex interactions within this genre between Propertius 1.6 and 1.8, and Gallus' *propemptika* to 'Caesar' and Lycoris. It is, of course, possible that 1.6,

---

41   Witches and philtres (*inter alia*) characterized Thessaly for all three surviving Roman elegists: cf. Prop. 3.24.10, alluding to 1.1.19–24; Tib. 2.4.56; Ov. *Am.* 3.7.27–8. It would hardly be rash to assume that this topos also cropped up in Gallan elegy.

42   Cf. below, p. 205 n. 53, and Index II s.v. ends of earth.

43   Above pp. 90, 162.

in addition to drawing on Gallus, harks back to Helvius Cinna's famous *propemptikon* for Asinius Pollio (frr. 1–5 Courtney); but it has to be said that none of the surviving fragments of Cinna's *propemptikon* shows any resemblance to Propertius 1.6.

Elegy 1.7 seems to announce its Gallan ancestry loudly by placing *militiae* (2) in first position and by following it up with *carminibus* (4, cf. above, pp. 171–2) in second position. Third position is occupied by the trisyllable *dominam* (6) – Gallus' *domina* features in the Qaṣr Ibrîm papyrus (fr. 2.7 Courtney) – while plausibly Gallan *ingeniis* (22) stands in antepenultimate position. Such a grouping of attested or highly probable Gallan terms in these locations, together with the content of 1.7 – an elegist's polemic against an epic poet – must indicate a debt to Gallus, certainly for language, and probably for content, since the omnipresence of such polemic in Augustan poetry, and its especially high profile in Propertius, cannot but be indebted to Gallus' Heliconian advent and to his other possible initiation.

With elegy 1.8 we are again on sure ground, since its emulation of Gallus' *propemptikon* to Lycoris is certain.[44] This permits confident interpretation of its greater quantity of polysyllabic pentameter endings.[45] *Illyria* (2) in first position is annunciatory, and *canitiem* (46) in ultimate position footnotes the elegy as Gallan. The Gallan associations of two of the other polysyllabic endings – *Vergiliis* (10) and *aequoribus* (20) – have already been discussed. The one remaining such ending in 1.8, *obsequio* (40), probably relates to Gallus' conception of Lycoris as his *domina*,[46] but the only other example of it as a pentameter ending (Ovid *Tristia* 5.6.30)[47] offers no further insights. 1.8 continues the literary polemic concerning the genre *propemptikon* begun in 1.6: on the one hand it reclaims for the elegiac tradition the Gallan propemptic theme which Virgil had appropriated for bucolic in *Eclogue* 10, something 'footnoted' by *Vergiliis* (10). But, on the other hand, Propertius' 'real' target is Gallus, whom he emulates by claiming to be a more successful, and hence a better, love-elegist than his predecessor in elegy. The proof of Propertius' claim is, as has already been proposed, the effectiveness of his *propemptikon* in

---

44 See Fedeli (1980) 204–5, and above, pp. 114–15.
45 Additionally the quinquesyllabic *Hippodamiae* ends a hexameter (1.8.35).
46 Gallus must have developed further the topos of *servitium amoris*, already implicit in Catullus and derived from Greek models. On the Greek derivation see Murgatroyd (1981), correcting Lyne (1979).
47 *hoc est cum miseris solum commune beatis,/ ambobus tribui quod solet obsequium* (29–30).

contrast with that of Gallus: whereas Gallus' mistress abandoned him and went off with her soldier, Propertius succeeds in dissuading Cynthia from doing likewise.

In contrast with 1.8, 1.9 contains only one polysyllabic pentameter ending, *blanditias* (30) in antepenultimate position, an ending repeated three times by Propertius but unparalleled elsewhere (see above, pp. 196–7). But, because it is erotodidactic and the sequel to 1.7, Gallan input must equally be suspected. *libera verba* (1.9.2) has already come under suspicion as a Gallan phrase (above, p. 96), and two other lines of 1.9 which have a marked resemblance to lines from Virgil's *Eclogues*, but which do not seem to derive from Virgil, have been independently tagged as Gallan.[48] Cf.:

> **Chaonias** dicunt aquila veniente **columbas**   (Virgil *Eclogue* 9.13)
>
> non me **Chaoniae** vincant in amore **columbae**   (Propertius 1.9.5)

> Daphnis et **Armenias** curru subiungere **tigris**   (Virgil *Eclogue* 5.29)
>
> tum magis **Armenias** cupies accedere **tigris**   (Propertius 1.9.19)[49]

1.10 resembles 1.9 in containing a single polysyllabic ending, *laetitiae* (12) on which see below, plus one trisyllabic ending, *lacrimis* (2). The latter is certainly in first position, but that in itself, and in isolation, is hardly a strong indication of Gallan influence. And yet, like 1.5 which it resembles in its paucity of polysyllabic endings, 1.10 is addressed to Gallus, and it probably reports an episode from Cornelius Gallus' *Amores*, perhaps in some detail. An explanation will be offered below, pp. 216–18.

In even sharper contrast with 1.10, elegy 1.11 returns to the world of multiple polysyllabic pentameter endings: in first position, the much-used *litoribus* (2), focus of a Gallan verbal complex, in second position *nobilibus* – as clear a Gallan pointer as could be found. The other quadrisyllabic endings do not form a sequence but are dispersed throughout the elegy: *carminibus* (8), *compositam* (14), *laetitiae* (24) and *discidium* (28).[50] The Gallan credentials of *carminibus* have already been discussed (pp. 171–2). *laetitia* is found twice as a

---

48   By Du Quesnay (1976–7) 33–4.
49   I hope to follow up the sources of 1.9 in a future publication.
50   *Qua* pentameter ending *discidium* is paralleled only at Cat. 66.22: *sed fratris cari flebile discidium*, where the *discidium* is caused by death.

polysyllabic pentameter ending in Catullus and four times in Propertius:

expulit ex omni pectore **laetitias**	(Catullus 76.22)
haec illi fatuo maxima **laetitia** est	(Catullus 83.2)
accipe commissae <u>munera</u> **laetitiae**	(Propertius 1.10.12)
omnia t u n o s t r a e <u>tempora</u> **laetitiae**	(Propertius 1.11.24)
illa tamen, longae conscia **laetitiae**	(Propertius 1.15.14)
turpia sub *tacita* condita **laetitia**	(Propertius 2.6.32)

The Catullan examples have nothing in common with those of Propertius except their endings in a form of *laetitia*. But *munera laetitiae* in Propertius 1.10.12 (addressed to Gallus) and *tempora laetitiae* in Propertius 1.11.24 could be Gallan or be variants of the same original in Gallus – of the sort visible in the derivates of his *historiae*. If 1.11 and 1.12 are a single elegy,[51] then *Eridano* (1.12.4) and *servitio* (1.12.18), in penultimate position, join the polysyllabic pentameter endings of 1.11+1.12. The Eridanus (Po) was a boundary river. Gallus was interested in such geographical features, and the Hypanis of the Caucasus, which Gallus is known to have written about from his own fr. 1 Courtney, *uno tellures dividit amne duas*,[52] appears in the same Propertian line (1.12.4): *quantum Hypanis Veneto dissidet Eridano*. A little later the couplet 1.12.9–10 *an quae/ lecta Prometheis dividit herba iugis* again concerns the Caucasus, and line 10's *dividit* echoes that same term in Gallus fr. 1 Courtney. The conjecture that Gallus, as well as Calvus, wrote about Io crossing continents was mentioned earlier. 1.12.10 hints that in his account of Io Gallus introduced Prometheus and brought Io into contact with him – cf. Aeschylus *Prometheus Vinctus* 561–886; and it also suggests that Gallus' line about the Hypanis came from that narrative. In the light of this and of other suspected Gallan material in 1.12,[53] it would be a bold sceptic who would deny the presence in it of Gallus. *servitio*

---

51   See above, p. 201 n. 40.
52   See also above, p. 199 and n. 33.
53   For a more extended discussion of the Io/Prometheus interaction see Cairns (1993) 112–14. The full range of Propertian passages where the Caucasus and/or Prometheus feature by name or by implication is: 1.12.9–10 (both); 1.14.6 (C.); 2.1.69–70 (both); 2.25.14 (both); 3.5.7–8 (P.). Virg. *Ecl.* 6.42 (*Caucasiasque refert volucres furtumque Promethei*) connects the topic with Gallus. Also thought-provoking are *Georg.* 2.440; 4.37–2; *Aen.* 4.366–7.

(1.12.18, cf. also 1.4.4) has already been suggested as Gallan (above, p. 201, cf. also p. 191); and three of the six quadrisyllabic endings of 1.11+1.12, including one highly likely to be Gallan in inspiration (*Eridano*, 1.12.4, see above), appear in learned geographical passages. As a Callimachean topic[54] rivers would have been a highly attractive subject for Gallan elegy, and Gallus' interest in them, as well as focussing on fabulous and boundary rivers, may have extended to waters nearer home. Two other passages of the Monobiblos hint in combination that it did: 1.11.1–4 sketches, in language linkable with Gallus (above, p. 118), elements of the mythical geography of the Baiae area, including its waters; and 1.20.7–10 (addressed to Gallus) contains similar material (cf. below, p. 227). 1.11.9–14, which describe Cynthia as swimming, boating and lying on the beach, have further water references (*Lucrina ... aqua*, 10; *tenui Teuthrantis in unda*, 11, *lympha*, 12) and could be indebted to the same Gallan source(s).[55]

Another elegy addressed to Gallus follows (1.13), and a pattern which by now is becoming familiar recurs: 1.13 contains only a single trisyllabic pentameter ending (*manibus*, 16), and no polysyllabic endings at all (although *heroinis* occurs at a hexameter ending, 31). Polysyllabic pentameter endings are better represented in 1.14, addressed to Tullus, and they occupy some significant locations towards its end, although there are no conspicuous sequences. Three of them belong to Gallan complexes already discussed: *arboribus* (6) in third position, *divitiis* (8) and *aequoribus* (12, cf. above, p. 170). Others, viz. *textilibus* (22) in penultimate position,[56] and *despicere* (24) in ultimate position and so perhaps 'footnoting' the elegy as of Gallan inspiration, are unparalleled at pentameter end.[57] Of the two trisyllabic endings, *opere* (2) is unique, while *Venere* (16) is also found in Tibullus (1.10.66, but cf. above, p. 185). In addition to belonging to a Gallan complex, *arboribus* (6) ends a line in which that prominent Gallan theme, the Caucasus, is mentioned, and *aequoribus*

54   Cf. Callim. frr. 457–9 Pf.
55   The common pentameter ending *litoribus* may also reflect Gallan interest in waters.
56   In classical Latin poetry the form is found elsewhere only at the beginning of a hexameter: *textilibusque onerat donis, ac talia fatur* (Virg. *Aen*. 3.485).
57   The overlap between Prop. 1.14.23–4 (*non ulla verebor/ regna vel Alcinoi munera despicere*) and the latter part of *quis non Antiphaten Laestrygona deuouet aut quis/ munifici mores improbat Alcinoi?* (Ov. *EP* 2.9.41–2) is suggestive of a common source, all the more so since the pentameter (42) has one of Ovid's few polysyllabic endings (repeated by him at *EP* 4.2.10: *Alcinoo*).

(12) exemplifies yet again Gallus' hypothesized interest in waters – note too the Tiber scenes of 1.14.1–4. The river Pactolus, which featured earlier at 1.6.32, also addressed to Tullus, then reappears in 1.14.11, followed by the Red Sea (12).[58]

The highest concentration of polysyllabic pentameter endings so far encountered now follows in elegy 1.15: one quinquesyllable and eleven quadrisyllables. There are also two trisyllables,[59] so that 14 out of the elegy's 21 couplets – two thirds of the total – end with a word longer than a dissyllable. They occupy first (*perfidia*, 2) and third (*desidia*, 6) positions, as well as antepenultimate (Gallan *nequitiae*, 38), penultimate (*luminibus*, 40), and ultimate (*blanditiis*, 42) positions. There is also a sequence of three polysyllabic pentameter endings from line 20 to line 24. Two of the polysyllabic endings of elegy 1.15 are unparalleled (*desidia*, 6[60] and *inciderit*, 28), whereas *hospitio* (20) is paralleled in the most Gallan of all Propertius' elegies, at 1.20.10, as well as at Valgius Rufus fr. 4.2 Courtney (*hospitiis*); cf. also *hospitibus* (Martial 5.62.4). Three others reappear more than once in Propertius but not elsewhere: *perfidia* (2, 34), *luminibus* (40), and *blanditiis* (42). A case has already been made (p. 197) for *blanditiae* being a Gallan quasi-synonym for love-elegy. The three appearances of *luminibus* in Propertius at pentameter end are:

luna moraturis sedula **luminibus**	(1.3.32)
et fletum invitis ducere **luminibus**	(1.15.40)
respiciens udis prodita **luminibus**	(2.7.10)

These lines in themselves perhaps would not justify the conclusion that this ending is Gallan, although one of Ovid's two elegiac uses of the term strongly suggests it. *luminibus* features in Ovid's self-defence against the charge of 'teaching adultery' addressed to Augustus:

luminibusque tuis, *totus* quibus utitur *orbis*,
scaenica vidisti lentus *adulteria*   (*Tristia* 2.513–4)

---

58   Cf. also Prop. 3.13.6; Tib. 2.4.30; [Tib.] 3.8.19–20.
59   *thalamo* (18, cf. Prop. 2.15.14; Cat. 68.104), and the common *manibus* (36).
60   Cf. the antecedent Lucr. *DRN* 5.48: *desidiaeque*. It is hard to know what weight to give to *desidiae* as a pentameter ending at [Senec.] *Epigr.* 41.4 Prato.

The couplet terminates in quinquesyllabic *adulteria*, already suspected of Gallan associations, and it contains Gallan *totus orbis*. The hypothesis coheres with Ovid's seeming self-identification in exile with Gallus.[61] As for *perfidia* in *hac tamen excepta, Cynthia, perfidia* (1.15.2), the theme of 'perfidy' is probably Gallan (below), and the term's reappearance in line 34, again at a pentameter ending (*per quos saepe mihi credita perfidia est*), gives it a special role in this elegy.

Finally four polysyllabic pentameter endings of 1.15 belong to already established Gallan verbal complexes, viz. *aequoribus* (10), *laetitiae* (14), *pudicitiae* (22) – and not least *historia* (24), preceded by *nobilis*: *tu quoque uti fieres nobilis historia*! Such a high proportion of polysyllabic pentameter endings must be significant, and they presumably tag much of the subject-matter of 1.15 as Gallan. Three elements of the elegy present themselves as likely candidates for this status:

1.   The account of Cynthia making herself up and decking herself with jewels (5–8) is reminiscent of 1.2.1–6, where Cynthia was warned against this sort of behaviour. Indications of Gallan inspiration, including fairly explicit internal claims, have already been observed in 1.2.

2.   1.15 includes an extended series of four mythical paradeigmata (9–22) which contains four polysyllabic pentameter endings. These are often found in paradeigmatic passages of Propertian elegy, and the influence of Gallus on Propertian *exempla* has several times been suspected both for general and for specific reasons.

3.   *perfidia* is a standard topos of the *propemptikon*,[62] although it is much more widespread.[63] There is no hint of it in Virgil's reprise of Gallus' *propemptikon* to Lycoris in *Eclogue* 10, but it surfaces in Propertius' imitation of Gallus' *propemptikon* (1.8), where Propertius calls Cynthia *periura* (17). This makes it very likely that Propertius

---

61   Despite the textual uncertainties of the hexameter, comparison of *non aliquid dixive, elatave lingua loquendo est,/ lapsaque sunt nimio verba profana mero* (*Tr.* 3.5.47–8), part of an address in self-defence by Ovid to Augustus, along with a couplet from another such address: *non fuit opprobrio celebrasse Lycorida Gallo,/ sed linguam nimio non tenuisse mero* (*Tr.* 2.445–6) reveals beyond doubt that Ovid in his exile was comparing/contrasting himself with Gallus, and supports some earlier conclusions on this topic: cf. Index III s.v. Ovid, and Gallus; Rohr (1994).

62   Cf. *GC* 57, 150.

63   *Inter alia* its prominence in Cat. 64 (esp. 132–3, in Ariadne's lament) assured it of a vigorous *Nachleben* in erotic contexts in later poetry.

found the theme in Gallus. If so, Propertius' application of the term *perfidus* to Gallus in himself under different circumstances (*at non ipse tuas imitabor, perfide, voces* (1.13.3) will be calculated ironic humour at Gallus' expense. Gallus' *voces* there also, of course, recall the *alternis vocibus* of Gallus and his girl-friend at 1.10.10, the reference in both cases being presumably to what Gallus expressed in his *Amores*.

A pattern of polysyllabic pentameter endings similar to that of 1.15 reappears in 1.16: one quinquesyllable and ten quadrisyllables, but this time accompanied by even more (seven) trisyllables. Hence of 1.16's 24 couplets, 18, i.e. three quarters, end in a word longer than a dissyllable. Once again significant locations are occupied, first position by quinquesyllabic *pudicitiae* (2), second position by quadrisyllabic *supplicibus* (4) and third position by trisyllabic *manibus* (6). Of the end positions, antepenultimate is filled symmetrically by *manibus* (44), penultimate by *alitibus* (46) and ultimate by *invidia* (48). This final sequence is preceded by *gradibus* (42). Not only are sequences of endings of more than two syllables formed both at the beginning and end of the elegy, but internal sequences are found too. One consists of four quadrisyllables: *carminibus* (10), *luxuria* (12), *excubiis* (14) and *blanditia* (16), which are followed by trisyllabic *foribus* (18). Another matching internal sequence contains rather more trisyllables: *cardinibus* (26), *auriculas* (28), *chalybe* (30), *lacrimis* (32), *Zephyro* (34) and *muneribus* (36). The terms involved are the usual mixture: the unparalleled quadrisyllables *supplicibus* (4),[64] *excubiis* (14) and *cardinibus* (26); those with some history, namely *luxuria* (12),[65] *auriculas* (28),[66] *alitibus* (46)[67] and *invidia* (48);[68] and finally those which can be reckoned as of likely Gallan origin: *pudicitiae* (2), *carminibus* (10), *blanditia* (16), *foribus* (18) and *muneribus* (36).

The implications of the many polysyllabic endings of 1.16 are clear enough. 1.16 is a *komos* of an unusual type, with its main speaker a door, and part of the door's narration is the reported speech of an excluded lover. This immediately makes 1.16 comparable to

---

64   But see Cat. 116.8, ending in *supplicium*, with, of course, a quite different sense.
65   It recurs at pentameter endings: Prop. 1.2.32 (in an elegy of Gallan inspiration); Mart. 2.63.4 (*luxuria est*).
66   Above, p. 156.
67   Above, p. 173.
68   Cf. *Catalept.* 11.8, where *invidia* ends the final pentameter of an epigram believed by some scholars to be a genuine work of Virgil; and many examples from Martial.

Catullus 67, another unusual *komos* also in the form of a dialogue between a door and an interlocutor who, on the surface at least, is not a komast. Both elegies also have in common that their doors purvey scandal about goings-on – mainly inside (Catullus), and mainly outside (Propertius) – their houses. On the level of detailed content, however, the two elegies are dissimilar; and, out of all the numerous polysyllabic pentameter endings of 1.16 only one overlaps with an ending in Catullus 67: Propertius' *auriculas* (1.16.28) = Catullus' *auriculam* (67.44). It is, therefore, hard to believe that 1.16's only model was Catullus 67. Since both general considerations and specific indications have made it is very likely that Gallus too worked in this genre, which was both a Leitmotiv and a quasi-equivalent of love/ love-elegy itself, we are probably seeing in Propertius 1.16 a heavily 'footnoted' reworking by Propertius of a Gallan *komos* or *komoi* in which Gallus had in turn reworked Catullus 67.

With 1.15 and 1.16 the high point of polysyllabic pentameter endings in the Monobiblos has been reached. With the exception of 1.20, which will be treated in Chapter 7, and the final two brief 'epigrams' (1.21 and 1.22), the remaining elegies of Book 1 do not display major concentrations of polysyllabic pentameter endings, although some such endings do continue to play a significant role. Elegy 1.17 has only three of them, but one, *alcyonas* (2), occupies first position, and another, *litoribus* (28, with Gallan associations) ultimate position; the third is *Tyndaridas* (18). Although *alcyonas* and *Tyndaridas* are unparalleled, the use of polysyllabic endings in the two most significant locations in the elegy looks very much like an initial announcement and an ultimate footnoting of a model.[69] Elegy 1.17 seems redolent of hellenistic treatments of myth; and, if this impression is not misleading, we might hypothesize that a hellenistic Greek model stands at some remove from it. This would bring 1.17 into harmony with 1.18, behind which lies ultimately Callimachus' Acontius and Cydippe *aetion*. It might also be surmised that, just as Gallus produced his own version of the Callimachean *aetion*,[70] he also rehandled the Greek model of 1.17. In that case Propertius could have

---

69   The hypothesis of a specific model and the elegy's membership of the genre *epibaterion* (cf. *GC* 59–69; Fedeli (1980) 400–1) are not incompatible. For an interaction of this type in Ovid see Cairns (1979b).

70   Cf. esp. Rosen and Farrell (1986). The nature of Gallus' rehandlings of his predecessors is unclear. That he sometimes did impersonate the heroes of his models' myths rather than simply narrate those myths is likely enough in view of *Eclogue* 10, but it is unlikely that Propertius always followed Gallus in all particulars of his treatments.

drawn on Gallus' rehandling of his Greek model, or, as in 1.18, have exploited both Gallus' elegy and its Greek model.[71]

What myth, then, might the Greek model of 1.17 have treated? It presumably told of a lover who left his beloved against her will, and who ended up shipwrecked. Since the Homeric archetype of the inverse *epibaterion* comes in the storm-scene which led to the shipwreck of Odysseus,[72] that narrative must be considered a possibility. Odysseus is in some senses a lover, and it is not beyond the bounds of imagination that Gallus/Propertius was familiar with an account of Odysseus, of his abandonment of Calypso(?) and of his arrival at Phaeacia (or Ithaca) which had been hyper-eroticized by a hellenistic intermediary. After all, Tibullus 1.3, which is close in its narrative outline to Propertius 1.17, and which shows Tibullus separated from Delia and sick at Corcyra, calls Corcyra 'Phaeacia' (3), thus reinforcing Tibullus' self-characterization as an Odysseus figure. Similarly Propertius' *Cassiope* (1.17.3) has been interpreted as a reference to the port of that name on Corcyra.[73] But there is another possibility, namely that Odysseus' circumstances were transferred by a hellenistic poet to a minor or an invented mythical figure. This is where the annunciatory polysyllabic pentameter ending *alcyonas* (2) might help. Is it pointing to the story of Ceyx, who left his wife Alcyone, sailed off, and was shipwrecked?[74] This apparent pointer might seem illusory since Ceyx was drowned at sea, whereas in 1.17 Propertius, although shipwrecked, has reached land safely. Propertius is, however, much taken up with imagining his death (1.17.8–24), and he even envisages for himself the typical drowned sailor's grave in the sand: *haecine parva meum funus harena teget?* (8). In any case mythical characters and backgrounds can mutate when a subjective elegist maps himself and his circumstances onto a hellenistic myth: in 1.18, for example, Propertius puts himself into Acontius' shoes, but Cynthia is no Cydippe! And the fate of Ceyx may not always have been narrated exactly as Ovid narrates it in *Metamorphoses* 11.

The story of Ceyx and Alcyone was handled by Cicero (in his

---

71   It will be argued that he also did so in 1.20: see below, pp. 237–49.

72   Hom. *Od.* 5.299–312: cf. *GC* 61–3.

73   Fedeli (1980) 402–3. The identification is very plausible, although it does not imply that the term necessarily has literary implications: Propertius may just be referring to the normal first port-of-call for Romans sailing to Greece.

74   For the variants of the myth see Fantham (1979). Alcyone's speech to Ceyx at Ov. *Met.* 11.421–43 is a *propemptikon*: cf. Yardley (1979); Fantham (1979) 336 n. 29. The connection between the myth and the genre may be older than Ovid.

youth?) in a poem perhaps named *Alcyones*. Cicero fr. 1 Courtney relates the parentage of Ceyx: he was the son of Phosphoros/Lucifer, who was also Hesperus:[75] *hunc genuit claris delapsus ab astris/ praevius Aurorae, solis noctisque satelles*. The second of these two hexameters inspired Ovid *Heroides* 18.112: *praevius Aurorae Lucifer*. Several earlier discussions of *Hesperus* and *Lucifer* in connection with Gallus are perhaps worth recalling in this context,[76] as is the phrase *aequoreae formosa Doride natae* at 1.17.25: Doris makes one of her other (infrequent) appearances at *Eclogue* 10.5, two lines before and two lines after namings of Gallus.

Despite the fact that 1.18 draws on a Gallan reworking of Callimachus' tale of Acontius and Cydippe (*Aetia* frr. 67–75 Pf.), it has few pentameter endings longer than a dissyllable: in third position the quadrisyllables *principium* (6) – cf. *principiis*, also found as a pentameter ending at Propertius 2.6.16 – and (unparalleled) *corticibus* (22), along with the seemingly Gallan trisyllables *lacrimis* (16) and *foribus* (24). *principium* is not uncommon from Catullus on at other line positions in elegy. Propertius' use of it twice at a pentameter ending might imply that it appeared in this position with some contextual significance in a predecessor.[77] But on the whole there is little metrical sign-posting of Gallus in 1.18. Callimachus' Acontius and Cydippe *aetion* was very well known,[78] and Gallus' reworking of it must have been correspondingly familiar; so Propertius may not have wanted to labour the obvious, but rather to emphasize his own novel contributions to the theme.

With its single example *exsequiis* in second position (4), elegy 1.19 represents a new low point in polysyllabic pentameter endings in the Monobiblos. It was argued (above, p. 180) that the use of *exsequiae* in pentameter endings by all three surviving Roman elegists, but not by Catullus, makes it likely that Gallus had exploited it in this

---

75   Courtney (1993) ad loc. and [Hyginus] *Fab.* 65: *Ceyx Hesperi sive Luciferi et Philonidis filius*. I note the (?)coincidental start of [Hyginus] *Fab.* 64 with *Cassiope* (cf. Prop. 1.17.3), which there is a variant on the name of Andromeda's mother, and the further (?)coincidence that Propertius names Andromeda four times: 1.3.4; 2.28.21; 3.22.29; 4.7.63.

76   Above, pp. 97–9, 143, 162. Parthenius *Erot. Pathem.* 27 tells the story of another Alcyone: see Lightfoot (1999) General Index s.vv. Alcyone; Ceyx. It is probably irrelevant that the father of Cydippe seems at Callim. *Aet.* fr. 75.28 Pf. to be called Ceyx.

77   Lucretius ends many hexameters with enhanced forms of *principium*, but is unlikely to be that predecessor.

78   The indirectness of Catullus' allusion to Cydippe at 65.19–24 is perhaps proof enough of this.

way. If so, the exemplum at 1.19.7–10 could indicate that Gallus had introduced it into an account of Protesilaus and Laodameia. Catullus also handled this theme in poem 68, but differently from Propertius in 1.19.[79] The papponymic/ethnic *Phylacides* by which Propertius designates Protesilaus (1.19.7) is not found in Catullus, but Ovid employed it three times (*Amores* 2.6.41; *Ars Amatoria* 2.356; 3.17), so it too may have featured in Gallus. Nothing much else[80] in this elegy brings Gallus to mind.[81]

After 1.20, in which polysyllabic pentameter endings are once more prominent (see below, pp. 234–5), 1.21 and 1.22, both of ten lines, each have three endings longer than a dissyllable: 1.21 places *aggeribus* (2) in first and Gallan *militiae* (4) in second position; the seemingly Gallan trisyllable *lacrimis* (6) then follows in third position. *aggeribus* (2) also ends a pentameter at Propertius 2.13.48 and that line, like 1.21.2, contains *miles*:

> **miles** ab Etruscis saucius **aggeribus** (1.21.2)
>
> Gallicus Iliacis **miles** in **aggeribus** (2.13.48)

The form *aggeribus*, employed by Virgil six times in hexameters,[82] is not found elsewhere in a pentameter, although Ovid uses it once, in a hexameter apparently unrelated to the Propertian lines: *velat et aggeribus factis a milite forti* (*Metamorphoses* 15.592). *agger* is, of course, a military technical term, and that may fully explain Ovid's recombination of it with *miles*, and indeed its overall distribution.[83] 1.22 contains quinquesyllabic *amicitia* (2) in first and *temporibus* (4) in

---

79 Fedeli (1980) 444 thinks it probable that Propertius is alluding to Catullus' treatment of the myth, but on slight grounds.

80 The only other noteworthy (hexameter) line-ending in 1.19 is *heroinae* (13). For Propertius' uses of this term in other hexameter endings (1.13.31 and 2.2.9), always (naturally) in mythical/heroic contexts, see above, p. 158.

81 Fedeli (1980) 439 declares, on the basis of Prop. 2.34.91–2, that the key concept underlying 1.19, namely that love persists after death, was 'ignota anche a Cornelio Gallo'. But only if that water is from Lethe, which Propertius does not specify, would Propertius be denying the persistence of Gallus' love. If the *inferna aqua* (of Euphoronic/Parthenian inspiration) with which Gallus washes his erotic wounds at 2.34.91–2 (see also above, p. 81 n. 56) is either, as Fedeli maintains, the water of the Styx, or like Euphorion's water, that of the Cocytus, then the opposite conclusion could be drawn, and a Gallan thematic link with 1.19 could be asserted.

82 *Georg.* 3.354; *Aen.* 2.496; 6.830; 9.70; 9.784;10.24.

83 Another (highly fragile) possible pointer to a Gallan origin for *aggeribus* as a pentameter ending is the adjective *Gallicus* attached by the Propertian MSS to *miles* in Prop. 2.13.48. However most editors of Propertius emend *Gallicus* or place it in *cruces*.

second position, both of likely Gallan origin. In ultimate position, and hence as the last word of the Monobiblos, stands *uberibus* (10). Propertius ends pentameters twice with this form:

me genuit terris fertilis **uberibus**   (1.22.10)

missus et impressis haedus ab **uberibus**   (2.34.70)

2.34 is also the final poem of its book, although its line 70 is nowhere near its end. But 2.34.70 falls within the section of Propertius 2.34 which – reversing Virgil's *deformazione* of Gallan elegy into bucolic in *Eclogue* 10 – transforms Virgil's *Eclogues* into (Gallan?) elegy; and that same section contains many polysyllabic pentameter endings (below, p. 215). Most of these have good Gallan credentials, and it might reasonably be supposed that *uberibus* does too.

Various other aspects of 1.21 and 1.22 have been discussed in earlier chapters. These include some of their polysyllabic endings and the presence in 1.21 of another (dead) man called Gallus (7), argued to be the same person as the *propinquus* of Propertius mentioned at 1.22.7.[84] Propertius addresses his second epilogue, 1.22, to Volcacius Tullus, just as the Monobiblos prologue (1.1) was addressed to him, and 1.22 appropriately stresses the *amicitia* of Propertius and Tullus, (*inter alia* their relationship as *cliens* and *patronus*) in a reminiscence of Gallan *amicitia*. This presence of Propertius' other *amicus*, Cornelius Gallus, at the end of the Monobiblos, albeit obliquely through allusion, is appropriate, and his homonym in the first of the epilogue elegies (1.21.7) naturally also recalls him; further references to Gallus' work in both epilogues, possibly even extending to short quotations, have already been noted. It can be presumed that, as fellow-patrons of Propertius, Tullus and Gallus were on good terms, and Propertius well knew that Gallus had been a friend of Virgil and dedicatee of some of his *Eclogues*. The carry-over of the striking line-ending *uberibus* from the final elegy of Book 1, where it is addressed to Gallus' fellow-patron Tullus, to the final elegy of Book 2, where it is applied to Virgil (and where it precedes by twenty lines Propertius' posthumous tribute to Gallus), may therefore be a tactful reminder in the latter elegy of the friendship between Virgil and Gallus.

The situation as regards polysyllabic (and trisyllabic) pentameter endings in Book 2 can be summarized more briefly. The prologue and

---

84   See above, pp. 49–50 and nn. 56, 58.

epilogue elegies (1 and 34) reveal fairly high totals: 2.1 has one quin-quesyllable and 6 quadrisyllables, and 2.34 has two quinquesyllables, 9 quadrisyllables, and two trisyllables (mainly clustered). But, since these are lengthy elegies (2.1: 78 lines; 2.34: 94 lines), the proportions of their pentameter endings longer than a dissyllable are not high. 2.1 and 2.34 celebrate Propertius' arrival in the circle of Maecenas.[85] However, instead of rejecting his poetic past and his links with Cornelius Gallus, Propertius makes them plain in both elegies: in 2.1 he alludes directly to Gallus' *historia* ending at line 16 and to his *arti-ficem* ending at line 58, and he lays stress on a number of other Gallan terms and themes.[86] And there are even more numerous Gallan reminiscences in 2.34, which include the only open reference in all Propertius' work to Gallus *qua* poet, to Gallus' suicide, to his mistress (by name), and to his poetry:

> et modo formosa quam multa Lycoride Gallus
> mortuus inferna vulnera lavit aqua (2.34.91–2)

Propertius then immediately closes 2.34 and Book 2 with a couplet containing his own name and referring to his own mistress and poetry, and in this way he explicitly claims for himself the mantle of Gallus:

> Cynthia †quin etiam† versu laudata Properti,
> hos inter si me ponere Fama volet. (2.34.93–4)

Of the other elegies of Book 2, 2.6 and 2.16 each have one quinquesyllable and 3 quadrisyllables, but the rest display fewer or none. Some of the terms used as polysyllabic endings in Book 2 are familiar and/or belong to Gallan complexes, some are unparalleled. Annunciatory first position is occupied in 2.5 (*nequitia*) and also in 2.20 (*Andromeda*), in which the final word too is a polysyllable. 2.6, 2.14, 2.32 and 2.33 show polysyllables in second position, and, in addition to 2.20, elegies 2.30 and 2.32 have polysyllables as their final word. The analytic techniques exemplified in this and the preceding chapter could also be applied to the polysyllabic endings of Book 2, and this might reveal new links with Gallus and help to confirm earlier hypotheses about such links. The fact remains, however, that Book 2 as a whole has moved strongly away from such endings. The

---

85 See below, pp. 260–6, 326–37, and Chapter 9.
86 See below, pp. 266–7.

deteriorating and subsequently condemned status of Cornelius Gallus must in part be responsible for this, but the influence of literary fashion as it developed over the twenties BC should not be underestimated. There are naturally no elegies addressed to Gallus in Book 2, but there is nothing to suggest that his new patron Maecenas frowned on Gallan *imitatio* by Propertius.[87] Already in the Monobiblos Propertius was asserting an independent elegiac stance, which he did there mainly by privileging his own elegy over that of Gallus. It may be that, as time went on, Propertius' increasing confidence in his own status as an elegist made it less and less necessary for him to compare and contrast himself with Gallus. Gallus never disappears from Propertian elegy, but over the remainder of his career Propertius was increasingly swimming with the tides, both literary and political; that in essence is why in his last two books there is a mere handful of polysyllabic endings – 11 in Book 3, with only one in *-ibus*, and 6 in Book 4.

If indebtedness to, and a wish to refer to, Gallus is the primary motive for Propertius' polysyllabic pentameter endings, what governs their proportions? This is a difficult question, and a firm answer to it cannot be given. Earliness has been suggested as a prime factor,[88] and it is not out of the question that those elegies with the highest proportions (1.3; 1.15; 1.16; 1.20) are among Propertius' earliest. Thus 1.3, with its nine polysyllabic endings (including two triple sequences), and five trisyllabic endings, could reflect a period when Propertius was totally under the spell of Gallus; and, of course, we must suspect that, if Propertius had not been a protégé of Gallus, his initial metrics might have been more like those of Tibullus. But on the other hand 1.3 is a very elaborate and sophisticated *komos*, and its relationship with Gallus' predecessor *komoi* might not have been obvious if Propertius had not provided copious confirmation of his debts to him. Similarly 1.15 and 1.16 could be among Propertius' first essays into elegy, when his excitement about the works of his predecessor encouraged him towards closer adherence to Gallus' style and language than he practised later. Contrariwise, however, Propertius may be emulating the work of Gallus and subjecting it to *deformazione* throughout these two elegies, and hence constantly drawing attention to what he is doing.

---

87   The presence in Book 3 of the *kletikon* to Tullus (22) also guarantees that Maecenas was not personally hostile to Propertius' former patrons.
88   By Skutsch (1963).

The question why the proportions of polysyllabic pentameter endings in Monobiblos elegies differ becomes most acute in the four addressed to Gallus, since of these 1.20 contains a large number of such endings, while the other three have remarkably few: 1.5 has only two, 1.10 only one, and 1.13 none (although it has one trisyllable). With the latter three it might be conjectured that, because Gallus is actually addressed in them, Propertius felt no need to highlight his indebtedness to Gallus by introducing polysyllabic pentameter endings except in near or actual quotations from Gallus. That might explain why he limited himself in 1.5 to *Thessalia* (6) and *imaginibus* (24) – in a quotation? – and in 1.10 to *laetitiae* (12), again plausibly in a quotation from Gallus. Another possible explanation might be that, just as Propertius emulates Gallus in these three elegies and subjects him to *deformazione* by playing *magister amoris* to his master in elegy, so Propertius was treating Gallus' metrics in the same way by 'translating' the language of Gallan elegy into his own (more 'modern') elegiac language with its fewer polysyllabic endings. There would be a nice irony in this, and it would be a new aspect of Propertius' constant attempts to assert himself on all levels in his relationship with Gallus while maintaining due respect for him as a senior elegist. But such an explanation does not account for the anomalous 1.20, also addressed to Gallus but packed with polysyllabic pentameter endings and hence very different in this respect from 1.5, 1.10, and 1.13. For 1.20 an alternative hypothesis is required: it will again suppose detailed and annotated *deformazione* of Gallus, but will also take account of Gallus' Greek original and Propertius' simultaneous homage to it (see below, pp. 237–49).

In elegies where polysyllabic pentameter endings are employed with reasonable restraint by Propertius the question of proportions does not really arise, and the relationship between the polysyllabic endings and Gallan influence is usually clearer. For example, it is generally accepted that 1.1 with its myth of Milanion and Atalanta is highly indebted to Gallus. Propertius' six polysyllabic and one trisyllabic pentameter endings, including one in first position, are obviously designed to acknowledge that indebtedness – and Propertius will have had additional motivation in that 1.1 was his first self-presentation to his public as an emulous pupil of Gallus. Elegy 1.2, with its diagnostic *nudus amor formae non amat artificem* (8), its five polysyllabic pentameter endings, one in ultimate position to footnote the debt to Gallus, and its two trisyllabic endings, is similar to 1.1.

Again, the five polysyllabic endings of 1.8, plus its use of first and ultimate positions, are enough to declare its derivation from and opposition to Gallus' *propemptikon* for Lycoris. The last two elegies of the Monobiblos are yet again modest in their polysyllabic endings, although clear in their declaration of poetic dependence on Gallus. In an elegy like 1.17 Propertius perhaps judged that the annunciatory first position and the ultimate position, plus quinquesyllabic *Tyndaridas* at line 18, sufficed to point to Gallus, especially if the underlying myth was well known to have been handled by Gallus. This certainly seems to be the case with the indubitably Gallan 1.18 in which positional pointers to Gallus are absent, although there are two polysyllabic (6, 22) and two trisyllabic (16, 24) endings. Where polysyllabic pentameter endings are virtually lacking but there are other strong indications of the presence of Gallus (as in 1.9), Gallan influence may have been so patent to Propertius' contemporaries that it required no underlining. In cases such as 1.19 where those other indications are also absent judgement must be suspended.

CHAPTER 7

Propertius 1.20, Gallus and
Parthenius of Nicaea

Propertius 1.20, addressed to 'Gallus', presents a striking admixture: on the one hand out of all Propertius' elegies it most notably exemplifies those features which previous scholarship and earlier chapters have argued to be characteristic of the work of its addressee, the poet C. Cornelius Gallus; on the other hand 1.20 is replete with hellenizing language, content, and ethos, and must ultimately be indebted also to a Greek model. The present chapter will follow up both sides of this admixture: it will aim first, through an examination of the Gallan elements of 1.20, to illustrate further the approaches and conclusions of Chapters 3–6; and it will then explore the implications of the hellenizing aspects of 1.20.

The uniqueness of 1.20, not just in the Monobiblos but in Propertius' first three books, is a useful point of departure. This elegy is unique in its combination of two factors: the virtual absence of any reference to Propertius' own personal concerns, and its concentration on a single myth. 1.20 says nothing about Propertius' love-life, and of his other preoccupations it highlights only his relationship with Gallus, given pride of place in the explicit and introductory *pro continuo ... amore* of line 1. In keeping with this emphasis 1.20 focuses completely on Gallus, and on Gallus' love affair with a boy whose name, Hylas, is also that of Hercules' beloved. The first fourteen lines enlarge on a difficulty which Gallus is likely to experience in his love affair: like his mythical namesake, Gallus' boy-friend Hylas is liable to stray.[1] In the case of Gallus' friend, the danger comes from the charms of 'Italian nymphs', that is, young Italian women (11–12) – this is, of course, a witty allusion to the poet Gallus' interest in

---

[1] Marathus, the beloved of Tib. 1.8 and 1.9, similarly strays from the poet to a girl.

mythical nymphs of all sorts.[2] The final couplet (51–2) will return to
the theme of Gallus and his peril. But the bulk of 1.20 narrates a single
myth, the story of how Hercules lost his Hylas during the Argonautic
expedition. There are of course other elegies of Propertius' first three
books in which one of the two characteristics of 1.20 can be identified,
and indeed elegies where Propertius' personal concerns are downplayed, or are virtually absent, are a characteristic of Book 3: ready
examples are 3.7, the *epikedion* for Paetus, or 3.22, the recall of Tullus
to Italy. But those elegies do not devote a high proportion of their
lines to one myth. Only 3.15, where the myth of Dirce occupies the
bulk of the elegy, parallels 1.20 in its high concentration on a single
myth.[3] But in 3.15 the Dirce myth is linked unequivocally with
Propertius' own love affair and with his own erotic past and present,
whereas in 1.20 the Hylas myth relates not to Propertius' love life but
to a potential erotic predicament of his addressee.

It has already been emphasized that even some scholars who do
not accept the identification of the 'Gallus' of the Monobiblos as the
poet C. Cornelius Gallus nevertheless admit that 1.20 shows the influence of Cornelius Gallus, or even that its 'Gallus' is the poet.[4]
There is, of course, an additional and highly specific reason for
accepting that the 'Gallus' of 1.20 is the poet, namely that C. Cornelius Gallus wrote a Hylas poem. As several scholars have recognized,
that is the plain implication of Virgil *Eclogue* 6.43–4.[5] One factor internal to 1.20 might appear to stand squarely against the identification:
our sources tell us that C. Cornelius Gallus wrote love-poetry about a
mistress called Lycoris, and it seems that the historical C. Cornelius
Gallus had a relationship with the celebrated contemporary courtesan
and mime-actress Volumnia Cytheris, upon whom he based his literary mistress; in contrast, the Gallus of 1.20 is engaged in an affair
with a young boy. One solution to this inconsistency might be to claim
that Cornelius Gallus wrote love-poems both to his mistress Lycoris
and, otherwise unbeknown to us, to a boy. After all Catullus had
Iuventius, and possibly others, as (at least literary) boy-friends, while
Tibullus devoted one tranche of his first book of elegies to Delia and
another to Marathus. So why should Gallus not have included homo-

---

2   See Index II s.v. Hamadryas etc.
3   Cf. Fedeli (1980) 455.
4   Above, p. 78 n. 38.
5   Cf. Fedeli (1980) 455; earlier Skutsch (1906) 145; Ross (1975) 75–81; *contra*, however,
     Lightfoot (1999) 467.

erotic as well as heterosexual love-poems in his *Amores*?[6] One scholar concluded from Virgil *Eclogue* 10 that Gallus 'may have treated homosexual love ... as well as his love for Lycoris', asserting that in *Eclogue* 10.37–41, lines which reflect Gallus' poetry, 'Gallus is presented as bisexual', and holding that this characterization is confirmed by Horace *Epode* 11, with its clear signs of elegiac and Gallan influence and with a similar move on the part of its speaker from heterosexual to homosexual love.[7]

This may be the correct explanation, but another possibility is worth considering: this is that Gallus did not write homosexual love-poetry, but that Propertius was subjecting the poetry of Gallus to *deformazione* in 1.20 by suggesting that he did. Propertius could have taken his cue from Virgil's similar treatment of Gallus in *Eclogue* 10,[8] and particularly from his imposition upon Gallus in lines 37–41 of a bucolic attitude to love – one tending more to homosexuality. The notion that Propertius misrepresented Gallus in this respect sits well with Propertius' misrepresentations of Virgil's *Eclogues*, *Georgics* and *Aeneid* in elegy 2.34 (see below, pp. 313–14). Moreover, the depictions of Gallus in the other elegies of the Monobiblos addressed to him (1.5, 1.10, and 1.13) contain elements inconsistent with each other and with the otherwise known portrait of Gallus as the constant lover of Lycoris. Hence at least two of them, and probably all three, must employ *deformazione*: in 1.5 Gallus is characterized as an aspiring lover of Cynthia, in 1.10 he is the newly successful lover of a girl who is presumably not Cynthia; and in 1.13 he is a former serial seducer who is now uniquely in love with one girl, again presumably not Cynthia. It has been proposed that in 1.5, 1.10 and 1.13 Propertius is misrepresenting Cornelius Gallus for various literary-polemical purposes.[9] The attribution to Gallus of a boy-love in elegy 1.20 could, then, be a further 'polemical' misrepresentation of the same type.

An advantage of this approach is that the distortions in all the Monobiblos elegies addressed to Gallus could now be explained on one and the same hypothesis. This is that in his *Amores* Gallus had written about various mythical heroines and beautiful boys who were love-objects (among them Hercules' Hylas), and that Propertius is pretending to believe that these characters of myth were disguises for

---

6   On this title, see below, pp. 230–2.
7   Du Quesnay (1979) 60–1; cf. also Kennedy (1982) 380.
8   Cf. pp. 106–7 and Ch. 4 *passim*.
9   See Cairns (1983a) 91–5 and above, pp. 113, 116–18.

real-life sexual partners of Gallus.[10] Given the known penchant of poets of that time, including Gallus and Propertius himself, to map themselves and their emotions onto the mythical personae of their poetry, Propertius' pretence to such a belief would easily have been understood. Contemporaries would also have recognized these Propertian fantasies about Gallus' love-affairs as a metaphrased version of recent literary history, i.e. as comments on the development of Roman elegy from being 'objective' to being 'subjective', something which could fairly be credited, at least in part, to Cornelius Gallus.[11] This approach also sits well with, and confirms, the old view, discussed earlier,[12] that Propertius 1.10 and 1.13 do not record that Propertius played the voyeur when Gallus was making love to a girl-friend, but rather refer to Propertius having read a poem by Cornelius Gallus in which Gallus described his own love-making.

GALLAN FEATURES IN 1.20

Now that this potential objection to the identification with the poet has been scotched, the features of 1.20 which point to Cornelius Gallus can be considered. To start with diction: the language of 1.20 is markedly more elevated than that of any other elegy of the Mono-biblos;[13] and numerous aspects of it appear to reflect the influence of Gallus' poetry. Many of these reflections of Gallus have been high-lighted by other scholars, especially by Ross,[14] and more can be added. First, those proposed by earlier scholarship (with addenda where necessary).

Hamadryads/Adryads/Dryads (12, 32, 45)
The manuscript readings at lines 12 and 32 are corrupt, but it seems

10   Popular belief, based on the *Eclogues*, that Alexis was Virgil's boy-friend (cf. Horsfall (1995) 6) provides a parallel. Mart. 8.55.12–18, adding that on acquiring Alexis Virgil lost interest in Galatea and Thestylis, further exemplifies the tendency.
11   This is not to say, however, that Catullus' elegies are wholly 'objective', or that hellenistic Greek elegy did not contain 'subjective' elements: cf. *THPR* Ch. 9; Butrica (1996b).
12   Above, pp. 116–17.
13   'Es gibt im I. Buch kaum eine Elegie, in der so sehr eine ungewöhnliche Sprachform gesucht ist wie in I, 20 ...' (Tränkle (1960) 15).
14   See Ross (1975) 75–81, with references to earlier work. Monteleone (1979) and Fabre-Serris (1995) argue (diversely) for the influence of both Gallus and Virgil. Murgatroyd (1992), in a valuable survey of all six versions of the Hylas myth, opts (91–3) for Theocritus *Idyll* 13.

clear, and this is confirmed by the uncorrupted *Dryades* of line 45, that Hamadryads/Adryads are involved. Ross, and more extensively Kennedy,[15] have shown that these nymphs have a special link with Gallus and that their reappearance in later poets is a pointer to Gallan influence.[16] It may be added that, since the phrase *Dryades* ... *puellae(as)* of 1.20.45 recurs at *Eclogues* 5.59, *Georgics* 1.11, and *Culex* 116, it is particularly likely to be Gallan in origin.

The 'wilderness area' (13–14)
Ross[17] highlights *duros montes, frigida saxa* and *expertos lacus*, and he sees this 'wilderness area' as 'exactly corresponding to Propertius' (originally Gallus') desolate solitude in <Propertius> 1.18 (especially lines 27–8, *pro quo divini fontes et frigida rupes/ et datur inculto tramite dura quies)*'. The concept that the 'wild surroundings'/'wilderness area' so popular in post-Gallan Roman poetry derives from a model in Gallus was discussed above (pp. 136–40).

The description of Pegae (33–8)
According to Ross,[18] this passage owes much to Gallus' description, derived from Euphorion, of the Grynean Grove.

Various grammatical, syntactical and stylistic features of 1.20
These are noted by Ross, who describes them as archaic, or 'neoteric', and therefore considers them Gallan. They are:

1. In lines 1–6, 'the neoteric placement of attribute and substantive' in 1–3, 'the similar placement of the two proper names' in 4, 'the two-and-a-half foot *Theiodamanteo*' in 6 (cf. Propertius 3.14.14; 4.9.1), and 'the elaborate periphrasis' of 5–6 (75 n.2).
2. 'the geographical periphrases in 1.20.7–10' and the anaphora of *sive* (76).
3. 'allowing Helle <(1.20.19)> only her patronymic' (77).
4. 'the archaic use <(18)> of the genitive' (77).
5. 'the words which introduce the *exemplum, namque ferunt olim* <(17)>' (77–78).

15   Ross (1975) 95 and n. 4; Kennedy (1982) 377–89.
16   The original inspiration may come from Cat. 61.21–5.
17   Ross (1975) 77, cf. also 92–6.
18   Ross (1975) 79–80.

6. 'In lines 23–4 the infinitive is used with a verb of motion to express purpose … this is a pure archaism' (78).
7. 'the dative form *nullae* <(35)> … must be archaic-poetic' (78–79).
8. The couplet (31–2) making 'the transition from the attack by Zetes and Calais to the *ekphrasis*' contains (31) an 'elaborate periphrasis'; it has a spondaic ending; and it terminates in a 'Greek proper name'. Line 32 contains '*a*, the neoteric exclamation'; it ends with *Hamadryasin*; and it probably echoes a line of Gallus (80).

Naturally it could be objected that most of the grammatical, syntactical, and stylistic features mentioned by Ross are neoteric in general rather than Gallan in particular, and hence do not constitute proof that Propertius was imitating Gallus rather than any other lost Roman writer or writers of the 60s, 50s, or 40s BC. While the strength of this objection must be admitted, nevertheless Ross's perceptions of the presence of Gallus in 1.20 are likely to be substantially correct when taken in context and as a group – especially given the limited scope of the elegiac tradition. Moreover, Ross's proposals can be reinforced by new, additional suggestions about Gallan features of 1.20. These supplementary proposals, which again assume that Propertius 1.5, 1.10, and 1.13 are also addressed to Cornelius Gallus, must, of course, be evaluated both as addenda to the proposals of Ross (and Tränkle), and cumulatively. Only in this way can their mutually supportive nature be appreciated. They concern:

amore (1)

> hoc pro continuo te, Galle, *monemus* **amore**   (1.20.1)

The metrical, verbal, and sound patterns of this, the first line of 1.20, in which Propertius begins to address Gallus, are close to those of the first line of Virgil's address to Cornelius Gallus in *Eclogue* 10 (the five previous lines of *Eclogue* 10 address Arethusa):

> incipe: sollicitos Galli *dicemus* **amores**   (*Eclogue* 10.6)

The obvious conclusion to be drawn is that one of Cornelius Gallus' own lines lies behind both of them.

animo (2)

> hoc pro continuo te, Galle, monemus amore,
> id tibi ne vacuo defluat ex **animo**   (1.20.1–2)

The terms *animus* and *anima* are common enough in Latin poetry, especially in Lucretius, but they seem to have been associated in a special way with Gallus.[19] Two further passages of the Monobiblos addressed to 'Gallus' support this association:

> illa feros **animis** alligat una viros (Propertius 1.5.12)
>
> vidi ego te toto vinctum languescere collo
>   et flere iniectis, Galle, diu manibus,
> et cupere optatis **animam** deponere labris (Propertius 1.13.15–17)

The Monobiblos contains only two cases of *animus* and two of *anima*. Three of them thus come in addresses to Gallus and refer, directly or indirectly, to Gallus' own *animus/anima*. The fourth comes at 1.6.26, in an address to Gallus' fellow patron, Tullus, and it concerns Propertius' *anima*. Ovid offers further indications that the terms were associated with Gallus: in the *propemptikon* for Gaius Caesar in *Ars Amatoria* 1, where Gallan influence seems certain, there is notable interest in '*animi*'.[20] Presumably Gallus had made play with his *animus/anima* in his *Amores*.

Hylae (6), silvae (7)

The Greek-Latin etymology implicit in these two terms, and 'marked' by their positioning at successive line-ends and by *non nomine dispar* (5), has recently been observed, and linked with the Gallan inspiration of 1.20.[21] Naturally, not all such etymologies are necessarily of Gallan provenance. For example, the analogous

> abstulit **Hylonome**, qua nulla decentior inter
> semiferos altis **habitavit** femina **silvis**.
>   (Ovid *Metamorphoses* 12.405–6)

where *habitavit ... silvis* similarly glosses a Greek proper name beginning with *Hyl-*, looks to be autonomous, as may possibly be (although *antro* (140) raises a question) the glossing of 'Hylaeus' in

> non aliter **silvas** umeris et utroque refringens
> pectore montano duplex **Hylaeus** ab antro
> praecipitat (Statius *Thebaid* 4.139–41)

---

19 See Index II s.vv.
20 See below, pp. 424–5.
21 See Petrain (2000).

But at least two other parallel etymologies do seem to derive from Gallus. The first is found in Martial 7.15:

> quis puer hic nitidis absistit Ianthidos undis?
> effugit dominam Naida numquid **Hylas**?
> o bene quod **silva** colitur Tirynthius ista
> et quod amatrices tam prope servat aquas!
> securus licet hos fontes, Argynne, ministres: 5
> nil facient Nymphae: ne velit ipse cave.

Here Hylas appears, along with a Naiad and Hercules featured as *Tirynthius*. Argynnus, another legendary drowned boy-beloved, also makes an appearance. Argynnus is a rare figure: in the whole of Latin poetry he is found only here and at Propertius 3.7.21–2: *sunt Agamemnonias testantia litora curas,/ quae notat Argynni poena minantis aquae* – in the company of Gallan *notat, testor, litora* and *curas*! Martial's interest in Gallus has already aroused comment,[22] and the very rarity of Argynnus hints that Propertius too got him from Gallus. The other etymological parallel, also from a Flavian writer, clinches the argument. In his *Argonautica* Valerius Flaccus retells the story of Hylas; he calls Hercules *Tirynthius* at 3.590, and a few lines later he repeats the etymology: *rursus Hylan et rursus Hylan per longa reclamat/ avia; responsant silvae et vaga certat imago* (3.596–7). This etymology comes three lines before line 600: *grata rudimenta; Herculeo sub nomine pendent*, which in Chapter 12 will for quite different reasons be cited as part of a proposed Gallan verbal complex, its derivation being signalled in this particular line by Gallan *nomine* (on which see also below).

nomen (5), nomen (50)

An important group of terms related etymologically by Romans, viz. *nomen, notus, nota, noscere,* and *nobilis*, has already featured largely in earlier chapters.[23] Not only does Cornelius Gallus seems to have been fond of these terms, but later poets associated them especially with him. Propertius' two uses of *nomen* are both in proximity to apostrophes of Gallus (1, 51).

---

22   See above, p. 87 and Ch. 5, esp. pp. 165–7.
23   For these (and later) discussions see Index II s.vv.

The waters of Baiae (7–10)
Lines 7–10 depict Gallus as enjoying himself at Tibur (8), Baiae (9) or
'wherever' (10). This passage places heavy emphasis on rivers and a
lake (*flumina*, 7; *Aniena* ... *tinxerit unda*, 8; *litoris*, 9; *fluminis*, 10),
and it mentions a coastal site near Baiae rich in myth (*Gigantea* ...
ora, 9). Inevitably the thought arises that 1.20.7–10 incorporate a
hitherto unrecognized example of the ancient convention, well known
to Propertius, whereby a poet is said to do what he writes about.[24] If
so, 1.20.7–10 may refer to the same Gallan elegy or elegies as do
1.11.1–4 and 9–14, where the waters of Baiae are detailed (*Herculeis*
... *litoribus*, 2; *aequora*, 4; *Lucrina* ... *aqua*, 10; *tenui Teuthrantis in
unda*, 11; *lympha*, 12) – cf. above, p. 206.

Hercules' error (15) and Hylas' errorem (42)
On the basis of several passages of Virgil and Ovid, and Propertius
1.1.11, Ross[25] claimed that various examples of *errare* in Augustan
poetry where the verb describes the actions of 'mad' lovers (*amens* is
the associated adjective) are Gallan in inspiration. He did so despite
knowing that Cicero *Aratea* 420–1 reads: *ut quondam Orion manibus
violasse Dianam/ dicitur excelsis errans in collibus amens*. Ross's
argument is perhaps strengthened by the discovery that in at least one
other celebrated case (that of *carmina digna*)[26] Gallus, rather than its
first inventor Lucretius, vectored the diffusion of an expression
throughout Augustan and later poetry.[27] Another pertinent point is that
at 1.13.35 Propertius calls Gallus' infatuation with his girl-friend a
novus ... *error* – a typical example of his playful interactions with the
elegies of his predecessor.[28] The two occurrences of the noun *error* in
Propertius 1.20 may well, then, derive from a similar vectoring by
Gallus of a phrase devised in essence by Cicero. The first occurrence
comes accompanied by *ignotis* ... *in oris* (15); *oris* is Gallan (see
below, pp. 228–9), and *ignotis* is part of the Gallan *nomen* group (see
Index II s.v.). *error* is also immediately preceded by the Gallan
Hamadryads (11–12), the 'wilderness area' (13–14), and the second

---

24   E.g. Thuc. 1.5.2; Moschus *Epitaph. Adon.* 81–4; Virg. *Ecl.* 6.45–6, 62–3; Hor. *Sat.*
      1.10.36–7; 2.5.40–1; Stat. *Silv.* 2.7.77–8. Propertian examples are: 2.30.19–22; 3.3.40–2.
      See also Coleman (1988) 84–5 and below, p. 232.
25   Ross (1975) 62–4; cf. Rosiello (2002) 437.
26   Cf. Anderson, Parsons and Nisbet (1979) 144; Hinds (1983); Cairns (1993) 108–15.
27   See above, pp. 91–3.
28   Cf. *errata* used of Ponticus' parallel infatuation at Prop. 1.9.33. For a recent wide-ranging
      exploration of *error* in this and related senses in Roman poetry see Rosiello (2002) 435–46.

invocation of Gallus (14). All this further supports the inference that *error/errare* is derived from Gallus. The fact that *error* in line 15 is qualified by *miser* suggests, but does not prove, that the evolution of *miser* in Augustan poetry from 'wretched in love' to 'lover' *simpliciter* owes at least something to Gallus. The second example of *error* in Propertius 1.20 at line 42 occurs within the phrase *nescius ... imaginibus*; its terms have already been noted as Gallan (cf. Index II s.vv.) and more will be said about *imaginibus* below (p. 230).

fleverat (16)

The surprising tears of Hercules at 1.20.16 surely require explanation. A plausible account can be offered by reference to a practice of Cornelius Gallus in his depiction of elegiac characters. It has been pointed out that, in Ovid and Virgil respectively, Milanion and Orpheus are said to have wept.[29] These are both heroes of Gallan elegy too,[30] and the similarities of expression between Ovid *Ars Amatoria* 2.188: *flesse sub arboribus* (describing Milanion), and Virgil *Georgics* 4.508–9: *rupe sub aeria .../ flesse* (used of Orpheus) indicate that both the phraseology and the sentiment are Gallan.[31] This assessment of Milanion's and Orpheus' tears is confirmed by the presence in the Ovidian passage of *arboribus*, a form already linked with Gallus (cf. Index II s.v. and below, p. 229). The tearful Hercules of 1.20 can, therefore, be added to the list of lachrymose Gallan heroes. Hercules' tears are located close to Propertius' second direct address to Gallus (14), and in the same couplet as *miser, ignotis, error* and *oris*, all terms which have just been noted as independent pointers to Gallus. It is both amusing and illuminating to observe that one of the actions which Propertius attributes no less than four times to this poet so interested in weeping heroes is weeping: 1.5.15 *fletibus*; 30 *flere* (along with Propertius himself); 1.10.2 *lacrimis*; 1.13.16 *flere*.

constitit oris (21)

In all Latin poetry prior to the fourth century AD this *iunctura* appears only here and, in the same *sedes*, at *Aeneid* 8.331. This is not likely to be an accident, and imitation of Virgil by Propertius can almost certainly be excluded since the Monobiblos appeared before the compo-

---

29   Nicastri (1984) 19.
30   Cf. Index II s.vv.
31   So Nicastri (1984) 19. *flesse* is a rare form in Augustan poetry, the only other examples being at Ov. *AA* 3.38 and *Met.* 6.404.

sition of the *Aeneid* was properly under way. Imitation of Propertius by Virgil is also unlikely; and the two passages in which the combination occurs do not overlap in any other way. It can therefore be plausibly conjectured that the coincidence is due to imitation of the same Gallan hexameter ending by both Propertius and Virgil.

arboribus (36)
The Gallan origin of *arboribus* at the end of pentameters, a *sedes* in which it is found on only three occasions besides this in Augustan poetry,[32] has already been discussed.[33] All four examples exhibit further metrical and semantic congruences and by now known Gallan terms:

roscida *desertis poma* sub **arboribus**	(Propertius 1.20.36)
urgetur quantis *Caucasus* **arboribus**	(Propertius 1.14.6)
cui *dulcia poma*	
Delia selectis *detrahat* **arboribus**	(Tibullus 1.5.31–2)
*poma*que *non notis* legit ab **arboribus**	(Tibullus 1.7.32)

Propertius 1.14.6 mentions the Caucasus, an area linked elsewhere with Gallus, and it comes two lines before *nescit Amor magnis cedere divitiis*, a line with recognized Gallan associations.[34] The use of *arboribus* in the two Tibullan pentameters gives them – fairly exceptionally for Tibullus – quadrisyllabic endings, and the second Tibullan example (1.7.32) also contains a term from the Gallan *nomen* group, i.e. (*non*) *notis*.[35] In view of all this, and of the Gallan associations of both Propertian passages, the best explanation for the congruences between Tibullus and Propertius is that offered above (p. 171): imitation by both poets of an influential line of Cornelius Gallus rather than imitation of one by the other. Finally it should be noted that the same combination of preposition and noun, *sub arboribus*, found in Propertius 1.20.36 reappears in a different *sedes* at Ovid *Ars Amatoria* 2.188 in a line (quoted above, p. 228) which may also derive from Gallus.

---

32   Cf. also Martial's *de Nomentanis sed damus arboribus* (13.42.2).
33   Above, pp. 170–1. Since different features of the relevant lines were emphasized there, they are reprinted here for convenience.
34   Cf. Index II s.vv. Amor etc., Caucasus, cedo, divitiae etc., nescio etc.
35   Compare further Prop. 1.20.15: *ignotis ... in oris*, and, for the additional possible Gallan association of final *oris*, see above, pp. 228–9 on Prop. 1.20.21: *constitit oris*.

imaginibus (42)

The three lines of classical Latin poetry[36] which present *imaginibus* in final position in the pentameter were studied earlier:[37]

> *nescius* undis
> *errorem blandis* tardat **imaginibus**   (Propertius 1.20.41–2)
>
> *nescit Amor* priscis *cedere* **imaginibus**   (Propertius 1.5.24)
>
> vanum nocturnis fallit **imaginibus**   ([Tibullus] 3.4.56)

Propertius 1.5.24, addressed to 'Gallus', has long been recognized as indebted to Cornelius Gallus,[38] and with it has been compared *nescit Amor magnis cedere divitiis* (1.14.8). Curiously earlier scholarship does not seem to have linked 1.20.41–2 with the other two lines ending with *imaginibus*, possibly because in those other lines the meaning of *imaginibus* is different. But they clearly belong together; again Gallan imitation seems virtually certain, and, as suggested above (p. 81), Propertius 1.5.24 is probably a direct or close quotation from Cornelius Gallus.

amores (51)

In the first line of 1.20 Propertius used *amore* to refer to his affection for Gallus. The penultimate line of 1.20 (*his, o Galle, tuos monitus servabis amores*, 51) was clearly intended to help provide symmetrical closure within the elegy's ring-compositional structure. This is obvious not just from the echo *amore/amores* but also from the concomitant matching of *monemus* (1) and *monitus* (51).[39] In line 51 *amores* has as its primary meaning not 'loves' but 'boy-friend', and it designates Gallus' beloved, Hylas. But there may be more to *amores*.[40] Servius' remark *Gallus ... amorum suorum de Cytheride scripsit libros quattuor* (ad *Ecl.* 10.1) was generally assumed until recently to mean that *Amores* was the title of Gallus' four books of elegies. But of late this has been denied, and it has been asserted that Roman poets

---

36   The ending also occurs at Mart. 2.90.6; 9.47.2.
37   Above, pp. 79–80, 160.
38   Cf. above, p. 79 n. 50.
39   Petrain (2000) 419–20 usefully associates the three other forms of *monere* found in the Monobiblos (two in poem 1) with these two. His point that the forms create a link between poems 1 and 20 can be extended: they also reinforce the Gallan flavour of both 1.1 and 1.20.
40   For the suggestion below, see also Petrain (2000) 419.

and critics could refer to love-poetry as *amores* with no necessary implication that this was a book-title.[41] I do not share this new view. The opening of Virgil's sustained treatment of Cornelius Gallus in *Eclogue* 10: *incipe: sollicitos Galli dicemus amores* (6), a line mentioned earlier as close in structure to 1.20.1 (cf. also *Naides, indigno cum Gallus amore peribat?*, *Eclogue* 10.10), speaks for the positive case, as does *Eclogue* 10.52–54: *certum est in silvis inter spelaea ferarum/ malle pati tenerisque meos incidere amores/ arboribus: crescent illae, crescetis, amores*, where similar allusion to a Gallan title '*Amores*' has been hypothesized.[42] Phanocles' title Ἔρωτες ἢ Καλοί has also been noted as a possible precedent,[43] and there has been some discussion of the *Ars Amatoria* couplet in which Ovid seems to have recorded the title of his own earlier amatory works as '*Amores*', although these lines have perhaps not been taken full account of in the controversy over Gallus' book-title:

> deve tribus libris, titulo quos signat AMORVM,
> elige, quod docili molliter ore legas.   (3.343–4)

The text of the couplet, printed here as by McKeown (1987), is disputed.[44] But what is not in dispute is that the couplet contains one or other form of *titulus* (the MSS offer either *titulo*, or *titulos*, or *titulus*), one of two forms of *amor* (the MSS read either *amorum* or *amoris*), and the verb *signat* (in all MSS). On any sensible combination of these readings Ovid's topic cannot be the contents of his book, but must be its title – at least, that is, the title of his second edition. So hesitation is out of place: Ovid did call his love-elegies *Amores*, and it would be no surprise if he did so to associate himself with the 'first inventor' of Roman elegy, Gallus,[45] whose influence on Ovid's later metrics has already been seen.[46] Propertius 1.20.51 does not seem to

41 By Gauly (1990) 33–40, cited with approval by Fantham (2001) 191 n. 19. Cf. also McKeown (1987) 103–7, assembling valuable additional evidence about '*Amores*' as a book-title possibly used by various writers, including Gallus, but not committing to either view.

42 By Ross (1975) 73, citing Skutsch (1901) 21–2, and referring also to *Ecl.* 10.34: *vestra meos olim si fistula dicat amores* (with Gallan *dicere*); Puelma (1982) esp. 221.

43 McKeown (1987) 105–6.

44 See McKeown (1987) 103 for details of alternative readings and references to earlier scholarly discussions; and, more recently on the text and interpretation, Gibson (2003) 237–8.

45 Cf. McKeown (1987) 104, referring to Puelma (1982) 221 n. 1. On *molliter* (344) as indicative of Gallus, see below.

46 See above, pp. 167, 170, 176, 178, 206 n. 57, but also p. 193.

have played any part in the controversy over Gallus' title, but it should certainly join the evidence for the view that the title of Gallus' elegiac poems was *Amores*: *amores* is placed prominently at the end of the penultimate line of 1.20; can it be doubted that it is in part a source-citation, and in part a reminiscence of its use (again as a source-citation) at *Eclogue* 10.54?

It was maintained earlier in this chapter that Cornelius Gallus wrote about Hylas. His Hylas poem might be expected, like his treatments of Milanion and Orpheus, to have been part of his *Amores*. A confirmation of this is perhaps detectable in the last line of Propertius 1.20. On a literal level line 52 – *formosum Nymphis credere visus Hylan* – sums up 1.20's earlier strictures on Gallus' lack of caution (2–3) and means 'you <Gallus> have been seen to entrust <your> beautiful Hylas to the nymphs <i.e. to Italian girls>'. But if Propertius is once again exploiting the ancient poetic convention whereby a writer can be said to do what he writes about (see above, p. 227), then 1.20.52 could refer additionally to Hercules' equal lack of caution and mean: 'you have been seen to write about how <Hercules> entrusted <his> Hylas to the nymphs'. On that interpretation, line 52 would also be a direct pointer to the tale of the mythical Hylas as it appeared in Gallus' *Amores* (cf. *amores* in line 51). This would give added significance to *tuos* (51), and line 52 would constitute a second source-citation confirming the earlier citation in *amores* (51), both of them placed at one of the most appropriate and most popular locations for source-citations, the end of a poem. Finally, *visus* (52) may exemplify that other poetic convention which has cropped up several times in connection with Gallus, namely that 'seeing something' equals 'reading about it',[47] and so may actually inform us that Propertius read about Hylas in the work of Gallus.

mollis/durus

mollis/durus is characteristic of Propertius:[48] the terms play a key role in the conceptual development of several Propertian elegies of the Monobiblos, in particular 1.6 and 1.7, and they also feature impor-tantly in other poems of all four Propertian books.[49] *mollis/durus* has already been noted in earlier chapters as probably derived from

---

47   See above, p. 117.
48   Cf. Ross (1975) 62 n. 2, 77; Cairns (1984b).
49   Cf. Cairns (1984b), esp. 214–17.

Gallus,[50] and the pair may have been widely recognized as emblematic of his work.[51] This is further suggested by 1.20, which presents not only *ne tibi sit duros montes et frigida saxa* (1.20.13), but also *mollia composita litora fronde tegit* (1.20.22),[52] as well as by 1.5, also addressed to 'Gallus', which offers *molliter irasci non sciet illa tibi* (8). Indeed the adverb *molliter* seems particularly diagnostic of Gallus: in addition to Propertius 1.5.8, it appears in the mouth of the Virgilian Gallus of *Eclogue* 10: *o mihi tum quam molliter ossa quiescant/ vestra meos olim si fistula dicat amores* (33–4), in proximity to one of those instances of *amores* at line-end which plausibly allude to Gallus' title.[53] Further confirmation comes from the many appearances of *molliter* in Propertian (7) and Ovidian elegy (11), in contrast with its infrequency in other Augustan poetry, where there is only a single secure example (Horace *Satires* 2.2.12).[54] Moreover some of the other Propertian uses occur in contexts where the presence of Gallus has already been suspected on other grounds: 1.3.12 (a Gallan(?) *komos*), 1.11.14 (on a 'shore' and close to Gallan 'waters'), and 1.14.1 (addressed to Tullus, Gallus' fellow-patron), where *molliter* comes early in a sentence which includes *Caucasus arboribus* (6) and ends with *nescit Amor magnis cedere divitiis* (8). In *Eclogue* 10.33, *o mihi tum quam molliter ossa quiescant*, Virgil's Gallus must be saying something close to what Cornelius Gallus wrote. Gallus' formulation may have been *molliter ossa cubent*, which Ovid repeats three times, applying it once to himself:

ut mea defunctae **molliter** *ossa* <u>cubent</u>	(*Amores* 1.8.108)
et senis Anchisae **molliter** *ossa* <u>cubent</u>	(*Heroides* 7.162)
dicere Nasonis **molliter** *ossa* <u>cubent</u>	(*Tristia* 3.3.76)[55]

---

50   See Index II s.v.

51   Cf. also Cairns (1984b) 220–1, arguing on the basis of *Ecl.* 10.42–5, where Virgil's Gallus is also the speaker.

52   Monteleone (1992) 91–124 connects some passages of Propertius 1.20 with Catullus and with Virgil's *Eclogues*. Propertius indubitably knew and imitated both, but allowance must be made for Gallan vectoring of Catullus and for a common origin in Gallus for material shared by Virgil and Propertius.

53   See above, p. 231 and n. 42.

54   The *Appendix Vergiliana* presents two further examples, both elegiac and of disputed date: *Eleg. in Maecen.* 1.92; *Catalept.* 9.17.

55   All *CLE* examples of the hemistich *molliter ossa cubent/cubant* (428.15, 1327.14, 1458.1, 2127.8) would seem to derive from Ovid.

If so, Virgil will have accommodated it to his hexameter by replacing *cubent* with *quiescant*; and Propertius' *molliter et tenera poneret ossa rosa* (1.17.22) will represent a freer variation.

Metrics

A final aspect of Propertius 1.20 worthy of study in relation to Cornelius Gallus is its metrics: of the twenty-six pentameters of 1.20 less than 50% (twelve) end in dissyllables; three of the other fourteen end in trisyllables, eight in quadrisyllables, and three in quinquesyllables. Hence of all the elegies in Propertius' four books 1.20 has the most couplets with endings longer than a dissyllable.[56] It was observed (above, p. 217) that the other elegies addressed to 'Gallus' (1.5; 1.10; and 1.13) do not employ numerous polysyllabic endings, and it was suggested that this is in part because Propertius is polemicizing against Gallus in those elegies *inter alia* by flaunting his own, more 'modern', metrics, and thus implicitly contrasting them with those of Gallus, whom he flatters elsewhere in the Monobiblos by employing a higher proportion of 'Gallan' polysyllabic endings. But 1.20, also addressed to 'Gallus', does contain numerous polysyllabic pentameter endings; so a different explanation is required. Some of the many polysyllabic endings of 1.20 are Greek proper names. Probably too various lines of 1.20 are closely modelled on lines from Cornelius Gallus' version of the myth of Hylas, some of which will have been pentameters ending in polysyllables.[57] An even more useful observation is that in 1.20 polysyllabic endings are not distributed evenly throughout. Instead seven quadrisyllable and quinquesyllable pentameter endings are concentrated in two successive episodes from the Hylas myth, the assault of the Boreads, and the *ekphrasis* of the spring (30, 32, 34, 36, 38, 40, 42), where there is an unbroken run of polysyllabic endings.[58] Of the remaining polysyllabic endings of 1.20 four are found in direct or indirect references to the rape of the mythical Hylas (4, 10, 12, 16). The result is that, with the possible exception of lines 10 and 12, the polysyllabic endings appear mainly in those parts of 1.20 in which Gallus does not appear in person. In microcosm, therefore, 1.20 reflects the same phenomenon as was observed overall in the Monobiblos: a lower proportion of

---

56   Proportions cannot be invoked here since 1.21 and 1.22 have a higher proportion of such endings than 1.20, but each is only ten lines long.
57   The polysyllabic hexameter ending *Orithyiae* (1.20.31) is also suggestive.
58   It is followed by a pentameter ending in a trisyllable (44).

polysyllabic endings is employed where Gallus is explicitly present, a higher proportion where his presence is implicit.

The polysyllabic pentameter endings of 1.20 are not noticeably different in nature from those found elsewhere in Propertius' work. Among the four and five syllable endings there are Catullan usages: *insidias* (30) and *officio* (40);[59] others are shared with other elegists, sometimes including Propertius himself. Of these, two come from Gallan verbal complexes: *arboribus* (36) and *imaginibus* (42). Another, *hospitio* (10), is paralleled in Propertius 1.15.20 and Valgius Rufus fr. 4.2 Courtney (*hospitiis*),[60] which might suggest that it too was Gallan. One proper noun ending (*Hamadryasin*, 32) is found elsewhere only in Propertius' *laudatur facilis inter Hamadryadas* (2.34.76), and there are some *unica*: the proper nouns/adjectives *Ascanius/Ascanio* (4, 16); *Adryasin* (12), *Thyniasin* (34), and the common noun *papaveribus* (38). The known Gallan associations of the nymphs referred to in *Adryasin* and *Hamadryasin* have already been remarked on (cf. Index II s.vv.); *papaveribus* as a form is unique in extant Latin literature. 1.20 is unremarkable in its placement of polysyllabic endings in significant locations. In this area Propertius appears to have consciously practised self-restraint. *Ascanius* comes in second position (4), concluding the first quatrain, with *ex animo* (2) preceding it at the end of the first couplet; this combination was perhaps enough to provide metrical confirmation of Gallan influence on 1.20. No other significant location in 1.20 exhibits a polysyllable pentameter ending. In this metrical aspect too 1.20 conforms by understatement with the practice of the other elegies addressed to 'Gallus'.

THE HYLAS MYTH

Although the majority of the polysyllabic pentameter endings of 1.20 are concentrated in its mythical portions, the reverse is true of many of the Gallan verbal echoes hypothesized in the preceding paragraphs: these have tended to come in sections of 1.20 addressed to 'Gallus'. A priori it can be surmised that the myth of Hylas does not in fact lack further reflections of Cornelius Gallus' work, among them the generalized 'neoteric' features identified by Ross. But it is nevertheless

---

59   For details, see above, pp. 156–7.
60   Cf. also *hospitibus* (Mart. 5.62.4).

intriguing that more specifically Gallan features are harder to find in the myth of 1.20, particularly since we know that Gallus actually wrote about Hylas. One possible explanation is that, as well as Gallus' Hylas poem, the Greek source of 1.20 has contributed largely to its account of the myth of Hylas. All scholars who have worked on Propertius 1.20, irrespective of whether or not they have concentrated on Gallus' role in it, and irrespective of how they have identified the 'Galli' of the Monobiblos, have felt the presence in the elegy of such a Greek source. The overwhelming likelihood is that in his Hylas poem Gallus had exploited the same Greek model, and that, although Propertius will also have had independent access to it, he utilized Gallus' version of it too. On these assumptions 1.20 will be commenting on Gallus' prior handling of their common model and be attempting to improve on Gallus' treatment of it. What, then, was that model? While Propertian scholars have been in agreement about its existence, there has been considerable debate about its identity. The main difficulty is, in the words of Virgil, *cui non dictus Hylas*? (*Georgics* 3.6).[61] Naturally Roman writers who had previously treated Hylas – Varro of Atax was one, and there must have been others – can be excluded right away:[62] the scholarly consensus that the postulated additional model was Greek is supported by the overwhelmingly hellenistic ethos of Propertius 1.20, and it will gain more strength in the discussion below. Incidentally, the impact of that Greek source on Gallus' myth of Hylas may have further induced Propertius to follow in 1.20 Gallan metrical practice, which was clearly closer to the Greek norm in its high tolerance of polysyllabic endings.

Models have been proposed for 1.20 in Greek versions of the Hylas myth. Two major ones survive, Theocritus *Idyll* 13 and Apollonius Rhodius *Argonautica* 1.1207–1272. Then there is a third, that of Nicander in his *Heteroioumena* (fr. 48 Schneider),[63] which can be reconstructed from Antoninus Liberalis 26; it was substantially the same as that of Theocritus.[64] Euphorion too may have treated the

---

61   For the implications of Virgil's question cf. Thomas (1988) II.38; Fedeli (1980) 455–8.

62   Varro of Atax's version of the Hylas story in his *Argonautae*, a translation of Apollonius' *Argonautica*, could nevertheless have contributed to those of Gallus and Propertius. Varro's choice of the name 'Leucadia' for his mistress might indicate the influence on him of Parthenius, who wrote a work called Λευκαδίαι (fr. 14 Lightfoot) – see below.

63   Cf. Gow and Scholfield (1953) 205–8, esp. 207.

64   Cf. the discussion of possible Greek sources by Fedeli (1980) 454–8, on which this paragraph is based. However, as Wijsman (1993) 316–7 points out, Nicander probably mentioned the river Ascanius, whereas other surviving accounts earlier than Prop. 1.20 do not. Nicander has therefore a claim to be at least an ultimate source for Propertius.

Hylas myth.[65] Fedeli draws some interesting parallels between the versions of Apollonius and Propertius, and these will be revisited below, but he notes that there are also significant differences between Apollonius' and Propertius' versions. Fedeli perceives analogies between Theocritus *Idyll* 13 and Propertius 1.20, and fewer diversities, but he does not claim that Theocritus is Propertius' Greek source. Fedeli also rejects, correctly in my view, various other scholars' proposals about Propertius' Greek source, namely that he was Philetas, or Euphorion,[66] or Callimachus. Fedeli continues, however, to adhere strongly to the notion that Propertius did have an (unknown) Greek source; as evidence he points to the mentions of the '*Adryades*' in line 12, and of Mt Arganthus in line 33, and also to the uniqueness of the episode of Hylas' conflict with the Boreads in lines 25–30, an episode found in no writer except Propertius.

Under these circumstances a new candidate for the Greek source of Gallus and Propertius may be proposed, namely the poet and scholar Parthenius of Nicaea, who has already surfaced[67] as teacher to Virgil, Gallus, and possibly also Propertius. Parthenius was brought as a captive to Rome from Bithynia at some time in the 70s or 60s BC and was manumitted, and he may have been active there until around 30 BC.[68] Apart from instructing Virgil, whose *Eclogues* and *Georgics* are indebted to him, and Gallus, to whom he dedicated his *Erotika Pathemata*, Parthenius' poetic influence probably extended to Varro of Atax and certainly to Helvius Cinna. Parthenius may also, although this can only be surmised, have instructed Catullus and Asinius Pollio.[69] The possibility that Parthenius taught the young Propertius arises from Propertius' tribute to him in the first elegy of the Monobiblos, but this could simply be an imitation of an earlier tribute by Gallus, or/and a genuflection to Virgil's allusion to his Greek master in the *Eclogues*.[70]

There is no direct evidence that Parthenius ever treated the Hylas myth.[71] But Parthenius' not very extensive fragments and testimonia

65 Frr. 79–81 van Groningen; cf. Ardizzoni (1967) 259.
66 However, Monteleone (1992) 120–2 continued to see in Euphorion a source for Gallus.
67 See above, esp. pp. 110–11, 131–4.
68 The date of Parthenius' arrival in Rome is disputed and the date of his death is unknown: see Lightfoot (1999) 9–16.
69 The sorts of instruction and assistance which such learned Greeks gave their Roman pupils are usefully set out by Francese (1999).
70 Cf. above, pp. 110–11, 131–4.
71 POxy. 3723 refers to Hylas as the beloved of Heracles, but Lightfoot (1999) 27 n. 42 stopped short of attributing it to Parthenius.

contain two works in which the Hylas myth could appropriately have featured: he wrote a *Heracles* (frr. 19–22 Lightfoot),[72] where the myth of Hylas would have been germane, and he also composed *Metamorphoses* (fr. 24 Lightfoot), which again could have included the transformation of Hylas. The only tale known for certain to have formed part of Parthenius' *Metamorphoses* is that of Scylla. But Nicander had included the Hylas myth in his *Heteroioumena*; so Parthenius could easily have done the same in his *Metamorphoses*. The relationship of Parthenius with Gallus as his teacher and *cliens* – for the dedication to Gallus of Parthenius' *Erotika Pathemata* implies *clientela* – would have provided background and motive for Gallus' use of a Parthenian myth. Moreover Propertius 1.20 contains pointers to Parthenius, both general and particular. The examination of them which follows will also note in passing further proofs that 1.20 must have had a specific, and indeed Greek, source in addition to Gallus, and it will attempt to elucidate more of the learned elements of the elegy. But attention will be given mainly to indications of the presence of Parthenius in Propertius 1.20.

The first point to be emphasized is that Parthenius was a Bithynian and that the myth of Hylas is narrated in Propertius 1.20 specifically as a Bithynian myth: this is made quite explicit when the nymphs who seize Hylas are characterized as 'Bithynian nymphs' – *Nymphis ... Thyniasin* (34). The other known toponym in the same couplet (33–4), *mons Arganthus*, was located above the Bithynian coastal city of Cius;[73] and the Ascanius, already named twice (4, 16), is a river or lake in the same vicinity. Bithynia was said to have been inhabited originally by Mysians,[74] and the boundaries of Bithynia and Mysia were fluid in antiquity. So it is no surprise that both Bithynia and Mysia laid claim to the area around Cius – and also to the myth of Hylas. Evidence of a real-life assertion cum 'proof' of the Mysian claim has survived: the Mysian women called ritually on Hylas as 'the Mysian'.[75] The dispute over Hylas between Bithynia and Mysia was certainly much discussed,[76] and among hellenistic poets it seems to have featured both in Alexander Aetolus and Euphorion. Strabo

72   Lightfoot (1999) 111–12, 160–4.
73   On the problem of Pege/Pegae, and on the form Arganthus, see Fedeli (1980) 477.
74   The claim goes back to Skylax of Karyanda (6th–5th century BC): see Strabo 12.4.8.
75   ἐπιβοᾷ τὸν Μύσιον· ὅταν θρηνῶσιν αἱ Μυσαί, τὸν Μύσιον [τὸν] Ὕλαν ἀνακαλοῦνται (Hesychius ε 4645).
76   See the texts cited by Magnelli (1999) 93–4, 218–23.

appears to have thought (14.5.29) that Alexander's lines favoured the Mysian claim:[77]

Οἳ καὶ ἐπ' Ἀσκανίων δώματ' ἔχουσι ροῶν
λίμνης Ἀσκανίης ἐπὶ χείλεσιν, ἔνθα Δολίων
υἱὸς Σειληνοῦ νάσσατο καὶ Μελίης.
(Alexander Aetolus fr. 6 Magnelli)

They whose homes are by the Ascanian streams on the lips of Lake Ascania, where Dolion, son of Silenus and Melie, lived.

Euphorion (like most writers) also definitely adopted the Mysian claim by asserting that the Ascanius is Mysian: Μυσοῖο παρ' ὕδασιν Ἀσκανίοιο (Euphorion fr. 74 van Groningen),[78] cf. Ascanius amnis est Mysiae (Servius auctus ad Georg. 3.269) – in these two passages the Ascanius is a river – and there are further echoes of this approach in other accounts of the rape of Hylas which place it in Mysia, e.g. those of Dionysius Periegetes Orbis Descriptio 805–8 and [Hyginus] Fabulae 14.25.

Nevertheless Propertius' Greek source for 1.20 clearly (and probably exceptionally) opted for Bithynia, which by Parthenius' time controlled the relevant area. This suits the idea that Propertius' source was Parthenius, a native Bithynian poet who started his poetic career there.[79] Such concentration on epichoric material of interest to local cities or rulers is a standard feature of hellenistic literature. The one mention of Mysia in Propertius 1.20 does not conflict with the elegy's choice of Bithynia as the location of the myth. Rather it too is part of the polemic, and was intended to forestall the Mysian claim to Hylas. The Argonauts, we are told, landed on the cliffs of Mysia (20); but then Hylas was taken by Bithynian nymphs (34): therefore he must have strayed from Mysia into Bithynia. The landing in Mysia thus explains away the Mysian claim, while the placement of the event in Bithynia disproves it. Who else but a Bithynian poet would have written in this way? And what other Bithynian poet's work would have ranked more highly in the minds of Gallus and Propertius than that of Parthenius? It should be added that there is an important

77   Although he might have been wrong if 'Melie' is not just a 'Dryad' but the name of the Bithynian nymph of Apollon. Rhod. Argon. 2.4: cf. Magnelli (1999) 222–3.

78   Cf. also Χθιζόν μοι κνώσσοντι παρ' Ἀργανθώνιον αἶπος (Euphorion fr. 80 van Groningen), suggesting Euphorion's further interest in the area.

79   Cf. Lightfoot (1999) 9–13.

learned background to the Mysia/Bithynia dispute. According to legend the eponyms of the two areas, Mysos and Thynos, were brothers, and sons of Arganthone, a heroine who will recur shortly in this discussion. As noted, Propertius twice names the 'Ascanius' (4, 16). Commentators have asked whether Propertius is referring to the river Ascanius near the city of Cius, or to Lake Ascanius – the λίμνη Ἀσκανία.[80] The river flowed out of the lake.[81] The ambivalence of Latin 'Ascanius', which has troubled Propertian scholars, would not have existed in Greek since 'river' is masculine in Greek while 'lake' is feminine. But the ambiguity may have been welcomed by Propertius (and Gallus?), since, as well as referring primarily to the river Ascanius (as it most likely does), the name would also have evoked the λίμνη Ἀσκανία (modern 'Lake of Iznik'), on the eastern shore of which Parthenius' probable native city Nicaea stood; so it would have had the additional function of alluding to Parthenius and his work. Another observation revolves around the two adjectives attached by Propertius to the 'Ascanius', viz. *crudelis* and *indomitus*:

crudelis Minyis dixerit **Ascanius**   (4)

Ascanius, harsh to the Argonauts, could attest this.

quae miser ignotis error perpessus in oris
    Herculis indomito fleuerat **Ascanio**   (15–16)

the suffering the unhappy lover, Hercules, wandering in strange lands, bewailed to the savage Ascanius.

It could of course be argued that these adjectives do no more than express the poet's indignation – reflecting in turn the feelings of Hercules and of the poem's reader – at the part played by the Ascanius in Hylas's rape and retention. But it is curious that the two epithets also seem to evoke a Greek etymology associated with a bye-name of 'Ascanius'. The trail begins with two successive entries in the *Etymologicum Magnum*. The fact that they are successive seems to be significant in this particular case, and it may reveal a common origin and/or transmission in scholia or lexicography:[82]

---

80   Strabo 12.4 discusses Bithynia, with awareness of historical changes; cf. also 14.5.29. On the Ascanius see Fedeli (1980) 459–60; Lightfoot (1999) 83 n. 275.
81   So Strabo 14.5.29.
82   How far sequence is generally significant in lexica is unclear, but for another instance where it appears to be see Cairns (1995) 612–13.

Ἀσκάνιος· Ὁ υἱὸς Αἰνείου τοῦ Τρωός. Εἴρηται δέ, ὅτι Αἰνείας ἐπιγαμίᾳ χρησάμενος ἀπ' Ἀσκάλωνος, ὑπό τε Ἀσκάλου τοῦ τότε βασιλεύοντος τῆς χώρας ξενισθείς, διὰ τὴν πρὸς αὐτὸν φιλίαν τὸν υἱὸν Ἀσκάλιον προσηγόρευσεν· ὃς τῇ Ῥωμαίων διαλέκτῳ Ἀσκάνιος ὠνομάσθη.

Ἀσκάλαφος· Παρὰ τὸ ἀσκαλὲς τῆς ἀφῆς, ὁ λίαν σκληρός. (p. 154 ll. 19–26 Kallierges)

The first entry tells us that 'Ascanius' is the Latin equivalent of Greek 'Askalios', and it explains the nomenclature of Aeneas' son. He was called Askalios after Askalos, king of Askalon, who had hosted Aeneas there. The second entry derives another name, 'Askalaphos', from τὸ ἀσκαλὲς τῆς ἀφῆς meaning something like 'the toughness/ harshness of the grip' (possibly a reference to wrestling); 'Aska-laphos' is then glossed as 'excessively harsh'. We are not far from *crudelis* and *indomitus*. Further etymologies in the Theocritus scholia of ἄσκαλα and ἀσκάλευτον(α) from negated σκαλίς, which produce such glosses as ἀναροτρίαστα, ἀκατέργαστα, ἀκόσμητα, ἀγεώργη-τον, and ἠμελημένα,[83] bring to mind the use of Greek ἡμερόω and Latin *domare* in agricultural contexts. Propertius seems to have repro-duced a Greek etymology which appeared in his Greek source, and which is reflected in these two lexicon entries. Of course other Greek writers, from Homer on, mention 'Ascania' and 'Ascanius'. But a writer who was Bithynian would have been more likely than most to interest himself in the etymology of 'Ascanius', particularly in the context of the rape of Hylas.

A Bithynian writer like Parthenius, who was brought as 'spoil' to Rome, and who then built himself a new life and career there as a poet and grammarian in the highest social circles, would have had an additional motive for spreading knowledge of the Bithynian Ascanius. The remark of the *Etymologicum Magnum* about the Roman and Greek forms Askalios/Ascanius fits very well with the intellectual climate of Rome in the late Republic, when learned Greeks were assuring their Roman pupils that Latin was a form of Greek.[84] The further remark of the *Etymologicum Magnum* about the association of the name Ascanius with Aeneas' son suits a context even closer to Parthenius – and to Cornelius Gallus: Cornelius Gallus was an adherent and military subordinate of C. Iulius Caesar, who in the 50s

---

83 Schol. Theocr. *Id.* 10.14. a–b, e–g Wendel.
84 On this theory's proponents, and on opposition to it, see Maltby (1993).

and 40s BC was publicizing the Trojan origins of his family, the derivation of his *nomen* 'Iulius' from Ascanius' later appellation Iulus, and his own direct descent from Aeneas and Ascanius.[85] The promotion of a link between the name of Aeneas' son and the Bithynian lake and river name Ascanius would have served the interests of Parthenius, of Gallus, and of Caesar. That the link became familiar to Romans is assured by its mention in Servius: *sciendum est autem hunc primo Ascanium dictum a Phrygiae flumine Ascanio, ut est 'transque sonantem Ascanium'* (ad *Aeneid* 1.267). One wonders if Parthenius propagated it, and whether Julius Caesar's early residence at the court of the Bithynian king Nicomedes IV is also relevant.[86]

A last point about the Ascanius: there is a possibility that Parthenius was popularly known in Rome as, or described himself as, something like 'the man from Askania', i.e. Bithynia. The evidence for this assertion comes from the first couplet of an elegiac epigram most probably composed by the emperor Hadrian, whose advanced cultural level makes it less likely that he employed a Greek epigrammatist to write it for him. This epigram was discovered in the Renaissance on the restored tomb of none other than Parthenius.[87] His tomb had been damaged by flood-water and it was then rebuilt by the philhellene Hadrian, who had the epigram inscribed upon it. The epigram was copied inaccurately in the Renaissance, and hence has required considerable restoration. But the key words are accepted by all editors:

[.......... ἀ]ριδείκετον [ἀν]δρὸ[ς] ἀοι[δοῦ,
[γαῖ]α τὸν Ἀ[σ]κανίη [γ]είνατο Πα[ρθέ]νιο[ν   (1–2)

the glorious (?name/?tomb) of the poet, Parthenius whom the Ascanian land bore

The use in line 2 of [γαῖ]α ... Ἀ[σ]κανίη to indicate Parthenius' birthplace is unlikely to have been casual, given Hadrian's learning. It may well indicate that Parthenius himself had described his native Bithynia as 'the Ascanian land', and indeed that he had done so when identifying himself in a *sphragis* or similar significant passage. If this is so, Propertius' (Gallus') two references to the Ascanius in 1.20 would amount to a 'hellenistic footnote' specifying his Greek source for the Hylas myth as Parthenius.

85   Cf., e.g., Weinstock (1971) 15–18, 253–4.
86   Cf. Sueton. *Iul.* 49.
87   Lightfoot (1999) 5–6 (Test. 4), 82–4.

Another indication that Parthenius was the Greek source for the Hylas poems of Gallus and Propertius is indirect but powerful. Propertius 1.20 introduces a second major geographical feature of Bithynia, Mt Arganthus (or 'Arganthon'), which Propertius specifically associates with the 'Thynian' nymphs:[88]

> hic erat Arganthi Pege sub uertice montis
> grata domus Nymphis umida Thyniasin   (33–4)

Here was Pege, beneath the peak of Mt Arganthus, a watery home pleasing to the Thynian nymphs.

Mt Arganthus specifies the locus of the rape of Hylas, but it may also again point to Parthenius. No poetic treatment of Arganthus by Parthenius is known. But in his Ἐρωτικὰ Παθήματα (36) Parthenius recounts the myth of Arganthone, the eponym of Mt Arganthus(on). Her story was aetiological, explaining the nomenclature of a major Bithynian mountain standing above an important Bithynian coastal city, Cius; it was also part of the foundation legend of Bithynia, since the founder, Thynos, was one of Arganthone's sons.[89] The legend of Arganthone stands in final position in the Ἐρωτικὰ Παθήματα, presumably because it had a special significance for the Bithynian Parthenius. This suggests that the mountain is named by Propertius because he found it either in an elegy of Gallus rendering Parthenius, or in a work of Parthenius himself. Moreover, and even more important, the Arganthone myth climaxes in an episode which is remarkably similar to the finale of the Hylas myth. After the rape of Hylas, Hercules wandered around the entire area calling on Hylas by name (e.g. Propertius 1.20.15–16, 49–50). This, as is well known, is another aetiology, that of ritual practices carried out in the area where Hylas disappeared.[90] In the myth of Arganthone as told by Parthenius she had a love affair with Rhesus who then went off to the Trojan War and was killed. Learning of his death Arganthone 'went back again to the place where she first made love with him and wandering around it called out constantly the name of Rhesus'.[91] This detail conjures up the vision (although it is very speculative) of a section of Parthenius'

88   Cf. Fedeli (1980) 447.
89   Cf. Lightfoot (1999) 363–4, 552–8.
90   Cf. Butler and Barber (1933) 185–6.
91   Cf. Lightfoot (1999) 557.

Metamorphoses in which Bithynian myths,[92] including those of Arganthone and Hylas, were juxtaposed.[93]

There are also some indications within the very small corpus of fragments of Parthenius that various expressions, topics, and interests of Propertius 1.20 (and Gallus) are not alien to Parthenius. None of them constitute a definite direct link between Parthenius and Propertius; rather they show congruity of material. Hence they will simply be listed with minimal commentary in the order in which they appear in Parthenius' fragments.

1. τὸν Ζέφ(υρον)· ἐκείνῳ γ(ὰρ) ἐγαμήθη ἡ Ἶρις (Zephyrus, for Iris married him) (fr. 2 Lightfoot: schol. 11–14 ad 15)

Possibly this scholion reveals interest in winds on Parthenius' part. The Boreads play a significant role in Propertius 1.20 (25–31), and their mother Orithyia is named and her rape by Boreas in Attica is evoked there (31).

2. Γρύνειος Ἀπόλλων (Grynean Apollo) (fr. 10 Lightfoot)

This fragment from the *Delos* of Parthenius shows that, at the very least, Parthenius had an interest in Grynean Apollo.[94] It thus counters to some extent the assumption sometimes made on the basis of Servius ad *Eclogue* 6.72 that the god and his grove were exclusively Euphorionic. So it may throw light on Gallus' famous poem on the Grynean Grove, suggesting that perhaps there too Parthenius was an influence.[95]

3. ἀμφοτέροις ἐπιβὰς Ἅρπυς ἐληΐσατο (with both feet planted on him <Love> the Harpy looted him) (fr. 13 Lightfoot)

In this line from Parthenius' *Crinagoras*, the Ἅρπυς is Eros and the metaphor is from 'straddling a fallen enemy/wrestling' – so Lightfoot. The attack is marginally similar to that of the Boreads on Hylas in Propertius 1.20, and the phraseology and underlying concept are close to those of Propertius 1.1.4: *et caput impositis pressit Amor pedibus*. It is generally acknowledged that behind Propertius 1.1.1–4 lies the first quatrain of an epigram of Meleager (*AP* 12.101.1–4).[96] However, particularly in view of the allusion to Parthenius which follows in

---

92   A substantial amount of Bithynian myth and geographical material survives from antiquity
      – for an interesting exploitation of it see Larson (1997). Parthenius must have contributed
      to its survival.
93   It must be said, however, that in the *Erotika Pathemata* her story ends not with a meta-
      morphosis but with her death from grief and from not eating and drinking.
94   Cf. Lightfoot (1999) General Index s.v. Grynium/Grynean Grove.
95   *Pace* Lightfoot (1999) 150.
96   Cf. Fedeli (1980) 62–3.

1.1.11, this Parthenian fragment hints that Parthenius and also Gallus influenced the opening two couplets of the Monobiblos as well as the following couplets.

4.] .. Ἀχιλλείων θῆκεν ἐπὶ σκοπέλων (placed them on the Achillean rocks) (fr. 27(a).7 Lightfoot)
]ς ἀλγεινοὶ παιδὸς εχ.. ι. [(painful ... of the boy) (fr. 27(a).9 Lightfoot)
Both lines probably come from an *epikedion* for a certain Timander (cf. fr. 27(a).4) and so are unlikely to be directly relevant. They involve a similar term (7, cf. Propertius 1.20.20: *scopulis*), and sentiment (9, loss of/longing for(?) a young person).

5. εἰσόκε μιν Κύπρις πηγὴν θέτο, μῖξε δ' ἔρωτι/ Κύδνου καὶ νύμφης ὑδατόεντα γάμον (until the Cyprian goddess made her a spring, and mingled in love the watery nuptials of Cydnus and the nymph) (fr. 28.4–5 Lightfoot)
This couplet, from an account of a different myth, probably that of Comaitho who fell in love with the river Cydnus and was turned into a spring, contains the terms πηγή and νύμφη, here seen conjoined by Parthenius in an erotic context. It is one of a number of fragments which show that Parthenius (like Gallus) had an interest in waters and littorals.[97]

6. αὐτὸς δ' ἐς νύμφας ὤχετ' ἐφυδριάδας (and it went to the water nymphs)
This line is not by Parthenius but is from the *Apollo* of Alexander Aetolus (fr. 3.22 Magnelli). It tells how (supposedly) a pitcher (αὐτός) fell into a well. The long fragment of Alexander Aetolus from which it comes is quoted by Parthenius in *Erotika Pathemata* 14. This shows that Parthenius was aware of a pentameter hemistich similar to the latter half of Propertius 1.20.32 (*ibat Hamadryasin* vel. sim.), and so raises the possibility that elsewhere Parthenius had altered Alexander's line into a more exact model for *ibat Hamadryasin* (and its Gallan predecessor?). Parthenius *Erotika Pathemata* 14 tells the tale of Antheus. It is of the 'Potiphar's wife' variety, and it differs in many of its details from the myth of Hylas. But, besides introducing in one version a vessel for carrying water, it also involves water (the well) and the immersion of the young man Antheus in it – and the errant wife is twice called νύμφη (fr. 3.8, 16 Magnelli).

97   Cf. also frr. 3.16 and schol., 11, 14, 23, 24(a), 24(b), 29, 32, 36, (?)54, (?)56.

The identification of Parthenius as the probable Greek source for the myth of Hylas in Gallus and Propertius enables a new approach to be taken to three couplets of Propertius 1.20 which have caused long-standing perplexities:

> hunc duo sectati fratres, Aquilonia proles,
>   hunc super et Zetes, hunc super et Calais,
> oscula suspensis instabant carpere palmis,
>   oscula et alterna ferre supina fuga.
> ille sub extrema pendens secluditur ala
>   et volucres ramo summovet insidias.   (Propertius 1.20.25–30)

Two brothers followed him, sons of the North Wind, both Zetes above him and Calais above him; their hands in mid-air, they pressed upon him to snatch kisses, and one after the other rushed to seize kisses from his uplifted face. He, hanging beneath a wing-tip, is shielded and with a branch wards off the winged ambush.

These complex and difficult lines describe a scene which precedes the rape of Hylas by the nymphs of the spring. Fedeli provided a defence of the transmitted readings, along with a comprehensive account of earlier interpretations of them.[98] The scene is unparalleled in ancient literature, and this fact raises two questions: who invented it, and with what inspiration? Addressing the latter question Butler and Barber usefully noted a resemblance between these lines and a depiction on a vase of 'a boy pursued or carried off by a two-winged figure, perhaps a representation of the story of Zephyrus and Hyacinthus'.[99] This pointer to representational art was shrewd: Propertius is an intensely visual poet,[100] and the Propertian lines indeed have the air of an *ekphrasis* of a work of art. More specifically the grotesque physical interactions between the Boreads and Hylas, and the bodily contortions in which the participants in the Propertian scene engage, are reminiscent of various Hellenistic and later works of visual art which exploit the flexibility of the human body in ways virtually

---

98 Fedeli (1980) 472–6. While certain difficulties remain, Fedeli's account is sufficiently persuasive to render otiose the heavily emended text subsequently printed by Goold (1990) 106 = (1999) 94: *hunc duo sectati fratres, Aquilonia proles/ (nunc superat Zetes, nunc superat Calais),/ oscula suspensis instabant carpere plantis/ oscula et alterna ferre supina fuga./ ille sed extrema pendentes ludit in ala/ et volucris ramo summovet insidias.* (The words underlined are emendations).

99 Butler and Barber (1933) 184–5. For a more exact and detailed discussion of such scenes on vases see Di Stefano (1992/93) 240–1.

100 Cf., e.g., Keyssner (1938); Di Stefano (1992/93).

unknown in earlier periods. In the sculptural field, one thinks, for example, of certain *symplegmata*, of the crucified Marsyas, of the dying Galatians, and of many other so-called 'grotesque' or 'baroque' pieces of hellenistic statuary.[101] However, little can be done to relate the Hylas myth to hellenistic art beyond noting the general congruence of the Boreads' attempt on Hylas with hellenistic visual tastes: *LIMC* s.v. Hylas offers nothing comparable. Enlightenment must, then, be sought elsewhere, and it will not be found in another description of the same event, since, as noted, none exists. But there does exist a Greek description of another episode from the rape of Hylas which embodies the same kinds of physical contortions, Apollonius Rhodius *Argonautica* 1.1234–9. This passage has frequently been discussed in connection with the assault on Hylas by the nymphs,[102] but its relevance to the Boreads' attempt on Hylas has not been observed:

> αὐτὰρ ὅγ᾽ ὡς τὰ πρῶτα ῥόῳ ἔνι κάλπιν ἔρεισε
> λέχρις ἐπιχριμφθείς, περὶ δ᾽ ἄσπετον ἔβραχεν ὕδωρ   1235
> χαλκὸν ἐς ἠχήεντα φορεύμενον, αὐτίκα δ᾽ ἥγε
> λαιὸν μὲν καθύπερθεν ἐπ᾽ αὐχένος ἄνθετο πῆχυν,
> κύσσαι ἐπιθύουσα τέρεν στόμα, δεξιτερῇ δὲ
> ἀγκῶν᾽ ἔσπασε χειρί· μέσῃ δ᾽ ἐνὶ κάββαλε δίνῃ.

But as soon as he dipped the pitcher in the stream, leaning to one side, and the plentiful water rang loud as it poured against the sounding bronze, straightaway she laid her left arm above upon his neck yearning to kiss his tender mouth; and with her right hand she drew down his elbow, and plunged him into the midst of the eddy. (tr. R.C. Seaton, adapted)

This is Apollonius' account of the seizure of Hylas by a (single) water-nymph, an event which is described less graphically by Propertius (43–8), at any rate as far as his (plural) nymphs' behaviour is concerned. What is striking about Apollonius' lines, themselves plausibly ekphrastic of a work of art, is that, like Propertius' account of the Boreads' attempt on Hylas, they involve gratuitously odd physical posturings. In Apollonius the boy Hylas, when he approaches

---

101 Cf., e.g., R. R. R. Smith (1991) 99–126. On the artistic background to representations of Hylas in vase-painting and mosaic see Di Stefano (1992/93) 236–45; on some later Hylas mosaics showing interlacings of limbs cf. also Muth (1999) esp. 112–17.

102 Cf., e.g., Fedeli (1980) 456, 479–80 using λέχρις ἐπιχριμφθείς (*Arg.* 1.1235) to illustrate *innixus* (Prop. 1.20.44).

the stream to fill his κάλπις,[103] bends over sideways (1235). Both the
adverb λέχρις and the verb ἐπιχρίμπτω are rarities, and the participle
ἐπιχριμφθείς is seemingly unique here in the sense 'lean over' or
'lean towards'.[104] Similarly Apollonius goes out of his way to sketch
in vivid detail the corporeal interactions of his water-nymph and
Hylas, portraying her with her left hand above Hylas' neck, and her
right hand grasping his elbow (1236–9). Moreover, in the context of
Propertius 1.20 Apollonius' κύσσαι ἐπιθύουσα τέρεν στόμα (1238)
can usefully be compared with Propertius' oscula ... instabant carpere
(27, of the Boreads), and his detail ἀγκῶν' (1239) is also worth comparing (although the correspondence is less exact) with Propertius' sub
extrema ... ala (29), again from the passage about the Boreads. Unfortunately, however, although the two poets have certain details in
common in these two passages, Apollonius' account of the nymph's
seizure of Hylas has limited value in explicating Propertius' account
of the Boreads' attempt on his Hylas. It is very likely that Apollonius,
among others, influenced Propertius' Greek model. But the features
shared by Apollonius and Propertius have been blurred in the
transmission, and Fedeli's exegesis still remains on the whole the best
guide to Propertius 1.20.25–30.

At the same time, once it is realized that the episode of the
Boreads is a doublet of the episode of Hylas' rape by the nymph, its
genesis can be hypothesized. It is highly improbable that either Gallus
or Propertius extrapolated the episode of the Boreads' preliminary
attack on Hylas directly from Apollonius' account of the actual Rape
of Hylas. There is too much in Propertius (Gallus?) that is too unlike
Apollonius, and yet the impression of a Greek source for 1.20 remains
ineluctable. But, if the Boreads episode is indeed the invention of a
Greek source, then the fact that it is unparalleled elsewhere in ancient
literature suggests strongly that it was invented not long before
Propertius wrote 1.20. Had it been an early hellenistic invention, it
would probably have found an echo in some other Greek text. As for
its failure to reappear in any later Latin (or indeed Greek) text, this
exemplifies the falling out of fashion of the Hylas legend among the
Augustans, the most striking proof of which is that the myth of Hylas
is conspicuously absent from the Metamorphoses, although perfectly

---

103 On this implement, and on the comment upon it of the scholia, see Ardizzoni (1967) 259–
     60.
104 On λέχρις see Ardizzoni (1967) 265; Fedeli (1980) 456, 479–80; on ἐπιχρίμπτω and its
     meanings, LSJ s.v.

appropriate in subject-matter. The easiest conclusion, then, must be that Parthenius was the creator of the incident of the Boreads. The linguistic and conceptual complexity of Propertius 1.20.25–31 also argues strongly for Parthenius, although of course Gallus too could well have narrated the episode in his Hylas poem, having taken it from Parthenius.

The upshot of this discussion is, then, that the Boreads episode was most likely calqued upon the later rape of Hylas by Parthenius, an acute reader of Apollonius Rhodius who wanted to recount as a preliminary to the successful rape of Hylas an unheard of, and unsuccessful, attempted rape of Hylas. Parthenius will have wanted to balance his narrative of the actual rape and to add fresh interest to it by prefacing the well-known success story of the nymph(s)' seizure of Hylas with a novel failed prior attempt by the Boreads, whose hereditary tendency to such activities might plausibly be deduced from the behaviour of their father, Boreas.[105] This sort of creativity in the multiplication of incidents and characters has perhaps been studied most intensively in the works of Parthenius' best pupil, Virgil, in whose *Aeneid* in particular single Homeric characters and incidents are frequently multiplied in this way.[106] Inevitably one might speculate that Parthenius taught this technique to his pupils as well as employing it in his own works.

---

105   Cf. Prop. 1.20.31, where the Boreads are described as *Pandioniae ... genus Orithyiae* as an allusion to their mother's rape by Boreas. The phrase may reproduce Parthenius' Greek.
106   On this feature of Virgil's compositional technique see especially Knauer (1964) Register s.v. Vergils Homerumformung etc. – dédoublement, Aufspaltung v. Personen u. Szenen.

CHAPTER 8

Maecenas

The Monobiblos makes no mention of Maecenas, and its only reference to the future Augustus (*Caesaris enses*, 1.21.7), although not hostile, merely precludes any implication that in 40 BC his troops killed a 'Gallus' argued above (pp. 49–50) to have been a *propinquus* of the poet. Book 2, however, provides a sharp contrast: it begins with a long, encomiastic *recusatio* addressed to Maecenas, which links Maecenas with 'his' Caesar (*tui* ... *Caesaris*, 2.1.25, i.e. Augustus),[1] and names 'Caesar' again twice (26, 42); and succeeding elegies of Book 2 contain further eulogies of Augustus.[2] Simultaneously, the patrons of the Monobiblos, Volcacius Tullus and Gallus, disapppear from Propertius' œuvre[3] except for a brief but significant notice of the death of C. Cornelius Gallus at 2.34.91–2,[4] and the *kletikon* recalling Tullus to Italy in Book 3 (3.22).[5] It is thus made abundantly clear that Propertius has entered the new patronage of Maecenas,[6] and so indirectly of Augustus, between the appearance of the Monobiblos and that of Book 2.[7]

C. Maecenas was a controversial figure in his own day and he has remained so.[8] The controversies start with his very nomenclature. The

1   It is impossible to date elegies on the basis of their choice of name for Augustus since elegies of Book 3, certainly completed after 27 BC, continue to call him Caesar.
2   Referred to both as Caesar (2.7.5; 2.16.41; 2.31.2; 2.34.62), and Augustus (2.10.15).
3   Bassus (1.4) and Ponticus (1.7; 1.9) also disappear. These two poets were clearly part of Propertius' literary milieu, and it might be conjectured, especially in view of the paral-lelisms between Prop. 1.4 (addressed to Bassus) and 1.5 (addressed to Gallus) that they too were associated with C. Cornelius Gallus and the younger Volcacius Tullus.
4   Cf. above, pp. 81, 112, 144, 213 n. 81, 215.
5   Cf. also above, pp. 76–7 and below, pp. 352–4.
6   *PIR*² M 37; *RE* s.v. Maecenas 6) (Stein).
7   The question whether Book 2 is a single entity or not (cf., e.g., Lyne (1998) with earlier bibliography) is therefore irrelevant.
8   On ancient criticism of Maecenas see the summary of Schoonhoven (1980) 40–4. On the Younger Seneca's hatred of him see Byrne (1999).

status of 'Maecenas' is clear: it is a *nomen* probably formed from a place-name (so Varro *De Lingua Latina* 8.84).[9] Hence Maecenas is unlikely ever to have been officially 'Cilnius Maecenas'.[10] 'Cilnius' has often been claimed as his metronymic – from an important family of Arretium, although this view has been attacked.[11] But it cannot be doubted that Maecenas was related to the Cilnii,[12] and the easiest hypothesis remains that his mother was a Cilnia.[13] In the twentieth century the fascination exercised by Maecenas on historians and literary critics of antiquity alike made him the subject of two scholarly monographs[14] and many contributions to periodicals and collections.[15] Indeed so much is known, or has been conjectured, about Maecenas that this chapter must confine itself strictly to those aspects of his life, personality, and aspirations which impinged upon Propertius.

With Roman poets changes of patronage are infrequent, and in each case an explanation is required.[16] Among the Augustans the only parallel involves Virgil, whose entry into Maecenas' circle in 38 BC can be attributed to the retirement from public life in that year of his former patron, Asinius Pollio, and to Virgil's continuing desire for a protector active at the forefront of politics. But there the parallelism ends. Despite his retirement Pollio remained all his life a prominent and powerful figure; but Cornelius Gallus committed suicide and the Volcacii seem to have fallen from prominence and even from grace (see above, pp. 74–7), and this appears to have been the cause of

---

9   Cf. Schulze (1904) 529; Simpson (1996) 394.
10   As his name appears at Tac. *Ann.* 6.11.3. Cf. *RE* s.v. Maecenas 6) coll. 207–8 (Stein).
11   *Positive*: (e.g.) Sordi (1981) 56; Graverini (1997) 232, with earlier bibliography; *negative*: Simpson (1996).
12   On whom see Torelli (1969) 291–2; Harris (1971) Index s.v.; Maggiani (1986); Fatucchi (1995); Steinbauer (1998).
13   *Pace* Simpson (1996) Tac. *Ann.* 6.11.3 and Macrob. *Sat.* 2.4.12 in combination cannot be ignored. Even if Tacitus was liable to the sort of error attributed to him by some moderns, the notion that in *Cilniorum smaragde* (from Augustus' letter to Maecenas as reported by Macrobius) Augustus was referring to a generalized distinguished Etruscan family is unconvincing: it takes no account of individual Etruscan family pride as documented in the Tarquinii *elogia*. Moreover, Horace's explicit reference at *Satires* 1.6.2–3 to Maecenas' *avus ... maternus* as well as his *<avus> paternus* having commanded legions points not just to Etruscan emphasis on matrilineal descent but also to the importance of Maecenas' maternal ancestors.
14   Avallone (1962); André (1967).
15   The bibliography over most of the twentieth century is surveyed by Graverini (1997); cf. also Evenepoel (1990).
16   The movement discussed by Williams (1990) 263–70, when a protégé transferred from his patron's protection into that of his patron's patron (as Virgil, Horace, and Propertius eventually moved from the *clientela* of Maecenas into that of Augustus) is both different and more frequent. Williams also (266 n. 16) collects a few cases of genuine transfer.

Propertius' enrolment by Maecenas. If both Propertius' previous patrons had incurred imperial displeasure, he and his family must have been relieved when he was invited to join Maecenas' circle, and the markedly fulsome tone of elegy 2.1 may mirror this. Some links between the Propertii and the family of Maecenas which perhaps facilitated the move have already been remarked on (above, pp. 20–2), namely the kinship of Maecenas' wife Terentia with Seianus, Seianus' adoption into the Aelii Galli, and the marriage of Aelia Galla to Propertius Postumus. Evidence that Maecenas may also have been related (possibly again through Terentia) to his fellow Etruscans, the Volcacii Tulli, comes from a funerary inscription of the late first century BC or early first century AD, probably from Rome or nearby.[17] It contains the names (some now partly deleted) of two slaves and two freedmen. The layout is somewhat irregular, but the names, according to the first editor, are:

> (?)Eros Senecio Terentiae [C.] Maecenatis
> C. Maecenas Nicia
> C. Volcacius) l. Metrodorus
> Benaea Methe

Senecio was thus a slave of Maecenas' wife Terentia, so in all likelihood he died before 12 BC, when the couple divorced finally;[18] and Nicia was a freedman of Maecenas himself, freed therefore before Maecenas' death in 8 BC. Metrodorus was the freedman of a Volcacia whose father was a C. Volcacius. Volcacia will therefore have been the daughter more probably of Caesar's lieutenant (on whom see above, pp. 45–6), or less probably of Propertius' first patron, the younger Tullus.[19] The recording on the same stone of the burials of these individuals is not coincidental: we are seeing here the sharing of a tomb by freedmen and slaves of related *gentes*,[20] i.e. of the families of Maecenas and/or his wife and the Volcacii. This relationship could

---

17   See Hammond (1980) with full discussion.

18   On the divorces of Maecenas and Terentia see *RE* s.v. Maecenas 6) col. 215 (Stein); Martini (1995).

19   Prop. 3.22, written in the late 20s BC, speaks of his former patron Tullus' *spes ... venturae coniugis* (42). This perhaps makes it less likely that Volcacia was Tullus' daughter, since a daughter of this marriage might not have been old enough to have freedmen by the date of the inscription. However, she could have been the issue of an earlier marriage of Tullus.

20   This is probably also the explanation of the shared use by several families of the large chamber tomb near Umbrian Vettona (modern Bettona) – this tomb also had major Etruscan content (cf. Verzar (1976) 119–20).

have further eased the transfer of Propertius as a *cliens* from the Volcacii to Maecenas.

The circle of Maecenas not only offered Propertius greater possibilities of literary support and promotion, but also the protection of a man who, although of equestrian status, was wealthier and more powerful than most senators, and who was more central to the rise of Augustus than any other potential patron of Propertius. The Maecenates of Arretium had, it seems, been attached to the Marian/Caesarian cause for generations.[21] The C. Maecenas who appears in Cicero *Pro Cluentio* 153 among the *robora populi Romani* opposed to Drusus in 91 BC was probably the Augustan magnate's grandfather.[22] Another Maecenas accompanied Sertorius to Spain and fought for the Marian cause there.[23] The home town of the family, Arretium, was a hive of Caesarian partisans,[24] and it was partly for this reason that it was chosen in 49 BC by Julius Caesar as one of his principal Italian bases in the Civil War, with M. Antonius detailed to hold it for him.[25] Later Arretium was similarly selected by Octavianus as his base, first after Julius Caesar's murder and again later, during the Perusine War.[26] Following Julius Caesar's death the family had no hesitations about where their allegiance lay: a Maecenas, either the Augustan magnate himself or more likely his father L. Maecenas,[27] was among the first supporters to rally to Octavianus in 44 BC and to offer him resources.[28] If this early adherent was L. Maecenas, his son will either have accompanied him, or have met Octavianus soon after. The family wealth of the Maecenates must have derived in part from that of the Cilnii, who had been rich and important in Etruria for centuries.[29] The toponymy of Arretium preserves the confines of the vast estates of the Cilnii in the form of multiple occurrences of the praedial 'Cignano' = *Cilnianum*, and the same place-name is found in the territories of

---

21 Harris (1971) 212–29 is, however, sceptical about identifying anti-Drusans with Marians.
22 Nicolet (1966–74) II.933–4 (No. 210); *PIR²* M 37 (p. 131).
23 *RE* s.v. Maecenas 2).
24 Sordi (1995) 154. The town's multiple maltreatment by Sulla (cf. Harris (1971) 258–9, 261–3, 269–70, 275–84; Poma (1995) 161–4) will have contributed to this enthusiasm.
25 Cf. esp. Zecchini (1998) 238.
26 Sordi (1972) 3–14; (1985) 310–11; Foresti (1996) 10 n. 16.
27 His father's name is guaranteed by *CIL* 6.21771, cf. *PIR²* M 37 (p. 131). For scholarly opinions on which of the two was involved in the approach to Octavianus see Graverini (1997) 233.
28 Cf. Zecchini (1998) 242–3.
29 Cf. Livy 10.5.13; Maggiani (1986), assembling Etruscan inscriptions of the family; Fatucchi (1995).

neighbouring Italian towns too.[30] All these estates subsequently belonged to Maecenas, and he also owned the immensely valuable Arretine potteries, again seemingly inherited from the Cilnii; this possession allowed Augustus to tease Maecenas by referring to him as a 'potter'.[31] His services to Octavianus after 43 BC were rewarded further. Octavianus' gift to Maecenas of the property of the senator M. Favonius is recorded.[32] Maecenas in fact obtained vast land and property holdings throughout the Roman world. Evidence of his Egyptian estates survives;[33] and a *vinum Maecenatianum* was produced in Gallia Cisalpina, which indicates Maecenas' ownership of vineyards there.[34] There is also another 'Cignano' in the territory of Brescia, and yet another south of the Po at Piacenza. Both areas are wine-producing, both have easy access to river transport on the Po, and both were centuriated in 40 BC.[35] These indications of Maecenas' wealth are only the tip of the iceberg. A hint of the numbers and *esprit de corps* of Maecenas' former slaves who passed into imperial ownership after his death comes from the tombstones naming them '*Maecenatiani*'.[36]

Maecenas is the dedicatee of Propertius Book 2 (he is addressed in 2.1 and named twice), and the addressee of 3.9, where his name appears four times. This new presence of Maecenas is one overt result of Propertius' entrance into his *clientela* – although even at the beginning of his relationship with Maecenas Propertius had either been instructed to give precedence as subject-matter to Augustus, as he does over the whole of Books 2 and 3, or was tactful enough to do so without instruction.[37] Maecenas had further effects on the content of Propertian elegy. To begin with, whereas the Monobiblos bears the hallmark of Gallan influence throughout, Propertius' literary indebtedness to C. Cornelius Gallus begins to wane in Book 2 and it reduces

---

30   Fatucchi (1995).
31   Fatucchi (1995) 195–6. Because he was therefore a 'potter', the reading *ficulorum/figulorum* in the letter of Augustus to him partially preserved by Macrob. *Sat.* 2.4.12 should not be emended to *Iguvinorum*, as is sometimes done.
32   *RE* s.v. Favonius 1) col. 2076 (Münzer).
33   Cf. *PIR*² M 37 (p. 134); Capponi (2002), referring (182 n. 11) to Parássoglou (1978), where Maecenas' known Egyptian estates are listed (79–80) and discussed – cf. also Parássoglou's Index II Persons and Places s.v. Maecenas etc.
34   Cf. Plin. *NH* 14.67.
35   Fatucchi (1995) 203–4.
36   *CIL* VI.4016, 4032, 4095, 4723, 19926; *AE* 1921.69. This onomastic practice was not, of course, confined to ex-slaves of Maecenas.
37   On the situation in Book 4, see below.

further in Book 3. As well as documenting Propertius' increasing confidence in his own status as an elegist, this reduction must to some extent reflect Gallus' fall from Augustus' favour, which will inevitably
have imposed discretion upon Propertius' enthusiasm for Gallus'
poetry. Whatever misbehaviour on Gallus' part brought about his fall,
it and his subsequent suicide clearly embarrassed Augustus greatly,[38]
and no doubt Augustus' feelings on this point were conveyed by Maecenas to his new *cliens*. On the other hand Propertius was clearly in no
way prohibited from imitation of Gallus. Gallan influence remains
significant in certain poems of Book 2 (see Chapters 3–6), and,
although some of these were perhaps written before Propertius entered
Maecenas' circle, Book 2 was published with Maecenas' approval
after his entry, and its prologue contains two prominent Gallan reminiscences, while its epilogue mentions Gallus and his death (see below,
pp. 266–7). Moreover Gallus is still sometimes an important presence
in Book 3: elegy 3.4, for example, which is highly laudatory of
Augustus, can now be seen to reflect a triumph poem of Gallus (see
Chapter 12). Obviously Gallus was too powerful an elegiac force to be
ignored by any successor elegist, and Maecenas may well have admired Gallan elegy.[39] But, even if he did not, Maecenas' patronage
was not such as to constrain his protégés' choices of literary influence.

Maecenas' input can perhaps be seen more clearly on another
front: presumably he can be credited with Propertius' gradual move
away from purely personal erotic elegy to elegies embracing moral,
social, and political themes. Maecenas was of course (again) too wise
to attempt to dampen Propertius' erotic ardour straightaway, and
indeed he would not have wanted to wean him off love-elegy all at
once. Maecenas appears to have wanted many areas of literature,
including erotic elegy, to be represented among his poets; so he could
have had little objection to Propertius' continuing engagement with
love-poetry over most of Book 2, much of Book 3, and even some of
Book 4. In any case Maecenas could have had a personal liking for the
Monobiblos, given that both his own life-style[40] and his literary
concerns and preferences were not too distant from those of the early

---

38   Following Gallus' suicide Augustus *vicem suam conquestus est, quod sibi soli non liceret*
     amicis, quatenus vellet, irasci (Sueton. *Aug.* 66.2).
39   See below, and nn. 40–3.
40   For material bearing on the overlap between Maecenas' way of life and that of Propertius'
     elegiac *persona* see Firpo (1998) 287–98; Rosati (2005) 137–40. The turbulent marital
     history of Maecenas – for which see Martini (1995) – is analogous to certain experiences of
     the elegiac lover.

Propertius. Thus Maecenas' own verses display 'Callimachean' interest in 'original' etymological meanings of words, and also in 'double-images'.[41] Again, Maecenas' poetic work shows the influence of Catullus, as does that of Propertius.[42] An even more significant area of literary confluence between the pair can perhaps be detected in Maecenas' self-indulgently 'baroque' style, which went to extreme lengths and hence encountered hostility in antiquity, beginning with Augustus' implied critique.[43] Propertius too was constantly tempted by linguistic excess, although he resisted this temptation more effectively than his patron. Maecenas cannot be blamed (or praised) for Propertius' mannered style since it was already fully developed in the Monobiblos, published before Propertius entered Maecenas' patronage; but Maecenas will hardly have discouraged it. A grafitto found on an external wall of the so-called 'Auditorium'[44] associated with the villa of Maecenas on the Esquiline perhaps confirms and expands the sphere of literary interests shared by the two men, as well as hinting at the sort of literary activity that went on there:[45] it is an epigram of Callimachus, and specifically one of his erotic komoi.[46]

But, although Maecenas' probable liking for the sorts of elegy which dominate the Monobiblos may have been one motive for bringing Propertius into his clientela, Propertius' writings under Maecenas' patronage began to move noticeably more towards themes of greater public and patriotic interest, and with growing success over Books 2–4. This movement may have resulted in part from tactful redirection by Maecenas and in part from Propertius' feelings of gratitude for his inclusion in Maecenas' circle and his consequent wish to take up new themes of known or supposed interest to his new amicus and to Maecenas' even more powerful amicus. Propertius' change of direction will certainly have pleased Augustus, who seems himself more and more to have become Propertius' chief patron. The ways in which Propertius showed ever-increasing willingness to accommodate Augustus' interests and ideology will be examined in Chapter 10. For the moment one minor point may be made about Book 2 before further impacts of Maecenas upon Propertius are

41   Avallone (1962) 128–33, with Citti (1966) 42–4.
42   Avallone (1962) 296–308, with Citti (1966) 45.
43   Cf. Lieberg (1996) 11–13; Graver (1998).
44   On this structure see Häuber (1990) 59–63; Sartorio (1996) 35–8; Coarelli (2004) 107, re-asserting its function as an auditorium.
45   Cf. Murray (1985) 43 and n. 16 with earlier bibliography; Sartorio (1996) 44.
46   Epigr. 42 Pf. (AP 12.118, 8 Gow–Page).

considered. Of all Propertius' four books Book 2 presents Propertian scholarship with the greatest problems of length, unity and textual integrity. If it is indeed a single book,[47] its length, which is out of line with that of other Augustan poetry books, can perhaps be related to his change of patronage and its effects on his publishing plans. Some elegies of Book 2 must already have been composed while Propertius was still with his first patrons. It may be debated whether many ancient poets destroyed their own work as readily as Ovid did.[48] But in any case, as his comparatively slender output reveals, Propertius did not share Ovid's facility as a writer; and yet Propertius greatly aspired to leave a poetic legacy.[49] Presumably, then, when he moved into the circle of Maecenas Propertius salvaged as many of his earlier and as yet unpublished compositions as he could, deleting or replacing addresses to his former patrons and their circle as part of the process. This supposition could help to explain why the elegies of Book 2, although more numerous than those of the Monobiblos, have so few named addressees,[50] why two (2.21; 2.22) are addressed to pseudo-nymous characters who cannot be identified,[51] and why so many address Cynthia, sometimes by name and sometimes not. However, in Book 2 Propertius also had to compose elegies for his new patron(s) (e.g. 2.1; 2.34). This combination of pressures might without much further ado explain the inordinate length of Book 2.[52]

In thinking about the stimuli which led to Propertius' changes of literary direction in Books 2–4, we inevitably and rightly concentrate on the personalities and aspirations of Maecenas and Augustus. But Propertius' responses to his patrons were also conditioned by the new literary, cultural, and social possibilities which opened up to him after his move into the protection of Maecenas. Around 30 BC Maecenas constructed a magnificent mansion and an adjacent tower on the Esquiline, which had formerly been an unhealthy quarter containing a decayed cemetery. His tower provided panoramic views of Rome and the surrounding countryside and an observation platform for its

---

47   Cf. also above, p. 194 and n. 20, and below, pp. 266 n. 88, 279 n. 139.
48   *Tr.* 4.10.61–4. Virgil left instructions that the unfinished *Aeneid* be destroyed, but only after his death.
49   *sat mea sat magna est, si tres sint pompa libelli* (2.13.25).
50   Prop. 2.8 may be a particularly diagnostic case, in that it is addressed to an unidentified 'friend' (*amice*, 2), whereas elsewhere in Propertius' œuvre *amice* addresses an individual named, at least pseudonymously, in the same elegy: cf. 1.10.14 and 1.13.18 (Gallus); 2.34.16 ('Lynceus').
51   2.34 addresses 'Lynceus', who is argued in Ch. 9 to be the poet Varius Rufus.
52   For further discusson of this topic see Ch. 10.

astrologically inclined owner.[53] It has been suggested that Maecenas chose the Esquiline for his house in part because of its associations with King Servius Tullius,[54] a figure said to have been identified by Etruscan sources with the Etruscan 'Mastarna'.[55] Servius Tullius was credited with having built his palace on the Esquiline, with having integrated the Esquiline into Rome, and with having constructed there an *aedes* of the goddess *Fortuna* (the Roman version of Etruscan *Nortia*), as well as the *agger*, part of which was incorporated into Maecenas' own construction.[56] These suggestions are confirmed by Horace's pointed reference to Servius Tullius at *Satires* 1.6.9 in a discourse directed to Maecenas. Maecenas' house and tower were prominent landmarks in the topography of Rome. They passed into imperial hands on Maecenas' death, and there are several notices of their use by Augustus and his successors.[57] The only known residence of Propertius at Rome was also on the Esquiline, and its precise location has been ingeniously reconstructed. Propertius' house probably stood in the vicinity of the modern Piazza S. Martino, close to the gardens of Maecenas and only a few hundred metres from the house of Maecenas.[58] It can hardly be doubted that the poet's house was either a 'grace and favour' residence or an outright gift of Maecenas. The physical proximity of Propertius to Maecenas within Rome should be borne in mind by any scholar tempted to claim that Propertius was semi-detached from Maecenas and his circle.[59] Certainly Propertius never achieved the intimacy which Horace apparently enjoyed with Maecenas; and mere proximity of residence need not imply constant association. But it implies something: at the very least Propertius had

---

53   On Maecenas' tower see Häuber (1990) 36–43; Ampolo (1996); Perrin (1996), who proposes that Maecenas built it on the plan of the Pharos of Alexandria, which would make it complementary to Augustus' mausoleum, which matched the tomb of Alexander. As Ian Du Quesnay points out to me, the tower may also have advertised Maecenas' Etruscan origins since a contemporary etymology claimed that the 'Tyrrhenoi'/'Tyrsenoi' (i.e. the Etruscans) were 'dwellers in towers' (τύρσις = *turris*); cf. Dion. Hal. 1.26.2.

54   Häuber (1990) 21, 66–7; Ampolo (1996).

55   The identification and its sources rest on the testimony of the emperor Claudius, credible in view of his researches on Etruria and his possible knowledge of Etruscan: see Cornell (1995) 133–41.

56   Häuber (1990) 21, 66–7; Ampolo (1996), who also draws attention (31) to Seianus' link with Servius Tullius' *aedes Fortunae*. This assumes even more interest in the light of the various relationships between Maecenas, Seianus, and the Propertii, on which see above, pp. 20–2, 252–3.

57   See Ampolo (1996) 29. The most notorious use was that of Nero, who allegedly sang from the tower as Rome burned.

58   See Rodríguez-Almeida (1987) 420; Häuber (1990) 65 n. 184; Grüner (1993) 39–53.

59   E.g. Lyne in G. Lee (1994) x–xiv.

the possibility of contact with many of the poets of Maecenas' circle, especially since others of them also seem to have resided in this area. According to Suetonius/Donatus, Virgil's Roman residence was adjacent: *habuitque domum Romae Esquiliis iuxta hortos Maecenatianos*. Horace also had a house there, and he was buried later in the gardens of Maecenas; Albinovanus Pedo was another resident.[60] Others of Maecenas' writers may also, unknown to us, have lived in a veritable 'poets' quarter'. We can surely on this basis imagine Propertius interacting freely within the multifarious intellectual ambience of the great *domus* of Maecenas on the Esquiline, and, as time went on, with the life of Augustus' establishment on the Palatine too.

Inevitably, the majority of known members of Maecenas' circle are poets, the best attested being Virgil, Horace, and Propertius himself. The elegy (2.34) in which Propertius celebrates his newfound entrée into the circle (cf. Chapter 9) unfortunately adds little firm historical detail, and for documentation we must rely mainly on Horace.[61] Virgil's two literary executors, L. Varius Rufus and Plotius Tucca, were clearly prominent members of the circle, as were the poets C. Valgius Rufus, Domitius Marsus, Quintilius Varus, Aristius Fuscus, Aemilius Macer, Sabinius Tiro,[62] and possibly C. Fundanius. Men of learning other than poets, or who added poetry to other accomplishments, must have been even more numerous, but it is not easy to identify many of them. Quintilius Varus seems to have been a critic as well as a poet, and Aristius Fuscus both a *grammaticus* and a literary man. If Horace *Satires* 1.10.82–8 provides another window into the circle of Maecenas, we might add at least some of those mentioned ('Octavius', the two Visci, 'Bibulus', 'Servius', and 'Furnius' – among *complures alii*') as members of mixed or non-poetic accomplishments. Another, although of lower birth than those named earlier, was C. Melissus,[63] a *grammaticus* who also wrote comedies. An Umbrian from Spoletium, he was born free, exposed, brought up as a

---

60   *Virgil*: *VSD* 13, received sceptically by Horsfall (1995) 8, but probably without justification. *Horace*: Rodríguez-Almeida (1987) 416–20; Häuber (1990) 65 n. 184; Grüner (1993) 53–4; Sueton. *De Poet.* c) 88–9 Rostagni. *Pedo*: Mart.10.20.10–11, cf. Rodríguez-Almeida (1987) 420; Grüner (1993) 54–5.

61   For a comprehensive discussion and documentation of the membership of the circle, and for remarks on Maecenas' influence on their work, see Avallone (1962) Ch. 5 esp. 177–218; for the flavour of Virgil's earlier ambience of the 40s BC, Gigante (1990).

62   I.e. if the work on horticulture which he dedicated to Maecenas (Plin. *NH* 19.177) was in verse.

63   Sueton. *De Vir. Illustr.* (*De Gramm. et Rhet.*) fr. 21 Reifferscheid, cf. E. Coli (1996) 270–1; more fully Kaster (1995) 24–5, 214–22.

slave, and given to Maecenas. When his mother claimed that he was free, Melissus chose to remain in slavery, presumably valuing his link with Maecenas more highly. Subsequently freed by Maecenas, Melissus was eventually employed directly by Augustus to organize the libraries of the *Porticus Octaviae*, a memorial to Octavia's son Marcellus who died in 23 BC.[64] Yet another freedman of Maecenas was Aquila, who expanded the shorthand system of Cicero's freedman Tiro;[65] and there must have been many other such freedmen, not to speak of learned Greek and Etruscan free dependants of Maecenas, all of whom Propertius would have had the chance of meeting and knowing on the Esquiline. The milieu which Propertius entered in 26 BC and in which he remained for the rest of his poetic career should colour our perceptions of the *doctrina* of his latter three books. It should also inform our thinking about the genesis of some elegies of those books, and help us to perceive (to take only a few examples) 2.31, Propertius' *ekphrasis* of Augustus' new temple of Apollo on the Palatine, his Actium elegy (4.6), and his account of the aetiology of the *spolia opima* (4.10)[66] as commissioned eulogies.

The Propertian elegies which address Maecenas (2.1 and 3.9), both of them *recusationes*, reveal Maecenas' major impact on Propertius, and the first of them does so with an immediacy which must have been startling in its time. The Roman reader who already knew the Monobiblos and who then took up Propertius' new elegy book was confronted in its prologue by two fresh dominant personalities, those of Maecenas and Augustus. That reader also encountered a way, new to Propertius, of treating contemporary persons and events. In 2.1 Maecenas and Augustus and their doings stand revealed concretely, directly, and in detail. The novelty of this treatment can be grasped by contrast with the presentation of real people and historical events in the Monobiblos. Two real individuals featured there are Bassus (1.4) and Ponticus (1.7; 1.9). Because virtually nothing is known about either from independent sources (cf. above, pp. 65–6), and because Propertius reveals little more, they are unidentifiable. Again, the most prominent addressees of the Monobiblos are Tullus and 'Gallus'. But, if the Monobiblos was our sole source of information about Tullus and

---

64   This progression from Maecenas to Augustus is reminiscent of the paths taken by Virgil, Horace, and Propertius.
65   Sueton. *De Vir. Illustr.* fr. 106 Reifferscheid.
66   For Augustus' personal and practical interest in this topic see Liv. 4.20.5–11 with Ogilvie (1965) 563–7.

his uncle, it would be hard to make any definitive statement about Tullus, so conventional and undetailed is his portrait. He might even be classed with the praetor of 1.8, 2.16, and 3.20 as of questionable reality, and his consular uncle considered imaginary. As for the 'Gallus' of the Monobiblos, his identity is still being debated after two thousand years. His Propertian portrait is fluid and 'generic'; and, if as this book asserts, he is C. Cornelius Gallus, it seems to be compounded from a set of wilful misrepresentations of Gallan elegy.[67] Historical events too, if they appear at all in the Monobiblos, assume blurred shapes: 1.21 and 1.22 treat the Perusine War, but only elliptically, and they have proved very difficult to interpret. Naturally Propertius' contemporaries, especially those living in Rome and *au fait* with the talk of the town, would have made more of the people and events of the Monobiblos than we can. But this cannot be the full story. Propertius must have felt some need for tact and discretion in his handling of individuals and historical events in the Monobiblos: it appeared at a time when the perils and uncertainties of the Civil Wars were still a fresh memory, and Propertius had as yet no broad public mandate or function for his elegy.[68] If, as seems likely, both his own family and the Volcacii had, at least initially, been on the losing side in the Perusine War (see above, pp. 46–9), that particular experience may have increased his caution. The subject-matter of the Monobiblos is therefore to a large extent the universe of literature and of literary stereotypes; and even when a *persona* like the *vir militaris* Tullus intersects with the real Volcacius Tullus the younger, the intersection draws more on stereotypes than reality. Only in the two final *sphragis* elegies of the Monobiblos (1.21 and 1.22) does near-contemporary political and historical reality intrude, and even there it is not permitted to take truly concrete shape. It is notable too that elsewhere in the Monobiblos hardly a shred of Roman history or of the politics of the Roman past shows itself.[69]

Elegy 2.1, then, contrasts starkly with the Monobiblos in its treatment of contemporary personalities and events. Propertius begins 2.1 by explaining that love-poetry is his forte, and that he turns the most trivial of his erotic adventures into 'Iliads' and 'Histories' (1–16).

---

67 See above, esp. pp. 220–2.
68 Tibullus' clearer references to Messalla's achievements in the same period presumably reflect both his own background and the status of his patron Messalla.
69 Even the 'Tarpeia' referred to at Prop. 1.16.2, although out of early Roman history, is cryptic in context.

Propertius next enters the realms of hypothesis: if the fates had made him an epic poet, he would not be writing a Gigantomachy, Thebaid, or Troy poem, or one on the Persian War, the foundation of Rome, Rome's wars with Carthage, or the victories of Marius (17–38). Instead his epic would celebrate the wars of Augustus and Maecenas' part in them. This fantasy allows Propertius to devote a substantial section (25–38) to detailing the victories and triumphs of Augustus, and to associating Maecenas with them (25–6, 35–8). Propertius mentions in succession the battles of Mutina (43 BC) and Philippi (42 BC), and the naval campaign around Sicily which led to the defeat of Sextus Pompeius by Agrippa at Naulochus in 36 BC and to Sextus' subsequent flight to Asia in 35 BC. Then come military operations in Etruria and the capture of Alexandria (30 BC). Propertius next refers to the triple triumph of Octavianus in 29 BC, recalling that in it the conquest of Egypt (30 BC) and the defeat of M. Antonius and Cleopatra at Actium (31 BC) were celebrated. The lines (25–6, 35–8) which enclose this account of the 'wars and victories of your Caesar' (*bellaque resque tui ... Caesaris*, 25) imply that Maecenas was present at all the battles mentioned, although in fact his participation in some of them has been questioned.[70]

Apart from this possibly tendentious implication and one historical detail requiring explication, the account is clear and factual. Its only unclear detail comes in line 29, where Propertius writes of *eversosque focos antiquae gentis Etruscae* as among the military activities and victories of Augustus in which Maecenas played a part. This line has generally been read as a reference to the Perusine War of 41–40 BC,[71] and it has even been interpreted as a reversal of Propertius' previously expressed attitudes to that campaign in the Monobiblos (1.21 and 1.22).[72] It could be the case that line 29 refers to the Perusine War, although this would not imply that Propertius had changed his view of the war: the line would simply be cataloguing the fall of Perusia as among the military achievements of Augustus, and Maecenas' presence there (if he was present) as further proof of Maecenas' *fides*. However, there is no independent evidence that Maecenas was at the siege and surrender of Perusia, episodes well documented in our

---

70   On his disputed presence at Actium see the summary of Woodman (1983) 238 n. 1 (with bibliography). It is hard to believe that *Epode* 1 would imply that Maecenas was at Actium if he was not.

71   Rothstein (1920–4) and Enk (1962) ad loc.

72   Reitzenstein (1896) 186. On the problem see now Fedeli (2005) 67–8.

sources. Moreover, a reference by Propertius to Maecenas' participation in those tragic and notorious events in his own Etruria (if he did
participate) might have been tactless.[73] Finally, if line 29 describes the
Etruria of 40 BC, it introduces a breach of chronological order into
Propertius' account of Augustus' military successes, which otherwise
– except for the slight temporal reversal of the conquest of Egypt and
the battle of Actium (31–4) – is observed by Propertius throughout
lines 26–34. This last objection is not in fact particularly significant,
given that achronicity is sometimes a characteristic of Propertian
historical catalogues.[74] But if the arguments about lack of evidence
and tactlessness carry any weight, an alternative interpretation of line
29 is available which also, for what this is worth, removes the chronological distortion. This is to understand line 29 as a reference to the
suppression of the unrest in Etruria which continued in the aftermath
of the Perusine War and which came to an end in 36 BC.[75] That would
both account for line 29's juxtaposition with line 28, which refers to
Naulochus (36 BC), and it would fit one of Maecenas' roles at the
time of the Sicilian War, to control and pacify Rome and Italy for
Octavianus.[76] Maecenas' activities at that time must have included
operations in his native territory, including securing his own estates
and possessions in Etruria. On this interpretation the destruction in
Etruria (*eversosque focos*) is being attributed by Propertius not to the
actions of Maecenas but to those of the Etruscan insurgents.[77] If this is
what is happening here, Propertius is employing the same technique –
attacking an acknowledged evil arising from conflict and implicitly
blaming it on the other side – as Virgil deploys in the *Eclogues*, where
he makes his rustic characters inveigh against the consequences of
civil strife, while he simultaneously contrives to absolve his own
patrons of any blame for them.[78]

As noted, the passage detailing Augustus' and Maecenas' military

---

73 Hence the conclusion drawn from this line and the rest of the passage by Stahl (1985) 165–
    7, namely that in 2.1 Propertius retains his attitude of 1.22.
74 Cairns (2002).
75 Cf. Dio 49.15.1, claiming that unrest in Etruria ended with the arrival of the news of
    Octavianus' victory at Naulochus. However, App. *Bell. Civ.* 5.132 reports continuing
    brigandage in Italy and Rome.
76 App. *Bell. Civ.* 5.99, 112; Dio 49.16.2; *Eleg. in Maecen.* 1.14, 27, with Schoonhoven
    (1980) on 1.27.
77 In this case the agent to be understood with *eversos* (29) is different from the agent to be
    understood with *capta* (30); (hellenistic) 'Subjektswechsel' is common in Roman poetry of
    this period, and such an occurrence would have to be explained in analogous terms.
78 Cf. *Ecl.* 1 esp. 64–78; 9 esp. 2–29.

exploits is preceded (23–4) by three episodes from older Roman history – the 'first kingdom of Remus', i.e. the foundation of Rome, the Punic Wars, and the defeat of the Cimbri by Marius. This emphasis on earlier Roman history is again a novelty in Propertian elegy, and, although he rejects these as epic subjects, Propertius clearly introduces them to make a specific point: all three are emblematic of Augustan pretensions. Romulus (on the assumption that, as sometimes happens, Remus is named here for metrical convenience but only in order to bring Romulus to mind) was claimed by Augustus as an ancestor and exemplar, *inter alia* by his selection of the name Augustus; the defeated Hannibal was equated with M. Antonius;[79] and Marius was the leader of the political movement later headed by Julius Caesar. Simultaneously, however, these subjects can, with one slight change of emphasis, be seen to fit the same thematic pattern as all the rejected epic subjects of 2.1.19–24 – one also central to Augustan ideology. For if *Remi* is additionally intended to make us think of Remus and his behaviour, then all (or almost all) of the epic subjects are linked by the notion of *hybris*, sometimes violent and often barbarous, followed by just punishment and the restoration of order.[80] This theme covers the challenging of the gods by the Titans (19–20), the destruction of Troy by the Greeks, whose descendants paid the price (21), Xerxes' impiety in trying to tame the sea (22), Remus' impious behaviour towards Romulus (23), Carthage's wars against Rome (23), and the invasion of the Cimbri (24). The failed first expedition of the 'Seven against Thebes' (21) – *veteres Thebas* makes that distinction – could fit the same pattern, if it is not simply included as a mandatory epic subject. Another archetypal Augustan concept appears in line 42, where in a brief recusatory couplet Propertius claims that he is unfit to write an epic 'tracing back Caesar's name to his Phrygian ancestors'. In the circle of Maecenas it would have been understood that Propertius was not only publicizing Augustus' Julian genealogy but hinting at Virgil's fitness to write such an epic.[81]

Not only does 2.1 dedicate Book 2 to Maecenas, but in its final lines (71–8) Propertius depicts himself explicitly as Maecenas' *cliens*. Again, this contrasts with Propertius' treatment of his patrons in the

---

79 Cf. Cairns (1983b) 85–90.
80 For these concepts, their cosmic dimensions, and their importance for Augustan ideology, cf. esp. P. R. Hardie (1986).
81 This is one of the many links between 2.1 and 2.34, where Virgil's forthcoming *Aeneid* is heralded (61–6) and praised as 'greater than the *Iliad*' (66): see below, pp. 313, 318.

Monobiblos. There Tullus was treated with respect, but in 1.6 he was ranked second to Cynthia when Propertius supposedly had to choose whether or not to accompany Tullus to Asia. Similarly in the Monobiblos Gallus was subjected to much literary polemic, including massive *deformazione*. Contrariwise in 2.1 Maecenas is the 'hope' of Propertius' youth and the 'glory' of Propertius both in life and in death (2.1.73–4). Propertius does re-emphasize in the final line of 2.1 that he remains a love-poet (78), a stress in keeping with the elegy's genre (*recusatio*), but the implication is that he does so with Maecenas' permission. No parallel dependence on either of his former patrons was asserted anywhere in the Monobiblos. Propertius has now moved to a protector at the highest level of power, and he genuflects publicly in acknowledgement of this. Presumably Maecenas was not displeased with Propertius' conspicuous show of respect, and indeed he may have expected it: Horace's posture towards Maecenas in *Satires* 1.6 and elsewhere is not dissimilar. Likewise Maecenas will have expected Propertius to meet his requests for coverage of certain topics; the changed subject-matter and attitudes visible in Books 2 and 3 are in part the consequence.

It is, of course, currently unfashionable to believe that Augustan poets wrote the types of poems their patrons wanted them to write.[82] Such a proposition affronts modern notions of artistic independence; and the water is seriously muddied by the conventions of the *recusatio*, in which ancient poets were able to affect a sturdy independence by refusing to write what their patrons never asked them to write in the first place. Such is the power of fashion that even some scholars perceptive enough to recognize that the poets did actually produce the sorts of poems their patrons asked of them fall back on claims of 'implicit ridicule'[83] and so forth in order (so they think) to restore to a poet a few rags of self-respect. All that is needed in this area is common sense.[84] We cannot seriously imagine, as we might be encouraged to do by deceptive poetic *recusationes*, that Maecenas lined up Horace, Propertius, and the rest, and demanded an epic from each of them (see also above, p. 41). And yet scholars who take Augustan *recusationes* seriously are, perhaps unwittingly, subscribing to such a supposition. Next, it must be remembered that the *pessimum*

---

82 On patronage in general and in relation to poets see above, pp. 35–42.
83 Stahl (1985) 164, in an analysis of Prop. 2.1 (162–71).
84 As exemplified, e.g., by Williams (1990).

exemplum of Alexander the Great and Choerilus[85] was at the forefront of Augustan patrons' minds. Above all they wanted quality work from their poets, and this entailed their showing respect for poets' artistic integrity, and conducting a dialogue with them, to which the poets doubtless contributed as much or more than the patrons. At the same time, however, a patron's poet was ultimately in the same situation as his painter, his musician, or his tailor: if a poet would not or could not write the sort of poems his patron wanted, his place would be taken by someone else who would offer to do so. And it is unrealistic to imagine that a poet could successfully pretend to produce the poetry a patron had requested while saving his own self-esteem by importing irony, 'implicit ridicule', and the like. Men of the calibre of Maecenas and Augustus would not have fallen for such foolish tricks; and even if they had been so undiscriminating, they did not lack friends and other clients to awaken their awareness.

But, for all that Maecenas is so prominent in 2.1, the Propertius of 2.1 (and of the whole of Book 2) remains the poet of the Monobiblos: even in 2.1 there are two unmistakable reminders of Cornelius Gallus to balance his death-notice in the book's final elegy (2.34.91–2). They appear immediately before the two sentences of 2.1 in which Propertius apostrophizes Maecenas (17, 73). The first is *maxima de nihilo nascitur historia* (2.1.16), a reminiscence of Gallus fr. 2.3 Courtney from the couplet *fata mihi, Caesar, tum erunt mea dulcia, quom tu/ maxima Romanae pars eri<s> historiae* (2–3).[86] The second Gallan reference comes in lines 69–70, where, in the last of a series of six couplets each containing a mythological exemplum, Prometheus is to be loosed *Caucasia ... de rupe* (69): the theme of the Caucasus in Propertius almost certainly derives from Gallus.[87] These Gallan references in a prologue addressed to Maecenas are unlikely to be fortuitous. Another elegy of Book 2, 2.13, which has certain characteristics of a 'proemio al mezzo',[88] and which in its initial couplet refers to Maecenas' Etruria, also contains clear echoes of Gallus, which start from that initial couplet. Such obtrusive references to Gallus in these contexts may well be indications by Propertius that his loyalty to his

---

85   See below, p. 320 and n. 3.
86   On *historia* and *maximus* as indicative of Gallan influence, see Index II s.vv.
87   See Index II s.v.; Cairns (1993) 113–14.
88   In view of its literary-programmatic content 2.10 could also qualify for this description. As has already been implied (above, pp. 194 and n. 20, 257), I remain to be convinced that Book 2 was originally published as two books.

previous patrons, although superseded, has not turned into hostility; Propertius thus proclaims his personal probity as a *cliens*, and at the same time advertises Maecenas' liberal attitude as a *patronus*. Propertius' sorrowful reference to Gallus in 2.34, and his eventual recall of Tullus to Italy (3.22), both undoubtedly with Maecenas' express leave, and the latter doubtless with the approval of Augustus too, conform to the same pattern.

Propertius' second *recusatio* to Maecenas (3.9) is just as detailed, straightforward, and explicit in its treatment of the personality of Maecenas as is 2.1. Its initial hexameter (*Maecenas, eques Etrusco de sanguine regum*, 1), which eulogizes both Maecenas' Etruscan ethnicity and his 'royal' descent (on which see below, pp. 271–4), is immediately qualified in the succeeding pentameter (*intra fortunam qui cupis esse tuam*, 2) by emphasis on Maecenas' well-known 'modesty', i.e. his refusal of high office. The essence of the man, his high pretensions to non-Roman rank and his refusal of Roman *honores*, is thus encapsulated in a single couplet. Propertius' subtly encomiastic argument throughout this second *recusatio*[89] is that, just as Maecenas has rejected high office and military commands, so too Propertius, a client who has accepted his patron's moral choices as guides for his own, should be permitted to decline the composition of epic. This line of argument is implicit in the first section of the elegy (1–20), but it becomes explicit at lines 21–2; and the central section of the elegy (23–34) expatiates on the theme of the first couplet, expanding on Maecenas' modesty and refusal of high civil and military rank, and, as in 2.1, highlighting Maecenas' loyalty to Augustus. Emboldened by Maecenas' values Propertius then categorically excludes certain epic subjects from his poetic agenda (37–42) before proclaiming his proper poetic role as a love-elegist and follower of Callimachus and Philetas (43–6). But Propertius goes on to take a further cue from Maecenas' loyalty to Augustus, at the same time exemplifying his own previously expressed willingness to live by Maecenas' values: he asserts that he will write on epic themes other than those rejected in lines 37–42 – but only if Maecenas gives him a lead (47–56). The words *te duce*, with which line 47 begins, have proved controversial. Some have understood them in purely literary terms, i.e. Propertius will attempt certain epic themes if Maecenas inspires him (*qua* Muse figure) to do so.

---

89   Fedeli (1985) 303 denies that 3.9 in its entirety is a *recusatio*, accepting this classification only for ll. 35–46. But explicit literary *recusatio* is already present in ll. 3–4 and the entire elegy revolves around it.

Others see Propertius expressing willingness to attempt epic if Maecenas gives him a lead by accepting high status in the public sphere.[90] The logic of the entire elegy speaks in favour of the latter interpretation. Only line 52, *crescet et ingenium sub tua iussa meum*, provides any comfort to the former view, and this line could just as easily be explained as a generalized compliment to Maecenas as patron, or as an oblique hint that Maecenas already had 'ordered' another of his poets (Virgil) to tackle the epic themes outlined in lines 47–56.[91]

One noteworthy difference between 2.1 and 3.9 lies in the identity of the epic subjects which Propertius rejects out of hand or considers hypothetically possible in each. Self-imitation with variation and 'self-correction' are visible here. In both elegies Propertius refuses to treat two topics from the traditional epic repertoire: Thebes (2.1.21 = 3.9.37–8) and Troy (2.1.21 = 3.9.39–40). In both he fantasizes about composing an epic on the recent Civil War won by Augustus (2.1.25–38 = 3.9.53–6). But in 3.9, out of the traditional stock epic topics Propertius accepts Gigantomachy as a possible theme (3.9.47–8), whereas he had rejected it as unsuited to him at 2.1.19–20. Perhaps by the late 20s BC Propertius had a better understanding of the role of Gigantomachy in the self-imaging of the principate, particularly as Virgil was exploiting it in his *Aeneid*,[92] and as Horace had exploited it in Odes 3.4.[93] In addition Propertius is willing in 3.9 at least to imagine himself writing an epic on the foundation of Rome (49–51), a subject which he had excluded absolutely in 2.1.23. Again, a better grasp by Propertius of the underlying concerns of the developing *Aeneid* may lie behind his growing appreciation of the Augustan nature of this theme. One or two small details of 3.9's account of the Civil War which are additional to that of 2.1 show Propertius increasingly confident in his handling of historical content: the suicide of M. Antonius is mentioned at 3.9.56, and 3.9.54 represents as a military victory what was probably a peace made with the Parthians in 30 BC.[94] Habitués of Maecenas' salon in the 20s BC will naturally have echoed the 'official' representation of what had happened in the previous decade.

2.1 ended with a piquant combination: an acknowledgement by

90   For viewpoints and arguments see Fedeli (1985) 326–8.
91   Cf. Virg. *Georg.* 3.41: *tua ... iussa* (of Maecenas).
92   Cf. esp. P. R. Hardie (1986). The theme was, of course, already a commonplace in the self-representation of hellenistic monarchy.
93   The Horatian parallel is all the more cogent given Propertius' interactions with the 'Roman odes' in Book 3.
94   Cf. Fedeli (1985) 330–1.

Propertius of his dependent status vis-à-vis Maecenas followed by a declaration of his elegiac independence. After saluting Maecenas as the 'hope of his youth, and his glory in life and death' (73–4), Propertius – on the assumption that he would end his life as a lover, and indeed die of love – imagined Maecenas as accepting this by saying over his grave (reading from his epitaph?): '*huic misero fatum dura puella fuit*' (78). In 2.1, then, Propertius was explicit about his erotic commitment, as he also was about his dependence on Maecenas, but he did not relate his prospective poetic activity to the personality and future life-choices of Maecenas. Elegy 3.9 presents a subtly altered stance. Throughout 3.9 Propertius' poetic goals are linked to Maecenas' ethics and to Maecenas' public ambitions (or rather lack of them), while Propertius' aspiration to continue in the life of love is conveyed only in the two final couplets (57–60) and only in the 'keyword' *mollis* (or *mollia*) (57)[95] plus the implications of *coeptae ... iuventae* (57). Moreover even in 57–60 emphasis on Maecenas' control over Propertius is dominant. The metaphors of lines 57–8, whatever their exact significance,[96] illustrate Maecenas' absolute power over Propertius and his destiny; and Propertius follows them up in 59–60 with an outright declaration of personal and poetic dependence upon Maecenas: 'You permit me to achieve this celebrity, and you allow me to be accounted as one of your dependants'. The final phrase of the elegy – *in partis ipse fuisse tuas* (60), equivalent to *in partes ivisse tuas*[97] – overtly states that Propertius belongs to the *clientela* of Maecenas. This is virtually the only element of Propertius' programme to survive unaltered from 2.1.

In other elegies of Book 2 a similar tone of devotion to the regime and a parallel technique in the handling of historical realities are visible. For example, in his brief but glittering *ekphrasis* of Augustus' new temple of Apollo on the Palatine (2.31), Propertius is highly specific about the occasion for which the elegy was composed (the opening of the attached portico) and about the temple's layout and

---

95 The MSS read *mollis*, which some editors have retained; others accept the emendation *mollia*: cf. Fedeli (1985) 332–3, who favours the emendation. Whichever reading is correct, the same point is made: for *mollis* as a Propertian 'keyword' see Cairns (1984b), and below, Index II s.v. *mollis*.

96 Interpretation of the couplet is not aided by a textual problem: in l. 57 N offers *factor*, FLP *faustor*. Editors print the corrrection *fautor* (made by a second hand in F); the term is appropriate to the context, but less obviously helpful to the coherence of the metaphors.

97 On the imagery of ll. 57–8, and on the significance of ll. 59–60 and of *in partis ipse fuisse tuas* (60), cf. esp. Fedeli (1985) 332–4.

sculptures. This new concreteness in the description of people and events which resulted from Propertius' changed patronage ambience remains in force throughout Books 3 and 4. Interestingly, its novelty is thrown into relief by contrast not only with the older, less precise mode of the Monobiblos but also with those elements of Propertius' earlier practice which survive into Book 2. Elegy 2.16 is particularly interesting in these respects because it exemplifies both Propertius' old and his new approaches. The old approach is present because 2.16 resumes the narrative of 1.8, and features once again the 'praetor' of 1.8. This man has now returned from his province loaded with wealth, and he is once more eager to oust Propertius from Cynthia's favours. But he remains the shadowy figure that he was in the Monobiblos. The scenario of 1.8 and 2.16 is patently fictitious, with no one individual standing behind the praetor.[98] It is, after all, very unlikely that Propertius, particularly in Book 2, published as it was under Maecenas' aegis, could, even in his guise of 'insane' poet-lover, have stigmatized an identifiable contemporary Roman ex-magistrate as *barbarus* (2.16.27), or referred to him in such grossly contemptuous terms as *maxima praeda* (2.16.2) and *stolidum ... pecus* (2.16.8). Nor is it credible that Propertius could publicly have urged Cynthia, once she has exhausted a recognizable ex-praetor's resources, to tell her victim to sail back to the *Illyrias* (2.16.10), or that Propertius could have wished a hernia on him (2.16.14), or have implied that he was a second M. Antonius (2.16.37–40), fit to be contrasted with the victorious bringer of peace, Augustus (41–2). Such humiliating attacks on major named or/and otherwise identified public figures were made in the society of Catullus, and they recur in the 30s BC in the interchange of insults between protagonists of the Civil Wars. But even in the 30s Horace was selecting the victims of his satirical and iambic poetry with greater care, and in the age of Augustus there is no poetic parallel for such treatment of a real ex-magistrate.

The fact that 2.16 is a sequel to 1.8, and so continues a narrative begun in the Monobiblos, probably explains the continued elusiveness of its narrative plot and vagueness of its unidentifiable praetor. But 2.16 also shares the tendency of many other elegies of Books 2, 3 and 4 to treat contemporary and earlier Roman history in a specific and detailed way: it stigmatizes M. Antonius and mentions Actium (36–40), and it eulogizes Augustus, alluding to his closure of the gates of

---

98   For further reflections along these lines see Fedeli (2005) 472–4.

the Janus temple in 29 BC (41–2). These passages, and perhaps also 19–20, which is less specific but is nevertheless allusively eulogistic of Augustus, bear the hallmarks of Maecenas' patronage. The elegy is thus an attractive candidate for transitional status between Propertius' two patronage situations. Other elegies of Book 2 where pseudonyms may hide or replace the names of real people, or/and where the plot scenario is vague, might also tentatively be dated to before Propertius' change of patronage. To this category belong, for example, 2.21 with its mysterious 'Panthus' and 2.22 with its almost equally opaque 'Demophoon'.[99]

It was argued above (pp. 60–2) that, although Propertius characterizes himself clearly as Umbrian, he was nevertheless possibly of part-Etruscan descent. Already in elegies 21 and 22 of the Monobiblos an Etruscan theme, the siege and fall of Etruscan Perusia and its aftermath, is prominent, unsurprisingly given the influence on Book 1 of his patrons, the Etruscan Volcacii Tulli of Perusia, his own possible kinship with them, the proximity of his native Asisium to Perusia, and Asisium's involvement in the events of 41–40 BC. But that is the sum of Propertius' expressed interest in matters Etruscan in the Monobiblos. However, his work as a whole shows him more committed to Etruria than any other Augustan poet,[100] so much so that at one point he can even characterize himself as a *haruspex*![101] Leaving aside earlier influences, that of Maecenas must loom large in the explanation of this. Maecenas seems to have been a dedicated Etruscan.[102] His un-Roman personal behaviour, dress, actions, and literary style, which attracted the criticism of Seneca, can best be seen as ostentatious expressions of his background in Etruria.[103] As an Etruscan of high birth on both sides of his family, possibly with some knowledge of the Etruscan language,[104] and certainly heir to a culture already largely Romanized but still sufficiently differentiated to preserve its own values and attitudes, Maecenas, especially when at home in Arretium or on the Esquiline, will have felt no more need to conform to Roman

---

99 Cf. above, p. 69.
100 Cf. esp. Newman (1997) Ch. 2 ('Etruria'), embracing however some material of uncertain relevance to Propertius. I have not annotated disagreements of detail with this work, but, as will emerge, my own criteria are more restricted. Sordi (1981) usefully notes Propertius' interest in female lineage in two contexts, 4.1.89–90 and 97 (66) and 4.11.31 (56).
101 Prop. 3.13.59. But, *pace* Feichtinger (1991) 189, his *patria* in this context is Rome.
102 André (1967) 55–60; Foresti (1991); (1996).
103 On his *turris* as possibly another see above, p. 258 n. 53.
104 On the replacement of Etruscan by Latin see Foresti (1996) 7–8, with bibliography.

expectations of his private life than to adopt the standard Roman view that the best career was the one leading to magistracies and army commands. Maecenas was not just content to live as an Etruscan; he also indubitably wanted to project not just his equestrian status but also his Etruscan origins as essential elements of his self-image: Horace, and to a lesser extent Propertius, harp as much on his ethnicity as on his remaining an *eques*.[105] Moreover Etruria was clearly central to the political thinking of Maecenas at the moral level,[106] and in practical terms: for example, when he formed the praetorian guard, Maecenas recruited from Umbria, Etruria, Latium and old Latin colonies;[107] and it is no accident that the Etruscans Seius Strabo and his adoptive son Seianus, related both to Maecenas and to Propertius (see above, pp. 20–1), turn up later as its commanders. Maecenas must, then, have welcomed the readiness of poets of his circle to treat Etruscan material and to do so in positive terms.[108] As regards Propertius, it cannot be fortuitous that his Books 2–4 display both Etruscan subject-matter and a pro-Etruscan attitude, and Maecenas will surely have inspired them to a significant degree. An observation which might at first seem to play against this hypothesis in fact strengthens it: elegy 3.22 is Propertius' *kletikon* to Tullus, his former patron who, like Maecenas, was an Etruscan. 3.22 parades the *laudes Italiae*, but there is a strange absence of mention of Etruria or of any Etruscan location, all the more strange because 1.22 had already asserted Tullus' ethnic origins.[109] Instead the main emphasis in 3.22 is on Rome and Latium. It is almost as though all cultural proprietary rights over Etruria have now been claimed by Maecenas.

Maecenas' wish and willingness to be identified as an Etruscan and as of Etruscan royal descent[110] can best be seen from the works of Horace, who raises the ethnic and rank issues most frequently, and who presumably did so advisedly (he never does it in the *Epodes*):

105 *RE* s.v. Maecenas 6) 208–9. Simpson (1996) 397 has interesting reflections on Horace's characterization of Maecenas as an *eques*.
106 Cf. esp. Sordi (1995).
107 Tac. *Ann.* 4.5.5; Sordi (1985) 13–17; (1995) 152–5.
108 Cf. MacFarlane (1996) 248–52; Firpo (1998), usefully surveying Etruscan influence on Augustan poets but (256–86) exaggerating Horace's 'criticisms' of Etruria and Etruscans.
109 Contrast Prop. 1.22, and indeed, through proximity, 1.21.
110 For some of the context of these claims see Cornell (1976). Their reality, at least on the Cilnii side, is underlined by the 'royal' nomenclature of a late fourth/early third-century BC *luvχume cilnie* (= Lucumo Cilnius) recorded from a now lost Etruscan inscription, probably of Tarquinia: see Maggiani (1986) 176–7, 187.

Maecenas <u>atavis</u> <u>edite</u> <u>regibus</u>   (*Odes* 1.1.1)

Maecenas, sprung from royal ancestors

care Maecenas *eques*,[111] ut <u>paterni</u>
<u>fluminis</u> ripae simul et iocosa
redderet laudes tibi Vaticani
    montis imago.   (*Odes* 1.20.5–8)

dear knight Maecenas, so the playful echo of your paternal river-bank
along with the Vatican hill repeated the acclamations back to you.

<u>Tyrrhena</u> <u>regum</u> <u>progenies</u>, tibi
non ante verso lene merum cado
    cum flore, Maecenas, rosarum   (*Odes* 3.29.1–3)

Etruscan descendant of kings, for you a smooth wine from an unbroken
cask with the blossom, Maecenas, of roses

Non quia, Maecenas, <u>Lydorum</u> quidquid <u>Etruscos</u>
incoluit finis, nemo <u>generosior</u> est te,
nec quod avus tibi maternus fuit atque paternus
olim qui magnis legionibus imperitarent   (*Satires* 1.6.1–4)

Not because, Maecenas, no-one is nobler than you among the Lydians
who have occupied the land of Etruria, nor because your maternal
ancestor and your paternal ancestor were once commanders of great
legions

Interestingly these topics are absent from Virgil's works; the four
places where he addresses Maecenas (only in the *Georgics*[112]) lack all
traces of either. Possibly Virgil did not wish to associate Maecenas as
patron of the *Georgics* with any particular part of Italy so as to allow
him to stand above local identifications and thus be the inspirer of a
poem celebrating the agriculture of Italy as a whole. As for Propertius,
his two elegies addressed to Maecenas give unequal weight to
Etruscan matters. Elegy 2.1 does not even mention them in direct
association with Maecenas, although *eversosque focos antiquae gentis
Etruscae* (29) would have evoked thoughts of Maecenas' origins in
the minds of those aware of them, irrespective of the historical
reference of the line (discussed above, pp. 262–3). The very first line
of elegy 3.9, however, attaches Etruria, royal blood, and equestrian
status explicitly to Maecenas' name:

111 Cf. *Od.* 3.16.20: *Maecenas, equitum decus.*
112 *Georg.* 1.2; 2.41; 3.41; 4.2.

Maecenas *eques* Etrusco de sanguine regum (3.9.1)[113]

A number of other Propertian elegies handle specifically Etruscan topics, and these merit discussion, since the volume of Etruscan material appearing in Books 2–4, although not to be exaggerated, is fairly substantial, and sometimes the Etruscan dimension helps to solve old problems of interpretation. The relevant poems will be treated in order, but one topic common to them and to the elegies addressed to Maecenas already discussed, namely those moral qualities claimed by contemporary Etruscan culture which were identical with the virtues of old Rome,[114] will be reserved for treatment in final position. The first noteworthy elegy is 2.13: in all the main Propertian MSS it begins:

> Non tot Achimeniis[115] armatur Etrusca sagittis
> spicula quot nostro pectore fixit Amor   (1–2)

Literally rendered this would mean: 'An Etruscan woman is not equipped with as many Achaemenian arrows as Love has fixed points in my breast'. Since the concept of an 'Etruscan woman' being equipped with arrows seems to be unparalleled and is difficult to make sense of,[116] editors often place *Etrusca* within cruces.[117] Many emendations, usually geographical terms, have also been proposed in place of *Etrusca*, but none has proved generally acceptable.[118] The notion that a geographical term is required here seems plausible since 2.13 displays multiple literary-geographical interest.[119] In the early lines come the Hesiodic 'Grove of Ascra' (4), Pieria, birthplace of the Muses (5), Ismaros, a location associated with Orpheus (6), and Linus' place of birth, Argos (8). Then *Phthii ... viri* ('the hero of Phthia', 38) identifies Achilles by his birthplace; and the final section of 2.13 offers first *Gallicus*[120] *Iliacis miles in aggeribus* (48), which, whatever

---

113   Cf. also *Eleg. in Maecen.* 1.13 (addressed to the now dead Maecenas): *regis eras, Etrusce, genus*, with Schoonhoven (1980) 98–9, 103–4; Augustus ap. Macrob. *Sat.* 2.4.12.
114   Cf. esp. Sordi (1995).
115   This is either an orthographical variant for *Achaemeniis* or a trivial error.
116   However Newman (1997) 500–1 understood it so.
117   E.g. Enk (1962); Barber (1953); Fedeli (1984); Fedeli (2005) 360, who goes on (365) to characterize attempts to defend the MSS reading as unworthy of discussion.
118   For the conjectures see Smyth (1970) 47.
119   On the relationship of this passage to Virg. *Ecl.* 6.64–73 and to lost works of C. Cornelius Gallus see Ross (1975) 118–120, and above, pp. 124–5.
120   *Gallicus* has been much emended, but it does not affect the point.

else it implies, at least points clearly to Troy; then Mt Idalium in Cyprus, where Adonis met his death (54), is mentioned.[121] This concentration of geographical terms encourages the notion that an ethnic or toponym stood in line 1 where the MSS proffer *Etrusca*. Indeed it suggests that *Etrusca* itself deserves further consideration as just such an ethnic, particularly since 2.13, although not addressed to Maecenas, shares with 2.1 (in which Book 2 is dedicated to him) both its literary concerns and its recusatory content, so that *Etrusca*, functioning as an initial reference to Etruria in this quasi-'proemio al mezzo' would be a further compliment to Maecenas.

Naturally 2.13.1–2 cannot be understood sensibly in the exact form in which it stands in the Propertian MSS: a minor emendation, or rather correction, already made by the humanists and accepted by most modern editors irrespective of their verdict on *Etrusca*, is necessary if an acceptable meaning is to be extracted. It amounts to no more than altering *armatur* (1) to *armantur*. The syntax remains slightly contorted, but with this small change the received text has been defended, and has been rendered as: 'Non, les flèches étrusques ne sont pas autant hérissées de pointes achéméniennes que l'Amour n'en a fichées dans mon cœur',[122] a rendering supported by the parallel: *libet Partho torquere Cydonia cornu/ spicula* (Virgil *Eclogues* 10.59–60). The only difficulty with this ingenious approach, which takes *sagitta* as an 'arrow-head' and *spiculum* as the 'shaft' of an arrow, is that, whereas the notion of 'Persian' = 'Parthian' (the two terms were regarded as synonymous in Propertius' day) arrow-heads is comprehensible enough, 'Etruscan shafts' seems a less plausible concept.[123] But, if the combination is reversed and *sagitta* and *spiculum* are given their normal senses of 'arrow' (i.e. 'shaft') and 'point' (i.e. 'arrow-head') respectively, and *armantur* means 'are fitted to', then the couplet can be translated as: 'Love has fixed in my heart more arrow-heads than there are Etruscan arrow-heads fitted to Persian (i.e. Parthian) shafts'. This makes more sense: 'Parthian shafts' are a commonplace, and Etruria was one of the finest producers of metal work in antiquity[124] – and well known as such in the ancient world.

---

121 On Adonis in Parthenius (and Gallus) see above, pp. 81 n. 56, 144 and n. 132, 145, 213 and n. 83.
122 By Verdière (1965) 23–5, 24.
123 Plin. *NH* 16.161 records that reeds from the river Rhenus at Bononia (Bologna), originally an Etruscan city, make the best arrows. This falls short of a justification.
124 *RE* s.v. Etrusker coll. 760–2 (Skutsch).

Pliny writes of Etruscan statues being found everywhere, and, on the authority of Metrodorus of Scepsus, of the Romans looting two thousand bronze statues after the fall of Volsinii.[125] Again, Greeks from the fifth century on were familiar with the high reputation of Etruscan metal-workers. Athenaeus (*Deipnosophistae* 28b.9–c.1) preserves a poem by Critias (B fr. 2 DK) in which the sources of various top quality products are listed; two lines (8–9) award the palm for metallurgy to the Etruscans:

> Τυρσηνὴ δὲ κρατεῖ χρυσότυπος φιάλη,
> καὶ πᾶς χαλκὸς ὅτις κοσμεῖ δόμον ἔν τινι χρείᾳ.

Best is an Etruscan beaten gold cup and all the bronze-ware that adorns a house for any purpose.

Another passage from Athenaeus (*Deipnosophistae* 700c.4–8) contains a quotation from a dramatist of Old Comedy (Pherecrates fr. 90 PCG) which illustrates the fame of Etruscan metal-workers:

> Φερεκράτης δὲ ἐν Κραπατάλλοις τὴν νῦν λυχνίαν καλουμένην
> λυχνεῖον κέκληκεν διὰ τούτων·
> Α. τίς τῶν λυχνείων ἡ 'ργασία; Β. Τυρρηνική.
> ποικίλαι γὰρ ἦσαν αἱ παρὰ τοῖς Τυρρηνοῖς ἐργασίαι, φιλοτέχνων
> ὄντων τῶν Τυρρηνῶν.

Pherecrates in *Good-for-Nothings* calls what is now called lychnia (lampstand or lantern) lychneion in these words: "A. What is the workmanship of these lampstands? B. Etruscan." Indeed manufactures were various among the Etruscans, devoted as they were to the arts. (tr. C. B. Gulick)

This passage continues (700c.8–11) with another quotation – from the *Knights* of Antiphanes, a dramatist of the Middle Comedy (Antiphanes fr. 109 PCG) – also concerning a lampstand. This quotation probably has nothing to do with the Etruscans, although curiously enough it mentions 'javelins' (literally 'little points' = *spicula*):

---

125 *signa quoque Tuscanica per terras dispersa qu<in> in Etruria factitata sint, non est dubium. deorum tantum putarem ea fuisse, ni Metrodorus Scepsius, cui cognomen a Romani nominis odio inditum est, propter MM statuarum Volsinios expugnatos obiceret.* (*NH* 34.34)

Ἀντιφάνης δ᾽ Ἱππεῦσι·
τῶν δ᾽ ἀκοντίων
συνδοῦντες ὀρθὰ τρία λυχνείῳ χρώμεθα

Antiphanes in *The Horsemen*: "We fasten three javelins upright together and use them as a lampstand." (tr. C. B. Gulick)

A further testimony – from the hellenistic poet Rhianus – perhaps brings us even closer to the path whereby this concept could have been transmitted to Propertius: a phrase from one of his poems – Ἀγύλλιον χαλκόν (*CA* fr. 48) – refers to bronze manufactured in the important Etruscan town of Agylla (Caere).

Roman poets of a hellenistic bent practised *aemulatio* of their models as a matter of course, and the conceit involved in 2.13.1–2 is perhaps best explained as the result of such poetic emulation. Cornelius Gallus either invented or popularized the practice of coupling a bow designated as the product of one geographical area with arrows attributed to another area; Crete and Parthia featured largely in the process. This conclusion can be drawn from: *libet Partho torquere Cydonia cornu/ spicula* (Virgil *Eclogues* 10.59–60, in a monologue of the love-lorn Gallus),[126] *Cnosia nec Partho contendens spicula cornu* (*Ciris* 299, from a poem known to have been influenced by Gallus),[127] and Virgil's later variation of the same conceit: *spicula torquebat Lycio Gortynia cornu* (*Aeneid* 11.773). Other Gallan material in Propertius 2.13 has been recognized independently.[128] I propose that Propertius' desire to emulate his predecessors (here especially Gallus) led him to differentiate geographically, not between a bow and arrows, but between two different elements of the arrow: so he made the shaft 'Persian' (*variatio* for 'Parthian'), and the barb 'Etruscan'.

Two explanations can be given for a Propertian variation from Cretan to Etruscan. Crete was a favourite place of origin for poetic arrows because of the age-old celebrity of Cretan archery.[129] Virgil (above), Ovid, Lucan, Statius, Valerius Flaccus, and Silius all use the toponym of Cretan Gortyn to signify 'Cretan' in archery contexts; Lucan and Silius combine Gortyn with a reference to 'eastern' arrows, thus alluding to the Parthian/Lycian bows of their poetic

---

126 Cf. esp. Rosen and Farrell (1986) 243–6.
127 For Gallan influence on the *Ciris* see Lyne (1978), 253, 312–13. For the (implausible) view that Gallus authored the *Ciris* see Skutsch (1901) esp. 61–102; (1906); the view has recently been revived by Gall (1999). On this particular *Ciris* passage cf. Connors (1991).
128 Ross (1975) 34–6, 118–120; Heyworth (1992) 48–53.
129 Cf. Nisbet and Hubbard (1970) 196.

predecessors.[130] It has even been proposed, on the basis of scholia to Lycophron *Alexandra* 805 and 806 which mention a 'Gortynaia' as a city of Etruria, that *Gortyna* should be read in place of *Etrusca* in Propertius 2.13.1.[131] However, rather than alter the text of Propertius we might credit him (or/and his model) with knowledge of the fact (or more probably fiction) of an Etruscan Gortynaia, and hypothesize here a learned substitution of 'Etruscan' for the expected 'Gortynian'.[132] A point in favour of this notion is that *Amor* had a 'Cnossian' quiver in a couplet of the preceding elegy (2.12.9–10) which also contains the *iunctura armata sagittis*;[133] hence Crete was seemingly in Propertius' mind at this point in Book 2[134] in circumstances linking love and archery. Paradoxically, if Propertius did intend a covert allusion to Crete in 2.13.1, his line would combine the same geographical elements as Virgil's *libet Partho torquere Cydonia cornu/ spicula*[135] and *Cnosia nec Partho contendens spicula cornu* (*Ciris* 299).

A second explanation not inconsistent with the first is that Propertius was aware of the unhistorical identification often made in antiquity between the Etruscans, who supposedly originated in Lydia, and the Lydians. A sign of Propertius' awareness is his high consciousness of Lydia/Lydians: the adjective *Lydus/Lydius* occurs six times in his elegies.[136] In one of these instances (3.5.17) the Lydian king, Croesus, in whose reign the Lydians and Persians clashed, is given his ethnic. He is also named in two further passages, 2.26.23 and 3.18.28, and in the former he is linked with the Persian king, Cambyses. Another Lydian/'Persian' collocation presents itself in Propertius 3.11.17–26, where the 'Lydian girl', Hercules' mistress Omphale (17–20), imme-

---

130 Ovid: *Gortyniaco ... arcu* (*Met.* 7.778). Lucan: *iam dilecta Ioui centenis uenit in arma/ Creta uetus populis Cnososque agitare pharetras/ docta nec Eois peior Gortyna sagittis* (*BC* 3.184–6); *Gortynis harundo* (*BC* 6.214). Statius: *Gortynia .../ cornua* (*Theb.* 3.587–8); *Gortynia .../ spicula* (*Theb.* 5.361–2). Valerius Flaccus: *plenisque redit Gortyna pharetris* (*Argon.* 1.708). Silius: *Gortynia .../ tela* (*Pun.* 2.90–1); *nec se tum pharetra iactauit iustius ulla/ Eois quamquam certet Gortyna sagittis* (*Pun.* 2.100–1); *Gortynia ... harundo* (*Pun.* 5.447).
131 By Boucher (1961) 239–40.
132 Some of the arguments of Boucher (1961) could be used to support this hypothesis.
133 *et merito hamatis manus est armata sagittis/ et pharetra ex umero Cnosia utroque iacet* (2.12.9–10).
134 This would not, of course, apply if those who believe that 2.13 is the proem to a new book and 2.12 a stray are correct!
135 *Aen.* 11.773; for this combination cf. also *Parthus sive Cydon telum inmedicabile torsit* (*Virg. Aen.* 12.858).
136 1.6.32; 3.5.17; 3.11.18; 3.17.30; 4.7.62; 4.9.48 (of Omphale, like 3.11.18). By contrast there are no examples in Tibullus, and only three in the more voluminous elegiac writings of Ovid.

diately precedes Semiramis (21–6), foundress of Babylon which Propertius calls a 'city of the Persians' (21). This is the only mention by name in Propertius of the 'Persians'. Along with the 'Medes', who occur twice in Propertius,[137] the Persians were in subjection to the Parthians in Propertius' day, and both subject peoples were frequently equated in Augustan poetry with the Parthians, who are named ten times by Propertius.[138] All in all, then, the Persian-Etruscan combination of 2.13.1–2 is fully in place in Propertius, and *Etrusca* should not be emended. It is highly appropriate that, in a programmatic poem[139] in which Propertius is once again establishing his credentials as the successor in elegy to Gallus, he should start by combining a challenging display of *aemulatio* of his poetic master and former patron with a compliment to his new patron, Maecenas.

In Book 4 Propertius gives much attention to Roman aetiology, which by its nature admits Etruscan material only when relevant to a specific *aetion*. Moreover Propertius had by this time come under the protection of Augustus, who is the patron of Book 4 (in which Maecenas does not appear), just as Augustus is the patron of the *Aeneid* and of Horace *Odes* 4.[140] Nevertheless Etruscan interest is a fairly major element in Book 4. This shows that Propertius had a continuing concern for things Etruscan, and it hints that his relationship with Maecenas still remained significant; we know that this was the case with Horace too after Augustus had become his main patron. Maecenas could also have continued to be a source or channel for Propertius of information about things Etruscan. The question whether Maecenas did or did not fall from Augustus' favour in the years following 20 BC seems now to have been answered in the negative;[141]

---

137 3.9.25; 3.12.11 (*Medae ... sagittae*).

138 2.10.14; 2.14.23; 2.27.5; 3.4.6; 3.9.54; 3.12.3; 4.3.36, 67; 4.5.26; 4.6.79.

139 Cf. esp. Wilkinson (1966); Heyworth (1992). The fact that 2.13 is programmatic does not, however, lend much comfort to the notion that it began a new book: it resembles more a 'proemio al mezzo'.

140 As evidenced by Augustus' request to Horace to address him in his poetry (Sueton. *Vit. Horat.* c) 44–7 Rostagni). Although patron of Prop. Book 4, Augustus is never directly addressed in it by Propertius, but only by the deified Julius Caesar at 4.6.38 (cf. P. White (1991) 138). Was elegy perhaps not 'respectable' enough for direct address by Propertius to the *princeps* to be encouraged – even though it had happened once before (*Auguste*, 2.10.15)? Or is it just that the address by Julius Caesar is more encomiastic?

141 Cf. esp. P. White (1991); Williams (1990) had recanted his earlier support for the notion. It must be said, however, that Maecenas' public activities do appear to have diminished in the teens BC: Sallustius Crispus seems to have taken over his security role, and, as noted by Foresti (1996) 11 n. 26, in 16 BC the departing Augustus appointed the elderly Statilius Taurus, not Maecenas, to take charge of Rome and Italy in his absence, even though Maecenas had held this position twice in the 30s BC.

the strong presence of Etruria in Propertius Book 4 perhaps adds an iota of support to the case against this now discredited notion.

Elegy 4.1 contains two passing Etruscan references. At line 8 the river Tiber is given the learnedly paradoxical description *nostris advena bubus*. Since it was the arriving Trojans and their cattle who were actually 'new-comers' to the Tiber, this paradox must have been meant to foreground the Etruscan associations of the Tiber, which in Augustan and later poetry is *par excellence* the 'Etruscan' river,[142] and which was in fact an ancient boundary between the Etruscans and other races of Italy. Another fleeting Etruscan reference comes at 4.1.29, which introduces an Etruscan ally of Romulus who fought and died in Rome's struggle against the Sabines (29). Propertius' account of this alliance is consonant with Virgil's representation in the *Aeneid* of the Etruscans, with the exception of the renegade Mezentius, as faithful allies of Aeneas; Maecenas' influence on both poets can be assumed in such references. At Propertius 4.1.29 Romulus' Etruscan ally features one line before Romulus' temporary enemy and subsequent ally, the Sabine Titus Tatius (4.1.30). Propertius may be making a point about the priority of the alliance between Rome and Etruria, while of course in no way demeaning the Sabine connection.[143] In the Propertian MSS Romulus' ally is 'Lygmon' (N Vo) or 'Ligmon' (F P L D V). This is a unique form, and the humanist emendation 'Lycmon', although also an *unicum*, may be preferable for a number of reasons: first the name is clearly related to 'lucumo', the Latinized form of an Etruscan term for 'king', and 'Lucumo' is what Cicero actually calls this same person.[144] Second, Propertius follows up his reference to Romulus' ally by noting (31) that he gave his name to the *Luceres*, one of the three tribes into which Romulus was said to have divided the Romans; this aetiology was a standard element of accounts of 'Lucumo'. Finally at 4.2.51 Propertius refers to the same person as 'Lycomedius'.[145] So an initial Lyc- seems more plausible. It must have been metrically convenient for Propertius to have available the alter-

---

142 E.g. *Tuscum Tiberim* (Virg. *Georg.* 1.499); *dum Tiberis liquidas Tuscus habebit aquas* (Ov. *Ib.* 138, cf. *Met.* 14.614–5; *Fast.* 4.47–48; 6.714); *castra super Tusci si ponere Thybridos undas* (Luc. *Phars.* 1.381, cf. Sil. *Pun.* 17.14–15).

143 On the (originally Sabine) Claudii and their contemporary representatives, see below, p. 287.

144 *Rep.* 2.14, cf. also Dion. Hal. 2.37–43 (Λοκόμων). Livy 1.34–40, Dion. Hal. 3.46–8, and Strabo 5.2.2 offer an account of a different 'Lucumo'/Λοκόμων/Λουκούμων who came to Rome from Tarquinii in the reign of Ancus Martius and ended up as king L. Tarquinius Priscus.

145 On this name see Rothstein (1920–4) II.197, 226.

native forms 'Lygmon'/'Lycmon' and 'Lycomedius', and that may be
the end of the story. But since aetiology and *doctrina* go together, this
individual's nomenclature could have been a subject of learned debate
among Propertius' contemporaries.[146] If so, Propertius' references are
meant to display his *doctrina*, and they may 'correct' his predecessors,
possibly on the basis of privileged information derived from Maecenas
or one of his Etruscan associates.

The learned and substantial (64–line) elegy 4.2 most extensively
reflects the Etruscan interests of Propertius in Book 4,[147] since it is devoted entirely to the Etruscan god Vertumnus,[148] who speaks throughout and who impacts on Rome through his statue there,[149] which, he
claims, antedated Numa in its original wooden form (60).[150] In line 3
Vertumnus calls himself an Etruscan, and he asserts an origin among
the Etruscans, *Tuscus ego Tuscis orior*, having already mentioned in
line 2 his *signa paterna*, i.e. presumably primarily 'Etruscan', but
possibly there is more to the adjective – see below (p. 283–4). Immediately after this, Vertumnus specifies that he came to Rome from
(Etruscan) Volsinii during a time of war, adding that he does not
regret his move (3–4). This last remark is not a repudiation of his
Etruscan ties but rather embodies an underlying theme of 4.2, the present harmonious coexistence in Rome of things and persons Etruscan
and Roman.[151] There follows a reference to the Tiber, now named 'Tiberinus' (7),[152] which recalls and reinforces the allusive significance
of *Tiberis ... advena* of 4.1.8.[153] Then Vertumnus speaks specifically

146 That the topic in general was debated cannot be doubted: e.g. Varro similarly gives the
     name 'Lucumo' to the eponym of the Luceres (*LL* 5.55), but identifies Romulus' ally as
     Caele Vibenna (*LL* 5.46).
147 On 4.2 see Boldrer (1999), drawing on much previous scholarship and with full biblio-
     graphy. Among important earlier contributions are Pillinger (1969) 178–81, and especially
     Pinotti (1983), illustrating in particular 4.2's 'Alexandrian' and hymnic features.
148 Vertumnus is his Roman name, and the etymologies of it proposed in antiquity (for which
     see *LALE* s.v.) all involve Latin *verto*, as do those which the god mentions in 4.2 (see
     below, p. 287). For a suggestion about the Etruscan name of Vertumnus see below, p. 282
     n. 154.
149 For an explanation of Propertius' concentration on this statue, rather than on Vertumnus'
     temple on the Aventine, see Pinotti (1983) 81–2.
150 This is probably a reference to Numa's proverbial association with antiquity: cf. Sutphen
     (1901) 255, citing for 'Numa as a type of antiquity' Mart. 3.62.2; 10.39.2; 10.76.4.
151 Cf. esp. Pinotti (1983), and also Firpo (1998) 288–92.
152 Cf. Boldrer (1999) 92–3, and, on the implications of the varied nomenclature of the Tiber,
     which will not have been lost on Propertius, Cairns (ftc.).
153 See above, p. 280; the dual nomenclature parallels that of Lygmon/Lycmon (4.1.29) and
     Lycomedius (4.2.51) discussed above, pp. 280–1, where Etruscan antiquarian material is
     probably again involved.

of 'his' Etruscans (*meis* ... *Tuscis*) at line 49, and in line 50 he mentions the *Vicus Tuscus*, the street in Rome where (appropriately) his statue stood. The next couplet (51–2) expands on lines 49–50 and reintroduces a topic already treated more briefly at 4.1.29–30 – the assistance given to Romulus by an Etruscan leader (there Lycmon, here Lycomedius) in his war with the Sabines. When Vertumnus mentions *praemia* given to the Etruscans in return for their assistance he presumably means the naming of one of the original Roman tribes '*Luceres*' after the Etruscan leader (this was already made explicit at 4.1.30), as well as the naming of the *Vicus Tuscus* (50). Vertumnus may also be thinking of the *praemia* as including the presence of his own statue in Rome in its second, bronze incarnation (61–4), and the worship which he receives there.

These indubitable Etruscan pointers are impressive, but, if a new proposal about 4.2 is correct, the elegy contains further and hitherto unrecognized information about Vertumnus' Etruscan aspects. Lines 33–4 (in the text of N) read:

> cassibus impositis venor; sed harundine sumpta
> Favor plumoso sum deus aucupio.

Put nets on me, and I am a hunter. But when I take up the reed I am the god Favor, catcher of feathered birds.

To date no editor of Propertius has printed *Favor*, all having preferred various emendations. But Martianus Capella in his *De Nuptiis Philologiae et Mercurii*, when locating Etruscan deities under Latin names in various parts of the heavens, refers three times (1.48, 50, 55) to *Favor* and once to *Favores* (1.45) as the Latin name(s) of an Etruscan god or gods. Hence it has been proposed that *Favor* should be retained at 4.2.34, and that Propertius is equating Vertumnus with 'Favor'.[154] Part or all of the passage in which Vertumnus describes his mutations would therefore be a genuine account of Etruscan religious beliefs.

There is, however, an obstacle to this approach: the first syllable of the Latin common noun *favor* is short, but, if *Favor* is read at 4.2.34, its first syllable must be long. There are various ways in which this obstacle might be bypassed: one would be to suppose that *favor* and *Favor* are etymologically unrelated, and do in fact differ in

---

154 By de Grummond (ftc.), who goes on to identify Vertumnus/Favor as the Etruscan god Thufltha, and to suggest possible representations of Vertumnus/Thufltha *qua* fowler in Etruscan art.

quantity; that would make the pair parallel to *fatuus* ('stupid') with short *a*, and *Fatuus*, another name of a 'deity', with long *a*.[155] Another way would be to hypothesize that *Favor* is derived from the perfect stem of *favere*, i.e. *favi*, with long *a*. A third way would be to suppose that Propertius is simply varying the quantity of *favor/Favor* in Book 4 – he has *favore* with short *a* at 4.6.12. Roman elegists, including Propertius, do sometimes employ the same word with varied scansion, but variation in the quantity of the first closed vowel of a dissyllable seems to be unparalleled.[156]

If the quantity of the *a* of *Favor* is not an impediment to retaining it in line 34, then Vertumnus is identifying himself with Favor there. Some additional features of 4.2 may both reinforce this new approach and further assure Propertius' accuracy and informedness. At 4.2.39 Vertumnus describes another of his guises; in all the MSS this line begins with the difficult *pastorem ad baculum possum curare*, but most editors print *pastor me ad baculum possum curvare*,[157] i.e. with Ayrmann's emendation *pastor me*, and the recentiores' *curvare*. Whether *pastorem* or *pastor* is read, this word, like *Favor*, occupies initial position in its line; and one of Martianus' references to *Favor* is as *Favor pastor* (1.55). Again, at another point Martianus writes of *Favores opertanei* (1.45). No plausible explanation of *opertanei* has been proposed, but in ll. 19–20 Vertumnus declares that he knows the 'correct' etymology of his own name; the first word he uses after this declaration is *opportuna* (21), which looks as though it might somehow be connected with *opertanei*. Finally, near the beginning of 4.2 Vertumnus speaks of his *signa paterna* (2). Propertian scholarship has long debated the significance of these words, and a slew of emendations has resulted.[158] Undoubtedly the correct approach is to retain the transmitted text and to understand *signa* as 'notae quibus Vertumnus agnosci potest', and to take *paterna* as designed 'ad originem designandam'.[159] But, as often in Propertius, there may also be a subsidiary sense or implication. At 1.50 Martianus characterizes Pales

---

155 From *fari*: Varro *LL* 6.55, cf. 6.52; Walde–Hofmann I.464.
156 See Platnauer (1951) 50–5.
157 Rothstein (1920–4) II.224 and Schuster (1958) 190 defended *curare* by claiming that it means 'pastoris partes agere'. Fedeli (1965) 114 rejected their defence and upheld the emendation *pastor me*, printed by Fedeli (1984). For discussion and further emendations see Boldrer (1999) 120–1.
158 Cf. Smyth (1970) 133; Fedeli (1984) 224; Boldrer (1999) 84–5.
159 So Fedeli (1984) 224.

and Favor as *'filii Iovis'*.[160] If Vertumnus is Favor, and hence *'filius Iovis'*, this would explain why he is so emphatic in describing his *signa* as *paterna* near the beginning of the elegy (2): his *paterna signa* would be those of the son of the greatest god of Etruria, Tinia (= Roman Jupiter). Vertumnus would thus not just be announcing his own name in line 2, but also allusively providing his patronymic. Vertumnus' filiation would also illuminate his sudden appeal to Jupiter at lines 55–6 as *divum Sator*: if Vertumnus/Favor is *'filius Iovis'*, he is calling on Jupiter not just as the 'father of the gods' in general, but as his own father.

When Vertumnus appears in subsequent Latin poetry (Ovid *Metamorphoses* 14.642–97, 765–71; *Fasti* 6.409–10, [Tibullus] 3.8.13–14) the information given about him seems to derive almost entirely from Propertius 4.2. So these passages neither support nor detract from the above suggestions.[161] Nor is Varro's brief account of Vertumnus helpful,[162] and his claim that Vertumnus is the chief god of Etruria (*is deus Etruriae princeps*) is positively misleading, since the chief god of Etruria was, as noted, Tinia = Jupiter.[163] But there are also earlier references to Vertumnus/the Vicus Tuscus in the works of another protégé of Maecenas, Horace, and one of them,[164] *Satires* 2.3.226–32, has some interesting and perhaps underexploited overlaps with Propertius 4.2.[165] These certainly reflect information shared by the two poets, although it is unclear whether Propertius is imitating Horace, or whether both had observed the same phenomena in their walks about Rome, and had learned in the circle of Maecenas how to interpret them. The truly interesting overlaps come in the first lines of the Horatian 'edict' of the prodigal heir (*Satires* 2.3.226–32):

160 The fact that the (plural) *Favores opertanei* (plurality being another characteristic of Etruscan deities) attend Jupiter in region 1 of the heavens (1.45) may confirm this.

161 Including Ovid's Vertumnus disguised as an old woman (*anus*), which merely 'reverses' Propertius' *indue me Cois, fiam non dura puella* (4.2.23), and including the curious recurrent emphasis in all three accounts on *decor*: *decorus* (Prop. 4.2.22); *decenter* (Prop. 4.2.45); *decoris* (Ov. *Met.* 14.684); *decenter* ([Tib.] 3.8.14), cf. *Decor* ([Tib.] 3.8.8); *decet* ([Tib.] 3.8.9).

162 *LL* 5.46.

163 If Vertumnus was identified with Favor *filius Iovis* (cf. above, p. 282–4), Varro might have been misled by a garbled source which had started out by stating that Vertumnus was the son of the *deus Etruriae princeps*.

164 The others are *Sat.* 2.7.13–14 and *Epist.* 1.20.1.

165 Cf. O'Neill (2000) 267–8, concluding that the Vicus Tuscus was a 'center of prostitution' (268), and bringing Hor. *Sat.* 2.3.226–32 to bear mainly on Prop. 4.2.23–4, where Vertumnus is a *non dura ... puella*, and 4.2.38, where she sees (270) an allusion to the sexual promiscuity of pedlars; Boldrer (1999) 114 had already remarked on the presence of the *piscator* and *auceps* in both texts.

hic simul accepit patrimoni mille talenta,
edicit, piscator uti, pomarius, auceps,
unguentarius ac Tusci turba inpia vici,
cum scurris fartor, cum Velabro omne macellum,
mane domum veniant. quid tum? venere frequentes,   230
verba facit leno: 'quidquid mihi, quidquid et horum
cuique domi est, id crede tuum et vel nunc pete vel cras.'

The trades mentioned here are those of a fisherman = fish-seller, a fruiterer, a bird-catcher = vendor of wild birds, a perfumer, the *turba impia* – probably sexual providers, parasites, a poulterer, a butcher, and a *leno*. Grammatically the description *Tusci ... vici* (228) attaches to the *turba impia*, but Horace was clearly linking all the trades in a general way with the *vicus Tuscus*; and some of them exactly echo the guises of Vertumnus. Thus fisherman = fish-seller corresponds with *piscis calamo praedabor* (4.2.37), a bird-catcher = vendor of wild birds with *harundine sumpta/ Favor plumoso sum deus aucupio* (4.2.35–6), and sexual providers with Vertumnus in Coan silks as a *non dura puella* (4.2.23), i.e. a *facilis puella* – a *meretrix*. Of the rest the fruiterer has no direct parallel among the guises of Vertumnus, although he appears as the *insitor* of 4.2.17 who makes a dedication to the god's statue at the end of a six-line account of offerings of fruit (13–18); and there is much emphasis too on Vertumnus' other agricultural roles (25–8, 39, 41–6: horticulture is his *maxima fama*, 41). Nor does the perfumer have an exact parallel in 4.2, although one of Vertumnus' guises there is as a florist (4.2.39–40), and his statue also wears floral crowns presumably dedicated to him by a florist (45–6). Horace's poulterer, butcher, and *leno* (unless Propertius' *meretrix* implies a *leno*) are unrepresented in 4.2, perhaps in part because their trades were more unsavoury. Many occupations are mentioned by Propertius and fewer by Horace, but the correspondences cannot easily be brushed aside as coincidence. Vertumnus was clearly the patron god of the trades which flourished in the area around his statue, and perhaps each of his humble votaries represented the god bearing the accoutrements of his own trade.

The fact that the Vicus Tuscus was *inter alia* an area in which prostitutes and their pimps operated has been interpreted to mean that Propertius was somehow undermining his patrons by portraying Vertumnus and his ambience.[166] This is not an acceptable conclusion:

166 O'Neill (2000).

prostitution was only one of the trades practised in the Vicus Tuscus, and both Horace and Propertius characterize it as a bustling centre of retail activity of many sorts. If any of the trades carried out there has special relevance to Propertius 4.2, it is the clothing industry, for which this area was particularly noted:[167] that is what lies behind Vertumnus' many disguises. Apart from this, Maecenas was no prude, and as one who rejected high office he may even have affected an affinity with the common man; at all events the lower-life aspects of the Vicus Tuscus are unlikely to have troubled him. Maecenas was moreover, as his writings show, himself learned in the Alexandrian tradition, and he will have appreciated that in representing a 'humble god' in 4.2 Propertius was following in the wake of Callimachus' *Iambi* 7 and 9.[168] *Iambus* 9 is a particularly significant parallel for Propertius 4.2 because in it Hermes speaks and (like Vertumnus) declares himself to be Etruscan in origin.[169] Callimachean learning and 'Etruscanizing' meet once more in the person of Vertumnus, who, as a small (Etruscan) god of small (Roman) people will undoubtedly have been a subject pleasing to Maecenas, whether in Horace's *Satires* or in Propertius 4.2.[170] It has already been suggested that some of the guises of Vertumnus may be grounded in Etruscan religion, and, if we were better informed, yet others might turn out to be.[171] At the very least Propertius knew more about Vertumnus and his functions within Etruscan culture and religion than any other surviving Roman writer. He could, of course, have used written sources, and, if he did, it must be suspected that Maecenas or other Etruscans of his household guided Propertius to them. If he had oral sources, these too are most likely to have come from the circle of Maecenas. It would be no surprise if the statue of Vertumnus was of keen interest in that milieu, and if the aetiology of the statue and of the cult which it received on the Vicus Tuscus had been researched by Maecenas' associates.[172]

---

167 *LTUR* s.v. Vicus Tuscus (E. Papi); Boldrer (1999) 7.
168 Cf. Boldrer (1999) 42–3. Priapus and similar deities are favourites in this class: for these see Herter (1926); (1932).
169 Diegesis VIII.37–8.
170 Cf. also Foresti (1996) 20–6, usefully examining the analogies between Maecenas' behaviour and lifestyle and the attributes and activities of Vertumnus. Both are represented in terms of Etruscan stereotypes.
171 The general point can be made that the male/female ambivalence of Vertumnus is a characteristic of a number of Etruscan divinities: cf. De Grummond (ftc.).
172 The same has already been surmised about Propertius' accounts of 'Lycmon' (4.1.29)/ Lycomedius (4.2.51), although in that instance Etruscan sources would not have been

The 'integrationist' aspect of 4.2 has already been mentioned, that is, its portrayal of Vertumnus and his Etruscan background as harmoniously embraced by Rome from the beginning. In consonance with this theme all the etymologies of Vertumnus' name proposed in 4.2 (9–12, 47–8) are Latin etymologies from *verto*; and, when the god confirms the 'truth' of the derivation of 'Vertumnus' from *vertor* and *omnes* (47), he does so in terms of '*patria lingua*', which can only be Latin.[173] The god, then, is aware that 'Vertumnus' is not his Etruscan name but his name in the language of his adopted *patria*, Rome. Another, non-Etruscan, Italic 'integrationist' note may be sounded by the *tellus* ... *Osca* (62) in which the sculptor of Vertumnus' statue is buried;[174] and the reference two lines earlier to Numa, who was of Sabine origin (60), and for whom Mamurrius Veturius created the *ancilia* as well as Vertumnus' cult statue at Rome, acknowledges the Sabine element in early Rome, which had already featured at 4.2.52. Elegy 4.2 thus reinforces the Sabine reference of 4.1 (above), and Sabine emphasis will reappear on a larger scale in 4.4, whose hero is the Sabine king Titus Tatius, and again in the fleeting but emphatically final reference of 4.9.74. It can hardly be irrelevant to this highlighting of the Sabines in Book 4 that from 23 BC on the two young stepsons of Augustus, the Claudii Tiberius and Drusus, from a family with a known and vaunted ancient Sabine origin, began to win victories on the frontiers of the *imperium*, to advance through the *cursus honorum*, to be eulogized openly in Horace's *Epistles* and *Odes* 4, and to be hinted at more discreetly in Virgil's *Aeneid*.[175] Propertius will have wanted to add his own indirect eulogies, especially in view of the connections between Tiberius and his associates and Asisium.[176] Maecenas was obviously content for poets of his circle to undertake these tasks, and Augustus will have approved.

Among the later elegies of Book 4, Propertius 4.9 contains a quatrain with an indirect connection to Etruria and a direct connection to Maecenas. It is Hercules' description of his enslavement to Omphale,

---

essential given the versions of Cicero and Dionysius of Halicarnassus (see above, p. 280 and n. 144).

173 On the etymologies, and for *patria lingua*, see Boldrer (1999) 19–26.
174 Cf. Boldrer (1999) 145; an alternative view is that its reference is more general: 'Italian soil'.
175 The appellation *Tiberinus* accorded to the Tiber at Prop. 4.2.6 is *inter alia* an allusion to Virgil's mode of eulogizing Tiberius in the *Aeneid*, on which cf. Cairns (ftc.).
176 See above, Ch. 1, esp. pp. 24–5.

his performance of feminine tasks for her, and his transvestism under
her influence:[177]

> idem ego Sidonia feci servilia palla
> officia et Lydo pensa diurna colo,
> mollis et hirsutum cepit mihi fascia pectus,
> et manibus duris apta puella fui.   (4.9.47–50)

I also performed servile tasks wearing a Sidonian dress and spun my
daily measures of wool with a Lydian distaff. A soft breastband
restrained my hairy chest, and with my rough hands I was a plausible
girl.

Other implications of this quatrain apart, its allusion to Omphale's
Lydian ethnicity (48) attracts attention, if only because *Elegiae in
Maecenatem* 1.69–80 recounts this same episode in direct relation to
Maecenas, laying stress on Hercules' effeminate garb (77–8), and
referring twice (75, 77) to Omphale as '*Lydia*':

> impiger Alcide, multo defuncte labore,
>   sic memorant curas te posuisse tuas,   70
> sic te cum tenera multum lusisse puella
>   oblitum Nemeae iamque, Erymanthe, tui.
> ultra numquid erat? torsisti pollice fusos,
>   lenisti morsu levia fila parum;
> percussit crebros te propter Lydia nodos,   75
>   te propter dura stamina rupta manu,
> Lydia te tunicas iussit lasciva fluentes
>   inter lanificas ducere saepe suas.
> clava torosa tua pariter cum pelle iacebat,
>   quam pede suspenso percutiebat Amor. (69–80)

Vigorous Alcides, they say that, retired from your great toil, you put
aside your cares so. They say you so made love often with a young girl,
now forgetful of Nemea and of you, Erymanthus. Was there something
more? You twisted spindles with your thumb, with your mouth you
softened threads to smoothness – but not enough! Because there were
many knots the Lydian woman beat you; she beat you because of the
threads snapped by your rough hands. The randy Lydian woman commanded you often to trail flowing robes among her spinners. Your

---

177 This passage has aroused considerable scholarly interest over the past two decades: cf.,
     e.g., Cairns (1992a) 89–90; Lindheim (1998); Fox (1999) 167–76; Janan (2001) 142–5;
     Debrohun (2003) 158–65; and the further bibliography below, p. 363 n. 8.

knotty club lay idle along with your lion skin, which Love used to smite with lifted foot.

This passage is part of a defence of Maecenas' luxurious way of life:[178] Bacchus, Hercules, and Jupiter all first won their victories and then enjoyed luxury and love; so did Maecenas.[179] Many aspects of these mythical comparisons are controversial, as indeed are almost all aspects of the *Elegiae*, but plausible reasons why their author thought to link Hercules' servitude with Maecenas can be proposed. First, the Lydian setting must have been intended to evoke the (false) theory current in antiquity that the Etruscans originated in Lydia. Second, and more important, since the *Elegiae* poet, whatever his date, is clearly well disposed to Maecenas, he must have thought that applying this macabre mythical episode to Maecenas was in order. He would have had unassailable justification for doing so if Maecenas himself had already analogized his Etruscan way of life with the Lydian life-style of Hercules under Omphale's sway, possibly in his *De cultu suo*.[180] If he did so, then Propertius' introduction of the same episode into 4.9 will reflect his knowledge of Maecenas' tastes in mythology, his self-imaging through myth, and his writings.

The last elegy of Book 4 with a reference to Etruria is 4.10, which belongs to the ultimate period of Propertius' poetic career, when his services were directly at the call of Augustus. It treats the *spolia opima*, a topic of considerable interest to Augustus, who had person-ally intervened in 29 BC to deprive M. Crassus of the signal honour of making this offering to Jupiter Feretrius.[181] The pretext for the denial, namely that to dedicate the *spolia* a commander must not only per-sonally kill the enemy leader but must do so while fighting under his own auspices (Crassus was fighting under those of Imperator Caesar), is unobtrusively underlined by Propertius in *omine quod certo dux ferit ense ducem* (46). Of the three historical figures who did win this honour and who are celebrated in 4.10, two have clear associations

---

178 See now Rosati (2005) 137–40 on Maecenas' '"soft" elegiac life-style' (139), and for the view that in the *Elegiae* he is represented as an elegiac poet (138).

179 On this and other aspects of Maecenas' self-image and life-style see Firpo (1998) 288–9 n. 123, with bibliography. For an important analysis of Velleius Paterculus' portrait of Mae-cenas in its representational context see Woodman (1983) 239–44.

180 Fr. A) II – André (1967) 149. Nigro (1998) 139 ingeniously suggests that Omphale repre-sents Maecenas' wife Terentia.

181 Cf. Liv. 4.19–20 with Ogilvie (1965) 563–4; Rich (1996), who, however, believes that Crassus did not claim the right to offer *spolia opima* (see above, p. 74 and n. 26); Harrison (2005) 127–8.

with Augustus: the first, Romulus, indirectly provided him with his name 'Augustus' and usefully functioned as part of his public image, while the third, M. Claudius Marcellus, was the ancestor of Augustus' nephew Marcellus. Another link between the *spolia* and Augustus is that the mysterious *lapis silex* of the *fetiales* was also kept in the temple of Jupiter Feretrius: Augustus was a *fetialis*, and he had declared war on Egypt in 32 BC in this capacity.

All this is perhaps explanation enough of how 4.10 served Augustus' ends; and yet the amounts of text assigned to the three dedicators of *spolia opima* raise questions. There is no problem about Romulus and his victory being given the most extensive treatment (eighteen lines, 5–22): he prefigured Augustus. To explain why M. Claudius Marcellus, who dedicated *spolia opima* after killing a Gallic chieftain at the battle of Clastidium (222 BC), is awarded only six lines (39–44) one might invoke hellenistic compositional technique, with its tendency to asymmetry in poetic structures, often involving the abbreviation of later sections.[182] But this very high disproportion is striking, and it is rendered all the more so by the allocation to the remaining dedicator, the fifth-century BC A. Cornelius Cossus,[183] of sixteen lines (23–38). A first consideration is that the star of the Claudii Marcelli had set when Augustus' nephew and heir presumptive, the last male representative of his family, died in 23 BC during his aedileship. Clearly this was a tragedy for the family of Augustus, and some tributes survive: Virgil's famous lines at *Aeneid* 6.861–86 and Propertius' *epikedion* (3.18).[184] But by the mid-teens BC the Claudii Marcelli no longer mattered in practical terms, and Augustus' sister Octavia, the mother of Marcellus, went into seclusion after her son's death, thereby further reducing the residual impact of his memory. Moreover in the years when Propertius' Book 4 was being composed (approximately 21–15 BC) another branch of the Claudii, the Claudii Nerones, was becoming ever more ascendant in the persons of Tiberius and Drusus, seconded by their mother Livia. This may go some way towards explaining why Propertius was comparatively reticent about the feat by which the third-century BC Claudius Marcellus had won *spolia opima*.

The sixteen lines of 4.10 allocated to A. Cornelius Cossus also

---

182   Cf. *THPR* Ch. 8, esp. 202–13.
183   Kl. P. s.v. Cornelius I.17.
184   The work dedicated to Octavia by Athenodorus Calvus (Plut. *Public.* 17.5) might also have been consolatory.

call for an explanation. Augustus' refusal in 29 BC to allow M. Crassus to dedicate *spolia opima* was underpinned by an inscription said to have been found in the temple of Jupiter Feretrius upon Cossus' dedication: the inscription allegedly proved that Cossus fought under his own auspices.[185] This may sufficiently explain why Cossus is given such prominence in 4.10. It may also, however, be relevant to call attention to a contemporary of Propertius, a young Cornelius whose use of 'Cossus' (originally a *cognomen*) as his *praenomen* was clearly intended to claim descent from the dedicator of *spolia opima*.[186] This man (Cossus Cornelius Lentulus *PIR*² C 1380), became consul in 1 BC, and was subsequently proconsul of Africa, *praefectus urbis*, and an intimate of Tiberius. But in 16 BC he was only around eighteen years of age, and one might wonder how his existence could have contributed towards inducing Propertius to give so much space to his 'ancestor'. The answer could be that Cossus Cornelius Lentulus was related to the very well-connected Cornelia[187] whose *epikedion* is the next, and final, elegy of Propertius Book 4. Her connections, and those of her husband (Paullus Aemilius Lepidus – another man with a *cognomen* for a *praenomen*) reveal them as high in the Augustan power structure at the time of her death (see below, pp. 358–61). Presumably Cornelia speaks truthfully when she claims to be *univira* (4.11.68),[188] so the young Cossus cannot have been her son by a previous marriage,[189] but he was possibly her nephew or cousin.

Whatever other motives Propertius had for giving the fifth-century BC A. Cornelius Cossus sixteen lines of 4.10, one is secure: Cossus' exploit, for which he won the *spolia opima*, was the killing in single combat of Tolumnius, king of Etruscan Veii. Here, then, was an opportunity for Propertius to introduce yet another substantial item of Etruscan interest into his Roman aetiology book. Tolumnius' death preceded the destruction of Veii by over a generation, but in the centrepiece of his narrative Propertius looks forward in time to that event in a lament for the ruined town:

---

185 See above, p. 289 n. 181.
186 Pinotti (2004) 215 pertinently refers to his coinage (before 12 BC) as *IIIvir monetalis*, which shows an equestrian statue of a figure carrying a *tropaion*.
187 Her families can be traced through Syme (1986) Index of Persons s.v. Cornelia, wife of Paullus the Censor.
188 Horace tendentiously implies this status for Livia (*Od.* 3.14.5), but does not actually claim it.
189 This is unlikely in any case since Cossus was probably the son of Cn. Cornelius Lentulus cos. 18 BC (*PIR*² C 1378).

> heu Veii veteres! et vos tum regna fuistis,
> et vestro posita est aurea sella foro:
> nunc intra muros pastoris bucina lenti
> cantat, et in vestris ossibus arva metunt.   (27–30)

Alas, old Veii, you too were a kingdom then, and a golden throne was placed in your forum. Now within your walls the horn of the slow shepherd sounds, and they reap the fields over your bones.

As already noted,[190] Cato wrote of a *rex Propertius* of Veii. The lament may thus recall the alleged former status of the Propertii themselves as Kings of Veii. The evident pathos of these lines would be enhanced by the poet's reference to the kingdom (*regna*, 27) once ruled by his family, and to the royal throne (*aurea sella*, 28) once occupied by his ancestors. Lines 29–30 might seem to be no more than a continuation of Propertius' lament for Veii, its desolation made more pitiful by the thought of its urban space now a pasture and the bones of its inhabitants now lying under cultivated fields. However, Veii was actually refounded by Augustus.[191] The process was probably complex, and firm dates are not to be had;[192] but it looks as if Propertius was either aware of a refoundation (as he must have been if it had occurred earlier), or was at least conscious of plans in that direction. His use of the adjective *veteres* (27) is unlikely to be casual; it should distinguish 'old Veii' from Augustus' new Veii, and thus turn the couplet into an implicit eulogy of Augustus either for having refounded Veii, or at least for planning to do so. An advantage of this proposal is that it would provide a conceptual parallel for the interpretation of 4.1.127–30 offered above, pp. 54–9: there Propertius' mention of the loss of his lands in 40 BC was interpreted as an allusion to the restoration or replacement of lands of the Propertii at Asisium.

Another very important dimension of Maecenas' Etruscanizing influence on Propertian elegy, retained for that reason to a late point in this chapter, can be seen in the virtues which Propertius attributes to Maecenas in the two elegies addressed to him (2.1 and 3.9).[193] These are not merely traditional Roman qualities: they were an integral part

---

190   Above, p. 10 n. 54.
191   Kl. P. s.v. I. Bitto in AA.VV. (1972) 154–5, referring to earlier work, underlined a motive in Augustan ideology for the refoundation.
192   Cf. Harris (1971) 310–11.
193   Virg. *Georg.* 2.532–5, referring to the preceding lines and attributing a life of virtue to the Sabines, early Rome and *fortis Etruria* (533), similarly reflects the influence of Maecenas.

of Maecenas' self-image, and they were associated by him with Etruria.[194] The evidence that Maecenas saw himself in these terms comes from the *Elegiae in Maecenatem*, which drew on Maecenas' own writings (cf. above, pp. 288–9). In the first of the *Elegiae* Maecenas' *fides* (1.12) and *simplicitas* are lauded (1.22), and he is called *miles et Augusti fortiter usque pius* (1.40, cf. 1.43; 1.46). A link with Etruria, and a further link with Maecenas, is provided by the formula[195] used in the honourable discharge diplomas of the praetorians,[196] a body organized by Maecenas and recruited exclusively from areas near Rome, including prominently Etruria.[197] This formula – *fortiter et pie militia functi* – is verbally close to *Elegiae in Maecenatem* 1.40, and so covers all the categories under which Maecenas is praised there: his military activities (*miles*), his courage (*fortiter*), his *fides* (implied by *usque*) and his *pietas* (*pius*).[198] Propertius weaves these same categories (and *simplicitas*) more subtly into his elegies addressed to Maecenas, but his encomia are in essence identical: Maecenas' association with Octavianus' wars (2.1.25–38) demonstrates his *pietas* and courage; Maecenas' constant and conspicuous fidelity is stated in *et sumpta et posita pace fidele caput* (2.1.36), and is illustrated mythologically in the succeeding couplet (cf. also *Maecenatis erunt vera tropaea fides*, 3.9.34); and finally Maecenas' *simplicitas* is revealed by his refusal of high civil and military offices (3.9.2, 21–32). Propertius also tries to depict Maecenas as his own morally superior guide in life – not an easy task, given what we know, and what was generally known in his own time, about Maecenas' private life.[199] Propertius contrives to do this in 2.1 and 3.9 (see above, pp. 261–9) by implying much while actually saying very little: 2.1.71–8 contrasts the young lover Propertius doomed to an early death with Maecenas, who will outlive him and is his hope in life and his glory in life and death; 3.9.57–60 offers a complementary picture of Maecenas directing Propertius' endeavours and conferring distinction on him by allowing him to be his follower.

Elegy 2.1 ended with thoughts of the poet's death, and death was certainly a concern shared by Propertius and Maecenas. But it is

194   Sordi (1995), a thorough treatment which permits the topic to be handled briefly here.
195   So Sordi (1995) 150.
196   See N. Criniti in AA.VV. (1972) 150–1.
197   See above, p. 272 and n. 107.
198   For analyses of the defence of Maecenas in the *Elegiae in Maecenatem* see Schoonhoven (1980) esp. 39–56; Nigro (1998).
199   Cf. above, pp. 271, 287–9.

uncertain whether, and (if so) to what extent, Maecenas influenced Propertius' treatment of this topic. Maecenas' celebrated preoccupation with death[200] may have been due to his Etruscan background, or to a personality disorder, or both. What part Epicureanism played in it can only be conjectured: the school promoted its tenets as an antidote to the fear of death, but Maecenas' Epicureanism might also have encouraged his morbidness. Some commentators have seen a similar tendency in Propertius, but there is little to connect what Propertius wrote about death with Maecenas' unhealthy concern with it, or with the death-interest allegedly endemic among the Etruscans, or with Epicureanism (cf. below, p. 317). Horace, who did make a genuine effort to respond to Maecenas' concerns when addressing him about death, the afterlife, and philosophical matters, provides the benchmark here.[201]

Propertius' intellectual independence in this area goes hand in hand with his general lack of interest in philosophy, a feature of his poetry which stands out by contrast with the work of Horace, and indeed Virgil, both of whom were ready in their different ways to engage with the Epicurean side of Maecenas. In only a single elegy (2.34), which will be treated in Chapter 9, can Propertius be seen making a real attempt to come to grips with Epicureanism, and he is not completely successful. Apart from 2.34, Propertius' only philosophical thoughts come in his aspirations for his old age in 3.5.23–46. Some scholars have seen in these lines a profession by Propertius of attachment to Epicureanism, and certainly Maecenas will not have found them uncongenial. But the soundest assessment of 3.5 regards its philosophical content as commonplace: 'l'opinione di Properzio sembra accordarsi con la *communis opinio* dei rappresentanti della cultura, indipendentemente dalla loro etichetta filosofica.'[202]

---

200 This is a much discussed subject: cf., e.g., André (1967) 32–9.
201 For the interactions between Horace and Maecenas cf. esp. Lefèvre (1981), and the Indices Nominum s.v. Maecenas of Nisbet and Hubbard (1970) and (1978), and of Nisbet and Rudd (2004).
202 Fedeli (1985) 175 (with further internal references at 176).

CHAPTER 9

The Circle of Maecenas in Propertius 2.34

In Chapter 8 some remarks were made about the impact upon Propertius of membership of Maecenas' circle. The present chapter concentrates on Propertius 2.34, over half of which (1–54) is concerned
with another poet whom Propertius calls 'Lynceus'. Especially if one
scholarly hypothesis about Lynceus' identity is correct, this elegy
offers an insight into Propertius' presence within the circle of
Maecenas and his interactions with some of his fellow members. 2.34
is the epilogue of Propertius' longest book, and it is one of his longest
elegies,[1] as well as being one of his most complex. For these reasons,
every aspect of 2.34 merits detailed attention. To date, however, Propertian scholarship has focused mainly on comparatively few of them,
especially the numerous textual and interpretational problems of 2.34,
its passage celebrating Virgil's *Eclogues*, *Georgics* and forthcoming
Aeneid (61–82), and the figure of Lynceus. These are all, of course,
topics which must be addressed in any thoroughgoing treatment of
2.34, as they will be addressed in part or whole in this chapter. But
they should not be allowed to deflect attention, as they have often
done, from a significant dilemma that faces us as readers: how should
we characterize the nature and ethos of the communication between
Propertius and 'Lynceus'? And in what terms and on the basis of what
presuppositions does Propertius venture to confront and rebuke in
such a magisterial way Lynceus, a poet to whom the elegy devotes
more space (1–54) than to Virgil (61–82), so that he appears to be, not
just on a par with Virgil, but even of higher status than Virgil, at least
within the conceptual framework of this particular elegy?

---

1 This chapter assumes the unity of Prop. 2.34 against many dissentient voices; for unitarian
   arguments cf. R. E. White (1964) 61–8; Lefèvre (1980), esp. 127; Stahl (1985) Ch. 7. The
   description of Book 2 as the 'longest book' presumes that it is indeed a single book: see
   above, pp. 194 and n. 20, 266 n. 88, 279 n. 139.

This chapter will offer some suggestions about how to cope with that dilemma, but it must take as its starting-point the much discussed problem of the identity of 'Lynceus'. On the sensible assumption that Propertius would not have given an imaginary epic poet more space than Virgil, Lynceus has often been interpreted as a pseudonym for another contemporary writer, and a strong case was made decades ago by J.-P. Boucher for identifying Lynceus as Virgil's life-long friend and joint literary executor, the epic and tragic poet L. Varius Rufus.[2] There has been some sympathy for this identification,[3] but there is no current consensus in favour of it.[4] Under these circumstances it may be appropriate to approach the identity problem laterally via another question often asked about 2.34: what do Lynceus' behaviour, Lynceus' writings, and Virgil's poetry have in common which induced Propertius to weave them together to form the dominant portion of 2.34? One answer to this question was that Lynceus and Virgil are moving in contrary directions, Lynceus towards elegy, Virgil towards epic.[5] This is correct as far as it goes; but it does not go very far, particularly since Lynceus' move towards elegy looks like wishful thinking on Propertius' part. Some earlier commentators have noted hints of Epicureanism in 2.34,[6] or they have mentioned the circle of Philodemus at Naples in connection with it.[7] These hints will now be taken further: it will be suggested that the disparate personalities and themes of 2.34 are united primarily by their common Epicurean and Philodemean background in the *clientela* of the Epicurean Maecenas, a background which led Propertius to describe Lynceus' behaviour and writings and (to a lesser extent) the works of Virgil in consistently Epicurean terms. The proposals of this chapter do not absolutely

---

2   Boucher (1958).
3   Alfonsi (1963); Soubiran (1982) 266 n. 2; Cecchini (1984); D'Anna (1987) 436–8; Brugnoli and Stok (1991) 133–5 [Brugnoli].
4   Cf. the negative, uncommitted, or uninterested reactions of Nisbet and Hubbard (1970) 81 ('ingenious but implausible'); Wimmel (1983) 1583–5; Stahl (1985) 175 and 348 n. 6; Garbarino (1983) 130–1 n. 32; Newman (1997) 221. Most recently Fedeli (2005) 952–4, summarizing Cairns (2004a), my earlier revival of this view, stresses (954) that 'Lynceus' and 'Varius' are not syllabically and prosodically interchangeable. The equal metrical intransigence of tribrach 'Varius' (on which see below, p. 299) and any interchangeable name may answer this objection.
5   Advanced by Stahl (1985) over 177–8, and associated there with other considerations. The concept had already been formulated for other purposes by Alfonsi (1944–5) 118–20.
6   Esp. Boucher (1958) 312–13, remarking on Varius' Epicurean interests and describing him in Prop. 2.34 as 'l'épicurien amoureux'; cf. also Alfonsi (1963) 273–4. Rostagni (1959) collected Epicurean material in the fragments of Varius but did not relate it to Prop. 2.34.
7   Brugnoli and Stok (1991) 137 [Brugnoli].

require that Lynceus be Varius; he could be another contemporary poet, or theoretically – although this is virtually impossible to credit – he could be imaginary. But Varius is the only other major epic poet of the period with Epicurean leanings who was associated with Virgil, and their association helps to unify 2.34 conceptually.[8] The ancient *Lives of Virgil* place Virgil and either Varius or (Quintilius) Varus together (in Naples) in the 40s BC as students of Epicureanism under Siro.[9] Their testimony is confirmed by two fragments of transcripts of lectures given by Siro's colleague Philodemus[10] in which he addresses Virgil and Varius by name along with Plotius (Tucca) and Quintilius (Varus):

> ὦ Πλώτιε καὶ Οὐά-
> ρ[ι]ε καὶ Οὐεργ[ί]λιε καὶ Κοιντ[ί-
> λιε   (PHerc. Paris. 2.21–3, cf. also PHerc. 253 fr. 12)
>
> O Plotius and Varius and Virgil and Quintilius

The other arguments in favour of the Lynceus/Varius identification, most of them already assembled by Boucher (1958), can be summarized as follows:

1. At *Satires* 1.10.43–4 and *Odes* 1.6.1–2 Horace represents Varius as a celebrated epic poet (although the Agrippa epic envisaged in the latter passage was never written). Varius' epic stature derived from his Epicurean hexameter poem *De Morte*, and possibly from a laudatory hexameter poem about Augustus.[11]

2. In addition to their being conjoined by Philodemus, Varius is linked with Virgil by Horace at *Satires* 1.6.55, 1.10.43–5, *Epistles* 2.1.245–7 and *Ars Poetica* 53–5; the pair are also found together elsewhere in Horace within a larger Epicurean group.[12]

---

8   Cf. also D'Anna (1987) 436–7.
9   *Vita Donati Aucti* 79 Brugnoli and Stok ('*Varum*'); *Vita Probiana* p. 198.6 Brugnoli and Stok (ambivalent '*Vari*' – but '*Quintilii*' appears earlier and separately, so '*Vari*' should be Varius?); cf. also Servius ad Virg. *Ecl.* 6.13 ('*Varus*'). Because of the ease with which the two names can be confused it is impossible to be sure whether the tradition referred to Varius or to Varus as Virgil's fellow-pupil. My own instinct (perhaps not shared by the editors of these texts) is to opt for Varius as the better known figure. For a full discussion of the presence of Varius and Virgil in the Epicurean circle at Naples see Sider (1997) 18–23.
10 This is the correct perception of Philodemus' works offered by Armstrong (1995) 219–20. See also Sedley (1998) 104–9, discussing Epicurus' *On Nature* and Aristotle's *Physics* as lecture courses.
11 On which see below, p. 312.
12 *Sat.* 1.5.40–2; 1.10.81.

3. *varius* is the adjective attached to *lynx* at Virgil *Georgics* 3.264: *quid lynces Bacchi variae?*,[13] and also at [Hyginus] *Fabulae* 259 (of Lyncus king of Sicily): *ob quam rem irata Ceres, eum convertit in lyncem varii coloris, ut ipse variae mentis extiterat.* Euripides' βαλιαί τε λύγκες (*Alcestis* 579) is not only the equivalent Greek phrase but is phonetically analogous to *variae lynces*. Moreover lynxes are implicitly associated with the keen-eyed mythical Lynceus in: *peregrinae sunt <et> lynces, quae clarissime quadripedum omnium cernunt* ('lynxes too are foreign animals: they have the keenest sight of all quadrupeds', Pliny *Natural History* 28.122).

4. In line 83 the words *minor ore canorus* do not appear in N and must be supplemented from the other MSS. Otherwise the couplet 83–4 reads in the (unpunctuated) text of N:

> *nec* minor his animis aut sim minor ore <u>canorus</u>
> <u>anseris</u> indocto <u>carmine</u> cessit <u>olor</u>

The textual problems of these lines make it impossible to be confident about Propertius' exact meaning.[14] But it is clear that they allude to Virgil *Eclogue* 9.35–6:

> nam *neque* adhuc Vario videor *nec* <u>dicere</u> Cinna
> digna, sed <u>argutos</u> inter strepere <u>anser olores</u>.

For I do not think that I yet sing songs worthy of Varius or Cinna, but cackle as a goose among clear-voiced swans.

and, since Cinna was long dead, Propertius' *olor* ('swan') is likely to allude primarily to Varius.

5. Finally, an important discovery of Giorgio Brugnoli:[15] he perceived that line 67 of Propertius 2.34:

> **tu canis umbrosi** subter pineta Galaesi

> You sing (*canis*) beneath the pine-woods of shady Galaesus

---

13   Cf. Soubiran (1982) 266 n. 2.
14   The transmitted text is, however, defensible, as e.g. by Stahl (1985) 183–4, punctuating after *canorus*, and separating *in* and *docto*. On the textual problems of the couplet, see now Fedeli (2005) 1,002–4.
15   Brugnoli and Stok (1991) 133–4.

(where Propertius begins his description of Virgil's *Eclogues*) not only alludes to *Georgics* 4.126 *qua niger humectat flaventia culta Galaesus*[16] ('where dark Galaesus irrigates the yellow cornfields'), but also wittily echoes Varius *De Morte* fr. 4.1 Büchner:

> **ceu canis umbros**am lustrans Gortynia vallem
>
> Like a Gortynian bitch (*canis*) quartering a shady valley.

It may be added that the deliberateness of this echo is doubly assured by its implied reference to the famous pseudo-etymological derivation of *canis* ('dog') from *canere* ('to sing') first found in Varro *De Lingua Latina* 5.99; 7.32.[17] As an echo of Varius as well as Virgil, Propertius' line forwards our understanding of the assimilative agenda being followed in his treatment of Lynceus and Virgil. But more importantly the echo is decisive in favour of the identification of Lynceus as Varius.

Stahl sensibly demanded 'a plausible motive for the use of a pseudonym'.[18] The motive cannot simply be metrical, although, as a tribrach, nominative *Varius* might sometimes have been awkward; nor can it only be the possibility, however real, of confusion between forms of *Varius* and *Varus*. Rather, the motive relates to a practice of the Epicurean circle at Naples – the use of pseudonyms. Philodemus was, it seems, called Socrates (and perhaps also Socration), his wife or partner was Xantho, or Xanthippe, or Xanthion, or Xantharion; Siro was apparently Silenus, and Virgil was Parthenias.[19] All this suggests that Varius' nickname among the Epicureans at Naples was 'Lynceus'. In addition to the *varius/lynx* wordplay, Lynceus perhaps refers punningly to Varius as keen-sighted,[20] probably metaphorically *qua* critic or commentator.[21] His joint editorship of the *Aeneid* may, in

---

16   Cf. Thomas (1988) ad loc.
17   Cf. *LALE* s.v.
18   Stahl (1985) 348 n. 6.
19   For the copious evidence see Sider (1997) 20, 23–4, 34–8.
20   There seems to be no connection with the other mythical Lynceus, the husband of Hypermnestra, or with the historical hellenistic writer on cookery, Lynceus, brother of Douris of Samos.
21   Cf. the terminology of vision applied to literary criticism in two passages unconnected with Varius: *erat optimum, sed certe sint grandia et tumida, non stulta etiam et* acrioribus oculis intuenti *ridicula, ut, si iam cedendum est, impleat se declamator aliquando, dum sciat etc.* (Quint. *Inst. Orat.* 2.10.6); *sed qui altius haec non* perspexerunt *grammatici, hoc putant metrum decurtato pentametro factum, ut reddita syllaba fiat [pentametrum] tale etc.* (Caesius Bassus *GL* VI p. 268 l. 24 Keil).

addition to reflecting his status as both an epic poet and an old friend of Virgil, have been due to his recognized critical acumen. One motive, then, for Propertius' use of the pseudonym will have been that Lynceus was Varius' 'nom de philosophie'. If a further reason is needed, it may lie in the fictitious scenario of 2.34, in which Lynceus is ostensibly at fault. Although informed hearers would not have taken this scenario seriously, uninformed readers might have done so. Hence it may have been felt more discreet not to use Varius' real name. The Lynceus/Varius identification will, therefore, be adopted here as a working hypothesis, and it will gain further strength as this chapter proceeds. Adoption of it does not, however, imply support for various scholars' attributions to Varius (on the basis of Propertius 2.34) of a number of otherwise unattested poetic works.[22]

In his Monobiblos Propertius showed no interest in Epicureanism. He may possibly echo Virgil's *Eclogues* there in a number of places,[23] although some of these references are more probably to passages of Cornelius Gallus which also influenced Virgil. Virgil himself appears only once in the Monobiblos (1.8.10) in an allusive metrically anomalous reference to the Pleiads as *Vergiliae*.[24] The reason why things are so different in 2.34 lies in the development in Propertius' career which has already been discussed.[25] Propertius first entered the patronage of Maecenas around 27/26 BC, and he first mentioned Maecenas in 2.1; as a new member of the circle of Maecenas Propertius will have been anxious to establish himself solidly within it. This explains his fulsome praise of Maecenas in the prologue to Book 2, and also the prominence given in this, the epilogue of Book 2, to Varius and Virgil, the two most eminent and long-serving poets in Maecenas' circle, both also ex-pupils of the great Philodemus, whom Maecenas, himself a committed Epicurean, must have admired.

Although a number of scholars have correctly characterized some of the personal and poetic interactions of 2.34,[26] the ambiguity of the critical terminology used to describe poems like 2.34, i.e. 'literary programme', '*recusatio*' and 'polemic', can still give rise to misunder-

---

22   For such suggestions see Bickel (1950); Boucher (1958). In contrast Cova (1989) esp. Chs. 1; 3 presents a restricted view of Varius' œuvre: cf. Jocelyn (1990). Other accounts of Varius include Hollis (1977); Wimmel (1981); (1983); Rocca (1989) 37–64; Hollis (1996).
23   Lanzara (1990) assembles all possible imitations of Virgil by Propertius.
24   Cf. Hubaux (1957) 38, and see Index II s.v.
25   Above, pp. 74–7 and cf. Cairns (1983a) 89–91.
26   For good accounts of these aspects of Prop. 2.34 see Garbarino (1983) 130–9; D'Anna (1987).

standings of their real tone and implications. Such poems can be genuine, and even vituperative, rejections of one type of poetry by a practitioner of another type, as when Callimachus in *Aetia* fr. 1 Pf. spurns Homericizing epic,[27] or when Catullus expresses distaste for the verses of such writers as Volusius or Suffenus. But genuine disapproval and real literary battles need not be presumed in all cases. In particular Augustan writers of the poetic generation after Catullus often seem simply to be locating themselves within their own individual literary context without such rancour when they take issue with the practitioner of another type of poetry. Their overt rejection of poetry different from their own may even amount to covert or open praise of their supposed literary opponents and their works.[28] A more elusive aspect of literary programmes, *deformazione*, was discussed in earlier chapters; this is when a poet deliberately gives an inaccurate account of another poet's writings which may assimilate them to his own, or simulates the style or vocabulary of another type of poetry in order (supposedly) to attack it, or otherwise presents a false account of a fellow-writer's work. Cases discussed elsewhere in this book are the bucolicization of Cornelius Gallus by Virgil in *Eclogue* 10, and Propertius' treatment of three addressees of the Monobiblos: his iambic threats to his friend Bassus, a writer of iambs (1.4), his elegiac transformation of another friend, the epic poet Ponticus, into a lover who abandons epic and becomes a humble adherent of Propertian erotic elegy (1.7 and 1.9), and his portrayal of his patron Cornelius Gallus as at different times a philanderer with designs on Cynthia (1.5), a former seducer now in love (1.10; 1.13), and the lover of a boy (1.20).[29]

2.34 too contains prominent instances of *deformazione*; and Propertius' polemic in it against Lynceus and his writings is, as a number of scholars have realized,[30] a mock attack, analogous to his assaults on Bassus, Ponticus and Gallus; indeed in every case the publicization by Propertius of a friend's or patron's œuvre through apparent polemic is in fact complimentary. The Lynceus/Varius of 2.34 is represented in terms reminiscent of these three other poets: like Bassus and Gallus he has tried to damage Propertius' erotic relationship, like Gallus he has attempted to seduce Cynthia, and like Ponticus he is an epic poet who

---

27 Cameron (1995) esp. Ch. 10, believes that Callimachus is attacking earlier narrative elegy.
28 This point may seem laboured; but Prop. 2.34's lines about the *Aeneid* are sometimes regarded as 'implicit criticism': so, for example, Mitchell (1985) 52.
29 Cf. above, pp. 113, 116–18, 221–2.
30 See above, p. 300 n. 26.

has fallen in love. Virgil is not subjected to the same sort of head-on attack, but Virgil's *Eclogues* are systematically misrepresented so as to approximate them to Propertian elegy (see below, pp. 313–14). Propertius is just as well disposed to Varius and Virgil as he was to Bassus, Ponticus and Gallus in Book 1: as noted, even in Book 1 he had paid Virgil an oblique compliment.[31] Moreover it will emerge that a major part of Propertius' positive portrait of Varius and Virgil in 2.34 involves bringing to the fore in a laudatory fashion their shared Epicurean interests. Touches of irony are indeed also present, and Varius is seemingly reproached; but equally Propertius directs many barbs against himself. Furthermore it is possible, although unsure, that Propertius' use of Epicurean concepts in his polemic with Lynceus was intended to seem technically inept, and thus to undermine his own position. Finally, the overall scenario of 2.34 is, like those of the elegies involving fellow-poets in Book 1, fictional and intended to be recognized as such, and Cynthia herself, as she appears in Propertian elegy, is fictionalized and stereotypic;[32] so the notion developed in 2.34 that Varius has tried to seduce her[33] is as fantastic as the idea put about in the Monobiblos that Gallus had tried to do so. Varius could at some point have expressed an interest in writing elegy, and this might have been Propertius' starting point. But there is probably no more substance to Varius' conversion to love and love-elegy than there is to Propertius' impertinent asssertion (2.34.81–2, assimilating Virgil to a *magister amoris*) that all Virgil's work will be equally pleasing to expert lovers and novices in love.

Before a detailed reading of 2.34 in Epicurean terms can be attempted, two preliminary points should be made to forestall possible objections: (1) certain Epicurean attitudes were, of course, shared by some or all other philosophical schools, but that does not make them any less specifically Epicurean when they appear in an Epicurean context; (2) since we cannot be sure that all, or indeed any, readers outside the circle of Maecenas would have grasped the sometimes recondite Epicurean allusions of 2.34, it must be assumed that the

31   See Index II s.v. *Vergiliae*.
32   Cf. above, pp. 66–8.
33   The nonsensical account of *VSD* 10: *vulgatum est consuesse eum* <i.e. Virgil> *et cum Plotia Hieria. sed Asconius Pedianus adfirmat, ipsam postea maiorem natu narrare solitam, invitatum quidem a Vario ad communionem sui, verum pertinacissime refutasse* (a derivative, even more muddled tale about 'Varus' can be found in Serv. ad *Ecl.* 3.20) looks like a distortion of the scenario of 2.34. But it should not be concluded from the presence of Lynceus/Var(i)us in these texts that he was in fact given to this sort of activity.

elegy was aimed primarily at this inner circle, although of course on many levels the elegy is perfectly comprehensible, and has often been understood, without any reference to Epicureanism.

Elegy 2.34 starts by sketching a friendship between Propertius and Lynceus which requires mutual *fides*. There is strikingly repetitious emphasis on this theme: *credat* (1), *fidelis* (3), *cognatos*, *amicos* (5), *bene concordes* (6), *hospes* and *hospitium* (7). But Lynceus has breached this type of friendship by attempting to seduce Cynthia; and Propertius' reproaches culminate in an accusation of treachery addressed directly to Lynceus in *perfide* (9). Presumably this elegy was first recited in Maecenas' house on the Esquiline, and Varius may or may not have been present at the recital. In either case Propertius' original audience will have recognized Varius under his pseudonym Lynceus. So they will have understood that Propertius was treating Lynceus not just as a friend but as an Epicurean φίλος, and was thus evoking the circle of Philodemus, to which several members of Maecenas' circle, including the protagonists of 2.34, had belonged. As Cynthia's would-be seducer, Lynceus falls below the standards required specifically of an Epicurean friend.[34] In *De Finibus* Cicero is polemicizing against Epicureanism; but, in conceding the natural goodness of Epicurus and his followers, he uses some phrases which are curiously similar to expressions employed by Propertius here and later (2.81): *et ipse bonus vir fuit et multi Epicurei et fuerunt et hodie sunt et in amicitiis fideles et in omni vita constantes et graves* ('[Epicurus] was a good man, and many Epicureans have been and are today faithful in their friendships and constant and high-principled throughout life'). Cicero may be mimicking the language in which Roman Epicureans expressed their ideals.

The situation in 2.34 becomes even more intriguing from line 11 on. A friend treated perfidiously by his friend in antiquity might have been expected to respond with fierce hatred and a keen desire for revenge. The vicious inverse *propemptikon* attributed variously to Archilochus or Hipponax is the archetype for such a reaction: it ends with the explanatory: ὅς μ' ἠδίκησε, λ[ὰ]ξ δ' ἐπ' ὁρκίοις ἔβη,/ τὸ πρὶν ἑταῖρος [ἐ]ών[35] ('he who wronged me, and trampled on his oaths, he who before was my friend'). But Propertius reacts very differently, much as he had behaved towards another friend of Virgil,

---

34 For Epicurean friendship in general see Long and Sedley (1987) II.126–7 and 132–3 (with the corresponding original texts in I), 137–8.
35 (?)Hipponax fr. 194.15–16 Degani. For the attributions see Degani int. to fr. 194.

Cornelius Gallus, who in the Monobiblos also supposedly attempted to seduce Cynthia. Apart from noting ironically that Cynthia, in implicit contrast to Lynceus, has shown *constantia* and has been *certa* (11) – another curious overlap with *De Finibus* 2.81 quoted above – Propertius is mainly concerned about the *flagitium* (12), in this case the loss of esteem from his friends and consequent pain, which success with Cynthia would have brought upon Lynceus. Concepts similar to Propertius' *flagitium* appear in the fragmentary treatise of Philodemus *Περὶ Παρρησίας* (*On Frank Speaking*), where the term ἀδοξία ('ill repute') is used. Fr. 3.7–11 speaks of the 'ill repute in the eyes of the public and ... separation from one's family'[36] (suffered by the object of frank criticism) as topics already treated by Philodemus. Again Col. XIXb.1–5 declares '<[for they think that it is the part of a friend to apply frank criticism and to]> admonish others, but that to do oneself what is deserving of rebuke is a disgrace and crime.'[37]

Strikingly, despite Lynceus' offence against him, Propertius is still willing to regard Lynceus as his *socius vitae* and *socius corporis* and as the *dominus* of his possessions (15–16); and he continues to address Lynceus as *amice* (16). In this couplet echoes of Epicurean aspirations to a communal life-style shared with a group of like-minded friends can be heard, and *socium vitae* (15) may perhaps even recall Epicurus' demand that friends should commit themselves completely to their friends even to the point of dying for them: καὶ ὑπὲρ φίλου ποτὲ τεθνήξεσθαι ('and on occasion he will die for a friend', fr. 590 Us. = Diogenes Laertius *Vita Epicuri* 120).[38] Propertius' willingness to forgive Lynceus' offence may reflect yet more Epicurean precepts: Epicurus said that one should never give up a friend: cf.: τύχῃ τ' ἀντιτάξεσθαι, φίλον τε οὐδένα προήσεσθαι ('he will take his stand against fortune and never give up a friend', fr. 584 Us. = Diogenes Laertius *Vita Epicuri* 120). Epicurus also seems to have encouraged forgiveness. His preserved precept on this topic relates to slaves, but presumably his tolerance extended even more to free friends: οὐδὲ κολάσειν οἰκέτας, ἐλεήσειν μέντοι καὶ συγγνώμην τινὶ ἕξειν τῶν

---

36   καὶ πε/[ρ]ὶ τῆς ἀδοξίας τῆς παρὰ/ [τοῖς] πο[λ]λοῖς κα[ὶ] περὶ τοῦ/ τῶν οἰκείων ἀ[πο]σπασ/μοῦ. This was an esoteric treatise, being a summary of Zeno's lectures in Athens (see Konstan et al. (1998) 8). The translations printed here and in other quotations are those of Konstan et al. (1998). In this specific instance, however, τῶν οἰκείων might, I suggest, refer to the offender's circle of Epicurean friends rather than to his family.

37   [φιλικὸν μὲν γὰρ οἴονται τὸ παρρησί]/[α]ν ἐπι[φέρειν καὶ τὸ νου]/θετεῖν ἄλλους, τὸ δ' αὐτὸν ἄ/ξια ποιε[ῖ]ν ἐπιπλήξεως, ἀ/δοξίαν καὶ κατάγνω[σ]ιν.

38   The translations of Diogenes Laertius are those of R. D. Hicks, usually adapted.

σπουδαίων ('nor will he punish his servants, but rather show compassion and forgive a servant of good character', fr. 594 Us. = Diogenes Laertius *Vita Epicuri* 118).

Doubtless Propertius hoped that, as an Epicurean, Varius would be suitably grateful for being corrected for his offence: cf. another precept of Epicurus: καὶ ἐπιχαρήσεσθαί τινι ἐπὶ τῷ διορθώματι ('and he will be grateful to anyone correcting him', fr. 592 Us. = Diogenes Laertius *Vita Epicuri* 120).[39] Indeed, Epicureans were very much concerned with frank criticism within their own circle.[40] This was the topic of Philodemus' Περὶ Παρρησίας (*On Frank Speaking*, mentioned above). Such frankness was considered a virtue opposed to the vice of flattery, and therefore as an integral and essential element of Epicurean friendship.[41]

Along with Propertius' remarkable seeming tolerance of Lynceus goes self-accusation. Propertius describes himself as jealous (17–18) and says that he is *stultus* because his jealousy frequently causes him to tremble with *stultus timor* (19–20). As the opposite of *sapiens*, *stultus* can in philosophical contexts mean 'unphilosophical'.[42] Since fear was regarded in antiquity as a form of mental pain, and since avoidance of unnecessary pain was a cardinal Epicurean precept, Propertius, by describing himself as *stultus*, characterizes himself as, in Epicurean terms, morally as well as philosophically defective. This couplet may also contain a witty allusion to Epicurean teaching about death in words relevant to Varius' *De Morte*, and perhaps even quoting from it. In *quod nil est, ... umbras* ('[my] shadows, which are nothing', 19) *umbras* means 'shadows', but *quod nil est* seems to be evoking — via Lucretius' maxim *nil igitur mors est ad nos* ('so death is nothing to us [Epicureans]', *De Rerum Natura* 3.830) — the other meaning of *umbrae*, 'ghosts', and the standard Epicurean denial that *umbrae* persist after death. Propertius goes on (apparently) to exonerate Lynceus further when he offers an excuse for Lynceus' offence: Lynceus was drunk when he approached Cynthia (21–2).[43] But, of course, an Epicurean sage should not talk nonsense in his cups: cf.

---

39 For this theme cf. also Gigante (1983).
40 PHerc. 1082 (Philodemus) Col. II.1–14 distinguishes between frank criticism addressed to 'intimate associates' and to 'all men': see Konstan et al. (1998) 7.
41 See esp. Konstan et al. (1998) 5–7.
42 E.g. Cic. *Paradox.* 2.19; *De Fin.* 1.57; 1.61; 3.60; *Tusc.* 4.14; 5.54; Hor. *Epist.* 1.1.41–2.
43 Curiously Ovid (*Tr.* 2.1.445–6) represents C. Cornelius Gallus, that other alleged would-be seducer of Cynthia (in Prop. 1.5), as having fallen from the favour of Augustus because he did not hold his tongue when drunk.

Epicurus' precept οὐδὲ μὴν ληρήσειν ἐν μέθῃ φησὶν ὁ Ἐπίκουρος ἐν τῷ Συμποσίῳ ('Epicurus in the *Symposium* says that the sage will not drivel when drunken', fr. 63 Us. = Diogenes Laertius *Vita Epicuri* 119). Line 23 looks like a touch of renewed asperity: Propertius will never again be fooled by a stern (i.e. by implication philosophic) appearance: *ruga vitae severae*.[44]

Line 24, *omnes iam norunt quam sit amare bonum* ('everybody knows what a good thing it is to love'), could be taken as a jest against all brands of philosophy if *bonum* is regarded as a philosophic *terminus technicus* in general. But the wit is at the expense of Epicureanism in particular if the Epicurean *summum bonum*, ἡδονή ('pleasure'), is being identified as *amare*, since of course Epicureans did not approve of love (see below, p. 307). That line 24 draws on a specific, and possibly a well-known, canard against Epicureanism, is suggested by a couplet from Petronius' *Satyricon* – if the emendations *doctos* and *amare* are acceptable:

> ipse pater veri doctos Epicurus amare
> iussit et hoc vitam dixit habere τέλος   (132.15.7–8)

The father of truth himself, Epicurus, taught his sages to love and said that it was the goal of life.

In line 7 the manuscript tradition of the *Satyricon* offers *doctus*, which is unmetrical, and *in arte*, which is feeble. Some older editors attempted to retain these manuscript readings, but it is hard to see how *doctos* can be resisted, and, once *doctos* is read, the adoption of *amare* is almost inevitable.[45]

In lines 19–24 Propertius may also be undercutting his own position by revealing himself as an unworthy and doctrinally shaky Epicurean – if indeed he is one at all. As well as jealousy driven by fear, Propertius also nurtures rancour, despite his earlier show of forgiveness. It could be argued that, since Propertius readily admits these faults, his confession might in Epicurean terms serve both as mitigation and therapy, this being the standard doctrine of the school.[46] But Propertius' novice status *qua* Epicurean is made evident throughout, and this implies that his criticism of Lynceus, although in one dimension an act of Epicurean friendship, is in another dimension

---

44 Cf., e.g., Cic. *Post. Red. in Sen.* 15; Petron. *Satyr.* 132.15.1–2.
45 Cf. Kragelund (1989) 449–50. Both emendations are accepted in the most recent Teubner text (K. Mueller).
46 See Konstan et al. (1998) 8.

impertinence. Although it was normal in Epicurean communities for 'the care of souls' not to be 'restricted to a few members invested with pre-eminent authority',[47] and although Epicurean teachers were sometimes themselves in need of criticism,[48] nevertheless Propertius must have intended his criticism of a well-known Epicurean of long standing to be seen as intrinsically out of order.[49]

Line 25 builds upon what has gone before: we are told that Lynceus, who is still being spoken of in avowedly friendly terms by Propertius as *Lynceus ... meus*, is 'mad with a belated love'. The obvious point of criticism of Lynceus here is that he has fallen in love, which an Epicurean sage should not do: ἐρασθήσεσθαι τὸν σοφὸν οὐ δοκεῖ αὐτοῖς· οὐδὲ (Us., p. 332, 15) ταφῆς φροντιεῖν· οὐδὲ θεόπεμπτον εἶναι τὸν ἔρωτα ('[the Epicureans] do not think that the sage will fall in love, nor that he will be concerned about burial, nor that love is divinely inspired', fr. 574 Us. = Diogenes Laertius *Vita Epicuri* 118, cf. Lucretius *De Rerum Natura* 4.1058–192). Moreover Philodemus *Περὶ Παρρησίας* fr. 57.1–5 refers to someone (probably an Epicurean teacher) not catching people in love but inferring that they are in love.[50] Clearly this was for Epicureans a standard situation calling for criticism. In Propertius' eyes Lynceus' falling in love is partly an excuse for his behaviour; but more importantly it allows Propertius to claim Lynceus in line 26 as a convert to his own erotic way of life and poetry. Thus Lynceus can be misrepresented from line 31 on as a (potential) love-poet.

There is another more recondite and more telling attack on Lynceus in Epicurean terms. It involves an idea which, although it cannot be shown to be certainly or exclusively Philodemean, surfaces clearly in *On Choices and Avoidances*, probably a work of Philodemus. This text proclaims that people who postpone pleasure become 'faithless'.[51] Cf.:

---

47 Konstan et al. (1998) 23–4.
48 Konstan et al. (1998) 8; *Περὶ Παρρησίας* frr. 40, 46.
49 There is, of course, some irony implicit in this situation in which Propertius was doctrinally, although not socially, justified in his criticism. There is incidentally no hint in Prop. 2.34 that Lynceus is annoyed by Propertius' criticism, as 'old men' are said by Philodemus to be annoyed by frankness (*Περὶ Παρρησίας* Col. XXIVa.7–15).
50 [κἂν μὴ]/ κατειλήφηι ἐρ[ῶν]ταϲ/ ἢ καταϲ[χ]έτουϲ κακίαιϲ/ τιϲίν, ἀλλὰ ϲημειωϲά/ μενον. ('even if' {it is the case that} he has [not] caught them in love or possessed by some vices, but has inferred {it} from signs.').
51 For this meaning see, in addition to LSJ s.v. II, Danker³ (2000) s.v.

... κατὰ δὲ τὴν φορὰν γινό-
μενο[ι τ]αύτην ὑπό τε τοῦ παρὰ π[ροσ]δοκίαν ἐξαπιναίου
τυπ[τόμ]ενοι τελέ{ξε}ως ἐ-
ξίστανται. πρότερον δὲ πά-
σης ἀπολαύσεως ἑαυτοὺς στε-
ρίσκουσιν, ἵνα δὴ διαρκέσῃ τὰ-
ναγκαῖα πρὸς τὸν βίον αὐ-
τοῖς· καὶ πρὸς ἀναβολὴν [ζ]ῶ-
σιν ὡς ἐξεσ[ό]μενον αὐτοῖς
ὕστερον ἀγαθῶν μετασχεῖν·
κᾆτα διὰ παντὸς ἀσύνθε-
τοι διατελοῦ[σιν]. καὶ διδόασιν
αὐ[τοὺς εἰς] πόνο[υς πολλούς
            (Col. XIX.12–21 Indelli and Tsouna-McKirahan)

... thus, carried away by this line of thought and struck against
expectation by something sudden, they are entirely beside themselves.
But even before, they deprive themselves of every enjoyment in order
that the essentials of life will suffice for them. And they live delaying
(pleasures), under the impression that they will have the chance of
having a share of good things later. And from that point on they pass
their lives as faithless (ἀσύνθετοι) men. And they devote themselves to
great labors ... (tr. by Jeff Fish, based on that of Indelli and Tsouna-
McKirahan)

This is exactly Lynceus' situation: he has become faithless (*perfide*, 9)
because he has left love until late (*seros ... amores*, 25). He is now
mad (*insanit*, 25), like the people of whom Philodemus says that they
have been 'struck against expectation by something sudden' and are
'beside themselves'. Propertius is of course teasing his Epicurean
friend by applying this maxim in a philosophically outrageous way.
Love, as opposed to sex, is not a pleasure in which an Epicurean
should indulge. Indeed it is more akin to the 'great labours' of which
Philodemus spoke. Propertius does not harp on about the troubles that
Lynceus will suffer in love, as he did with Bassus, Gallus and
Ponticus in the Monobiblos. But the implications are there from line
45 on. Philodemus and his teaching seem, then, to enter the elegy in
full force at line 25.

    It may be that this is not the only reference to Philodemus in this
part of the elegy. 'Socrates' can stand for philosophy in general since
many philosophical schools claimed to be Socratic, and commentators
on line 27 have usually taken *Socraticis ... sapientia libris* (27) as

generalized 'philosophic books'. But we cannot fail to remember that Philodemus probably bore the nickname 'Socrates' (and possibly also 'Socration') in his own Neapolitan circle (see above, p. 299). Hence *Socraticis ... sapientia libris* could well refer to the works of Philodemus.[52] In line 28 Lynceus is not reading but writing (*dicere*). The allusion could be to a past opus of Varius involving physics. If so, it need not be anything other than his well-known Epicurean hexameter poem *De Morte*, which presumably introduced physics to explain Epicurean doctrine on the non-immortality of the soul. But *posse* might signal a potential not a past work: it would be natural to represent an Epicurean poet as likely to compose, for example, a *De Rerum Natura*.

The proper name or adjective of line 29 is uncertain. Neapolitanus (N), the Propertius MS which usually offers a superior text, reads *Erechti*, while the descendants of A, copied from the same archetype as N but defective at this point, present an anagram of *Erechti*, namely *Crethei*. *Crethei* is hard to sustain: the only eligible Cretan poet is Epimenides, who wrote *Katharmoi*, a title also employed by Empedocles, a strong influence upon Lucretius. But that would be a somewhat labyrinthine path. Many arbitrary emendations of *Erechti* have been proposed, with, for example, Turnebus and Scaliger suggesting *Lucreti*, and others a wide variety of other proper names. Newman recently went further and emended more widely *exempli gratia*, producing *aut quid nunc Triquetri prosunt tibi carmina lecti*, and in this way introducing Empedocles.[53] Certainty is impossible here, but the least intrusive approach is perhaps preferable, i.e. to replace the misspelled and unmetrical *Erechti* with the correct form, *Erecthei*, so that the line reads: *aut quid Erecthei prosunt tibi carmina lecta*. That leaves us with an 'Athenian'. Might *Erecthei* have suggested itself to Propertius during the process of composition because he had just written *Socraticis* in 23?

If Propertius did write *Erecthei*, what poet (poet-philosopher?) had he in mind? Again, certainty is unattainable, but the question is worth pursuing. First of all, it is very unlikely that Propertius was thinking of the historical Socrates. Socrates may have written some

---

52   Similarly Hor. *Od.* 3.21.9–10, *Socraticis* .../ *sermonibus*, might refer to Philodemus' lectures, since the ode is addressed to Messalla Corvinus, an Epicurean if Momigliano (1941) 153 is correct. At Cic. *Tusc.* 3.43 'Socratic' dialogues would seem to refer to Socrates.

53   Newman (1997) 221–3. For a discussion of the emendations proposed see now Fedeli (2005) 966–7.

verses in his last confinement, but they were not one of his claims to fame.[54] Plato, another Athenian philosopher, also wrote verses, but again he would hardly have been thought of as a poet by Propertius. Yet another philosopher who was an Athenian citizen (for all that he was born on Samos), Epicurus, who resided most of his life in Athens and who looms large in the rest of 2.34, must be ruled out because he wrote no poetry.[55] There remains a candidate who was certainly both a celebrated poet and an Epicurean philosopher, but who at first sight seems excluded because he was not Athenian, namely the teacher of both Virgil and Varius, Philodemus, who was born in Gadara. However, Philodemus moved, perhaps even as a youth, to Athens, and he probably spent a long time there in the philosophical schools.[56] The shared elements in the lives of Socrates, Epicurus and Philodemus cannot fail to have been observed by Philodemus' pupils, particularly because of Philodemus' seeming nicknames Socrates/(?)Socration. Might such a nickname and the immigrant status of both Epicurus and Philodemus, combined with Philodemus' long residence in Athens, have led his pupils, in the hothouse atmosphere of the Neapolitan circle, to describe him as 'the Athenian'? A special factor could have helped by making his original ethnic 'Gadarene' uncongenial to Philodemus: Gadara had been conquered and probably forcibly judaized in Philodemus' early years by the Jewish king Alexander Jannaeus,[57] so that a Greek, particularly in a Roman context, might well have wanted to distance himself from this ethnic. There is a parallel to what is being proposed here about Philodemus in the case of a fellow-Gadarene, Theodorus of Gadara, who taught the young Tiberius on Rhodes: he 'preferred to be called Theodorus of Rhodes', doubtless for the same reason.[58] It is not a valid objection to this hypothesis, or to the earlier suggestion that *Socraticis ... sapientia libris* (27) refers to the works of Philodemus, to claim that many Epicureans had a poor opinion of Socrates. Dirk Obbink has discussed this problem with

---

54   Cf. Plat. *Phaedo* 60c–61b. Two fragments are attributed to Socrates at Diog. Laert. 2.42.

55   Some other (non-philosophical) candidates, including Solon, on whom cf. Soubiran (1982), are mentioned by Cecchini (1984) 155, who goes on to argue (156) that *carmina lecta* might refer to a set of philosophical maxims, and therefore might denote Epicurus' κύριαι δόξαι. Ingenious though this argument is, it depends too much on special pleading: *lecta* means most obviously 'read' not 'selected' and *carmina* are a world away from prose *sententiae*.

56   On the life of Philodemus see Sider (1997) 3–10.

57   Sider (1997) 4–5.

58   *Theodorus Gadareus, qui se dici maluit Rhodium* (Quint. *Inst. Orat.* 3.1.17–18).

great care.[59] His conclusion, namely that this was an early attitude and that 'Plato's Socrates ... was rehabilitated' among Epicureans by the mid-first century BC (379), would allow Philodemus to have been reasonably comfortable with Socratic associations woven around himself by his school. Nothing, of course, is thereby implied about Philodemus' commitment to Socratic positions.

If 'the Athenian' of line 29 is also Philodemus, then the two couplets 27–8 and 29–30 refer to his philosophic works and to his poetry respectively. Philodemus' *carmina* (his epigrams) are indeed 'unhelpful in a great love' (30), since they conform with Epicurean views of poetry and of personal relationships.[60] The form in which this statement is made, i.e. their author 'does not help at all' (*nil iuvat*, 30) negates another Epicurean joke: the literal meaning of Epicurus' name ('helper', 'ally') seems to have been played upon among Epicureans.[61] Horace employs the same joke at *Satires* 2.6.32: *hoc iuvat et melli est* ('that gives pleasure and is as good as honey') – again in an Epicurean context. Moreover, if the Athenian is Philodemus, *vester senex* (30) acquires an appropriateness which is otherwise hard to understand, since for Varius, Virgil and the Epicureans of the Neapolitan circle he was indeed their revered master.[62] A last thought: if Philodemus is the main subject of lines 27–30, then the insistence of these lines upon books (*libris*, 27) and reading (*lecta*, 29) becomes more meaningful in the context of the Epicurean library at Herculaneum.

Lines 31–8 describe poems which Propertius says it would be better for Lynceus in his new role as lover to write, *rursus* (33) meaning not 'again' but 'on the contrary'.[63] They turn out to be Philetan/ Callimachean *Aetia*. Lines 39–40 have been misunderstood and have caused improper speculation about an epic *Thebais* by Varius for which there is no other attestation. The subjunctive *prosint* indicates that this work is hypothetical: 'it would do you no good to write a Thebaid', i.e. now you are a lover. Propertius is not attributing a Thebaid to Varius: he mentions a Thebaid only because this is a typical epic subject, and so stands for all epic. Propertius may be seeking here

59   Obbink (1996) 379–80, 509–14, 542–6. Cf. also Sider (1997) 37.
60   Cf. Sider (1997) 24–40.
61   Cf. Gale (1994) 137 and n. 32; O'Hara (1998) 69–71.
62   The term is appropriate for a literary predecessor. In *Aet.* fr. 75 Pf. Callimachus calls his admired source Xenomedes γέρων (66) and πρέσβυς (76). Euhemerus is similarly addressed (*Iambi* fr. 191.11 Pf.), although he is being criticized there. For further literary 'old men' see Thomas (1992) 51–8.
63   *OLD* s.v. 6.

to gloss over a slight oddity in Varius' literary career. Varius was an epic poet in that he wrote hexameters. But, as far as we know, his hexameter poetry consisted solely of his *De Morte* (and his possible 'panegyric' on Augustus),[64] and he wrote no narrative epics. Propertius' mention of an imaginary epic may be intended to obscure the fact that Varius' hexameter compositions were epic only in this attenuated sense.[65]

Lines 41–2 indicate through *desine* (41) that we are back in the world of reality. The couplet refers to a literary form which Varius certainly did compose – tragedy. Varius' *Thyestes*, written to celebrate Augustus' victory at Actium,[66] was rewarded by the *princeps* with a million sesterces.[67] Varius is now being told to abandon tragedy and to take up erotic elegy; compare the situation of Ponticus in Propertius 1.7 and 1.9. After this couplet modern editors begin to shuffle lines, but there is little point to this activity. Various reflections on Varius' poetic conversion lead to a description in 51ff. of the poetic subjects which girls do not like to hear about. One such is *ratio mundi* (51), reminiscent of *rerum vias* (28), and also of course of the typical Epicurean Περὶ Φύσεως/*De Rerum Natura*. Then come explanations of eclipses (52), survival after death (53) and thunderbolts (54). Among these typical Epicurean (and Lucretian) concerns the mention of survival after death certainly alludes to Varius' *De Morte*, which in all probability drew on (or even rendered) Philodemus' Περὶ Θανάτου.[68] That link provides yet another reason for thinking that Philodemus is the main subject of lines 27–30. The other Epicurean subject-matter can again be explained most economically either as further material from the *De Morte* or as prospective topics for an Epicurean poet.

64   A curious and obscure maxim, seemingly of Epicurus, that the sage οὐ πανηγυριεῖν ('will not panegyrize', Diog. Laert. 10.120) has no relevance to Varius' encomium: Porphyrio (ad Hor. *Epist.* 1.16.25) describes Varius' opus as a *panegyricus*, but in later Greek usage this simply means 'encomium'.

65   However, on the artificiality of such distinctions, see Gale (1994) Ch. 3, discussing whether *De Rerum Natura* is epic or didactic. The possible 'panegyric', which, as Courtney (1993) 275 argues, would actually have been entitled '*Laudes Augusti*', could, of course, have contained historical narrative.

66   The occasion of its performance is usually identified as the Actian games of 29 BC, but Jocelyn (1980) 391 n. 24 argues for the dedication of the temple of Apollo Palatinus in 28 BC.

67   Cova (1989) 9–24 is sceptical about the link between Varius' *Thyestes* and celebrations of the Actian victory; he even doubts its performance. But the notion that Augustus would have given 1,000,000 sesterces for a closet drama beggars belief. For a critique of Cova's views see Jocelyn (1990) esp. 599–600, referring to his own earlier writings.

68   See esp. Rostagni (1959) 386–94.

After a six-line cameo (55–60) depicting Propertius as *rex convivii* ('symposiarch'), a setting in which his elegiac genius makes him a favourite of the girls, Virgil is introduced at line 61 – under his real name. In contrast to Propertius Virgil might gladly (*iuvet*, 59) celebrate Augustus' Actian victory; and he is now composing the *Aeneid* (63–4). *Actia ... litora* (61) and *Caesaris rates* (62) manifestly bridge the transition from Varius to Virgil, since Varius had contributed so notably to the post-Actian celebrations.[69] The references to Actium may also be intended to credit Virgil with a prospective analogue of Varius' panegyric of Augustus, if it ever existed.

The use of Virgil's real name rather than a pseudonym must be linked with two other differences between Propertius' treatments of Varius and Virgil. First, and in contrast to Varius, Virgil is accorded great respect as a past and future epic poet: there are no suggestions that he should or might abandon epic, the *Georgics* are handled without irony, and Propertius' account of Virgil's future *Aeneid* is accurate for its time, straightforward and highly laudatory. Propertius was aware that he could not jest publicly with Virgil over works involving Maecenas and Augustus. But in lines 67–76 Virgil's *Eclogues* are treated in a more light-hearted but complex way which is reminiscent of Propertius' approach to Varius: Propertius transforms the *Eclogues* into elegies, and he distorts them and parades his learning by importing Theocritean material into his account of them.[70] But here Virgil as an individual is hardly visible, his 'love-life', if present at all, is hinted at briefly under the mask of Corydon, and there is no interplay whatsoever between Virgil and the erotic life of Propertius. In any case the *Eclogues* sprang from Virgil's distant literary past, before he graduated to more elevated genres, and before he entered the patronage of Maecenas and Augustus.

The second divergence between Propertius' treatments of the two poets involves Epicureanism: in contrast to the repeated emphases on

69   Lines 63–4 definitely reveal Propertius' foreknowledge of the main theme of the *Aeneid* and of its opening lines; for further proof that Propertius knew those lines see Cairns (2003). Rothstein ad loc. suggested that lines 61–2 refer to a different epic poem which might succeed the *Aeneid*. Others claim that 61–2 reveal further access on Propertius' part to sections of the *Aeneid*, esp. to the end of *Aen.* 8, in pre-publication form. Given the bridging and equating functions of 61–2, such speculations concerning them seem pointless.

70   For discussions see, e.g., Alfonsi (1954) 210–21; D'Anna (1981) 289–92; Stahl (1985) 181–2. Thomas (1996) 241–4 = (1999) 263–6 offers an ingenious account of Propertius' 'summaries' of Virgil's works which includes the suggestion that each of the ten lines devoted to the *Eclogues* contains a reminiscence of the corresponding *Eclogue.*

Lynceus' Epicurean commitment, there is only one Epicurean (and Philodemean) touch in Propertius' account of Virgil – striking though it is. Among other misrepresentations of the *Eclogues*, Propertius claims (69–72) that Virgil describes his country folk as buying sex cheaply from girls with a gift of ten quinces or a goat. In fact this never happens in the *Eclogues*. There ten quinces are a gift for a boy (*Eclogue* 3.70–1) and there is no assumption that they will buy his favours; and yet Propertius harps on this theme over four lines. This particular Propertian *deformazione* has the effect of assimilating the *Eclogues*, where love is often homosexual, to the mainly heterosexual ethos of Propertian (and Gallan) elegy. Propertius is also reflecting on general Epicurean recommendations of *vulgivaga Venus*, on their role in Lucretius, and on Lucretius' description of such mercenary transactions in primitive country settings.[71] Propertius probably also had in mind the epigrams of Philodemus: among those which survive a number are concerned with *meretrices*,[72] and, if we had all Philodemus' epigrams, the theme might be even more prominent.

Apart from Propertius' misrepresentations of the *Eclogues*, among which this last is the only *deformazione* to involve philosophy, and apart also from Propertius' tongue-in-cheek claim that all Virgil's works are acceptable to lovers, experienced and inexperienced alike (81–2), Propertius' portrait of Virgil is that of a serious and minimally Epicurean figure. This is a *persona* which allows Virgil to be given his real name, and which may also represent the reality of Virgil himself in the mid-20s BC. Although Virgil was a pupil of Philodemus in the 40s BC, and although his work reveals knowledge of Epicureanism, it shows no signs of strong or exclusive commitment. Rather Virgil's keen interest in philosophy went hand in hand with a deliberate withholding of allegiance to any particular school – which also was the ostensible stance of Horace (*Epistles* 1.1.13–15). This attitude was cultivated by Romans for different reasons, among them the feeling that the *mos maiorum* should take precedence over Greek philosophy as a guide to life.[73] Another reason may be political. In the 60s–40s BC Epicureans could be found among both supporters and opponents of Julius Caesar: Cassius for example was a distinguished convert. But

71   *DRN* 5.962–5.
72   E.g. Nos 10, 11, 17, 18, 20, 21 (Sider). Nos 37, 38 (Sider) also fall into this category, but are probably not genuine.
73   See, e.g., Cairns (1989) 36–8.

there was a distinct tendency for Caesarians to be Epicureans;[74] and there is some evidence that other schools too attracted individuals of a particular political outlook.[75] Augustus, however, clearly rejected politico-philosophical sectarianism, ostentatiously attaching to himself leading Greek philosophers of several schools. These included the Alexandrian Areius Didymus, who specialized in the reconciliation of apparently conflicting philosophical traditions.[76] The public espousal by Virgil and Horace, both intimately connected with Augustus, of a broader philosophical openness may reflect imperial policy. Augustus' attitude perhaps sprang from his Italian bourgeois background; but it also made better political sense in a *princeps* for whom reconciliation with former political opponents was a primary imperative.

The final section of Propertius 2.34 moves away from Virgil to introduce other recent poets. First comes a renewed recall of Varius (the *olor* of 83–4, see above, p. 298), after which individual couplets are allocated to four elegists, their names placed at the ends of four successive hexameters. None of them is misrepresented and each is accompanied by his named beloved: Varro of Atax (85–6), Catullus (87–8), Calvus (89–90) and the recently deceased Cornelius Gallus (91–2). Calvus is additionally paired with Gallus via the theme of death – that of Calvus' wife or mistress Quintilia[77] and Gallus' own suicide. Then the concluding couplet proudly tacks Propertius himself onto the catalogue of poets, again at the end of the hexameter (93–4). It is clear that Propertius, having criticized Varius and 'polemicized' against Virgil, is now establishing a literary genealogy for himself as an elegist, with all the poets listed fitting roughly into this category. The difference between this list of 'elegists' and Ovid's canon of Roman elegists (Gallus, Tibullus, Propertius and himself)[78] is notable; neither poet is trying to write literary history, rather each is trying to present himself in the most acceptable light of the moment, and in both cases special pleading is manifest. Ovid sought to appear as a major adherent of a 'modern' school of major elegists who wrote

---

74   For a balanced discussion see Momigliano (1941) 151–7; also Griffin (1997) 101–9.
75   E.g. the Pythagorean and Pompeian Nigidius Figulus, and the Stoic Cato and the Academic Brutus with their republican sympathies. For Brutus' philosophical adhesion to the Old Academy see Sedley (1997).
76   Cairns (1989) 34, 37.
77   If Quintilia (*RE* Quinctilius 19) was a relative of Quintilius Varus (*RE* Quinctilius 5; *PIR*[1] Q 25), this would constitute a link between Calvus and the later circle of Maecenas – one of which Propertius might have been aware.
78   *Tr.* 4.10.51–4.

elegy exclusively, while Propertius wanted to dilute his enormous poetic dependence on his former patron, the recently disgraced Cornelius Gallus, without showing himself an ingrate and without denying what would have been known and obvious to his reading public. Hence Propertius promoted to the status of elegist three writers (Varro, Catullus and Calvus) who did write erotic elegy, but whose main contributions were not elegiac, in order not to have Gallus as his sole predecessor.

This adjustment of Propertius' literary past is not, however, the sole function of the final section of 2.34. Gallus, with whom its list of other elegists climaxes, as well as being the strongest poetic influence upon Propertius in the Monobiblos and probably one of his patrons,[79] had been a friend and poetic colleague of Virgil since the 40s BC. Indeed, according to ps.-Probus,[80] C. Cornelius Gallus was a fellow pupil (condiscipulus) of Virgil, presumably in the 40s BC.[81] There is no reason to doubt this testimony, or to locate the experience of Virgil and Gallus as fellow-pupils anywhere other than in the Naples area, where (incidentally) Propertius places the Gallus of the Monobiblos at 1.20.9. As well as evoking Virgil's old friendship with Gallus, and as well as providing Propertius with a bevy of Roman elegiac predecessors, the catalogue of elegists in 2.34 seems to recall another figure who was certainly influential upon Virgil, Gallus and Propertius,[82] and who may also have touched some of the other Roman writers who appear in 2.34. This is the Greek poet and teacher Parthenius, to whom both Virgil and Propertius allude by name.[83] As already observed, one of Parthenius' elegiac works (fr. 14 Lightfoot) was entitled Λευκαδίαι.[84] Varro of Atax's elegiac mistress (and elegy book), as Propertius specifically remarks, bore the pseudonym Leucadia (2.34.86), and this may indicate a debt to, or link with, Parthenius. Similarly Calvus is characterized by Propertius as (in effect) the author of an elegiac epikedion for his dead wife or mistress Quintilia (2.34.89–90), while Parthenius was famous as the author of an elegiac epikedion precisely for his wife Arete (frr. 1–5 Lightfoot), and he composed at least one other such epikedion (for Archelais, fr. 6

79   Cf. above, pp. 70–1, 74–7.
80   Comm. p. 328.2 Hagen.
81   Either of Philodemus or of Parthenius?
82   Cf. above, pp. 110–11, 131–4, 237–49.
83   Virg. Ecl. 10.57; Prop. 1.1.11; cf. Hubaux (1930) 96 n. 1.
84   See above, p. 236 n. 62 and Lightfoot (1999) 156–7.

Lightfoot).[85] Since Parthenius almost certainly introduced the *epikedion* to Rome, he very plausibly influenced Calvus' use of it, particularly since both poets employed the genre to honour their dead consorts. As for Gallus, it would hardly be necessary to argue that the dedicatee of Parthenius' Ἐρωτικὰ Παθήματα was influenced in his own elegiac *Amores* by Parthenius even without the further indications of this which exist.[86] This leaves Catullus unaccounted for among the 'elegists'. There is little evidence of indebtedness to Parthenius on Catullus' part, although it cannot be ruled out;[87] but, even if Catullus had no link with Parthenius, Catullus' elegiac cycle (65–68) was too important an elegiac precedent to be omitted by Propertius from the catalogue.

An attempt can now be made to sum up: as far as we know, Propertius himself had no Epicurean background and he does not give the impression of being deeply concerned with Epicureanism.[88] His entry into the circle of Maecenas was belated, and, although he seems to have remained associated with Maecenas until either his death or the end of his poetic career, he may not have felt completely at home in his circle, and he may not have proved congenial to all its members. Whether or not Propertius is the butt of Horace's wit at *Epistles* 2.2.99–100, where an unnamed poet is willing to award Horace the title Alcaeus in return for being himself hailed as Callimachus or Mimnermus,[89] there is a distinct absence of friendly poetic contact between Horace and Propertius[90] which contrasts strongly with Horace's poems addressed to Virgil and other Roman literati, including Tibullus – not even a member of Maecenas' circle. Elegy 2.34 looks very much like Propertius' attempt to establish his presence in the circle by courting Varius and Virgil, and in the case of Varius Propertius appears to have decided to pay homage to him by evoking the memory and teachings of his (and Virgil's) philosophical master, Philodemus. Many of Propertius' philosophical allusions may, of course, be generic Epicureanism rather than specific to Philodemus, but the

---

85   Lightfoot (1999) 34–5.
86   Cf. Lightfoot (1999) General Index s.v. Gallus, C. Cornelius, and above, esp. pp. 237–49.
87   See the discussion of Lightfoot (1999) 206; the key link may be through Euphorion, who influenced Catullus and was championed by Parthenius: cf. Lightfoot (1999) esp. 57–67.
88   His aspiration, stated at 3.21.26, to study Epicureanism in Athens is combined with further hopes to study Platonism (25), oratory (Demosthenes, 27) and New Comedy (Menander, 28). The entire package is thus manifestly both conventional and fictional.
89   For an assessment of this view see below, p. 325 n. 12.
90   Horace wrote an ode (2.14) for Postumus, plausibly Propertius' relative Propertius Postumus (see above, pp. 19–20); but this seems to have been a commissioned piece.

very fact that Virgil and Varius had been Philodemus' pupils would, for Propertius, have made everything Epicurean in 2.34 Philodemean.

After his tribute to Varius Propertius sets himself to sketching the works of Virgil, first lauding his forthcoming *Aeneid* without *deformazione* and then transforming Virgil's *Eclogues* into pseudo-elegies. This latter process cannot have failed to remind Virgil and others of how Virgil in *Eclogue* 10 had transformed Gallus' elegies into pseudo-bucolics. That train of reminiscence, once established, enabled Propertius to assert his own elegiac identity against its Roman background. In the course of doing so Propertius evoked a second Greek master, Parthenius, whose works and teaching had inspired Virgil in his *Eclogues*, so as to balance the prominence of Philodemus, Varius' inspiration in his Epicurean poetry. It was all the more advantageous to Propertius to evoke Parthenius since Parthenius had equally been the shaping force behind the work of Virgil's old comrade and Propertius' former patron, C. Cornelius Gallus, who – so Propertius implicitly asserts – had in turn transmitted the heritage of Parthenius to his protégé and successor, Propertius himself.

A final achievement of this long and lively elegy is the laudatory skills it displays. Overall it is an implicit eulogy of Maecenas, who, although unmentioned, shines in the reflected glory of his two great epic poets, Varius and Virgil, the leading figures of his circle. 2.34 also focusses in a witty way on Maecenas' Epicurean interests. It lures its reader into a sham situation in which Varius is accused of the unlikely crime of attempting to seduce Cynthia – doubtless nothing more than a metaphor for (supposedly) wanting to write elegiac poetry – and is then given a dressing-down in vivid Philodemean terms which reiterate his credentials as an Epicurean poet. Within Propertius' treatment of Virgil, his sober and high valuation of the *Georgics* (77–80), a work dedicated to Maecenas, stands out; and it preludes Propertius' unabashed praise of Virgil's forthcoming *Aeneid*. As for the *Eclogues*, works of Virgil's youth written under the patronage of others than himself, Maecenas, with his own elegiac life-style,[91] must have been amused to see them mutated into erotic elegy. Another encomiastic feature which Maecenas will certainly have valued is Propertius' open praise of Augustus, who is named and identified by implication as the encomiand of Virgil's future *Aeneid*, and whose ancestor Aeneas is said to be the main subject of it (61–4). This deft

91   See above, pp. 255 n. 40, 287–9.

insertion of a eulogy of Maecenas' *patronus* into a poem ostensibly devoted to quite other topics shows Propertius in full command of the techniques of the court poets of Alexandria. His credit for it with Maecenas will have been substantial. In carrying out this entire operation Propertius is impressively self-assertive in his own literary métier, an essential characteristic of an encomiast if he is to be taken seriously by his readers: not only does he lay a relentless elegiac veneer over Virgil's *Eclogues* but he claims for himself the principal elegiac role in Maecenas' circle,[92] lining up his poetic predecessors and climaxing his elegy and his book with a reiteration of his principal elegiac subject matter, Cynthia, and of his hope that his fame will rest on her.

---

92   C. Valgius Rufus, almost certainly a member of Maecenas' circle, also wrote elegies (frr. 2–4 Courtney), but in addition he composed hexameter poetry and possibly lyrics (frr. 5 and 1), and he may not have been regarded as primarily an elegist (cf. Courtney (1993) 287, noting that '*Pan. Mess.* 179–80 suggests him as a panegyrist').

CHAPTER 10

Augustus

Over the years 30–15 BC the poets of Maecenas' circle were in-creasingly drawn into a closer relationship with his more powerful 'friend' Augustus, and in consequence Maecenas gradually faded from their poetry while Augustus became more prominent in it. Propertius entered Maecenas' patronage in 27/26 BC, a decade or so after Mae-cenas had recruited Virgil, Varius, and Horace, and Augustus is already a major presence in his Book 2. Maecenas' impact never dis-appeared from the elegies of Propertius, but he eventually vanished from them as a named individual, being unmentioned in Book 4, where Augustus is the direct patron. As has already been emphasized,[1] this development does not imply a waning of the political influence of Maecenas, or a cooling in the relations between Maecenas and Pro-pertius.[2] Rather, as also with Horace and Virgil, it reflects Augustus' steadily growing confidence in the ability of Maecenas' protégés to eulogize him to contemporaries and posterity without risk of the unfortunate consequences suffered by Alexander the Great when he attempted to achieve immortality through poetry. Horace *Epistles* 2.1.229–50, addressed to Augustus, sketches for his imperial patron the two scenarios: Alexander's bad taste in poets and its deplorable results, and Augustus' contrasting good taste (Varius and Virgil are the chosen examples) and its predictable excellent outcome.[3] Horace's lines surely echo discussions of these matters in the house of Maecenas and in the Palace.

In this chapter it will be argued that, from the moment of his entry into Maecenas' circle, as throughout his subsequent poetic life,

---

1   Above, p. 279 n. 141.
2   Cf. esp. Williams (1990) 265–75, contextualizing this development.
3   See Brink (1982) 243–53, 483–7; Hor. *AP* 357–8, with Brink (1971) 365–6. Curt. Ruf. 8.5.7 mentions other inferior encomiasts of Alexander apart from Choerilus.

Propertius' literary services were fully at the disposal of the *princeps*. This argument necessitates some initial concentration on Book 2, in which Propertian scholarship has sometimes underplayed Propertius' commitment to Augustus.[4] This situation does not arise solely from the reluctance of some recent scholarship to acknowledge the realities of patron–poet relationships in antiquity, and from the resulting image of Propertius as a covertly seditious poet of 'opposition'.[5] Book 2 also presents its own special obstacles to modern understanding, the most confusing being the heavy smokescreen of elegiac independence laid down in it by Propertius, which can cause even some Propertian commentators who acknowledge that the Propertius of Books 3 and 4 was committed to the Augustan programme to hesitate over Book 2. The challenge to such under-assessments which follows implies rejection of an unspoken assumption underlying many interpretations of Propertius – that his elegies can be equated with confessional statements, or diary entries, or communications to a single addressee. On the contrary, Propertian elegy was always directed to a broader audience than its nominal addressee(s). This obviously does not mean that every single aspect of Propertian elegy (or of any ancient poetry) was equally accessible to all ancient readers. Some Augustan poems do contain esoteric elements: for example, a Roman reader ignorant of Maecenas' erotic interest in his contemporary *pantomimus* Bathyllus would not have realized that Horace is teasing Maecenas when he refers at *Epode* 14.9 to Anacreon's homonymous boyfriend. Again, if the 'Lynceus' of 2.34 is indeed Varius Rufus (cf. Chapter 9), readers outside the circle of Maecenas and not otherwise *au courant* presumably did not grasp this. But such esoteric features, although no doubt highly appreciated by those in the know, are supererogatory: the overall contents of the poems in which they occur are open to a wider public. On the literary front the business of Propertian elegy was *inter alia* to come to terms with its audience's expectations of elegy and of an elegiac poet. Propertius therefore needed to adopt and adapt a relevant elegiac *persona*, along with an appropriate set of elegiac conventions and content. As the direct poetic heir of Cornelius Gallus his solution was

---

4   It might seem otiose to treat this topic given that many correct verdicts on it have been offered: cf., e.g., among recent contributions, Álvarez Hernández (1997), summed up at 310–11; Newman (1997) 5–7; Lieberg (2002); André (2002). However old attitudes persist. They were championed most significantly by Stahl (1985) Ch. 6: 'No Epic for the Master of Rome (2.7, 2.10, and 2.1)', which reached conclusions diametrically opposite to those of this chapter; and there continue to be proponents of such views.

5   Cf. above, pp. 35–42.

to depict himself as an unhappy lover of an 'antisocial' cast, disliking war, reluctant to marry, and generally shirking civic obligations; Tibullus' poetic *persona* and declared attitudes fall within the same overall range. But the adoption of such a *persona* did not prevent the elegist from simultaneously praising patrons such as Augustus and Messalla who espoused the contrary, civic values of the Roman state. This was simply another aspect of the public functions of elegy.

Propertius' praise of Augustus cannot, of course, be shown to reflect his innermost thoughts any more than his elegiac *persona* can be shown to represent his life choices. Propertius may have had private reservations about Augustus, but there is no way of knowing whether he did or not, and in any case 'sincerity' is not a useful critical concept in the context of Roman elegy: does anyone believe that Propertius was in real life the unsuccessful elegiac lover he claims to be? All that can sensibly be said about Propertius' entry into Maecenas' circle and his subsequent laudations of the *princeps* is that his familial, urban, and regional connections were Caesarian to begin with,[6] and that (if 2.1 is anything to go by) the invitation by Maecenas, and hence by Augustus, to join their patronage circle in the circumstances in which he found himself around 27 BC[7] was seen by Propertius as a major and welcome opportunity. It is therefore perverse to regard Propertius' adherence to his new patrons as anything other than a decision to commit to the *princeps*. This is also implied by the prominence of Augustus and his concerns in Book 2, despite the space which Propertius also gives to sentiments appropriate to his role as elegiac lover.

Conversely, however, it was in the interests of Maecenas (and Augustus) that Propertius should continue to write love poems and, even in elegies evincing general approval of the Augustan regime, continue to voice the antisocial attitudes of his elegiac *persona* when they clashed with the regime's civic policies. Propertius could not in Book 2 have doffed the character which he had paraded in the Monobiblos without reducing his value to Maecenas as a literary acquisition; and Maecenas and Augustus were far too shrewd to squander their investment by pressuring Propertius to express views which would have discredited his as an elegist. Written as they were, Propertius' elegies of Book 2 attracted contemporary readers of all

6   See above, pp. 10, 15–16, 37–8, 44–50.
7   See above, pp. 74–7.

political outlooks whereas, if he had immediately set about writing pure and unconditional encomia of the *princeps*, he might have lost his audience. What Propertius could do without compromising his elegiac commitment was to demonstrate that even an erotic elegist whose *persona* was conventionally characterized by moral and social 'worthlessness' could nevertheless still recognize and laud the virtues of Augustus and the blessings of his moral, social, and political programmes (see below, pp. 325–6 on 2.7).

Some further relevant points can be added. First, after Actium the Caesarian leaders faced a difficult public relations task. They needed to persuade the Roman public that things had changed for the better and that there would be no more civil wars. They employed many devices to do this: one, which we tend to forget because we know that Augustus' reign ended on a gloomy note, was to inform citizens that, provided they stayed within the boundaries of licit pleasures, they could enjoy themselves and, as a bonus, do so without fear of civic unrest. That is the message of many of Horace's *Odes*; and it is also, up to a point, the message of Roman elegy, although elegy offered the further attraction of a hint of illicitness. A second point is that the important Augustan politicians who patronized poets had usually themselves tried their hands at various types of literature and so had an understanding of the dominating conventions of different literary types. They were also, many of them, individuals who in private enjoyed a relaxed cultural and sexual ambience far removed from the *gravitas* of their public *personae*. One only has to think of the private letters, and perhaps the private behaviour, of Augustus, and of the life of self-indulgence led by Maecenas. So a distinction must be made between the public profiles of Propertius' patrons and the faces they may have presented to him in ordinary social intercourse. There is no reason, then, to believe that Maecenas and Augustus would have disapproved of Propertius' elegies, or of his *persona*'s self-presentation, provided always that in those elegies their own images were delineated appropriately. A last point is that Propertius and other Augustan poets were free to decide whether or not they wanted to be included among the 'friends' of Maecenas and Augustus. Like Tibullus they could have opted for another patron, or, as Ovid seemingly did, they could have cultivated looser relationships with more numerous social superiors. But once an Augustan poet had joined the circle of a patron, he was obliged by *gratia* to show deference and respect towards his benefactor in his poetry and in his life, and this included acceding to a patron's reasonable requests for poetic eulogy and output. If Propertius had genuinely displayed the subversive attitudes and behaviour attributed to him by some modern critics, this would not have been regarded positively by his contemporaries as a mark of independence: instead it would have met condemnation as churlish ingratitude.

The deeply Augustan nature of Book 2 and the fact that Propertius' dependence on Maecenas entails his simultaneous attachment to Maecenas' more powerful 'friend' are proclaimed straightaway in the dramatic, linked, first-time appearances of Augustus and Maecenas in 2.1.[8] The two addresses to Maecenas by name in 2.1 (17, 73), assure his status as the dedicatee of 2.1 and indeed of Book 2 as a whole. But 2.1 gives far greater prominence to Augustus, who is denominated 'Caesar' three times (25, 26, 42), and whose superiority to Maecenas is made abundantly clear throughout.[9] The subordination of Maecenas to Augustus at the very beginning of the book is not an inevitable consequence of their rankings in the real world, and neither is it an essential ingredient of a poetic book dedicated to Maecenas: Horace's Odes open with a poem addressed to Maecenas (1.1) which does not even mention Augustus, who appears only in the succeeding ode. Because the two distinct Horatian odes treat distinct issues, 1.1 the 'personal' interactions of Horace and Maecenas qua poet and patron, and 1.2 the fate of the Roman imperium and Augustus' vital role in it, the relative rankings of Maecenas and Augustus are again clear in them, although implicit. But, since Propertius 2.1 is a single elegy which aims to assert the closest collaboration between Maecenas and Augustus, the rankings of the two men inevitably become an explicit element in it; and, of course, there is no reason to think that Maecenas would have been anything but delighted at his representation as the faithful and self-effacing lieutenant of Augustus.[10] And yet the repeated priority accorded to Augustus in 2.1, which is not wholly the product of its subject-matter, also reflects a deliberate choice on Propertius' part; and it initiates a trend which continues throughout Book 2, where Maecenas makes not a single further appearance, whereas Augustus is named and eulogized in 2.7, 2.10 (he is even apostrophized there at line 15), 2.16, 2.31, and 2.34. Furthermore these elegies feature major concerns of Augustus, as also do certain

8   On 2.1 see also above, pp. 260–7.
9   See above, pp. 262–4.
10   The relationship between Caesar/Augustus and Maecenas in the Georgics is parallel.

other Book 2 elegies. What this means is that already by the mid-20s BC Propertius is representing Augustus, in addition to Maecenas, as a patron of his elegies. This conclusion is worth stressing and exploring for at least two reasons. First, Propertian scholarship does not usually conceive of Augustus as Propertius' patron at this point in his career; and second, Propertius often seems to be regarded as an inferior or underprivileged member of Maecenas' circle, or one kept at a distance by Maecenas and the *princeps*.[11] Such judgements have no foundation, but are based mainly on arguments from silence,[12] in particular, from the lack of evidence of personal contacts between Augustus and Propertius, which contrasts with the testimonies of such contacts between the *princeps* and Virgil, Horace, and Varius. But the principal reason for this discrepancy could be that no trace of a *Life of Propertius* by Suetonius survives;[13] a subsidiary reason is that most of our information about the circle of Maecenas comes from Horace, who did not mention Propertius.[14]

After 2.1 Augustus next plays a central role in 2.7, an intriguing and controversial piece which seemingly attacks a measure proposed by him but either rescinded or not followed through. This legislation, whatever its nature,[15] would, so Propertius alleges, have affected the poet's private life by forcing him to abandon Cynthia and to marry. The crucial problem of 2.7 is whether Propertius offers in it genuine criticism of Augustus and his proposal, which seems unlikely given his obligations as a friend of Maecenas, or whether a Roman reader would have understood the elegy in quite different terms. The available solutions are diverse but convergent:[16] Propertius is probably exaggerating when he claims that the law would have forced him to

---

11 The location and presumed donor of Propertius' house (see above, pp. 258–9) should in itself put paid to this notion.

12 Horace's target at *Epist.* 2.2.91–101 has sometimes been identified as Propertius, and various biographical conclusions, *inter alia* about Propertius' lack of standing in Maecenas' circle, have been drawn. For the fragility of this entire structure see Brink (1982) 325.

13 It is dubious whether such a *Life* ever existed: cf. Rostagni (1964) Introd. XXIII.

14 All sorts of motives for this omission (literary, historical, and personal) might be speculated; but it could just be that Horace's circle of friends was formed in the 30s BC.

15 For a thorough treatment of Augustus' legislation on marriage etc. see Raditsa (1980); Fedeli (2005) 221–3 offers an equally exhaustive account of the scholarly debates about the nature and date of the measure to which Propertius refers. But whether the measure concerned was a *lex* advanced and then abandoned by Augustus or whether, with Badian (1985), it was a proposed triumviral enactment that met a similar fate, the interpretation of 2.7 is not materially affected.

16 For a detailed exposition of these solutions see Cairns (1979a). They are attacked at length, and an alternative reading is offered, by Stahl (1985) 141–56.

marry; he is also playing on the fears of his mistress, on his readers' expectations of the *persona* of the love-elegist, and on literary antecedents, especially in comedy, of the theme 'love versus enforced marriage'. Finally, and most relevant to the question of criticism of Augustus, Propertius couches 2.7 in the form of a rhetorical *progymnasma* (elementary exercise), the 'attack on a law'. Propertius' contemporaries expected such an 'attack' to be made along certain lines and to advance certain arguments. But 2.7 is so deliberately defective in its argumentation, so lame in its use of the expected commonplaces of the genre,[17] and so clearly antisocial in its attitudes that no Roman reader could have been expected – *qua* citizen – to be persuaded by it. By thus undermining his own position Propertius contrives to turn his 'attack on the law' into a eulogy of the law and of its author. Propertius also pretends to be compelled to counter an argument (in itself highly flattering to the *princeps*) from the high status of the enactment's proposer: *at magnus Caesar* ('but Caesar is mighty', 5). This he does by asserting the even more encomiastic: *sed magnus Caesar in armis:/ devictae gentes nil in amore valent* ('yes, but Caesar is mighty in war; the conquest of nations counts for nothing in love', 5–6). Such praise, supposedly wrung from the mouth of a social outcast, reinforces the eulogistic implications of the rest of 2.7. And indeed they touch again on the paradox behind Propertius' recruitment by Maecenas, that Propertius' ultimate value to the imperial establishment lay in no small part in his status as a poet conventionally dedicated to *nequitia*. If someone apparently so antisocial and so committed to a way of life antipathetic to the regime could nevertheless be forced by the manifest virtues of Augustus and his policies to make such admissions, their sincerity and their merit as arguments could hardly be challenged.

Augustus next features largely in 2.10, which introduces programmatic imagery drawn from the many Heliconian investiture scenes sketched by Propertius' poetic predecessors, starting with Hesiod, and including Callimachus, Philetas, and in large measure Cornelius Gallus (the plausibly Gallan term *choreis*[18] surfaces immediately in line 1). Although 2.10 eventually reveals itself as a *recusatio*, it begins with Propertius declaring unequivocally his intention to turn away from love poetry and to celebrate Augustus' wars. This represents an

---

17   On Prop. 2.7's use of the topos of the 'possible' see below, pp. 397–9.
18   Cf. above, pp. 120–31 and Index II s.v. *chorea*.

advance on his concessions to Augustus and Maecenas in 2.1, where his ability to compose an epic celebrating Augustus was dependent from the start on an unfulfilled condition (2.1.17–18, cf. 39–42). 2.10 also functions implicitly as a partial palinode to the literal drift of 2.7: it may be significant that *triumphus* and *castra*, terms which appeared in 2.7.13 and 15 respectively, recur in 2.10.15, and in 2.10.4 and 19, in very different contexts.

The literary-programmatic language of 2.10 presents a number of difficulties. If more of Cornelius Gallus' work survived, these might more easily be resolved, but for present purposes a simple, if not simplistic, reading of 2.10 will suffice to underscore its eulogies of Augustus. Propertius now (*tempus*, 1, 2; *iam*, 3) would like (*libet*, 3) to write poetry of a higher type. By this he means epic: *bella* (8) can hardly refer to anything else, given the contrast between war and love omnipresent in the standard epic/elegiac dichotomy.[19] However lines 5–6 introduce an obstacle: Propertius might lack the strength to make an actual attempt at epic: *quod si deficiant vires* (5). His dilemma resolves itself in the following couplet: youth, he says, should sing of love and old age of wars (7). The next line:

> bella canam quando scripta puella mea est   (8)

has often been misinterpreted by Propertian scholarship.[20] *quando* has been taken as causal, which yields a rendering such as: 'henceforth I will sing of wars, <u>since</u> my girl's praises have been penned'.[21] But the logic of the couplet demands the meaning: 'I will sing of wars <u>when</u> I have finished writing about my girl', i.e. it requires that *quando* be temporal and that *scripta est* should convey the sense of *scripta erit*. Since the incorrect rendering of 2.10.8 currently prevails, it may be worth noting that the phenomenon posited, the use of present for future, is common in Latin in a number of circumstances. One

---

19   Cameron (1995) esp. Ch. 10 argues that Callimachus' polemic in *Aetia* fr. 1 Pf. was not against epic, and (Ch. 18) that Augustan poets' references to it support this view. Few have been persuaded.

20   Exceptions include Birt (1882) 416 (who, however, coupled his rendering with a proposal for an unnecessary transposition, and whose view was rejected by Enk (1962) 157–8), Juhnke (1963) 286 n. 2, and Wimmel (1960) 194, 197–8. More recently Nethercut (1972) 87–8 and Tatum (2000) 406 have asserted that both renderings discussed below are possible. Fedeli (2005) 318–19 reasserts the causal interpretation of *quando*, but without additional argument.

21   Goold (1990) 151 = (1999) 133.

involves certain conditional clauses. As Hofmann–Szantyr point out,[22] while there is a general tendency for subordinate clauses with an indicative verb to employ the tense which represents their accurate temporal relationship with the main clause, this is not universal: when the subordinate clause is conditional and the main clause contains a future or a verbal form with a future sense, the present tense is often found instead of the future, especially in cases where the action of the verb in the conditional clause is conceived as simultaneous with the action of the verb in the principal clause. Temporal clauses, particularly when there is an element of conditionality, can behave in the same way. Ernst Neumann, the author of an old but useful dissertation on the language of Propertius, noted that, although elegant Latinity calls for a careful marking of the temporal relationships between the subordinate and the principal clause, Propertius sometimes does not follow that practice. Instead, where a future tense might be expected, he opts in certain cases for the present.[23] Three examples of this phenomenon (of which the third is perhaps closest to 2.10.8) were then cited by Neumann:

> altera me cupidis teneat foveatque lacertis,
> altera si quando non sinit esse locum   (2.22.37–8)

Let one girl hold and cherish me with eager arms whenever another girl does not [i.e. will not] oblige me.

> nam tibi victrices, quascumque labore parasti,
> eludit palmas una puella tuas   (4.1.139–40)

For whatever palms of victory you have won by your toil, one girl makes [i.e. will make] a mockery of them.

> at cum est imposta corona,
> clamabis capiti vina subisse meo.   (4.2.29–30)

But when a crown is put [i.e. will be put] on my head, you will cry out that the wine has gone to my head.

---

22 'Zur Beibehaltung der absoluten Zeitgebung in den indikativischen Nebensätzen ist zu bemerken, dass in Bedingungssätzen in Beziehung auf ein übergeordnetes Fut. oder eine Verbalform mit futurischem Sinn oft das Praes. statt des Fut. steht, besonders bei Gleichzeitigkeit der Handlung des Nebensatzes mit der des Hauptsatzes', Hofmann–Szantyr 549; cf. also Marx (1894) 177-8.

23 'Deinde poeta in sententiis subordinatis, cum rationes temporales in eleganti latinitate diligenter definiri soleant, interdum simpliciore forma anteposita futurum tempus neglegit', Neumann (1925) 60; for other Propertian uses of present for future see Uhlmann (1909) 61.

This reading of 2.10.8's *scripta ... est* further undermines the wide-spread tendency of Propertian scholarship[24] to fantasize in this line a *scripta puella* ('written girl') – a notion which has as much substance as would a 'put-on crown' (*imposta corona*) in 4.2.29. More significantly, the correct interpretation of this line clarifies the run of thought of the entire elegy (see also the schema below, p. 336). With it the first (implied) element of *recusatio* comes in lines 7–8, and it exactly matches the second element (21–4): Propertius retains his resolve to sing of Augustus' wars, but is caveating 'not yet'.[25] Nevertheless at line 9 the declaration *bella canam* of line 8 remains prepotent in Propertius' mind, and this makes him reiterate in lines 9–10 his aspiration of 1–2 to start writing epic 'now' (cf. *volo*, 9; *nunc*, 11, 12). Propertius' thoughts then turn to the actual subject-matter of the grand epic to which he aspires in general terms in 9–11: Augustus will conquer the East, and eventually the rest of the world (13–18), and these campaigns will be Propertius' theme, if only he lives long enough (19–20). The passage about the conquest of Parthia, India, Arabia, and the rest of the world (13–18), which modulates at line 15 into an apostrophe of Augustus, constitutes direct and unqualified eulogy of his patron. Then Propertius' prayer for long life for himself (20) harks back to his procrastinations of 7–8 and to their resolution there in terms of youth and age. The second time round, however, *recusatio* prevails in the images of the monumental statue (of a god?) which is too lofty to be crowned (21–2) and the humble sacral offerings of a poor man (23–4): at present Propertius has only such humble praise to give (i.e. 2.10 itself), but he gives it – as to a deity (21–24). The element of *recusatio* in 2.10 is therefore unmistakable, and doubly so. But it is not, as it was in 2.1, absolute: given time, Propertius is saying, he will sing of Caesar's wars. All *recusatio* tends to be laudatory since it affords the opportunity for praise, often indirect but sometimes, as in 2.10, also direct. Conditional *recusatio*, as found in 2.10, is even more laudatory, particularly if the condition amounts to no more than the passage of time.

The final couplet of 2.10 (25–6) sums up the elegy: the *Ascraeos ... fontes*, as yet unknown to Propertius' poetry, are contrasted with the *Permessi flumine* in which Love has 'recently' (or 'only') bathed it:

24   Cf. most recently Fedeli (2005) 319.
25   Cf. Mader (2003) 115–25, usefully placing Prop. 2.10 in its conceptual background, i.e. the linked concepts of *aetas*, *genus*, and propriety underlying Augustan literary theory.

nondum etiam Ascraeos norunt mea carmina fontes,
sed modo Permessi flumine lavit Amor.

These lines present at least two interpretational problems. One can be dealt with reasonably easily. The couplet manifestly alludes to *Eclogue* 6's account of Gallus' Heliconian initiation (64–73) and line 26 points directly to Virgil's *errantem Permessi ad flumina Gallum* (64). Similarly line 25 caps the next event in the Virgilian initiation of Gallus: *Aonas in montes ut duxerit una Sororum*. Virgil had described in *Eclogue* 6.64–5 how Gallus was 'wandering' by the river Permessus, i.e. he was on a lower geographical level where (by implication) he was composing his *Amores*, and how a Muse (doubtless Calliope) then led him up Helicon. Propertius expects his readers to know both Virgil's account and the Gallan poem which lay behind it; and it is a fair conjecture that, in addition to what Virgil has reported (or misrepresented) about Gallus' initiation, Gallus had recounted that he was given water from a spring or springs higher up on Helicon. So Propertius, placing himself in Gallus' footsteps, is making a distinction between the Permessus and some, presumably higher, spring(s).[26] In Propertius' case the Permessus is explicitly associated with his own erotic elegy, inspired by Gallus, since it is *Amor* who 'has bathed' Propertius in the Permessus.[27] Gallus may have designated his poetry written prior to his Heliconian initiation as erotic with similar explicitness.

The second problem of interpretation is more troublesome: why are Propertius' inspirational springs of line 25 'Ascraean', i.e. Hesiodic? Propertius' continuing allusion to Gallus' initiation as detailed in *Eclogue* 6, and also his reference to Gallus' presumed poetic account of his visit to Helicon, are both clear enough. According to Virgil the climax of Gallus' initiation was the priming of Gallus for his Grynean Grove poem: this was achieved through the presentation to Gallus by Linus of the Muses' gift – a set of pipes which they had earlier given *Ascraeo ... seni* (*Eclogue* 6.70), i.e. to Hesiod. Gallus' ascent and initiation on Helicon thus symbolized his transition from love-elegies about Lycoris to Callimachean aetiological poetry.[28] However, when

---

26   Ross (1975) 119–120 claimed that 'the *Ascraeos fontes* and the *flumine Permessi* are the same waters' (120 n. 1). The present discussion assumes that this counter-intuitive claim is incorrect.

27   *Amor* might also allude to Gallus' title, *Amores*, on which see above, pp. 230–2.

28   Cf. Clausen (1994) 200.

Propertius writes in 2.10.25 of *Ascraeos ... fontes*, there is nothing in 2.10 to indicate that he is thinking of a similar move to aetiology; so Hesiod must represent something else. There is no particular difficulty in seeing Hesiod as standing for different sorts of poetry in different Augustan contexts, especially in view of the tricks and misrepresentations perpetrated by ancient poets practising *deformazione* on their fellows in literary programmes and polemics. Indeed, since the Ascraean/Hesiodic grove on Helicon was subsequently a locus for the initiation of other poets than epicists, Hesiod even seems to stand in another passage of Book 2, 2.13.3–8 (with some contortions and caveats, see above, pp. 124–5) for a modified version of love-elegy.[29] There Apollo tells Propertius to 'live in the grove of Ascra' (4) but simultaneously orders him 'not to despise slender Muses' (3) and to remain a love-elegist (7). But the significance of *Ascraeos ... fontes* at 2.10.25 is not so easy to pin down.

Since the *alia cithara* ('other lyre') which Propertius' Muse is teaching him (2.10.10) is one apt for epic, a natural assumption might be that Propertius' *Ascraeos ... fontes* are 'epic' springs, albeit ones with a Gallan tinge. But this has been denied by some scholars,[30] who translate *nondum etiam* in line 25 (*nondum etiam Ascraeos norunt mea carmina fontes*) as 'not even': e.g., 'So far my songs have not even known the springs of Ascra'.[31] Behind this approach lies the view that Propertius in line 25 is envisaging three stages – 1) the Permessus, 2) *Ascraeos ... fontes* and 3) epic – and indeed that Propertius was thinking of Virgil's triple œuvre, *Eclogues*, *Georgics*, and *Aeneid*, and was characterizing himself as not yet having reached even the second level, i.e. the (certainly Hesiodic) *Georgics*, let alone the epic *Aeneid*.[32] However, this rendering finds no support in Latin usage: *nondum etiam* never means 'not even'. It is an emphatic equivalent of *nondum* – 'not (as) yet',[33] and it refers to the second stage of a binary process. This is obvious in Propertius' other use of it:

> hanc ego, nondum etiam sensus deperditus omnes,
> molliter impresso conor adire toro   (1.3.11–12)

---

29   Cf. now Fedeli (2005) 269–70. Propertius may be distinguishing between his own Hesiodic aspects and others attributed to Hesiod, possibly by Gallus (cf. above, pp. 121–5).

30   E.g. '... the Ascraean fountains cannot stand for epic on Roman, Augustan themes: to credit Propertius with such an unparalleled poetic solecism is intolerable ...' (Ross (1975) 119).

31   Stahl (1985) 156; so also, in effect, earlier Ross (1975) 120.

32   Cf. Stahl (1985) 160.

33   So, e.g. Goold (1990) 151 = (1999) 135; Tatum (2000) 393–4.

I had not yet lost all my wits, and I tried gently by getting on to the couch to approach her

where 'not even' would plainly be nonsensical. Similarly 'not even' would make no sense in Silius *Punica* 6.164: *nondum etiam toto demersus corpore in amnem* ('with his body not yet fully submerged into the stream'). The same is also true of the comic, elegiac, and prose examples of the phrase.[34]

Propertius' *Ascraeos ... fontes* must then be 'epic' springs, from which Propertius has 'not yet' drunk. But how can this further example of Hesiodic polyvalence be explained? Certainly not on the same basis as Hesiod's iconic statuses in *Eclogue* 6.69–73 (aetiology) and in Propertius 2.13 (love-elegy): there Virgil/Gallus and Propertius actually had in mind Hesiod's follower 'Callimachus Hesiodeus'. For, although Hesiod wrote in epic hexameters, Callimachus and his successors saw him as antithetic to Homer; and Hesiod's archetypal meeting with the Muses in the *Theogony* contextualized Callimachus' elegiac encounter with the Muses in *Aetia* fr. 2 Pf. and their assumption of the roles of interlocutors in *Aetia* Books 1 and 2.[35] Analogously, the influential love stories of the *Aetia* transformed Callimachus in Roman eyes into a love-elegist.[36] A different consideration must be invoked to explain Hesiod's epic status in Propertius 2.10.25: this is simply that, as a hexameter poet, Hesiod was by definition an epicist, and one more palatable than Homer to Propertius the elegiac disciple of Callimachus and Gallus, and so more acceptable to Propertius as a future potential model for epic.

This may be enough to explain Hesiod's role in 2.10.25. But, if more explanation is needed, another aspect of Hesiod's work would reinforce his plausibility as an epic forebear for Propertius, especially given the themes which Propertius has in mind for his future epics, the victorious campaigns of Augustus. Of those envisaged by Propertius in 2.10.13–16 as potential epic subject-matter, two (the wars with Parthia and Arabia) were real possibilities. Indeed Aelius Gallus' irruption into Arabia in 26 BC may already have been in train or at

---

34   E.g. Plaut. *Pers*. 174; Ter. *Hecyr*. 745; Lucil. H32 Charpin; Cic. *Pro Rosc*. 23; Sall. *BJ* 31.20; Ov. *Am*. 1.14.19; Fronto 1.7.1; Aul. Gell. 2.28.1; 3.12.2; 4.1.2; 16.11.2; 17.9.17; Apul. *Apol*. 33. Only in Cic. *Pro Rosc*. 23 might some doubt seem to arise; but it is dispelled by the temporal limit of nine days allocated by Romans to funerary arrangements.
35   Cf. Reinsch-Werner (1976).
36   Cf., e.g., McKeown (1998) 73–4 on Ov. *Am*. 2.4.19–20.

planning stage when 2.10 was being composed.[37] But Augustus surely never in reality contemplated extending his military operations to India. Indian delegations did visit Augustus twice in the 20s BC (once in 25 BC, and again in 20 BC), and they probably inspired the interestingly numerous mentions of India and the Indians in Propertius (see below, p. 340). But the reference to India in 2.10.15 (as in 3.4.1) is due to its mythico-historical significance. Propertius starts not from current military planning but from the notion of world-conquest: this is made explicit in lines 17–18, where Augustus is characterized as (ultimately) a world-conqueror. India crops up in line 15 because it featured in the exploits of one mythical (Dionysus) and one historical (Alexander the Great) world-conquering predecessor of Augustus, the latter always in Augustus' mind as a model and forerunner. Dionysus and Alexander were also prototypes of the *triumphator*, and it is no accident that line 15 unites India and triumphs: *India quin, Auguste, tuo dat colla triumpho.*[38] When wars between West and East/civilized and barbarian are under discussion in Augustan writings these themes of world-conquest and triumphs often mesh with another Augustan stereotype, that 'particularly Augustan obsession',[39] Gigantomachy/ Titanomachy.[40] Antiquity saw this as one of Hesiod's most sublime and most truly epic subjects: 'his <Hesiod's> accounts, in the Theogony, of the generation of the cosmic deities out of Chaos, and of the awesome struggles of Titanomachy and Typhonomachy, represented a level of epic grandeur higher even than the wars of gods and men in the *Iliad*.'[41]

If Propertius was envisaging Augustus' forthcoming wars against the forces of the East as a species of Gigantomachy, then Hesiod's major treatment of the Titanomachy in his *Theogony* may further explain Propertius' reference to *Ascraeos ... fontes* in 2.10.25. It has

---

37 Propertius' relationship by marriage with Aelius Gallus (see above, pp. 20–1, 24) could have further impelled him to mention this particular campaign.

38 Another similar mythical figure, Hercules, is not mentioned or alluded to in 2.10, although his labours and his links with Bacchus made him too a contributor to the world conqueror/ *triumphator* stereotype. The fact that both Dionysus and Heracles were venerated as ancestors by the Ptolemies, and were celebrated as such by poets of the Ptolemaic court, additionally explains their importance in Augustan poetry. For further reflections of, and bibliography on, the linked figures mentioned in this paragraph see Indexes II and III s.vv.

39 So P. R. Hardie (1986) 87 n. 6; cf. also his detailed remarks at 86–8.

40 The terms 'Gigantomachy' and 'Titanomachy' overlap and are sometimes used inter-changeably in what follows. The participation of Hercules as an auxiliary of the gods in the Gigantomachy (see also above, n. 38) further unites the two stereotypes.

41 So P. R. Hardie (1986) 7 – in a discussion unrelated to Propertius.

been abundantly demonstrated that Gigantomachy was fundamental to poetic conceptualizations of such conflicts, both of hellenistic kings and of Augustus, with forces outside the 'civilized' *oikoumene* of the Greeks and Romans, as well as to poetic representations of Augustus' control of the Roman world, and that it is these associations which make it such a widespead theme in Augustan poetry.[42] The familiarity of this entire conceptual complex to Augustan poets is well demonstrated by Ovid *Ex Ponto* 4.8.51–64. Ovid starts with the standard proposition that poetry confers immortality upon its subjects, exemplifying this from the Trojan and Theban epics (51–4). Then he advances a bolder claim: *di quoque carminibus, si fas est dicere, fiunt/ tantaque maiestas ore canentis eget* ('the gods too, if it is not impious to say, come into being through songs, and such majesty needs the voice of the singer', 55–6), before launching into a series of 'proofs' of this proposition (57–64):

> Sic Chaos ex illa naturae mole prioris
>   digestum partes scimus habere suas;
> sic adfectantes caelestia regna Gigantes
>   ad Styga nimbifero vindicis igne datos;   60
> sic victor laudem superatis Liber ab Indis,
>   Alcides capta traxit ab Oechalia,
> et modo, Caesar, avum, quem virtus addidit astris,
>   sacrarunt aliqua carmina parte tuum.

Even so, we know, from the mass of its former nature Chaos separated into the parts it has; even so the Giants who sought after the realms of heaven were thrust down into the Styx by the cloud-bearing fire of the liberator; even so Bacchus was lauded as victor after his conquest of the Indians, and Hercules received praise for his capture of Oechalia. And of late, Caesar, songs to a degree deified your grandfather, whose virtue added him to the stars.

The ease with which Ovid moves through the tralatician stereotypes, transposing from Chaos (another Hesiodic topic), to Gigantomachy, to Dionysus and Hercules, and finally turns smoothly to Augustus (here the *avus* of Germanicus), is both remarkable and instructive.

Propertius, like other contemporary and later poets, makes overt use of Gigantomachy in his other *recusationes*.[43] It appears in 2.1 as a

---

42   Esp. by P. R. Hardie (1986); cf. also Innes (1979).
43   See the examples collected at P. R. Hardie (1986) 87 n. 6; cf. also 87 n. 8, which remarks valuably on the contrasting handling of this theme in Prop. 2.1 and Prop. 3.9.

rejected theme both at the beginning (19–20) and towards the end (39–40) of an elegy in which Propertius gave conditional acceptance to the idea that he would in the future write an epic on the deeds of Augustus. Even more significantly, at 3.9.47–8 Gigantomachy heads the list of epic themes deemed treatable by Propertius, the others being the foundation of Rome and Augustus' triumphs and victories. In some later *recusationes* Gigantomachy 'becomes associated allegorically with the exploits of Augustus'.[44] Hence an implicit presence of Titanomachy/Gigantomachy in the final couplet of 2.10's reference to Hesiod is not unlikely; and perhaps, as seemingly in other such cases, Propertius' understanding of this Augustan concept derived from discussions in the circle of Maecenas.[45] Moreover – although this is a mere supplementary suggestion whose failure would not detract from the arguments already made – there could be further support for the presence of Gigantomachy at the end of 2.10 if a parallel theme can correctly be identified near its beginning. Line 2 mentions a 'Haemonian', i.e. Thessalian, horse. The line has been correctly understood as alluding to a widespread topos of programmatic *recusationes* – the contrast between the unimpeded plain or highway used by many (= epic) and the narrow or untrodden path used by few (= non-epic);[46] and Thessaly was famous for its horses, including prominently its warhorses, another symbol of epic.[47] If more can legitimately be extracted from *Haemonio*,[48] the term might allude to the 'Thessalian' Lapiths, traditionally the first tamers of horses for riding,[49] and thus indirectly to the celebrated battle between the Lapiths and the Centaurs. That battle, well represented in ancient visual art, is generally regarded, for example in its appearances on the metopes of the Parthenon and on the west pediment of the temple of Zeus at Olympia, as symbolizing the fifth-century BC repulse of the Persians by the Greeks, another war emblematic of the conflict between civilization/order and barbarism/

44 So P. R. Hardie (1986) 87.
45 For suggestions about other such discussions see Cairns (2002) 34–5, 44, and above, p. 320, below, p. 340.
46 The *locus classicus* is Callim. *Aet.* fr. 1.25–8 Pf. Massimilla (1996) 219–22 notes copious earlier and later parallels.
47 Cf. (in a literary programme) Prop. 3.3.40: *nec te fortis equi ducet ad arma sonus*, with Fedeli (1985) 146–7; and now Fedeli (2005) 315, considering also the possibility that *Haemonio* might point to Achilles and hence to Homeric epic.
48 The attractive suggestion of Hendry (1997) esp. 601 that mention of '*Haemonia*' here, as elsewhere, evokes αἷμα (blood) is consonant both with the notion of a 'war-horse' and with the further associations suggested below.
49 Cf. Virg. *Georg.* 3.115–17 with Thomas (1988) II.60–1 and Mynors (1990) 199.

disorder[50] – and, of course, Persians were often synonymous with Parthians in Propertius' day.[51] If *Haemonio* does carry this further implication, and if the earlier arguments about *Ascraeos ... fontes* are correct, then the initial and final couplets of 2.10 are neatly linked by learned allusions in both to conflicts between order and disorder.

An important additional underpinning for the interpretations of 2.10 offered above, namely the elegy's elaborate conceptual and verbal symmetry, should not pass unremarked. Complex and detailed patterning of the type found in 2.10 is not, of course, unusual for Propertius,[52] but it is particularly helpful to note it in the case of 2.10 because it strengthens the view that the final couplet contrasts elegy and epic.[53]

A1	1–4	It is time for me to write epic; I want to celebrate the wars of Augustus.
B1	5–8	I might turn out to lack the strength, but even an attempt would be praiseworthy. Elegy is for a young poet, epic for his later years.
C1	9–12	I want now to move to the higher plane of epic; Muses, cooperate!
D	13–18	Present and future triumphs of Augustus (addressed by name in line 15 at the conceptual centre of the elegy)
C2	19–20	These will be my great epic theme.
B2	21–4	But for now I can only offer small (i.e. elegiac) homage.
A2	25–6	As yet I have no epic inspiration but only that of (Gallan) elegy.

The partial asymmetry characteristic of hellenistic and post-hellenistic ring-composition is visible here, with A2 and C2 offering only a single couplet in contrast with the two couplets of A1 and C1, so that the reprise contains only eight lines in all as against the twelve of the first sequence of themes. In addition the verbal patterning of 2.10 to some extent reinforces its ring-structure, and the central section (D) has, as often, elements in common with the two outermost sections (A1 and A2):

---

50   Cf. P. R. Hardie (1986) General Index s.vv. Athenian use of myth in political symbolism; Persians; *OCD*[3] s.vv. Centaurs; Persian-Wars tradition.
51   See above, p. 279.
52   Nor for ancient poetry in general: for a detailed discussion of symmetrical composition, and 'cross-cutting' see *THPR* Ch. 8.
53   For a different, and contrasting, thematic analysis see Stahl (1985) 159–60.

A1	*tempus* (1, 2), *iam* (2, 3)	A2	*nondum* (25), *modo* (26)
B1	*laus, in magnis* (6), *canat* (7), *canam* (8)	B2	*laudis* (23), *in magnis* (21), *carmen* (23)
C1	*carmine* (11), *magni* (12)	C2	*canendo* (19), *magnus* (20)
D	*iam, equitem* (13), *Auguste* (15)	A1	*iam* (2, 3), *equo* (2), *turmas* (3), *ducis* (4)
D	*postmodo* (18)	A2	*modo* (26)

However, verbal continuity, which includes much 'cross-cutting' when vocabulary works against the ring-structure, is an even more pronounced feature of 2.10. Thus a string of temporal nouns and adverbs runs through large sections of it: *tempus* (1, 2); *iam* (2, 3); *quando* (8); *nunc* (9, 10); *iam* (11); *nunc* (12); *iam* (13); *postmodo* (18); *diem* (20); *nunc* (23); *nondum* (25); *modo*(?) (26). Other strings of related terms refer to wars, camps and cavalry: *equo* (2); *proelia* (3); *turmas* (3); *castra* (4); *tumultus* (7); *bella* (8); *equitem* (13); *castra* (19, twice); and yet others repeatedly evoke poetry under a number of guises: directly through *memorare* (3); *dicere* (4); *canat* (7); *canam* (8); *mea Musa* (10); *carmine* (11); *Pierides* (12); *oris* (12); *vates* (19); *canendo* (19); *carmen* (23); and *carmina* (25); and less directly in *choreis* (1); *procedere* (9); *citharam* (10); *fontis* (25), and *Permessi flumine lavit* (26). *magnus* too is repeated to emphasize the 'greatness' of epic (*in magnis*, 6; *magni*, 12; *magnus*, 20; *in magnis*, 21), and epic is associated with the *campus* of Thessaly (2), and with becoming *gravior* (9) and acquiring *vires* (11). Contrast the lowliness and weakness of elegy: *deficiant vires*, 5; *ex humili*, 11; *inopes*, 23; *pauperibus sacris* and *vilia tura*, 24; and the presumably small stream of Permessus (26). One or two further 'cross-cuttings' underscore specific arguments: thus *aliis* (1) = *aliam* (10); and Propertius' volition is repeatedly stressed in *libet* (3), *audacia* (5), *voluisse* (6) and *dat* (15) = *damus* (24). The purpose of these strings of concepts and terms, and even of the frequent cross-cutting, is not so much to challenge the thematic structure as to give the impression that the elegy propounds a flawless and unbroken sequence of logical reasoning.

Two further elegies of Book 2, 2.15 and 2.16, while not naming Augustus, briefly introduce topics of relevance and concern to him. A six line passage of 2.15 (41–6) interrupts a love-poem in which Propertius describes one of his rare successes with Cynthia; it does so in order to reflect on the Actian War and on Rome's military successes in general. Propertius muses that, if everyone were willing to engage in a life of love and wine, then weapons and warships would not exist and the Actian sea would not be churning 'our bones' (41–4);

he further remarks that in this case Rome's conquests would not so often have caused her to mourn (45–6).[54] The elegiac poet is of course by his nature a lover of peace, as Love is the god of peace (3.5.1), so these lines could be taken as a straightforward expression of that topos. But the specific mention of the Actian War is arresting, and it inevitably raises the question whether Propertius might be engaging in criticism, indeed overt criticism, of Augustus. On one level it could be argued that Propertius is simply putting into elegiac language that abhorrence of civil war which was expressed by other adherents of Augustus such as Virgil and Horace; after all, was it not Augustus who had put an end to the evil of civil war?[55] But precisely because the sentiments come from a lover, i.e. a degenerate, and also because they are generalized and could potentially cover military actions which Roman citizens would have regarded as right and proper, it is more likely that they were intended to have an impact analogous to that of 2.7. The 'good citizens' who would have regarded 2.7 as a ridiculously weak and self-defeating attack on Augustus' 'law' were confronted in 2.15 with an elegiac lover in a state of post-coital euphoria congratulating himself on a night of vinous (*mero*, 42) sexual satisfaction with a *meretrix*. No doubt those same 'good citizens' enjoyed the mildly pornographic aspects of Propertius' account (as they will have enjoyed their own personal nocturnal excesses with *meretrices*), but they would not have expressed open agreement with Propertius' 'moralizings'. The views of an elegiac *amator*, a stereotype of disgraceful living, on the Actian War were not going to impress his fellow citizens; and this, it must be remembered, is the same poet who in the preceding elegy (2.14) had declared that a night with Cynthia was for him more significant than a victory over the Parthians and a consequent triumph (23–4): fine words for a poet-lover, but no sentiments for a self-respecting Roman!

Any lingering doubts left by 2.15 are allayed by 2.16. This is Propertius' inverse welcome to the praetor who was first mentioned in 1.8.[56] This individual, loaded with wealth on his return from his province, immediately ousts Propertius from Cynthia's favours, and Propertius has many things to say about this; eventually he makes an

---

54   A reading in l. 44 and the interpretation of l. 45 are both open to question; these paraphrases are intended as a 'catch-all' compromise.
55   If this was Propertius' intention, then ll. 45–6 will also refer to civil strife.
56   For the genre see *GC* General Index s.v. prosphonetikon; and 204–8 (on Prop. 2.16). On 2.16 cf. also above, pp. 270–1.

explicit attack on M. Antonius and utters a contrasting laudation of 'Caesar'. Propertius is able to introduce these topics because at lines 35–6 he had suddenly felt shame and disgust at being in the thrall of a disgraceful love – *turpis amor* (36). This leads him to compare himself with M. Antonius, whom *infamis amor* (39) compelled to run away and seek refuge in Egypt (37–40). These two couplets attacking M. Antonius are followed by a single couplet praising Augustus not just for his victory at Actium but for returning the world to peace (41–2). In these two lines Augustus is twice named as '*Caesar*' – M. Antonius was simply *ducem* (37). Propertius makes the link between his own disgraceful love and that of Antonius explicit, but does not mention Antonius' notorious drunkenness. However, the juxtaposition of this passage with 2.15.42, where Propertius had implicitly stigmatized himself as a drunk, also brings this parallelism between poet and triumvir to mind.[57] Readers to whom it occurred might also have reflected that the Antonius of 2.16.37–40, like the Propertius/Antonius of 2.15.41–6, would of course have preferred to wish away his defeat at Actium! And they might have followed up this reflection by concluding that the elegiac life of wine, love, and erotic servitude shared by Propertius and M. Antonius was not only responsible for Antonius' defeat at Actium but also for the outbreak of the Civil War in the first place.

Other love-elegies of Book 2 introduce yet more topics close to Augustus' heart but without naming him or referring to him. One such recurrent Propertian theme is world-conquest, an aspiration-cum-fantasy given full expression in 2.10. Britain features largely in the fantasy: already in 2.1 Maecenas was imagined driving *esseda ... Britanna* (76); and in 2.18, where line 23 initiates an attack on Cynthia for using cosmetics,[58] criticism of her also alludes to current frontier policy. Cynthia, so Propertius claims, is imitating the Britons by applying make-up (23); he goes on to say that 'Belgic' colour is a disgrace on a Roman face (26), referring not to the Belgae of continental Europe but to those of southern Britain. The *Britanni* then resurface at 2.27.5 along with the Parthians: *seu pedibus Parthos sequimur seu classe Britannos*;[59] and Propertius 2.10.17 probably also refers to Britain (unnamed). These references, like Horace's frequent

---

57 Cf. also Stahl (1985) 227–31, with additional argument that Propertius identifies himself with M. Antonius in these two passages, but with different conclusions.
58 A standard topos of amatory poetry: cf. Prop. 1.2 with Fedeli (1980) 88–96.
59 Prop. 4.3.9 reiterates the same topic.

contemporary mentions of the Britons as possible targets of Augustus' future military operations,[60] reflect inconclusive plans in imperial circles to assume direct control of those portions of Britain conquered by Julius Caesar and currently under indirect Roman sway.[61] The Parthians, more realistic potential objects of Roman aggression in the 20s BC, were certainly discussed as such by Augustus and his advisors, and Propertius reflects this interest. In Book 2 the Parthians appear at 2.14.23, at 2.27.5 (coupled with the Britons), and (extensively) in 2.10, as well as in later books.[62] Finally there are the Indians, whose embassies to Augustus in 25 and 20 BC[63] and the gifts they brought clearly captured Propertius' imagination. As well as asserting tendentiously that India submits to Augustus (2.10.15), Propertius fantasizes that he himself might have been soldiering there (2.9.29),[64] and in Book 2 he also shows interest in Indian gems (2.22.10) and in India as the 'home' of Aurora (2.18.11). Books 3 and 4 continue the interest with remarks on Indian gems (3.18.19–20) and gold (3.13.5), on Bacchus' conquest of India (3.17.22), and on the dark skin of Indians (4.3.10).[65] Perhaps contemporaries thinking in terms of an '*imperium* without bounds' saw India as an eventual possible acquisition, and India will undoubtedly have featured in discussions around Augustus. But, as noted, Propertius' claim that Augustus is planning war against India (3.4.1) is an exaggeration.

It can be assumed that Propertius' insertion into erotic elegies of the political topics so far treated was motivated by a desire to gratify Augustus, and that it was done either on the advice or with the consent of Maecenas. But in only one case (2.31) can an elegy of Book 2 be securely regarded as commissioned. The temple of Apollo Palatinus, dedicated in 28 BC, was one of Augustus' major contributions to his new Rome, and its proximity to his house underscored the closeness

---

60   *Od.* 1.21.13–16; 1.35.29–30; 3.4.33; 3.5.3–4; 4.14.47–8.

61   For Rome's indirect control, at least of southern England, and at least from the reign of Augustus on, see Creighton (2000). *RG* 32.1 records two British *reges* who fled as refugees to Augustus; and Strabo 4.5.3 writes of British embassies to him, of British chieftains having made Britain virtually Roman property, and of direct occupation being uneconomic (echoes of high policy discussions derived from conversations with his patron, Aelius Gallus?).

62   By name at 3.4.6; 3.9.54; 3.12.3; 4.3.36, 67; 4.5.26; 4.6.79.

63   Kienast (1982) 277 n. 61; cf. also Bosworth (1999) 3 and n. 17, 15 and nn. 92–4.

64   The 'ends of the earth' topos is overtly in play here since Propertius links India with the opposite 'end', Britain (*aut mea si staret navis in Oceano*, 2.9.30), and since the topos is present in many Augustan poetic references to Britain.

65   Cf. also the earlier 1.8.39.

of his ties with the god. Propertius seemingly memorializes not the dedication of the temple itself but the subsequent opening of the attached portico of the Danaids.[66] But the connection of the portico to the temple permits Propertius to offer an *ekphrasis* of the temple and its statuary which is pure eulogy of Augustus from start to finish.[67] Propertius artfully employs the pretext that Cynthia has reproached him for being late when coming to make love with her,[68] and that this elegy is his answer. The implication of Propertius' lateness, namely that he had chosen to visit the portico and temple of Apollo Palatinus instead of going directly to his mistress, should not be missed. Propertius' priorities *qua* elegiac lover ought to have dictated that he kept his erotic appointment with Cynthia punctually, leaving all other attractions aside. But in fact, and preternaturally, Propertius has given precedence over his mistress to the portico and temple and to their builder, his patron Augustus. This is a high honour on the part of an elegist: *mutatis mutandis* we might contrast 1.6, where staying with Cynthia is Propertius' priority rather than going abroad with his earlier patron, Volcacius Tullus. Elegy 2.31 fulfils its supposed excusatory function by evincing rapt, universal and uncritical awe of what Propertius has seen: the golden portico opened by 'great Caesar' (2),[69] lovely with its Punic marble columns and its statues of the fifty Danaids – which must in fact have been an amazing spectacle; the image of Apollo Citharoedus more beautiful to Propertius than the god himself; the four life-like oxen of Myron which stood around the altar: the temple, built of marble and dearer to Apollo than his birthplace, Delos; the Chariot of the Sun standing over it; and the doors of ivory representing Apollo's defeat of the Gauls at Delphi and his sister Diana's destruction of the children of Niobe. The elegy climaxes with the cult image of Apollo between those of Diana and Latona. It is small wonder that those who believe Propertius to be either consistently 'subversive', or a late and reluctant encomiast of the Augustan regime, have little to say about 2.31.

The final elegy of Book 2 (34) was discussed in detail in Chapter 9; if the approach taken there is correct, the epilogue of Book 2, like

---

66 On the dating and subject-matter of the elegy cf. now Fedeli (2005) 870–4.
67 Augustus is 'Caesar' at l. 2 but this has no necessary dating implication.
68 For this specialized sense of *venire* see Pichon (1902) s.v.
69 *magnus* here, at Prop. 2.1.26, and (twice) at Prop. 2.7.5 apparently echoes the use of *Caesar Magnus* as an appellation for the future Augustus after Actium (on the analogy of 'Pompeius Magnus'?): cf. Du Quesnay (1995) 177 with n. 263.

its prologue, revolves around Maecenas in that it showcases his circle. But, unlike 2.1, 2.34 does not name Maecenas. Instead a six-line passage anticipating Virgil's future *Aeneid* names 'Caesar' i.e. Augustus and his 'ancestor' Aeneas as the main subjects of the *Aeneid*. There can be no doubt about Propertius' openly encomiastic attitude towards Virgil and the two heroes of his epic:[70]

> Actia Vergilio custodis litora Phoebi,
>   Caesaris et fortis dicere posse rates,
> qui nunc Aeneae Troiani suscitat arma
>   iactaque Lavinis moenia litoribus.
> cedite, Romani scriptores, cedite, Grai!
> nescio quid maius nascitur Iliade.   (61–6)

Virgil's choice is the power to sing of the Actian shores of Phoebus the Watcher and of the valiant ships of Caesar, Virgil who now arouses the arms of Trojan Aeneas and the city he founded on the Lavinian shores. Give way, Roman writers, give way, Greeks! Something greater than the Iliad is coming into being.

If it is the case that, as was suggested (above, p. 257), Propertius had in hand unpublished poems when he entered the circle of Maecenas, it is all the more remarkable that so much of Book 2 is devoted to his new patrons and their concerns. Certain poems – among them 2.1, 2.7, 2.10, 2.31 and 2.34 – were clearly written *ab integro* for this purpose, thus swelling the book to its greater length. It is less easy to identify poems altered to suit Propertius' new patronage context. A tempting approach would be to suppose that love elegies containing sections in praise of, or subject-matter congenial to, Augustus and Maecenas originally lacked these passages, which were subsequently inserted.[71] But equally Propertius' new engagement with these two powerful patrons might have caused him to reflect, even in his erotic writings, on public topics of interest to them, as he would not have done earlier. At all events the major difference between the Monobiblos and Book 2 (cf. above, pp. 261–4, 270–1), i.e. the absence from the former and the presence in the latter of contemporary and past Roman history, is not just an indication of the emergence of a 'new Propertius' in Book 2, but a useful marker of works from the period of his new patronage.

---

70   *Pace* Stahl (1985) 190, who manages to find irony in the passage.
71   E.g. 2.13.1; 2.15.41–6; 2.16.37–42; 2.18.23–6; 2.27.5–6 – most of them already discussed here.

By the time Propertius was composing the elegies of Book 3 in the later 20s BC his poetic aspirations were clearly moving towards a more overt Callimacheanism and a diminished mediation of Gallan erotic elegy; such are the clear implications of the programmatic cycle 3.1–3, and in Book 4 these tendencies become even stronger. Moreover, as the years went by and Propertius gained experience in the circle of Maecenas he also became more politically engaged. These factors influenced the elegiac *persona* adopted by Propertius in Books 3 and 4, which shifts increasingly away from that of the irresponsible lover, although erotic interests never fully depart. This modulation embarrasses scholars who espouse the theory of a subversive Propertius and leads them to over-emphasize the presence of the old elegiac lover in Books 3 and 4, to downplay the poet's new historical and aetiological interests, and to try to undermine the antiquarianism by contrasting it over-sharply with the eroticism.[72] However, all sides of Propertius' elegiac *persona* in Books 3 and 4 are appropriate for the '*Romanus Callimachus*', whose model was at once a courtier, a learned writer, and a lover. And it should be stressed once more that we shall not find Propertius' personal views in his elegies: Propertius is fulfilling a public role for his patrons within the conventions of his chosen poetic form. Some of the advantages for Augustus and Maecenas in possessing an encomiast who was a self-confessed nonconformist member of society have already been mentioned. Not least among them was the attractiveness to potential readers of the risqué life-style and erotic adventures claimed by the elegiac poet, who, once he had gained the interest and the confidence of his audience by such means, could then direct their attention towards the praise of his patrons. An interesting and partially parallel situation in the Arabic poetry of early Islam was described in the early twentieth century in the language of the times:

> The satire in old times and the eulogy at all times start with some amatory verses; ... The purpose of these erotic prologues is indicated by their name, "setting alight"; the poetic flame must be kindled by something, and this was done by imagining a situation likely to set it alight. ... Once it has been kindled, the difficulty is to direct it from the imaginary beloved to the very real hero or *mamduh* (object of eulogy)

---

72 E.g. Stahl (1985) 195: 'For my own interpretation, I must emphasize the increasing abyss between what has by now become public adulation and, on the other hand, the proud, but disguised denial of any common ground with the adulated.' Stahl thus convicts his Propertius of both sycophancy and hypocrisy!

who is waiting to hear himself admired. Probably the commonest method is to say that the ill-treatment which the poet has received from the disdainful fair one forces him to take refuge with some one, and so he seeks the Protector of all the World; at times the poet cuts the knot, and simply drops the subject of his love-affairs and turns abruptly to the subject of the ode. (D. S. Margoliouth, *Mohammedanism* (London and New York 1911) 231–2)

Propertius' commitment to Augustan ideology in Books 3 and 4 is on the whole better understood than his posture in Book 2, although doubts have continued to be raised.[73] Fundamental to his thought-processes in Book 3 is the antithesis which also underlies so much of his earlier work, that between war/epic on one hand and love/elegy on the other, with the 'war of love' playing an intermediate role. This antithesis was already established in the work of Cornelius Gallus, as its presence in *Eclogue* 10 implies and as the Qaṣr Ibrîm papyrus confirms; and it appears also in the elegies of Tibullus and Ovid. In his to-ing and fro-ing between the twin poles of love and war Propertius assumed that his readers were aware of them as conventional conceptual substructures; and much of his readers' enjoyment sprang from observation of the poet's deft manipulation of the conventions. Interpretation of Propertian elegies goes awry when commentators fail to identify the intellectual games which the poet is playing: much, for example, has been wrongly concluded from the contrast between the first line of the overtly pro-Augustan 3.4 and the first line of 3.5:[74]

<u>Arma</u> **deus** *Caesar* dites meditatur ad Indos   (3.4.1)

The god Caesar is planning war against the rich Indians

<u>Pacis</u> *Amor* **deus** est, <u>Pacem</u> veneramur *amantes*   (3.5.1)

Love is the god of peace, we lovers reverence peace

Propertius was perfectly conscious of the initial clash of *Arma/Pacis*, of the contradiction between *deus Caesar* and *Amor deus*, and probably also of the partial assonance of <u>Arma</u> and <u>Amor</u>. But it is incorrect to see these oppositions as constituting a snub to Augustus. This particular conceptual see-saw is not limited to 3.4 and 3.5. It

---

73   E.g. by Stahl (1985) Chs. 8, 10, 12.
74   E.g. by Stahl (1985) 195–9.

actually begins in 3.3, where Propertius was expressly told by both Apollo and Calliope to abstain from epic and to cultivate love elegy, and where the epic subjects from which they deterred Propertius were mainly bellicose (39–46). But what happens next, at the start of 3.4, if taken seriously, amounts to a partial rejection of the gods' advice, since *Arma deus Caesar dites meditatur ad Indos* introduces an elegy anticipating the victorious war of Augustus against the Parthians. But, of course, since scholars do not take Apollo and Calliope seriously, and do not agonize over their advice to Propertius or Propertius' reaction to it, they do not comment on how 'subversively' Propertius is behaving towards these deities and their counsels. But those same scholars – taking Augustus and Propertius' implied attitudes to him over-literally and over-seriously – claim that Propertius is subverting his encomium of Augustus in 3.4 by starting 3.5 with *Pacis Amor deus est, pacem veneramur amantes*. They should rather have observed that in 3.5.1, as well as neatly capping the first line of 3.4, Propertius is alluding to his own earlier Callimachean couplet of 3.1.17–18 in which, addressing Rome, he had stated: *sed quod pace legas opus hoc de monte Sororum/ detulit intacta pagina nostra via* ('but this, something for you to read in peace, my page brought down from the mountain of the Sisters by an untrod path'). In addition Propertius is looking in 3.5.1 to Calliope's instructions of 3.3 and to the *amantes* (also in final position in the hexameter there) whom she told him to sing of: *quippe coronatos alienum ad limen amantes/ nocturnaeque canes ebria signa fugae* ('you will sing of garlanded lovers at doors not their own, and of the drunken traces of nocturnal rout', 3.3.47–8).

A closer examination of 3.5 reveals rather its impeccably Augustan (and Maecenatian) credentials. To begin with, Pax was a major Augustan deity, whose importance for Augustus is shown by his later dedication in 9 BC of the *Ara Pacis* as the centrepiece of his monumental complex on the Campus Martius.[75] In addition Pax was associated with Livia: Augustus chose to dedicate the *Ara Pacis* on her birthday, and there is epigraphic and numismatic evidence linking Livia closely with Pax.[76] Augustus' Pax was, of course, not the anaemic 'peace' of modernity, but *parta vic[torii]s pax* ('peace won through victories', *Res Gestae* 13). Again, the Pax of Propertius 3.5.1

---

75 For the significance of the Ara Pacis and its roles in the construction of the regime's self-image see Galinsky (1996) General Index s.v.

76 For Livia's birthday as an important date, and for her associations with Pax, see Purcell (1986) 92–3.

must somehow be linked with the subject-matter of 3.5.25–46. There Propertius fantasizes that he will spend his old age on the study of philosophy, with particular attention to the physical sciences. Since the description of his current life-style as set out in 3.5.19–22 is clearly meant to equate with the love-elegy he is now writing, his later philosophical studies of 3.5.25–46 ought also to equate with a (future) poetic work – a philosophical epic. By implication that epic too will be something *quod pace legas*, something very different, however, from his Book 3, which Propertius was programmatically presenting to Rome in 3.1.17–18. His projected philosophical epic is Virgilian, as well as Lucretian/Varian, in its conception, and its philosophy is more commonplace than Epicurean,[77] but Propertius' sketch of it will have pleased both Maecenas the Epicurean and Augustus with his more catholic approach to philosophy.[78] Only at one point in 3.5 might it be thought that Propertius is casting doubt on Augustus' programme of world conquest:[79]

> nunc maris in tantum vento iactamur, et hostem
> quaerimus, atque armis nectimus arma nova. (3.5.11–12)

> Now we are tossed by the wind into such an expanse of sea, and we go looking for an enemy, and we weave new wars onto wars.

Outwith its context, this couplet might be understood thus. But the section of 3.5 (3–18) in which it appears is a *psogos ploutou*, a rhetorico-philosophical attack on wealth made up of commonplaces strung together in the manner of a diatribe cum declamation; and indeed a concept analogous to that of lines 11–12 can be found later in a philosophical passage of Seneca.[80] Hence there can be no justification for plucking this commonplace out of its context and interpreting it as having specific reference to Augustan military policy, particularly since 3.5 is principally concerned with Propertius' personal life-choices, which equate with his poetic choices, and since Propertius is declaring in it that, at least for the present, he remains dedicated to his life of love/love-poetry (cf. esp. 3.5.19–22). This declaration, anticipated in 3.5.2, explains Propertius' flaunting in 3.5 of that antithesis between love and war which is the life-blood of love-

---

77   Cf. also above, p. 294.
78   For this trend in Augustan poetry see above, pp. 313–15.
79   So Stahl (1985) 199.
80   *NQ* 5.18.5, quoted by Fedeli (1985) 182.

elegy's self-representation: an elegist committed by his literary/life choices to outrageous elegiac attitudes can of course in lines 11–12 view the socially accepted good of expanding the *imperium Romanum* as the mere pursuit of personal wealth. But when Propertius goes on to write, as he does in the final couplet of 3.5 (47–8), not about the imaginary world of elegiac conventions but about the real world of Augustan politics and warfare, then everything changes. Propertius now addresses the same army which he had eulogized, along with Augustus, in 3.4; by ending the last hexameter of 3.5 with *arma* he glances back to the incipit of 3.4; and he endorses at the end of 3.5 the same military policy he had endorsed in 3.4:

> vos, quibus arma
> grata magis, Crassi signa referte domum. (47–8)

> You who prefer warfare, bring home the standards of Crassus.

More can be said (and will be said in Chapter 12) about 3.4 *qua* laudation of Augustus than could have been concluded before the publication of the Qaṣr Ibrîm papyrus.[81] In brief – and in anticipation of Chapter 12 – the poem from which Gallus' lines came initiated a distinct poetic tradition of propemptic encomium of a 'Caesar' about to go to war with Parthia. Recognition of this tradition, of which 3.4 forms part, helps both to dispel misinterpretation of 3.4[82] and to reveal it (like 2.31) as a commissioned eulogy. Ovid continued the Gallan tradition in his *propemptikon* for Gaius Caesar in *Ars Amatoria* 1, a further indication that this type of imperial panegyric was both standard and desiderated. Gallus had, in effect, established a 'brand', and Augustus obviously wanted from Propertius in 3.4 a sequel to Gallus' *propemptikon* to his 'father'. It seems obvious that similar requests from Augustus lie behind 3.18 and 4.11. Propertius' *epi-kedion* for Marcellus (3.18), itself clearly a commissioned piece, will have led to a further commission for a funerary commemoration (4.11) of Cornelia, who at the time of her death was located at the centre of a network of powerful families, including that of Augustus himself (see below, pp. 360-1).

Rather than continuing to parry misinterpretations of more elegies

---

81 However, my earlier generic analysis of Prop. 3.4, for which see *GC* Index of Genres and Examples s.v. PROPEMPTIKON, remains valid.

82 E.g. by Stahl (1985) 193–5.

from Book 3, it may be more profitable at this point to highlight some aspects of Book 3 which clearly reveal its Augustan character. First, although Cynthia features in it, on the whole she receives less attention than in Books 1 and 2.[83] Her first appearance comes in 3.6[84] – contrast Books 1 and 2 where she was already present in the first elegies. Thereafter she appears (or is implied) in elegies 8, 10, 11, 15, 16, 19, 20, 21, 23, and 24/25. This adds up to almost half the elegies of Book 3, which may seem an impressive total. However, in some cases Cynthia makes only a cameo appearance, and/or she is more a peg on which to hang a rhetorical theme than the real focus of the elegy. Thus 3.11 mentions Cynthia as *femina* in its first line, but thereafter Cynthia vanishes and the elegy becomes a tirade against bad women which reaches its climax with Cleopatra (see below, p. 350–1). Similarly the bulk of 3.15 (11–42) is concerned with the myth of Dirce, which is certainly relevant to Cynthia's behaviour at the beginning (1–10) and end (43–6) of the elegy, but which, on the face of it, is told for its own sake. 3.19's first couplet mentions Cynthia's frequent jealousy, which Propertius rebuts; twenty-six lines then expatiate on mainly mythical feminine licence in general. In 3.21 Propertius is proposing to leave Rome for Athens to escape his love; ten lines announce and explain his proposal, and another twenty-four imagine the journey and its result. 3.23 is an 'advertisement' through which Propertius seeks to recover his lost writing-tablets. The elegy transparently anticipates the *renuntiatio amoris* of 3.24+25, and it contains (12–18) sample messages that Propertius might have hoped to receive from Cynthia; but Cynthia does not appear in person in 3.23. The diminution of Cynthia's importance in Book 3 must not, of course, be exaggerated, since she remains a powerful presence in elegies 6, 8, 10, 16, 20, and 24+25. But it is real nevertheless.

Hand in hand with the reduced importance of Cynthia in Book 3 goes an increased number of elegies dedicated to imperial and public themes. In 3.1.15 Propertius addresses '*Roma*' as his audience for the first time in his œuvre.[85] There are more such addresses to Rome by the poet in his own person in Book 3,[86] and this is not fortuitous: they

---

83   Where a mistress who is not named appears in a Propertian elegy, I assume that she is Cynthia (if this matters).

84   An unnamed *puella* (Cynthia?) too insubstantial to be worth counting appears fleetingly at 3.2.2 (cf. 17) and 3.4.15.

85   The address to Rome found in some texts of Propertius at 1.12.2 is the product of unjustified emendation of the MSS reading *faciat* to *facias*.

86   3.11.36, 49; 3.14.34; 3.22.20.

show Propertius self-consciously speaking as a public mouthpiece of the regime;[87] the trend will continue in Book 4.[88] Later in 3.1 Propertius draws a lengthy parallel between poetic accounts of matters Trojan and Roman, and proudly proclaims that Rome will grant him posthumous fame (25–36). Then 3.3 contains a large element of Roman history, first its summary of the themes – the kings of Rome and various military victories – which Propertius claims were treated by Ennius (3–12),[89] and then two couplets celebrating more recent Roman achievements in war, namely Marius' crushing of the Teutones (43–4) and a later victory (45–6), plausibly that of Julius Caesar in 58 BC over Ariovistus and a German force which included the Suevi.[90] The mention here of the Caesarian icon Marius is one of four in Propertius, and all are laudatory:

> Cimbrorumque minas et bene facta Mari (2.1.24)

The threats of the Cimbri and the victories of Marius.

> aut quibus in campis Mariano proelia signo
> stent et Teutonicas Roma refringat opes (3.3.43–4)

Or on what fields pitched battles take place under the standard of Marius, and Rome smashes the forces of the Teutones.

> victor cum victo pariter miscebitur umbris:
> consule cum Mario, capte Iugurtha, sedes. (3.5.15–16)

Victor with vanquished will alike be joined to the shades. You, captive Jugurtha, will sit with the consul Marius.

> iura dare et statuas inter et arma Mari (3.11.46)

And to give judgements amid the statues and arms of Marius.

What makes these four references all the more interesting is that Marius turns up only once in Virgil, never in Horace,[91] never in Tibullus, and only once in the voluminous works of Ovid (at *Ex Ponto*

---

87 Contrast the only such address in Tibullus, at 2.5.57 (on the triumph of Messalinus), where it is placed in the mouth of the Sibyl.
88 Viz. 4.1.67 and 4.10.10. Other speakers than Propertius also address Rome: 3.11.55 (Cleopatra); 4.2.49 (Vertumnus); 4.4.35 (Tarpeia); 4.11.37 (Cornelia).
89 On the problems of this passage see Cairns (2002).
90 For this interpretation see Fedeli (1985) 151. Other commentators have related the couplet to a victory of C. Carinas over the Suevi in 29 BC.
91 The Marius of Hor. *Sat.* 2.3.277 is someone else.

4.3.47).[92] Marius' role as leader of the political faction later headed by Julius Caesar and Augustus cannot be the only factor which stimulated Propertius' mentions of him; otherwise plural references to Marius might have been expected in Virgil and Horace too. Asisium's proximity to Etruria and Propertius' own Etruscan interests must also have contributed to his frequent commemorations of Marius, who had a major following in Etruria.

Attention needs now to be directed towards some as yet untreated elegies of Book 3 with overt Augustan content. 3.11 begins by describing Propertius' *servitium amoris* (1–8). His subjection to Cynthia then becomes a peg on which he hangs a sequence of *exempla* of domineering mythical women: Medea, Penthesilea, Omphale and Semiramis (9–26). After a transitional couplet of disputed import (27– 8),[93] Propertius arrives at the principal subjects of his elegy – Cleopatra, blisteringly attacked, and in contrast Augustus, who is ardently eulogized as the saviour of Rome (29–72). Within this passage lines 59–70 treat Roman history, cataloguing various Roman victories which climax in the defeat of Cleopatra at Actium. Propertius' view of Actium and Cleopatra and of the final phase of the Civil Wars is closely analogous to that of Horace in *Odes* 1.37 and Virgil in *Aeneid* 8.671–713, and it clearly represents the official Augustan version of recent history. Two notable features of it are the sympathetic treatment of Pompeius Magnus (33–8) and the virtual suppression of the role of M. Antonius at Actium – but note the earlier *coniugis obscaeni* (31).[94] Once Magnus' son Sextus Pompeius was dead, the feelings of gratitude of those, including Livia and her son Tiberius, who had been saved by Sextus from the triumviral proscriptions, and the old loyalties of 'republicans' and former supporters of Pompeius Magnus could be respected by Augustus without danger. The scant emphasis on M. Antonius is characteristic of Augustus' own way of rewriting recent history: Antonius, like Brutus and Cassius (and indeed Sextus Pompeius), is unnamed in the *Res Gestae*, and all his actions and achievements in the period 44–31 BC go unmentioned. This general trend recurs, and not accidentally, in the accounts of Actium by Virgil and by Propertius himself. Virgil names M. Antonius only once (*Aeneid* 8.685), and all his emphasis is on Antonius' Eastern forces and his *Aegyptia coniunx* (688). Propertius too names M. Antonius only once

92   Virg. *Georg.* 2.169; Ov. *EP* 4.3.47. Cf. also Manil. *Astron.* 4.45.
93   For the various interpretations see Fedeli (1985) 369–71.
94   On the correctness of this reading see Fedeli (1985) 372–3.

in his entire œuvre (at 3.9.56), and refers to him in slighting terms in
3.11 (above). But M. Antonius is neither named nor referred to in 4.6,
Propertius' twenty-fifth anniversary celebration of Actium; instead 4.6
once again places all the stress on Cleopatra. Any attempt to read 3.11
as 'subversive' is therefore based on *petitio principii*.[95]

The public and political aspects of 3.14 and 3.17 will be treated in
Chapter 11. 3.18, Propertius' *epikedion* for M. Claudius Marcellus,
nephew, son-in-law, and putative successor of Augustus until his pre-
mature death in 23 BC, is patently, as noted (p. 347), a commissioned
piece. It can usefully be contrasted with Propertius' other *epikedion* of
Book 3, elegy 7, which laments the drowning at sea of Paetus. On a
number of grounds it is likely that Paetus was related to Propertius,[96]
and this helps to explain the extraordinary amount of seeming moralizing criticism of the dead man in 3.7: particularly when relatives are
speaking, reproaches of the dead for abandoning the living are a commonplace of the death genres.[97] Propertius' treatment of Marcellus is
markedly different in this respect from his treatment of Paetus: criticism is not directed at Marcellus, but Baiae, the place of his death, is
reproached (8–9). The greater part of 3.18 combines encomium of
Marcellus (11–16), which includes two laudatory mentions of Marcellus' mother, Augustus' sister Octavia (11–12, 14), and consolatory
commonplaces (17–30).[98] Its final quatrain (31–4) similarly unites
praise with consolation by referring to a catasterism of Marcellus on a
par with that of Julius Caesar and (allegedly) Marcellus' ancestor, M.
Claudius Marcellus, five times consul, victor over the Gauls, winner
of the *spolia opima*, and conqueror of Sicily.[99]

Baiae enters 3.18 because Marcellus died there. But Propertius
makes much in lines 1–4 of the coast and waters of Baiae, which he
had described earlier in 1.11.1–4 and 9–12. His emphasis on this topic
in both elegies may well have been similarly motivated:[100] in 37 BC
Agrippa cut through from the Lucrine Lake to Lake Avernus to create
the *portus Iulius*, a safe harbour for Octavianus' fleet in its operations

---

95 But cf. Stahl (1985) Ch. 10 for such an attempt.
96 See above, pp. 20–1.
97 Alexiou (1974) Indexes II: Index of motifs and images s.v. reproach: of mourner to dead.
98 Esteve Forriol (1962) 120–1 (incorrect, however, *re* the genre of 3.18); Fedeli (1985) 542–
    68.
99 Fedeli (1985) 566–7.
100 Since Baiae and its waters probably also featured in Gallan elegy (cf. Index II s.v. Baiae),
     this too will have encouraged Propertius to dwell on them.

against Sextus Pompeius.[101] Both mentions of the *portus* are thus implicitly laudatory of Agrippa.[102] Propertius' genuflection to Agrippa in his *epikedion* for Marcellus also brings us close to contemporary politics. At the time of Marcellus' death Agrippa was married to Marcella, the sister of Marcellus. If 3.18 was written soon after the death of Marcellus, the allusion to the *portus* could have been intended to flatter Agrippa *qua* brother-in-law of the dead man. However, Agrippa subsequently divorced Marcella and married Marcellus' widow, Augustus' daughter Julia, thus becoming the unchallengeable natural successor to Augustus. If 3.18 was written after Agrippa's divorce and remarriage had been decided on, then Agrippa was an even more useful man to puff. The divorce and remarriage was a matter of public policy, and Maecenas is alleged to have advised it (as one alternative).[103] Whenever the elegy was written, then, honorific allusion in the *epikedion* for Marcellus to Agrippa's great achievement at Baiae will have been approved by Maecenas. More compliments can be detected in the joint mention of Hercules and Bacchus[104] in lines 3–6. Especially in combination, these model predecessors are emblematic of the triumph, and they are often found in Augustan poetry in triumphal contexts.[105] Their presence here amounts to indirect eulogy of Marcellus through his homonymous *triumphator* ancestor. But it bears more directly on Augustus, another *triumphator* openly destined for deification.

The last elegy of Book 3 with major Augustan content which will be treated as a unit in this chapter is poem 22, Propertius' *kletikon* to the younger Tullus, recalling him to Rome from his residence in Cyzicus. Its roles as a public announcement of Tullus' future social acceptability at Rome, as a manifesto of Propertius' loyalty as *cliens* (albeit to a former patron), and as a sign of Maecenas' liberality as Propertius' current *patronus*, have already been discussed.[106] Here a few further aspects of 3.22 can usefully be foregrounded. It is a formal piece closely related to the (later) rhetorical prescription for its genre, perhaps appropriately since Tullus had been, like the addressee of the model *kletikon*, a 'governor'.[107] Only a few minor touches personalize

---

101 Fedeli (1985) 546–8.
102 Cf. the explicit encomium of the *portus* at Virg. *Georg.* 2.161–4.
103 Dio 54.6.5.
104 For confirmation that the *deus* of ll. 5–6 is Bacchus see Fedeli (1985) 550.
105 See Index III s.vv. Bacchus, Dionysus, Hercules.
106 Above, pp. 76, 267.
107 For the prescription see Menander Rhetor 424.4–430.8 (Spengel).

the generic material: *desiderio ... meo* (6), mention of Umbria and of Propertius' favourite haunts on the Clitumnus (23–4), and the final quatrain sketching Tullus' potential future at Rome (39–42). Thus the standard down-grading of the place where the addressee currently resides (1–5) is followed by a detrimental comparison of other places which Tullus might visit with the place to which he is invited (7–18), Italy. Then come Propertius' so-called '*laudes Italiae*' (19–38), a passage replete with 'Augustan ideology' in which Propertius is close in tone and content to Virgil *Georgics* 2.136–76. The description '*laudes Italiae*' is, however, something of a misnomer: although Propertius mentions a number of Italian locations, he anticipates his listing with an implicit characterization of them as part of the *Romana ... terra* (17), in this way propagating the Augustan view that Rome was now co-extensive with Italy.[108] To confirm the identification of Italy with Rome, Propertius goes on to address *Roma* in line 20: *famam, Roma, tuae non pudet historiae*. The reminiscence in this line of Cornelius Gallus' *maxima Romanae pars eri<s> historiae*[109] may well recall the close association of Tullus and Gallus in Book 1.

For Propertius the *Romana terra* is superior to other lands on four main grounds:

A1:	17–18	the 'marvels' of other lands pale beside its 'marvels';[110]
B1:	19–22	it is the land of Roman virtue both in arms and in civic life;
A2:	23–26	it has <marvellous> beauty-spots;
B2:	27–38	it is free of various unseemly monsters and mythical horrors of the Greek world.

The argument is thus antithetic in form, and the positive moral pronouncements of B1 embody standard themes of Augustan ideology: Rome is powerful in arms but does not stoop to treachery, and this is Rome's proud claim to fame; Rome's power and stability are based on *pietas* as much as on force, and Roman victory is followed by Roman *clementia*.[111] There is a strong Virgilian flavour to Propertius' *laudes* as a whole, and especially to B1, which is reminiscent of the words of Anchises in *Aeneid* 6.851–3.[112] Some of the monsters

108 For the concept and its implementation see Syme (1939) Ch. 20.
109 Fr. 2.3 Courtney. See Index II s.vv. *historia, Roma* etc.
110 For the surviving Greek thaumatographic texts see Giannini (1965); on Virgil's and others' interest in such themes, P. R. Hardie (1996) esp. 108–9; Thomas (1999) 95–8, 155–6.
111 For this interpretation (esp. of l. 22) cf. Fedeli (1985) 643–5.
112 These ideals must have been discussed in Maecenas' circle. However, Propertius could have known of Anchises' words, since *VSD* 32 recounts that, after Marcellus' death, Virgil read Books 2, 4, and 6 of the *Aeneid* to Augustus, and that Marcellus' mother Octavia, who

and horrors then detailed by Propertius in B2 also have obvious moral implications, which become clearer as his list proceeds; they additionally function as symbols of barbarism contrasted with civilization.[113] Further moralizing, possibly connected with Augustus' earlier attempt at 'moral' legislation[114] and with the *Leges Iuliae* and *Lex Papia Poppaea* to come, then appears in the final couplet (41–2): Tullus is to return to Rome *inter alia* in order to marry and have children. The overlaps between this Propertian emphasis, the attacks on immorality of Horace *Odes* 3.6.17–48,[115] and Horace's later *Carmen Saeculare* 17–20 of 17 BC, with its explicit reference to the *Leges Iuliae*, imply that there was continuing interest in this subject in the imperial circle throughout the 20s BC; indeed the mentions of it suggest a publicity campaign by Maecenas' poets. In the penultimate couplet (39–40) Tullus is offered the prospect of seeking *honos* (i.e. *honores*, magistracies) appropriate to his 'worthy family', and in the final couplet (41–2) he is also imagined as practising public oratory, probably as a means thereto.[116] These activities characterize the good Roman citizen of the highest class; hence Propertius' inducements to Tullus have further moral implications. 3.22 takes a positive view of Tullus' future throughout; but, as already noted, nothing more is heard of him and the Volcacii virtually disappear from the historical record.[117] Tullus may of course have died shortly after returning, or he may have decided to remain absent from Italy; if he lived and returned to Italy, he chose obscurity there – or it was chosen for him. Interpretation of the scant evidence depends very much on how cynically one evaluates the implication of 3.22 that Propertius (speaking for Maecenas and Augustus) expected Tullus to return and to resume his position in Roman society.

Two more features of Book 3 plausibly contribute to an Augustan reading of it as a whole. The first, already partially exemplified, is the frequency of its moralizing passages, which appear in elegies both unconcerned and concerned with Cynthia; and the second is its ending with a *renuntiatio amoris* (3.24–25).[118] Moralizing unconnected with

---

was present, fainted when Virgil recited 6.884 (but for apparent scepticism see Horsfall (1995) 19).
113 Cf. Fedeli (1985) 647–54 for detailed analysis of the legends and their significance.
114 As documented in Prop. 2.7.
115 Cf. Nisbet and Rudd (2004) 98–100.
116 As explained by Fedeli (1985) 656.
117 Cf. also above, p. 77 and n. 30.
118 With Fedeli (1985) 672–4 I take these to be a single elegy.

Cynthia can be seen prominently in the *propemptikon* for Postumus (3.12) and the *epikedion* for Paetus (3.7), and it has just been analysed in the *kletikon* to Tullus (3.22). Some of the elegies which do introduce Cynthia are even more moralistic in tone and content. These start from 3.11 (above, pp. 350–1) and continue with 3.13, which contains a long and fierce attack on female *avaritia*, and its result, female immorality. In 3.13 the climax of Propertius' sententiousness comes when he proclaims himself a neglected *haruspex*:[119]

> proloquar – atque utinam patriae sim verus haruspex! –
> frangitur ipsa suis Roma superba bonis.
> certa loquor, sed nulla fides ...   (59–61)

> I shall speak out – and may I be a true diviner for my country – proud Rome is broken by her own resources. I speak the truth, but there is no credence ...

before comparing himself to Cassandra. The 'professional' tone of this proclamation recalls Horos' claims in 4.1, but 3.13 does not similarly insinuate that Propertius' preaching should be disregarded. Another elegy of Book 3 which also uses Cynthia as a peg and advances a moral view is 3.15, and yet another is 3.19,[120] a tirade against female lust again conveniently draped upon Cynthia. Indeed the moralizing trend of the Cynthia elegies continues right up to the end of Book 3. Elegy 20 unveils the shabby finale of the mini-drama whose earlier acts were 1.8 and 2.16. Here, however, although Cynthia is described at one point as 'stupid' for not comprehending her true situation (5–6), Propertius' assault is not so much on Cynthia as on his rival, who has abandoned her; and, far from wanting to give up Cynthia, Propertius is overjoyed at recovering her (esp. 13–24). But the psychological truth of Propertius' self-emancipatory progress is upheld when in the very next poem (3.21) he plans to free himself from his love for Cynthia by going to Athens (1–2) – a reversal of the theme of 1.6. Then in 3.23 Propertius has lost his writing-tablets, which, with their imagined love messages (13–18), manifestly stand for his amatory relationship and his erotic elegy. Book 3 then ends with a clinching confirmation of its poet's Augustan civic commitment: in its epilogue (24–25) Propertius renounces Cynthia amid a flurry of topoi recalling those of 1.1: the

---

119 For the context of Propertius' choice of this Etruscan role see above, pp. 271–4.
120 *Pace* Fedeli (1985) 571.

former anti-social lover has now rounded off and ended his amatory life and has conformed to the norms of Roman citizenship.

All this said, however, Propertius' moralizing in Book 3 and his closing *renuntiatio amoris* still require nuanced assessment as indicators of Augustanism. Propertius has a moralistic streak throughout his entire œuvre: even in the Monobiblos he can adopt a posture of injured virtue vis-à-vis Cynthia (e.g. in 1.15), and he moralizes at some length in many of the Cynthia elegies of Book 2 (2.5; 2.6; 2.17; 2.18; 2.19; 2.20; 2.21; 2.24; 2.32; 2.33). At the same time, there is nothing in Book 2 to compare with the sustained bitterness and censure found in many of the elegies addressed to Cynthia in Book 3. As for the *renuntiatio* of 3.24–25, on the one hand it did not exclude Cynthia from Book 4; but on the other hand 4.7 is about the ghost of Cynthia, who was dead before the completion of Book 4, and 4.5 and 4.8 look back to the time-frame of Books 1–3. So from the viewpoint of Propertius' erotic pseudo-biography the *renuntiatio amoris* of 3.24–25 was indeed final.

Nowadays there should be little doubt about the genuinely Augustan character of Book 4. Its central poem (6), once controversial and once even thought by some to be undermining its own literal sense, has now shaken off this interpretation.[121] The only resource seemingly left to anyone wishing to view Propertius as 'subversive' in Book 4 is to depict him there as, in effect, a cowed and beaten panegyrist of Augustus writing under duress![122] This is a parody of the truth: in Book 4 Propertius displays more confidence in his personal and poetic stature than ever before. 4.1 is the most egotistical elegy in his entire œuvre, and, while enlarging his field of competence to include Roman aetiology on a Callimachean scale, it also stoutly upholds Propertius' credentials as a Callimachean erotic elegist. This allows love-interest to continue in Book 4 not just in the three elegies focussed on Cynthia, but in others (see below). And, although the aetiological elegies of Book 4 do manifestly promote an Augustan programme, there are no grounds for thinking that Propertius subscribed to it involuntarily. The re-creations of early Rome in which Augustan literature is so rich were, of course, close to the *princeps'* heart in their multiple functions – political, moral, cultural, and even religious; and it is clear that Augustus and his advisers were

---

121 For an 'Augustan' interpretation of Prop. 4.6 see Cairns (1984a).
122 Cf. Stahl (1985) Chs. 11 and 12.

designedly seeking to mould the consciousness of their times by reviving past glories. Roman history, often labile and adaptable, was to be exploited as the model and inspiration for Rome's present, and Rome's founders were to become archetypes for Augustus' nomenclature and self-presentation.[123] Doubtless poets and patrons consulted together on these matters, but the huge success which the literature of the Augustan age enjoyed both among contemporaries and with posterity puts paid to any notion that events from the past, or interpretations of the past, were being imposed on writers against their will. The richness, variety, interest, and multiplicity of Augustan antiquarianism sprang not from oppressive dictation by the *princeps* but from genuine personal commitment on the part of the writers together with a proper sense of gratitude for the benefits which they had received from Augustus. The ultimate proof that Propertius was still in command of his literary destiny in his aetiological poems is that they are distinctly his own, those of a former love-elegist. Thus, for example, Propertius is sensitive to the erotic possibilities of Vertumnus' transvestism (4.2.21–24), and his Tarpeia (4.4) not only falls in love with an enemy leader, as did so many heroines of similar hellenistic and earlier foundation myths,[124] but is permitted a long soliloquy of unfulfilled amatory fantasizing (4.4.31–66). The Hercules of 4.9 has fewer comic, and more numerous serious, aspects than was once thought.[125] But there can be no doubting the underlying influence of the erotic *komos* on the scene of Hercules' exclusion from, and violent intrusion into, the grove where he established the *Ara Maxima*; nor can we ignore the relish with which Propertius makes Hercules speak of his transvestism in Lydia with Omphale, and of the feminine tasks which he carried out there (4.9.47–50) – for all that this episode too has an analogue in ritual.[126] 4.10 is a sterner elegy which lacks erotic elements, but its lament for Veii (27–30) fulfils that other proper function of elegy, to mourn for the dead.

The multiple traditional interests of the elegist, including the continuing commitment of Propertius to erotic themes, can also be seen in Book 4 in poems which are both non-aetiological and unengaged with Cynthia. As already observed,[127] 4.3 is a reworking of

123 On the processes and materials see Galinsky (1996) esp. Chs. III, IV, VI.
124 Cf. Lightfoot (1999) General Index s.v. princess in love with enemy commander.
125 See the bibliography below, p. 363 n. 8.
126 Cf. also Cairns (1992a) 89–90, and above, pp. 287–9.
127 Above, p. 19 n. 93.

3.12, an example of self-emulation with variation: whereas 3.12 portrays two specific contemporary Romans, the Greek names of the protagonists of 4.3 (Arethusa and Lycotas) generalize the elegy, making it about any idealized wife of any idealized Roman officer, and so a 'patriotic' piece offering a moralizing template for the attitudes and behaviour of any upper-class Roman *matrona* with a husband in the Roman army. But additionally, and whatever the relationship of 4.3 with the *Heroides*,[128] like them 4.3 is thoroughly imbued with erotic-elegiac sentiments. Similarly 4.11, placed in the mouth of Cornelia, who died in 16 BC, primarily fulfills elegy's mourning role but simultaneously draws on the erotic dimensions of Propertian elegy. Since Cornelia was a *matrona* of the highest class, Propertius had to be discreetly cautious when depicting her emotions, but he nevertheless contrived to represent her very effectively as a loving and loyal wife. Propertius did this in part by concentrating on her husband, L. Aemilius Paullus, and on his feelings of loss for her: his tears and vain supplications of the gods of the underworld (1–8); his anguish which he must hide dry-eyed from their children (79–80); his sleepless nights and dreams of Cornelia (81–2); and his words addressed in solitude to her statue (83–4).

But when Cornelia speaks of herself in 4.11, she conforms in all respects to the Augustan ideal of a *matrona*. She asserts her marital fidelity and lack of moral blemish (15–18), and she then reinforces her assertions through a series of underworld scenes climaxing with the Danaids (27–8). Here Propertius is evoking one of the multiple significances of the Danaid statues placed by Augustus in the portico attached to his Apollo temple[129] – the fidelity to her husband of Hypermnestra and the contrasting lack of such fidelity on the part of her sister Danaids. Then in 35–6 Cornelia proclaims that she is *univira*, i.e. that Paullus was the only husband she ever had; she will later urge this same related Roman ideal upon her daughter (68). Wifely chastity and decency remain a persistent theme over 37–56, with 41–2 expressing it explicitly: ... *me neque censurae legem mollisse neque ulla/ labe mea nostros erubuisse focos* ('... that I never diluted the censorship's law, nor did the family hearth ever blush for a failing of mine'). The 'censorship' here, as at line 67, is, of course, a complimentary allusion to Paullus' tenure of that office in 22 BC, and this

---

128   For a succinct account of this question see Knox (1995) 17–18.
129   For these cf. Galinsky (1996) 220–2.

glance at the public sphere draws further attention to the regime's concern for female marital fidelity. Propertius manifestly has Augustus' marriage legislation, the *Leges Iuliae* of 18 BC, in mind throughout 4.11,[130] and in his 'Cornelia' he is representing a member of the imperial family (see below, pp. 360–1) who is a conspicuous embodiment of the morality that the *Leges Iuliae* sought to promote. Augustus was later to suffer two public relations disasters because of the 'adulteries' of his daughter and granddaughter; 4.11 illustrates tellingly by contrast the seriousness of these debacles. In two other respects Propertius' Cornelia also adheres to the spirit of the *Leges Iuliae*. Cornelia makes much of her children: her two sons, Lepidus and Paullus, are named in line 63, and her daughter, born in 22 BC appears (unnamed, but undoubtedly an Aemilia)[131] in line 67; and at lines 97–8 Cornelia declares that all her children survived her. Not only, then, was she fruitful, but she and her husband had achieved the *ius trium liberorum*, another Augustan aspiration enshrined in the *Leges Iuliae*. Finally, although Cornelia envisages that her husband might remain unmarried after her death[132] – another pathetic touch is his portrayal in his old age as alone except for his children (91–8) – Cornelia has already gone out of her way to authorize his remarriage and to encourage her children to accept their new stepmother:

> seu tamen adversum mutarit ianua lectum,
> sederit et nostro cauta noverca toro,
> coniugium, pueri, laudate et ferte paternum!
> capta dabit vestris moribus illa manus.
> nec matrem laudate nimis: collata priori
> vertet in offensas libera verba suas. (85–90)

But if the door has a changed bed opposite, and a cautious stepmother sits on my couch, praise and endure, children, your father's marriage: captivated she will surrender to your good behaviour. Nor should you praise your mother overmuch; if compared with her predecessor, she will treat your free speech as insults to her.

For a man of Paullus' class remarriage was more or less mandated by

---

130 For the context and functions of Augustan marital legislation of 18 BC cf. Galinsky (1996) 128–40. For 4.11's links with it cf. Harrison (2005) 128–9.
131 Hence, perhaps, the couplet laudatory of the (also unnamed) *Vestalis Maxima* Aemilia (4.11.53–4, cf. Val. Max. 1.1.7).
132 In fact he did not: for his second marriage (to Marcella Minor) see Syme (1986) 147–51.

the *Leges Iuliae*.[133] Propertius has not failed to show Cornelia dutiful in her acceptance of this legal obligation upon her husband, however much she might have been expected not to welcome it. Cornelia's fidelity and fertility preceded, as well as followed, the enactment of the *Leges Iuliae* in 18 BC, so she had already conformed to the letter and spirit of Augustus' legislation before it was enacted. No doubt one of Augustus' arguments for the *Leges Iuliae* was that they did no more than enact into law the pre-existent attitudes and practices of good Roman citizens.

The obvious commissioned status of 4.11 has already been mentioned, as has the probability that the commission resulted from the success of Propertius' *epikedion* for Marcellus (3.18).[134] 4.11 confirms that by 16 BC Propertius had been fully assimilated into the innermost circles surrounding the imperial family. Cornelia was no ordinary upper-class Roman *matrona*.[135] She was the daughter of Scribonia, first wife of Augustus, by an earlier husband, a P. Cornelius, who was probably P. Cornelius Scipio, suffect consul in 35 BC. Scribonia is mentioned at 4.11.55 as *mater Scribonia*. Cornelia was therefore the half-sister of Julia, Augustus' daughter by Scribonia. At the time of Cornelia's death Julia was the wife of M. Agrippa and the mother of several children by him. Two of these, Gaius and Lucius, had just been adopted in 17 BC by Augustus as his intended successors. Julia is referred to at 4.11.59 as *sua* (Augustus') *nata*, and Augustus[136] himself is said to have mourned and wept for Cornelia (4.11.58, 60). Cornelia claims descent maternally from the Scribonii Libones (31–2), and paternally from Scipio Africanus and (incorrectly) Scipio Aemilianus (37–40). Her brother P. Cornelius P.f. Scipio was *consul ordinarius* in the year of her death (cf. 4.11.65–6), yet another indication of her own family's prominence at this time. Further distinction accrued to Cornelia through her husband Paullus Aemilius Lepidus, with his very successful public career. Proscribed by the second triumvirate (although a nephew of the triumvir Lepidus), he became an adherent of Brutus and Cassius; but he had joined Octavianus by 36 BC and was rewarded with a suffect consulship in 34 BC. Paullus was later proconsul, most likely of Macedonia, censor in

---

133 Cf. Kienast (1982) 137–9.
134 Above, pp. 347, 351–2.
135 What follows may be documented from Syme (1986) Index of Persons s.vv. Cornelia, wife of Paullus the Censor; Aemilius Lepidus, Paullus (*suff.* 34).
136 The casualness of the reference to him as *deo* at 4.11.60 is worth noting.

22 BC (4.11.41, 67), and (probably) an *arvalis*. Of his two sons, both mentioned at 4.11.63–4, one, L. Aemilius Lepidus, married Augustus' granddaughter Julia in 5 or 4 BC – another sign of the closeness of Paullus' family to that of Augustus. This was the kinship group for which Propertius wrote 4.11, in which he impersonated and spoke for a woman who had been at the heart of it, making her an epitome of and spokeswoman for Augustus' 'moral' legislation. Propertius' last words to his public, placed in the mouth of Cornelia, are thus those of a fully committed supporter of the regime.

A Lighter Shade of Praise?
Propertius 3.17 and 3.14

Elegies of Books 2, 3 and 4 which overtly laud the *princeps*, his policies and his actions were clearly intended to serve Augustus' ends. This chapter raises the question whether certain other elegies from these books which modern scholarship has treated as humorous or frivolous[1] might have done so in a more subtle and indirect way. This is not an easy question to answer: Propertian 'humour' is complex and variegated,[2] and much indebted to his hellenistic Greek heritage. Among hellenistic writers whose work survives to any extent, Callimachus, one of Propertius' proclaimed masters, and Theocritus, whose major influence entered Latin poetry through Virgil's *Eclogues*, cultivated 'irony', 'distancing', 'self-undermining' and grotesquerie in large measure.[3] These para-serious techniques were aimed at more than providing amusement: they were a means of exposing and exploring the complexities and contradictions which the poets perceived in themselves and in their literary and political ambience. The hellenistic intelligentsia looked back with appreciation and sympathy, but also with a certain sense of superiority, to the literature of the preceding classical and archaic periods, revelling in a subtly pleasurable sense of simultaneous engagement and disengagement with it. The Greek lands had expanded hugely through the conquests

---

1 Commentators may, of course, vary in their assessment of the tone of particular elegies, and indeed of Propertius' seriousness or lack of it in general: the poet's chameleon-like qualities are amply illustrated in the different impressions of him conveyed by Lefèvre (1966), Stahl (1985) and Papanghelis (1987).
2 For Propertius cf. esp. Lefèvre (1966), treating 'Ironie' (Chs. 2, 4), 'Phantasie' and 'Irrealität' as prerequisites of humour (Ch. 3); 'Distanz', along with irony (Ch. 4); and Propertius' self-vision and his varying modes of self-presentation, including self-undermining (Ch. 5). Propertius' individual brand of humour is summated in Chs. 6–7.
3 Cf., e.g., G. Giangrande (1975); Hutchinson (1988).

of Alexander, but the intellectual and political hellenism of the age demanded that poets continue to view their new world through the eyes of the past. Augustan Rome belonged to the same ongoing hellenistic culture, and the 'Romanus Callimachus' deployed the same battery of 'humorous' techniques as his Greek predecessors for the same purposes. Antiquity was, of course, aware of the possibility of combining humour with seriousness: one category covering such a combination was the '*spoudogeloion*',[4] while the looser and even less prescriptive concept of '*charis/charites*'[5] seems to have embraced a whole range of para-serious effects. However, this chapter is not concerned with labelling or re-labelling the humorous aspects of Propertius,[6] but with discovering whether some Propertian elegies which modern critics have thought unserious might, alternatively or additionally, have had political, moral, cultural, and even religious purposes germane to the Augustan enterprise – without devaluing their lighter side if they genuinely have one. This is part of an ongoing enquiry: Propertius' Actium elegy (4.6), which used to be mistaken for an attempt at humour, has already been reclaimed,[7] as have the politically significant aspects of his more light-hearted account of Hercules' visit to Rome (4.9), which of course also contains major elements of genuine humour.[8] To forward the enquiry this chapter will examine two further Propertian elegies where non-serious content has seemed prevalent, but where reassessment is necessary: a brief analysis of 3.17 will reveal it as conforming to elegiac conventions but not lacking serious elements, while a more detailed treatment of 3.14

4   Diog. Laert. 9.17 describes a Heracleitus as a σπουδογέλοιος, and Strabo 16.2.29 applies the term to Menippus of Gadara. Stephanus *Ethnica* 357.3 refers to Blaesus of Capri as a 'poet of *spoudogeloia*' (σπουδογελοίων ποιητής). L. Giangrande (1972) discusses the origins and meaning of the term and its applications both to the mixing of the serious and humorous and to humorous works with serious intent.

5   Demetr. *De Composit.* 127–69.

6   Lefèvre (1966) starts appropriately (11–21) with a terminological discussion which deprecates over-precision.

7   See Cairns (1984a), documenting (131–2) the opinions of the 1960s and 1970s before offering new perspectives. These were accepted by Isager (1998). Gurval (1995) 167–87 reverts to older approaches.

8   For its para-serious elements see esp. Anderson (1964), linking it with (erotic) *komoi*, on which cf. esp. Copley (1956); *GC* General Index s.v. komos; Pinotti (1977); Yardley (1978). Further treatments of Prop. 4.9 are McParland (1970), criticized in part by Warden (1982), who treads a measured path but regards the elegy as in essence humorous, as do – but only to an extent – Lindheim (1998) and Debrohun (2003) Ch. 4. For stress on the serious functions of 4.9 see Piccaluga (1964); Holleman (1977); Cairns (1992a); Janan (2001) Ch. 8, usefully underlining 4.9's interest in *Romanitas*; Harrison (2005) with further bibliography.

will acknowledge its substantial elegiac humour, but will also argue that it is not the unbridled fantasy that scholarship has judged it to be, and that it was written, possibly on commission, to honour Sparta within a specific historical context.

3.17, Propertius' hymn to Bacchus, combines prayer, praise, and vows in standard hymnic fashion.[9] If its praise and vows were read in isolation from its prayer, they could easily be taken completely seriously. But Propertius' prayer is for release from love, and particularly from sleeplessness, the result of frustrated love and a condition virtually synonymous with love in antiquity; and Propertius hopes that his release will be achieved through wine, the gift of Bacchus. Hence the major commentary on 3.17 speaks of the 'presenza di un tono sottilmente ironico' and a 'vena sottilmente ironica'.[10] Is, then, Bacchus the object of humorous, albeit gentle, mockery in 3.17? The implications of such a judgement would be thorough-going: the solemn and formulaic address *o Bacche* (1) (cf. also *Bacche* at lines 5, 13, and 20) and the Roman divine appellative *pater* (2) would be self-undermining; and similarly *humiles* (1) and the entire hymnic panoply of the elegy would be parodic. The multiple appearances of formulaic *Du-Stil*[11] (*tu* 3, *tuo* 4, *te ... te* 5, *tu* 6, *te* 7, *tuis* 8, *tua* 10, *tuis* 13, *te ... tua* 19, *tuae* 20, *tibi* 27, *tuum* 28, *tua* 38, *tu* 41) would each serve to underscore the pastiche; and Propertius' vows – to plant vines and make wine (15–18), and to celebrate Bacchus in dithyrambic vein (19–40) as his poetic priest (37–8)[12] – would reside only in the realms of fantasy. Indeed the former vow is highlighted by Fedeli (1985) as 'una burlesca enfatizzazione della supplica ben più normale, da parte dell'innamorato, di bere vino per dimenticare le proprie pene' (514).[13]

Prayer-parody is, of course, common enough in ancient literature.[14] But 3.17 is not a convincing example of it. To begin with,

---

9   On the hymnic aspects of 3.17 see Norden (1913) 154; Littlewood (1975) 664–9; Swoboda (1977) 131–6; Fedeli (1985) 512–4, 517 (on the correction *pacatus*, 2); La Bua (1999) 247–53.

10   Fedeli (1985) 513, 514 (also quoted below). The tendency to see 3.17 as humorous is marked in Littlewood (1975), and present in J. F. Miller (1991). Mader (1994) analyses 3.17's style and content from a formal viewpoint, and locates it within the structure of Book 3.

11   Cf. Norden (1913) 143–63.

12   This description of Propertius assumes that the MSS' *crater antistitis auro* (37) should, with Heinsius, be corrected to *cratere antistes et auro*. For arguments in favour of the correction see Fedeli (1985) 536–7.

13   'a burlesque exaggeration of the more standard prayer of the lover to drink wine in order to forget his troubles'.

14   On 'Gebetsparodie' see Kleinknecht (1937), where Prop. 3.17 does not feature.

Propertius actually carries out his promise to write Dionysiac poetry: lines 21–40 are a 'self-fulfilling undertaking', a typical Pindaric device[15] which is 'footnoted' in the common hellenistic manner by the mention of Pindar in line 40. Again, although Propertius can certainly be ironic in literary programmatic mode when he is undermining his 'opponents' and their pretensions, and although he can practise *deformazione* in a tendentious way which is not intended to be taken seriously,[16] nevertheless Propertius is always essentially serious when presenting and promoting himself as a poet, and this is what he is doing in 3.17. Lines 21–8, where Propertius compiles a catalogue of hellenistic myths, are particularly emblematic of his *doctrina*, an inseparable element of that self-definition as a poet which is the subject of lines 21–40[17] – a passage, incidentally, which makes up almost half the elegy. If, then, we should not take as parodic Propertius' undertaking to hymn Bacchus in the second half of the poem, why should we think that Propertius' earlier, parallel vow to be a viticulturalist and wine-maker[18] is parodic? There is certainly an element of fantasy in his vow, as there is in the similar aspirations expressed by Tibullus,[19] but parody is not the aim of either poet. The real-life Propertius (and Tibullus) would not have engaged personally in the menial labour of vine-pruning or wine-making,[20] but the estates of both will have included vineyards, along with slaves to do the work for them. Viticulture was a respectable occupation in antiquity, and Propertius had good reasons for promoting it in an Augustan context (see below). More generally, the notion that the apparatus of hymnic style in 3.17 aims purely to provide the reader with amusement is unsustainable, since it would have been pointless for an Augustan poet to mock Bacchus in the way hypothesized.

A better approach to this and to other Augustan treatments of Bacchus starts from the 'religious' difficulties which were a legacy of

---

15 *GC* 97. Lefèvre (1991) sees in 3.17 imitation of Horace, and thinks that when Propertius writes 'Pindar' he means Horace.

16 E.g. when he misrepresents Virgil's *Eclogues* in 2.34.67–76: see above, pp. 313–14.

17 On the sources of Propertius' catalogue see Fedeli (1985) 514, citing earlier scholarship.

18 In antiquity the two activities were not dissociated, as they may be today.

19 *ipse seram teneras maturo tempore vites/ rusticus et facili grandia poma manu;/ nec Spes destituat, sed frugum semper acervos/ praebeat et pleno pinguia musta lacu* ('As a countryman, I myself would plant young vines in due season and tall fruit trees with adept hand. Nor would Hope cheat me, but would always provide heaps of grain and rich musts in a full vat.' 1.1.7–10).

20 Similarly few would imagine that the real Propertius was genuinely sleepless through love and was resorting to wine as a soporific.

the final Civil War. Apollo was disputed territory.[21] Two other 'gods' (Bacchus and Hercules) had been hijacked by the Antonian side, and conscious efforts were subsequently made by Augustan poets to reintegrate them into the post-Actium consensus. M. Antonius had represented himself in the Greek East as the 'New Dionysus', he had strongly emphasized Dionysus' aspect as 'liberator' (Lyaeus), and in his Egyptian episodes he had traded on the commonplace identification of Osiris with Dionysus in order to represent Cleopatra (the 'living Isis') and himself as the twin divine rulers of Egypt.[22] This made Bacchus initially a problematic deity for Augustan poets.[23] A similar difficulty subsisted with Hercules since the Antonii claimed descent from Anton, a son of Hercules, and M. Antonius had paraded Hercules on his coins.[24] From an Augustan viewpoint these problems were by no means trivial. Bacchus and Hercules both had a god (Jupiter) for father and a mortal woman for mother; both had achieved divinity through their virtues and their services to mankind; and both were 'saviours' of the human race. Cults and cult-associations of Dionysus/Bacchus were widespread in the Graeco-Roman world and were for many people from all ranks of society the focus of belief in a blessed afterlife to be achieved through initiation and ritual founded on the god's own sufferings and achievements.[25] Finally, Bacchus and Hercules were both world-conquerors and *triumphatores*. Augustus needed the pair as precursors of his own status as the 'son' of the deified Iulius, as a 'saviour', as a world conqueror and *triumphator*, and as a future 'god'. Bacchus and Hercules were too important to be left in a cultural and religious limbo.[26]

---

21   For Augustus' well-known interest in Apollo see, e.g., Zanker (1987) 57–61, 338 = (1988) 49–53, 347. On the 'republican' side Sulla's devotion to Apollo is secure (cf., e.g., Plut. *Sulla* 19.6; 29.6–7), as is that of Brutus: cf. Moles (1983), and also, for Apollo's symbols on the coins of the Liberators, Zanker (1987) 57 = (1988) 49. It is not clear whether the republicans used 'Apollo' as their watchword at the second battle of Philippi, as did the Caesarians: cf. Moles (1983) esp. 249–51. C. Sosius' Apollo temple falls outwith this discussion since the Antonians were also fundamentally Caesarians.

22   For Antonius' interactions with Dionysus/Bacchus see Zanker (1987) 54–8, 65–6, 338–9 = (1988) 46–7, 57–8, 347–8; Pelling (1988) Indexes I: Names s.v. Dionysus; Marasco (1992) with bibliography.

23   In Roman terms Bacchus had been problematic long before M. Antonius took him up, with the *Senatus consultum de Bacchanalibus* of 186 BC signalling how easily a cult with Eastern overtones and attractive to women could become politically and morally suspect.

24   Zanker (1987) 53–4, 67–8, 338 = (1988) 45–6, 59–60, 347; Pelling (1988) Indexes I: Names s.v. Heracles/Hercules; Marasco (1992) esp. 541–5.

25   See, e.g., Dickie (1995) – with bibliography – for the growing evidence in this area.

26   Cf. Du Quesnay (1984) 31 and 204 n. 55; Du Quesnay (1995) 177–8 on Augustus' identification with Hercules; it embraced (notably) the cult of Hercules at the *Ara Maxima*. The

The reintegration of Bacchus into the Augustan consensus was in part achieved by presenting him not as an Eastern deity but as the Italian and Roman agricultural Bacchus/Liber; this is how he resurfaces in Augustan literature, cleansed of his Antonian associations. He makes frequent appearances in Horace's first three books of *Odes*, published in 23 BC. One ode (1.18) strikes a note comparable to that of Propertius 3.17.15–18: Horace starts it with a 'motto' translated from Alcaeus:[27] *Nullam, Vare, sacra vite prius severis arborem* ('Plant no other tree, Varus, before the holy vine', 1). There is a good reason for this coincidence: Horace's injunction to 'plant vines' and Propertius' vow to become a viticulturalist relate to contemporary events.[28] Rome's vital supply needs started with two items of produce, corn, and the 'second basic item of nourishment after bread',[29] wine. In 22 BC Augustus took responsibility for the corn-supply.[30] But Suetonius *Divus Augustus* 42.1 has Augustus refusing to supply Rome with wine even though the city suffered genuine shortages in the 20s BC, with public protests resulting.[31] It is improbable that Augustus was unaware that wine was (*inter alia*)[32] a nutritional element in the ancient diet almost as essential as grain. What his refusal to take responsibility for its provision shows is that he understood the logistics of the two commodities.[33] As owner of Egypt Augustus could virtually guarantee the corn-supply, but the sources of wine were too varied and dispersed to be controlled. However the Augustan regime did give

analysis of Virgil's treatment of Hercules by Binder (1971) 141–9 has rightly been influential; cf. also Cairns (1989) General Index s.vv. Heracles; Hercules. Schmitzer (2002)'s extensive treatments, 'Bacchus und Augustus' (147–66) and 'Hercules und Augustus' (166–86) are fundamental.

27 μηδὲν ἄλλο φυτεύσῃς πρότερον δένδρεον ἀμπέλω ('plant no other tree before the vine', fr. 342 Voigt).

28 Nisbet and Hubbard (1970) 229 remark (intro. to *Od.* 1.18): 'It may be asked what the ode is about' and conclude that 'he <Horace> is elaborating variations on an old commonplace which praised the moderate, but not excessive use of wine'. They go on to say 'A poem of this sort makes little appeal to moderns'. The political circumstances outlined here perhaps provide a supplementary answer to the question.

29 'Second aliment de base après le pain' (Tchernia (1986) 188). On the matters mentioned cf. Tchernia (1986) 177–9, 188–9. Naturally Tchernia was aware of, and did not intend to undervalue, the almost equal importance of oil in the ancient diet.

30 Kienast (1982) 92–3.

31 Augustus supposedly referred to the aqueducts of Rome provided by his son-in-law Agrippa as sufficient to ensure that no-one there went thirsty. If accurate, this dates the event to after 23 BC, when Agrippa married Julia.

32 Wine had a second, equally essential, use in antiquity: to become vinegar for clearing calcium carbonate from stone aqueducts. This was vital for the functioning of Roman conurbations; see Fahlbusch (1991).

33 On Domitian's two edicts about viticulture see Tchernia (1986) 221–9.

strong literary encouragement to viticulture: in addition to Horace *Odes* 1.18, Virgil *Georgics* 2 handles this theme; and Propertius 3.17 should be read as another such manifesto about wine production, and as a contribution to the rehabilitation of Bacchus as a precursor of Augustus. This latter task was taken up by Horace in other odes besides 1.18, where (incidentally) the god is also addressed as *Bacche pater* (6). Bacchus/Liber appears in a more mystic role in *Odes* 2.19, the final lines of which (29–32) hint at his sway over the underworld; and in *Odes* 3.25 the god's power to inspire poetry is linked with Horace's own ability to celebrate the apotheosis of Augustus (2–6). Horace is usually careful in his sympotic odes to sanitize Bacchus by distinguishing between the right and wrong uses of his gift of wine (1.18.7–16; 1.27.1–8), but this does not imply that his attitude to wine was puritanical: cf., e.g., *Odes* 2.7.21–8, which presents Horace in a less self-restrained and more bibulous frame of mind. Finally, in two further odes Horace explicitly rehabilitates Bacchus in contrasting ways. The later *Odes* 3.3.9–16 lists Pollux, Hercules, Augustus, Bacchus – pointedly described as *te merentem* and (again) addressed as *Bacche pater* (13), and Quirinus; Augustus is thus placed in the centre of these successful candidates for deification. In *Odes* 1.12, a self-consciously Pindaricizing and probably earlier piece,[34] Horace's technique is different and may reflect some misgivings about his first broaching of these themes. Although the same line-up of deified heroes – Bacchus, Hercules, and the Dioscuri – appears, it is stiffened by the insertion of full-blown gods, Pallas and the siblings Apollo and Diana; then Romulus heads a roll-call of great Romans which ends with Augustus. Another interesting feature of *Odes* 1.12 is the slight obliqueness with which both Bacchus and Hercules are introduced – as the Italian 'Liber' (22) and as 'Alcides' (25) respectively.[35]

Propertius' Pindaric reference of 3.17.40 may bow to Horace's *Odes* (above, p. 365); at the very least it reveals that Propertius, like Horace, understood the value of Pindaric poetry as a cultural matrix for the glorification of the *princeps*; and Propertius is also manifestly following the pattern of rehabilitating Bacchus observed in Horace. 3.17 takes the form it does because Propertius had to handle Bacchus in a manner appropriate to elegy. This in effect meant that the hymn to

---

34   On which cf., most recently, A. Hardie (2003).
35   Cf. the even more oblique *iunctura* of *Od.* 1.7.22–3 (describing Teucer): *uda Lyaeo/ tempora populea fertur vinxisse corona*, where wine = Bacchus, and the white poplar = Hercules.

Bacchus had to conform to elegy's erotic mode,[36] and that is why Propertius approached his subject through one of the standard topoi linking wine and love, namely 'wine is a cure for love',[37] and via the near-synonymity of Bacchus and wine in ancient life and literature.[38] As a result lighter material inevitably entered 3.17; but this does not detract from the serious purposes of the elegy. The two elements co-exist in it, and both should be recognized. Finally, an official occasion at which Propertius 3.17 might have been publicly performed should be recollected: Propertius 3.17, Horace *Odes* 3.25, Ovid *Tristia* 5.3, and later literary and archaeological evidence have been used to re-construct a Roman '*festum poetarum*' held every year at a shrine of Bacchus on the Palatine, close to the temple of the Magna Mater and the house of Augustus.[39] This annual event, which was clearly part of the regime's programme to rehabilitate Bacchus, certainly dates from before Ovid's exile, and, if it was already established in the late 20s BC, then it could help account for the many Bacchic odes of Horace; it is even possible that Propertius 3.17 was written for it.

The second, more substantial attempt to show that a Propertian elegy with undeniable non-serious elements may also have a serious purpose confronts an extreme case, which has almost universally been thought to be purely frivolous. Propertius 3.14 describes Sparta as a city where naked and semi-naked girls exercise along with males and where more mature women are freely available to their lovers. On the face of it, 3.14 is one of the most outré of Propertius' elegies, and the consensus of scholarship has seen Propertius' Sparta as an elegiac utopia detached from reality, constructed out of the poet's erotic imagination, voyeuristic fantasy, and wishful thinking.[40] But before 3.14 can be dismissed as nothing more than an elaborate joke shared by Propertius' sophisticated Roman audience,[41] two questions must be

---

36 Anacr. fr. 4 PMG anticipated the Propertian combination in lyric, as did *AP* 12.49 (Meleager) in epigram. [Tib.] 3.6 reworks the same themes, again elegiacally: cf. also Navarro Antolín (1996) 463–4.
37 Cf. Navarro Antolín (1996) 460–2, with earlier bibliography.
38 As is piquantly shown by Lucretius' usage at *DRN* 3.221 and by his discussion at *DRN* 2.655–60 esp. 656.
39 See *LTUR* s.v. Bacchus (Palatium) (E. Rodríguez-Almeida).
40 E.g. Lana (1948); Lefèvre (1966) 137–8; Nethercut (1970) esp. 100–1; La Penna (1977) 79.
41 Cf. 'il poeta si diverte ... un *lusus* elegante e raffinato' (Fedeli (1985) 451). Fedeli correctly rejects (449–50) the attempt of Alfonsi (1949) 97–8 to endow Propertius' description of Spartan female gymnastics with moralizing intent; Greek texts linking the nudity of Spartan girls (and boys) with moral rectitude are irrelevant to Rome, where even male athletic nudity was deemed shocking, not morally uplifting: cf. Ennius *ap.* Cic. *Tusc.* 4.70; Dion. Hal. *Ant. Rom.* 7.72.2–4; Tac. *Ann.* 14.20.6.

asked. The first, and more important, is: what did the poet's contemporaries believe about the Sparta of their day? If Propertius' depiction of Sparta in 3.14 is out of line with their belief, then he is manifestly fantasizing, presumably with humorous intent. But, if Propertius' Sparta accords in large part with the Augustan Roman view of Sparta, as I shall argue it does, then that conclusion needs to be modified. The second question is: what sorts of activities were actually going on in Augustan Sparta? This is intrinsically the less important question, but the answer to be proposed, i.e. that at least some of what Propertius describes and which modern scholarship regards as fantasy was really happening in Augustan Sparta, has some preemptive utility. It helps to parry the possible objection that, despite general Augustan belief about Sparta, Propertius and his elite audience were better informed, and so were engaged throughout 3.14 in a humorous conspiracy of privileged knowledge. If the points outlined above, namely that Propertius' Sparta conforms to a large extent with contemporary belief about Augustan Sparta and even with the facts about Sparta, are sustainable, then a more rounded approach to the light-hearted side of Propertius 3.14 is manifestly required. This is not to say, of course, that the elegy contains no elements of humour. Quite the contrary: it has major humorous aspects, and they will be analysed in the final part of this chapter; but first the proposals made above about Augustan Romans' view of Sparta and about what actually went on in Augustan Sparta must be substantiated.

Examination of Propertius 3.14 can begin with its account of Spartan female athletics (1–20). Although there is no modern consensus concerning the real-life physical education of Spartan girls,[42] ancient belief about female athletics at Sparta is more readily accessible. Many of the girls' activities described by Propertius were an established part of the popular image of Sparta in antiquity. Euripides specifies that Spartan maidens practised running and wrestling (cf. 3.14.1, 7).[43] Critias and Plato characterize their exercises

---

42   For earlier bibliography (mostly of broader scope) see Jüthner (1965) 101–2 and n. 294; Arrigoni (1985) 176–8. Arrigoni (1985) 65–95 (with notes) provides a detailed treatment of Spartan female athletics. Other discussions, some covering a wider area, include: Harris (1964) 179–86; Cartledge (1981) 90–3; Bernardini (1986/7); (1988); Scanlon (1988), with bibliography at 206 n. 1; Blundell (1995) 151–2; Kennell (1995) 45–6; Thommen (1999) 135–8; Ducat (1999) 57–9; Millender (1999) 367–9; Hodkinson (1999) 150–2; Pomeroy (2002) 12–29.

43   Eur. *Andr.* 599. On the texts discussed here cf. Fedeli (1985) 450–3 and esp. Thommen (1999).

as gymnastics in general,[44] and Aristophanes speaks of gymnastics and high-kicking dancing, possibly competitive.[45] Xenophon writes of competitions in running (cf. 3.14.7) and in 'strength' without giving further details, although 'strength' should imply wrestling.[46] Plutarch, who employed hellenistic sources,[47] lists running, wrestling, discus, and javelin throwing (cf. 3.14.10).[48] Finally, a fragment of early Roman tragedy quoted by Cicero speaks of Spartan women engaging in wrestling (*palaestra, pulvis*, cf. 3.14.1, 4), (?)running (*sol, Eurota*, cf. 3.14.17),[49] combat sports (*labor, militia*), i.e. *pancration* (cf. 3.14.8), boxing (cf. 3.14.9), and weapons-training (cf. 3.14.8-9, 10-11):

> quod Spartiatae etiam in feminas transtulerunt ...
>
>   apud Lacaenas virgines,
>   magis *palaestra Eurota sol pulvis labor*
>   *militia* in studio est quam fertilitas barbara.   (*Trag. inc.* 205–7 R)
>
> ergo his *laboriosis exercitationibus* et dolor intercurrit non numquam, *impelluntur feriuntur abiciuntur cadunt*, et ipse labor quasi callum quoddam obducit dolori. (Cicero *Tusculans* 2.36)

The Spartiates applied the same rule to women ... 'Spartan girls,/ whose cares are wrestling, Eurotas, sun, dust, toil,/ drill far more than barbarous fecundity.' So pain sometimes intervenes in these toilsome exercises. They are pushed, struck, thrust aside, they fall, and the toil of itself puts a sort of callus over the pain.' (tr. J. E. King, adapted)

The fragment thus equates Spartan women's events with all the sporting activities of Spartan men; and Cicero follows up his quotation with present-tense remarks which suggest that he himself had witnessed them at Sparta (see below, p. 380 and n. 87). His picture is very close to that of Propertius; and, while Cicero may be idealizing, he is certainly not fantasizing or being ironic. Finally a passage of

---

44 Critias B fr. 32 DK – from his *Constitution of the Lacedaimonians*; Plat. *Leg.* 806a.
45 Aristoph. *Lysistr.* 82, 1310. On the latter event (*bibasis*) see Arrigoni (1985) 88–9; Scanlon (1988) 215 n. 74.
46 Xen. *Resp. Lac.* 1.3–4. For wrestling as a 'strength' event (κατ' ἰσχύν) cf. Plat. *Leg.* 833d.
47 Kennell (1995) 23–5, 102–14, arguing also that Plutarch's *Laconian Institutions* 1–17 derives from a lost work of Sphaerus indebted to his master Zeno. If correct, this gives greater weight to Plutarch's evidence.
48 δρόμοις καὶ πάλαις καὶ βολαῖς δίσκων καὶ ἀκοντίων (*Lycurg.* 14.2). Theocr. *Id.* 18.22–5 (cited below, p. 384 n. 106), which draws on archaic models, also describes the races of Spartan girls of Helen's time. Philostratus *De Gymnastica* 27 refers to Spartan girls' 'public racing'. See also Scanlon (1988) 186–8; Thommen (1999) 137.
49 In *Tusc.* 2.36 *Eurota* probably refers to girls' races (cf. Theocr. *Id.* 18.22–4, cited below, p. 384 n. 106), whereas in Prop. 3.14.17 *Eurotae* is associated with boxing and horse-racing.

Athenaeus (and more dubiously one of Plutarch) might possibly refer to girls driving chariots either in processions or competitively:[50] cf. 3.14.11, which describes either horse-riding, or, in view of the plural *equis*, chariot driving.[51] Equitation, if it is this, could also fall under Cicero's *militia*;[52] and in fact both horse and chariot riding by Spartan women are historically well attested (see also below, pp. 382–3 and n. 102), and there is good reason to think that they also engaged personally in chariot races.[53] That leaves three of the sports mentioned by Propertius otherwise unattested as female activities at Sparta. These are the ball game (5), the spinning of hoops (6), and hunting (15–16). But Propertius does not actually portray the Spartan girls as playing at ball and with hoops (cf. below, pp. 380–1, 393); and the idea that Spartan girls went hunting may simply reflect a confusion in or caused by Propertius' source.[54] All in all then, Propertius' account of the events constituting Spartan female gymnastics corresponds reasonably closely to ascertainable ancient belief about what went on in Sparta.

But what of Propertius' notion that Spartan girls exercised in the presence of males (3.14.3–4)? Again there is evidence, not copious but adequate, of ancient belief that Spartan girls did so. The earliest text is Euripides *Andromache* 595–601:

οὐδ' ἂν εἰ βούλοιτό τις   595
σώφρων γένοιτο Σπαρτιατίδων κόρη,
αἳ ξὺν νέοισιν ἐξερημοῦσαι δόμους
γυμνοῖσι μηροῖς καὶ πέπλοις ἀνειμένοις
δρόμους παλαίστρας τ' οὐκ ἀνασχετοὺς ἐμοὶ
κοινὰς ἔχουσι. κᾆτα θαυμάζειν χρεὼν   600
εἰ μὴ γυναῖκας σώφρονας παιδεύετε;

Nor, if one of the Spartan girls wished to be chaste, could she be; they leave their homes, and, in the company of youths, with naked thighs and loose robes race and wrestle along with them, things unendurable to me. And must one then marvel, if you do not bring up chaste women? (tr. T. A. Buckley, freely adapted)

50   Athen. *Deipn.* 139f. Contrariwise, Plut. *Agesilaus* 19.5 seems to envisage girls being transported.

51   Arrigoni (1985) 190 n. 150 insists that chariot driving is meant, but it is too sweeping to condemn as an 'errore' the view that l. 11 refers to horse-riding: a Roman poet always has the option of employing 'singular for plural'.

52   Plat. *Rep.* 452c also speaks of female guardians bearing arms and riding horses.

53   See Arrigoni (1985) 92–5.

54   It is suggested below (p. 395) that Propertius had a source or sources in thaumatography for his Sparta material.

ξὺν νέοισιν (597, 'in the company of youths'), in combination with κοινάς (600, 'along with them'), indubitably asserts that the girls and boys raced and wrestled in each other's presence at Sparta. But neither Euripides nor Propertius necessarily claims that Spartan girls competed in wrestling with boys, although the phraseology of both authors could prompt this deduction.[55] Euripides was, of course, propagandizing against the Athenians' arch-enemy during the Peloponnesian War, but he must have had some basis for his allegation, if only in popular belief. It has been claimed that Euripides is contradicted by Xenophon on this matter,[56] but this is only the case if Euripides is really alleging that the sexes competed one against the other.[57] Xenophon says that Lycurgus 'first directed that women should train physically no less than men' and 'then he set up contests in running and strength, just as for the men, in which women could compete among themselves'.[58] So Xenophon is not addressing the question whether men and women competed with each other, or even whether they exercised in each other's company. Plutarch's contribution to this topic, based on a hellenistic source, goes some way towards confirming that Euripides' story corresponded to popular belief. Immediately after describing the Spartan girls' gymnastics and their eugenic functions, Plutarch tells us that 'He (Lycurgus) freed them from softness and delicacy and all effeminacy by accustoming the maidens no less than the youths to take part in processions naked and to dance and sing naked at certain festivals with the young men present as spectators'.[59] This text brings the girls and young men together, but not in the context of gymnastic exercises. A little later Plutarch writes: 'Moreover, these things were incentives to marriage – I mean the

---

55 Cartledge (1981) 91 understands Euripides' attack on Sparta as meaning that the two sexes wrestled together naked. Apart from the possibility that Euripides may not be alleging competitions between the sexes, Euripides' girls are wearing short chitons.
56 So Fedeli (1985) 450.
57 Fedeli (1985) 450 takes Euripides to be asserting this. He also claims that Paus. 5.16.2–3 attests single-sex events at Sparta. In fact Pausanias is not dealing with Sparta at that point: he is concerned with the races of Elean women in the Heraia at Olympia; these were indeed limited to maidens, divided into three separate age-groups. Paus. 3.13.7 does document the (single-sex) races of the Spartan female 'Dionysiades'.
58 πρῶτον μὲν σωμασκεῖν ἔταξεν οὐδὲν ἧττον τὸ θῆλυ τοῦ ἄρρενος φύλου· ἔπειτα δὲ δρόμου καὶ ἰσχύος, ὥσπερ καὶ τοῖς ἀνδράσιν, οὕτω καὶ ταῖς θηλείαις ἀγῶνας πρὸς ἀλλήλας ἐποίησε (Xen. Resp. Lac. 1.4).
59 ἀφελὼν δὲ θρύψιν καὶ σκιατραφίαν καὶ θηλύτητα πᾶσαν οὐδὲν ἧττον εἴθισε τῶν κόρων τὰς κόρας γυμνάς τε πομπεύειν καὶ πρὸς ἱεροῖς τισιν ὀρχεῖσθαι καὶ ᾄδειν τῶν νέων παρόντων καὶ θεωμένων (Lycurg. 14.2, tr. B. Perrin, adapted). Plutarch continues with an account of insults and praise directed by the girls at the boys: cf. Lycurg. 14.3.

processions of maidens and their nakedness and their contests where young men were looking on – for the latter were drawn on by necessity, 'not geometrical, but erotic' as Plato says'.[60] When he writes of 'their contests' Plutarch could of course be referring only to the girls' dance and song competitions, but, given the general belief that Spartan girls also competed in athletics, it is impossible to exclude the possibility that 'their contests' also covers athletic events. All in all, then, there are reasonable indications of ancient belief that girls and boys exercised in each others' presence at Sparta.[61]

What, then, of Propertius' description of his Spartan female athletes as nude (4, 7, 11) or topless (13, cf. 19)? From the fifth century on at the latest male athletic nudity was universal in the Greek world, and it was taken for granted by Greeks.[62] Ancient ideas about what Spartan girls wore or did not wear for their exercises varied and they are difficult to pin down because of the notorious ambiguity of Greek γυμνός and Latin *nudus*,[63] particularly troublesome in this context since the everyday garb of young Spartan girls in the classical period was a short chiton slit at the sides and worn without a belt.[64] Since Propertius indubitably characterizes his Spartan girl athletes as nude or topless, the question is whether antiquity in general thought that this was how Spartan girls exercised and competed. The two passages of Plutarch just quoted show that, in the view of Plutarch and his hellenistic source, public female nudity existed at Sparta; but the main emphasis of those passages is not gymnastic. However, as his

---

60   ἦν μὲν οὖν καὶ ταῦτα παρορμητικὰ πρὸς γάμον· λέγω δὲ τὰς πομπὰς τῶν παρθένων καὶ τὰς ἀποδύσεις καὶ τοὺς ἀγῶνας ἐν ὄψει τῶν νέων, ἀγομένων οὐ γεωμετρικαῖς, ἀλλ' ἐρωτικαῖς, ὥς φησιν ὁ Πλάτων, ἀνάγκαις· (*Lycurg.* 15.1, tr. B. Perrin, adapted).

61   On the question whether Sparta had one or two *dromoi* (running tracks) in the pre-imperial period see Arrigoni (1985) 73–5, arguing in detail that there were two, one within the city for ephebes and one on the banks of the Eurotas for girls. Scanlon (1988) 190, 197 asserts that there was only one and that both girls and boys used it.

62   Crowther (1982) provides a general oversight of the question, and of the puzzling account given by Thucyd. 1.5–6.

63   They may mean either 'lightly clad' or 'naked' depending on their context. γυμνάζω too is ambiguous: 'to train in gymnastics' or 'to strip naked'.

64   This costume afforded the viewer glimpses of thigh, which led to the girls being described as 'thigh-flashers'; for references and discussion see Cartledge (1981) 91–2 and n. 46; this is the garb of the Spartan girls in Eur. *Androm.* 598. For various artistic representations of girl runners in short chitons see Jüthner (1965) Taf. VII; (1968) Taf. XII b); Arrigoni (1985) Tavv. 2–3; Scanlon (1988) 214 n. 62. One such representation, a copy of a fifth-century BC bronze original (Arrigoni (1985) 159–60 and Tav. 6), is of a female runner with one breast bare, which corresponds with Pausanias' account of the races of Elean maidens at Olympia: see Serwint (1993); Scanlon (1988) 186 and n. 4. Another, which is classical, hellenistic, or a copy (Arrigoni (1985) 160–1 and Tav. 7), is of a running girl with both breasts exposed. On Spartan female clothing see also Thommen (1999) 138–40.

discussion continues Plutarch raises the associated moral problem: 'Nor was there anything disgraceful in the nudity of the maidens, for modesty attended them, and wantonness was banished; rather it produced in them habits of simplicity and an ardent desire for health and beauty of body. It gave also to woman-kind a taste of lofty sentiment, for they felt that they too had a place in the arena of bravery and ambition'.[65] Plutarch's final words, like those of the second of his two passages quoted above, suggest, although they do not prove, that gymnastic competitions were in his mind as well as processions, etc. At all events, Plutarch's moral comments make it clear that he, like Propertius, is writing about nudity rather than about the wearing of short chitons. Another attestation of ancient belief in female nudity, this time athletic, at Sparta comes from Theocritus *Idyll* 18.23 (see below, p. 384 n. 106), and further indications will emerge when what actually happened at Sparta is discussed (below, pp. 383–5).

From a more general viewpoint belief in nude female gymnastics was perhaps easier to hold in antiquity than might be imagined. Theopompus' fictional Etruria, with its women who exercise nude and are immoral,[66] combines the two themes of Propertius 3.14; and, closer to the issue, Plato twice envisages female athletic nudity, and indeed military training, in his ideal societies. In the *Republic* Socrates leads Glaucon to admit that female guardians should receive exactly the same education as male guardians, including gymnastics and military training (451e–452a). Next Glaucon says that he thinks it would be ridiculous for women, young and old, to exercise nude along with men in the wrestling schools (452a–b). But he is then forced to agree that male gymnastic nudity had 'only recently' been regarded as shocking and ludicrous but was now not so regarded (452c–d). Eventually Socrates draws the discussion to a conclusion: 'Our women Guardians must strip for exercise, then – their character will be all the clothes they need. They must play their part in war and in all other duties of a guardian, which will be their sole occupation; only, as they are the weaker sex, we must give them a lighter share of these duties than men. And any man who laughs at women who, for these excellent reasons, exercise themselves naked is, as Pindar says, 'picking the

---

65   ἡ δὲ γύμνωσις τῶν παρθένων οὐδὲν αἰσχρὸν εἶχεν, αἰδοῦς μὲν παρούσης, ἀκρασίας δὲ ἀπούσης, ἀλλ' ἐθισμὸν ἀφελῆ καὶ ζῆλον εὐεξίας ἐνειργάζετο, καὶ φρονήματος τὸ θῆλυ παρέγευεν οὐκ ἀγεννοῦς, ὡς μηδὲν ἧττον αὐτῷ καὶ ἀρετῆς καὶ φιλοτιμίας μετουσίαν οὖσαν. (Plut. *Lycurg.* 14.4, tr. B. Perrin, adapted).

66   Athen. *Deipn.* 517d.

unripe fruit of laughter' – he does not know what he is laughing at or what he is doing'.[67] In his second ideal society of the *Laws* Plato's Athenian stranger links all the exercises he recommends for his ideal city with training for war (832d). He prescribes running for girls but he is more concerned with decorum than Plato's 'Socrates': pre-pubertal girls should run naked, he says, but older girls, up to age 18–20, should wear 'suitable garb' (833c–d). There follows a series of approved exercises for men: not 'strength events', but fighting in armour (833d–e). Then the Athenian stranger adds: 'these regulations should apply to women until their marriage' (834a), thus indicating that all these events are mandatory for girls too. Another series of exercises follows: peltast contests to replace *pancration*, (possibly) horse-racing, mounted archery, and mounted javelin-throwing (834a–d). The Athenian refuses to make these obligatory for girls, but he allows girls to practise them if they wish (834d). His underlying concern in all these regulations was revealed earlier at 785b, where he proposed that some women should be given suitable military duties up to the age of fifty. At another point in *Laws* we find the proposal that, in order to promote marriages and dispel ignorance: 'boys and girls should dance for recreation, looking on and being looked on by each other, in an orderly way and as their age offers suitable occasions, both sexes naked so long as prudent modesty is observed by each.'[68] Plato uses the feminine as well as the masculine form here (i.e. γυμνοὺς καὶ γυμνάς) in order to make his meaning inescapable. Whether Plato was influenced by what he believed went on at Sparta or/and whether his works influenced later belief about Sparta and Spartan practice, the inclusion of such arrangements in his two ideal societies at least shows that he thought them feasible. So there is nothing intrinsically flawed in the notion that Propertius was reporting a widely held belief that Spartan girls exercised naked.

67   ἀποδυτέον δὴ ταῖς τῶν φυλάκων γυναιξίν, ἐπείπερ ἀρετὴν ἀντὶ ἱματίων ἀμφιέσονται, καὶ κοινωνητέον πολέμου τε καὶ τῆς ἄλλης φυλακῆς τῆς περὶ τὴν πόλιν, καὶ οὐκ ἄλλα πρακτέον· τούτων δ' αὐτῶν τὰ ἐλαφρότερα ταῖς γυναιξὶν ἢ τοῖς ἀνδράσι δοτέον διὰ τὴν τοῦ γένους ἀσθένειαν. ὁ δὲ γελῶν ἀνὴρ ἐπὶ γυμναῖς γυναιξί, τοῦ βελτίστου ἕνεκα γυμναζομέναις, ἀτελῆ τοῦ γελοίου σοφίας δρέπων καρπόν, οὐδὲν οἶδεν, ὡς ἔοικεν, ἐφ' ᾧ γελᾷ οὐδ' ὅτι πράττει· (Plat. *Rep.* 457a–b, tr. H. P. D. Lee). Halliwell (1993) 142–3 contends that Plato does not mean female nudity; but the parallel with male nudity drawn by 'Socrates' (452c–d) has no point if female nudity is not at issue.
68   ... χρὴ καὶ τὰς παιδιὰς ποιεῖσθαι χορεύοντάς τε καὶ χορευούσας κόρους καὶ κόρας, καὶ ἅμα δὴ θεωροῦντάς τε καὶ θεωρουμένους μετὰ λόγου τε καὶ ἡλικίας τινὸς ἐχούσης εἰκυίας προφάσεις, γυμνοὺς καὶ γυμνὰς μέχριπερ αἰδοῦς σώφρονος ἑκάστων. (771e–772a).

Propertius also claims that Spartan women were sexually liberated (21–8). Again, although scholarship is divided on the historicity of such allegations,[69] there is no doubt that from the fifth century BC on Spartan women were believed to be sexually loose. The entire speech of Euripides' Peleus (above, p. 372), focussing as it does on Helen and her infidelity, demonstrates this; and a casual remark of the Athenian to the Spartan in Plato's *Laws*: 'the looseness of your women' (τὴν τῶν γυναικῶν παρ' ὑμῖν ἄνεσιν, 637c) provides confirmation. Various sexual practices scandalous to the outside world were thought in antiquity to be institutionalized at Sparta: according to Polybius, polyandry was both 'an ancestral custom' and 'current practice' there; and when a man's wife had given him enough children, it was acceptable for him to hand her on to a friend.[70] Xenophon *Constitution of the Lacedaemonians* 1.7 fills out the picture: an older husband with a young wife could invite a younger man into his house to beget a child on his wife, this being an institution supposedly established by the Spartan lawgiver Lycurgus! Xenophon's language may even indicate that he thought it was mandatory. Similarly, according to Xenophon, it was a Lycurgan law that a man who did not wish to marry could select a suitable married woman and try to persuade her husband to allow him to impregnate her;[71] these topics resurface in Plutarch *Lycurgus* 15.6–10. Then Xenophon mentions women keeping two households and men adopting children (from the context presumably those of their wife by other men) into their own households.[72] Finally, Spartan women were said in antiquity not to be closely guarded (cf. 3.14.23);[73] and they supposedly offered themselves to strangers;[74] it is easy to see how they gained a reputation for promiscuity.[75]

Paradoxically, then, it turns out that, elegiac posturing apart, much

---

69 For a thorough study of the evidence see Cartledge (1981); cf. also MacDowell (1986) Ch. 4; Thommen (1999); Millender (1999) 356–63; Pomeroy (2002) 37–8, 44–7.

70 Cartledge (1981) 102, citing Polyb. 12.6b.8; cf. also Thommen (1999) 142–3.

71 Xen. *Resp. Lac.* 1.8; cf. Plut. *Lycurg.* 15.7.

72 Xen. *Resp. Lac.* 1.9. Historically trial marriages, terminable if the woman did not conceive, may have been permitted at Sparta; see Cartledge (1981) 102 and n. 108.

73 Cartledge (1981) 102 and n. 109; Xen. *Resp. Lac.* 1.7 notes that Lycurgus' enactment about old husbands and young wives was intended to prevent women being guarded. Cf. also Plut. *Lycurg.* 15.8.

74 Cartledge (1981) 102.

75 Cf. Thommen (1999) 142 n. 71. It may seem paradoxical that, if all this was going on, Plutarch could make a Spartan man claim that adultery was non-existent at Sparta (*Lycurg.* 15.10; *Mor.* 228b–c). But adultery at Sparta was clearly a matter of definition.

of what Propertius says about Spartan females was standard ancient belief, which would still have been current in Augustan Rome. So, as indicated earlier, if the conclusion that Propertius was not engaging in personal fantasy and exaggeration throughout 3.14 is to be evaded, the only remaining argument against it would be that, although Propertius' account corresponds with ancient beliefs about Sparta in general, he and his audience somehow knew better and were laughing at the stereotype of Sparta and at the simpletons who took it seriously. It would be difficult under any circumstances to prove complicity of this type between poet and readers, but such facts as can be established about the women of historical Sparta make it even harder. Getting at those facts is not easy: as noted, modern scholarship has reached no consensus over them, with verdicts ranging from acceptance of virtually all the ancient sources' claims to more or less complete scepticism. This is not surprising since the vast majority of the sources are literary and therefore misleading in various different ways,[76] while some are also antiquarian rather than historical in emphasis; and in many cases it is unclear to which period information refers. Individual scholars' preconceptions therefore largely influence their judgements of what is and is not historical. There is, of course, additional archaeological and epigraphic evidence, but the overall difficulty persists because only the literary sources, which are bedevilled by these inherent problems, offer a conceptual framework.

The background to Spartan athletics of the Augustan age lies ultimately in the quasi-mythical 'Lycurgan' *diaita* of the archaic and classical periods,[77] which broke down in the early third century BC, and was revived in the 220s BC by King Cleomenes III through the agency of the Stoic philosopher Sphaerus. Sphaerus' new system, then or later called the *agoge*,[78] was clearly an antiquarian reconstruction: his main qualification for the task was his role as a specialist in the history of Sparta, who had access to the full text of Aristotle's '*Constitution of the Lacedaemonians*', the works of Xenophon and Critias on the same topic, and the *Republic* of his own teacher Zeno of

---

76   On the 'constraints ... of the evidence' cf. esp. Ducat (1999) 43–52.
77   See Kennell (1995) 98–100. Much of what follows can be documented additionally via the Index of Kennell (1995), even when that work is not specifically cited.
78   On the revived *agoge* see Cartledge and Spawforth (1989) 202–7, and esp. Kennell (1995), whose Ch. 5 assembles the evidence about Sphaerus' role.

Citium, based on Lycurgan Sparta.[79] Sphaerus' *agoge* only endured for some twenty years, but, when in 146 BC Rome defeated the Achaean League with Sparta as her ally, Sparta was awarded her freedom and the *agoge* was restored in something close to Sphaerus' form. It consisted mainly in militaristic physical education and competitive events, and it was not just the all-enveloping educational and training system for young people aged 14–20 and beyond but also the most significant single communal activity of the Spartan state.[80] In the Augustan period the *agoge* was a flourishing institution: the altar of Artemis Orthia, at which one of the central and culminating events of the *agoge* took place, was improved during his reign through stone seating; and the theatre on the side of the acropolis, another focal point for the *agoge*, was built in the same period.[81]

The Spartan athletic events described by Propertius correspond in the main[82] with known elements of the post-146 BC *agoge*. Attestations of them normally involve male competitors, so the key question is whether females also practised them. In general the evidence is encouraging: the physical education of girls was as much part of the *agoge* as that of boys,[83] and there is epigraphic evidence of female athletic events as well as dancing from the post-146 BC era. A ritual race was held for girls named for this purpose '*Dionysiades*'.[84] It was organized by the same board of magistrates, the *bideoi*, which supervised the training of young men. Girls also competed in the 'Livian' games, introduced under Tiberius or Claudius.[85] Much of the literary evidence already adduced to demonstrate ancient beliefs about Sparta also has some historical value for this period. Plutarch's testimony

79   The chronological relationship between Cleisthenes' commission and Sphaerus' '*On the Laconian Constitution*' and '*On Lycurgus and Socrates*' is unknown: cf. Kennell (1995) 99.

80   The official who controlled the *agoge* and the young people in it, the *patronomos*, was also the eponymous magistrate of Sparta.

81   For the altar see Kennell (1995) 50; for the theatre see below, p. 389 and n. 130.

82   For several possible misunderstandings or confusions on Propertius' part see below, pp. 392–5.

83   On female participation in the revived *agoge* and on its details see Cartledge and Spawforth (1989) 205–6. A Spartan female wrestler competing with a man allegedly appears in Schol. Juv. 4.53, but Arrigoni (1985) 88 and H. M. Lee (1988) 113–14 question the authenticity of this notice, regarding it as a renaissance interpolation. Scanlon (1988) 187 usefully asssembles evidence to show that the girls formed groups similar to those of the boys in the *agoge*.

84   See Arrigoni (1985) 76–84 on 'running for Dionysus' and other Dionysiac activities at Sparta.

85   Cartledge and Spawforth (1989) 102–3 date their foundation either to AD 29 (Livia's death) or AD 42 (her deification).

reproduces hellenistic sources,[86] and hence shows that wrestling and the throwing of discus and javelin were then practised by Spartan girls, as well as running, singing, dancing, and processions. Cicero's present-tense comments on Spartan female gymnastics at *Tusculans* 2.36 (above, p. 371) look like those of a spectator. He visited Sparta in 79 BC, and at *Tusculans* 2.34 and 5.77 he confirms his autopsy of some events of the *agoge*.[87] If, as seems likely, Cicero also witnessed Spartan militaristic female exercises, his account of them is factual.

Which, then, of the specific events mentioned by Propertius could a visitor to Augustan Sparta have seen? Male wrestling (cf. 3.14.1–4) was certainly one, and, on the evidence so far assembled, wrestling bouts involving Spartan females before mixed audiences can be added. Mixed-sex wrestling is much less likely, although not absolutely impossible, and Propertius is probably not describing this anyhow.[88] Propertius 3.14.5 probably refers to the Spartan game of 'Battle-ball', which was held in the theatre on the side of the acropolis.[89] The teams were males who just had completed the *agoge*, and this was the liminal event which signalled their transformation from ephebes to adults. Girls did not take part in 'Battle-ball', but (as noted above, p. 372), Propertius does not say that they did; nor does

---

86   Cf. Kennell (1995) 23–5. In Propertius' day female athletics were apparently still rare enough to be startling, whereas they were commoner by Plutarch's time (later first and early second centuries AD) and can be attested elsewhere in Greece: see Cartledge and Spawforth (1989) 206. But this should not automatically call into question Plutarch's statements about an earlier epoch of Sparta.

87   *Spartae vero pueri ad aram sic verberibus accipiuntur, 'ut multus e visceribus sanguis exeat,' non numquam etiam, ut, **cum ibi essem**, audiebam, ad necem* ('At Sparta the boys are so flogged at the altar "that much blood flows from their innards" – sometimes even (as I heard when I was there) to their death.' 2.34); *pueri Spartiatae non ingemescunt verberum dolore laniati. adulescentium greges Lacedaemone **vidimus ipsi** incredibili contentione certantis pugnis calcibus unguibus morsu denique, cum exanimarentur prius quam victos se faterentur* ('The Spartiate boys do not let out a groan when they are torn by pain of the whips. I myself at Sparta saw the herds of youths competing with incredible tenacity with fists, feet, nails and even teeth, when they were ready to die rather than admit themselves defeated.' 5.77).

88   See also below, pp. 392–4. If Schol. Juv. 4.53 (above, p. 379 n. 83) is interpolated, Athen. *Deipn.* 566e ('And on the island of Chios it is very pleasant just to walk to the gymnasia and running-tracks and watch the young men wrestling with the girls', tr. C. B. Gulick) is the only ancient text which unambiguously refers to non-mythical, mixed-sex wrestling. If credible, the practice could have been introduced from Sparta by Laconizers; cf. also Plutarch's assertion that on Chios youths spectated the games(?) and dances of the maidens (*Mor.* 249d), and, on the gymnastic interests of Chiote girls, Arrigoni (1985) 112–14. For non-Spartan vases showing Peleus and Atalanta wrestling together see Jüthner (1965) 101–2. Arrigoni (1985) 87 rejects the idea of male-female wrestling at Sparta; cf. also H. M. Lee (1988), limiting possible mixed competition to musical events.

89   Kennell (1995) 60–2.

he say that they exercised with hoops (6). Rather lines 5–6 treat events happening at roughly the same time as those of 1–4 (cf. *cum*, 5). Nothing is known about exercises with hoops at Sparta, perhaps because they were not normally a competitive sport but a form of training.[90] Girls' races (cf. 3.14.7) were an element of the *agoge*, as of the *diaita*. The evidence starts with Euripides and Plato, and for the post 146 BC period there is also the epigraphic and historical testimony already mentioned.[91] So a visitor to Augustan Sparta would certainly have been able to see girls race. The title of another element of the *agoge*, *gymnopaediae* ('naked games'), in which choruses, but only of boys and ephebes, competed, may have influenced Propertius' emphasis on nudity, but (cf. below, pp. 383–5) naked female runners at Sparta are not an impossibility. A striking correspondence between 3.14.7 and a Spartan inscription has been noted:[92] since the *extremas metas* (7) are the second, 'final', finishing-line, Propertius is describing a woman who has completed the *diaulos*, and the inscription celebrates a Spartan woman who won the *diaulos* in real life.

Lines 8–12 introduce mainly militaristic exercises. If Plato's prescriptions for his ideal societies reflect earlier Spartan practice, then hand-to-hand combat was part of the original *diaita*; as for the later *agoge*, it is known that military trainers and drill instructors were engaged in it, and evidence continues down to Roman times.[93] But Propertius is not describing armed combat here, nor is he foregrounding another, very famous, event of the Spartan *agoge*, 'the whips', 'the contest of endurance' (ὁ τῆς καρτερίας ἀγών), in which the ephebes were flogged at the altar of Artemis Orthia to stain it with human blood – even though *patitur* in line 8 clearly alludes to it.[94] Line 8 refers to *pancration* and line 9 to boxing. Propertius' source may have introduced these events to take sides learnedly in a conflict

---

90   See Harris (1972) 133–41, esp. 138, for details of κρικηλασία as an exercise; the evidence for any competitive element in its use is little and late. The *trochus* first appears in Latin poetry at Hor. *Od.* 3.24.57, where it is 'Greek' and is treated derogatively; it recurs in other Augustan lists of (mainly) physical activities, viz. Hor. *AP* 380; Ov. *AA* 3.383; *Tr.* 2.486; 3.12.20, which presumably look to Greek models.

91   Cf. Kennell (1995) 45–6.

92   *SEG* XI.830 (second century AD), cf. Arrigoni (1985) 68–9.

93   See Kennell (1995) 46–7. The ephebes even fought a species of battle (without weapons) at the plane tree: Kennell (1995) 55–9.

94   The ephebes were expected to suffer in silence, and prizes were awarded to those who displayed the most endurance (καρτερία – *patientia*). Horace also alludes to 'the whips', using the same term (*patiens*) and reinforcing *percussit* at *Od.* 1.7.10–11: *nec me tam patiens Lacedaemon/... percussit*: cf. Moles (2002) 102.

of traditions. One tradition held that *pancration* and boxing were prohibited at Sparta, another that the Spartans invented boxing; there is in
fact evidence that some form of boxing was practised at Sparta, and
there are epigraphic references to the *pancration* from the Roman
period.[95] Female *pancration* and boxing are not specifically attested at
Sparta by any writer other than Propertius, and Propertius might be
convicted of fantasizing on this point[96] were it not for Cicero's *im-
pelluntur, feriuntur, abiciuntur, cadunt* (*Tusculans* 2.36). What can
these 'pushes, blows, throws and falls' be if not wrestling, combat
sports, i.e. *pancration* and boxing, and perhaps also weapons-training?

Discus-throwing is the subject of line 10: women's participation
in this sport at Sparta is claimed by Plutarch *Lycurgus* 14.2, and there
is no reason to doubt it.[97] Lines 11–12 deal with horse or chariot
racing and with weapons-training. Horsemanship was a key concept
within the Spartan *agoge*:[98] the elite group of ephebes was known as
hippeis ('horsemen') even though they did not fight on horseback, and
they were closely linked with the mythical duo who appear in 3.14 a
few lines later, Castor and Pollux, heroes who were the focus of the
agoge and indeed of the entire Spartan state as the 'divine counterparts
and guarantors of the city's double kingship'.[99] For the ephebes the
Dioscuri were models embodying their ideals, and their status as
horsemen was vital to this role: Theocritus, when summarizing their
attributes, does not fail to include 'horsemen' – ἱππῆες (*Idyll* 22.24,
cf. 136 ταχύπωλε 'swift-horsed', addressed to Castor). A vivid demonstration of the key role of horses and horsemen in the *agoge* came
with the discovery in the sanctuary of Artemis Orthia of more dedications of horses and horsemen than of all other animals put together.
Propertius will also introduce Helen in the company of her brothers
(19–20); and a relief found there shows a priestess (presumably a representative of Helen) standing between two nude horsemen,
doubtless the Dioscuri.[100] Even more interesting for present purposes

---

95 On this question see Hodkinson (1999) 157–9.
96 Cf. Arrigoni (1985) 90–1, denying that Spartan women actually practised *pancration* and
boxing.
97 Arrigoni (1985) 89–90 is inclined, despite the lack of corroborative evidence, to accept
Plutarch's testimony.
98 For what follows see Kennell (1995) 138–42.
99 So Kennell (1995) 138–9. Propertius' introduction of Castor and Pollux also contributes to
the network of verbal connections within 3.14: thus Pollux's *pugnis* (18) picks up the
boxing of 9 (and is echoed irrationally in *pugnasque*, 33), while Castor's *equis* (18) picks
up *equis* (11): for such connections, see also below, p. 402.
100 Kennell (1995) 142.

because contemporary with 3.14, *stelai* of the Augustan period from the temple of Castor and Pollux recording sacred banquets depict the Dioscuri along with Helen; and a joint priesthood of Helen and the Dioscuri is attested from the age of Augustus on.[101] That Spartan women regularly rode horses is unquestionable: excavations in the Menelaion (the shrine of Menelaus and Helen) revealed large numbers of late archaic equestrian figures, the majority of which are definitely female. Given the location of the finds, it is certain that they are connected with the cult of Helen as a rider, and they may also be linked with local horse-races by women.[102] Female weapons-training (11–12) falls within Cicero's description. Hunting (15–16) was an integral part of the *agoge* as a preparation for war, and it was the means whereby ephebes and Spartiates made contributions to their communal messes.[103] But there is no evidence that Spartan women hunted, and, if Propertius was not just extrapolating from male practice, lines 15–16 may result from a confusion in his source (see below, pp. 394–5).

To sum up: most of the athletic activities attributed by Propertius to Spartan women can be documented as an integral part of the physical education of Spartan males. There is also evidence that the majority of them were practised by Spartan females, while others not specifically attested for women may fall under one of the more general headings under which our texts class some female gymnastics. Hence Propertius' contemporaries could, so it seems, have watched Spartan women participating in most of the events in which Propertius claims they participated.

This still leaves open the question whether Spartan girls really performed their athletic activities naked or semi-naked in public, as Propertius claims. Modern scholarly opinion has perhaps been more divided on this point than on any other.[104] Sparta was so different from other Greek cities in its attitudes to women, and much else, that scepticism may be out of place even here. Douglas MacDowell's

101 Cartledge and Spawforth (1989) 99, 195.
102 Cf. Arrigoni (1985) 92–3. If, however, line 11 refers rather to chariot-riding or chariot-racing, it can be linked with evidence for Spartan women processing in chariots, and entering chariots in races: cf. Arrigoni (1985) 94–5, stressing the prestige acquired in the fourth century BC by Spartan women who won Olympic victories with chariots owned by them but driven by others.
103 Kennell (1995) 52–4, 76–7.
104 Bömer (1980) 194–5 collects material and bibliography on this topic. For a range of recent views see, e.g., Arrigoni (1985) 86–8; Scanlon (1988) 186–98, 203–4; Stewart (1997) 29–31, 108–16; Millender (1999) 367–9; Pomeroy (2002) 25–7.

words are perhaps to the point: 'In studying Sparta it is not safe to dismiss a particular social arrangement as impossible merely on the ground that it seems preposterous to us'.[105] Theocritus imagines the girl companions of Helen as 'oiling themselves in male fashion' before running at Sparta.[106] If this reflects what happened at Sparta in his own day, then it argues that the Spartan girls raced naked. A practical point about wrestling can be added: in the ancient sport the body was covered with oil, which makes the wearing of clothes virtually impossible.[107] On vases depicting Atalanta wrestling with Peleus (none of them Spartan) she sometimes wears a dress, sometimes a bikini, but she is most often topless and wears only a *perizoma* or trunks, which were presumably the practical maximum.[108] The same mythical pair may be depicted on a well-known *kalix* from Locri Epizephyrii which shows a naked youth standing in the *palaestra* together with a girl clad only in a bikini bottom and carrying a strigil. Again, sports like discus and javelin-throwing cannot easily be combined with the wearing of loose clothing.

Another more general reflection may be relevant here: by the first century BC, Sparta had become a popular tourist venue, for Romans among others.[109] It seems *a priori* likely that the Spartans stimulated their tourist trade by spreading heightened reports of the sights of Sparta: hence, for example, stories about the large number of fatalities in the annual whipping contest at the altar of Artemis Orthia.[110] There may have been an occasional death there; but would well-to-do Spartan parents have routinely stood by watching their sons being flogged to death for the amusement of tourists? Stories about naked Spartan girl athletes and about their exercising along with naked youths could be taken as similarly exaggerated products of the same publicity

---

105 MacDowell (1986) 80.
106 ἄμμες δ' αἱ πᾶσαι συνομάλικες, αἷς δρόμος ωὑτός/ χρισαμέναις ἀνδριστὶ παρ' Εὐρώταο λοετροῖς,/ τετράκις ἑξήκοντα κόραι, θῆλυς νεολαία ('and we, who are all her contemporaries who run the same race, oiled in male fashion, by the bathing-places of Eurotas – four times sixty girls, young maidens …', *Id.* 18.22–4). Cf. also above, pp. 373–6. Arrigoni (1985) 72 admits their nudity but excludes male spectators. Scanlon (1988) 197 usefully notes that the turtles and frog found under the feet of some archaic nude female bronzes from Laconia may allude to the girls' sports on the banks of the Eurotas.
107 So Jüthner (1965) 101.
108 See, for these and the *kalix* mentioned below, Jüthner (1965) 101–2; Scanlon (1988) 193; Ley (1990), who provides a wide variety of illustrations; *LIMC* II.2.695–9.
109 On tourism at Sparta see Cartledge and Spawforth (1989) 207–11.
110 Kennell (1995) 149–61 collects all relevant material as Appendix 1: 'Testimonia on the Whipping Contest'. The notion that many boys died is persistent. The earliest surviving text to mention it is Cic. *Tusc.* 2.34.

machine, in which case Propertius and his audience will have been deceived. But Spartan parents might have been more willing to strip their daughters for the delectation of Roman tourists than to have their sons flogged to death, particularly if the girls' nudity was genuinely an old institution. It is interesting that, in the same passage in which Athenaeus talks about the wrestling of girls and boys on Chios, he writes of the Spartans: 'The Spartan custom, also, of stripping young girls before strangers is highly praised'.[111] As for the antiquity of female nudity at Sparta, it was certainly well established there in another context, dancing. In addition to Plutarch's testimony and the implications of Plato, there is early evidence of nude female ritual dances at Sparta in the form of pottery dedications;[112] and the practice is also attested, although for pre-pubescent girls, at Brauron in Attica.[113] Another strong argument for the historicity of female nudity under some circumstances at Sparta is that late archaic female nude figures from Laconia are fairly numerous at a time when they are seldom found elsewhere in the Greek world.[114] So public female nudity or semi-nudity cannot be dismissed as impossible in Roman Sparta.

What then of Propertius' last claim, that Spartan women enjoyed sexual freedom? The fact that historically bigamy was tolerated in one case at Sparta[115] and that trial marriages seem to have been permitted there[116] shows at once that the sexual *mores* of Sparta were not those of other Greek states. Again, the testimonies of Plato, Xenophon, Polybius, and Plutarch already mentioned cannot be taken as evidence of popular belief alone: wife-sharing and the other sexual practices prohibited elsewhere in Greece and ascribed to Sparta by these four authors must in some sense have been institutionalized among the Spartans in the archaic and classical periods, and perhaps even later.[117] There are also intermittent indications that female adultery committed

---

111 ἐπαινεῖται καὶ τῶν Σπαρτιατῶν τὸ ἔθος τὸ γυμνοῦν τὰς παρθένους τοῖς ξένοις. (*Deipn.* 566e, tr. C. B. Gulick).

112 Constantinidou (1998) 24–5, arguing that this dancing was a feature of the early cult of Artemis Orthia.

113 Arrigoni (1985) 101–4; Scanlon (1988) 186; Thommen (1999) 138.

114 Cartledge (1981) 92 and n. 47; Scanlon (1988) 191–7, 203–4 (= Appendix 1: 'Naked female Bronzes'; but only 17 of the 26 listed are fully nude (194)).

115 Herod. 5.40.2; cf. Cartledge (1981) 102; MacDowell (1986) 82–8.

116 Cartledge (1981) 102.

117 Sphaerus, reinventor of the *agoge* (on whom see Kennell (1995) Ch. 5), was a pupil of Zeno of Citium, who believed that wives should be held in common; cf. also Plat. *Rep.* proposing community of wives and children (457c–d) and of houses and meals (συσσίτια, 458c). Could Sphaerus have revived wife-sharing as an 'old Spartan custom'?

without the husband's consent and resulting in the birth of illegitimate children was regarded quite differently in Sparta from elsewhere.[118] To all this may be added the economic freedom of Spartan women to inherit and own property, which must have given them an independence of mind unparalleled among female citizens of other Greek cities.[119] It is not known how much of this survived to Propertius' day. From Augustus to Severus an official (the *gynaikonomos*, with five junior *syngynaikonomoi*), whose duty it was to regulate female behaviour, is found epigraphically at Sparta.[120] But this does not prove that Spartan women were particularly badly behaved. Similar officials are found elsewhere; and even if the Spartans of Propertius' day were willing to maintain old traditions like 'the whips' and the naked girls, they will hardly have thrown their wives at tourists.[121] Hence the second half of 3.14 no doubt departs further from the facts about Sparta than the first half, although neither Propertius nor his audience may have been particularly aware of this.

The result, then, of applying the two yardsticks, the popular views of Sparta held in antiquity and the historical truth about Sparta, is that Propertius 3.14 is not out of kilter with ancient belief about Sparta and only partially at odds with the facts – and then only in minor details which probably stem from his source rather than being evidence of his own fantasizing. So the notion that the poet and his audience were sharing a joke at the expense of unsophisticates holding popular beliefs about Sparta fails. The emerging conclusion about 3.14 is therefore that its account of Spartan female activities is not intrinsically humorous or ironic; what gives it its undoubted humorous overlay is the poet's own intrusive elegiac personality and interests. The effects of this intrusion will be discussed below.

The verdict that Propertius' description of Sparta sticks fairly closely to ancient belief about Sparta and indeed to the facts about Sparta places 3.14 in a new light. In particular it helps to distinguish 3.14 from its associated elegy, 3.13, which contains a passage about

---

118 Cf. Herod. 6.68–9: king Demaratus questions his mother about his paternity, telling her that she would not be the first Spartan woman to commit adultery (68.3); Plut. *Alcib.* 23.7–8: the wife of king Agis admits that Alcibiades is the father of her child.

119 Cf. (with varying degrees of acceptance) Cartledge (1981) esp. 97–9; Hodkinson (1986) esp. 394–406; Hodkinson (1989); Dettenhofer (1993); Thommen (1999) 143–7; Millender (1999); Pomeroy (2002) Ch. 4.

120 On this and what follows see Cartledge and Spawforth (1989) 200–1.

121 Inscriptions from the Roman period praising the good moral qualities of Spartan women reveal these as at least an aspiration.

India, possibly from the same thaumatographic source as the Spartan material of 3.14. In both elegies Propertius describes and recommends non-Roman customs, and he calls them both *lex*: the *felix lex funeris* of 3.13.15–22 is suttee. But there the similarities end: despite the visits of Indian ambassadors to Augustus,[122] India was for Propertius and his audience a fabulous and far-off place, and Roman interest in India was naturally limited. This limitation is reflected in 3.13, where suttee and India actually occupy only eight lines of a sixty-six line elegy. In contrast, however, Sparta occupies the entire thirty-four lines of 3.14; and Sparta was no remote and alien location, but a place well known to and well visited by Romans, constantly linked politically with Rome in the second and first centuries BC, and of real interest to Propertius and his audience.[123] At the root of the relationship between Rome and Sparta stood two shared beliefs, that the Spartans and the Romans were blood kin, and that the Roman and Spartan constitutions were alike.[124] The latter belief gives a special piquancy to Propertius' final couplet (33–4), where he wishes that Rome had modelled its *iura* on those of Sparta. Although these beliefs had no historical foundation, they did have practical effects: they encouraged active Spartan adherence to the Roman cause in Greece in the second and first centuries BC,[125] and they even played a part (since the Jews also claimed relationship with Sparta) in the triangular foreign policies of Rome, Sparta and Judaea in the second century BC.[126] From at least 42 BC on Sparta was in the Caesarian camp and was prominent in every crisis.[127] She had been forced against her will to join the Pompeian side against Julius Caesar in 49–48 BC, but following Caesar's murder Sparta declared for the triumvirs, even though Brutus was in control of Greece at the time. Sparta then fought at Philippi on the side of the triumvirs against Brutus and Cassius and suffered the loss of 2,000 men, a significant number for a city of her size; she received additional territory as a reward for her support. In 33 BC, when

122 Propertius' concern with India in 3.13 of course obliquely compliments Augustus: on the visits to Augustus of Indian embassies cf. also above, p. 340 and n. 63.
123 With Propertius' intense interest in Sparta in 3.14 may be contrasted his treatment of Athens (not Augustus' favourite city) in 3.21. He expresses a wish to visit Athens, but he devotes only eight (23–30) out of thirty-four lines to the city, and these are mainly concerned with his own imagined future activities there.
124 Cf. Kennell (1995) 10–11, 173 n. 36.
125 Reflected in the construction at Sparta post-146 BC of a lodging reserved for official Roman visitors; see Cartledge and Spawforth (1989) 94, 251 n. 3.
126 See Cartledge and Spawforth (1989) Index s.v. Jews, etc.
127 For documentation of what follows see Cartledge and Spawforth (1989) 95–104.

Octavianus and M. Antonius were moving towards confrontation, Sparta was the only *polis* in Greece apart from Mantinea, her long-standing ally, to declare for Octavianus. The prime movers in this last decision were probably two of Sparta's prominent Caesarian partisans and leading citizens, Lachares and his son Eurycles, the founders of a dynasty which, although troubled, lasted for over one hundred and fifty years:[128]

Lachares
(executed by M. Antonius 31 BC)
|
Eurycles, later C. Iulius Eurycles
(*PIR*² I 301, instituted dynast by Augustus 31 BC, deposed by him 7–2 BC)
|
C. Iulius Laco
(*PIR*² I 372, restored by Tiberius after AD 14, deposed AD 33, restored by Caligula or Claudius)
|
C. Iulius Spartiaticus
(*PIR*² I 587, deposed by Nero *ca* AD 61)
|
C. Iulius Eurycles Herculanus L. Vibullius Pius
(*PIR*² I 302, owner of Cythera died *ca* AD 130)

Lachares attacked the supply ships of M. Antonius as they sailed passed Laconia in the run-up to the battle of Actium, and it was this which led to his execution by Antonius; his son now had an additional motive for hostility to M. Antonius. Eurycles went on to command his own warships on Octavianus' side at Actium; he captured one of Antonius' treasure ships and was subsequently given the island of Cythera as a personal gift from Augustus.[129] Sparta received a mark of high favour from Augustus in the early 20s BC when she was put in charge of the quinquennial *Actia* games celebrating his victory at Actium. These were held at Nicopolis in Epirus, the city founded by Augustus as a permanent memorial to his victory, and Sparta's leading role in them in effect gave her prime position among Greek cities.

128 The dynasty was first brought into focus by Bowersock (1961), who offers a more extensive family tree (118): cf. also *PIR*² IV.209.
129 Cartledge and Spawforth (1989) 97–8 suggest Lachares' execution for piracy had a foundation in fact; and (following Bowersock (1961) 116) they link the family's activities and its connection with Cythera to that trade. Augustus, however, must have regarded them as more than opportunistic pirates.

After Actium C. Julius Eurycles, as he now was through Roman citizenship, became, with Roman approval, formally ruler over the Spartans. Not surprisingly he was a major benefactor of his town: among other endowments he built a state-of-the-art theatre, very unusually of marble and up to the standards of Rome itself with its massively impressive and very complex stage machinery, and he held shows there.[130] *Stelai* from this period connected with the cult of the Dioscuri and Helen, all three of whom are shown on them, have already been mentioned; and the priest and priestess of Helen and the Dioscuri were related to Eurycles.[131] Eurycles was also the founder, and almost certainly himself the first high priest, of the imperial cult at Sparta, and he had a special relationship with Agrippa, his old commander at Actium. In 16 BC Sparta issued coins in honour of Agrippa, who was then on a tour of the East during which he visited Sparta. The year 16 BC had a special significance in the Augustan era, since it was celebrated as the 15th anniversary of the battle of Actium, and in that very year Propertius himself composed elegy 4.6, which memorializes that victory. A cult association, the *Agrippiastae*, is documented at Sparta, and may well date from Agrippa's visit in 16 BC. By that time Agrippa was, through his marriage to Augustus' daughter Julia, a full member of the imperial family, but Sparta's links with other family members go back to 40 BC and earlier. In 40 BC Livia, later wife of Augustus, was still married to her first husband, Tiberius Claudius Nero. She, her husband, and their infant son, the future Emperor Tiberius, all became refugees after the fall of Perusia to the forces of Octavianus. They eventually arrived in Sparta, where Livia was given refuge and the infant Tiberius was placed under the official protection of the Spartan state:[132] he was *Lacedaemoniis publice demandatus* (Suetonius *Tiberius* 6.2). Suetonius also gives the reason: *quod in tutela Claudiorum erant*; i.e. the patrician Claudii, the family to which both Livia and her husband belonged, were hereditary patrons of Sparta. Livia's marriage to Octavianus in 38 BC may have determined Sparta's later support of Octavianus rather than Antonius during the Actium campaign. Augustus' high regard for the city was shown in 21 BC, when Augustus and Livia visited Sparta together, a visit also

---

130 See Waywell (1999) 15–22, who dates the theatre to 30–20 BC, noting (15) that: 'Trial trenches ... have confirmed that the theatre as we have it was of one build.'
131 On this office cf. above, p. 383. For the relationship, and for Agrippa's visit (below) see Cartledge and Spawforth (1989) 99.
132 Cartledge and Spawforth (1989) 96.

celebrated by Eurycles with coin issues. On that occasion Augustus took part in the traditional Spartan common messes (so it was said),[133] apparently as a sign of his appreciation of the people of Sparta for the protection they had accorded Livia nineteen years before.

Propertius' third book appears to have been published in 21 BC, by which time Propertius had been in the *clientela* of Maecenas, and so indirectly of Augustus, for around six years. Sparta's links with Rome, with the Caesarian cause, and with Livia place 3.14 squarely in the political arena. They make it even more unlikely that Propertius would have devoted to Augustus' and Livia's favourite Greek city, the home of Agrippa's old friend and only Greek sea-captain in his fleet at Actium, an entire elegy which was nothing more than a silly fantasy. It is even less likely that Propertius would have done so around the very time when Augustus and Livia were visiting Sparta and when Sparta was in the news for this reason. Indeed that chronological coincidence hints at the reverse, a connection between the elegy and the historical context, and consequently a request to Propertius to celebrate Sparta in elegiac mode. If 3.14 was in fact commissioned, the commissioner cannot be identified. But a survey of possibilities is worthwhile since it illustrates further the importance of Sparta in Roman minds at that time. A request for 3.14 in connection with Augustus' visit to Sparta could have come indirectly from Maecenas or directly from Augustus; equally it could have come from a Roman friend of Eurycles, since Eurycles himself would probably not have been interested in Latin literature. Eurycles' friend Agrippa is a not impossible candidate: he had enough literary taste to be the willing recipient of a Horatian ode (1.6), and there is a curious overlap between Agrippa and elegy 3.14: in the late 20s BC the Campus Martius was provided by Agrippa with lavish gymnastic and other facilities, including a 'Laconian sudatorium/gymnasium' (Dio 53.27.1).[134] This was not a casual benefaction, nor a mere compliment to Sparta and its ruler. Rather Agrippa's building programme on the Campus was part of an imperial policy of encouraging Roman young men (not women) to engage in gymnastic exercises as a preparation for military service,

133 On the visit, Cartledge and Spawforth (1989) 199–200, who interpret the meal as a banquet with the magistrates.

134 Roddaz (1984) 278–80. This structure seemingly predated his Thermae, into which it was probably absorbed; for the details and problems see Fagan (1999) 107–10, esp. n. 11. Agrippa dedicated his new aqueduct (Aqua Virgo) on 9 June 19 BC; his building activities in the Campus must have been talked of in previous years.

which was the regime's real aspiration. Hints of this policy can be detected in Horace's *Odes*: in 1.8, which rebukes a *meretrix* for luring a young Roman away from his exercises on the Campus Martius (he should instead, so Horace insinuates via a mythological exemplum (13–16), be envisaging going into the army); and in 3.7, which warns a wife against a would-be seducer but concedes his good looks produced by exercises on the Campus (25–8). Propertius' account of the gymnastics of (mainly) Spartan girls is tangential to this interest but reflects it nevertheless; 3.14 starts by expressing admiration for the *iura* of the Spartan *palaestra,* and it ends by coupling the *iura* of the Laconians with their *pugnae* (33), i.e. their military prowess throughout Greek history.

Yet another possibility about a commissioner for 3.14 is worth entertaining briefly. Propertius' cousin Propertius Postumus saw warservice in the East in 21–20 BC, and it has been argued (see above, pp. 18–19, 22–4) that he participated in Tiberius' expedition to recover the Roman standards captured at Carrhae and settle Armenia. The precise route taken by Tiberius and his entourage on their way east is known: by ship across the Adriatic to Dyrrhachium and then by land over the via Egnatia to the Hellespont and so into Asia Minor and Syria.[135] Tiberius' return route brought him first to Rhodes.[136] Hence his return to Rome was necessarily in part, and possibly wholly, by sea.[137] There were two normal East–West sea routes in the Mediterranean: of these the northerly was 'by way of Cyprus, Myra, Rhodes, or Cnidos',[138] and it then involved rounding southern Laconia.[139] If Tiberius took this route, could he have failed to land at Gytheum, a standard stopping-off place, to be welcomed by Eurycles, son of the man whose protection had ensured the lives of his mother and himself? If such a visit took place, one might imagine it lying behind the elegy, with Tiberius' companion Postumus as the commissioner.

---

135 Hor. *Epist.* 1.3.1–5; Sueton. *Tiber.* 14.3.

136 Sueton. *Tiber.* 11.1: *Rhodum enavigavit, amoenitate et salubritate insulae iam inde captus cum ad eam ab Armenia rediens appulisset*; cf. also Quint. *Inst. Orat.* 3.1.17–18; Damascius *Vita Isidori* fr. 64 (p. 94 Zintzen).

137 This would be particularly likely if he is the honorand of *AP* 9.219, and if this epigram is dated to 20 BC; see Cichorius (1922) 299–300. Gow and Page (1968) II.265, however, while accepting that 'Nero' is Tiberius, refer the epigram to his return from Spain in 24 BC. Most recently Schmitzer (2002) 295 returns to Cichorius' dating.

138 Casson (1971) 297–9, esp 297; Lucian *Navigium* 7–9. This was the route of the Alexandrian grain-fleet.

139 There would be no particular reason for someone sailing from Rhodes to Rome to go to the Isthmus of Corinth, traverse it, and then resume a voyage to Italy.

Propertian scholarship acknowledges that elegies 3.12, 3.13 and 3.14 form a species of trilogy;[140] and that, like 3.14, 3.13 contrasts Roman and foreign *mores*. 3.12, the first item in the trilogy, is addressed to Postumus and lauds his 'military' achievements in the East. Tiberius' *comites* were a highly cultured group. Horace *Epistle* 1.3 emphatically characterizes them as such; and Tiberius himself had marked literary tastes,[141] specifically for Hellenistic Greek poets. Two named as his favourites by Suetonius[142] are Euphorion, a well-known influence on Roman elegy, and Rhianus.[143] The third and most recent poet favoured by Tiberius had lived into Tiberius' own lifetime;[144] he was Parthenius, teacher of Virgil, Cinna and not least of Gallus, Propertius' main elegiac model, and the recipient of a compliment from Propertius in his very first elegy (1.1.11).[145] The notion that Postumus might have asked his cousin the poet to produce a piece about Sparta for Tiberius and his *comites* would fit what we know of them.[146]

As already emphasized, 3.14 has genuinely light-hearted aspects. These do not, however, include Propertius' innocent reproductions of confusions which he found in his source. That Propertius had a specific source (or sources) for his Spartan female gymnastics has long been believed.[147] It was definitely Greek and probably hellenistic: the first part of 3.14 is spattered with Greek terminology: *palaestrae* (1), *gymnasii* (2), *trochi* (6), *pancratio* (8), *disci* (10), *gyrum* (11); more tellingly, all these Greek words are technical terms of sport, and 3.14 is the only elegy of Propertius in which Greek sporting vocabulary is found.[148] Two items from Propertius' account of Spartan female athletics are not only unclear, but they seem to have implications which are out of kilter both with ancient beliefs about girls' gymnastic activities at Sparta and with the facts. The first anomaly surfaces in lines 3–4:

140 See esp. Nethercut (1970).
141 See, most recently, Lightfoot (1999) 80–2 for a detailed discussion.
142 Sueton. *Tiber.* 70.2 = Lightfoot (1999) 4 Test. 3.
143 Lightfoot (1999) 80–1 regards Rhianus as 'surprising' in this role. One solution may be that his *Messeniaka* dealt with the revolt of Aristomenes against the Spartans and interested Tiberius for its Laconian content; after all, there were not many poems about Sparta.
144 Suda π 664 = Lightfoot (1999) 3–4 Test. 1.
145 For Parthenius see Indexes II and III s.v.
146 The hypothesis does, however, require that Propertius had considerable advance notice of Tiberius' intention (or aspiration) to visit Sparta. Tiberius' return to Rome took place in 19 BC, whereas Book 3 seems to have appeared by 21 BC.
147 Alfonsi (1949) 96 suggested that it was 'Alexandrian'. Boyd (1987) saw a resemblance between 3.14.17–18 and Callim. *Hymn* 5.23–5; but *Hymn* 5 is not Propertius' source.
148 Maltby (1999) 395.

> quod non infamis exercet corpore laudes
> inter luctantes nuda puella viros

since a naked girl among straining men wins with her body praise involving no ill repute.[149]

The Greek-Latin gloss[150] *luctantes ... viros* (4) = *palaestrae* (1) confirms that, in Propertius' mind, some male wrestling is going on in 3–4. But what does his other bilingual gloss *nuda puella* (4) = *virginei ... gymnasii* (2) imply? Are we to conclude that, within the context of this latter gloss, *exercet corpore* should be understood as referring to female wrestling, which in fact is an otherwise well attested activity of Spartan girls?[151] Or are the girls just exercising while the males wrestle? And, if the girls are in fact wrestling, are the two sexes wrestling separately, or are the females wrestling with the males? The succeeding couplet (5–6) offers no obvious illumination: it simply tells us that, at the same time as the events of lines 3–4 are going on, other Spartan athletes are taking part in a ball game while yet others are exercising with hoops. However, the very proximity of the ball game to the wrestling raises the possibility that the ball game might illuminate the unclarities of the wrestling. It is likely that the ball game was prominent in Propertius' source since the Spartans claimed to have invented ball games in general,[152] and, as already observed, they had a particularly celebrated ball game played by their ephebes called 'battle-ball' (*sphairomachia*)[153] or 'on the lime' (*episkyros*).[154] The lexicographer Pollux depicts this game as follows:

ἦν δὲ τῆς ἐν σφαίρᾳ παιδιᾶς ὀνόματα ἐπίσκυρος, φαινίνδα, ἀπόρραξις, οὐρανία. καὶ ἡ μὲν ἐπίσκυρος καὶ ἐφηβικὴ καὶ ἐπί-κοινος ἐπίκλην ἔχει, παίζεται δὲ κατὰ πλῆθος διαστάντων ἴσων πρὸς ἴσους, εἶτα μέσην γραμμὴν λατύπῃ ἑλκυσάντων, ἣν σκῦρον καλοῦσιν ἐφ' ἣν καταθέντες τὴν σφαῖραν, ἑτέρας δύο γραμμὰς κατόπιν ἑκατέρας τῆς τάξεως καταγράψαντες, ὑπὲρ τοὺς ἑτέρους οἱ προανελόμενοι ῥίπτουσιν, οἷς ἔργον ἦν ἐπιδράξασθαί τε τῆς

---

149 This rendering evades the problems of translation noted below.
150 For etymologizing through glossing cf., e.g., Günther (1994) 257–8; O'Hara (1996) 8–9, 64–5.
151 Eur. *Androm.* 599; Xen. *Resp. Lac.* 1.4 (implied); Plut. *Lycurg.* 14.2; Cic. *Tusc.* 2.36; and see above, pp. 370–3, 380, 382, 384, 385.
152 For these see Harris (1972) 75–111 (= Ch. 3); Kennell (1995) Index s.v. Ball games.
153 Pollux 9.107.
154 Harris (1972) 86–7; Kennell (1995) 60–1.

σφαίρας φερομένης καὶ ἀντιβαλεῖν, ἕως ἂν οἱ ἕτεροι τοὺς ἑτέρους ὑπὲρ τὴν κατόπιν γραμμὴν ἀπώσωνται. (Pollux 9.104).

The names of the ball games were "on the lime," "feigning," "dribbling," and "sky high." "On the lime" is also called the "ephebic game" and the "all-in game"; it is played in a crowd which has split into two equal sides. Then with white lime they draw a line down the middle which they call "the lime," and onto which they place the ball. After drawing another two lines behind each team, preselected team members throw the ball over the other team, whose job it was to catch hold of the moving ball and throw it back until one side pushes the other over the back line. (tr. N. M. Kennell)

On Pollux's account the players displayed both ball-skills and strength, since they were trying to push each other over the line. Their catching and throwing correspond well with line 5 of Propertius 3.14; and their pushing and shoving are reminiscent of line 4. Of course, when Propertius wrote *luctantes* ... *viros* in line 4 he meant 'wrestling men', but he could have found the original of this phrase in his source as a description of the teams playing battle-ball trying to push each other over the line.[155] There may be another vestige of Propertius' source in *fallit* (5): a different ball game played by the Spartans was called φαινίνδα ('feigning') and one (incorrect) ancient derivation of this term was from φενακίζειν (= *fallere*: 'to deceive').[156]

A second and similar muddle might be responsible for Propertius' later claim that Spartan girls go hunting:

> et modo Taygeti, crinis aspersa pruina,
> sectatur patrios per iuga longa canis   (15–16)

and now, her hair sprinkled with hoar-frost, she follows her native hounds over the long ridges of Taygetus

There is no other testimony to hunting by Spartan girls, although it was an integral part of the activity of Spartan males.[157] One might try to bridge this gap by characterizing hunting as a 'military' exercise in the broader sense, since in antiquity hunting was regarded as a

---

155 This hypothesis may also explain why Propertius starts line 5 with *cum*.
156 Pollux 9.105; Harris (1972) 88–9. If Propertius was implying that σφαιρομαχία took place in the *palaestra*, this would be an error: it was held in the main theatre of Sparta, and, like the whipping at the altar of Artemis Orthia, it was one of the culminating events of the *agoge*: see Kennell (1995) 59–62.
157 Kennell (1995) 76–7.

preparation for war.[158] This would allow us to imagine that Propertius' source listed it along with other militaristic exercises of Spartan girls, although hunting would still sit uneasily with the Spartan girls' other activities as Propertius details them. Alternatively one might surmise that Propertius or his source simply extrapolated from the hunting of Spartan males. But there is a better possibility, namely that Propertius' source was not referring to hunting at all, but to another competition held at Sparta – a danced or mimed hunt originally called 'The Hunter' (Κυναγέτας).[159] There is no evidence that girls ever performed 'The Hunter'; but there is copious evidence that dancing was one of the main activities of Spartan maidens,[160] which might have made it easier for Propertius' source to link girls with 'The Hunter'.

A reasonable guess can be made about the general identity of Propertius' source. Cicero *Tusculans* 5.78 praises Indian women who compete to commit suttee; and this passage has been duly noted in connection with the previous elegy of Propertius (3.13), where lines 15–22 deal with suttee in a similar way.[161] It does not, however, seem to have been observed that in *Tusculans* 5.77, immediately before his introduction of suttee, Cicero treats two other topics: the endurance of Spartan boys in the 'whips'[162] and *pancration*, and the 'nude sages' of India who endure cold and fire. This is not to say that Propertius' source was Cicero; indeed, it has been independently and plausibly proposed that Propertius derived his lines about Indian suttee in 3.13 from thaumatography, and ultimately from Onesicritus.[163] So, given the recognized status of Propertius 3.13 and 3.14 as paired elegies,[164] and given the combination of topics found in *Tusculans* 5.77–8, it seems probable that Propertius (like Cicero) derived material for both 3.13 (suttee) and 3.14 (the 'whips', *pancration* and possibly nudity) from a thaumatographic source.

158 For Horace it was the *Romana/ ... militia* (*Sat.* 2.2.10–11). For Roman attitudes to hunting see Aymard (1951) esp. 91–3, 469–81.
159 Kennell (1995) 52–4.
160 See Constantinidou (1998). Arrigoni (1985) 188 n. 131 suggests that Helen's helmet at Prop. 3.14.12 is a confused residue of an 'athlete's cap', as frequently represented in statuary and vases; if so, Propertius' source will again be responsible.
161 Fedeli (1985) 424–5, referring to Heckel and Yardley (1981).
162 On Propertius' fleeting allusion to the 'whips' see above, p. 381 n. 94. His source (like that of *Tusc.* 5.77) clearly combined 'the whips' with *pancration*.
163 See Heckel and Yardley (1981).
164 Cf. Nethercut (1970), with many perceptive observations on the cycle 3.12–3.14 and on the links between 3.13 and 3.14.

The genuinely humorous aspects of 3.14 can now be considered; they start with its genre, which is well enough known. Camps wrote of 'an affinity ... with the *laus legis*',[165] and Underwood specified more precisely that 3.14 is mainly modelled on the elementary rhetorical exercise (*progymnasma*), 'praise of a law'.[166] Hence it is a laudation of Spartan institutions. Its latter section draws on another elementary exercise, the *comparatio*,[167] in this case a comparison of the laws or customs of Sparta and Rome. Propertius includes in his first line two clear verbal signals intended to alert the reader to the presence of a rhetorical *progymnasma*, namely *multa* and *miramur*,[168] which are commonplace terms in the elementary exercises of the schools. Another pointer to the elegy's genre in line 3 has been emended away by some scholars, viz. *laudes*, an allusion to the *progymnasma*'s Latin title, '*laus legis*'. The reason given for emending is: '*laudes* = *res laude dignas* is defensible in itself: ... *non infames* ... *laudes*, again, might be justified ... But *in toto* the expression is implausible, and *ludos* an entirely satisfactory correction'.[169] But 'keywords' like *laudes* are a standard way in which poets confirm that they are writing in a particular genre;[170] and the emendation *exercet* ... *ludos* produces a banality. Nor is it easy to see why Propertius should be permitted one refinement of poetic language but not two. Possibly, in addition to a standard sense of *exercere*, 'practice' (*OLD* s.v. *exerceo* 1), Propertius had in mind the technical meaning 'exact' (e.g. of taxes, *OLD* s.v. *exerceo* 9). *non infamis exercet corpore laudes* would then mean something like 'earns reputable praise for her physical exercises'/'wins with her body praise involving no ill repute'.

As befits a poet, Propertius is cavalier in his treatment of the *laus legis*.[171] In particular Propertius' 'law' is somewhat Protean. It starts in line 1 as *iura palaestrae* (the customs(?), rules(?), rights(?) of the wrestling school), and mutates by implication in line 2 into the *iura* of

---

165 Camps (1966) 121.
166 Underwood (1971) 72–8, considering only Latin evidence. *Legum laus* is found at Quint. *Inst. Orat.* 2.4.33. For the various titles found in the Greek rhetorical tradition see Cairns (1979a) 193 n. 20.
167 So Underwood (1971) 76–7.
168 Cf. Underwood (1971) 75, cf. 26–7, 31, 33–4, 42. However Fedeli (1985) 451, comparing Prop. 3.10.1 and referring to his own commentary on that line, believes that *mirari* indicates epigrammatic influence.
169 Shackleton Bailey (1956) 183, followed by Fedeli (1985) 453–4.
170 E.g. phrases like 'you will go' to signal a *propemptikon* or mentions of the door to indicate a *komos*/*paraclausithyron*.
171 See Underwood (1971) 72–8.

the virgins' gymnasium which produce *tot bona*. Then in line 21 we
encounter a 'Spartan law' (*lex ... Spartana*) regulating the behaviour
of lovers. Finally at line 33 come *iura ... Laconum*, presumably the
entire socio-legal system of the Spartans, and especially those elements highlighted by the poet. Propertius is also cavalier in his
handling of further commonplaces of the 'praise of a law'. But in this
case he has a distinct, and humorous, message to convey. If 3.14 had
been a standard school example of the *laus legis*, it would have evaluated Spartan institutions under the regular headings used to praise or
blame laws in antiquity. These vary from prescription to prescription,
but four appear in every case and these may have been the only four
used in Propertius' time – legality, justice, utility, and possibility.[172]
Some of these topics seem to appear early in 3.14, although they are
not clearly distinguished: line 2's insistence that the Spartan virgins'
gymnasium produces *tot bona*, cf. *bono* (34), implies the 'usefulness'
of the *iura* of Sparta's *palaestra*, and also probably their 'legality'.
Lines 3–4 then claim that a Spartan girl, albeit naked, *non infamis exercet corpore laudes*. The theme here is the 'just', and possibly again
legality; and the final, comparative, section from line 29 on may also
imply 'the just'. But the fourth topic, 'the possible', is entirely missing
from 3.14. That its absence is significant is guaranteed by the role of
the 'possible' in another Propertian elegy (2.7) which is based on the
'attack on a law', the *progymnasma* with an 'inverse' relationship to
the *laus legis*.[173] In 2.7 Propertius ostensibly criticizes an enactment
about marriage which (the later) Augustus proposed or introduced
before 28 BC and then abandoned or revoked.[174] However, Propertius
admits that the marriage law is just, useful, and fitting. He attacks it
only on the ground of possibility, and only because he personally finds
it impossible to obey, since he is an elegiac poet committed to love,
who therefore cannot marry. Because Propertius, when composing the
sister genre in 2.7, concentrated all his negative remarks on 'the possible', his omission of 'the possible' from 3.14 must be meaningful. It
is a tacit and self-mocking admission that, despite his warm advocacy
of Spartan customs as a model for Rome, Propertius knows that his

---

172 For ancient variation in the number of headings see Cairns (1979a) 193–4 and n. 22. Theon
has the most (8) headings: for his full version (in part recovered from the Armenian
translation) see Patillon and Bolognesi (1997) 95–102.

173 For an analysis in these terms see Cairns (1979a).

174 From a generic point of view it is unimportant whether the proposed enactment was a 'law'
or a triumviral edict, as was argued by Badian (1985). Indeed Propertius' public 'rejection'
of it would make even more sense on the latter hypothesis.

recommendations do not fall within the realm of the 'possible' and hence could not be implemented; and, of course, it must have been obvious to anyone encountering 3.14 at the time that its Rome full of naked exercising girls of the free classes was a ludicrous proposition. Similarly a Rome where all free women and girls were open and accessible to the advances of lovers and where no protection was provided for them was an equally utopian idea. Propertius' aspirations in these directions are thus revealed as nothing more than the wishful thinking of the elegiac poet, that creature of self-admitted *nequitia*.[175]

Some further minor indications of Propertius' awareness that he is arguing humorously for an impossibility are worth noting briefly. The elegy as a whole, with its basis in the 'praise of a law' and its emphasis on rights/rules and law, has an air of pseudo-legality; and Fedeli noted the legalisms *vetat* (21), *licet* (22), *tutela* (23) and *poena* (24);[176] possibly *cura* (28) can be added.[177] There may also be a sly legal joke in Propertius' mentions of *via* (30) and *iter* (32). *via* (a 'roadway', i.e. the right to drive a vehicle) and *iter* (a 'pathway', i.e. the right to walk or ride) were in Roman law two of the four oldest 'rustic praedial servitudes' – another was *actus* (a 'driveway', i.e. the right to drive animals). These servitudes could be transferred from one Roman citizen to another only through *mancipatio*, the purely Roman method of conveying property,[178] and as such they were matters of interest to Roman citizens, and would have been especially familiar to a former law student like Propertius.[179] When Propertius qualifies *via* with *angusta*, he may be referring to juristic opinions (which employ *angustus*) about how wide the way had to be for these various rights to be acquired:

> Pomponius libro quarto decimo ad Quintum Mucium. Si tam **angusti** loci demonstratione facta **via** concessa fuerit, ut neque vehiculum neque iumentum ea inire possit, **iter** <magis quam> **via** aut actus adquisitus videbitur: sed si iumentum ea duci poterit, non etiam vehiculum, actus videbitur adquisitus. (Justinian *Digest* 8.1.13 pr.)

---

175 The view of Lana (1948) 44 that 3.14 is an attack on Augustus' 'moral' legislation (he cites Sueton. *Aug.* 44.3 where Augustus bars women from spectating male athletes) does not take account of the impossibility of Propertius' proposals.
176 Fedeli (1985) 461, 462.
177 Cf. *VJR* s.v. *cura*. For the legal implications to be felt, N's *adoratae* and O's *domi* would have to be retained in line 28.
178 Kaser² (1971) I.143, 441.
179 Cf. Prop. 4.1.133–4.

Pomponius *On Quintus Mucius Book 14*: If a roadway has been granted, but such a narrow space has been allocated to it that neither a wagon nor a beast of burden can go in through it, a pathway rather than a roadway or driveway will be deemed to have been acquired; but, if a beast of burden can be taken through it but not a wagon too, a driveway will be held to have been acquired.

Paulus libro quinto decimo ad Sabinum. **Via** constitui uel latior octo pedibus uel **angustior** potest, ut tamen eam latitudinem habeat, qua vehiculum ire potest: alioquin **iter** erit, non **via**. (Justinian *Digest* 8.3.23 pr.)

Paul *On Sabinus Book 15*: A roadway can be constituted which is either broader or narrower than eight feet, as long as it is broad enough for a wagon to go through it; otherwise it will be a pathway, not a roadway.

This joke would be in keeping with Propertius' witty exploitations of legal jargon elsewhere.[180] Propertius' light-hearted references to legal matters are thus another element of genuine humour in 3.14.

Other amusing aspects of 3.14 are its shameless hyper-eroticism and hyper-elegiacism. In the first half Propertius deliberately titillates his readers with lascivious emphases on mixed-sex nudity, inviting them to imagine themselves in sexually arousing situations, and compounding his suggestiveness through double-entendres.[181] *quod non infamis exercet corpore laudes* (3) inevitably hints – particularly in the phrase *exercet corpore* – at something more lubricious; so does *inter luctantes nuda puella viros* (4), where a naked girl placed among men 'making an effort' conjures up a second, even more indecent, picture. The steady reiteration of female nudity or semi-nudity with men looking on is also manifestly intended to be erotically stimulating: the *nuda puella* of line 4, the *pulverulenta femina* of line 7, covered with dust and therefore a naked runner as runners normally were in antiquity, the bare breasts (*nudatis mammis*) of the Amazons (13) and of Helen (*nudis papillis*, 19), and not least the *niveum latus* of line 11, given the special attractiveness of thighs to ancient audiences, always open to homoerotic interest. The repetition of these concepts is intended to rack up the audience's sexual engagement, but in doing so

---

180 E.g. Propertius 2.29A contains a tissue of comic legalisms; see Cairns (1971).
181 Cf. also Galán (1996) 38–9, 42, although perhaps slightly exaggerating this element. Propertius' source(s) may well already have shown marked interest in the erotic: on this aspect of Phylarchus (a source for Plutarch's Spartan material) see Powell (1999) esp. 401–4.

the elegist adopts a detached narrative tone which implies his ironic amusement at the effect he is contriving.[182] Then in the second half of the elegy Propertius sustains the erotic atmosphere of the first half when he repeatedly invokes absolutely unimpeded physical closeness between the Spartan lover and his mistress (21–6). He also flaunts his identity as an elegist by couching his description of love at Sparta in terms specific to a genre central to Roman erotic elegy (and Greek epigram), the *komos/paraclausi-thyron*.[183] In this genre the speaker often attempts to persuade the beloved to admit him or come out to him, and it employs a number of commonplaces which Propertius duly negates here: lovers dally at the crossroads (22); guards are not placed upon the girl (23) by her jealous *vir* (24); delays and rejections are not endured by the lover at the hands of the beloved (25–6), and (by implication) the lover does not suffer outside the beloved's closed door (28). All this creates a hyper-elegiac atmosphere throughout the second half of 3.14; and the numerous topoi of the *komos/paraclausithyron* amusingly introduce into Sparta sophisticated activities more appropriate to great cities like Alexandria and Rome. Together the two trends make 3.14 one of the most erotic elegies extant.

Helen, whose role as an exemplum of the gymnastics and the revealing clothing of Spartan girls goes back to Euripides,[184] is a key figure in 3.14's hyper-eroticism and hyper-elegiacism, but her role in the elegy, and in particular in its argumentation, perhaps needs to be clarified if the true conceptual structure of 3.14, which is subtler than it first seems, is to emerge.[185] In one set of terms the elegy divides at line 21, with 1–20 covering the physical activities of Spartan girls, and the remaining fourteen lines the consequent (*igitur*, 21) beneficial results for the love-lives of Spartan women, which contrast with the state of affairs at Rome. This division accords with the literal flow of the elegy, in which lines 15–20 compare the Spartan girl *qua* huntress to Castor and Pollux, and Helen is mentioned at lines 19–20 as an adjunct to her brothers. But if the entire passage from lines 12 to 20 is perceived as a unit, Helen acquires a more important role: the Spartan

---

182 Cf. Fedeli (1985) 450–1.

183 For this genre and the topoi mentioned, see the bibliography listed above, p. 363 n. 8.

184 See above, pp. 372–3. In Eur. *Androm*. Peleus refers slightingly to Helen (591–5) before denouncing all Spartan girls (595–601), naming Helen (602), and attacking her again (602–9).

185 Lines 15–16 are frequently transposed, either to after l. 10 or to after l. 12 (cf. Fedeli (1985) 457). These transpositions affect the current argument only minimally.

girl practises arms (11–12) as does Helen (19–20); she hunts (15–16) as do the Dioscuri (17–18). Helen now becomes, not just a companion to her brothers, but the archetypal Spartan girl gymnast. Moreover, Helen is also emblematic of the second aspect of Sparta sketched by Propertius, female sexual freedom. Like his free-loving women of lines 21–6, Helen would later elope with a lover, in her case Paris. *futurus* in line 18, although properly it refers to the Dioscuri, also hints at Helen's 'future'. Propertius might well have felt that all aspects of the freedom which he attributes to contemporary Spartan women also applied in Helen's case. If he was thinking of Helen's story in the context of that freedom, then his implications could be that Helen was able to get close to Paris since she was not under guard (cf. 23), that Menelaus did not punish Helen when he recovered her from Troy because at Sparta no terrible punishment from a puritanical husband awaits a girl (cf. 24), that no-one stood between Paris and Helen when they first met since at Sparta no intermediary is placed between lovers (cf. 25–6), and that Helen was easily seduced by Paris because at Sparta a lover gets the answer 'Yes' in double-quick time (cf. 26). All this would probably have been obvious to an ancient reader, particularly since the notion that immodest Spartan female gymnastics led to Helen's infidelity was already explicit in Euripides *Andromache* 592–604,[186] as indeed was the combination of *komos/paraclausithyron* and sexual licence which recurs in Propertius 3.14.[187]

Overall the structure of 3.14 is ring-compositional: the initial couplet (1–2) is generally laudatory of Spartan gymnastics; eight lines (3–10) treat female athletic training and sports at Sparta; a ten line central section (11–20) handles the more militaristic training of Spartan girls, eight lines (21–8) describe the free love-lives of Spartan women, four (29–32) compare the restricted experiences of Roman women; and the final couplet (33–4) awards Sparta the palm over Rome. Within the central section there is a miniature ring in which the Spartan girl training in arms (11–12) is balanced against Helen in armour (19–20); then the next innermost couplets contain two mythical paradeigmata illustrating two of the Spartan girl's activities: Amazons for her riding and arms drill (13–14), and the Dioscuri for

---

186 See also above, pp. 372–3. The notion that mixed gymnastics etc. have an erotic function and intention is already found at Plat. *Rep.* 458d and it recurs in Plut. *Lycurg.* 15.1.
187 Ἑλένην ἐρέσθαι χρὴ τάδ᾽, ἥτις ἐκ δόμων/ τὸν σὸν λιποῦσα Φίλιον ἐξεκώμασεν/ νεα-νίου μετ᾽ ἀνδρὸς εἰς ἄλλην χθόνα ('you must ask this of Helen, who, leaving your house-hold, went from home on a *komos* with a young man to another land', Eur. *Andr.* 602–4).

her hunting (17–18). That leaves as 3.14's central couplet the Spartan girl's hunt: *et modo Taygeti crinis aspersa pruina/ sectatur patrios per iuga longa canes.*

Verbal and conceptual repetitions reinforce this structure. The last couplet multiply echoes the first: *iura* appears in lines 1 and 33; *pugnas* (33) equates with *palaestrae* (1);[188] *Sparte* (1) is matched by *Laconum* (33), while *bona* (2) corresponds to *bono* (34) and *tuae* (1) to *tu* (34). There are further verbal/conceptual links throughout 3.14: *inter quos* (19) recalls *inter luctantes viros* (4); *harenis* at 17 (a virtually certain emendation)[189] literally means the sandy banks of the Eurotas, but the term also evokes the combative sports of the arena mentioned elsewhere in the elegy; *nudis papillis* (19) echoes *nuda puella* (4); *pugnis* (18) and *capere arma* (19) again equate with *palaestrae* (1); more covertly, *pugnis* (18) implies its 'etymological' derivation from *pugnas* (33);[190] *nec ... erubuisse* (20) picks up *non infamis* (3); *nudatis mammis* (13) = *nudis papillis* (19); *ense revincit* (11) and *cavo aere* (12) = *capere arma* (19); and there are others too.[191]

In formal terms the ring-compositional structure can be set down as follows:

A1	(1–2)	Praise of the Spartan palaestra and female gymnasium
B1	(3–10)	The naked gymnastics of the Spartan girls
C	(11–20)	The militaristic training of Spartan girls
		(11–12) **a1** the Spartan girl training in arms
		(13–14) **b1** compared to Amazons
		(15–16) **c1** The Spartan huntress
		(17–18) **b2** compared to the Dioscuri
		(19–20) **a2** Helen in armour
B2	(21–32)	Love at Sparta (21–8), the result of the naked or topless activities of B1 and C, and contrastingly love at Rome (29–32), with its *Tyriae vestes* (27)
A2	(33–4)	Rome should follow Sparta in her athletic (and by implication, erotic) practices

---

188 Cf. Fedeli (1985) 465–6.
189 N offers *habenis*, possibly influenced by *equis* (18).
190 See *LALE* s.vv. pugna; pugnus.
191 E.g. *qualis* (13) anticipating *qualis et* (17); *equis* (11 and 18); *Spartana* (21) = *Sparte* (1), *Laconum* (33); *patrios* (16, the specific 'Spartan' breed). For ring-compositional structures and 'cross-cutting' verbal correspondences of the types discussed here se *THPR* Ch. 8, with bibliography.

For all its seemingly casual development, the elegy uses this structure to advance a clear, logical argument in a detached and amused tone: Spartan institutions are excellent because they bring young women and young men together naked in the wrestling school, gymnasium, and school of arms. This means that in later life lovers in Sparta have free and easy access to their girlfriends. What a sad contrast Rome provides!

CHAPTER 12

Three Propemptika *for 'Caesar'*

Earlier chapters have tried to relate Propertius' œuvre to his familial and educational background, to the changing networks of patronage which supported him personally and politically, and, not least, to that characteristically Roman and highly sophisticated literary form of elegy which came to maturity in Propertius' own lifetime and to which he himself contributed so much. The attempt to place him in his elegiac setting necessitated a quest for the elusive but seemingly all-pervasive influence upon Propertius of C. Cornelius Gallus. This chapter returns to that quest, not to recapitulate or reargue positions already advanced, but to seek fresh profit from the fact that three of the four Roman elegists (Gallus, Propertius, Ovid) wrote *propemptika* for a 'Caesar'. These pieces, as well as sharing membership of a well-documented genre,[1] all handle the projected triumph of their 'Caesar', and those by Propertius and Ovid manifestly have in mind their elegiac predecessor(s). They thus constitute a three-tier elegiac sequence which embodies a continuous strand of the history of Roman elegy, and which invites diachronic analysis; this will further illuminate the place within the elegiac tradition not only of Propertius but of Ovid.[2]

Of the three *propemptika* Propertius 3.4 offers the best starting point.[3] As emphasized earlier,[4] Propertius' third elegy book, composed in its entirety in the later 20s BC, was the work of an

---

1 For the *propemptikon* and for documentation of subsequent statements about it see *GC* General Index s.v.; on Prop. 3.4 as a *propemptikon*, *GC* 185–8.
2 Wildberger (1998) 60–76 also treats these three texts as part of her analysis of Ovid's *Ars Amatoria*, and offers useful insights. Schmitzer (2002) 287–304 concentrates mainly on the Ovidian text but also introduces Prop. 3.4, and provides a valuable account of the historical and literary contexts of the two *propemptika*.
3 Naturally, Gallan aspects of Prop. 3.4 were immediately recognized by Anderson, Parsons and Nisbet (1979) 152.
4 Above, pp. 343–7.

established member of Maecenas' coterie. Whereas in his second book Propertius had only begun to move away from the celebration of his mistress Cynthia and to include praise of Maecenas and imperial panegyric, his Book 3 is much more unequivocally elevated and public in its styles and its choices of subject-matter. Its first three poems are literary programmes in which Propertius proclaims his poetic links with the Alexandrian poets Philetas and Callimachus, thus designating himself a court poet in the service of a 'king', who, like the Ptolemies in their literary manifestations, is wide-ruling and quasi-divine. Immediately after this extended prologue cycle, analogous in some of its functions to the 'Roman Odes' of Horace's third book, comes Propertius 3.4, which begins:

> Arma deus Caesar dites meditatur ad Indos,
>   et freta gemmiferi findere classe maris.
> magna, viri, merces: parat ultima terra triumphos;
>   Tigris et Euphrates sub tua iura fluent.   (3.4.1–4)

The god Caesar is planning war against the rich Indians, and to cleave with his fleet the straits of the gem-bearing sea. Great is the reward, men! The last of lands prepares triumphs; Tigris and Euphrates will flow under your jurisdiction.

The first three words are pregnant with confident implications: *arma* is the subject-matter of epic,[5] and (as Propertius already knew) the subject – and first word – of Virgil's forthcoming *Aeneid*: references to the *Aeneid* incipit continue in *viri* (3) and *cano* (9), with each term in its Virgilian order and *sedes*.[6] Immediately after *arma* in 3.4.1 comes *deus Caesar*, an open proclamation of the forthcoming and current divinity of Augustus, and an allusive reminiscence of Augustus' 'father', *divus Iulius*. In 3.4 Propertius is bidding farewell to the Roman expeditionary force setting off against Parthia in 21 BC, but he concludes his first line with the grandiloquent claim that the Romans are marching against India, one of the ends of the earth. Because India had formerly been conquered by two of the archetypal *triumphatores*, Bacchus and Alexander the Great,[7] both 'gods', Propertius' claim

---

5   The commonplace use of 'arms', 'war', and the like as shorthand for 'epic' goes back at least as far as Callim. *Aet.* fr. 1.4 Pf.: cf. Massimilla (1996) 204.

6   For Propertius' knowledge of the *Aeneid* incipit prior to its 'publication', and for his allusions to it in 3.4, see Cairns (2003).

7   Cf. *GC* 187; Du Quesnay (1976–7) 32–3; *THPR* 43–4. On 'Alexander panegyric' see esp. Bosworth (1999); Schmitzer (1990) 110; (2002) 294, with earlier bibliography; on the

anticipates the triumph prophesied for *deus Caesar* later in the elegy.[8] Given the status of its addressee (see below, pp. 413–14), this particular *propemptikon* naturally includes no element of *schetliasmos*:[9] there is no attempt, that is, to dissuade Augustus and his armies from setting out on their journey. Instead it anticipates their victorious return,[10] loaded with spoils, and the triumph which Augustus will then celebrate in Rome (11–18). Propertius imagines himself as a spectator at that triumph in the arms of his girlfriend (15, 22). There is the unspoken implication in this last fantasy that, because he is an unwarlike lover, Propertius' personal participation in the expedition is out of the question. A small 'excusatory' touch may be visible here,[11] but significantly, even in this highly encomiastic elegy Propertius adheres to the conventions of elegy which opposed love and war, and which represented the lover as unfit and unwilling for the military life.[12]

The authoritative tone of 3.4, which continues almost to its end, has something in common with the confidence in his poetic status expressed by Propertius in the three preceding elegies, but the voice of 3.4 is even more self-assured. Something of this tone derives from the *persona* adopted in 3.4 by Propertius, that of *augur*.[13] But another element is present too, which was revealed only on publication of the Gallus fragment from Qaṣr Ibrîm (fr. 2 Courtney); at least some of its lines (quoted below, p. 408) come from a similar propemptic address to another Roman army, and they provide a further explanation of Propertius' tone, namely that it derives in part from the predecessor elegy by Gallus, who because of his personal military achievements and experience had a greater right to be authoritative about such matters. While it is not certain that Gallus wrote for another Parthian expedition, a plausible argument has been made to that effect (see below, p. 408); and it would be unsurprising if Propertius was imitating a closely matched exemplar, given that Roman incursions into

---

ambivalent partial identification of Augustus with Alexander in this context see esp. Sidari (1982) 7–50.

8   Augustus in fact refused a triumph for the return of the Parthian standards, as he did all triumphs after 27 BC; on his policies in this area see Hickson (1991) esp. 137.

9   On *schetliasmos* in *propemptika* see *GC* General Index s.vv. schetliasmos, schetliastic.

10   On such anticipation as a feature of the *propemptikon* see *GC* 159–60, 186–7.

11   On excusatory *propemptika* see *GC* 11–13, 15–16, 116–17, 162–3, 246 n. 17.

12   For these conventions see esp. Spies (1930); Murgatroyd (1975). For further bibliography, Pianezzola (1987) 135–6, esp. n. 11. Among the surviving elegists Tibullus (esp. 1.7.9–12 and 1.10) comes nearest to breaching them, although he is a reluctant warrior.

13   Cf. *GC* 185, and, for another augural speaker in a *propemptikon*, *GC* 189–92.

Parthia were no novelty.[14] Rome first came into conflict with Parthia, the power which controlled the valleys of the Tigris and the Euphrates, in the last century of the Republic, over Armenia, a buffer state culturally akin to Parthia which Rome wanted to keep detached from Parthia but which Parthia constantly sought to control. Since the family sport of the Parthian royal house was murder, and since most Parthian kings came to power by making away with their father and/or brothers, Parthia was frequently unstable, and this provided a recurrent opportunity for Roman interference. Surprisingly, however, the first serious clash between Rome and Parthia came as late as 53 BC. In that year Marcus Crassus, attempting to emulate the military achievements of his fellow triumvirs, Julius Caesar and Pompeius Magnus, marched his army deep into Parthian territory, and was disastrously defeated at the battle of Carrhae. Crassus and his son were killed, 30,000 Roman soldiers died or were captured, and the standards of the Roman legions fell into Parthian hands. For Rome this was a national disaster, which impressed itself indelibly on the Roman psyche and created a strong desire for vengeance and the recovery of the lost standards. In 45/44 BC Julius Caesar was planning to march east for these purposes. His murder on the Ides of March 44 BC terminated that project. M. Antonius did invade Parthia in 36 BC. He found the Parthians as dangerous as ever, incurred heavy losses, and had to save what remained of his army by a hasty retreat. When the future Augustus assumed sole power in 31 BC, the Parthian situation was still unresolved, and early Augustan poetry is full of envisagements of the vengeance which Augustus will take on the Parthians for Carrhae.[15] In fact, the Parthian question was settled peacefully in 20 BC. The expedition to which Propertius bids farewell in 3.4 was a show of force, and negotiation achieved the return of the lost Roman legionary standards and prisoners. Augustan poets celebrated this event as a military victory, and the senate voted Augustus a triumph, which he refused; but the settlement was in fact the product of realism, since neither side had any prospect of completely dominating the other.

When the Qaṣr Ibrîm Gallus fragment came to light, some lines of it were recognized as celebrating the proposed or imminent departure of a military expedition, and as having influenced Propertius 3.4:

14 For surveys of interactions between Rome and Parthia in the relevant period see Sidari (1977–8) 35–48; Sherwin-White (1984) 218–26, 279–90, 298–337; *CAH* 9.402–3 (T. P. Wiseman); *CAH* 10.13, 21–4, 28, 30–4 (C. Pelling); 158–63 (E. Gruen).
15 For Horace's contributions cf. Seager (1980).

> fata mihi, Caesar, tum erunt mea dulcia, quom tu
> maxima Romanae pars eris historiae
> postque tuum reditum multorum templa deorum
> fixa legam spolieis deivitiora tueis.   (fr. 2.2–5 Courtney)

Its first editors believed that these lines were written about Julius Caesar's projected war against Parthia of 45/44 BC.[16] Other scholars have argued that '*Caesar*' in line 2 is the future Augustus,[17] and they have proposed various other occasions for the lines, including the Illyrian campaign of Octavianus, his war against Sextus Pompeius, and the Actian War, with consequent dates for the elegiacs ranging from 36 BC to 31 BC (or even later).[18] The evidence in any direction is slight, and consensus is unlikely ever to be reached; my own view, however, is that its first editors decided correctly in favour of Julius Caesar as the addressee of Gallus' poem, and that they rightly connected it with Julius Caesar's planned but abortive Parthian expedition of 45/44 BC.[19] There is, I believe, further support for the first editors' conclusions in the high level of intertextuality which will emerge in this chapter, not just between Propertius 3.4 and the lines of Gallus, but between both texts and the third elegiac *propemptikon* to be discussed, which, like Propertius 3.4, was again definitely for a Parthian expedition: Ovid's farewell to C. Caesar (*Ars Amatoria* 1.177–228). The multiple connections[20] between these three texts which address different men called 'Caesar' – C. Julius Caesar, his adopted 'son' Octavianus (Augustus)[21] and Augustus' grandson and 'son' by adoption, C. Caesar – make more sense if all are *propemptika* for Parthian campaigns: that of Gallus for Julius' planned expedition which never took place, that of Propertius for Augustus' show of force

---

16   Anderson, Parsons and Nisbet (1979) 151–2. (See above, p. 83, for the translation by P. J. Parsons and R. G. M. Nisbet.) It is perhaps worth recalling that, several years before the discovery of the Qaṣr Ibrîm papyrus, Du Quesnay (1976–7) 33–4 had already hypothesized that Gallus wrote a poem for the quadruple triumph of Julius Caesar in 45 BC.

17   For summaries of opinions on these and other questions, and for bibliography on the Qaṣr Ibrîm Gallus, see, e.g., Marioni (1984) 88–91, Nicastri (1984) 102–8; Courtney (1993) 259–70; Manzoni (1995) esp. 59–92.

18   It has even been proposed that the date is 30–29 BC and that the lines express opposition to Augustus' 'solution' to the Parthian problem: for details see Marioni (1984) 90 n. 9.

19   Even in the unlikely event that at some point in the future the first editors' conclusions were disproved by new evidence, this would not affect the literary arguments that follow.

20   By contrast there is a lower level of overlap between Prop. 3.4 and Ovid's other descriptions of triumphs, i.e. *Tr.* 4.2; *EP* 2.1; *EP* 3.4.

21   The future Augustus' *praenomen* was also C., but it is not recorded as used by him after his adoption. His known style thereafter is *Imperator Caesar divi f.*

of 21/20 BC and that of Ovid for the campaign of 2/1 BC led by C. Caesar.

The Gallan lines have been commented upon extensively, and many of their links with Propertius 3.4 have been covered by previous scholarship; hence the connections can be presented economically, with the addition of only a few new points. What is immediately striking is that *Caesar* appears in the same *sedes* in the second (possibly the first propemptic?) line of the Gallus papyrus, the first line of Propertius 3.4, and the first line of Ovid's *propemptikon*, and that in all three *Caesar* is preceded by two words of exactly the same shape and metrical value. Moreover, even the initial letters of some words of Gallus' line, *d* and *m*, have influenced the lines of Propertius and Ovid:

> <u>fata mihi</u>, **Caesar**, tum erunt **m**ea **d**ulcia, quom tu
> (Gallus fr. 2.2 Courtney)
>
> <u>Arma **d**e**us**</u> **Caesar d**ites **m**editatur ad Indos (Propertius 3.4.1)
>
> <u>Ecce **parat**</u> **Caesar d**omito quod **d**efuit orbi
> (Ovid *Ars Amatoria* 1.177)

The line of Gallus has also affected later lines of Propertius 3.4. Gallus' vocative *Caesar* is reflected in Propertius' vocative *viri* (3), and his mention of *fata* (2) not only influenced Propertius' *omina fausta* (9) and Propertius' prayer to Mars and Vesta that he would live long enough to see Augustus' triumph (11–13),[22] but also inspired Propertius' specific choice of *fatalia* (11). This imitative pattern is paralleled in the generous combination of Gallan terms from the Qaṣr Ibrîm papyrus which peppers a passage of an earlier elegy of Propertius, 2.1.15–19 (quoted and analysed below, p. 411). Next there is the striking correspondence between Gallus' line 3 and Propertius 3.4.10:

> maxima *Romanae* pars eris *historiae* (Gallus)
>
> ite et *Romanae* consulite *historiae* (Propertius)

where the identical words *Romanae* and *historiae* occupy the same *sedes* in both cases, and where *historiae* gives both pentameters a

---

22 Particularly if Gallus' *fata* is an anticipatory reference to his own death: for this interpretation cf. Newman (1980) 84.

quadrisyllabic ending (see Chapter 5).[23] Again, Propertius has picked up *legam* and *spoliis* from Gallus' line 5 (*fixa legam spolieis deivitiora tueis*) and has placed them in different and separate contexts within his own *propemptikon*:

> inque sinu carae nixus spectare puellae
> incipiam et titulis oppida capta **legam**   (15–16)

And leaning on my dear girl's bosom I begin to spectate and read on placards the names of captured cities.

> ante meos obitus sit precor illa dies,
> qua videam **spoliis** oneratos Caesaris axis   (12–13)

May that day come, I pray, before my death, on which I see the chariot-wheels of Caesar loaded with spoils.

In the latter passage *spoliis* occupies the same *sedes* as in Gallus, although in a hexameter not a pentameter. Gallus' *deivitiora* (5) is indirectly reflected in Propertius' initial description of the Indians as *dites* (3.4.1). Varro had derived *dives* from *divus*: *dives a divo qui ut deus nihil indigere videtur* ('*dives* [rich] is derived from *divus* [deified person], who, being a *deus* [god] seems in need of nothing');[24] so *dites* both etymologizes *deus* (1), applied by Propertius to Augustus, and confirms his allusion in *deus Caesar* to *divus Iulius*.

It is clear, then, that Propertius has exploited what survives of his Gallan model. Inevitably the question arises whether there was once more of that model, and this in turn introduces the most troublesome dilemma posed by the Gallus papyrus: are its four quatrains (1, 2–5, 6–9, 10–12) independent epigrams, or is each an extract from a different elegy, or are all, or some of them, parts of the same elegy? In favour of the idea that the papyrus contains epigrams or extracts from different elegies is the presence in it of division marks and of extra space between the quatrains. One of the papyrus' first editors opined that 'the quatrains i 2–5 and i 6–9 ... could ... be construed as part of a continuous text with i 1; and might indeed be thought less jejune in context than in isolation', but he finally concluded that the 'very wide spacing ... indicates a major division: that is, between poems'.[25] But

---

23   For other Propertian imitations (with variations) of the same Gallan line, always with allusive force, see Index II s.v. *historia*.
24   *LL* 5.92; see also *LALE* s.vv. dives, deus.
25   Anderson, Parsons and Nisbet (1979) 129.

the fact that there are connections between the different quatrains, despite their badly mutilated state, makes the question worth revisiting. The first edition observed that *tristia* (1) was the opposite of *dulcia* (2),[26] which could link the first and second quatrains, and also pointed out that *Tyria* (11) might refer to the *triumphator*'s purple cloak;[27] this would connect the second and fourth quatrains. Nevertheless the first edition's commentary refers to 'epigrams' throughout.[28] There is more to be said: part of Propertius 2.1 (15–19) contains multiple verbal reminiscences extending over lines 2–8 of the Qaṣr Ibrîm Gallus.[29] These reminiscences therefore link Gallus' second and third quatrains indirectly:

Propertius 2.1.15–19	*Gallus*
seu quidquid **fecit** sivest quodcumque locuta,	fecerunt (6)
maxima de nihilo nascitur **historia**.	maxima ... historiae (3)
quod **mihi** si tantum, Maecenas, **fata** dedissent,	fata mihi (2)
ut **possem** heroas **ducere** in arma manus	possem ... deicere! (7)
non ego Titanas canerem, non Ossan Olympo	non ego (8)

Then there is another, seemingly unnoticed, possible connection between the second quatrain (the anticipation of the triumph of 'Caesar') and the third.[30] In the third quatrain the collocation *idem tibi* in].*atur idem tibi, non ego, Visce* (8) at first sight looks unremarkable. But in extant Latin poetry prior to the fourth century AD *idem tibi* is found elsewhere only once – in the *Panegyricus Messallae*. There too it is combined with *non*, although this time *non* precedes *idem tibi*, whereas *non* follows *idem tibi* in Gallus:

non idem tibi sint aliisque triumphi ([Tibullus] 3.7.136)

This line also contains *triumphi*, and it introduces a long passage

26 Anderson, Parsons and Nisbet (1979) 141, 149.
27 Anderson, Parsons and Nisbet (1979) 147. *Tyria* is not printed as part of the fragment by Courtney (1993), although he mentions it as a word surviving in isolation (264).
28 Anderson, Parsons and Nisbet (1979) 140–8. Subsequently several other scholars have attempted to reinforce this position, or to argue that the lines are 'amoebean verse': for details see P. A. Miller (2004) 76–80.
29 Most of these reminiscences are assembled by J. F. Miller (1981), referring to earlier scholarship; he regarded the fragment as a single elegy (a *recusatio*): cf. also Newman (1980) 93–4.
30 Anderson, Parsons and Nisbet (1979) 149 lists many stylistic connections between 'the epigrams', but none of these constitute arguments for the quatrains being part of a single elegy.

dealing with Messalla's victorious campaigns and triumphs. Similarly Propertius' *historia* of 2.1.16 introduces a lengthy catalogue of epic themes which culminates at 2.1.33–4 in Augustus' Actian triumph. All this hints at a link between the second and third quatrains of the Gallus papyrus, suggesting that the third quatrain too was part of Gallus' account of the triumph of 'Caesar'. The connection of thought might have been that, with the triumph of 'Caesar' as their subject matter (quatrain 2), Gallus' verses would at last be worthy of his mistress (6–7, quatrain 3). Another hint that the third quatrain was part of the triumph of Caesar derives from the presence of Propertius' mistress at the envisaged triumph of Augustus (3.4.15): cf. Gallus' mention of his *domina* at line 7. There is, then, at least a fair possibility that all the quatrains of the Qaṣr Ibrîm papyrus come from the same Gallan elegy; and yet another indication of this will emerge later.

At this point the Gallus papyrus might seem to have exhausted its ability to throw more new light on Propertius 3.4, or on the ongoing development of propemptic and triumphal themes in Roman elegy. However, the *propemptikon* for C. Caesar at Ovid *Ars Amatoria* 1.177–228, which manifestly draws both on Propertius 3.4 and on its Gallan predecessor, might provide further insights into Gallus' influence on his successors; and, even should this hope prove illusory, the Ovidian *propemptikon* may at least reveal how Ovid saw Propertius 3.4. Ovid's piece was composed in 2 BC, when, after two decades of comparative quiet, new family murders within the Parthian royal house had once more disturbed the peace with Rome. This time C. Caesar, as the designated successor of Augustus, was sent east with an army.[31] Rome and Parthia once again settled their differences peacefully, but C. Caesar became involved in subsequent military operations in Armenia, was wounded, and eventually died of his wound in AD 4. Ovid's *propemptikon*, which like its predecessors prophesied its addressee's triumphal return to Rome after a victorious military campaign, was probably written before C. Caesar's departure from Rome; there is a *prima facie* case for suspecting that it first existed as an independent elegy and was subsequently incorporated into the *Ars Amatoria*, probably with alterations and certainly with witty additions designed to integrate it into its new context.[32]

---

31   For the public and dynastic context of the expedition see Schmitzer (2002) 284–7.
32   Cf. Pohlenz (1913) 3: 'Der Abschnitt … hebt sich von seiner Umgebung merkbar ab und ist wohl eine nachträgliche Einlage'; Syme (1978) 13–14: 'Along with the Naumachia, the digression about C. Caesar patently interrupts the sequence of operations in the chase for

Before *Ars Amatoria* 1.177–228 can be exploited to illuminate its predecessors, those of its elements which are derived from the rhetorical tradition of the *propemptikon* must be distinguished from those influenced by, or drawn from, earlier poetic *propemptika*. This distinction can be made without too much difficulty, although it requires a brief digression on the genre. A *propemptikon* is a farewell poem or speech; its speaker is the person remaining behind and its addressee is the person or persons departing. It is very well exemplified: the first poetic *propemptika* appear in Homer, and others were composed through the archaic, classical and hellenistic periods of Greek poetry. By around 60 BC Roman poets were being taught by Greek teachers how to write up-to-date poetic *propemptika* in Latin. Such a teacher was (notably) Parthenius of Nicaea, who had himself written at least one *propemptikon*, and who may well have introduced the genre to Rome.[33] Romans of this period were also studying the *propemptikon* along with other epideictic genres under rhetoricians.[34] The surviving prescription for the *propemptikon* by the late Greek rhetorician Menander Rhetor preserves many of the precepts taught for centuries in the schools of rhetoric.[35] Near its beginning Menander warns about the heterogeneous nature of the *propemptikon*: 'There are many types of *propemptikon*' (395.4–5 Spengel). Menander then distinguishes three types, using Aristotelian categories (395.5–26 Spengel):

1. the *propemptikon* of superior to inferior, especially characterized by advice.
2. the *propemptikon* of equal to equal, especially characterized by affection.
3. the *propemptikon* of inferior to superior, especially characterized by encomium.

The type of *propemptikon* most familiar to modern scholarship is the second, that of equal to equal. It includes '*schetliasmos*' (attempts to deter the departing addressee from doing so) followed by resignation, good wishes for the journey, and sometimes an anticipation of the

---

women. Not merely a digression, but an addition.' (14); Jenkyns (1993) 120. This is not to say that Ovid has failed to integrate it properly: cf. Wildberger (1998) 60–1.

33 Parthenius fr. 26 (Lightfoot), and Lightfoot (1999) General Index s.v. *propemptikon*. On Parthenius see also Indexes II and III s.v.

34 For Octavianus' early experience of the *propemptikon* and *syntaktikon* see Du Quesnay (1981) 65–6.

35 395.1–399.10 Spengel.

traveller's return. However the other two types of *propemptikon*, which do not include *schetliasmos*, are no less members of the same genre. Ovid's *propemptikon* for C. Caesar and its two Roman elegiac predecessors belong to Menander's third type, that of inferior to superior. Menander's examples of this type are speeches addressed to a governor or official who is leaving because his term of office has come to an end, or who is going from one city to another (395.24–6 Spengel). C. Caesar was a very important 'governor', and he was leaving Rome to take control of the Eastern provinces of the empire and to deal with the Parthians. According to Menander, the third type of *propemptikon* consists almost wholly of praise (395.21–2 Spengel).

The two commentators on *Ars Amatoria* 1, Hollis (1977) and Pianezzola (1991), note some of the propemptic commonplaces used by Ovid.[36] Hollis specifies as such:[37]

i. a prayer to the gods for the traveller's safety and success (203–4)
ii. a promised offering upon his return (205)
iii. the joyful anticipation of festivities when the wanderer rejoins his countrymen (213 ff.).

Pianezzola adds:[38]

iv. La profezia del ritorno vittorioso rientra nella typologia del *propemptikon* ('the prophecy of the victorious return belongs to the typology of the *propemptikon*').

These are in origin and essence poetic topoi. But the Ovidian passage also contains six further rhetorical commonplaces, which can be detected with the aid of Menander's prescription. As noted, Menander emphasizes that encomia will be a very prominent feature of this particular type of *propemptikon*. Ovid is not sparing in his encomiastic treatment of C. Caesar, and much of it is remarkably similar to what Menander prescribes.

1. Ovid devotes ten lines (181–90) to underlining his addressee's youthfulness, while Menander's addressee in his *propemptikon* prescription is characterized throughout as a young man (cf. esp. 396.2; 397.17–18; 398.15–23 Spengel).
2. Ovid compares his addressee to Bacchus and Hercules and he

---

36   They refer to *GC* for these topoi.
37   Hollis (1977) 65.
38   Pianezzola (1991) 213, referring to *GC* 185–6.

classes the 'Caesars', among them C. Caesar, as 'gods' (183–90); Menander applies to his propemptic addressee the Homeric phrase 'a hero like unto the gods' (399.8 Spengel, cf. *Odyssey* 13.89).

3.   Ovid addresses C. Caesar as *pulcherrime rerum* (213), 'fairest in the world'. This phrase, found elsewhere only in an erotic context at *Heroides* 4.125, has aroused comment. Hollis remarks 'a surprisingly informal mode of address' (81); and Pianezzola explains this 'espressione affettiva' by reference to C. Caesar's youth (214). Two passages of Menander's *propemptikon* prescription provide further illumination. In one Menander prescribes detailed description and praise of the physical beauty of his addressee (398.15–23 Spengel). In another Menander takes great pains to explain the prime role of affection in all *propemptika*. He does, of course, say that only one of his three types of *propemptikon* (the second) is specifically characterized by affection, but he also declares that no *propemptika* lack affection and that the propemptic speech always rejoices in the emotions of love (395.26–9 Spengel).[39]

Ovid makes a show of his rhetorical training both in these hellenizing commonplaces, and in three more rhetorical topoi which are shared with non-specialized encomium, viz.:[40]

4.   When Ovid starts his *propemptikon* by referring to Augustus as 'Caesar', and when he later emphasizes that Augustus is C. Caesar's 'father', and that they are both 'Caesars' (177–8, 181–4, 191–8, 203–4), Ovid is not simply justifying C. Caesar's youthful military command on the grounds of his 'divine' descent: Ovid is also covering two major standard topics of rhetorical encomium, the family and upbringing of the encomiand.

5.   The case is similar when Ovid, in a striking personification, says that *iusque piumque* will take their stance before C. Caesar's standards (200).[41] Here Ovid claims that Rome's cause is just: but he also evokes the two Greek abstractions τὸ δίκαιον (justice) and τὸ εὐσεβές (piety). In doing so Ovid introduces yet another commonplace of rhetorical encomium, the attribution to the addressee of the virtues

---

39   λέγω δὲ ταῦτα οὐκ ἀποστερῶν οὐδένα τῶν προειρημένων τρόπων τῆς προπεμπτικῆς τῶν ἐρωτικῶν παθῶν – χαίρει γὰρ ἡ προπεμπτικὴ πανταχοῦ τούτοις – ἀλλ᾽ ἐνδεικνύμενος ὅτι ὅπου μὲν μᾶλλόν ἐστιν αὐτοῖς καταχρῆσθαι, ὅπου δὲ ἐπ᾽ ἔλαττον.

40   These may be documented from, e.g., Volkmann² (1885) 314–61; Martin (1974) 177–210.

41   The phrase also occurs, although not in a personification, at Ov. *Her.* 8.4, and it is imitated, again less strikingly, by the author of the *Consolatio ad Liviam*: *et quoscumque coli est iusque piumque deos* (24).

of justice and piety. The fact that piety is 'justice concerning the gods'[42] further integrates the phrase *iusque piumque*, and of course 'justice' can stand as shorthand for virtue in its entirety,[43] i.e. for all four cardinal virtues which it was almost obligatory to attribute to rhetorical encomiands.

6. Finally, rhetorical encomium required that the encomiand's virtues be demonstrated through a description of his achievements, which was often organized under the categories 'in war' and 'in peace'. Much of Ovid's *propemptikon* covers the themes of C. Caesar's achievements in war (his future success against the Parthians) and in peace (his anticipated triumph on his homecoming). These are of course both prospective achievements, since as yet C. Caesar has not actually done anything. But temporal variation of this type, far from being a problem, is actually a standard feature of ancient generic composition.[44] Interestingly too, Menander's propemptic addressee, who is similarly at the beginning of his career (although as a rhetorician, not a general), is handled in much the same way. Menander prescribes description of his addressee's achievements – 'if you have any to describe' (397.25–6 Spengel). But for the most part Menander concentrates on what his propemptic addressee will achieve in the future: among these feats the addressee will be 'useful to the emperors when his virtue is recognized' (397.27 Spengel). In sum, then, Ovid's *propemptikon* for C. Caesar sits very well within Menander's third, encomiastic type, and it has many features indebted to Ovid's rhetorical training.

Against these rhetorical features must be set what Ovid owes to his poetic predecessors – in addition, of course, to the four poetic topoi noted by the commentators. Here modern scholarship is in a fortunate position: Ovid's technique, both in imitating poetic forebears and in self-imitation, is better known than that of many other ancient poets,[45] and it is similar in both cases: he selects a single principal model and loots it mercilessly for raw material, which he then recombines, amplifies, alters, or negates; and into this new creation Ovid freely weaves commonplaces, groups of topoi, and verbal borrowings from further sources, both poetic and rhetorical.

---

42   Cf. the summarizing 'Platonic' definition: [Plat.] *Def.* 412e.14; also Plat. *Euthyph.* 12e.5–7.
43   The *locus classicus* is Aristot. *Nic. Eth.* 1130a–b.
44   *GC* 127–8.
45   Ovid's self-imitation is particularly instructive since his source is certain: for his practice in the *Amores* and *Ars Amatoria* see, e.g., Cairns (1979b); Merkle (1983).

Sometimes the borrowed material is easily recognizable, and that will have been intentional. Ovid wanted his audience to follow up such overt clues and so come to appreciate the skill and tact of his other, less easily recognizable, borrowings. The result, despite – or perhaps because of – the varied sources upon which Ovid draws, is usually a fresh and original treatment.

Ovid's imitative technique in his *propemptikon* for C. Caesar turns out to be characteristic. His primary model is Propertius 3.4,[46] which, because it is a briefer and more concentrated *propemptikon*, affords Ovid the opportunity for his favourite practice of *amplificatio*. Ovid's indebtedness goes far beyond his echoing of *arma deus **Caesar** dites meditatur ad **Indos** ... magna, viri, **merces*** (Propertius 3.4.1–3) at ***Eoas** Latio **dux meus** addat **opes*** (*Ars Amatoria* 1.202),[47] and the general inspiration which he took from the parallel scene at Propertius 3.4.11–18 for his vision of the lover in the company of his girlfriend at a triumph (*Ars Amatoria* 1.217–28).[48] Borrowings start right at the beginning of Ovid's *propemptikon*, where (see also above, p. 409) he proclaims Propertius 3.4 as his primary model by mimicking the rhythm and word-shapes of its first hemistich (as well as the initial *d* of *deus* and *dites*), by placing *Caesar* (by whom Ovid too probably means Augustus rather than C. Caesar)[49] in the same metrical *sedes*,[50] and by glossing *ad Indos* as an end of the Roman-controlled world.

> Arma deus **Caesar d**ites meditatur ad Indos   (Propertius 3.4.1)
>
> Ecce parat **Caesar d**omito quod **d**efuit orbi
> (Ovid *Ars Amatoria* 1.177)

Borrowing continues in the *Crassi* of Ovid's injunctive third line (*Crassi gaudete sepulti, Ars Amatoria* 1.179), who derive (with variation) from Propertius' injunction to the departing army of Augustus *Crassos clademque piate* (Propertius 3.4.9);[51] in both cases the names *Crassi/Crassos* are in the same *sedes* and are accompanied by a second person plural present imperative. And there is yet more of Propertius 3.4 in Ovid's *propemptikon*, as fuller comparison of the first quatrains of the two *propemptika* reveals:

---

46 Hollis (1977) 65.
47 Hollis (1977) 78.
48 Hollis (1977) 65, 81.
49 So Hollis (1977) 73, followed by Pianezzola (1991) 210.
50 Pianezzola (1991) 210.
51 Pianezzola (1991) 210.

> ecce, <u>parat</u> Caesar domito quod defuit orbi
> addere: nunc, **Oriens <u>ultime</u>**, noster eris.
> **Parthe**, dabis poenas: **Crassi** gaudete **sepulti**,
> **signaque** barbaricas non bene passa manus.
> *(Ars Amatoria* 1.177–80)

Look, Caesar prepares to complete the conquest of the world! Now, furthest Orient, you will be ours! Parthian, you will be punished! Rejoice, buried Crassi, and you, Roman Eagles who spurned barbarian hands.

> Arma deus Caesar dites meditatur ad Indos,
> et freta gemmiferi findere classe maris.
> magna, **viri**, merces: <u>parat</u> **<u>ultima</u>** terra triumphos;
> *Tigris* et *Euphrates* sub tua iura fluent;
> (Propertius 3.4.1–4, tr. on p. 405)

Ovid employs four vocatives (emboldened) to emulate Propertius' single vocative, *viri* (3); and Ovid will later repeat twice his apostrophe of 'the Parthian' (211–12). Ovid moves Propertius' *parat* (3) up to his own initial line (177), changing its subject and sense; he also transforms Propertius' *ultima terra* into *Oriens ultime*, and he will later pick up Propertius' reference in 3.4.1 to 'the Indians' with a line describing Bacchus' effect on them: *cum timuit thyrsos India victa tuos* (190). Again, Propertius' prophetic assertion (3.4.4) that the two rivers of Mesopotamia will come under Roman rule is wittily reworked by Ovid at 223–4:

> hic est *Euphrates*, praecinctus harundine frontem:
> cui coma dependet caerula, *Tigris* erit.

'This is the Euphrates, forehead crowned with reeds; the one with blue hair hanging down will be the Tigris.'

where pictures of the conquered Tigris and Euphrates (in reverse order) will be carried in C. Caesar's triumphal procession – so Propertius' prophecy will finally be fulfilled! Propertius' later reference to the Parthian practice of shooting their arrows in flight, <u>tela fugacis</u> <u>equi</u> *et bracati militis arcus* (17), is reprised by Ovid in:

> tergaque Parthorum Romanaque pectora dicam,
> <u>telaque</u>, ab averso quae iacit hostis <u>equo</u>.
> qui <u>fugis</u> ut vincas ... Parthe ...   (209–11)

I will sing of the backs of Parthians and the breasts of Romans and the
arrows the foe shoots from retreating horse. You who flee to conquer,
Parthian ...

with amplification (including no less than three references to an
etymology of *Parthi*),[52] and with removal of the Parthians' trousers.
Ovid possibly found the very concept of trousers inelegant, and, since
bracae is in any case a Gallic word, his Latin linguistic purism (on
which see also below, p. 420 and n. 56) was perhaps another factor in
his avoidance of it, and in his implied criticism of Propertius for
having used it. Ovid may also have felt that the term's Gallic origin
made it even more inappropriate when applied to Parthians.[53]

Again, there are many further minor verbal imitations and echoes
of Propertius by Ovid which can be reported summarily. When the
corresponding terms also appear in the same *sedes*, this is indicated by
an asterisk (*):

Propertius 3.4	Ovid *Ars Amatoria* 1.177–228
arma (1, cf. *armigeri* 8)	*arma* (191, 197), *armis* (201)
*Caesar** (1), *Caesaris* (13)	*Caesarque* (177*, 203*), *Caesaribus* (184)
iura (4)	*iura* (196), *iusque* (200)
Partha (6)	*Parthe* (179, 211, 212), *Parthi* (201), *Parthorum* (209)
*equi** (8), *equos** (14), *equi* (17)	*equo** (210), *equis** (214)
omina (9)	*omen* (212)
piate (9)	*pia* (199)
Mars pater (11)	*Marsque pater Caesarque pater* (203), cf. *patris* (191, 192), *pater ... patris* (196), *genitor patriae* (197), *parente* (198) – and see below, p. 420.[54]
*oneratos** (13)	*onerati** (215)
*puellae** (15)	*puellae** (217)
*tela** (17)	*tela* (199), *telaque** (210, see above)
duces (18, cf. *ducite* 8)	*duces* (215, 227), *ducem* (181), *dux* (202)

Then there are the conceptual equivalences between the two poets
where different terms are used. Ovid's *opes* (202) does duty for

---

52 See *LALE* s.v. Parthi, where the term is equated with *exules*. Presumably all Augustan
poetic passages associating the Parthians with *fuga* allude directly or indirectly to this same
etymology.

53 Phraates' sons, then living in Rome, are referred to at *AA* 1.195–8. Their presence must
have enhanced Roman awareness of things Parthian.

54 For useful comments on Mars and *pater* in this context see Schmitzer (2002) 290.

Propertius' *merces* (3), *spoliis* (13) and *praeda* (21). Ovid refers to the Roman standards lost at Carrhae, but by now restored, and to C. Caesar's standards using Latin *signa – signaque* (180), *signis* (200) – whereas Propertius had used the Graecism *tropaea* allusively of the Parthian arms which Augustus' forces would capture and dedicate to Jupiter (6). Propertius' *omina fausta cano* (9) reappears in two different Ovidian passages as *auspiciis* (191, 192) and *auguror* (205). *regum* stands in Ovid (219) for Propertius' oriental *duces* (18), although Ovid also employs *duces* twice (215, 227) when referring to the same or a similar group. Elegance and love of *variatio* seem to have dictated most of Ovid's verbal substitutions. His failure to use *tropaea* may be accidental since elsewhere he was untroubled by it, as were many Latin poets, starting with Accius and including most of Ovid's contemporaries.[55] The fact that *tropaea* is not found in Tibullus, another poet linked, like Ovid, with that lover of correct latinity Messalla Corvinus,[56] could, however, mean that Tibullus was practising an even more rigorous Latin linguistic purism.

In small numbers such verbal overlaps and equivalences might be judged the result of shared subject-matter, and hence insignificant. But in the numbers found here they rather illustrate one of Ovid's major skills, his ability to exploit the work of his predecessors in order to add layers of meaning and allusiveness. Ovid had clearly selected Propertius 3.4 as his principal source of inspiration, and, in accordance with his standard practice, he drew more widely on the works of the poet who had composed his chosen model; moreover, and again in conformity to his usual pattern, Ovid inserted additional material from a number of other sources: these range from the Arval Hymn, whence he and Propertius drew their invocations of *Mars pater*, to the work of near-contemporaries such as Virgil and Horace.[57]

Some of the features of Propertius 3.4 imitated by Ovid go back ultimately to Gallus, as Ovid was, of course, aware. Thus the resemblances already noted between the first lines of Propertius' and Ovid's *propemptika* and the second line of the Gallus papyrus are not just the result of Propertius imitating Gallus, and of Ovid then imitating Propertius. Rather Ovid has 'looked through' Propertius to his Gallan

---

55   Cf. *OLD* s.v. *tropaeum*.
56   The evidence for Messalla's linguistic purism is collected by Valvo (1983) 1676.
57   For all these literary debts see Hollis (1977) 65–82; Pianezzola (1991) 209–16.

model.[58] This is shown in particular by the subtle partial overlap of *quom* (Gallus) and *quod* (Ovid):

fata mihi, Caesar, tum erunt mea dulcia, quom tu
                                    (Gallus fr. 2.2 Courtney)

Arma deus Caesar dites meditatur ad Indos   (Propertius 3.4.1)

ecce parat Caesar domito quod defuit orbi
                                    (Ovid *Ars Amatoria* 1.177)

Similarly the four vocatives which Ovid places in his first and second couplets (*Oriens ultime* in the first; *Parthe, Crassi sepulti* and *signaque* in the second), as well as paying homage to Propertius' one vocative (*viri*, 3) of his second couplet, also hark back to Gallus' vocatives: *Caesar* (2), *Visce* (8) and *Kato* (9).[59] Yet again, Gallus' thematically closer mention of his *fata* (2), as well as Propertius' *fatalia* (3.4.11), may have prompted Ovid's *ergo erit illa dies* (213), itself independently suggestive of Gallus.[60]

If Ovid's use of these elements of the Qaṣr Ibrîm Gallus is indeed semi-independent of Propertius, then a possible new approach, both to the Gallus fragments and to Ovid's *propemptikon*, is indicated. On the hypothesis that Gallus' propemptic second quatrain anticipating Caesar's triumph is part of a longer elegy containing further propemptic and triumphal elements, then we might look in Ovid's *propemptikon* for reminiscences of the lost portion of that elegy of Gallus. Some encouragement for this approach might come from an apparently unobserved overlap between the Gallus fragments and Ovid's *propemptikon*, provided, of course, that it is deemed significant. They share two further terms utterly banal in themselves but with powerful associations: *carmina* (Ovid 205 = Gallus 6) and *dignus* (Ovid 188) = *digna* (Gallus 7). These words together make up Gallus' famous phrase *carmina* .../... *digna* (6–7), so often imitated by subsequent Roman poets.[61] The difference in case and number between

---

58   This practice (variously named) was first identified, and ancient consciousness of it demonstrated, by Du Quesnay (1976) 55 and n. 213, 99. For further documentation, bibliography, and examples see *VAE* 194–5; Nelis (2001) General Index s.vv. double allusion; looking through.

59   Provided, of course, that Gallus 8–9 are part of the same poem as 2–3.

60   Cf. also Virg. *Ecl.* 4.53–4, preceding a passage of acknowledged Gallan content (Orpheus, Linus, Calliope, Pan), and *Ecl.* 8.7–9, verbally closer to Ovid (esp. *en erit umquam/ ille dies*, 7–8), and again reminiscent of Gallus: cf. *totum ... per orbem* (9).

61   See, e.g., Anderson, Parsons and Nisbet (1979) 144; Hinds (1983); Cairns (1993); Index II s.vv.

dignus (Ovid 188) and *digna* (Gallus 7) might be thought to detract from the value of *dignus* as an echo of Gallus; but grammatical variation does not significantly weaken an argument for imitation in ancient poetry.[62] The fact that the terms are so widely separated in Ovid and come in reversed order presents a greater difficulty: indeed, if *carmina digna* were not so absolutely diagnostic of Gallus, and if Ovid's *propemptikon* were not the linear descendant of the Qaṣr Ibrîm fragment, the Ovidian repetition of *carmina* and *dignus(a)* could comfortably be dismissed as a coincidence.

But, as things are, this possible signal of the further presence of Gallus in Ovid's *propemptikon*, which would also provide a new argument for the third Gallan quatrain having being part of his triumph poem, cannot be abandoned without further thought, particularly since Ovid's attitude to Gallan *imitatio* was not straightforward, as can be illustrated by a less fragile Ovidian case which also both assists with the *carmina/dignus* problem and leads to a new Gallan verbal complex. A couplet from Ovid *Heroides* 17 offers, in inverse order and split between its two lines, the Gallan phrase *iudice te vereor* (9):

> sic illas *vereor*, quae, si tua gloria vera[63] est,
> *iudice te* causam non tenuere duae.   (*Heroides* 17.243–4)

Ovid's re-use of this Gallan phrase is clearly no coincidence: and the line immediately preceding this couplet is

> parta per arbitrium <u>bina</u> **tropaea** TUUM   (*Heroides* 17.242)

which contains the military/triumphal term *tropaea* in the same form and *sedes* as in Propertius 3.4.6:

> assuescent Latio Partha **tropaea** <u>Iovi</u>.   (Propertius 3.4.6)

This collocation of *vereor* .../ *iudice te* with *tropaea* in *Heroides* 17 again links Gallus' third quatrain indirectly with his second, triumphal quatrain, and, of course, it suggests that *tropaea* appeared in Gallus' *propemptikon* for 'Caesar'. A listing of the other examples of *tropaeum* in pentameters strengthens this suggestion:

---

62   Cf., e.g., the variation *viri* (Prop.) = *virum* (Virg.) in Prop. 3.4's anticipation of the *Aeneid* incipit (above, p. 405).

63   *vera* has the look of being an 'etymology' of *vereor*; if so, it is otherwise unattested.

regiaque Aemilia vecta **tropaea** rate.	(Propertius 3.3.8)
Maecenatis erunt vera **tropaea** fides.	(Propertius 3.9.34)
differat in pueros ista **tropaea** SUOS	(Propertius 4.6.82)
si cui fama fuit per avita **tropaea** decori.	(Propertius 4.11.29)
et refer ad patrios <u>bina</u> **tropaea** <u>deos</u>	(Ovid *Remedia Amoris* 158)
ponite de nostra <u>bina</u> **tropaea** domo	(Ovid *Heroides* 4.66)
et tulit e capto nota **tropaea** <u>viro</u>	(Ovid *Heroides* 9.104)
ingenii videas magna **tropaea** TUI	(Ovid *Heroides* 21.214)

stentque super vinctos trunca **tropaea** <u>viros</u>
(Ovid *Ex Ponto* 3.4.104)[64]

All these lines use the form *tropaea*, and they all place it in the same *sedes* as in Propertius 3.4.6 and *Heroides* 17.242. Other similarities appear when *tropaea* is followed by a pronominal adjective, or by forms of *vir* or *deus*, or by a god's name. All this seems indicative of an influential forebear who used *tropaea* in this *sedes* – and he could hardly be other than Gallus. Even the three placements of *bina* before *tropaea* may be not of Ovid's own devising, if Virgil *Georgics* 3.30–3, part of his description of the imaginary temple memorializing Octavianus' victories, can be relied upon. This Virgilian passage is certainly not the inspiration for the triumphal *propemptika* under discussion, but it nevertheless also proffers the motifs of 'two *tropaea*' and 'Parthians shooting arrows in flight':

> addam urbes Asiae domitas pulsumque Niphaten
> fidentemque fuga Parthum versisque sagittis;
> et <u>duo</u> rapta manu diverso ex hoste **tropaea**
> <u>bisque</u> triumphatas utroque ab litore gentis.

I will add Asia's vanquished cities, the routed Niphates, the Parthian, whose trust is in flight and backward-shot arrows, the two trophies torn perforce from far-sundered foes and the nations on either shore that yielded twofold triumphs. (tr. H. R. Fairclough)

---

64 Cf. also the Ovidian hexameters: *digna Giganteis haec sunt delubra tropaeis* (*Fast.* 5.555); *deque tropaeorum, quod sol incenderit, auro* (*EP* 2.1.41).

It thus confirms the impression given by the pentameter *tropaea* group that Gallus lies behind the reappearances of this motif, both in his elegiac successors and in *Georgics* 3.33–4. Indeed it is hard to resist the further speculations that Gallus too in his *propemptikon* for 'Caesar' wrote of 'twin *tropaea*' – Virgil's *bisque* being an indirect hint at the form (*bina*) used by Gallus, which Ovid simply followed – and that Gallus too had exploited the 'Parthians shooting arrows in flight' topos to which Propertius (3.4.17) and Ovid (209–11) both refer in their own *propemptika*. In sum, then, what can be deduced from *Heroides* 17.242–4 also gives further encouragement to the view that the joint appearance of *carmina* and *dignus* in Ovid's *propemptikon* is more likely to be the product of design than chance.

To enable further progress in detecting traces of Gallus in Ovid's *propemptikon* those techniques established vis-à-vis Propertius in earlier chapters must be recalled to duty. Gallus' strong interest in a group of words associated by ancient etymological theory, *nomen*, *nota*, *notus* and other parts of *noscere*, has already been documented;[65] and Gallan input into Ovid's *propemptikon* is shown in its use of such terms. *nescire* too appears in Ovid as part of this word-group, which further confirms that *nescire* (and *nescius*) were Gallan:[66]

> tale rudimentum tanto sub **nomine** debes (193)
>
> atque aliqua ex illis cum regum **nomina** quaeret (219)
>
> et quae **nescieris**, ut bene **nota** refer (222)
>
> ille vel ille, duces; et erunt quae **nomina** dicas (227)

Also visible in Ovid's *propemptikon* is another Gallan verbal complex (*animus/anima*), earlier linked with Gallus on the basis of Propertius 1.5.12, 1.13.17 and 1.20.1–2, all from elegies addressed to Gallus.[67] The Ovidian lines are:

---

65   See Index II s.vv. *nomen* (*nomina erunt*), *nosco/nota* (*notus*).
66   For the appearances of *nescius* and *nescire* in Propertian lines associated with Gallus, and especially that of *nescire* in an almost certain Gallan quotation (*nescit amor priscis cedere imaginibus*, 1.5.24), see Index II s.v. *nescio/nescius* (*nescit amor*).
67   Cf. Index II s.v. *anima/animus*. The strong Lucretian flavour of *animus* and *anima* is not a counter-argument to the notion that they have a special Gallan association; indeed in this they parallel the diagnostic Gallan *carmina ... digna* collocation, which also has a Lucretian analogue (and probably origin): cf. Cairns (1993) 108–11 and Index II s.vv. *carmen* (*carminibus*), *dignus* (*carmina digna*).

auspiciis **animisque** patris, puer, arma movebis,
et vinces **animis** auspiciisque patris   (191–2)

o desint **animis** ne mea verba tuis   (208)

diffundetque **animos** omnibus ista dies   (218)

In lines 191–2 the Gallan complex usefully argues for the readings *animisque* (191) and *animis* (192) against the alternative readings *annisque* and *annis*.[68] Additional support for *animisque* and *animis* may come from three poetic collocations of *auspicium* with *animus* which seem to imply that these terms were somehow associated in augural contexts:

nunc ab auspicio bono profecti,
mutuis **animis** amant amantur   (Catullus 45.19–20)

en huius, nate, auspiciis illa incluta Roma
imperium terris, **animos** aequabit Olympo   (Virgil *Aeneid* 6.781–2)

nunc fateor; volui revocare **animusque** ferebat;
substitit auspicii lingua timore mali   (Ovid *Heroides* 13.85–6).[69]

A final possible Gallan import into Ovid's *propemptikon* is the striking term *rudimentum*, which appears in one of the four Ovidian lines containing *nomen* quoted above (193). Propertius does not employ *rudimentum*, which is found only in hexameters and which overall has an epic rather than an elegiac flavour. But the pattern of its distribution in classical Latin poetry up to the end of the first century AD is consistent with the hypothesis that Gallus introduced it into poetry, or at least employed it conspicuously:

dura **rudimenta**, et nulli exaudita deorum   (Virgil *Aeneid* 11.157)

tale **rudimentum** tanto sub nomine debes
                                            (Ovid *Ars Amatoria* 1.193)

turpe **rudimentum**, patriae praeponere raptam
                                            (Ovid *Heroides* 5.97)

prima **rudimenta** et iuvenes exegimus annos   (*Ciris* 45)

---

68   Pianezzola (1991) 22 printed *animisque* and *animis*, Hollis (1977) 8 *annisque* and *annis*. For earlier contributions to the problem see Pianezzola (1991) 211–12. Most recently Schmitzer (2002) 295–6 has noted factors which would speak for *annisque* and *annis*.
69   Plaut. *Asin.* 374–5 might constitute another example (*nomen* appears in 374!).

grata **rudimenta**; Herculeo sub nomine pendent
(Valerius Flaccus *Argonautica* 3.600)

nava **rudimenta** et primos in Marte calores   (Silius *Punica* 1.549)

clara **rudimenta** et castrorum dulce vocaret   (Statius *Silvae* 5.2.9)

cruda **rudimenta** et teneros formaverit annos
(Statius *Achilleid* 1.478)

The *sedes* of *rudimentum*(*a*) is the same in all these examples, and it is always preceded by an adjective in agreement. The *sedes*, of course, results from its metrical intransigence, and so is no argument for anything, but the very unmanageability of *rudimentum/a* sharpens the question why these poets troubled to employ it. Particularly significant are the examples from the *Aeneid*, given the close relations between Gallus and Virgil, and from the *Ciris*, given the heavy and acknowledged influence of Gallus on certain poems of the *Appendix Vergiliana*, including *Ciris*. Ovid's use of *rudimentum* at *Ars Amatoria* 1.193 would be an additional point favouring a Gallan origin for it, even if it did not occur there in combination with Gallan *nomine*.

Another interesting aspect of *rudimentum*(*a*) is that the adjectives accompanying it often appear to be commenting on it, whether or not this amounts to full-blown 'etymologizing' by synonym or antonym.[70] This does not happen in *Ars Amatoria* 1.193, but Virgil's *dura* (*dur*-reversing *rud*-?) and *Heroides* 5.97's *turpe* seem to illustrate the first element of *rudimentum*, as does *Achilleid* 1.478's *cruda*, which also incorporates it, while *Ciris* 45's *prima* glosses the whole word. Contrariwise Valerius Flaccus' *grata*, Silius' *nava* (but cf. *primos*) and *Silvae* 5.2.9's *clara* are in their different ways antonymic. Such varied linguistic comment[71] confirms that *rudimentum/a* held a special value for poets employing it; and it suggests both that they knew who had introduced it into Latin poetry, and that it had arrived there similarly commented. A further point emerges from an unlikely source: Valerius Flaccus' *grata rudimenta; Herculeo sub nomine pendent* (3.600), like Ovid's *tale rudimentum tanto sub nomine debes*, combines *rudimentum/a* with *sub nomine*. This might have been dismissable as a

---

70   Cf. Cairns (1996) 27: 'Etymology: Type 3'; O'Hara (1996) 64–6; Michalopoulos (2001) 11–12.

71   The fact that it became a technical term for initial military service (cf. Lyne (1978) 120), which many young Romans of the upper classes performed, must have stimulated this interest.

coincidence but for the *Argonautica* context: Valerius Flaccus is describing Hercules' frantic search and calls for the lost Hylas. The poet then relates that the Argonauts are delaying resumption of their voyage not because they like the youthful Hylas (although they all do), but because they are missing Hercules with his great reputation: *morae est nec parvus Hylas, quamquam omnibus aeque/ grata rudimenta; Herculeo sub nomine pendent* (3.599–600). It cannot be a coincidence that *rudimenta* and *Herculeo sub nomine* present themselves in combination in the very myth which Propertius too had narrated in his highly Gallan elegy 1.20 – a myth for which Propertius certainly drew on Cornelius Gallus and which very probably came to Gallus (and to Propertius) from the works of Gallus' poetic master, Parthenius.[72] It can, then, be proposed with some confidence that *rudimentum/a* was employed by Gallus, probably with linguistic comment, and that Augustan and later poets knew this and reintroduced it as a specifically Gallan term.

Beyond this only thematic comparisons can reveal more about the possible impact of lost portions of Gallus' triumphal *propemptikon* on those of Propertius and Ovid, and, as already emphasized,[73] in this area even greater caution is needed than when verbal influence is being sought. A minor item first: Propertius imagines himself watching the triumph of Augustus, but his role at that future date will be restricted to applauding (3.4.22). Ovid on the other hand undertakes to compose celebratory verses in high epic style for C. Caesar's triumphal return in accordance with a vow: *votivaque carmina reddam/ et magno nobis ore sonandus eris* (205–6). This topic is certainly an addition to Propertius' repertoire, and as such may be suspected of deriving from Gallus. Indeed Ovid's *reddam* might hint at Gallus' surviving *reditum* (fr. 2.4 Courtney). No ancient etymological text links *reddo* and *redeo* or their cognates, but elsewhere Ovid does juxtapose them: *si perstas certare, locum redeamus in illum;/ redde hostem vulnusque tuum solitumque timorem* (*Metamorphoses* 13.77–8). Horace too employed this combination conspicuously in connection with the return of Augustus from a foreign military expedition: *maturum reditum pollicitus patrum/ sancto concilio, redi./ lucem redde tuae, dux bone, patriae* (*Odes* 4.5.3–5), and the trend continues

---

72   Cf. Ch. 7.
73   Above, pp. 104–7.

in subsequent poetry.[74] All this gives ground for thinking that 'etymology' rather than mere assonance was involved, and again Gallus seems a good fit for the predecessor who influenced his successors.[75] There could, then, be both a conceptual and a verbal reminiscence of Gallus in Ovid's *votivaque carmina reddam*. Indeed, if Gallus promised verses for the triumphant return of his 'Caesar', these could be the same verses – but only if his claim is made retrospectively from a future standpoint – which allowed Gallus to claim that 'the Muses have finally composed *carmina* worthy of my mistress' (fr. 2.6–7 Courtney).[76]

Ovid's *propemptikon* handles *in extenso* two further themes touched on only briefly by Propertius. These deserve attention for their intrinsic interest as well as for their possible Gallan origin. The first is the divinity of 'Caesars'. Propertius begins (3.4.1) by referring in a single word – *deus* – to 'the god Caesar', by whom he means Augustus. But Ovid gives more space to the divine aspects of C. Caesar, and of the imperial house in general (181–90, 203–4). Ovid starts with the allusive and topical *ultor* ('avenger') of line 181 (the temple of Mars Ultor in the Forum Augustum was dedicated in the same year, 2 BC. He then proceeds to characterize implicitly all the 'Caesars', starting no doubt with Julius Caesar, as 'gods' (183–4). Next *ingenium caeleste* ('a divine mind', 185) reiterates the notion of divinity and so provides a transition to Ovid's specific comparisons of C. Caesar with Hercules and Bacchus in lines 187–90. When Ovid resumes the same theme (203–4), it is again to link Augustus with Mars and so cap his earlier allusive *ultor* of line 181, and to hail Augustus explicitly as a future god. It could be argued that the difference between Ovid's treatment and Propertius' highly honorific but brief *deus Caesar* is due simply to Ovid's love of *amplificatio*. But, on the other hand, talk of Julius Caesar's divinity was very much in the air in 45/44 BC,[77] and so would have been germane to the historical context within which, on the view accepted in this chapter, Gallus' lines were composed. Hence it was possibly a prominent topic of Gallus' *propemptikon* for Julius Caesar. Again, Ovid's comparisons

---

74 E.g. *ira frater abiecta redit/ partemque regni reddit et lacerae domus/ componit artus teque restituit tibi*. (Senec. *Thyest.* 431–3); *sed moti redeunt iubente uento/ reddunturque sibi* ... (Mart. 10.83.4–5).
75 Lucretius does not exemplify this word-play/etymology.
76 The alternative, suggested above, p. 412, is that Gallus' words refer to the *propemptikon* for Caesar in which they occur.
77 Weinstock (1971) esp. 186–8.

of C. Caesar to Hercules and Bacchus are specific to a triumphal context. The pair were not just heroes deified for general services to mankind: Bacchus was a world-conqueror and *triumphator*, and Hercules was emblematic of his 'descendant', Alexander the Great, another archetypal *triumphator*.[78] Hence Bacchus and Hercules may well have been mentioned by Gallus in connection with the future triumph of Julius Caesar.

The second theme which Ovid's *propemptikon* handles at greater length (213–28) and in greater detail than does Propertius in 3.4 (13–18) is the future triumph. Ovid may have taken his cue here from Gallus, and there are some contextual indications that elements of Ovid's expansive account do hark back to Gallus: three of Ovid's four evocations of Gallus' *nomen* interest – *nomina* (219), *nota* (222) and *nomina* (227)[79] – appear within his triumph description. A rare collocation adds further support to this proposal: whereas *erit* and *nomen* are often juxtaposed in Roman poetry, the plurals *erunt* and *nomina* are very infrequent in combination. Apart from Ovid's line 227 (*ille vel ille duces, et erunt quae nomina dicas*) and Plautus *Asinaria* 131–2, a passage with no connection to Ovid 227, *erunt* and *nomina* are found together only twice: in *haec tum **nomina** erunt, nunc sunt sine **nomine** terrae* (Virgil *Aeneid* 6.776), and in *iunctaque semper erunt nomina nostra tuis* (Ovid *Amores* 1.3.26). Of these two, the *Aeneid* passage has no known link with Gallus, but *Amores* 1.3.26 is the final and climactic line of an elegy with numerous other strong associations with him.[80] Allusion to a Gallan use of combined *erunt* and *nomina* can therefore be hypothesized with some security in Ovid's description of the triumphal procession of C. Caesar.

Gallan influence alone cannot, however, fully explain the greater length and detail of Ovid's account. Ovid needed to integrate his originally independent *propemptikon* into *Ars Amatoria* 1, which at this point was recommending public shows as opportunities to pick up girls; so he will have needed to expand his earlier version so as to highlight the triumph as an occasion on which young men would be able to associate with *puellae* and to impress them. There is certainly humour in this passage, and it may have been introduced during Ovid's rewriting, but its precise meaning and implications are curiously hard to pin down. The *puellae* watching the triumph along

---

78   Cf. above, p. 405 n. 7.
79   Also *nescieris* (222), if it belongs to this complex.
80   Cf. Cairns (1993).

with the young men (217) will ask them the names of the captured Parthian 'kings' (*regum*, 219; cf. *duces*, 227) who are being paraded in the procession, and of the 'places' (*loca*),[81] 'mountains', and 'waters' which are being carried past in representation (220)[82] – or the young men will give the *puellae* unsought information (221). Why do the girls need to ask what is represented (a question, incidentally, not posed by commentators)? As Ovid knew, the images of towns, and probably of all significant items in triumphal processions, were accompanied by placards naming them.[83] An obvious answer might be that the girls are illiterate: although elegiac *doctae puellae* like Propertius' Cynthia were cultivated and literate,[84] this cannot be assumed about all erotically available Roman girls,[85] so Ovid was perhaps making a sly joke at female expense. But what follows reopens the question. Ovid invites the young men to invent the answers when they do not know them (222), as he does again in lines 227–8, without explaining why they might not know them. Line 222 could refer to details other than the names of the processional items, but line 227 definitely specifies names (*nomina*). So why should the young men sometimes be able, and sometimes be unable, to give the correct names? And might Ovid have become so careless in his quest for humour that, when amusing himself further at the expense of the *puellae* by hinting that any invented answer will satisfy them, he failed to realize that this joke was inconsistent with the partial male literacy implied by him a few lines before?

Such carelessness on Ovid's part is implausible, particularly since everything in this area suggests very careful composition. Ovid reiterates in 223–7 the topics of 219–20 with painstaking use of chiasmus, and he rounds off each segment with an invitation to the

---

81 In Ovid's reprise of this passage in lines 223–7 one of the 'places' is *Danaeia Persis* (225), which should be that region of the Parthian empire (although P. R. Hardie (2002) 310 takes *Danaeia Persis* as 'the Persians descended from Danae'), and another is a city (*urbs*, 226); so *loca* would seem to cover both regions and towns.

82 For the triumphal procession see *RE* s.v. Triumphus coll. 502–10 (W. Ehlers).

83 For *tituli* displayed at triumphs, and for the representations of individuals, towns, tribes, mountains, rivers, etc. carried in triumphal processions, see Fedeli (1985) 168–9, and esp. *RE* s.v. Triumphus coll. 502–3 (W. Ehlers), assembling the ancient evidence. Placards identifying the booty can be seen in the relief-sculptures of triumphal processions on the Arches of Titus and Trajan: see below, p. 432 n. 88.

84 Cf. Prop. 1.2.27–30; 2.3.21–2.

85 Ovid's claim (*AA* 1.31–4, cf. *Tr.* 2.247–52, 303–4; *EP* 3.3.49–58) that his *Ars* is concerned only with affairs with *meretrices* is patently disingenuous, but prostitutes undoubtedly featured largely in the erotic life of young Roman men, and they are the *puellae* of this context.

youths to invent what they do not know. The equations become exact
if we assume either that *Armenios* (225) implies *Armenios montes* (cf.
220) or that Ovid is thinking of the Armenians as 'mountain-
dwellers'; the pattern is:

a1	'kings/leaders' (219)
b1	*loca* (220)
c1	*montes* (220)
d1	*aquae* (220)
	et quae nescieris, ut bene nota refer (222)
d2	*Euphrates, Tigris* (223–4)
c2	*Armenios* (225)
b2	*Danaeia Persis, urbs* (225–6)
a2	'kings/leaders' (227)
	si poteris, vere, si minus, apta tamen (228)

Such meticulousness in the ordering of material is inconsistent with
conceptual sloppiness; and another of Ovid's self-imitative reworkings[86] of the triumphal section of his *Ars Amatoria propemptikon*,
Tristia 4.2, poses the same problem with no mention of *puellae*. There
lines 19–20 declare without qualification that the entire *populus* will
read the triumphal placards:

> ergo omnis populus poterit spectare triumphos,
> cumque ducum titulis oppida capta leget.

So all of the people will be able to view the triumphs, and along with
the placards of the leaders will read <the names of> captured cities.

However, a few lines later the same reading difficulty and invention of
answers recur – without gender discrimination:

> quorum pars causas et res et nomina quaeret,
> pars referet, quamvis noverit illa parum.   (*Tristia* 4.2.25–6)

Some of them will ask about the reasons and the objects and the names,
and others will tell, although they know too little.

Tristia 4.2 then continues, slightly surprisingly, with a long, detailed,
and rather well-informed account of the imagined triumphal

---

86   *Tr.* 4.2; *EP* 2.1; 3.4. For a recent treatment of Ovid's triumph poems from another
viewpoint see P. R. Hardie (2002) 307–13.

procession (27–56) given by a member of the *populus*, although the information about the *duces* (27–36) does not include their names but only their relative statuses and their 'crimes' against Rome.

It might be suggested that *Tristia* 4.2.25–6, being a reminiscence of Ovid's own earlier account of a triumph in the *Ars Amatoria*, is not fully integrated into its new context. That, however, would be a despairing verdict.[87] A better approach might be to see Ovid reflecting in both elegies the confused and confusing real-life experience of spectators at a Roman triumph: the illiterates among the crowds (including many females) cannot read the labels identifying the exhibits, and so they ask their neighbours for information; other, mainly male and literate, attendees nevertheless have problems discerning the *tituli* because they are too far back in the crowd. No actual triumphal placard has survived from antiquity, but, on the presumption that those depicted in the triumphal reliefs on the Arches of Titus and Trajan[88] are to scale – a presumption confirmed by the scale accuracy of the Menorah also represented on the Arch of Titus[89] – then distant spectators would indeed have found the *tituli* difficult to read, even though formal Roman processions moved slowly.[90] Another relevant factor is the strange Parthian (and German) names on Ovid's placards.[91] Aided by iconography the young men of *Ars Amatoria* will easily identify the Euphrates (223) and Tigris (224) as those rivers; and similarly they will conjecture the identity of the 'Armenians'/ 'Armenian mountains', and will recognize 'Persia' (225), again probably helped by a representation of Danaë. But when it comes to the barbarous nomenclature of the *urbs* of line 226 and of the Parthian leaders (227), recognition and pronunciation will become more problematic. That could explain why the youths are urged at 222 to make up what they do not know, and why, although they are in effect reminded at 227 that the names will be there on the placards for them to scrutinize, they are nevertheless told to utter something plausible

---

87   Especially in view of the heavily Gallan content of these lines: see below, p. 433.
88   For illustrations see: (Arch of Titus) Pfanner (1983) Tafel 54, 55.1, 59.1, 61.1, 5, 66.4; Beilage 3; (Arch of Trajan at Beneventum) Rotili (1972) 109–11; Tav. CXLV.5; CXLVI.1, 5, 6, 7, 10; CXLVII; CXLVIII.2, 4; CXLIX.3.
89   Yarden (1971) 8–11 reaches the conclusion that the dimensions and the height/breadth ratio of the Menorah offered in rabbinical literature are 'largely confirmed by the relief on the Arch of Titus' (9).
90   Cf. Cic. *De Off.* 1.131.
91   A number of ancient texts, including Ov. *Tr.* 4.2.19–20 (below, p. 433) show that the names of captured *duces*, and not just their status, appeared on the placards: cf. *RE* s.v. Triumphus coll. 502–3 (W. Ehlers).

(228): similar difficulties with foreign, this time German, names could help explain the parallel inconcinnity between *Tristia* 4.2.19–20 and 25–6. Because no-one likes to admit ignorance, correct and incorrect information no doubt circulated equally freely at triumphs amid babble and confusion.

However, this cannot be the whole story: apart from wondering why Ovid set about achieving a humorous effect in these two passages in such a roundabout way, we might note that, both in *Ars Amatoria* and *Tristia* 4.2, the relevant lines send out Gallan signals, namely 'reading' and ostentatious *nomen* panoply:

> atque aliqua ex illis cum regum **nomina** quaeret,
> quae loca, qui montes, quaeve ferantur aquae,
> omnia responde, nec tantum si qua rogabit;
> et quae **nescieris**, ut bene **nota** refer.   (*Ars Amatoria* 1.219–22)

> ille vel ille, duces, et erunt quae **nomina** dicas,
> si poteris, vere, si minus, apta tamen.   (*Ars Amatoria* 1.227–8)

> ergo omnis populus poterit spectare triumphos,
> cumque ducum titulis oppida capta **leget.**   (*Tristia* 4.2.19–20)[92]

> quorum pars causas et res et **nomina** quaeret,
> pars referet, quamvis **noverit** illa parum.   (*Tristia* 4.2.25–6)

This language sends us back to Propertius 3.4, where the poet, envisaging himself in a parallel situation, claims without qualification that he will 'read (*legam*, 16) <the names of> captured (Parthian) towns on the placards':

> inque sinu carae nixus spectare puellae
> incipiam et titulis oppida capta **legam**,
> tela fugacis equi et bracati militis arcus,
> et subter captos arma sedere duces.   (15–18, tr. on p. 410)

Ovid may have reflected wryly that even the *doctus poeta* Propertius might have found such reading less easy to do than he imagined. More importantly, Ovid must also be referring to the Gallan antecedent of Propertius' lines. The Propertian commentators have been troubled by the complexities of 3.4.15–18, which also relate to that antecedent.

---

92   The pentameter is, as P. R. Hardie (2002) 309 n. 65 points out, an imitation of Prop. 3.4.16 imitating Gallus fr. 2.4–5 Courtney.

Apart from the word order of 17–18 the main issue is whether *legam* (16) can legitimately govern *tela* and *arcus* (17) as well as *oppida capta* (16). The verdict of the major commentary was negative: it held that *tela* and *arcus* are objects to *spectare* ...*/ incipiam* (15–16) – this phrase to be understood in the sense of *spectem.*[93] A contrary verdict would presuppose that enemy weaponry carried conspicuously as booty in triumphal processions was labelled like any other booty,[94] and so could be 'read', like the 'captured cities' of line 16. Propertian scholarship has also decreed that line 18 (*et subter captos arma sedere duces*) cannot be the object of *legam*, and hence must be governed by *spectare* ... / *incipiam* (15–16).

Whatever is ultimately concluded on these matters, the level of convolutedness found here, compounded as it is by the word-order of line 18, demands an explanation, which must start from the inescapable fact that Propertius' *legam* (16) responds directly to Gallus' *legam*:

> postque tuum reditum multorum templa deorum
> fixa **legam** spolieis deivitiora tueis.   (fr. 2.4–5 Courtney)

The struggles of modern scholarship to make sense of this Gallan couplet demonstrate both its obscurity and the difficulty of determining its motivation.[95] One explanation of Propertius' complexities might be that he is attempting to outbid Gallus' crypticism, just as Ovid's elaborate joke could be seen as capping both his predecessors' contortions. The Gallan couplet certainly caused heart-searchings in antiquity: the author of the *Consolatio ad Liviam* used parts of *legere* three times in diverse contexts to offer 'interpretations' of Gallus' *legam*. To make it clear that he was referring to Gallus the *Consolatio* poet accompanied those parts of *legere* with other Gallan lexemes, and in the third of the passages quoted below he further clarified his intentions by introducing triumphal concepts, plus an allusion to Propertius' earlier reprise of the same Gallan material in 3.4. The

---

93   Fedeli (1985) 168–9.
94   This is not in itself unlikely: the details of the procession were at the discretion of the *triumphator*: cf. Plin. *NH* 5.37 and Sueton. *Iul.* 37.2 (cited by Fedeli (1985) 168–9); and Lucullus' display of captured Armenian arms in the Circus Flaminius at his triumph in 63 BC must surely have been placarded, as perhaps too were the captured cataphracts and scythed chariots exhibited in his triumphal procession: for these cf. Plut. *Lucull.* 37.2–4.
95   See, e.g., Schoonhoven (1983) with earlier bibliography, and noting the *Consol. ad Liv.* passages treated below.

Consolatio poet's explanations seem to be that Gallus was envisaging (1) reading about Caesar's deeds in a history or poetry book, or (2) reading dedicatory inscriptions upon temples, or (3) reading placards during a triumphal procession:

1.   pars erit ⌐historiae⌐ totoque **legetur** in aevo
       seque opus ingeniis carminibusque dabit.
                                   (*Consolatio ad Liviam* 267–8)

2.   nec sua conspiciet (miserum me) munera Drusus
       nec sua prae ⌐templi⌐ **nomina** ⌐fronte⌐ **leget**.
                                   (*Consolatio ad Liviam* 287–8)

3.   nec meritis +quicquam illa iuvant magis+ afuit illis,
          mater, honos: ⌐titulis⌐ **nomina** plena vides.
       consul et ignoti victor Germanicus orbis,
          cui fuit heu mortis publica causa, **legor**:
       cingor Apollinea victricia tempora lauro
       et sensi exsequias funeris ipse mei,
       decursusque virum notos mihi donaque regum
       cunctaque per ⌐titulos⌐ oppida **lecta** suos.
                                   (*Consolatio ad Liviam* 455–62)

Gallus probably wanted to convey something like 'when I will read <the *tituli* on the> temples of many gods hung with your trophies, and made the richer by them'.[96] In his mind Gallus had moved ahead in time of the imagined triumph to the post-triumphal situation in which the spoils, along with their descriptive *tituli*, would be dedicated in temples and would be on show for him to see and read: *titulus* can also designate a label attached to a temple offering.[97] The first of the *Consolatio* poet's notions, then, that Gallus was thinking about reading a history (or poetry) book, should be rejected outright; the two other possibilities are both closer to Gallus' meaning, although neither hits the mark. Gallus was not imagining himself reading the names of his Caesar upon a temple, as in the second passage, but of reading the triumphal labels on spoils deposited in temples; nor was Gallus thinking of doing his 'reading' during the actual triumphal procession, as in the third.

Propertius was clearly addressing the same Gallan *Streitpunkt* in

---

96 So, in effect, both Putnam (1980) 53 and Schoonhoven (1983) 78, whose translation is adapted here.
97 E.g. Ov. *Am.* 2.13.25–6 with McKeown (1998) 291; *Met.* 9.791–4. On *tituli* in general see Daremberg-Saglio s.v. *titulus* (Cagnat); Tandoi (1992) 451–3.

3.4, but he seems to have 'corrected' or misrepresented Gallus rather than interpreting him; and the *Consolatio* poet was perhaps misled by Propertius' intervention into offering his third explanation in line 462. Propertius first sets the scene firmly at Augustus' future triumph, and he then confirms his intention by adding *titulis* to *legam* (16).[98] Propertius 'will read' placards carried in the triumphal procession – a clear *deformazione* of the Gallan couplet. Propertius had already tacitly negated the notion of 'reading' a history book – the *Consolatio* poet's first explanation – when he placed his reference to Gallus' *Romanae ... historiae* separately and earlier in 3.4, at line 10. Then Propertius tries to ensure that his audience will grasp his allusion to Gallus: he mimics Gallus' linguistic and conceptual contortedness in his next couplet (17–18) while sticking tenaciously to his own preferred 'interpretation' of Gallus' couplet. The *tela* and *arcus* of Propertius 3.4.17 will be displayed during, not after, the triumph, and 3.4.18 reiterates that the entire scene comes from a triumph and that the 'captured leaders' who sit beneath their arms are also being transported in the triumphal procession.

The current views of Propertian scholarship on the syntax of lines 15–18 were set out above, p. 434: *spectare .../ incipiam* (15–16), not *legam* (16) governs *tela* and *arcus* (17), as well as the clause of line 18. But, if that approach is correct, *legam*, the key term in the intertextual relationship between Propertius and Gallus, has little impact on the sentence. Giving *legam* more of a role would admittedly strain the syntax, but perhaps not unacceptably, particularly if the force of *spectare .../ incipiam* were allowed to continue *pari passu*: first Propertius 'will read <the names of> the cities on the placards' (16). Then (in asyndeton) he 'will (see and?) read <the names of, i.e. the designations of> the *tela* of the *fugax equus* and the *arcus* of the *bracatus miles*' (17), since such items (see above) were labelled in triumphal processions. Finally, if *legam* (with copula *et*) can continue to govern line 18, Propertius 'will see (and read?) that captured leaders are sitting beneath their weapons', the reading being perhaps the reading of a label indicating that the individuals in this situation are 'captured leaders'. The shift from nouns as the objects of *legam* to an accusative and infinitive clause as its object is not intolerable, since *lego* can be followed either by a direct object or by an accusative and

---

98   At *Tr.* 4.2.19–20 (quoted above, p. 433) Ovid opts, following Propertius, for the same 'solution'.

infinitive clause;[99] and the possible implied shift from the sense 'read' in lines 16–17 to the sense 'recognize' in line 18 might indicate that Propertius was thinking either of ἀναγιγνώσκειν, the Greek equivalent of *legere*, which starts off by meaning 'to recognize' before developing the more specialized meaning 'to read',[100] or of a more basic sense of *legere* itself, i.e. 'to pick out' (*OLD* s.v. *lego* 5), which was highlighted by Varro in *De Lingua Latina* 6.66: *legere dictum, quod leguntur ab oculis litterae* ('*legere* [to read] has this meaning because letters *leguntur* [are picked out] with the eyes'). At all events Propertius' two couplets are evidently his grammatical 'correction' of Gallus' single couplet. For Propertius 'reading temples made richer etc.' seemed too harsh an expression, while his own extended combination of 'seeing' and 'reading' is harsh enough to evoke Gallus, but smooth enough to pass muster.

At this point it is perhaps appropriate to enquire exactly what Propertius is describing in these lines. Most commentators draw the obvious conclusion that the *oppida capta* (3.4.16) being carried in procession are models or paintings of cities.[101] But there is no consensus about lines 17–18. The *tela* and *arcus* of line 17 are usually seen as real weapons captured as booty, although line 17 is taken by one commentator to refer to a painting of a battle.[102] Line 18 (prisoners sitting beneath *arma*) is interpreted either as a description of actual leaders being processed in this condition, or (again) as referring to a painting or effigy.[103] The couplet (17–18) as a whole has correctly been related to stock artistic and numismatic representations of bound captives sitting on the ground beneath a trophy hung with arms in the aftermath of a Roman victory, and the lower section of the *Gemma Augustea* has been mentioned as one such illustration.[104] I have argued elsewhere[105] that in fact Propertius is envisaging in this couplet not two items in the procession but a single item, one which is

---

99   *TLL* s.v. 2. lego col. 1129.5–59.
100 LSJ s.v.
101 The parading at triumphs of paintings, models, and effigies was standard: see *RE* s.v. Triumphus (W. Ehlers) coll. 502–3; Ov. *EP* 2.1.37–8; Appian *Mithr.* 117. For the most part Fedeli (1985) does not treat the topics which follow.
102 Rothstein (1920–4) II.32, citing Ov. *EP* 2.1.39–40.
103 *Actual leaders*: Hertzberg (1843–5) III.2 (IV). 269; Butler (1933) 269; Camps (1996) 71. *Effigy*: Paley² (1872) 152. *Painting*: Rothstein (1920–4) II.32, citing Ov. *EP* 3.4.104.
104 By Richardson (1977) 332; cf. Paley² (1872) 152; Rothstein loc. cit. (n. 102); Butler (1933) 269. For discussions and illustrations of *tropaia* see Wölcke (1911); Picard (1957); *RE* s.v. τρόπαιον (F. Lammert).
105 Cairns (2005).

illustrated on a contemporary frieze from the temple of Apollo *in circo* (the so-called Apollo Sosianus/Apollo Medicus temple).[106] That frieze depicts the procession at the triple triumph of Octavianus in 29 BC: two bound barbarian prisoners are shown seated beneath and either side of a trophy hung with arms. Prisoners and trophy are mounted upon a *ferculum*,[107] which eight bearers (four on each side, although one is missing where the frieze is broken off) have just set down. The *tela* and *arcus* of line 17 are therefore wholly or partly synonymous with the *arma* of line 18; as for the *captos duces* (18), the Apollo Sosianus frieze and similar later representations do not make it clear whether live captives or effigies are involved.

In linguistic terms Propertius is following up his Gallan *legam* (16) with a cryptic couplet intended to match that of Gallus, and therefore couched in deliberately contorted language. Propertius' puzzle has, however, a simpler solution than its Gallan forebear: his readers would easily have concluded that he was introducing a motif linked, first in coinage and then in triumphs, with the Marian/ Caesarian cause, i.e. a *tropaion* with one prisoner (eventually two prisoners) kneeling (eventually sitting) beneath it. The exact scene in its developed form (two seated captives beneath a trophy) appears on Julius Caesar's coin issues of 46–45 BC, and then on C. Sosius' coinage, as well as on his frieze. The same variant reappears in imperial coinage and sculpture, where, at least in some examples, it continues to evoke the Marian-Caesarian association.[108] C. Sosius' frieze testifies that at least one *ferculum* containing a trophy, with beneath it (?)effigies of two seated prisoners, was processed at the triple triumph of Octavianus in 29 BC. Propertius' couplet (17–18) doubtless refers to that feature of the triumphal procession of 29, which he will have witnessed in person. His prophecy that a similar *ferculum* will be carried in Augustus' forthcoming triumphal procession is therefore a complimentary allusion to Augustus' earlier triumphs, and it is made all the more complimentary by the Caesarian

---

106 Zanker (1987) 78 (Ill. 55) = (1988) 70 (Ill. 55).
107 The *fercula* illustrated in Roman art are flat rectangular trays with low sides and with long carrying-handles at their four corners, i.e. in effect open litters. *TLL* s.v. II pompaticum, seems to equate *ferculum* (incorrectly) with *sella* and *currus*; *OLD* s.v. *ferculum* 1 offers the correct meaning.
108 For evidence of the Marian/Caesarian associations of this motif, and for details of the relevant coin issues and sculpture, see Cairns (2005). Ov. *EP* 3.4.103–4 represents the same scene, again in a triumph: *scuta sed et galeae gemmis radientur et auro,/ stentque super vinctos trunca tropaea viros* ('let the shields and the helmets glitter with gems and gold, and let felled trophies stand over bound men').

flavour of the motif, of which Propertius will certainly have been aware. There may be even more to the couplet: as noted, the icono-graphical theme in its fully developed form is first seen on coins of Julius Caesar minted in 46–45 BC, and the quadruple triumph of Julius, in which the future Augustus participated, took place in 45 BC. It is a small step to surmise that one or more *fercula* bearing a trophy and two seated captives were carried in Julius Caesar's triumphal processions. In that case the presence of such a *ferculum* or *fercula* at the triple triumph of Octavianus in 29 was a deliberate reminiscence of his 'father's' triumphs of 45, as well as a further ostentatious dis-play of a Marian/Caesarian motif; and, if such *fercula* did participate in Julius' triumphs of 45, might Gallus similarly have prophesied their participation in that fresh triumph over the Parthians which his verses anticipated for Julius Caesar? If so, Propertius will be matching Gallus' *legam* using another Gallan topic from the same context.

Like Propertius, Ovid was aware of the Gallan dilemma addressed by the *Consolatio* poet, and he knew too of Propertius' earlier con-tribution in 3.4 to the problem of Gallus' *legam*. Ovid's approach in the *Ars Amatoria* is, however, more tangential: he does not employ a form of *legere*,[109] although, like Propertius, he creates his own puzzle to parallel that of Gallus – and that of Propertius. First Ovid varies upon, and probably 'corrects', Propertius' initially slightly opaque account of captured *duces* sitting under their arms (3.4.17–18): Ovid has his prisoners walking, as normal, loaded with chains in front of the triumphal procession (215–16). Then, in order to match his predeces-sors' challenges to their readers, Ovid develops his own fantasy about the *iuvenes* and what they should tell the *puellae* about the items of the triumphal procession. By concentrating on these items Ovid is indi-cating that, like Propertius, he believes that Gallus should have been concerned primarily with the *tituli* of his 'Caesar' during the actual triumph. But at the same time Ovid undercuts all the three solutions to the Gallan problem later proposed by the *Consolatio* poet, and indeed all such solutions: by casting doubt on the possibility of reading *tituli* accurately, Ovid implies that the answers to 'philological' problems such as those presented by Gallus' *legam* can licitly be, and in fact are, pure inventions anyhow.

A minor addendum may end this discussion: just as thematic

---

109   Although (as noted above, p. 436 n. 98) he does so, and is less tangential, in the triumphal scene of *Tr.* 4.2 (20) – apparently in an allusion to Prop. 3.4.16 as well.

comparisons with Propertius 3.4 have been used to reveal possible Gallan material in Ovid's *propemptikon*, so a reverse comparison can generate a parallel conclusion about Propertius 3.4. Propertius' *propemptikon* is much briefer than Ovid's, and yet it introduces several characters not found in Ovid: Propertius mentions Aeneas (20) and Vesta (11), and his combination in lines 11–12 of Vesta with Mars (who does appear in Ovid) evokes Romulus, son of Mars and Ilia, priestess of Vesta. Aeneas and Romulus were in vogue in the 20s BC as antecedents for Augustus, *inter alia* in the ongoing *Aeneid*, a work in which (as noted above, p. 405), Propertius shows special interest in this elegy.[110] But Aeneas and Romulus were also fashionable in the mid 40s BC, when Julius Caesar was actively publicizing the descent of the Iulii from Venus, Mars, Aeneas, and Romulus.[111] The *personae* who appear in Propertius 3.4 but not in Ovid's *propemptikon* could therefore derive from Gallus.

By their nature the techniques applied in this chapter cannot yield certainty at all points. But they hold out tantalizing hints about how Gallus might have influenced his successors, they help to reveal more about the tone and content of Propertius 3.4, and they offer something for Ovid too – a means of discriminating between what Ovid learned from Gallus and what he learned from his teachers of rhetoric, and better understanding of how Ovid imitated a principal model, in this case Propertius 3.4.

A summation may now be in order. This monograph (as I proposed in the Preface) tries to account for the individuality and nature of Propertian elegy. It begins by placing Propertius in some of his most significant but comparatively neglected contexts, starting with his origins in the leading family of Asisium and the pressures which brought this local aristocrat to Rome in the 30s BC and led him to pursue a literary career. Propertius' familial, social and regional origins, and the political background which came with them, determined the patronage which he enjoyed throughout his career, which in turn influenced heavily his literary development.

Propertius' first patrons, who loom large in his Monobiblos, were Volcacius Tullus, from a consular *gens*, and 'Gallus'. Particularly if, as I maintain, 'Gallus' is the accomplished soldier, equestrian first

---

110 Cf. Cairns (2003).
111 Cf. Weinstock (1971) Index I s.vv. Iulius Caesar C. (*cos.* 59) – descent from Ares and Aphrodite; Mars; Romulus; Venus.

'prefect' of Egypt and elegist, C. Cornelius Gallus, then those characteristics of Propertian elegy (and especially of the Monobiblos) which
distinguish it from other surviving Roman elegy become more explicable: they resulted from initial admiration, almost bordering on
obsession, on the part of Propertius for the works of his predecessor
elegist. Cornelius Gallus' influence on Propertian elegy is examined in
several chapters with the help of prior scholarship and notably of
heuristic techniques, both lexical and metrical, which greatly expand
the range of Gallan impact detectable in Propertius' works.

The changes in tone and subject-matter in Propertius Books 2–4,
again more easily explicable if the 'Gallus' of the Monobiblos is the
poet, are interpreted in terms of Propertius' altered patronage situation
from 27–26 BC on. The fall from Augustus' favour around 27 BC of
C. Cornelius Gallus, and seemingly also of the Volcacii Tulli, left
Propertius patronless; but he was taken up first by Augustus' associate
and confidant, C. Maecenas, and later directly by Augustus himself.
Once Propertius had come under the protection of Maecenas and
Augustus his poetry moved increasingly towards topics of public
concern, while never altogether abandoning its essential elegiac stance
and its continuing, although reduced, indebtedness to the work of
Cornelius Gallus.

Propertius' life-long politics and loyalties were Caesarian, his first
patrons were adherents of Augustus, and he ended up in direct dependence on Augustus. In view of this, Propertius' continued expressions
of elegiac attitudes and aspirations in Books 2–4 should be seen as
relating to literary canons, not as political. Further chapters analyse
how his new patrons placed their equally powerful imprints on Propertius' work, and document his progression to a more overtly political
role as an encomiast of the Augustan regime and a spokesman for the
recreation of the Roman past which it promulgated. A grasp both of
Propertius' political and patronal allegiances, and of his role as follower and successor of Gallus, allows exploration of the development
of Roman elegy from Gallus beyond Propertius to Ovid through the
analysis of a triple sequence of triumph poems by Gallus, Propertius
and Ovid which has been the topic of the present chapter.

It should now be clear that no sensible understanding of the works
of Propertius, or of the progress of elegy at Rome and his part in it,
can be achieved without a better grasp of the role of Gallus. But the
loss of most of Gallus' elegies imposes limits on how far the history of
Roman elegy can be reconstructed. Nevertheless the search for what

can sensibly be hypothesized about those lost elegies has at least pointed to the achievable limits of such reconstructions, as well as underlining the recalibrations which need to be applied to earlier attempts to elucidate the progress of elegy at Rome. A fundamental point is that one-to-one comparisons between Propertius Book 1 and Tibullus Book 1 aimed at asserting the priority or dependence of one poet on the other can never be convincing.[112] The massive presence of Gallus in the Monobiblos and the fact that it is not to be discounted in Tibullus' first book call into doubt every conclusion ever reached in that area.[113] Similarly, the notion that Ovid's originality and intentions as an elegist can be gauged simply by contrasting his *Amores* with Propertian and Tibullan elegy is untenable. By selecting '*Amores*' as his book title[114] Ovid is telling his readership something important about his literary allegiances, and his message must be that he has Gallus somewhere in the forefront of his mind. Ovid's later and more explicit revelations of interest in Gallus, as documented in Chapters 5 and 6, are not therefore an entirely new development but continue a trend which goes back to his earliest productions. All this is not to imply that the approaches followed in this book are intended only to undermine the assertions of past scholarship about the history of elegy. On the contrary, positive lines of enquiry about elegiac literary influence and imitation have been developed in Chapters 3–7 and in this chapter; and, if the methodologies offered there are valid, then the way is open for extended future applications, particularly since, as has often been exemplified in this book, insights gained through them are often mutually supportive. If Latinists can lose their fear of eliciting the unknown from the known, and can at last face up to Gallus, who is the great enigma of Roman elegy, then we may finally arrive at a history of Roman elegy in which Propertius is not an inexplicable oddity generated *e nilo*, and Ovid is not a mere afterthought, parodist, or element of decline.

A further essential prerequisite to a sensible understanding of Roman elegy is the abandonment of anachronistic modern attitudes to Roman patronage and politics. Scholars seeking to interpret the meaning and import of 'political' statements in Augustan poetry must

---

112 There have been many such attempts: see, most recently, Lyne (1998).
113 The possibility (cf. *THPR* 228) that Tibullus and Propertius were composing some of their first books within the same time-slot, and that they attended some of each other's recitations, makes such questions doubly unanswerable.
114 Cf. Index II s.v.

keep firmly in mind the real-life social situations in which Propertius and Tibullus flourished and in which Ovid eventually came to grief. Unthinking attempts to label Propertian elegy and much of Ovid's œuvre as 'subversive' cannot stand when viewed in the cold light of Roman history and Roman *mores*.[115] One of the more amusing aspects of such anachronistic assessments of Roman elegy is the exemption of Tibullus from the interpretative follies inflicted on his poetic contemporaries. Tibullus treats Messalla Corvinus and his son Messalinus very much as Propertius, and to some extent Ovid, treat Augustus. Yet no-one accuses Tibullus of harbouring a covertly subversive attitude towards Messalla, or of 'anti-Messallism'!

---

115 For a recent trenchant refutation of such fallacies in connection with Martial and Domitian see L. Watson and P. Watson (2003) 10–12.

Works Cited

Modern authors of texts, commentaries, notes, translations, and so forth, are described as their 'editor' (ed./eds.); subtitles and part-titles of such works are generally omitted. The titles of less well-known periodicals may be abbreviated less stringently than by L'Année Philologique. The earliest publication date is usually given, and reprints are not noted; this also applies to second and subsequent editions which are in fact reprints. Only the first place of publication is recorded. Edited collections have independent entries if more than one paper from them is cited.

AA.VV. (Gruppo di ricerca sulla propaganda antica) (1972). 'L'integrazione dell'Italia nello Stato romano attraverso la poesia e la cultura proto-augustea', in M. Sordi (ed.) *Contributi dell'Istituto di storia antica I.* Milan. 146–75.

Alexiou, M. (1974). *The Ritual Lament in Greek Tradition.* Cambridge.

Alfonsi, L. (1943). 'L'elegia di Gallo', *RFIC* 21.46–56.

—— (1944–5). 'Di Properzio II, 34 e della protasi dell'Eneide', *RFIC* 22–3.16–29.

—— (1949). 'Note properziane', *MH* 6.90–9.

—— (1954). 'Il giudizio di Properzio sulla poesia vergiliana', *Aevum* 28.205–21.

—— (1963). 'La 34ª elegia del II libro di Properzio e il poeta Lynceo', *Maia* 15.270–7.

—— (1964). 'Dal "lamento della fanciulla abbandonata" a Properzio', *Aegyptus* 44.3–8.

Álvarez Hernández, A. (1997). *La poética de Propercio (Autobiografía artística del 'Calímaco romano').* Propertiana 2. Assisi.

Ampolo, C. (1996). 'Livio I, 44,3: la casa di Servio Tullio, l'Esquilino e Mecenate', *Parola del Passato* 286.27–32.

Anderson, R. D., P. J. Parsons, R. G. M. Nisbet (1979). 'Elegiacs by Gallus from Qaṣr Ibrîm', *JRS* 69.125–55.

Anderson, W. S. (1964). '*Hercules exclusus*: Propertius IV, 9.', *AJPh* 85.1–12.

André, J.-M. (1967). *Mécène. Essai de biographie spirituelle*. Annales littéraires de l'Université de Besançon 86. Paris.

——— (2002). 'Politique, dirigisme augustéen et esthétisme chez Properce', in P. Defosse (ed.) *Hommages à Carl Deroux* I *Poésie*. Collection Latomus 266. Brussels. 13–28.

Ardizzoni, A. (1967). (ed.) *Apollonio Rodio. Le Argonautiche Libro 1*. Bibliotheca Athena 3. Rome.

Armstrong, D. (1989). *Horace*. New Haven.

——— (1995). 'The impossibility of metathesis: Philodemus and Lucretius on form and content in poetry', in D. Obbink (ed.) *Philodemus and Poetry: Poetic Theory and Practice in Lucretius, Philodemus, and Horace*. New York. 210–32.

Arrigoni, G. (1985). 'Donne e sport nel mondo greco. Religione e società', in G. Arrigoni (ed.) *Le Donne in Grecia*. Rome. 55–201.

Avallone, R. (1962). *Mecenate*. Naples.

Aymard, J. (1951). *Essai sur les chasses romaines: des origines à la fin du siècle des Antonins (Cynegetica)*. BEFAR 171. Paris.

Badian, E. (1985). 'A phantom marriage law', *Philologus* 129.82–98.

Balbo, A. (1999). 'Contributi ad un'edizione dei frammenti degli oratori romani dell'età imperiale: alcuni problemi relativi a testi di Cornelio Gallo e di Tito Labieno', in *Quaderni del dipartimento di filologia linguistica e tradizione classica «Augusto Rostagni»*. Pubblicazioni del Dipartimento di Filologia, Linguistica e Tradizione Classica. Università degli Studi di Torino 1999. Bologna. 241–54.

——— (2004). *I frammenti degli oratori romani dell'età augustea e tiberiana. Parte prima: Età augustea*. Minima Philologica. Serie Latina 1. Alessandria.

Bannon, C. J. (1997). *The Brothers of Romulus: Fraternal Pietas in Roman Law, Literature, and Society*. Princeton NJ.

Barber, E. A. (1953). (ed.) *Sexti Properti Carmina*. Oxford

Barchiesi, A. (1981). 'Notizie sul «nuovo Gallo»', *Atene e Roma* 26.153–66.

Barsby, J. A. (1974). 'Propertius' polysyllabic pentameters', *Latomus* 33.46–53.

Becker, W. A. (1898). *Gallus: or Roman Scenes of the Time of Augustus*, tr. F. Metcalfe, 2nd edn. London.

Benedum, J. (1967). *Studien zur Dichtkunst des späten Ovids*. Diss. Giessen.

Bernardini, P. A. (1986–7). 'Aspects ludiques, rituels et sportifs de la course féminine dans la Grèce antique', *Stadion* 12–13.17–26.

——— (1988). 'Le donne e la pratica della corsa nella Grecia antica', in P. A. Bernardini (ed.) *Lo Sport in Grecia*. Rome. 153–84.

Berry, D. H. (1996). (ed.) *Cicero: Pro P. Sulla Oratio*. CCTC 30. Cambridge.

——— (2003). '*Equester ordo tuus est*: did Cicero win his cases because of his support for the *equites*?', *CQ* 53.222–34.

Bickel, E. (1950). 'Varii Carmen Epicum de Actis Caesaris et Agrippae. Critica in Laudem Pisonis', *SO* 28.17–43.

Binder, G. (1971). *Aeneas und Augustus: Interpretationen zum 8. Buch der Aeneis*. Beiträge zur klassischen Philologie 38. Meisenheim am Glan.

Birt, T. (1882). *Das antike Buchwesen in seinem Verhältniss zur Litteratur*. Berlin.

Blundell, S. (1995). *Women in Ancient Greece*. London.

Bömer, F. (1980). (ed.) *P. Ovidius Naso. Metamorphosen. Buch X–XI*. Heidelberg.

(1982). (ed.) *P. Ovidius Naso. Metamorphosen. Buch XII–XIII*. Heidelberg.

Boldrer, F. (1999). *L'Elegia di Vertumno (Properzio 4.2). Introduzione, testo critico, traduzione e commento*. Supplementi di Lexis 4. Amsterdam.

Bonamente, G. (1984). 'Properzio, cosa "nostra"', in *Il Liceo classico di Assisi nel Bimillenario di Properzio*. Assisi. 121–8.

(2004). 'Properzio, un esponente dell'aristocrazia municipale di *Asisium* nella Roma di Augusto', in Santini and Santucci (2004) 17–74.

Bonamente, G. and G. Catanzaro (1996). (eds.) *Omaggio a Francesco Antonio Frondini nel 150° anniversario della morte*. I. *Museo Lapidario Asisinate*. Assisi.

Bonamente, G. and F. Coarelli (1996). (eds.) *Assisi e gli Umbri nell'antichità. Atti del Convegno Internazionale, Assisi 18–21 dicembre 1991*. Assisi.

Bonner, S. F. (1949). *Roman Declamation in the Late Republic and Early Empire*. Liverpool.

(1977). *Education in Ancient Rome. From the Elder Cato to the Younger Pliny*. London.

Bosworth, B. (1999). 'Augustus, the *Res Gestae* and hellenistic theories of apotheosis', *JRS* 89.1–18.

Boucher, J.-P. (1958). 'L'œuvre de L. Varius Rufus d'après Properce II, 34', *REA* 60.307–22.

(1961). 'Properce II, 13, 1–2', *Rev. Phil.* 35.232.

(1965). *Études sur Properce. Problèmes d'inspiration et d'art*, BEFAR 204. Paris.

(1966). *Caius Cornélius Gallus*. Bibliothèque de la Faculté des Lettres de Lyon 11. Paris.

Bowersock, G. W. (1961). 'Eurycles of Sparta', *JRS* 51.112–18.

(1965). *Augustus and the Greek World*. Oxford.

Boyd, B. W. (1987). 'Propertius on the banks of the Eurotas (a note on 3.14. 17–20)', *CQ* 37.527–8.

Bradley, G. (2000). *Ancient Umbria: State, Culture, and Identity in Central Italy from the Iron Age to the Augustan Era*. Oxford.

Bradshaw, A. (1989). 'Horace *in Sabinis*', in C. Deroux (ed.) *Studies in Latin Literature and Roman History* vol. 5. Collection Latomus 206. Brussels. 160–86.

Bramble, J. (1974). '*Cui non dictus Hylas puer?* Propertius 1. 20', in Woodman and West (1974) 81–93, 150–1.

Bright, D. F. (1981). 'Ovid vs. Apuleius', *ICS* 6.356–66.

Brink, C. O. (1971). *Horace on Poetry, II: The Ars Poetica.* Cambridge.

(1982). *Horace on Poetry, III: Epistles Book II: The Letters to Augustus and Florus.* Cambridge.

Brugnoli, G. (1983). 'C. Galli Fragm.', *Mus. Crit.* 18.233–6.

Brugnoli, G. and F. Stok (1991). 'Questioni biografiche III, IV, V', *GIF* 43.133–50.

Brunt, P. A. (1982). '*Nobilitas* and *novitas*', *JRS* 72.1–17.

Buck, C. D. (1904). *A Grammar of Oscan and Umbrian.* Boston.

Buckland, W. W. (1963). *A Text-Book of Roman Law: from Augustus to Justinian*, 3rd edn. rev. by Peter Stein. Cambridge.

Burckhardt, L. A. (1990). 'The political elite of the Roman republic: comments on recent discussion of the concepts *nobilitas* and *homo novus*', *Historia* 39.77–99.

Burgers, P. (1997). 'The Narbonensian colonial elite – 1958–1995', *Ancient Society* 28.89–106.

Butler, H. E. and E. A. Barber (1933). (eds.) *The Elegies of Propertius.* Oxford.

Butrica, J. L. (1996a). 'Two two-part poems in Propertius Book 1 (1.8; 1.11 and 12)', *Papers of the Leeds International Latin Seminar* 9.83–91.

(1996b). 'Hellenistic erotic elegy: the evidence of the papyri', *Papers of the Leeds International Latin Seminar* 9.297–322.

(1996c). 'The *Amores* of Propertius: Unity and Structure in Books 2–4', *ICS* 21.85–158.

Byrne, S. N. (1999). 'Maecenas in Seneca and other post-Augustan authors', in S. N. Byrne and E. P. Cueva (eds.) *Veritatis Amicitiaeque Causa: Essays in Honor of Anna Lydia Motto and John R. Clark.* Wauconda Ill. 21–40.

Cairns, F. (1969). 'Propertius i. 18 and Callimachus, Acontius and Cydippe', *CR* 19.131–4.

(1971). 'Propertius 2.29A', *CQ.* 21.455–60.

(1974a). 'Some observations on Propertius 1.1', *CQ* 24.94–110.

(1974b). 'Some problems in Propertius 1.6', *AJPh* 95.150–63.

(1977). 'Two unidentified *komoi* of Propertius. I 3 and II 29', *Emerita* 45.325–53.

(1979a). 'Propertius on Augustus' marriage law (II, 7)', *Grazer Beiträge* 8.185–204.

(1979b). 'Self-imitation within a generic framework: Ovid, *Amores* 2.9 and 3.11 and the *renuntiatio amoris*', in West and Woodman (1979) 121–41, 229–31.

(1983a). 'Propertius 1,4 and 1,5 and the 'Gallus' of the Monobiblos', *Papers of the Liverpool Latin Seminar* 4.61–103.

(1983b). 'Horace *Epode* 9: some new interpretations', *ICS* 8.80–93.

(1984a). 'Propertius and the battle of Actium (4.6)', in Woodman and West (1984) 129–68, 229–36.

(1984b). 'The etymology of *militia* in Roman elegy', in L. Gil and R. M. Aguilar (eds.) *Apophoreta philologica Emmanueli Fernández-Galiano a sodalibus oblata* II. Estudios Clásicos 24. Madrid. 211–22.

(1986). 'The Milanion/Atalanta *exemplum* in Propertius 1, 1: *uidere feras* (12) and Greek models', in F. Decreus and C. Deroux (eds.) *Hommages à Jozef Veremans*. Collection Latomus 193. Brussels. 29–38.

(1987). '*AP* 9, 588 (Alcaeus of Messene) and *nam modo* in Propertius 1, 1, 11', in *Filologia e forme letterarie: studi offerti a Francesco della Corte* I. Urbino. 377–84.

(1989). *Virgil's Augustan Epic*. Cambridge.

(1992a). 'Propertius 4.9: '*Hercules exclusus*' and the dimensions of genre' in K. Galinsky (ed.) *The Interpretation of Roman Poetry*. Studien zur klassischen Philologie 67. Frankfurt am Main. 65–95.

(1992b). 'The power of implication: Horace's invitation to Maecenas (*Odes* 1.20)', in Woodman and Powell (1992) 84–109, 236–41.

(1992c). 'Rhetoric and genre: Propertius 1.6.31–6, Menander Rhetor 398.29–32 – 399.1, and a topos of the propemptikon', *SIFC* 10.980–90.

(1993). 'Imitation and originality in Ovid *Amores* 1.3', *Papers of the Leeds International Latin Seminar* 7.101–22.

(1995). 'Callimachus the 'Woodentop' (*AP* XI 275)' in L. Belloni, G. Milanese and A. Porro (eds.) *Studia classica Iohanni Tarditi oblata* I. Milan. 607–15.

(1996). 'Ancient "etymology" and Tibullus: on the classification of "etymologies" and on "etymological markers"' *PCPhS* 42.24–59.

(2000). 'Allusions to *hunc ... meum esse aio* in Propertius?' *Res Publica Litterarum* 3.168–81.

(2002). 'Propertius the historian (3.3.1–12)?' in D. S. Levene and D. P. Nelis (eds.) *Clio and the Poets: Augustan Poetry and the Traditions of Ancient Historiography*. Mnemosyne Suppl. 224. Leiden. 25–44.

(2003). 'Propertius 3.4 and the *Aeneid* incipit', *CQ* 53.309–11.

(2004a). 'Varius and Vergil: two pupils of Philodemus in Propertius 2.34?' in D. Armstrong, J. Fish, P. A. Johnston and M. B. Skinner (eds.) *Philodemus, Vergil and the Augustans*. Austin Texas. 299–321.

(2004b). 'Variazioni su Ila in Properzio 1.20', in Santini and Santucci (2004) 75–98.

(2005). 'The triumphal motif of Propertius 3.4.17–18 and its political associations: sculptural and numismatic evidence', in C. Deroux (ed.) *Studies in Latin Literature and Roman History XII*. Collection Latomus 287. Brussels. 214–18.

(ftc.). 'The nomenclature of the Tiber in Virgil's *Aeneid*', in J. Booth and R. Maltby (eds.) *What's in a Name? The Significance of Proper Names in Classical Latin Literature*. Swansea.

Callegari, M. (1999). '*P.Oxy.* 2820', *Acme* 52.87–107.

Cameron, A. (1995). *Callimachus and his Critics.* Princeton NJ.

Campanile, E. (1996). 'I testi umbri minori', in Bonamente and Coarelli (1996) 181–92.

Campbell, B. (2000). (ed.) *The Writings of the Roman Land Surveyors.* Journal of Roman Studies Monograph No. 9. London.

Camps, W. A. (1966). (ed.) *Propertius. Elegies Book III.* Cambridge.

Capponi, L. (2002). 'Maecenas and Pollio', *ZPE* 140.181–4.

Carratello, U. (1991). 'Una curiosità properziana (1, 21, 9–10)', in *Studi di Filologia Classica in onore di Giusto Monaco* II. Palermo. 995–1000.

Carter, J. M. (1982). (ed.) *Suetonius: Divus Augustus.* Bristol.

Cartledge, P. (1981). 'Spartan wives: liberation or licence?', *CQ* 31.84–105 = Cartledge (2001) 106–26, 212–20.

Cartledge, P. and A. Spawforth (1989). *Hellenistic and Roman Sparta. A Tale of Two Cities.* London.

Casson, L. (1971). *Ships and Seamanship in the Ancient World.* Baltimore.

Catanzaro, G. and F. Santucci (2002). (eds.) *Properzio alle soglie del 2000. Un bilancio di fine secolo. Atti convegno internazionale. Assisi, 25–28 maggio 2000.* Assisi.

Ceccarelli, L. (2002). 'La metrica di Properzio', in Catanzaro and Santucci (2002) 133–76.

Cecchini, E. (1984). 'Properzio 2, 34', *RFIC* 112.154–66.

Cenerini, F. (1985). 'I *Caesii*: Prosopografia delle regioni VI, VIII e V', in G. Susini (ed.) *Cultura epigrafica dell'Appennino. Sarsina, Mevaniola e altri studi.* Epigrafia e antichità 8. Faenza. 203–32.

—— (1996). 'Il ruolo dei *Caesii* sui due versanti appenninici', in Bonamente and Coarelli (1996) 235–44.

Centroni, C. (1994). 'La Villa di Orazio a Licenza', in *Atti del Convegno di Licenza. 19–23 Aprile 1993.* Venosa. 107–16.

Cichorius, C. (1922). *Römische Studien. Historisches Epigraphisches Literaturgeschichtliches aus vier Jahrhunderten Roms.* Leipzig.

Citti, V. (1966). 'C. Cilnio Mecenate "poeta novello" e il libro di Riccardo Avallone', *Vichiana* 3.40–8.

Clausen, W. (1994). *A Commentary on Virgil Eclogues.* Oxford.

Coarelli, F. (1991). 'Assisi repubblicana: riflessioni su un caso di autoromanizzazione', *Atti Accademia Properziana del Subasio – Assisi* s. VI 19.5–22 + Pl. I–III.

—— (1996). 'Da Assisi a Roma. Architettura pubblica e promozione sociale in una città dell'Umbria', in Bonamente and Coarelli (1996) 245–63.

—— (2004). 'Assisi, Roma, Tivoli. I luoghi di Properzio', in Santini and Santucci (2004) 99–115.

Coleman, K. M. (1988). *Statius. Silvae IV. Edited with an English Translation, Commentary and Bibliography.* Oxford.

Coli, E. (1996). 'L'Umbria nell'elegia latina', in Bonamente and Coarelli (1996) 265–75.

Coli, U. (1964). 'L'organizzazione politica dell'umbria preromana', in *I problemi di storia e archeologia dell' Umbria. Atti del I convegno di studi Umbri, Gubbio 1963*. Gubbio. 133–59.

Connors, C. (1991). 'Simultaneous hunting and herding at *Ciris* 297–300', *CQ* 41.556–9.

Constantinidou, S. (1998). 'Dionysiac elements in Spartan cult dances', *Phoenix* 52.15–30.

Copley, F. O. (1956). *Exclusus Amator: A Study in Latin Love Poetry*. Philological Monographs published by the American Philological Association 17. Madison Wis.

Cornell, T. J. (1976). 'Etruscan historiography', *Annali della Scuola Normale Superiore di Pisa* ser. 3 6.411–39.

―― (1992). 'The effects of war on the society of ancient Rome', in G. Ausenda (ed.) *The Effects of War on Society*. San Marino. 131–48.

―― (1995). *The Beginnings of Rome. Italy and Rome from the Bronze Age to the Punic Wars (c. 1000–264 BC)*. London.

Courtney, E. (1991). (ed.) *The Poems of Petronius*. Atlanta GA.

―― (1993). (ed.) *The Fragmentary Latin Poets*. Oxford.

―― (1998). 'Echtheitskritik: Ovidian and non-Ovidian Heroides again', *CJ* 93.157–66.

Cova, P. V. (1989). *Il poeta Vario*. Scienze Filologiche e Storia, Brescia 2. Milan.

Creighton, J. (2000). *Coins and Power in Late Iron Age Britain*. Cambridge.

Crowther, N. B. (1982). 'Athletic dress and nudity in Greek athletics', *Eranos* 80.163–8.

D'Anna, G. (1981). 'Cornelio Gallo, Virgilio e Properzio', *Athenaeum* 59.284–98.

―― (1987). 'Verg. *ecl.* 9, 32–36 e Prop. II, 34, 83–84', in *Filologia e forme letterarie. Studi offerti a F. Della Corte*, II. Urbino. 427–38.

Danker, F. W. (2000). (ed.) *A Greek-English Lexicon of the New Testament and other Early Christian Literature*, 3rd edn. Chicago.

Day, A. A. (1938). *The Origins of Latin Love-Elegy*. Oxford.

De Albentiis, E. (1986). 'Brevi note di geografia storica sulle conche intermontane dell'Umbria', in G. L. Carancini (ed.) *Atti dell'Incontro di Acquasparta 1985 "Gli insediamenti perilacustri dell'età del bronzo e della prima età del ferro: il caso dell'antico Lacus Velinus". Palazzo Cesi, 15–17 novembre 1985*. Quaderni di Protostoria I. Perugia. 193–9.

de Grummond, N. (ftc.). 'Roman Favor and Etruscan Thuf(ltha): A Note on Propertius 4.2.34', *Ancient East and West*.

Debrohun, J. B. (2003). *Roman Propertius and the Reinvention of Elegy*. Ann Arbor.

Dettenhofer, M. H. (1993). 'Die Frauen von Sparta: Gesellschaftliche Position und politische Relevanz', *Klio* 75.61–75.

Di Stefano, D. (1992–3). 'Miti Properziani e arte figurativa', *Annali della Facoltà di Lettere e Filosofia, Bari* 35–6.221–59.

Dickie, M. W. (1995). 'The Dionysiac mysteries in Pella', *ZPE* 109.81–6.

Ducat, J. (1999). 'Perspectives on Spartan education in the classical period', in Hodkinson and Powell (1999) 43–66 (= Ch. 2).

Du Quesnay, I. M. Le M. (1976). 'Vergil's fourth *Eclogue*', *Papers of the Liverpool Latin Seminar* 1.25–99.

——— (1976–7). 'Virgil's fifth *Eclogue*: the song of Mopsus and the new Daphnis', *PVS* 16.18–41.

——— (1978). Review of Ross (1975), *CR* 28.276–7.

——— (1979). 'From Polyphemus to Corydon: Virgil, *Eclogue* 2 and the *Idylls* of Theocritus', in West and Woodman (1979) 35–69, 206–21.

——— (1981). 'Vergil's first Eclogue', *Papers of the Liverpool Latin Seminar* 3.29–182.

——— (1984). 'Horace and Maecenas. The propaganda value of *Sermones* I', in Woodman and West (1984) 19–58, 200–11.

——— (1992). '*In memoriam Galli*: Propertius 1.21', in Woodman and Powell (1992) 52–83, 225–36.

——— (1995). 'Horace, *Odes* 4. 5: *Pro Reditu Imperatoris Caesaris Divi Filii Augusti*', in Harrison (1995) 128–87.

Eck, W. (1995). 'Augustus und Claudius in Perusia', *Athenaeum* 83.83–90 + plate.

——— (1996). 'Cittadini e amministrazione statale nell'Umbria in età imperiale', in Bonamente and Coarelli (1996) 283–300.

Elisei, R. (1916). *Della città natale di Sesto Properzio*, 3rd edn. Rome.

Enk, P. J. (1946). (ed.) *Sex. Propertii elegiarum liber I (Monobiblos)* (2 vols). Leiden.

——— (1962). (ed.) *Sex. Propertii elegiarum liber secundus* (2 vols). Leiden.

Esteve Forriol, J. (1962). *Die Trauer- und Trostgedichte in der römischen Literatur untersucht nach ihrer Topik und ihrem Motivschatz*. Diss. Munich.

Evenepoel, W. (1990). 'Maecenas: a survey of recent literature', *Ancient Society* 21.99–117.

Fabre-Serris, J. (1995). 'Jeux de modèles dans l'Alexandrinisme romain: les hommages à Gallus dans la *Bucolique* X et l'élégie I, 20 de Properce et ses échos ovidiens', *RÉL* 73.124–37.

Fagan, G. G. (1999). *Bathing in Public in the Roman World*. Ann Arbor.

Fahlbusch, H. (1991). 'Maintenance problems in ancient aqueducts', in A. T. Hodge (ed.) *Future Currents in Aqueduct Studies*. Collected Classical Papers 2. Leeds. 7–14 and Pll. 1–3a.

Fairweather, J. A. (1974). 'Fiction in the biographies of ancient writers', *Ancient Society* 5.231–75.

——— (1981). *Seneca the Elder*. Cambridge.

——— (1984). 'The elder Seneca and declamation', *ANRW* II 32.1.514–56.

Fantham, R. E. (1979). 'Ovid's Ceyx and Alcyone: the metamorphosis of a myth', *Phoenix* 33.330–45.

(2001). 'Roman elegy: problems of self-definition, and redirection', in
    L'Histoire littéraire immanente dans la poésie latine. Fondation Hardt,
    Entretiens sur l'antiquité classique 47. Vandoeuvres–Genève. 183–211.
Fatucchi, A. (1995). 'Le tracce della *gens Cilnia* nel territorio dell'Etruria',
    Riv. Stor. Ant. (Convegno su Mecenate, Arezzo, novembre 1993) 25.187–
    205.
Fedeli, P. (1965). (ed.) *Properzio: Elegie: libro IV*. Pubblicazioni della Facol-
    tà di Lettere e Filosofia della Università degli Studi di Bari 1. Bari.
    (1980). (ed.) *Sesto Properzio: il primo libro delle elegie*. Accademia Tos-
    cana di Scienze e Lettere «La Colombaria»: Studi 53. Florence.
    (1981). 'Elegy and literary polemic in Propertius' *Monobiblos*', *Papers of
    the Liverpool Latin Seminar* 3.227–42.
    (1984). (ed.) *Sexti Properti Elegiarum Libri IV*. Stuttgart.
    (1985). (ed.) *Properzio: il libro terzo delle elegie*. Studi e commenti 3.
    Bari.
    (2005). (ed.) *Properzio: Elegie Libro II*. Arca 45. Cambridge.
Fedeli, P. and P. Pinotti (1985). *Bibliografia Properziana (1946–1983)*. Atti
    Accademia Properziana del Subasio s.VI. n. 9. Assisi.
Feichtinger, B. (1991). 'Properz, Vates oder Haruspex? Zu seinem politi-
    schen und poetischen Selbstverständnis', *Classica et Mediaevalia*
    42.187–212.
Firpo, G. (1998). 'La polemica sugli Etruschi nei poeti dell'età augustea', in
    L. Aigner-Foresti (ed.) *Die Integration der Etrusker und das Weiter-
    wirken etruskischen Kulturgutes im republikanischen und kaiserzeit-
    lichen Rom*. Österreichische Akademie der Wissenschaften. Phil.-Hist.
    Kl. Sitzungsberichte 658. Vienna. 251–98.
Flower, H. I. (1996). *Ancestor Masks and Aristocratic Power in Roman
    Culture*. Oxford.
Foresti, L. A. (1991). '*Quod discinctus eras, animo quoque, carpitur unum*
    (Maec., El., I, 21)', in M. Sordi (ed.) *L'immagine dell'uomo politico:
    vita pubblica e morale nell'antichità*. Contributi dell'Istituto di storia
    antica 17. Milan. 201–14.
    (1996). 'L'uomo Mecenate', *Riv. Stor. Ant.* 26.7–26.
Forni, G. (1977). 'Il ruolo della menzione della tribù nell'onomastica
    romana', in *L'Onomastique latine. Paris. 13–15 octobre 1975*. Colloques
    internationaux du Centre National de la Recherche Scientifique 564.
    Paris. 73–99 (discussion 99–101).
    (1982) (publ. 1984). 'Umbri antichi iscritti in tribù romane', *Bollettino
    della deputazione di storia patria per l'Umbria* 79.21–73.
    (1983). 'Un senatore romano misconosciuto verosimilmente da Assisi (*CIL*
    XI 4647)', *Bollettino della deputazione per la storia patria di Umbria*
    80.275–80.
    (1985). 'I Properzi nel mondo romano: indagine prosopografica', *Atti della
    Accademia Nazionale dei Lincei. Rendiconti. Classe di scienze morali,
    storiche e filologiche* s.viii 40.205–23 + tav. I–II.

Fortini, A. (1931). *Il più ardente poeta d'amore*. Assisi.

Fox, M. (1999). 'Propertius 4.9 and the toils of historicism', *MD* 43.157–76.

Francese, C. (1999). 'Parthenius *grammaticus*', *Mnemosyne* 52.63–71.

Frier, B. W. (1985). *The Rise of the Roman Jurists: Studies in Cicero's Pro Caecina*. Princeton NJ.

Frischer, B. D. (1995). 'Horazens Sabiner Villa. Dichtung und Wahrheit', in G. Alföldy, T. Hölscher, R. Kettemann, H. Petersmann (eds.) *Römische Lebenskunst. Interdisziplinäres Kolloquium zum 85. Geburtstag von Viktor Pöschl. Heidelberg, 2.–4. Februar 1995*. Heidelberg. 31–45.

Gabba, E. (1971). 'The Perusine war and triumviral Italy', *HSCPh* 75.139–60.

——— (1972). 'Urbanizzazione e rinnovamenti urbanistici nell'Italia centro-meridionale del I sec. a. C.', *SCO* 21.73–112.

——— (1986). 'Trasformazioni politiche e socio-economiche dell'Umbria dopo il 'Bellum Perusinum'', in G. Catanzaro and F. Santucci (eds.) *Bimillenario della morte di Properzio: Atti del convegno internazionale di studi Properziani. Roma–Assisi, 21–26 maggio 1985*. Assisi. 95–104.

Galán Vioque, G. (2002). (ed.) *Martial, Book VII*, tr. J. J. Zoltowski. Mnemosyne Suppl. 226. Leiden.

Galán, L. M. (1996). 'Gimnasia en Propercio (Elegia 3,14)', *Auster* 1.33–44.

Gale, M. R. (1994). *Myth and Poetry in Lucretius*. Cambridge.

Galinsky, K. (1996). *Augustan Culture. An Interpretive Introduction*. Princeton NJ.

Gall, D. (1999). *Zur Technik von Anspielung und Zitat in der römischen Dichtung. Vergil, Gallus und die Ciris*. Munich.

Garbarino, G. (1983). 'Epiloghi properziani: le elegie di chiusura dei primi tre libri', in *Colloquium Propertianum (tertium), Assisi, 29–31 maggio, 1981*. Assisi. 117–48.

Gauly, B. M. (1990). *Liebeserfahrungen. Zur Rolle des elegischen Ich in Ovids Amores*. Studien zur klassischen Philologie 48. Frankfurt am Main.

Georg, B. (2001). *Exegetische und schmückende Eindichtungen im ersten Properzbuch*. Studien zur Geschichte und Kultur des Altertums n.f. 1.17. Paderborn.

Giangrande, G. (1975). *L'humour des Alexandrins*. Classical and Byzantine Monographs 2. Amsterdam.

Giangrande, L. (1972). *The Use of Spoudaiogeloion in Greek and Roman Literature*. The Hague.

Giannini, A. (1965). *Paradoxographorum Graecorum Reliquiae*. Classici greci e latini. Sezione Testi e Commenti 3. Milan.

Gibson, R. K. (2003). (ed.) *Ovid Ars Amatoria Book 3*. CCTC 40. Cambridge.

Gigante, M. (1983). 'Filodemo sulla libertà di parola', in M. Gigante, *Ricerche Filodemee*, 2nd edn. Biblioteca della Parola del Passato 6. Naples. 55–113.

(1990). 'La brigata virgiliana ad Ercolano', in M. Gigante (ed.) *Virgilio e gli augustei*. Naples. 7–22.

Giordano, F. (1990). '*Nobilitas* in Ovidio', *Boll. St. Lat.* 20.344–59.

Gold, B. K. (1987). *Literary Patronage in Greece and Rome*. Chapel Hill.

Goold, G. P. (1990, rev. edn 1999). (ed.) *Propertius. Elegies*. Loeb Classical Library 18. Cambridge Mass.

Gow, A. S. F. and D. L. Page (1968). (eds.) *The Greek Anthology 2: The Garland of Philip and Some Contemporary Epigrams* (2 vols). Cambridge.

Gow, A. S. F. and A. F. Scholfield (1953). (eds.) *Nicander: The Poems and Poetical Fragments*. Cambridge.

Graver, M. (1998). 'The manhandling of Maecenas: Senecan abstractions of masculinity', *AJPh* 119.607–32.

Graverini, L. (1997). 'Un secolo di studi su Mecenate', *Riv. Stor. Ant.* 27.231–89.

Griffin, M. (1997). 'From Aristotle to Atticus: Cicero and Matius on friendship', in J. Barnes and M. Griffin (eds.) *Philosophia Togata II. Plato and Aristotle at Rome*. Oxford. 86–109.

Grüner, A. (1993). 'Zur Topographie des Esquilin in der frühen Kaiserzeit. Das Haus von Properz – Versuch einer Lokalisierung', *Boreas* 16.39–55.

Guarducci, M. (1979). '*Domus Musae*. Epigrafi greche e latine in un'antica casa di Assisi', *Atti della Accademia Nazionale dei Lincei. Memorie. Classe di Scienze morali, storiche e filologiche* s.viii 23.269–97 and Tavv. I–VII.

(1985). 'La casa di Properzio: nuove riflessioni sulla Domus Musae di Assisi e sulle sue epigrafi', *Atti della Accademia Nazionale dei Lincei. Rendiconti. Classe di Scienze morali, storiche e filologiche* s.viii 40.163–81.

Günther, H.-C. (1994). 'Tibullus Ludens', *Eikasmos* 5.251–69.

(1997). *Quaestiones Propertianae*. Mnemosyne Suppl. 169. Leiden.

Gurval, R. A. (1995). *Actium and Augustus: The Politics and Emotions of Civil War*. Ann Arbor.

Hall, J. F. (1996a). (ed.) *Etruscan Italy: Etruscan Influences on the Civilisations of Italy from Antiquity to the Modern Era*. Provo Utah.

(1996b). 'From Tarquins to Caesars: Etruscan governance at Rome', in Hall (1996a) 149–89.

Halliwell, S. (1993). (ed.) *Plato Republic 5*. Warminster.

Hammond, M. (1980). 'An unpublished Latin funerary inscription of persons connected with Maecenas', *HSCPh* 84.263–77.

Hardie, A. (2003). 'The Pindaric sources of Horace *Odes* 1.12', *HSCPh* 101.371–404.

Hardie, P. R. (1986). *Virgil's Aeneid: Cosmos and Imperium*. Oxford.

(1996). 'Virgil: a paradoxical poet?', *Papers of the Leeds International Latin Seminar* 9.103–21.

(2002). *Ovid's Poetics of Illusion*. Cambridge.

Harrauer, H. (1973). *Bibliography to the Augustan Poetry. II. A Bibliography to Propertius*. Hildesheim.

Harris, H. A. (1964). *Greek Athletes and Athletics*. London.

(1972). *Sport in Greece and Rome*. London.

Harris, W. V. (1971). *Rome in Etruria and Umbria*. Oxford.

Harrison, S. J. (1995). (ed.) *Homage to Horace. A Bimillenary Celebration*. Oxford.

(2005). 'Hercules and Augustus in Propertius 4.9', *Papers of the Langford Latin Seminar* 12.117–31.

Häuber, R. C. (1990). 'Zur Topographie der Horti Maecenatis und der Horti Lamiani auf dem Esquilin in Rom', *Kölner Jahrbuch für Vor- und Frühgeschichte* 23.11–107.

Heckel, W. and J. C. Yardley (1981). 'Roman writers and the Indian practice of suttee', *Philologus* 125.305–11.

Heiden, B. (1995). '*Sic te servato*: an interpretation of Propertius 1.21', *CPh* 90.161–7.

Helzle, M. (1989). (ed.) *Publii Ovidii Nasonis Epistularum ex Ponto liber IV. A Commentary on Poems 1 to 7 and 16*. Spudasmata 43. Hildesheim.

Hendry, M. (1997). 'Three Propertian puns', *CQ* 47.599–603.

Herter, H. (1926). *De Dis Atticis Priapi Similibus*. Diss. Bonn.

(1932). *De Priapo*. Religionsgeschichtliche Versuche und Vorarbeiten 23. Giessen.

Hertzberg, G. A. B. (1843–5). (ed.) *Sex. Aurelii Propertii Elegiarum Libri Quattuor* (4 vols). Halle.

Heyworth, S. J. (1992). 'Propertius 2.13', *Mnemosyne* 45.45–59.

Hickson, F. V. (1991). '*Augustus triumphator*: manipulation of the triumphal theme in the political program of Augustus', *Latomus* 50.124–38.

Hinds, S. (1983). 'Carmina digna. Gallus P Qaṣr Ibrîm 6–7 metamorphosed', *Papers of the Liverpool Latin Seminar* 4.43–54.

Hodkinson, S. (1986). 'Land tenure and inheritance in classical Sparta', *CQ* 36.378–406.

(1989). 'Inheritance, marriage and demography: perspectives upon the success and decline of classical Sparta', in A. Powell (ed.) *Classical Sparta: Techniques behind her Success*. London. 79–121.

(1999). 'An agonistic culture? Athletic competition in archaic and classical Spartan society', in Hodkinson and Powell (1999) 147–87 (= Ch. 6).

Hodkinson, S. and A. Powell (1999). (eds.) *Sparta: New Perspectives*. London.

Holleman, A. W. J. (1977). 'Propertius IV 9: an Augustan view of Roman religion', *Revue Belge de Philologie et d'Histoire* 55.79–92.

Hollis, A. S. (1977). (ed.) *Ovid: Ars Amatoria Book I*. Oxford.

(1977). 'L. Varius Rufus, *De morte* (frs. 1–4 Morel)', *CQ* 27.187–90.

(1990). (ed.) *Callimachus Hecale*. Oxford.

(1996). Virgil's friend Varius Rufus', *PVS* 22.19–33.

Holzberg, N. (2004a). *Die Römische Elegie. Gallus – Properz – Tibull – Ovid, Amores. Eine Bibliographie.* Munich.

(2004b). 'Impersonating young Virgil: the author of the Catalepton and his libellus', *MD* 52.29–40.

Hopkins, K. (1974). 'Elite mobility in the Roman empire', in M. I. Finley, (ed.) *Studies in Ancient Society.* London. 103–20 (= Ch. 5).

(1978). *Conquerors and Slaves: Sociological Studies in Roman History 1.* Cambridge.

(1983). *Death and Renewal: Sociological Studies in Roman History 2.* Cambridge.

Horsfall, N. M. (1981). *Poets and Patron. Maecenas, Horace and the Georgics, Once More.* Publications of the Macquarie Ancient History Association 3. North Ryde.

(1995). 'Virgil: his life and times', in N. M. Horsfall (ed.) *A Companion to the Study of Virgil.* Leiden. 1–25 (= Ch. 1).

Hubaux, J. (1930). *Les thèmes bucoliques dans la poésie latine.* Académie royale de Belgique. Classe des Lettres et des Sciences morales et politiques. Mémoires 8.29.1. Brussels.

(1957). 'Parthenius. Gallus. Virgile. Properce', in *Miscellanea Properziana, Atti Accademia Properziana del Subasio – Assisi* s.V 5.31–8.

Hubbard, M. (1974). *Propertius.* London.

Hutchinson, G. O. (1988). *Hellenistic Poetry.* Oxford.

Indelli, G. and V. Tsouna-McKirahan (1995). (eds.) *Philodemus: On Choices and Avoidances.* La Scuola di Epicuro 15. Naples.

Innes, D. C. (1979). 'Gigantomachy and natural philosophy', *CQ* 29.165–71.

Isager, J. (1998). 'Propertius and the *monumenta* of Actium. (IV, 6 as a topographical source)', in S. Dietz and S. Isager (eds.) *Proceedings of the Danish Institute at Athens.* Aarhus. II.399–411.

Janan, M. W. (2001). *The Politics of Desire: Propertius IV.* Berkeley.

Jenkyns, R. (1993). 'Virgil and the Euphrates', *AJPh* 114.115–21.

Jocelyn, H. D. (1980). 'The fate of Varius' *Thyestes*', *CQ* 30.387–400.

(1990). Review of Cova (1989), *Gnomon* 62.596–600.

Jones, H. (1992). 'The death of the paraclausithyron: Propertius 1.16', in R. M. Wilhelm and H. Jones (eds.) *The Two Worlds of the Poet. New Perspectives on Vergil.* Detroit. 303–9

Juhnke, H. (1963). *Das dichterische Selbstverständnis des Horaz und Properz.* Diss. Kiel.

Jüthner, J. (1965). *Die athletischen Leibesübungen der Griechen. I. Geschichte der Leibesübungen.* Österreichische Akademie der Wissenschaften. Philosophisch-Historische Klasse. Sitzungsberichte, 249. Band, 1. Abhandlung. ed. F. Brein. Graz.

(1968). *Die athletischen Leibesübungen der Griechen. II. Einzelne Sportarten. 1. Lauf-, Sprung- und Wurfbewerbe.* Österreichische Akademie der Wissenschaften. Philosophisch-Historische Klasse. Sitzungsberichte, 249. Band, 2. Abhandlung. ed. F. Brein. Graz.

Kaser, M. (1971). *Das römische Privatrecht 1. Das altrömische, das vor-klassische und klassische Recht*, 2nd edn. Rechtsgeschichte des Altertums 3.3.1. Munich.

Kaster, R. A. (1995). (ed.) *Suetonius. De Grammaticis et Rhetoribus*. Oxford.

Kennedy, D. F. (1982). 'Gallus and the *Culex*', *CQ* 32.371–89.

(1987). '*Arcades ambo*: Virgil, Gallus and Arcadia', *Hermathena* 143.47–59.

Kennell, N. M. (1995). *The Gymnasium of Virtue. Education and Culture in Ancient Sparta*. Chapel Hill.

Kenney, E. J. (1969). 'Ovid and the law', *YClS* 21.243–63.

Keppie, L. (1983). *Colonisation and Veteran Settlement in Italy: 47–14 BC*. London.

Kershaw, A. (1980). 'Emendation and usage: two readings of Propertius', *CPh* 75.71–2.

(1983). '*A!* and the elegists: more observations', *CPh* 78.232–3.

Keyser, P. T. (1992). 'The length and scansion of Propertius II as evidence of book division', *Philologus* 136.81–8.

Keyssner, K. (1938). 'Die Bildende Kunst bei Properz', in R. Herbig (ed.) *Würzburger Festgabe. Heinrich Bulle dargebracht zum siebzigsten Geburtstag am 11. Dezember 1937*. Würzburger Studien zur Altertumswissenschaft 13. Stuttgart. 169–89.

Kienast, D. (1982). *Augustus. Prinzeps und Monarch*. Darmstadt.

King, J. K. (1980). 'The two Galluses of Propertius' Monobiblos', *Philologus* 124.212–30.

Kleinknecht, H. (1937). *Die Gebetsparodie in der Antike*. Tübinger Beiträge zur Altertumswissenschaft 28. Stuttgart.

Knauer, G. N. (1964). *Die Aeneis und Homer: Studien zur poetischen Technik Vergils mit Listen der Homerzitate in der Aeneis*. Hypomnemata 7. Göttingen.

Knox, P. E. (1985). 'The old Gallus', *Hermes* 113.497.

(1995). (ed.) *Ovid. Heroides. Select Epistles*. Cambridge.

(2005). 'Milestones in the Career of Tibullus', *CQ* 55.204–16.

Kölblinger, G. (1971). *Einige Topoi bei den lateinischen Liebesdichtern*. Dissertationen der Universität Graz 15. Vienna.

Konstan, D., D. Clay, C. E. Glad, J. C. Thom and J. Ware (1998). *Philodemus On Frank Criticism. Introduction, Translation, and Notes*. Society of Biblical Literature, Texts and Translations 43, Graeco-Roman 13. Atlanta GA.

Kragelund, P. (1989). 'Epicurus, Priapus and the dreams in Petronius', *CQ* 39.436–50.

Krenkel, W. A. (1977a). 'Exhibitionismus in der Antike', *Wissenschaftliche Zeitschrift der Wilhelm-Pieck-Universität Rostock* 26.613–18.

(1977b). 'Skopophilie in der Antike', *Wissenschaftliche Zeitschrift der Wilhelm-Pieck-Universität Rostock* 26.619–31.

Kroll, W. (1959). (ed.) *C. Valerius Catullus*, 3rd edn. Stuttgart.

La Bua, G. (1999). *L'Inno nella letteratura poetica latina*. Drion. Studi sul mondo classico 1. San Severo.

La Penna, A. (1977). *L'integrazione difficile. Un profilo di Properzio*. Turin.

Lana, I. (1948). 'Sull'elegia III, 14 di Properzio', *RFIC* 26.37–45.

Lanzara, V. G. (1990). 'Virgilio e Properzio', in M. Gigante (ed.) *Virgilio e gli Augustei*. Naples. 111–76.

Larson, J. (1997). 'Astacides the goatherd (Callim. *Epigr.* 22 Pf.)', *CPh* 92.131–7.

Lavagne, H. (1988). *Operosa Antra: Recherches sur la Grotte à Rome de Sylla à Hadrien*. BEFAR 272. Rome.

Leach, E. W. (1992). 'Polyphemus in a landscape: traditions of pastoral courtship', in J. Dixon Hunt (ed.) *The Pastoral Landscape*. National Gallery of Art. Studies in the History of Art 36. 63–87.

Lee, G. (1982). (ed.) *Tibullus: Elegies*, 2nd edn. Liverpool Latin Texts (Classical and Medieval) 3. Liverpool.

Lee, G. with R. Maltby (1990). (ed.) *Tibullus: Elegies*, 3rd edn. Latin and Greek Texts 6. Leeds.

Lee, G. with O. Lyne (1994). (ed.) *Propertius. The Poems*. Oxford.

Lee, H. M. (1988). 'SIG³ 802: did women compete against men in Greek athletic festivals?', *Nikephoros* 1.103–17.

Lefèvre, E. (1966). *Propertius ludibundus. Elemente des Humors in seinen Elegien*. Heidelberg.

——— (1980). 'L'unité de l'élégie II, 34 de Properce', in *L'Élégie romaine. Enracinement—Thèmes—Diffusion*. Bulletin de la Faculté des Lettres de Mulhouse 10. 123–9.

——— (1981). 'Horaz und Maecenas', *ANRW* II.31.3.1987–2029.

——— (1991). 'Propertius Pindaricus. Der Sinn der Elegie 3,17 und ihr Verhältnis zu 3,18', in *Studi di Filologia classica in onore di Giusto Monaco* II. Palermo. 1001–5.

Lefkowitz, M. R. (1981). *The Lives of the Greek Poets*. London.

Leigh, M. (1994). 'Servius on Vergil's senex Corycius: new evidence', *MD* 33.181–95.

Leo, F. (1902). 'Vergil und die Ciris', *Hermes* 37.14–55.

——— (1907). 'Nochmals die Ciris und Vergil', *Hermes* 42.35–77.

Levi, M. A. (1998). '*Nobilis* e *nobilitas*', *REA* 100.555–9.

Lewis, N. (1975). '*P. Oxy.* 2820: whose preparations?', *GRBS* 16.295–303.

Ley, A. (1990). 'Atalante – Von der Athletin zur Liebhaberin. Ein Beitrag zum Rezeptionswandel eines mythologischen Themas auf Vasen des 6.–4. Jhs. v. Chr.', *Nikephoros* 3.31–72 Abb. 1–20.

Lieberg, G. (1996). 'Mecenate letterato', *Boll. St. Lat.* 26.9–18.

——— (1997–2000). '*Desertus* bei Properz und Catull', *Museum Criticum* 32–35.153–65.

——— (2002). 'Amor et Roma apud Propertium, Tibullum, Ovidium', *Hermes* 130.433–48.

Lightfoot, J. L. (1999). (ed.) *Parthenius of Nicaea. The Poetical Fragments and the Ἐρωτικὰ Παθήματα.* Oxford.

Lindheim, S. H. (1998). 'Hercules cross-dressed, Hercules undressed: unmasking the construction of the Propertian *amator* in Elegy 4.9', *AJPh* 119.43–66.

Lintott, A. (2001–3). '*Delator* and *index*: informers and accusers at Rome from the Republic to the early Principate', *Accordia Research Papers* 9.105–22.

Littlewood, R. J. (1975). 'Two elegiac hymns: Propertius, 3.17 and Ovid, *Fasti* 5.663–692', *Latomus* 34.662–74.

Long, A. A. and D. N. Sedley (1987). *The Hellenistic Philosophers* (2 vols). Cambridge.

Luque Moreno, J. (1994). *El dístico elegíaco. Lecciones de métrica latina.* Madrid.

—— (1995). 'Tibulo a través de Ovidio', *Emerita* 63.341–51.

Lyne, R. O. A. M. (1978). (ed.) *Ciris: A Poem Attributed to Vergil.* CCTC 20. Cambridge.

—— (1979). 'Servitium amoris', *CQ* 29.117–30.

—— (1998). 'Propertius and Tibullus: early exchanges', *CQ* 48.519–44.

MacDowell, D. M. (1986). *Spartan Law.* Scottish Classical Studies 1. Edinburgh.

MacFarlane, R. T. (1996). '*Tyrrhena regum progenies*: Etruscan literary figures from Horace to Ovid', in Hall (1996a) 241–65.

McKeown, J. C. (1987). (ed.) *Ovid: Amores. I. Text and Prolegomena.* Arca 20. Liverpool.

—— (1989). *Ovid: Amores. II. A Commentary on Book One.* Arca 22. Leeds.

—— (1998). *Ovid: Amores. III. A Commentary on Book Two.* Arca 36. Leeds.

McLennan, G. (1972). 'Arte allusiva and Ovidian metrics', *Hermes* 100.495–6.

Macleod, C. (1975). 'In line with Catullus', review of Ross (1975), *TLS* 1326 (7.11.75).

McParland, E. (1970). 'Propertius 4.9', *TAPA* 101.349–55.

Maddoli, G. (1963). 'Ancora sulla patria di Properzio', *Parola del Passato* 18.295–301.

Mader, G. (1994). 'Propertius' hymn to Bacchus (3,17) and the poetic design of the third book', in C. Deroux (ed.) *Studies in Latin Literature and Roman History VII.* Collection Latomus 227. Brussels. 369–85.

—— (2003). '*Aetas prima canat veneres*: Propertius and the poetics of age', *WS* 116.115–34.

Maggiani, A. (1986). '*Cilnium genus.* La documentazione epigrafica etrusca', *Studi Etruschi* 54.171–96 with plates L–LIV (including [193–6] Appendice, Le due iscrizioni aretine di probabile rinvenimento cinquecentesco, by Armando Cherici).

Magi, F. (1963). 'Le iscrizioni recentemente scoperte sull'obelisco Vaticano', *Studi Romani* 11.50–6.

Magnelli, E. (1999). (ed.) *Alexandri Aetoli Testimonia et Fragmenta*. Studi e Testi 15. Florence.

Maltby, R. (1993). 'Varro's attitude to Latin derivations from Greek', *Papers of the Leeds International Latin Seminar* 7.47–60.

—— (1999). 'Tibullus and the language of Latin elegy', in J. Adams and R. Mayer (eds.) *Aspects of the Language of Latin Poetry*. Proceedings of the British Academy 93. London. 377–98.

—— (2002). (ed.) *Tibullus: Elegies*. Arca 41. Leeds.

Manca, M. L. (1996). 'Le mura di «*Asisium*»', in Bonamente and Coarelli (1996) 359–74.

Manconi, D., P. Camerieri, V. Cruciani (1996). '*Hispellum*: pianificazione urbana e territoriale', in Bonamente and Coarelli (1996) 375–429.

Manzoni, G. E. (1995). *Foroiuliensis poeta. Vita e poesia di Cornelio Gallo*. Milan.

Marasco, G. (1992). 'Marco Antonio «Nuovo Dionisio» e il *De sua ebrietate*', *Latomus* 51.538–48.

Marina Sáez, R. M. (2003). 'Notas sobre la estructura métrico-verbal del final del pentámetro latino tardío', *Latomus* 62.648–63.

Marioni, G. D. (1984). 'Una reminiscenza di Cornelio Gallo nella *Consolatio ad Liviam* e il tema del trionfo negli elegiaci', in Tandoi (1984–5) I.88–98.

Mariotti, S. (1963). 'Intorno a Domitio Marso', in *Miscellanea di studi alessandrini in memoria di Augusto Rostagni*. Turin. 588–614.

Marshall, A. J. (1976). 'Library resources and creative writing at Rome', *Phoenix* 30.252–64.

Martin, J. (1974). *Antike Rhetorik. Technik und Methode*. Handbuch der Altertumswissenschaft 2.3. Munich.

Martin, R. H. (1998). 'Tacitus on Agricola: truth and stereotype', in J. Bird (ed.) *Form and Fabric: Studies in Rome's Material Past in Honour of B. R. Hartley*. Oxbow Monograph 80. Oxford. 9–12 (= Ch. 2).

Martini, R. (1995). 'Di una causa giudiziaria, inter Terentiam et Maecenatem', *Riv. Stor. Ant. (Convegno su Mecenate, Arezzo, novembre 1993)* 25.177–85.

Marx, F. (1894). (ed.) *Incerti Auctoris de Ratione Dicendi ad C. Herennium Libri IV [M. Tulli Ciceronis ad Herennium Libri IV]*. Leipzig.

Massimilla, G. (1996). (ed.) *Callimaco. Aitia. Libri primo e secondo*. Biblioteca di studi antichi 77. Pisa.

Meillier, C. (1979). *Callimaque et son temps. Recherches sur la carrière et la condition d'un écrivain à l'époque des premiers Lagides*. Publications de l'Université de Lille 3. Lille.

Merkle, S. (1983). 'Amores 3,2 und Ars Amatoria 1,135–162 – ein Selbstplagiat Ovids?', *Živa Antika* 33.135–45.

Merriam, C. U. (1990). 'The new Gallus revisited', *Latomus* 49.443–52.

Michalopoulos, A. (2001). *Ancient Etymologies in Ovid's Metamorphoses. A Commented Lexicon*. Arca 40. Leeds.

Millender, E. (1999). 'Athenian ideology and the empowered Spartan woman', in Hodkinson and Powell (1999) 355–91 (= Ch. 13).

Miller, J. F. (1981). 'Propertius 2.1 and the new Gallus papyrus', *ZPE* 44.173–6.

(1991). 'Propertius' hymn to Bacchus and contemporary poetry', *AJPh* 112.77–86.

Miller, P. A. (2004). *Subjecting Verses: Latin Love Elegy and the Emergence of the Real*. Princeton NJ.

Mitchell, R. N. (1985). 'Propertius on poetry and poets: tradition and the individual erotic talent', *Ramus* 14.46–58.

Moles, J. (1983). 'Fate, Apollo and M. Junius Brutus', *AJPh* 104.249–56.

(2002). 'Reconstructing Plancus (Horace *C*. 1.7)', *JRS* 92.86–109.

Momigliano, A. (1941). 'Benjamin Farrington, *Science and Politics in the Ancient World*', review article, *JRS* 31.149–57.

Monteleone, C. (1979). 'Cornelio Gallo tra Ila e le Driadi (Virgilio, Properzio e una controversia letteraria)', *Latomus* 38.28–53.

(1992). *Stratigrafie esegetiche*. Bari.

Morelli, A. M. (1985). 'Rassegna sul nuovo Gallo', in Tandoi (1984–5) II.140–83.

Morelli, A. M. and V. Tandoi (1984). 'Un probabile omaggio a Cornelio Gallo nella seconda Ecloga', in Tandoi (1984–5) I.101–16.

Murgatroyd, P. (1975). '*Militia amoris* and the Roman elegists', *Latomus* 34.59–79.

(1981). '*Seruitium Amoris* and the Roman elegists', *Latomus* 40.589–606.

(1992). 'Setting in six versions of the Hylas myth', in *Studies in Latin Literature and Roman History VI*. Collection Latomus 217. Brussels. 84–93.

Murray, O. (1985). 'Symposium and genre in the poetry of Horace', *JRS* 75.39–50.

Muth, S. (1999). 'Hylas oder "Der ergriffene Mann" : Zur Eigenständigkeit der Mythenrezeption in der Bildkunst', in F. de Angelis and S. Muth (eds.) *Im Spiegel des Mythos. Bilderwelt und Lebenswelt. Symposium, Rom 19.-20. Februar 1998 = Lo specchio del mito. Immaginario e realtà*. Palilia 6. Wiesbaden. 109–29.

Mynors, R. A. B. (1990). (ed.) *Virgil, Georgics*. Oxford.

Navarro Antolín, F. (1996). (ed.) *Lygdamus. Corpus Tibullianum III.1–6. Lygdami Elegiarum Liber*, tr. J. J. Zoltowski. Mnemosyne Suppl. 154. Leiden.

Nelis, D. (2001). *Vergil's Aeneid and the Argonautica of Apollonius Rhodius*. Arca 39. Leeds.

Nethercut, W. R. (1970). 'Propertius 3. 12–14', *CPh* 65.99–102.

(1972). 'Propertius, Elegy II, 10', *SO* 47.79–94.

Neumann, E. (1925). *De Cottidiani Sermonis apud Propertium Proprietatibus. Accedit Mantissa de Codicibus D et V*. Diss. Königsberg.

Newman, J. K. (1980). 'De novo Galli fragmento in Nubia eruto', *Latinitas* 28.83–94.

(1997). *Augustan Propertius: The Recapitulations of a Genre*. Spudasmata 63. Hildesheim.

Nicastri, L. (1984). *Cornelio Gallo e l'elegia ellenistico-romana. Studio dei nuovi frammenti*. Naples.

Nicolet, C. (1966–74). *L'ordre équestre à l'époque républicaine (312–43 av. J.-C.)* (2 vols). BEFAR 207. Paris.

Nigro, M. A. (1998). 'La prima *Elegia a Mecenate*. Apologia di un ministro e propaganda di regime', *Ant. Class.* 67.137–48.

Nisbet, R. G. (1939). (ed.) *M. Tulli Ciceronis: De Domo Sua ad Pontifices Oratio*. Oxford.

Nisbet, R. G. M. and M. Hubbard (1970). *A Commentary on Horace: Odes Book I*. Oxford.

(1978). *A Commentary on Horace: Odes Book II*. Oxford.

Nisbet, R. G. M. and N. Rudd (2004). *A Commentary on Horace: Odes Book III*. Oxford.

Noonan, J. D. (1991). 'Re-examining the text and meaning of the Gallus fragment', *Latomus* 50.118–23.

Norden, E. (1913). *Agnostos Theos. Untersuchungen zur Formen-Geschichte religiöser Rede*. Leipzig.

O'Hara, J. J. (1996). *True Names: Vergil and the Alexandrian Tradition of Etymological Wordplay*. Ann Arbor.

(1998). 'Venus or the Muse as "Ally" (Lucr. 1.24, Simon. Frag. Eleg. 11.20–22W)', *CPh* 93.69–74.

O'Neill, K. (2000). 'Propertius 4.2: slumming with Vertumnus?', *AJPh* 121.259–77.

Obbink, D. (1996). (ed.) *Philodemus On Piety: Part 1*. Oxford.

Ogilvie, R. M. (1965). *A Commentary on Livy Books 1–5*. Oxford.

Paci, G. (1986). 'Gli Albii del Lazio e il nome di Tibullo', in *Atti del convegno internazionale di studi su Albio Tibullo (Roma-Palestrina, 10–13 maggio 1984)*. Rome. 275–90.

Paley, F. A. (1872). (ed.) *Sex. Aurelii Propertii Carmina: The Elegies of Propertius with English Notes*, 2nd edn. London.

Palmer, R. E. A. (1989[1998]). 'Bullae Insignia Ingenuitatis', *AJAH* 14.1–69.

Papanghelis, T. D. (1987). *Propertius: A Hellenistic Poet on Love and Death*. Cambridge.

Parássoglou, G. M. (1978). *Imperial Estates in Roman Egypt*. American Studies in Papyrology 18. Amsterdam.

Parker, H. N. (1991). 'The bones: Propertius 1.21.9–10', *CPh* 86.328–33.

(1992). 'The fertile fields of Umbria: Prop. 1.22.10', *Mnemosyne* 45.88–92.

Pasoli, E. (1977). 'Gli *amores* di Cornelio Gallo nell'ecloga X di Virgilio e nell'elegia I,8 di Properzio. Riconsiderazione del problema', *RCCM* 19.585–96.

Patillon, M. and G. Bolognesi (1997). (eds.) *Aelius Théon: Progymnasmata*. Paris.

Pellegrino, C. (1995). 'Per l'interpretazione di Properzio I, 21', *Latomus* 54.613–24.

Pelling, C. B. R. (1988). *Plutarch. Life of Antony.* Cambridge.

Perkell, C. G. (1996). 'The 'dying Gallus' and the design of *Eclogue* 10', *CPh* 91.128–40.

Perrin, Y. (1996). '*Turris Maecenatiana*: une note d'histoire et de topographie', *Latomus* 55.399–410.

Petrain, D. (2000). 'Hylas and *silva*: etymological wordplay in Propertius 1.20', *HSCPh* 100.409–21.

Pfanner, M. (1983). *Der Titusbogen.* Mainz am Rhein.

Pianezzola, E. (1987). 'Il canto di trionfo nell'elegia latina. Trasposizione di un topos', in *Filologia e forme letterarie. Studi offerti a Francesco Della Corte* III. Urbino. 131–42.

Pianezzola, E. (ed.) with G. Baldo and L. Cristanti (1991). *Ovidio. L'Arte di amare.* Milan.

Picard, G. C. (1957). *Les trophées romains. Contribution à l'histoire de la religion et de l'art triomphal de Rome.* BEFAR 187. Paris.

Piccaluga, G. (1964). 'Bona Dea: due contributi all'interpretazione del suo culto', *Studi e Materiali di Storia delle Religioni* 35.195–237.

Pichon, R. (1902). *Index verborum amatoriorum*, repr. Hildesheim 1966 (= *De sermone amatorio apud Latinos elegiarum scriptores*, Diss. Paris (1902) 75–303).

Pillinger, H. E. (1969). 'Some Callimachean influences on Propertius, Book 4', *HSCPh* 73.171–99.

Pinotti, P. (1977). 'Propert. IV 9: Alessandrinismo e arte allusiva', *GIF* 29.50–71.

———(1983). 'Properzio e Vertumno: anticonformismo e restaurazione augustea', in *Colloquium Propertianum (tertium). Assisi, 29–31 maggio 1981. Atti.* Assisi. 75–96.

———(2004). *Primus Ingredior. Studi su Properzio.* Testi e Manuali per l'insegnamento universitario del Latino 84. Bologna.

Pizzani, U. (1996). 'Le vite umanistiche di Properzio', in Bonamente and Coarelli (1996) 483–516.

Platnauer, M. (1951). *Latin Elegiac Verse: A Study of the Metrical Usages of Tibullus, Propertius and Ovid.* Cambridge.

Poccetti, P. (1986). 'Sul nome preromano di Assisi, in margine alla restituzione testuale di Properzio IV 1,125', in *Atti Accademia Properziana del Subasio* s. VI 13.45–61.

Pohlenz, M. (1913). 'Die Abfassungszeit von Ovids Metamorphosen', *Hermes* 48.1–13.

Poma, G. (1995). 'Civis Romanus nell'Arezzo di Mecenate', *Riv. Stor. Ant. (Convegno su Mecenate, Arezzo, novembre 1993)* 25.157–67.

Pomeroy, S. B. (2002). *Spartan Women.* Oxford.

Poulsen, B. (1991). 'The Dioscuri and ruler ideology', *SO* 66.119–46.

Powell, A. (1999). 'Spartan women assertive in politics? Plutarch's Lives of Agis and Kleomenes', in Hodkinson and Powell (1999) 393–419 (= Ch. 14).

Prato, C. (1964). (ed.) *Gli Epigrammi attribuiti a L. Anneo Seneca.* Rome.

Prosdocimi, A. L. (1981). Review of E. Campanile and C. Letta, *Studi sulle magistrature indigene e municipali in area italica* (Pisa 1979), *Studi Etruschi* 49.548–63.

Puelma, M. (1982). 'Die Aetien des Kallimachos als Vorbild der römischen Amores-Elegie' I and II, *MH* 39.221–46, 285–304.

Pulgram, E. (1978). (ed.) *Italic, Latin, Italian 600 BC to AD 1260.* Heidelberg.

Purcell, N. (1986). 'Livia and the womanhood of Rome', *PCPhS* 32.78–105.

Putnam, M. C. J. (1980). 'Propertius and the new Gallus fragment', *ZPE* 39.49–56.

Raaflaub, K. A. and M. Toher (1990). (eds.) *Between Republic and Empire: Interpretations of Augustus and his Principate.* Berkeley.

Raaflaub, K. A. and L. J. Samons II (1990). 'Opposition to Augustus', in Raaflaub and Toher (1990) 417–54.

Raditsa, L. F. (1980). 'Augustus' legislation concerning marriage, procreation, love affairs and adultery', *ANRW* II.13.278–339.

Reinsch-Werner, H. (1976). *Callimachus Hesiodicus: die Rezeption der hesiodischen Dichtung durch Kallimachos von Kyrene.* Diss. Berlin.

Reitzenstein, R. (1896). 'Properz-Studien', *Hermes* 31.185–220.

Rich, J. W. (1996). 'Augustus and the spolia opima', *Chiron* 26.85–127.

Richardson, L., Jr. (1977). (ed.) *Propertius Elegies I-IV.* Norman Oklahoma.

Rix, H. (1998). 'Teonimi etruschi e teonimi italici', in *Etrusca disciplina e culti stranieri in Etruria. Atti dei Convegni IV e V (= Annali della fondazione per il museo «Claudio Faina» 5).* Orvieto. 207–29.

Rocca, R. (1989). *Epici minori d'età augustea.* Pubblicazioni del D. Ar. Fi. Cl. e T. n.s. 124. Genoa.

Roddaz, J.-M. (1984). *Marcus Agrippa.* BEFAR 253. Rome.

—— (1988). 'Lucius Antonius', *Historia* 37.317–46.

Rodríguez-Almeida, E. (1987). 'Qualche osservazione sulle Esquiliae patrizie e il lacus Orphei', in *L'Urbs. Espace urbain et histoire (Ier siècle av. J.-C. – IIIe siècle ap. J.-C.). Actes du colloque international organisé par le Centre national de la recherche scientifique et l'École française de Rome (Rome, 8–12 mai 1985).* Collection de l'École française de Rome 98. Rome. 415–28.

Rohr, F. (1994). '*Non fuit obprobrio celebrasse Lycorida Gallo* (Ovidio e la memoria di Gaio Cornelio Gallo)', *Sileno* 20.305–16.

Rosati, G. (2005). 'Elegy after the elegists: from opposition to assent', *Papers of the Langford Latin Seminar* 12.133–50.

Rose, H. J. (1927). ''Mox'', *CQ* 21.57–66.

Rosen, R. M. and J. Farrell (1986). 'Acontius, Milanion, and Gallus: Vergil *Ecl.* 10.52–61', *TAPA* 116.241–54.

Rosiello, F. (2002). 'Semantica di *error* in Ovidio', *Boll. St. Lat.* 32.424–62.

Ross, D. O., Jr. (1975). *Backgrounds to Augustan Poetry: Gallus Elegy and Rome.* Cambridge.

Rostagni, A. (1959). 'Il *De morte* di L. Vario Rufo', *RFIC* 87.380–94.

——— (1964). (ed.) *Svetonio De poetis e biografi minori.* Turin.

Rothstein, M. (1920–4). (ed.) *Die Elegien des Sextus Propertius*, 2nd edn (2 vols). Berlin.

Rotili, M. (1972). *L'Arco di Traiano a Benevento.* Rome.

Russell, D. A. and N. G. Wilson (1981). (eds.) *Menander Rhetor.* Oxford.

Saller, R. P. (1982). *Personal Patronage under the Early Empire.* Cambridge.

——— (1989). 'Patronage and friendship in early Imperial Rome: drawing the distinction', in A. Wallace-Hadrill (ed.) *Patronage in Ancient Society.* London. 49–62 (= Ch. 2).

——— (1994). Patriarchy, Property and Death in the Roman Family. Cambridge.

Salomies, O. (1992). *Adoptive and Polyonymous Nomenclature in the Roman Empire.* Commentationes Humanarum Litterarum 97. Helsinki.

Salvaterra, C. (1987). '*Forum Iulium* nell'iscrizione di C. Cornelio Gallo sull'obelisco Vaticano', *Aegyptus* 67.171–81.

Salvatore, A. (1965). 'La patria di Properzio ed aspetti del paesaggio Umbro nel tardo-antico', in *Ricorde sull'Umbria tardo-antica e preromanica – Atti del II convegno di Studi Umbri – Gubbio – 24–28 maggio.* Gubbio. 379–98.

Santini, C. (1966). '*Pun.* 8, 446–462: l'Umbria di Silio Italico', in Bonamente and Coarelli (1996) 517–30.

Santini, C. and F. Santucci (2004). (eds.) *Properzio tra storia arte mito. Atti del convegno internazionale. Assisi, 24–26 maggio 2002.* Assisi.

Santucci, F. (1976). 'Note di toponomastica assisana', *Bollettino della deputazione di storia patria per l'Umbria* 73.223–31.

Sartorio, G. P. (1996). 'Mecenate sull'Esquilino', *Riv. Stor. Ant.* 26.33–45.

Scanlon, T. F. (1988). 'Virgineum gymnasium: Spartan females and early Greek athletics', in W. J. Raschke (ed.) *The Archaeology of the Olympics: The Olympics and Other Festivals in Antiquity.* Madison Wis. 185–216 (= Ch. 12).

Scheidel, W. (1997). 'Continuity and change in classical scholarship: a quantitative survey 1924–1992', *Ancient Society* 28.265–89.

Schmidt, E. A. (1979). Review of Ross (1975), *Gnomon* 51.432–5.

Schmitzer, U. (1990). *Zeitgeschichte in Ovids Metamorphosen. Mythologische Dichtung unter politischem Anspruch.* Beiträge zur Altertumswissenschaft 4. Stuttgart.

——— (2002). 'Die Macht über die Imagination. Literatur und Politik unter den Bedingungen des frühen Prinzipats', *RhM* 145.281–304.

Schoonhoven, H. (1980). *Elegiae in Maecenatem. Prolegomena, Text and Commentary.* Diss. Groningen.

——— (1983). '... si parva licet componere magnis (a note on the new Gallus papyrus, ll.3–5)', *ZPE* 53.73–8.

(1992). (ed.) *The Pseudo-Ovidian Ad Liviam de Morte Drusi (Consolatio ad Liviam, Epicedium Drusi)*. Groningen.

Schork, R. J. (2004). 'Horatian meditation on Gallus' gold', *Latomus* 63.81–7.

Schulze, W. (1904). *Zur Geschichte lateinischer Eigennamen*. Abhandl. d. Königlichen Gesellschaft der Wissenschaften zu Göttingen, Phil.-Hist. Klasse, n.f. Bd. 5.5. Berlin.

Schuster, M. (1958). (ed.) *Sex. Propertii elegiarum libri IV*, 2nd edn, corr. F. Dornseiff. Leipzig.

Seager, R. (1980). '*Neu sinas Medos equitare inultos*: Horace, the Parthians and Augustan foreign policy', *Athenaeum* 58.103–18.

Sedley, D. (1997). 'The ethics of Brutus and Cassius', *JRS* 87.41–53.

(1998). *Lucretius and the Transformation of Greek Wisdom*. Cambridge.

Sensi, L. (1983). 'Assisi: Aspetti Prosopografici', in *Les «Bourgeoisies» municipales italiennes aux IIe et Ier siècles av. J.-C.: Centre Jean Bérard. Institut Français de Naples 7–10 décembre 1981*. Bibliothèque de l'Institut français de Naples 6. 165–73.

Serwint. N. (1993). 'The female athletic costume at the Heraia and prenuptial initiation rites', *AJA* 97.403–22.

Shackleton Bailey, D. R. (1956). *Propertiana*. Cambridge.

(1965). (ed.) *Cicero's Letters to Atticus vol. I. 68–59 B.C. 1–45 (Books I and II)*. Cambridge.

(1968). (ed.) *Cicero's Letters to Atticus vol. III. 51–50 B.C. 94–132 (Books V–VII. 9)*. Cambridge.

(1986). 'Nobiles and novi reconsidered', *AJPh* 107.255–60.

Sherwin-White, A. N. (1984). *Roman Foreign Policy in the East: 168 B.C.–A.D. 1*. London.

Sidari, D. (1977–8). 'Il problema partico nella poesia ovidiana', *Atti dell'Istituto Veneto di scienze, lettere ed arti. Cl. di scienze morali, lettere ed arti* 136.35–54.

(1982). *Problema partico ed imitatio Alexandri nella dinastia giulioclaudia*. Istituto Veneto di scienze, lettere ed arti. Memorie. Cl. di scienze morali, lettere ed arti 38.3. Venice.

Sider, D. (1997). (ed.) *The Epigrams of Philodemos*. New York.

Simpson, C. J. (1996). 'Two small thoughts on "Cilnius Maecenas"', *Latomus* 55.394–8.

Skutsch, F. (1901). *Aus Vergils Frühzeit*. Leipzig.

(1906). *Gallus und Vergil. Aus Vergils Frühzeit*. Zweiter Teil. Leipzig.

Skutsch, O. (1963). 'The structure of the Propertian *Monobiblos*', *CPh* 58.238–9.

Smith, K. F. (1913). (ed.) *The Elegies of Albius Tibullus: The Corpus Tibullianum Edited with Introduction and Notes on Books I, II, and IV, 2–14*. New York.

Smith, R. E. (1958). Service in the Post-Marian Roman Army. Manchester.

Smith, R. R. R. (1991). *Hellenistic Sculpture: A Handbook*. London.

Smyth, G. R. (1970). *Thesaurus Criticus ad Sexti Properti Textum*. Mnemosyne Suppl. 12. Leiden.

Solin, H. (1993). 'Zur Tragfähigkeit der Onomastik in der Prosopographie', in W. Eck (ed.) *Prosopographie und Sozialgeschichte. Studien zur Methodik und Erkenntnismöglichkeit der kaiserzeitlichen Prosopographie. Kolloquium Köln 24.– 26. November 1991*. Cologne. 1–33.

Sordi, M. (1964). 'Virgilio e la storia romana del IV sec. a. C.', *Athenaeum* 42.80–100.

—— (1972). 'Ottaviano e l'Etruria nel 44 a.C.', *Studi Etruschi* 40.3–17.

—— (1981). 'La donna etrusca', in *Misoginia e maschilismo in Grecia e in Roma. Ottave giornate filologiche genovesi, 25–26 febbraio 1980*. Pubblicazioni dell'Istituto di filologia classica e medievale 71. Genoa. 49–67.

—— (1985). 'La guerra di Perugia e la fonte del l.V dei *Bella Civilia* di Appiano', *Latomus* 44.301–16.

—— (1995). 'La centralità dell'Etruria nella politica di Mecenate', *Riv. Stor. Ant. (Convegno su Mecenate, Arezzo, novembre 1993)* 25.149–56.

Soubiran, J. (1982). 'Solon chez Properce (II, 34, 27–30)', *RÉL* 60.266–72.

Spadoni Cerroni, M. C. (1996). 'I bolli laterizi di *Caius Mimisius* di *Asisium*', *Epigraphica* 58.193–5.

Spies, A. (1930). *Militat omnis amans. Ein Beitrag zur Bildersprache der antiken Erotik*. Diss. Tübingen.

Stahl, H.-P. (1985). *Propertius: "Love" and "War": Individual and State under Augustus*. Berkeley.

Stein, A. (1950). *Die Präfekten von Ägypten in der römischen Kaiserzeit*. Dissertationes Bernenses historiam orbis antiqui nascentisque medii aevi elucubrantes 1.1. Bern.

Steinbauer, D. (1998). 'Zur Grabinschrift der Larthi Cilnei aus Aritim/Arretium/Arezzo', *ZPE* 121.363–81.

Stewart, A. (1997). *Art, Desire, and the Body in Ancient Greece*. Cambridge.

Stok, F. (1996). 'La genealogia umbra di Varrone', in Bonamente and Coarelli (1996) 571–94.

Strazzulla, M. J. (1983). 'Assisi: problemi urbanistici', in *Les «Bourgeoisies» municipales italiennes aux IIe et Ier siècles av. J.-C.: Centre Jean Bérard. Institut Français de Naples 7–10 décembre 1981*. Bibliothèque de l'Institut français de Naples 6. 151–64.

—— (1985). *Assisi Romana*. Atti Accademia Properziana del Subasio, s. VI.10. Assisi.

Suits, T. A. (1976). 'The iambic character of Propertius 1.4', *Philologus* 120.86–91.

Suolahti, J. (1955). *The Junior Officers of the Roman Army in the Republican Period: A Study on Social Structure*. Annales Academiae Fennicae ser. B.97. Helsinki.

Sutphen, M. C. (1901). 'A further collection of Latin proverbs', *AJPh* 22.1–28, 121–48, 241–60, 361–91.

Swoboda, M. (1977). 'De Propertii elegiis hymnos imitantibus', *Eos* 65.131–8.

Syme, R. (1938). 'The origin of Cornelius Gallus', *CQ* 32.39–44.

(1939). *The Roman Revolution*. Oxford.

(1978). *History in Ovid*. Oxford.

(1979). *Roman Papers* II, ed. E. Badian. Oxford.

(1986). *The Augustan Aristocracy*. Oxford.

Tandoi, V. (1984–5). (ed.) *Disiecti Membra Poetae. Studi di poesia latina in frammenti*. Foggia.

(1992). 'Il trionfo di Claudio sulla Britannia e il suo cantore (*Anth. Lat.* 419–426 Riese)', in F. E. Consolino, G. Lotito, M.-P. Pieri, G. Sommariva, S. Timpanaro and M. A. Vinchesi (eds.) *Scritti di Filologia e di Storia della Cultura Classica* I. Pisa. 449–508 = *SIFC* 34 (1962) 83–129, 137–68.

Tatum, W. J. (1999). *The Patrician Tribune: Publius Clodius Pulcher*. Chapel Hill.

(2000). 'Aspirations and divagations: the poetics of place in Propertius 2.10', *TAPA* 130.393–410.

Taylor, L. R. (1960). *The Voting Districts of the Roman Republic: The Thirty-Five Urban and Rural Tribes*. Rome.

Tchernia, A. (1986). *Le vin de l'Italie romaine: Essai d'histoire économique d'après les amphores*. BEFAR 261. Rome.

Thomas, R. F. (1979). 'New comedy, Callimachus, and Roman poetry', *HSCPh* 83.179–206.

(1988). (ed.) *Virgil: Georgics* (2 vols). Cambridge.

(1992). 'The old man revisited: memory, reference, and genre in Virgil *Georgics* 4.116–48', *MD* 29.35–70.

(1996). 'Genre through intertextuality: Theocritus to Virgil and Propertius', in M. A. Harder, R. F. Regtuit and G. C. Wakker (eds.) *Theocritus*. Groningen. 227–44.

(1999). *Reading Virgil and his Texts: Studies in Intertextuality*. Ann Arbor.

Thommen, L. (1999). 'Spartanische Frauen', *MH* 56.129–49.

Torelli, M. (1969). 'Senatori etruschi della tarda repubblica e dell'impero', *Dialoghi di Archeologia* 3.285–363.

Traill, D. A. (1994). 'Propertius 1.21: the sister, the bones, and the wayfarer', *AJPh* 115.89–96.

Tränkle, H. (1960). *Die Sprachkunst des Properz und die Tradition der Lateinischen Dichtersprache*. Hermes Einzelschriften 15. Wiesbaden.

Tuplin, C. (1976). 'Cantores Euphorionis', *Papers of the Liverpool Latin Seminar* 1.1–23.

Uhlmann, W. (1909). *De Sex. Properti Genere Dicendi*. Diss. Münster.

Underwood, J. T., Jr. (1971). *Locus Communis, Laus Legum and Laus Locorum: Rhetorical Exercises as a Model for Propertius, Book III*. Diss. Ohio State University.

Valenti, C. P. (2000). 'Storia ed istituzioni del *municipium* di Arna', *Bollettino della deputazione per la storia patria di Umbria* 97.185–222.

Valvo, A. (1983). 'M. Valerio Messalla Corvino negli studi più recenti', *ANRW* II.30.3.1663–80.

(1989). 'L'iscrizione a *Iuppiter Iurarius* dell'isola Tiberina (*C.I.L.* I², 990)', *Istituto Lombardo (Rend. Lett.)* 123.263–77.

van der Meer, L. B. (1987). *The Bronze Liver of Piacenza: Analysis of a Polytheistic Structure.* Amsterdam.

van Groningen, B. A. (1977). (ed.) *Euphorion.* Amsterdam.

Verdière, R. (1965). 'Propertiana', *Riv. Stud. Class.* 13.23–7.

Verzar, M. (1976). 'Archäologische Zeugnisse aus Umbrien', in P. Zanker (ed.) *Hellenismus in Mittelitalien: Kolloquium in Göttingen vom 5. bis 9. Juni 1974* I. Abhandlungen der Akademie der Wissenschaften in Göttingen, phil.-hist. Kl. (3 ser.) 97/1. Göttingen. 116–42.

Volkmann, R. (1885). *Die Rhetorik der Griechen und Römer*, 2nd edn. Leipzig.

Warden, J. (1982). 'Epic into elegy: Propertius 4, 9, 70f.', *Hermes* 110.228–42.

Watson, A. (1975). *Rome of the XII Tables. Persons and Property.* Princeton NJ.

Watson, L. and P. Watson (2003). (eds.) *Martial. Select Epigrams.* Cambridge.

Waywell, G. (1999). 'Sparta and its topography', *BICS* 43.1–26.

Weinstock, S. (1971). *Divus Julius.* Oxford.

West, D. (1978). Review of Ross (1975), *Latomus* 37.209–11.

West, D. and T. Woodman (1979). (eds.) *Creative Imitation in Latin Literature.* Cambridge.

White, P. (1991). 'Maecenas' retirement', *CPh* 86.130–8.

(1993). *Promised Verse: Poets in the Society of Augustan Rome.* Cambridge Mass.

White, R. E. (1964). 'The unity of Propertius 2.34 and 3.20', in M. F. Gyles and E. W. Davis (eds.) *Laudatores Temporis Acti: Studies in Memory of Wallace Everett Caldwell.* The James Sprunt Studies in History and Political Science 46. Chapel Hill. 63–72.

White, S. A. (1999). 'Callimachus Battiades (*Epigr.* 35)', *CPh* 94.168–81.

Wijsman, H. J. (1993). 'Ascanius, Gargara and female power (*Georgics* 3.269–270)', *HSCPh* 95.315–18.

Wildberger, J. (1998). *Ovids Schule der "elegischen" Liebe. Erotodidaxe und Psychagogie in der Ars Amatoria.* Studien zur klassischen Philologie 112. Frankfurt am Main.

Wilkinson, L. P. (1966). 'The continuity of Propertius ii. 13', *CR* 16.141–4.

Williams, G. (1990). 'Did Maecenas "fall from favor"? Augustan literary patronage', in Raaflaub and Toher (1990) 258–75.

(1995). '*Libertino patre natus*: true or false?', in Harrison (1995) 296–313.

Wills, J. (1996). *Repetition in Latin Poetry: Figures of Allusion.* Oxford.

Wimmel, W. (1960). *Kallimachos in Rom: Die Nachfolge seines apologetischen Dichtens in der Augusteerzeit.* Hermes Einzelschriften 16. Wiesbaden.

(1981). *Der tragische Dichter L. Varius Rufus. Zur Frage seines Augusteertums.* Akademie der Wissenschaften und der Literatur. Abhandlungen der Geistes- und Sozialwissenschaftlichen Klasse. Jahrgang 1981, 5. Mainz.

(1983). 'Der Augusteer Lucius Varius Rufus', *ANRW* II.30.3.1562–621.

Wiseman, T. P. (1964). 'Some Republican senators and their tribes', *CQ* 14.122–33 [= Wiseman (1987) 15–26].

(1969). *Catullan Questions.* Leicester.

(1971). *New Men in the Roman Senate 139 B.C.–A.D. 14.* Oxford.

(1974). *Cinna the Poet.* Leicester.

(1979). *Clio's Cosmetics: Three Studies in Greco-Roman Literature.* Leicester.

(1984). 'Two small boys with famous names: a study in social history', *Opus* 3(1).93–7.

(1985). *Catullus and his World: A Reappraisal.* Cambridge.

(1987). *Roman Studies: Literary and Historical.* Collected Classical Papers 1. Liverpool.

Wölcke, K. (1911). 'Beiträge zur Geschichte des Tropaions', *BJ* 120.127–235 and Taf. VIII-XII.

Woodman, A. J. (1983). (ed.) *Velleius Paterculus. The Caesarian and Augustan Narrative (2.41–93).* CCTC 25. Cambridge.

Woodman, T. and J. Powell (1992). (eds.) *Author and Audience in Latin Literature.* Cambridge.

Woodman, T. and D. West (1974). (eds.) *Quality and Pleasure in Latin Poetry.* Cambridge.

Woodman, T. and D. West (1984). (eds.) *Poetry and Politics in the Age of Augustus.* Cambridge.

Yarden, L. (1971). The Tree of Light: A Study of the Menorah: The Seven-Branched Lampstand. London.

Yardley, J. C. (1974). 'Propertius' Lycinna', *TAPA* 104.429–34.

(1978). 'The elegiac paraclausithyron', *Eranos* 76.19–34.

(1979). 'Ovid's other *propempticon*', *Hermes* 107.183–8.

(1980). 'Gallus in *Eclogue* 10: quotation or adaptation?', *Vergilius* 26.48–51.

Zanker, P. (1987). *Augustus und die Macht der Bilder.* Munich.

(1988). *The Power of Images in the Age of Augustus*, tr. A. Shapiro. Ann Arbor.

Zecchini, G. (1998). 'Cesare e gli Etruschi', in L. Aigner-Foresti (ed.) *Die Integration der Etrusker und das Weiterwirken etruskischen Kulturgutes im republikanischen und kaiserzeitlichen Rom.* Österreichische Akademie der Wissenschaften. Phil.-Hist. Kl. Sitzungsberichte 658. Vienna. 237–49.

Zetzel, J. E. G. (1977). 'Gallus, elegy, and Ross', review article of Ross (1975), *CPh* 72.249–60.

Zintzen, C. (1967). (ed.) *Damaskios. Vitae Isidori reliquiae.* Bibliotheca Graeca et Latina suppletoria 1. Hildesheim.

Indexes

I. INDEX LOCORUM

Emboldening indicates major discussions; page numbers include citations in footnotes.

This index contains only those items associated with Gallus which are discussed in this volume. Their Gallan status ranges from firm (i.e. when they are attested in surviving lines of Gallus) through plausible to speculative. Nouns and adjectives are generally lemmatised in nom. sing. masc., verbs in 1st pers. pres. indic. act.; form(s) and phrases commonly found may follow in parentheses. Proper names (and adjectives) are not italicized and are treated as concepts, even if they do feature, or may have featured, as words in Gallus. A reference to a page may also include the notes on that page.

The entries in this index are not necessarily highlighted as 'Gallan' on their every appearance in the text; hence those which are not highlighted may offer further subsidiary support for a word's or concept's Gallan status.

III. GENERAL INDEX

Modern scholars appear only when they are mentioned in the text. Only historical aspects of Sex. Propertius are indexed.